RECIPES FROM

LE MANOIR AUX
QUAT' SAISONS

ABOVE

*Tartelette soufflée aux framboises
(page 157)*

FACING PAGE

*Rable de lapin rôti aux graines de
moutarde et ses cuisses braisées au
jus d'estragon (page 195)*

RAYMOND BLANC

RECIPES FROM

LE MANOIR AUX
QUAT' SAISONS

Macdonald Orbis

A Macdonald Orbis BOOK

TEXT © RAYMOND BLANC 1988
PHOTOGRAPHY AND DESIGN OF THIS VOLUME
© MACDONALD ORBIS 1988

FIRST PUBLISHED IN GREAT BRITAIN IN 1988
BY MACDONALD & CO (PUBLISHERS) LTD
LONDON & SYDNEY

A MEMBER OF THE MAXWELL PERGAMON PUBLISHING
CORPORATION PLC

REPRINTED 1988

BRITISH LIBRARY CATALOGUING IN PUBLICATION
DATA

BLANC, RAYMOND
LE MANOIR AUX QUAT' SAISONS
1. COOKERY, FRENCH
I. TITLE
641.5944   TX719
ISBN 0-356-12077-5

FILMSET BY BOOKWORM TYPESETTING, MANCHESTER,
ENGLAND

COLOUR SEPARATION BY COLORLITO, MILAN

PRINTED AND BOUND IN GREAT BRITAIN BY PURNELL BOOK
PRODUCTION. A MEMBER OF BPCC PLC

ASSISTANT WRITER: JULIAN COLBECK
EDITOR: KATE WHITEMAN
DESIGN: IVOR CLAYDON/BOB HOOK
PHOTOGRAPHER: MICHAEL BOYS

MACDONALD & CO (PUBLISHERS) LTD
GREATER LONDON HOUSE
HAMPSTEAD ROAD
LONDON NW1 7QX

Contents

Preface

There are two reasons for which I consider this book to be very special.

There was a time when a chef had to be a Carême, Soyer or Escoffier for his published recipes to command attention. But in recent decades cookery books have flowed continuously, both here and abroad, from famous – recently even from lesser – chefs who, with almost no exception, have progressed by gathering experience in numerous kitchens during their career. Such cookery books, however excellent many of them are, reflect the well-tried, basic rules of the profession in which these authors are steeped. Their works are variations on time-honoured themes, at times brilliant, but with the common root of classical methods nevertheless. Originality is excessively rare.

Raymond Blanc, however, has not been hemmed in by such early influences of professional cuisine, however beneficial they are. The amazing fact is that he is totally self-taught: having come to England to learn the language at 22, he took a waiter's job, then began humble work in the kitchen of a hotel and, with absolutely no experience anywhere else, started his own restaurant in Oxford, rocketing to recognition and fame in a very few years.

This freedom from training and its rules is reflected in his recipes. Like pearls from oysters, they result from lonely, struggling effort, and also from intelligence and quite exceptional intuition.

But there is another, stronger factor that sets his book apart. The 'art' of cooking has become a greatly misused phrase. Outstanding artisans are many, but I reserve the term 'artist' for only a few in Europe. Among the long line of well-known painters, how many Turners have there been? Among present-day chefs in Britain, I could comfortably count 'artists', in the true sense of the word, on one hand, with fingers to spare. Vision, originality, constant flashes of imagination, with results I do not hesitate to call lyrical and akin to poesy, can all be found in Raymond Blanc's cooking.

Lucky are those of us who have experienced this exceptional man's art. Lucky will be many, many more who can now possess a record of it.

EGON RONAY

Foreword

Le Manoir aux Quat' Saisons is more English than French in feeling: a rambling gabled Cotswold house with rosebeds and croquet lawns, with deep armchairs and a faint suggestion of an old-fashioned house party.

You could be lulled into thinking that the slight young man in white with eager eyes and beaded brow has just popped in from tennis. Until you hear him talk. This is a zealot talking; talking about food in a way that makes you prick up your ears. His enthusiasm bubbles over. With missionary zeal he makes you want to taste every dish he is forming in the air with his hands as he describes it.

Raymond Blanc is an instinctive chef: perhaps the best such chef in England today. He is self-taught, sometimes iconoclastic, always uninhibited. He uses cookery as an artist uses light: to reveal his own vision of a world whose ingredients seem to him to be almost too wonderful to be true.

So preconceptions are put aside at Le Manoir. Preconceptions about wine as well as food. Classical restaurant wine-lists are heavily biased towards Burgundy and Bordeaux. To be fair to them they are merely playing safe: off-the-beaten track wines were often poorly made in the past, and frequently bottled and shipped without proper professional care. But we live in a new world of wine today, as we do in a new world of food. 'Regional' is no longer a term of faint praise. Technical competence is no longer confined to famous names. Ambition has reached out and touched the vine's remotest outposts.

There is real excitement in tasting for the first time the wine of an obscure valley in Savoie or Béarn (or Navarre or Friuli) – far more excitement than in yet another bottle of a name which has become a commercial cliché.

'Little' wines are often only little in price. It is typical of Raymond Blanc and his restaurant director, Alain Desenclos, that they direct their guests' attention first to the 'regional' wines at modest prices on their wonderful wine list. The senior bottles at stately prices are there for those who appreciate and can afford them. But there is no hint of stigma in spending less and being more adventurous.

I have been stimulated, often enthralled, by this new creative voice. Although authentically French, Raymond Blanc is himself stimulated and inspired by England.

When we meet it is not to drink Champagne but to find ways of characterizing an unknown vin de pays that one of us has found; a wine which fits no ready-made pigeon-hole, yet will shed new light on the flavour of a salmon.

Many such wines are suggested to accompany the dishes in this book. A list of their (present) suppliers is offered on page 275. I suggested to Raymond that such a list would soon become out of date. "But Hugh," he said, "'ow are we going to encourage people? They cannot all come to the Manoir." Alas.

HUGH JOHNSON

Introduction

FROM CHILD TO CHEF

I cannot claim that cooking has always been my passion. If credits are due, they go to my mother, grandmother, and various food-loving ancestors whose general attitude towards food and eating I have inherited; and possibly to God, whose dubious blessing it seems to have been that I should be kissed by the Muse of the Flambé and so enter the world of cuisine.

I was raised in a small village, where I went in search of wild mushrooms at four in the morning, spent enchanted nights hunting for frogs, or sunny afternoons gathering wild flowers, collecting snails, or fishing for trout. But at this stage I was not in the least interested in cooking the fruits of these adventures, simply in the thrill of the chase. However, these pursuits made me aware of the changing seasons, each with its unique offering of scents, colours and tastes, and taught me to respect the harmony and contrast of the seasons, all of which has had a tremendous influence on the development of my ideas in cooking.

In most French households life revolves around mealtimes, and my family was no exception. I too learned to respect all the rituals and customs of the table: the ceremonious placing of the soup tureen at the head of the table; my father (for he alone had this privilege) slicing chunks of deliciously fresh bread while we waited patiently for my mother to bring in those magical dishes from the kitchen; long, tedious conversations about religion, war and politics, which seemed interminable to a youngster with a sweet tooth eagerly anticipating the Grande Finale of the dessert.

These mealtimes gave me a feel not only for food itself, but for the whole event: how a meal is created, presented and received. Although I loathed helping out in the kitchen, I was always a fascinated spectator of my mother's culinary activities. But if my parents had ever suspected a chef in the making, my initial venture – during which the Pyrex dish containing my *crêpes Suzette* exploded on the hotplate – would certainly have dispossessed them of this idea.

When I was eighteen I left college. I knew then that I wanted to succeed in a creative field, although I didn't have a specific interest. By the age of nineteen I could feel my dreams slipping away. Then, on a warm summer's evening, right in the heart of busy Besançon, I saw my vision. Surrounded by majestic trees was the terrace of a restaurant, illuminated by the gentle light of gas lamps and flickering candles. The scene was stunning. Here was life at its best – elegantly dressed guests sat at tables covered with long, fine lace tablecloths and laid with glittering silver and fine china. And oh . . . the wonder of a fat capon studded with black truffles, surrounded by a ballet of the brightest red freshwater crayfish. Never could this capon have looked so good, even at the greatest and proudest moment of its life. Suddenly I knew where I could succeed.

The next day I returned to ask for an interview as an apprentice in the kitchen. I was refused because of my age but, instead, I was offered the position of *commis* waiter at a nearby restaurant, which I took, working for nearly two years under the guidance of a hard taskmaster, M. Belligat, President of the hôteliers in Franche-Comté. Here I learned about dealing with customers, about wine, various carving techniques . . .but my heart was still in cooking. I returned to the restaurant that had inspired me, as *chef de rang*. But there was no way I could enter the inner sanctum of *cuisine* even as the most humble servant. Ultimately, the high priest remains the head chef, as I discovered to my cost when I dared to voice my opinion on the heaviness or taste of his sauces. I resigned myself to being a restaurant manager.

Then came military service. There was not much to do and I began to think seriously about my professional life. Despite the fact that my English was practically non-existent, I decided to go to England, and worked ferociously at learning this impossible language!

I came to England for one year in 1972, to The Rose Revived, a pretty restaurant/hotel on the banks of the Thames where gourmets came to savour the famous *canard à l'orange*, and where, having befriended the chef, I was allowed to experiment with a few ideas in the kitchen. I married in 1974. Unfortunately, our marriage did not survive the daily pressure of our professional lives, but I am grateful for her contribution to our partnership. I have two wonderful sons, Olivier (13) and Sebastian (6).

In 1975 the chef of The Rose Revived and his

entire brigade walked out and I was offered the position of head chef, which I accepted without hesitation. I can still recall the feeling that my chef's clothes were just a disguise as, with much apprehension, I entered the kitchen flanked by two English Cordon Bleu chefs.

The adventure had begun. After two years The Rose Revived was rewarded by an entry in Michelin and one AA star. In 1977 my first restaurant, Les Quat' Saisons, was opened in Oxford, sandwiched between a ladies' underwear shop and Oxfam. It was an instant success, and won more coveted awards.

I then started to look for suitable premises. I had in mind a small house in the country, but in September 1983 fell in love with a much grander manor house, Great Milton Manor, set in 30 acres. With the help of a few friends, it was transformed into a most magnificent country house restaurant and hotel – Le Manoir aux Quat' Saisons.

I am self-taught, and proud of being so. What I may lack from not having had a master to guide me, I have gained in enjoying the freedom to indulge my curiosity. I strive to attain simplicity through complexity, freedom through restriction, harmony through conflict. But most of all I am motivated by the progression of a dish from the initial idea to its preparation and presentation, and the happiness of my guests. It is this enthusiasm and joy that I have tried to impart in this book. I hope that those of you who like to experiment, then present the results to your guests, will have as much fun and pleasure in doing so as I have had while working on this book.

COOKING IN BRITAIN – YESTERDAY

Fifteen years ago, at the time of my naive entry into the world of *cuisine*, I was astonished at the lack of service and poor quality of ingredients available in Britain, and soon realized that a long and arduous fight lay ahead of me. I still remember with horror the sight of those obese white ducks which needed hours of cooking just to melt their fat; the poor, tasteless, pellet-fed, hormone-ridden battery farmed chickens and the huge vegetables which the British grew with such pride.

My first goal was to find the right produce. I had heard of the famous Aylesbury ducklings and, since I lived near that town, I went in search of them, convinced that I should find farms bursting with these dream birds. Off I set, full of expectation, hopes high, dreaming of lovely ducks wobbling about on their short legs, happily pecking freely in the farmyard. But I searched in vain, trudging from butcher to butcher, and finally learnt that all the farms had long since been industrialized and now produced only the fat, nightmarish birds I sought to replace.

At first, my pride was hurt. No Frenchman likes to feel he has been taken for a ride, especially where food is concerned. More importantly, I realised that *regional* cuisine no longer existed in Britain, so life would bear little resemblance to what I had known in France.

In Britain, industrialization had largely squeezed the small home producer out of existence, bringing the dreaded 'rationalization' and 'standardization' and eliminating consumer choice. This, of course, bred a most unhelpful attitude to consumers, chefs and anyone concerned with quality of produce, as I discovered to my cost. When I asked for anything that had not come off a conveyor belt, I was stared at in disbelief and considered a thorough nuisance. It was the start of many arguments.

In this cycle of apathy, I observed, the consumer accepts unquestioningly, so the producer never bothers to improve – and so it goes on. It was staggering to encounter such appalling difficulties in obtaining the simplest ingredients for my culinary needs – and in a country which abounds in wonderful game, fish and meat.

I had ambitious plans for changing the world of vegetables and this also proved to be a struggle. I had to revolutionize the gardener before I could revolutionize the garden, but I was handicapped from the start. Mr Lay, the gardener in question, was built like a truck, whereas I am slight, even for a Frenchman. He was reluctant to grow 'unusual' and 'exotic' vegetables like celeriac, mange-tout and even French beans . . . and when harvest time came, all hell broke loose! I was bent on picking young vegetables – small, delicate tender shoots. (Mr Lay grew vegetables proportional to his considerable size and age.) I used to sneak out at night, armed with a torch, basket and courage, and steal the infant plants. Mr Lay suspected a raider and one night he chased me irately across the bean rows. Luckily, small Frenchmen run much faster than large Englishmen, but although I managed to escape from this particular gardener, his stick-in-the-mud attitude was all-prevailing and was reflected in the market and ultimately on the plate.

Talking of markets, where are they? I wandered from town to town without ever seeing the colourful market stalls where local farmers bring their offerings. In other European countries, the markets provide a constant turnover of fresh fruit and vegetables and the shopper comes to expect an abundance of local produce and choice. Here, I encountered such wondrous fruit and vegetables only in travellers' tales.

If finding fresh vegetables was a problem, what hope of fresh fish? While I realized that Oxford is relatively far from the coast, the so-called 'fresh' fish I found in the covered market truly horrified me – menacing rows of sunken-eyed, limp-bodied, long-dead fish that the customers happily bought, for they knew no better. And this on an island surrounded by a bounty of fish!

A bounty – yes, but transported around the country (often days after being caught) in unrefrigerated vans. The average 'fresh' fish available was at least three days old, conveying a lack of respect for the fish, the customer's palate and, worse, his health. Complaints were met with the same dead-eyed stare as that of the fish.

Needless to say, this attitude towards produce was mirrored in the restaurant world, where abysmally low standards of hygiene and lack of enthusiasm on the part of the staff, despite lavish expenditure on furnishings and decor, gave Britain's restaurants a worldwide reputation for mediocrity.

Working in a restaurant kitchen was just a job, not a profession. It imposed no strain on the imagination, engendered no curiosity, eagerness or pride. Much of the problem was due to a lack of training and the poor quality of students. Giving service with pride, elegance and sincerity, doing away with the hollow, fixed grin of the insincere, requires train-

ing. It *can* be taught, as pioneer chefs like Francis Coulson, George Perry-Smith and the Roux brothers demonstrated. They and others set about creating a new world, with a different awareness and attitudes – and so a new cycle began.

COOKING IN BRITAIN TODAY

Britain is said to be a very conservative country, where tradition is valued more highly than change. Yet in a relatively short space of time, much *has* changed in the fields of cooking and hotelery. Nowadays, those who aim for quality can achieve it. It is nice to know that I am no longer the odd man out. Now, there is a definite interest in food, a general desire for improvement and a constant flow of questions, answers and suggestions from all sides – growers, suppliers, restaurateurs and consumers – aimed at promoting a mutually beneficial understanding.

The hotel and restaurant industry is acquiring a new respectable image and is no longer regarded as a last resort for those who cannot think what else to do. *Nouvelle cuisine* sparked off many new trends and kindled so much interest in food that outlooks and attitudes have inevitably changed for the better. It is no longer true that if you wish to eat well in Britain, you must eat breakfast three times a day!

An abundance of high-quality home produce has emerged, or re-emerged in some cases. From Scotland come fresh chanterelles, no longer trodden underfoot, but picked and sold, and truly fresh fish – translucent langoustines delivered still alive, scallops caught by divers. Meat, which has always been of a basic high quality, is now matured and cut the way you want it – and all because there is finally a demand for such produce. How different from yesterday's nightmare.

These changing attitudes have given birth to a lively and exciting movement; young, gifted British chefs, working with motivation and a new-found passion, are becoming the stars of tomorrow, despite a lack of early education. There is a long way to go; most catering establishments still do not understand the *cuisine* of today and the importance of freshness and quality. But the process is in motion and we can look forward to tomorrow with pride, hope and confidence.

HOW TO USE THIS BOOK

Although this book has been written around the seasons, you will find that many of the dishes overlap and may be appropriate to the preceeding or following season. This is partly due to the happy abundance of year-round food supplies which can import the summer into the midst of our winter (by bringing us produce from California or South America, for instance). It is still rather a novelty to eat fresh raspberries or apricots whilst staring at a winter landscape – and they usually taste as good as they should.

Very often, readers skip the introductory and explanatory chapters of books like this one and head straight for the recipes. Please do not do this! I hope to convey the attitude towards cooking that you need to acquire before embarking on the recipes. It is important to understand how and why each step is done, so that you gain a feel and complete understanding of my kind of cooking; then even a tomato will become a subject for artful discussion at a dinner party and your shopping will become a different experience.

How to follow the recipes:
All ingredients should be weighed and prepared (ie: peeled, washed, diced if necessary) in advance.
Planning ahead points out which stages of the recipe can be done in advance without affecting the quality of the dish.
Variations and Chef's notes are there to point out any difficulties and show you how to overcome them.
For special ingredients and a list of wine merchants, see page 274.
Difficulty of recipes is indicated by the number of toques (🎩). One toque denotes an easy dish; three toques mean that the recipe is complex and often lengthy.
Menus At the end of each season, you will find seasonal menu suggestions; these will help you to plan a well-balanced meal.

HOW TO GIVE A SUCCESSFUL DINNER PARTY

We ought to look forward to giving dinner parties – but do we? Often, they become a dreaded test upon which lives, career promotions, marriages, divorces – perhaps even wars – depend. I often wonder to what extent the quality of a meal affects the decisions of world leaders. Might a terrible dinner lead to war and a wonderful meal bring world peace, no less?

Short of saving the world, let us merely aspire to saving face. Start by deciding not to panic at any cost! All you need is proper planning. Take your choice of courses; if your main course is a complicated dish requiring a lot of work and attention, make a cold starter and a simpler dessert, so that you avoid panic and a loss of confidence.

Plan ahead and order the ingredients in advance. Many of my recipes give you ample opportunity to prepare parts of the dishes well ahead.

Never test new dishes on your guests; they are not there as guinea pigs. Let your family or long-suffering and well-trusted friends help you with some honest criticism first. Your social life will then not suffer (family and friends soon forget, but a disastrous dinner party lingers long in the memory of disappointed guests). More importantly, you will be familiar with the recipe and find you can prepare it better and faster, knowing the pitfalls and difficulties.

Start by making some of the easier recipes (those with one 🎩). Read the recipes carefully before plunging in; you should be able to visualise the dish and yourself preparing it. Understand all the stages and get a feel for how they should turn out. You need not slavishly adhere to all the recipes. Consider them as a guide and feel free to leave out or substitute ingredients, especially if these are difficult to obtain.

Read the introductory chapters; they will help you to succeed and to select the right ingredients. Freshness is of prime importance; learn where to buy the freshest ingredients. I have included a list of reliable wine merchants and specialist food suppliers who will be only too pleased to advise you on the wine best suited to your menu. One more piece of advice – *nag*! – demand, blackmail if you must, but insist on quality service. Only constant nagging will promote the necessary changes in the food supply industry, so never be reticent – you deserve the best!

And so, to work. The whole process should be easy and fun, from planning to shopping and cooking. Your efforts will be well rewarded by the smiles of delight and admiration on the faces of your guests. Congratulations!

RAYMOND BLANC

Basic Recipes

AND TECHNIQUES

CHOOSING AND BUYING INGREDIENTS

Oil
Olive oil: Look for 'extra virgin olive oil, first cold press', which contains all the real fruit and flavour from the sunny Mediterranean.

Groundnut, corn and sunflower are all non-scented oils. They are best for searing meats, since they have no taste of their own and do not interfere with other flavours. Grapeseed oil is perfect for mayonnaise, as it does not congeal when cold.

Walnut and hazelnut oil are heavily scented and, used sparingly, can provide a wonderful flavour. It may be a good idea to mix them with non-scented oils to prevent them from overpowering a dish.

Vinegar
Never use malt vinegar.

For salads, use a good white or red wine vinegar.

Fruit-flavoured vinegars such as raspberry, blackcurrant or passion fruit are products of *nouvelle cuisine*. Frankly, some are rather 'faddy'. Use them sparingly, as they can be overpowering.

Butter
Always use the best unsalted butter.

Goose or duck fats
You can make your own by keeping cooking fat from the birds, but they can also be found in some delicatessens (see page 274).

Truffles
Black Périgourdine truffles are the 'black diamonds' of French cuisine, still somewhat shrouded in mystery, since no one has yet succeeded in cultivating them, although they can be encouraged to grow. Rare and outrageously expensive, they are in season from January to March. See page 274 for where to order them fresh. Stored in a sealed container in the fridge, they will keep for about 2 weeks. If you store truffles alongside eggs, their scent will permeate the porous shell and flavour the eggs. Prepare yourself for the most delicious scrambled eggs you will ever taste!

You can prolong the short truffle season by sterilizing and storing: clean the truffles under running water using a soft brush (to remove all traces of dirt) and rinse well. Boil 1 L/1¾ pt water with 100 ml/3½ fl oz port and 1 teaspoon salt. Skim, add the truffles and cook for 5 minutes (small ones), 8–10 minutes (medium), 15 minutes (large). Place in jars with their cooking liquid and sterilize for 20 minutes. Cool and keep refrigerated until needed.

White truffles from Piedmont are even more expensive and more exquisitely scented. Their season is from October to December. They must be used raw.

Caviar
When I first tasted caviar in my early cooking days, I was totally unmoved. But I persevered and after a long grind of caviar tasting, I have now acquired the taste. In fact I could live on it! Simply spread it on a slice of bread, with a little sour cream. The best caviar is Russian large-grain Beluga. It will keep for up to 1 month in the fridge.

Salmon and sea trout eggs have a rather unpleasant texture, although they are interesting and look pretty.

Snails and snail eggs
You would think that rainy England would be an ideal place to breed snails. But no – they are mostly imported from France, although there are some British snail farms. You can buy best quality tinned snails from most good delicatessens.

Stop Press! Snail hunting is now illegal in France, since Frenchmen with their large appetites have now made these molluscs an endangered species. We never learn.

Snail eggs: Only a Frenchman would have thought of this! In fact they are quite delicious. Be adventurous and give them a try.

Vanilla pods

Whenever possible use the real thing. Before you buy make sure that the pod is moist; pods that have dried out will have lost much of their flavour.

Buy up to 6 at a time and store them in sugar in an airtight container; this will give you vanilla sugar.

For the best results split the pod lengthways, scrape out the inside and add these scrapings to the liquid. Chop and add the pod. This may not be economical but it makes the most delicious custard.

For a lighter flavour, infuse a whole pod in the milk, then wash and dry it, and store it in caster sugar for further use. This way, a vanilla pod can be used at least two or three times. Split the pod when using it for the last time.

Vanilla flavouring: Never! Please avoid as it is too often associated with the worst kind of chemistry.

Vanilla essence: You may be able to find good quality vanilla essence. Check thoroughly before buying.

Star anise

These pretty, star-shaped, highly aromatic seeds can be bought in most delicatessens and in Chinese supermarkets.

Dried fennel

Fennel grows wild all over Provence. If you can't gather it yourself, you can find dried fennel in some delicatessens.

— FISH —

Before the health and diet revolution, fish eating was largely limited to Fridays. Now, however, many people are discovering how to cook this delightful source of protein. What better place for this, you might think, than Britain, surrounded as it is by water and an abundance of fish?

In my experience, there are two types of fish available – the first (though it ought to be the last) comes from trawlers, which can net up to 130 tonnes of fish in a single catch! This type of fishing destroys marine life and threatens several species of fish with extinction – and imagine what tons of bruised, frozen fish of dubious freshness come from these huge ships, often after 4 or 5 days' storage on ice. It is these fish which are most often found in shops under the guise of 'fresh fish'.

The other, less accessible, type (the truly fresh fish) comes from the tiny number of small boats operated by fishermen whose respect for the sea and its bounty is still intact. Their fish arrives in the market within one day, fresh and unbruised. Unfortunately, this type of fishing is considered expensive and exotic and most of the beautifully fresh catch ends up in France, although I buy my fish from a small network of fishermen in Cornwall, the Isle of Wight and Scotland. With luck, and your help, these small suppliers (a new addition to the British market) will continue to flourish.

Only when fish is really fresh can a chef apply his skill to create a delicate and beautiful dish, instead of fighting a losing battle with a bruised, dead corpse from the trawlers. Alas, nature will soon be replaced by aquaculture and, as ever, quantity and quick profit-making overrule quality. Thus fish farms often end up with much the same product as the trawlers, through pellet-feeding and overcrowding; farmed trout are a perfect example of tasteless failure. That being said, although I am against the cultivation of any living creatures, my curiosity has led me to compare the difference between farmed and wild turbot and salmon. I was amazed to find that some of the farmed fish were as good as their wild counterparts. Be aware, however, that the quality can vary; I shall stay with my faithful small suppliers and hope for their continued survival!

How to recognize fresh fish

In Japan, fish is only considered fresh when it jumps over the counter; our criteria are rather less stringent and we must rely on other indications of freshness. The appearance of a fish should be attractive; the eyes should be clear and bright – a glazed eye indicates that the fish has long departed from the land of the living. The scales should be shiny, steely and undamaged, the gills should be bright red and the flesh firm to the touch. There should be no unattractive odour. If the fish looks or smells unpleasant do not buy it – and tell your fishmonger why; quality and service will only improve if you are critical.

Shellfish

The shells must be tightly closed, or snap firmly shut at the slightest touch; if not the shellfish are probably dead – *do not buy them*. Dying shellfish close slowly and not tightly. Do not buy these either. Really fresh shellfish should be heavy with sea water. Less than fresh shellfish are not only unpalatable gastronomically – they can also cause food poisoning.

Crustaceans (especially lobsters, and langoustines): These should be bought alive, or the serum which holds the flesh together will slowly flow out and the flesh will quickly deteriorate and be like cotton wool when cooked.

Service

A final word about fishmongers. If customers receive poor service, it is because they do not demand any better. A good fishmonger should clean and open scallops and oysters for you and should cater for special requirements, such as boning, filleting, gutting and scaling – all at no extra charge. Always ask for special orders well in advance, and a smile always helps.

SHELLING A COOKED LOBSTER OR LANGOUSTINE

Twist off the claws and pincers and pull off the tail.

Using scissors, cut down the length of the tail, starting at the top.

Discard the black thread-like intestine from the centre of the tail and pull out the tail meat.

Gently crack open the claws with a mallet and extract the flesh.

OPENING OYSTERS

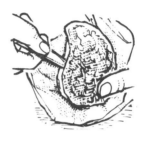

Hold the oyster in a tea towel, flat side up, over a bowl lined with a strainer to catch the juices. Push the tip of an oyster knife into the hinge and twist to prise the shells apart.

Lift off the top shell. Free the oyster with the knife.

Cooking fish

Avoid strong heat throughout the cooking process, except briefly for sealing or browning. Fish have fragile connective tissues with little fat content, so they must be subjected to only gentle heat and should be barely cooked – just to the point when the protein coagulates. If fish is cooked at too high a temperature or for too long, the flesh will dry out and disintegrate.

To keep fish moist and firm, it is generally cooked in 2 stages:

1. Cooking: During this stage, the heat penetrates the flesh, the fibres tense up and the fish is cooked only to medium rare.

2. Resting: Leave to rest in a warm place, covered so that it does not dry out. The residual heat will gradually penetrate the flesh and relax the muscle tissues. The flesh retains its taste and firmness and the delicious juices released are then added to the sauce.

How to tell when fish is cooked

Test by pressing the thickest part of the fillet with the inside of your finger; if the flesh is still springy and translucent, the fish is undercooked; if there is very little shrinkage and the flesh is smooth and opaque and feels firm and slightly supple with no sign of flakiness, it is correctly cooked. Overcooked fish will shrink and flake and have a dry taste and texture.

Seasoning is done in 2 stages

1. Just before cooking, using a little salt and a tiny amount of pepper.
2. Correct the seasoning after cooking. During cooking, most of the salt is diluted by the steam or the juices which flow out and does not penetrate the flesh, so season again afterwards. Taste a small piece of the fish, or press the back of your index finger against the flesh and taste; this will give you a good idea of the seasoning.

FILLETING ROUND FISH

Using a sharp knife, make an incision just below the head through the flesh to the bone, then cut off the fins and carefully cut along the backbone from head to tail. Lift off the fillet and repeat on the other side.

FILLETING FLAT FISH

Lay the fish on the work surface with its head away from you. Make an incision through to the bone along the central line from head to tail. Slide the knife under one fillet, tight to the bone, and cut the fillet free. Remove the other fillet, in the same way, turn the fish over and repeat.

SKINNING FLAT FISH

Cut off the fins or 'skirt'. Make an incision across the tail through to the bone. Use your fingers to loosen the skin at the sides of the fish. Salt your fingers to get a good grip, grip the skin tightly with one hand and pull it firmly away from you with the other hand.

— MEAT —

Britain can proudly claim to produce the finest quality meat, from lamb to the best of beef. However, the 20th century has brought intensive farming and it has become harder to find natural, unspoilt meat.

The quality of meat varies according to its breed, provenance and farming techniques, so what different butchers sell as fillet of beef may be as different as lumpfish roe is from caviar. It would be helpful to know where the butcher gets his supplies and thus have a vague notion of what to expect.

Alas, most British butchers (with some notable exceptions) have lost their skill and butchers' shops in this country are a pretty dispiriting sight, unless you are a confirmed vegetarian. Continental butchers spoil their customers for choice with arrays of neatly prepared and trimmed cuts; here, the choice is often dictated by how quickly you can escape the sight and smell of the shop. Do not feel shy about asking your butcher to trim off fat or prepare a cut to your requirements; if he is a professional, he will readily perform these services, and if he seems surprised or reluctant at first, remember that you are helping him to rediscover his craft.

All too often, you buy a prime cut of meat for Sunday lunch or a dinner party, and having followed a wonderful recipe with faith and precision, you end up with a tough, flavourless piece of meat and no praise for your efforts. Of course, you will blame your lack of understanding of cooking – have you ever considered blaming your butcher?

Most meat should be hung; through hanging, the meat loses water and matures somewhat, thus improving in flavour and tenderness. Most butchers in Britain do not hang their meat, so the customer judges quality by the vivid redness of unhung meat. This is for the convenience of the butcher, not the customer; hanging meat requires space and investment in a larger cold room – and water loss translates into weight loss, hence into money loss. Since customers believe that good meat is red meat, there is little incentive to change this practice, unless the customer demands better quality and threatens to withdraw his custom. It is important to realise how much power we have as customers; only by excercising this power can we alter and improve standards of service.

For example, by 1980, veal rearing in France had become so intensive and hormone-ridden and the meat so tasteless and unacceptable to the fussy food-conscious French that they decided to boycott all veal. This nearly bankrupted the veal producers, who were forced to rethink their farming policies, and all hormones are now forbidden by law. Once again, the French can enjoy their veal cutlets, proving that demands for quality can get results. If we were to adopt similar attitudes, perhaps butchers in Britain would once again become proud of their craft and the word 'butchery' would no longer carry such pejorative overtones.

— GAME —

Britain abounds in game, unlike France, where it is becoming extinct, due largely to the activities of little gumbooted men who shoot on sight anything which flies or jumps about, thus drastically reducing the wildlife population. Never trust a Frenchman with a gun!

Here, there is a staggering variety of game – wild duck, woodcock, teal, grouse, snipe, hare . . . . Yet despite this abundance, game farming has become big business nowadays. Farming spoils the quality; the delicate pink flesh of the red-leg partridge has, through cross-breeding, become strong and resistant to disease – but at the expense of taste and texture, since it ends up much like chicken. Beware of wild ducks built like chickens: they have done more running than flying and hence have long legs and strange bodies! Steer well clear of these Frankenstein monsters; they are anathema to any caring cook.

Hanging

Game usually has a distinctive, rather strong taste. Most must be hung for 1–3 days, so that the flesh relaxes, but,

generally speaking, if it is hung for too long, the flavour becomes coarse and over-assertive. The only game I hang for more than 3 days is venison, pheasant, partridge and wild boar. Grouse is so strong to start with that hanging would make it overwhelmingly pungent. Pheasant, on the other hand, which has white flesh and a rather faint taste, needs to hang for 8–10 days before being drawn and plucked, or it will taste like chicken. During hanging, the flesh develops a mature, distinctive flavour.

Choosing and cooking game

All game birds are delicious simply roasted. Deglaze the caramelized juices in the pan with a little water; you can hardly go wrong. Furred game, like venison or hare, always needs a sauce to match the original flavour. Never use farmed game; it is much cheaper, but not worth buying. (Venison is the only exception.) Do not be impressed by the mention of 'French red-leg' partridge; these birds no longer exist! They used to be a delicacy, but thanks to over-enthusiastic French hunters, they have mostly died out and the farmed substitute retains little more than the red leg. Far better to opt for its English counterpart, the grey-leg, which is much more the real thing.

Fresh game should have an attractive appearance and hardly any smell; any odour should not be unpleasant. The skin should be dry, not moist. Never buy birds which were shot in the breast, as the flesh will be inedible.

TRUSSING POULTRY AND GAME

Thread a trussing needle with fine string and push it through the lower part of the carcass, then through the lower part of one drumstick, through the breastbone and through the other drumstick. Tie firmly.

Re-thread the needle and push it right through the carcass above the wings. Turn the bird over and push the needle through one wing, thread it through the neck flap (it is important that this is properly secured) and push it through the other wing. Tie firmly.

— HERBS —

To me, herbs are a great source of wonder. They fire the imagination and inspire associations. Some have a deep, heavy scent; others are delicate and ephemeral, but all are somewhat mysterious.

Have you ever found yourself in a beautiful old walled herb garden? If so, you will know the strange and delightful experience of the all-pervading sensation of scents from the herbs of different character. As you reach curiously for a stem, the association with a season, an image of a face or a landscape appears and transports you to lands of childhood memories and all the associated colours and emotions. The scents are often stronger than the taste itself, sometimes pungent and spicy, almost overpowering; sometimes fragile, fresh and dainty.

Since time immemorial, herbs have been used medicinally, both for good and evil; those with a knowledge and understanding of their power were greatly revered or feared. While I am no expert in herbal medicine, herbs have always fascinated me. They can make or break a dish, round off the character or ruin the whole creation, or lift an otherwise uninteresting roast.

How to use herbs

Herbs fall into two categories: the stronger varieties (rosemary, thyme, sage, marjoram, bay) which diffuse flavour and can withstand long cooking without deterioration, and the more delicate varieties like chives, tarragon, basil and chervil, which must be added at the last moment, or they denaturate, especially when the sauce contains wine or any acid.

Certain herbs must be blanched before use to remove coarseness of flavour and texture. When I specify young tarragon in a recipe, for example, I mean the first shoots of the plant, added just as they are; older leaves need blanching or their strength will spoil the sauce. Use fresh herbs whenever possible; you will need less and get a more precise flavour. For where to buy fresh herbs, see page 274.

Dried herbs develop a more powerful and often bitter flavour and will ruin many a dish. Try to avoid them. Never over-use herbs; they can so easily become overpowering.

Do not shy away from experimenting with these challenging little plants. Try different combinations; the clever and imaginative use of herbs can give new, exciting character to a well-tried dish. My visit to Joel Rebuchon's famed establishment in Paris illustrates this well: out of the whole excellent meal one dish was outstanding – none other than the side salad, which was an innovative and delicious mixture of herbs which surprised my palate –almost disconcertingly simple, yet highly sophisticated. Although there was a generous grating of truffle adding its earthy scent, the originality came mostly from the unusual alliance of herbs.

— CHEESE —

Cheese should play an important part in a dinner party; whether you choose to serve it before or after the sweet being a matter of taste and tradition. My opinion is bound to be influenced by my early French education, and even after many attempts I still cannot enjoy cheese after the sweet. I find the transition from savoury to sweet and back to savoury again totally confusing and conflicting.

Whatever type you choose, try to buy craftsman produced, farmhouse cheeses, not synthetically-produced 'convenience' cheeses wrapped in plastic.

Until recently, apart from a few classic varieties which absorbed such creativity as there was, British cheese making concerned itself with colour more than taste. Today, however, we are witnessing a revival of hand-made farmhouse cheeses, with almost every region boasting its own particular style. We are almost spoilt for choice.

How to select

If pre-packed, only buy cheese labelled 'Farmhouse'.

Although the look will tell you a lot about the condition of the cheese, it is vitally important to taste before you buy, since too many cheeses have not matured properly.

It is always better to offer a small selection of cheeses (perhaps only two) – mature, and at their best – rather than a vast array of cheeses which have not reached their prime.

Storing

Do not buy too much cheese at a time. Generally, it does not benefit from being stored in the refrigerator for too long. If you must refrigerate cheeses, wrap them in clingfilm or foil and store at the bottom (the least cool part). If you have a cellar, this is the ideal place for storage.

Serving

Serve cheese at room temperature. Remove it from the refrigerator 1 hour before serving.

HOW TO PREPARE SALADS

Discard weathered leaves, then cut the base to free the leaves.

Wash the salads in cold water. Fragile salads such as lettuce should not be soaked in water for more than 5 minutes; leave firmer salads like curly endive, radicchio and batavia for up to 10 minutes. They will revive and take up some of their lost moisture.

Wash all salads in at least 2 changes of water. Use a large quantity of water at first so that all dirt and impurities fall to the bottom, then change the water and repeat with a smaller quantity.

To dry: Do not bruise the leaves. Remove all excess moisture, or it will interfere with the dressing.

To store: Wrap in a cloth and refrigerate until ready to use.

Add the dressing at the very last moment, as the vinegar will destroy the texture of the leaves.

HOW TO PREPARE TOMATOES

To peel: Using a sharp paring knife, cut off the stem and slit the skin. Plunge the tomatoes into plenty of boiling water for 2–5 seconds to loosen the skin (the precise time will vary according to ripeness). Remove with a slotted spoon, refresh in cold water for a few seconds and peel.

To segment or dice: Halve the peeled tomatoes, deseed with a teaspoon and remove the core (core and seeds can be kept for other uses). Cut into segments or dice.

HOW TO PREPARE MUSHROOMS

Cultivated button mushrooms: Cut off the base of the stalks and wash the mushrooms briefly in plenty of cold water. Pat dry with a tea towel.

Wild mushrooms: Cut off the base of the stalks and scrape the stems and cups very gently with a small paring knife. Only wash – briefly – if grit or dirt is plainly visible. If wild mushrooms are soaked in water and drowned their taste and texture will be ruined.

Morels are the exception; their conical, spongy caps hold a lot of earth and sand, so they must be washed in 2 or 3 changes of water.

Small insects and tiny worms often nest in these tasty fungi, especially the larger ones, so check carefully and discard any affected stalks.

Halve or quarter larger mushrooms so that they cook evenly.

PREPARING AND COOKING GLOBE ARTICHOKE HEARTS

Makes 8
Difficulty: 🎩
Total recipe time: 40 minutes

––––––– INGREDIENTS –––––––
1 onion, finely chopped

8 globe artichokes

2 lemons

2 teaspoons caster sugar

salt

8 white peppercorns, crushed

Snap off the artichoke stalks With a sharp paring knife, starting from the base, trim off the leaves until you are left with only a neatly-shaped heart. Rub the base with the cut side of a lemon.
Put the hearts into a pan with 1 L/ 1¾ pt water, the juice of the 2 lemons, chopped onion, sugar, salt and crushed peppercorns. Bring to the boil, then simmer, uncovered, for 15–20 minutes.
Leave to cool in the cooking liquid then remove the chokes with a teaspoon.

Storing
Do not expose the artichoke hearts to the air for too long, as they will discolour.
They can be kept in their cooking liquid in the fridge for 1–2 days; after this time, the acidity of the lemon juice will penetrate the flesh and damage the taste and texture.

CHLOROPHYLL
Vegetable extract

Special equipment: blender, fine conical sieve, muslin cloth

Chlorophyll of red peppers
(makes 3 tablespoons)
1 medium red pepper

500 ml/18 fl oz water

Remove stalk, halve, deseed and purée the pepper with the water until velvety smooth. Strain through a fine conical sieve, then through a muslin cloth into a small saucepan and gently bring to the boil. The rising temperature will coagulate the chlorophyll and the gentle boil will carry it to the surface where it can be scooped off with a tablespoon. You will obtain 3 tablespoons of pleasantly flavoured chlorophyll with a mild taste of red peppers.

Chlorophyll of spinach
(makes 2 tablespoons)
250 g/9 oz spinach

500 ml/18 fl oz water

Snap off the spinach stalks and wash the leaves in plenty of cold water. Liquidize with the water until very smooth and all the fibres have been broken down. Proceed as for chlorophyll of red peppers.

Storing
Chlorophyll will keep for 1–2 days in a covered container in the fridge or for 1–2 weeks in the freezer.

— STOCKS —

General rules for all stocks
Vegetables: Dice or chop them finely so that they release their flavour more quickly.
The wine must be boiled to remove the alcohol, then reduced to remove some of its acidity.
You must use *cold water* so that when the stock is brought back to the boil the heat will solidify all the impurities. These are carried to the surface during simmering and can be skimmed off.
The stock must be simmered, not cooked at full boil, or the impurities would be recycled and turn the stock cloudy again.
No salt is added to basic stock recipes since the meats already contain some and a stock is often reduced and used to enrich a sauce. Add salt then if necessary.

JUS DE VEAU/GLACE DE VEAU
Veal stock and glace

This stock is made from veal, poultry, vegetables, herbs and spices, slowly simmered so that the flavours mingle. This is a two stage process: first a lengthy simmering to fuse the flavours. This produces a light stock which is then reduced by boiling, to concentrate the taste and texture. It should have the consistency of a light sauce.

Makes 500 ml/18 fl oz
Difficulty: 🎩 🎩
Total recipe time: 40 minutes preparation, plus 2½ hours simmering and 40 minutes reducing

––––––– INGREDIENTS –––––––
1½ kg/3½ lb shin of veal, boned

1 kg/2¼ lb turkey legs or boiling fowl

Mirepoix

500 g/1lb 2 oz onions, roughly chopped

4 celery stalks, washed and cut into 2 cm/1 in lengths

200 g/7 oz carrots, washed, peeled and cut into 2 cm/1 in cubes

250 g/9 oz large field or button mushrooms, washed and chopped

200 ml/7 fl oz non-scented oil

350 g/12 oz Fondue de tomates (see Beurre de langoustines, page 25)

2 sprigs of thyme

¼ bayleaf

10 black peppercorns, crushed

small bunch of parsley, washed and finely chopped

1 sprig of chervil, washed and finely chopped

1 sprig of tarragon

300 ml/½ pt dry white wine

Planning ahead
The *fondue de tomates* must be made in advance.

1. Preparing the meats (10 minutes)
Shin of veal: Chop into four pieces.
Turkey legs: Cut at the joints to divide the drumsticks and thighs. (If using a boiling fowl, chop into 6 pieces.)

2. Searing the meats (15 minutes)
Place in a large roasting pan over high heat and sear in 100 ml/3½ fl oz oil until light golden brown, or brown in a hot oven for 40 minutes. Remove the meats, skim off most of the fat and pour in the wine. Bring to the boil and reduce by half. Scrape the bottom of the pan with a wooden spoon to incorporate the caramelized juices.

3. Searing the vegetables
(10 minutes)
Onions, celery and carrots: In a large thick-bottomed saucepan, sear in 90 ml/3 fl oz oil until lightly coloured. *Mushrooms*: In a small frying pan, heat 1 tablespoon oil until hot and sear the mushrooms until lightly coloured. Add them to the other vegetables.

4. Simmering and reducing the stock (2½-3 hours)
Rest the meats on the bed of vegetables, pour in the reduced wine from the roasting pan, add the *fondue de tomates* and 4 L/7 pt cold water. Bring to a brisk boil and skim. Throw in the thyme, bayleaf and crushed peppercorns and simmer for 2½-3 hours, skimming occasionally. Add the chopped chervil and tarragon towards the end.

5. Straining and reducing the stock (30 minutes)
Lift out the meats and reserve for another use (see Chef's notes). Using a ladle, force the vegetables and stock through a fine conical sieve to extract all the juices. Strain the liquid through a muslin cloth into a medium saucepan and reduce to 500 ml/18 fl oz flavourful veal stock.

Storing
The stock can be kept in a covered container for up to 3 weeks in the freezer, or for 1 week in the fridge.
When it cools the stock will jellify: refrigerate, then scrape off the fat which settles on the surface.

———— VARIATIONS ————
You can enrich this stock with 2 kg/4½ lb chopped veal bones roasted in the oven with the meats until golden brown. You will need 6 L/11 pt water.
Veal glace or essence is the quintessence of veal stock – deep, glazed and rich. It is highly flavoured, so use it very sparingly. To make *glace,* reduce the stock to 150 ml/5 fl oz by boiling for 30 minutes.
Add a few powdered or dried ceps for extra flavour.
To make these precious juices go further, thicken them with 1 tablespoon arrowroot or cornflour mixed with 100 ml/3½ fl oz water. Whisk into the stock and bring to the boil.

Chef's notes
Do not use veal stock in the hope of improving a characterless sauce. It should have a pleasant, *neutral* taste, and is generally used to improve the texture of a sauce without altering its flavour.
Modern sauces do not contain thickeners like flour or cornflour; instead, the juices from cooked meats are simply reduced to obtain an essence. However, this essence can sometimes become too concentrated and almost bitter and may completely overpower the flavours of the dish it accompanies.
A small quantity of veal stock added to the reduced juices will not dilute the essential flavour of a dish and will transform a rather too light and runny juice into a handsome, tasty, but still light-textured sauce.
Meat: I do not use calves' feet, as they make the reduced stock too gelatinous.
This is an expensive stock, but the cooked meat can be used for shepherd's pies, stuffed tomatoes or curries.
Vegetables: I use a large quantity of vegetables in the stock to 'round up' the flavours of the meats and contribute to the harmonious build-up of flavours.
Tomatoes: If you cannot find good ripe tomatoes, use Italian tinned Roma tomatoes.
Mushrooms: Field mushrooms give a better colour and taste than button mushrooms. Browning improves the flavour and colour of the stock.
Searing the meats: This is a vital stage. If the meats are not sufficiently browned, they will produce a rather pale, flavourless stock. Be careful, however, not to over-brown them or the stock will be bitter, especially

when reduced. Check from time to time that they do not catch or burn while searing.
Tarragon and chervil are added towards the end of cooking to preserve their delicate flavours.

FUMET DE POISSONS
Light fish stock

This light stock can be used for a variety of fish dishes where the flavour of the sauce needs to be heightened or intensified.
It can be stored to use as required, but try to make the stock from the bones of the fish you are using in the recipe. This will give the finished dish a unified flavour.

Makes 1 L/1¾ pt
Difficulty: 🍳
Total recipe time: 50 minutes

INGREDIENTS

500 g/1 lb 2 oz fish bones and heads

1 onion, finely diced

1 leek, washed and finely diced

1 carrot, peeled and finely diced

¼ celery stalk, finely diced

100 g/3½ oz firm white button mushrooms, washed and finely chopped

1 tablespoon unsalted butter

freshly ground white pepper

200 ml/7 fl oz dry white wine

a small bunch of parsley, wrapped in muslin

1 L/1¾ pt cold water

1. Preparing the fish bones and heads (20 minutes)
Cut off the gills with scissors. Roughly chop the bones and soak in cold running water for 2–3 minutes. Drain and reserve.

2. Cooking the stock (20 minutes)
Put all the prepared vegetables in a large pan with the butter, season with 8 turns of pepper and sweat for 1–2 minutes without colouring. Add the fish bones and heads and sweat for 1 further minute. Pour in the wine, boil for a few seconds to remove the alcohol, then add 1 L/1¾ pt cold water and the parsley. Boil for not more than 1–2 minutes and skim. Simmer gently for about 15 minutes, then strain the stock through a fine conical sieve into a large bowl, pressing the bones lightly with a ladle. Leave to cool before storing.

Storing
The stock will keep in a covered container for 2–3 days in the fridge, or for several weeks in the freezer.

VARIATIONS

For an essence or *glace de poissons*, reduce the strained stock to about 200 ml/7 fl oz. This can be used to strengthen any sauce which lacks character.

Chef's note
When you boil the wine, the stock will turn cloudy for a moment. This is perfectly normal; it will clear when you add the cold water.
The best fish stock is obtained from sole bones.

FUMET DE SOLE AU GEWÜRZTRAMINER
Fumet of sole with Gewürztraminer

This rich fish stock is highly concentrated and wonderfully aromatic thanks to the spicy taste of the Gewürztraminer.

Makes 500 ml/18 fl oz
Difficulty: 🍳
Total recipe time: 1 hour 10 minutes

INGREDIENTS

heads and bones of 4 sole

10 shallots, finely chopped

100 g/3½ oz firm white button mushrooms, finely chopped

1 tablespoon unsalted butter

400 ml/14 fl oz Gewürztraminer

400 ml/14 fl oz water or Light fish stock (left)

freshly ground white pepper

1. Preparing the fish bones (15 minutes)
Roughly chop the heads and bones and soak in cold running water for 2–3 minutes. Drain.

2. Cooking the stock (55 minutes)
In a large saucepan, sweat the chopped shallots in 1 tablespoon butter for 2–3 minutes without colouring. Add the mushrooms and the fish bones and heads and sweat for a further minute. Pour in the Gewürztraminer, bring to the boil, then add the 400 ml/14 fl oz cold water, skim and season with 4 turns of pepper. Simmer gently for 30 minutes.
Pass through a fine conical sieve, using a ladle to force through as much stock as possible.

Storing
Cool, then store in a covered container. The stock can be kept in the

fridge for 2–3 days, or for up to 2 weeks in the freezer.

By reducing this stock by two-thirds, you will obtain a concentrated essence or *glace de poisson*.
The equivalent weight of bones from turbot, brill or lemon sole can be used instead of sole.

Chef's note

Gewürztraminer is rich, fruity and spicy, but low in acidity, so it is not necessary to reduce it. The long cooking time will remove the alcohol.

FOND BLANC DE VOLAILLE

Light chicken stock

This subtle stock is mainly used to enrich and enhance the flavours of many dishes.

Makes 1 L/1¾ pt stock
Difficulty: 👨‍🍳
Total recipe time: 1 hour 20 minutes

— INGREDIENTS —
2 kg/4½ lb chicken wings or carcasses, or turkey legs or a plump boiling fowl

1 tablespoon unsalted butter

white of 1 small leek, finely chopped

1 small onion, finely chopped

1 small celery stalk, finely chopped

100 g/3½ oz button mushrooms, finely sliced

1 garlic clove, crushed

1 sprig of parsley

1 sprig of thyme

½ fresh bayleaf

10 white peppercorns, crushed

200 ml/7 fl oz dry white wine (optional)

1. The vegetables (15 minutes)
Mix together all the prepared vegetables.
Wash the parsley, shake dry and tie in a muslin cloth with the thyme and ½ bayleaf.

2. Cooking (1 hour)
In a large saucepan, sweat the chicken wings in 1 tablespoon butter for 5 minutes without colouring. Add the chopped vegetables and crushed peppercorns and sweat for a further 5 minutes. Pour in the wine, if using, and reduce by one-third. Cover with 150 ml/5 fl oz cold water, bring back to the boil, skim, throw in the parcel of herbs and simmer for 1 hour, skimming from time to time.
Strain through a fine sieve and leave to cool.

Storing
Cool and store in a covered container in the fridge for 3 or 4 days, or for up to 2 months in the freezer.

Chicken demi-glace: By reducing the stock by half, to 500 ml/18 fl oz, you will obtain an even more flavourful stock.
Chicken essence or glace: By reducing the stock further, to 200 ml/7 fl oz, you will obtain an essence of chicken. This must be used very sparingly since it is extremely concentrated; it will greatly improve a sauce which lacks character.

JUS BRUN DE VOLAILLE

Brown chicken stock

This golden brown stock can be used as an easy alternative to veal *demi-glace* (see page 18).

Makes 300 ml/½ pt (which can be reduced to 100 ml/3½ fl oz *glace*)
Difficulty: 👨‍🍳
Total recipe time: 1 hour 10 minutes

— INGREDIENTS —
1.5 kg/3–3½ lb chicken wings or carcasses

100 ml/3½ fl oz non-scented oil

6 black peppercorns, crushed

1 medium onion, finely chopped

1 garlic clove, crushed

1 sprig of thyme

½ bayleaf

4 medium tomatoes, plus 1 teaspoon non-scented oil

900 ml/1½ pt water

Planning ahead
This stock can be made in advance and kept in the fridge for 1 week or in the freezer for 3 weeks.

1. Preparing the vegetables and spices (5 minutes)
Preheat the oven to 230°C/450°F/gas 8.
Place the peppercorns, onion and garlic in a small bowl with the bayleaf and thyme. Wash the tomatoes, remove the stems, halve, oil lightly and put in a small ovenproof sauté pan.

2. Cooking the stock
(1 hour 5 minutes)
In a large roasting pan, heat 100 ml/3½ fl oz oil until smoking, then brown the chicken wings for 8–10 minutes, stirring occasionally with a wooden spoon.

Add the chopped onion mixture and cook for another 5 minutes, until lightly coloured. Cook in the pre-heated oven for 20 minutes, until the chicken wings and vegetables turn a rich brown.

Meanwhile, cook the tomatoes in the oven for 8–10 minutes until brown, then add them to the chicken wings.

Deglaze the pan with 200 ml/7 fl oz cold water, scraping up all the caramelized juices from the bottom of the pan. Bring to the boil, then return to the oven for 20 minutes.

Strain the juices into a small saucepan, bring to the boil, skim and reduce to about 500 ml/18 fl oz tasty clear brown stock. Allow to cool, then refrigerate. Remove any fat which has settled on the surface, then seal with clingfilm and store until needed.

Demi-glace de volaille: Reduce the juices by half.

Glace de volaille: Reduce the juices to 100 ml/3½ fl oz to obtain a rich and concentrated essence.

VARIATIONS

Although this seems a great deal of effort for so small a quantity of juices, such are the secrets of cuisine! You can, however, increase the yield by binding the juices with 2 level teaspoons arrowroot, diluted with 2 tablespoons cold water.

Chef's notes

See Chef's note on *veal glace or essence* page 19.

I prefer to keep this stock neutral tasting so that it will not interfere with the flavour of the sauce to which it is added, but if you wish you can add a touch of sharpness by deglazing with a glass of white wine or dry Madeira. The degree of browning will determine the taste and quality of the stock. If it does not have sufficient colour, add a teaspoon of soy sauce.

FUMET DE LEGUMES
Vegetable stock

This light vegetable stock is the base for many of my sauces. It has a wonderfully concentrated aroma of the garden and is very simple to make; prepare a large quantity and freeze it until needed.

Makes about 600 ml/1 pt
Difficulty: 🍳
Total recipe time: 20 minutes

INGREDIENTS

1 onion, finely chopped

1 large courgette, finely sliced

1 small leek, washed, trimmed and finely chopped

½ fennel bulb, finely sliced (optional)

1 garlic clove, finely chopped

1 tablespoon unsalted butter

2 sprigs of tarragon, chopped

a tiny bunch of chervil, chopped

freshly ground white pepper

In a medium saucepan, sweat all the vegetables in the butter for 2 minutes, without colouring. Cover with 600 ml/1 pt cold water, bring to the boil and simmer for 5 minutes.

Add the chopped herbs and simmer for a further 5 minutes. Season with 6 turns of pepper, but no salt.

Using the back of a ladle, force through a fine conical sieve into a small bowl or plastic container for freezing.

Chef's notes

Do not let the total cooking time exceed 15 minutes in order to preserve the freshness of flavour.

Vary the herbs according to the dish you are cooking; add them at the last moment to preserve their fragrance and flavour.

NAGE DE LEGUMES, HERBES ET CONDIMENTS
A clear, scented stock made from vegetables, herbs and spices

Makes 500 ml/18 fl oz
Difficulty: 🍳
Total recipe time: 30 minutes, plus 5–6 hours infusion

INGREDIENTS

½ onion, finely chopped

white of 1 small leek, finely chopped

1 carrot, peeled and finely chopped

¼ celery stalk, finely chopped

peelings of 1 fennel bulb, finely chopped or some fennel seeds

2 garlic cloves, finely chopped

4 pink peppercorns

1 star anise

zest of 1 lemon

zest of 1 orange

1 teaspoon coriander leaves, chopped or 6–8 coriander seeds

8 white peppercorns, crushed

a sprig of thyme

a small bunch of tarragon, chopped

a small bunch of chervil, chopped

500 ml/18 fl oz cold water

100 ml/3½ fl oz dry white wine

1. Cooking (15 minutes)
Put all the vegetables, spices and thyme into a large saucepan and pour in 500 ml/18 fl oz cold water. Bring to the boil and skim, then simmer for about 10 minutes. Add the chopped tarragon, chervil and coriander, pour in the wine and simmer for a further 2–3 minutes. The gentle acidity of the wine will 'lift' the stock.

2. Infusing (5–6 hours)

Take the pan off the heat and leave uncovered for 5–6 hours so that the flavours infuse.

Strain the stock through a fine conical sieve, pressing with a ladle, into a storage container and seal.

Storing

The stock will keep in a covered container for 2 or 3 days in the fridge or several weeks in the freezer.

Chef's note

This stock can be used as the basis for a sauce for steamed fish. Reduce 500 ml/18 fl oz stock by half. Add 2 tablespoons cream, then whisk in 40 g/1½ oz cold diced butter. Season and add lemon juice and your favourite herbs.

CLARIFICATION

This is necessary to produce the clearest possible stock for a consommé or jelly. Finely chopped raw fish or meat (depending on the main ingredient in the recipe) is mixed with egg white, vegetables, herbs and spices and added to the stock.

For clarifying 1 L/1¾ pt stock
Special equipment: whisk, fine sieve, muslin cloth

--- INGREDIENTS ---

1 L/1¾ pt stock or bouillon

100 g/3½ oz raw fish or lean meat, very finely chopped

herbs (according to taste and recipe), for flavouring

½ leek, washed and finely chopped

¼ celery stalk, finely chopped

1 tomato, finely chopped

1 carrot, peeled and finely chopped

3 egg whites

Lightly break the egg whites with 2 or 3 movements of the whisk. Add the chopped meat or fish, herbs and vegetables and mix thoroughly.

Whisk in all the clarifying elements and bring to the boil, stirring continuously.

Simmer for 30 minutes. Use a ladle to make a hole in the crust which forms on the surface at the point where the bubbling is strongest. Take the pan off the heat and leave to rest for a few minutes.

Pour the clear stock through a fine sieve lined with a damp muslin cloth. Leave to cool, cover and refrigerate.

Chef's notes

While the stock is simmering, the proteins in the meat, fish and egg white will coagulate and trap all the impurities present in the stock. The gentle simmering carries the solidified impurities to the surface, forming a light crust and leaving a completely clear stock. The hole in the crust prevents a build-up of heat and the stock will not boil over.

The addition of meat or fish compensates for the loss of flavour caused by clarifying.

I only clarify stocks as a last resort. I prefer to produce a very clear *bouillon* or jelly through careful, gentle simmering. (See also *Gelée de saumon*, page 65 and *Bouillon de poule*, page 220.)

GELEE DE VIANDE AU MADERE
Madeira jelly

Makes 1 L/1¾ pt
Difficulty: ♟
Total recipe time: 3 hours 40 minutes

--- INGREDIENTS ---

500 g/1 lb 2 oz shin of beef, cut into 100 g/3½ oz pieces

300 g/11 oz shin of veal, cut into 3 pieces

1 small boiling fowl, cut into 8 pieces, or 1 kg/2¼ lb chicken wings

1 calf's foot or 2 pig's trotters, quartered

150 g/5 oz carrot, peeled and diced

1 medium onion, diced

50 g/2 oz celery, diced

150 g/5 oz leek, washed and diced

150 g/5 oz tomatoes, peeled and diced

2 garlic cloves, lightly crushed

bouquet garni, made with ¼ bayleaf, 2 large sprigs of parsley and 1 sprig of thyme tied together

6 crushed black peppercorns

200 ml/7 fl oz dry Madeira

2 tablespoons soy sauce

2.5 L/4 pt cold water

1. Cooking and simmering the stock (3½ hours)

Combine all the ingredients in a large stockpot. Boil for about 5 minutes, skimming constantly, then cook at a gentle simmer for about 3 hours, skimming from time to time, until the stock is perfectly clear; it will not need clarifying.

2. Straining the stock (5 minutes, plus cooling and refrigerating)

Strain through a fine sieve lined with a damp muslin cloth into a large saucepan and allow to cool until just warm. Refrigerate for 3–4 hours, then skim off any fat which has settled on the surface.

--- VARIATIONS ---

A game jelly can be made by using game trimmings instead of meat. Use all chicken for a chicken jelly.

You can use up to 300 ml/½ pt Madeira for a stronger flavour.

A Sauternes jelly can be made by adding 100 ml/3½ fl oz Sauternes during the last 5 minutes of simmering instead of the Madeira.

Chef's notes

Use fresh, unhung meats. The large quantity of meats may seem expensive but this will produce a delectable jelly, far removed from the common aspic. The meats can be reused in curries, meatloaves or stuffed tomatoes, for example.

After the initial boiling, the stock must not boil again. Simmer it slowly or it will become cloudy and need clarifying.

Soy sauce is added for colour; if you want a pale jelly, omit it. For a darker jelly, sear the meats beforehand in a little oil or fat.

This jelly will keep, covered, for up to 1 week in the fridge. It is not necessary to add gelatine to set it, since the meat and calf's foot will release their own and the jelly will set naturally when cold.

BUTTERS

BEURRE BLANC
Butter sauce

Almost legendary, this classic star sauce still shines alongside lighter, modern sauces, despite its richness. Simple and delicious, it makes a wonderful accompaniment to any poached or grilled fish.

Serves 4
Difficulty: 🍳
Total recipe time: 15 minutes

INGREDIENTS

60 g/2 oz shallots, peeled and finely chopped

2 tablespoons white wine vinegar

3 tablespoons dry white wine

200 g/7 oz unsalted butter, chilled and diced

lemon juice

salt and freshly ground white pepper

In a small heavy-bottomed saucepan, combine the chopped shallots, vinegar and wine and boil until you have about 1 tablespoon syrupy liquid. If the liquid is not sufficiently reduced, the sauce will be too sharp. Add 2 tablespoons cold water (this extra liquid will help the emulsion) then, over a gentle heat, whisk in the cold diced butter, a little at a time until completely amalgamated. The finished sauce will be creamy and homogenous and a delicate lemon yellow. Season with a tiny amount of salt and pepper and enliven with a squeeze of lemon.

VARIATIONS

This mother sauce can produce many offspring; add a *julienne* of ginger, blanched for 15 minutes, or lemon or orange zest blanched for 3–4 minutes, or scent the sauce with shredded coriander, ginger, tarragon or other herbs.

Chef's notes

Beurre blanc is an emulsified sauce. The emulsion is made possible by the water in the butter, which helps the binding, then by fast whisking and finally the application of heat which stabilizes the emulsion.

Shallots have a tough fibrous second layer of skin – remove it, but leave the finely chopped shallots in the sauce for a pleasant, rustic flavour and texture.

Butter: The success of the sauce depends greatly on the quality of the butter. Use the best unsalted butter you can find.

If the butter is too soft, it will melt too quickly and not emulsify. Ideally, the temperature of the sauce should be 65°C/150°F when incorporating the butter. Test with your finger from time to time – the heat should be bearable. If the sauce is too cold, the butter will cream and separate. Try to maintain an even temperature.

Keeping the sauce: As there are no emulsifiers to stabilize the sauce completely, it will remain rather delicate and should be kept for no more than 1 hour in a warm bain-marie at 50°–60°C/122°–150°F. Whisk from time to time to maintain the emulsion.

Whisking: Constant whisking is extremely important to produce a smooth emulsion, especially at the beginning.

Problems

Too sharp: Add a little more butter or 1 tablespoon cream.

Separation: In a clean saucepan, bring to the boil 2 tablespoons whipping cream, then slowly whisk in the separated *beurre blanc*.

BEURRE NOISETTE
'Hazelnut' butter

Beurre noisette is butter which has been heated to a sufficiently high temperature for the solids contained in the butterfat to start cooking. This turns the butter a rich golden colour and gives it a distinct taste of hazelnuts.

Be warned, though; the stage beyond *beurre noisette* is *beurre noir*, which is black, rather nasty and pretty indigestible.

BEURRE DE LANGOUSTINES
Shellfish butter

This delicious butter is used to enrich shellfish sauces (eg: *Raviolis de homard*, page 124).

Makes about 450 g/1 lb
Difficulty: 🍳
Total recipe time: 35 minutes
Special equipment: food processor, fine conical sieve, muslin cloth

--- INGREDIENTS ---

450 g/1 lb langoustine or freshwater crayfish shells

50 ml/2 fl oz olive oil

100 ml/3½ fl oz Cognac

100 ml/3½ fl oz dry white wine

450 g/1 lb unsalted butter

a small bunch of tarragon

1 L/1¾ pt water

Fondue de tomates

½ medium onion, finely chopped

450 g/1 lb ripe tomatoes, deseeded and finely chopped

1 tablespoon olive oil

1 tablespoon tomato purée (optional)

2 sprigs of thyme

2 garlic cloves, crushed

a pinch of sugar (optional)

1. Fondue de tomates
Preheat the oven to 200°C/400°F/gas 6.
Sweat the onion in olive oil for about 5 minutes without colouring. Add the tomatoes, tomato purée (if using), thyme and crushed garlic and the sugar, if necessary. Bring to a brisk boil and cook uncovered in the preheated oven for 20 minutes.

2. Preparing, searing and cooking the langoustine shells (25 minutes)
Split the heads in half lengthways, discarding the intestine and the stomach which you will see at the base of the head. Sear in hot olive oil, then crush the carcasses in a food processor for a few seconds or pound them with a rolling pin. Place in a saucepan, add the Cognac and wine, boil and reduce over a high heat for 2 minutes. Add the butter, *fondue de tomates* and tarragon and simmer for a further 15 minutes.

3. Straining and removing the butter (10 minutes)
Using a ladle, force through a fine conical sieve, then strain the liquid through a muslin cloth into a jar or stainless steel bowl. Refrigerate for several hours until the butter rises to the top and solidifies. Scoop out the butter, scraping off any residue which remains attached to the underside.
Cut the butter into pieces, wrap each piece individually in clingfilm and place in a covered container; it will keep in the fridge for up to 1 week, or for 3–4 weeks in the freezer.

Chef's note
The slow simmering of all the ingredients is vital so that flavours are exchanged between the butter and langoustines.

BEURRE DE TOMATES CRUES
Tomato butter

Serves 4
Difficulty: 🍳
Total recipe time: 10 minutes

--- INGREDIENTS ---

400 g/14 oz ripe tomatoes

60 g/2½ oz unsalted butter, chilled and diced

salt and freshly ground white pepper

1 teaspoon caster sugar (optional)

Wash and halve the tomatoes and squeeze out the seeds and juices of half of them.
Purée finely in a food processor then, using a ladle, force through a fine conical sieve into a small saucepan.
Warm gently over low heat, (the purée must not boil) then whisk in the cold diced butter. Taste and season with salt and pepper. Taste again. If the tomatoes are a little too acidic add a pinch of caster sugar.

--- VARIATIONS ---
For an accompaniment to grilled or roast fish, replace half the butter with 1 or 2 tablespoons olive oil.
Add fresh basil or coriander, or try a clove of garlic.

Chef's notes
The puréed tomatoes must not boil or they will lose their freshness and the pulp will solidify. If this happens, force again through a fine conical sieve.
The seeds and juice of half the tomatoes are kept to give the sauce extra liveliness.
This sauce should be served just warm, not hot.

SAVOURY — SAUCES —

In a sauce, a chef can best express his style of cooking. Just as a poet chooses words which rhyme and express a very precise feeling, so a chef must assemble harmonious scents, tastes and colours with freedom and precision, with knowledge and a sure touch. He will marry the sweetness of honey with the tartness of vinegar, fiery ginger with bittersweet pink grapefruit, the exotic with the rustic, the earth with the sea, to conjure up a light witty juice or a richly textured sauce with subtle undertones. Sauce-making is like alchemy; sweet-scented vegetables and aromatic herbs are reduced to a magical essence.

Never allow a sauce to overpower the dish it accompanies. A sauce is an ally, not an oppressor; let it be the catalyst which brings out all the essential qualities the dish has to offer.

General advice on sauce making

Mirepoix: Diced vegetables form part of the build-up of flavours. The size of the dice varies according to the cooking time of the sauce.

Mushrooms: Use dark, open mushrooms for brown sauces; they have a strong flavour and add colour. Use white button mushrooms for light or clear sauces.

Browning the meats, vegetables or bones: This most important stage adds colour and flavour to a brown sauce. If the ingredients are not sufficiently browned, the sauce will be too light in taste and colour, but if they are too brown, the sauce may be too strong or bitter (although the colour will be good). Practice makes perfect! Make sure that the fat is hot before browning the meats.

Vinegar must be reduced completely. It should give the sauce a gentle acidity; if insufficiently reduced, the sauce will be too acid and difficult to correct.

Wine: The era of *coq au vin* cooked in

Chambertin is gone, alas, but do use a decent quality wine for a wine sauce. A good wine will lend its characteristics to the sauce – so will a bad one.

Unless otherwise stated in the recipe, always reduce wine by boiling to remove first the alcohol, then some of the acidity. Sweet wines do not need reducing, since they contain little or no acidity; boil only briefly to remove the alcohol but keep the flavour intact.

Red wine sauces: Always use a full-bodied wine with plenty of flavour and a deep colour, like a Rhône or good table wine.

White wine sauces: Use a dry white wine unless otherwise stated and reduce as above.

Port: Ruby port has a more pronounced flavour and colour than tawny.

Madeira: Use a dry Madeira, as a medium or sweet wine will often spoil the sauce.

Herbs: Some are robust enough to withstand long simmering (eg: thyme, rosemary, bayleaf) and can be added at the outset. More delicate herbs quickly denaturate, so add them at the end, a little at a time, tasting frequently so that they do not overpower the sauce.

Spices: Add sparingly at the beginning and adjust towards the end.

Moistening with stock or water: It is not always necessary to add stock if the meat has enough flavour of its own; I often use water, which does not interfere with the taste of the sauce.

The liquid must be added cold. As it heats, the impurities in the meat and bones rise to the surface and can be skimmed off. At this stage, the stock looks cloudy, but it will clarify through long simmering.

Brown sauces: A *demi-glace* is often added to give substance to a sauce, but it will not improve the flavour of an intrinsically bad sauce.

Salt: Since thickening agents are not much used nowadays, modern stocks often acquire their body through simmering and reduction. Their flavour is

often too concentrated and can overpower the dish, (meat and fish have a high sodium content) so add salt *after* the stock has been reduced if necessary.

Skimming: During the long simmering process, fats and impurities will rise to the surface of the stock, so skim frequently.

To correct a sauce: Sauces should be seasoned sparingly, first with salt, then pepper and finally with spices. It is more difficult to correct an over-seasoned sauce than one which is under-seasoned.

Too sharp: Add a dash of cream, whisk in a tiny quantity of butter or add a pinch of sugar, a touch of redcurrant jelly or honey.

Lacking acidity: Enliven with a tiny drop of vinegar, wine or a dash of orange or lemon juice.

SAUCE MAYONNAISE

Mayonnaise is an emulsified sauce which illustrates the magical power of egg yolks. Smooth and delicious, this classic sauce is very simple to make.

Serves 4
Difficulty: 🎩
Total recipe time: 10 minutes

——— INGREDIENTS ———
2 egg yolks
....
1 teaspoon Dijon mustard
....
250 ml/9 fl oz best quality non-scented oil
....
1 teaspoon white wine vinegar
....
2 teaspoons lemon juice
....
salt and freshly ground white pepper
....

In a large mixing bowl whisk together the egg yolks, mustard, 2 pinches of salt and 3 turns of pepper. Start adding the oil in a steady trickle, whisking energetically until the oil is absorbed and the mixture turns pale yellow and thickens (usually after adding 150 ml/ 5 fl oz oil). Loosen the consistency with 1 teaspoon wine vinegar and 2 teaspoons lemon juice, then whisk in the remaining oil. Taste and correct the seasoning if necessary.

Storing
In a covered container, mayonnaise will keep for 2 to 3 days in the lower part of the fridge.
If you are not going to use the mayonnaise immediately, make it with grapeseed oil, which prevents it from separating in the fridge.

VARIATIONS
Mayonnaise is a mother sauce from which others can be made – by adding tomato *coulis,* paprika, curry powder or saffron etc.
To make a light *rouille,* replace the non-scented oil with olive oil and add a pinch each of saffron and cayenne pepper, and 2 garlic cloves, crushed and puréed.

Chef's notes
All ingredients used must be at room temperature – especially the oil. If too cold, it will be difficult to incorporate.
Incorporating the oil: At first this must be done gradually, and with constant, vigorous whisking. The emulsion is created at this stage and the emulsifying agents within the egg yolk cannot cope with too much oil at a time. This is the most important stage of mayonnaise making. Once the sauce is emulsified it will be stable. The rest of the oil can be added in greater quantities and with less vigorous whisking.
If the mayonnaise separates, put 1 teaspoon Dijon mustard (which contains an emulsifier) in another bowl and gradually incorporate the mayonnaise, whisking vigorously.

SABAYON BASE FOR SAVOURY SAUCES

A *sabayon* is the lightest base used for binding sauces and creams and is the foundation for many of the sauces you will find in this book (eg: *Hollandaise,* page 28, *Huitres à la mangue,* page 228). Here is another example of egg yolk, acting this time as the emulsifier.

Serves 4–6
Difficulty: 👨‍🍳👨‍🍳
Total recipe time: 15 minutes

INGREDIENTS
3 very fresh egg yolks

4 tablespoons cold water

To achieve the lightest and best result, you must work in 2 stages:
1. Emulsifying the egg by whisking (this is easier in an electric mixer).
2. Coagulating by heat.

Stage 1 (5 minutes)
Combine the egg yolks and water, whisking continuously. The mixture will expand to 5 or 6 times its original volume and become light and foamy, but it needs heat to stabilize it.

Stage 2 (10 minutes)
The foam is composed of millions of little air bubbles wrapped in a film of egg yolk. While the yolk remains uncooked, the air will escape through its fragile walls, so you must now partially cook the protein wall (the yolk) to strengthen it. Do not use direct heat for this process, or you may end up with a nasty *sabayon* flecked with bits of solid egg yolk.
Set the mixing bowl in a hot bain-marie (with the water at about 80°C/ 175°F) so that the heat permeates the *sabayon* very gradually. Continue whisking vigorously for about 5 minutes at a constant temperature.

The mixture will now be firmer and have the consistency of lightly whipped cream.

When is it ready?
You may be tempted to remove the *sabayon* from the heat as soon as it begins to thicken, but this may be too soon and the mixture will quickly deflate and separate. If, however, you allow the temperature to rise above 80°C/175°F, the *sabayon* will be ruined and you will end up with scrambled egg; the first warning sign is the appearance of flecks of darker yellow solid yolk. Test the temperature by dipping your finger into the *sabayon*; the heat should be bearable.
I realize that all this sounds rather discouraging, but only practice will give you the confidence to recognize and 'feel' the precise moment at which the *sabayon* is ready – so be bold and start practising now!
An electric hand whisk is a good investment.

Keeping the sabayon
Keep warm in a bain-marie. If you are not using the *sabayon* immediately, cool it over ice, still whisking to minimize the loss of lightness. Since it is now fairly stable, the *sabayon* will keep for an hour or so before being used in your sauce.

SAUCE HOLLANDAISE
A lighter version of a classic hollandaise sauce

Serves 4
Difficulty: 🍳
Total recipe time: 20 minutes

INGREDIENTS

3 egg yolks

4 tablespoons water

150 g/5 oz clarified butter, warmed (see Chef's notes)

a pinch of salt

a pinch of cayenne pepper

juice of ¼ lemon

1. The sabayon base (10 minutes)
With the ingredients at room temperature, place the egg yolks in a *sabayon* bowl, add 4 tablespoons cold water and whisk vigorously until you obtain a beautifully light, bulky foam about 4 or 5 times its original volume. (Use an electric mixer with a whisk, which will make the beating much easier.) Place the bowl over a bain-marie (no hotter than 80°C/175°F) and continue whisking until the egg yolk is coagulated by the heat and the foam becomes stable.

2. Incorporate the clarified butter and seasoning (7 minutes)
Pour the warmed clarified butter into the *sabayon* in a steady trickle, whisking constantly. Taste, season with a tiny pinch of salt then a pinch of cayenne pepper and finally add most of the lemon juice. Taste again and add the remaining lemon juice if necessary.

VARIATIONS
You can use hollandaise as the basis for many sauces, eg:
Sauce mousseline: Add 100 ml/3½ fl oz whipped cream.
Curry sabayon (see *Huitres à la mangue*, page 228).

Chef's notes
You must use only the very best quality unsalted butter.
The clarified butter should not be hot, just warm. If too hot, it will raise the temperature of the *sabayon* too high and may cook the egg yolk.
This sauce can be prepared ½ hour before use and kept in a warm bain-marie (about 50°C/122°F). Cover with buttered greaseproof paper to prevent a skin from forming.

VINAIGRETTES

Much of the success of a salad lies in the harmony of its dressing, which should be neither too oily nor too thin, not overpowering nor too bland. These popular and contrasting vinaigrettes illustrate the range of flavours you can use.
Always add the vinaigrette to the salad at the last moment; the acid in the vinegar quickly attacks the colour and texture of the more fragile leaves.
All ingredients should be at room temperature. The quantities given here are for immediate use, but larger quantities can be made and stored in sealed bottles or jars at room temperature. Shake well before use.
All the vinaigrettes are quick and easy to make; they will serve 4–6 people.

VINAIGRETTE A L'HUILE D'OLIVE
Olive oil vinaigrette

. . . with all the evocative scents and flavours of sunny Provence.

INGREDIENTS

3 tablespoons extra virgin olive oil (see page 12)

1 tablespoon non-scented oil

1 tablespoon white wine vinegar

large pinch of salt

4 turns freshly ground white pepper

Mix all the ingredients together.

VARIATIONS
If you really adore olive oil, use 4 tablespoons and omit the non-scented oil.
Add a few shredded basil leaves.

VINAIGRETTE A L'HUILE D'ARACHIDE
A non-scented vinaigrette

If you do not enjoy scented oil, this vinaigrette is ideal and will not interfere with the flavours of the salad.

INGREDIENTS

3½ tablespoons non-scented oil

1 tablespoon white wine vinegar

a large pinch of salt

4 turns freshly ground white pepper

Mix all the ingredients together.

VARIATIONS
A few freshly chopped leaves of tarragon or chervil and a finely chopped shallot will give this vinaigrette a little more depth.

VINAIGRETTE A L'HUILE DE NOISETTE
Hazelnut oil vinaigrette

The most scented of all vinaigrettes.

INGREDIENTS
½ tablespoon hazelnut oil (see page 12)

3 tablespoons non-scented oil

1 tablespoon white wine vinegar

a large pinch of salt

4 turns freshly ground white pepper

Mix all the ingredients together.

Chef's note
Do not be tempted to increase the quantity of hazelnut oil; the vinaigrette will be too highly scented and overpower the salad.

VINAIGRETTE AU COULIS DE TOMATES
Tomato vinaigrette

The success of a tomato *coulis* depends on the ripeness of the tomatoes. Use fat, fleshy Marmande, olive-shaped Roma or sweet cherry tomatoes.

INGREDIENTS
200 g/7 oz ripe tomatoes

a large pinch of salt

a large pinch of caster sugar

a dash of white wine vinegar

2 tablespoons extra virgin olive oil (see page 12)

freshly ground white pepper

basil or coriander leaves, finely shredded (optional)

Halve the tomatoes and deseed with a teaspoon. Chop roughly and purée finely, then force through a fine conical sieve into a mixing bowl, using a ladle. Season with salt and sugar, add the vinegar then whisk in the olive oil until well emulsified. Finally, season with 4 turns of pepper and add the herbs, if using.

VINAIGRETTE AUX HERBES
Herb vinaigrette

Quite extravagant; quite delicious.

INGREDIENTS
300 ml/10 fl oz olive oil

1 garlic clove, crushed

4 sprigs of thyme

2 sprigs of marjoram

3 basil leaves

needles from a tiny sprig of rosemary

4 tablespoons white wine vinegar

150 ml/5 fl oz cold water

1¼ teaspoons salt

1 teaspoon freshly ground white pepper

1 teaspoon caster sugar

In a saucepan mix together the oil, crushed garlic, thyme, marjoram, basil and rosemary.
Bring to simmering point then draw off the heat. Cover and leave to stand at room temperature for 3 or 4 hours to allow the flavours to exchange.

Using a ladle force through a fine conical sieve into a mixing bowl. Whisk in the vinegar, water, salt, sugar and pepper. Taste and correct the seasoning if necessary.

VARIATIONS
Vary the fresh herbs according to your preference and the dish the vinaigrette is to accompany.

VINAIGRETTE A LA MOUTARDE ET AU POIVRE VERT
A powerful mustard vinaigrette with green peppercorns

INGREDIENTS
1 teaspoon green peppercorns

1 heaped teaspoon Dijon mustard

a large pinch of salt

5 tablespoons groundnut oil

1 tablespoon white wine vinegar

1 tablespoon hot water

Crush the green peppercorns to a paste with the blade of a knife and place in a bowl with the mustard and salt. Pour in half the oil in a slow trickle, whisking continuously until the mixture thickens (a folded tea towel under the bowl will help to keep it stable).
Add a little vinegar and slowly trickle in the rest of the oil. Finally, add the remaining vinegar and the hot water. Pass through a fine conical sieve.

Chef's notes
The green peppercorns can be replaced by a large pinch of freshly ground white pepper.
If the vinaigrette separates, put 1 teaspoon mustard in another bowl and whisk in the separated vinaigrette, a little at a time.

VINAIGRETTE A L'HUILE DE NOIX
Walnut vinaigrette

INGREDIENTS

2 tablespoons walnut oil (see page 12)

1½ tablespoons non-scented oil

1 tablespoon white wine vinegar

a large pinch of salt

4 turns freshly ground white pepper

Mix all the ingredients together.

Chef's note
Do not be tempted to add more walnut oil; its powerful flavour could unbalance the flavours of the dish it complements.

—SWEET SAUCES—

SWEET SABAYON

A delicate foam of beaten egg yolks flavoured with your favourite wine or liqueur.

Serves 4–6
Difficulty: 🍳 🍳
Total recipe time: 15 minutes

INGREDIENTS

4 egg yolks

50 g/2 oz caster sugar

200 ml/7 fl oz Champagne

In an electric mixer on full speed, cream together the egg yolks and sugar for a few seconds. Add the Champagne and continue whisking vigorously until very frothy and firm. Stand the bowl in a warm bain-marie and cook as for savoury *sabayon* until it has the texture of lightly whipped cream.

Turn into a serving bowl and serve warm, or remove the bowl from the bain-marie, whisk until the *sabayon* is just tepid, then turn into a serving bowl, cover with clingfilm and chill until needed.

Quick method
Whisk the egg yolks, sugar and one-quarter of the Champagne in an electric mixer at high speed until light and bulky.

In a small saucepan, boil the remaining Champagne for 1–2 seconds. Reduce the speed of the mixer, pour in the hot Champagne and mix until frothy and firm.

Keep warm in a bain-marie and serve within 15 minutes, or cool as above and serve within 2–3 hours.

VARIATIONS
Replace the Champagne with other sweet or dry white wines or sherry or Marsala. Vary the quantity of sugar accordingly. Other liqueurs can be added towards the end.

Although this *sabayon* is normally served as an accompaniment to certain desserts, it can easily become a dish in its own right.

Special Champagne sabayon: Place 8 or 10 deseeded grapes in the bottom of chilled glasses, enliven the *sabayon* with a little *marc de Champagne* and pour it into the glasses.

Beaumes-de-Venise sabayon: Replace the Champagne with Beaumes-de-Venise, grate the zest of 1 lemon into the *sabayon*, increase the lemon juice to 100 ml/3½ fl oz and fold in 200 ml/ 7 fl oz whipped cream when cold. Serve in chilled glasses.

COULIS DE FRUITS DE LA PASSION
Passion fruit coulis

A *coulis* is cooked or uncooked juice and pulp from puréed and sieved fruits or vegetables.

Makes 300 ml/½ pt
Difficulty: 🍳
Total recipe time: 15 minutes

INGREDIENTS

12 passion fruit

1 large orange

65 g/2½ oz caster sugar

50 ml/2 fl oz water

Planning ahead
This *coulis* can be made up to 3 days in advance and kept in a sealed container in the fridge.

Halve the passion fruit, remove the seeds and pulp with a teaspoon and reserve in a bowl.

Halve the orange, squeeze and strain all the juice into the passion fruit. Add the sugar and water and liquidize for 20 seconds. Boil the pulp in a small saucepan for about 2 minutes, skimming the froth from the surface.

Strain through a fine sieve, forcing the pulp through with a small ladle to extract all the juices.

Cool, cover with clingfilm and store in the fridge.

VARIATIONS
Add 65 g/2¼ oz ripe mango.

Chef's notes
Depending on the ripeness of the fruit, the *coulis* may need a little more sugar or a dash of lemon juice. Taste it cold before correcting. Heat enhances the flavours, so you will gain a false impression by tasting it hot.

Passion fruit contains a large amount of pectin which will thicken the *coulis* during cooking.

COULIS D'ABRICOTS
Apricot coulis

Makes 300 ml/½ pt
Difficulty: 🎩
Total recipe time: 15 minutes

——— INGREDIENTS ———

400 g/14 oz ripe apricots

150 ml/5 fl oz water

100 g/3½ oz caster sugar

juice of ¼ lemon

1 tablespoon kirsch

Planning ahead
The sauce can be made up to 3 days in advance and kept covered in the fridge.

Wash and drain the apricots, halve, stone and cut each half into 3.
Put the apricots in a medium saucepan with the water, sugar and lemon juice, cover and bring to the boil.
Reduce the heat and simmer for 5 minutes until the juice turns into a light golden syrup. Taste to see if the apricots are cooked, then leave to cool.
Purée and force through a fine sieve. Taste, correct with a little more sugar or lemon juice as necessary, then add the kirsch. Store in a covered container in the fridge.

——— VARIATIONS ———
This *coulis* can also be made with peaches, nectarines, pears or apples.

Chef's notes
Sugar: The quantity of sugar given is for use with *ripe* apricots. If slightly unripe, increase the sugar and halve the amount of lemon juice.
Cooking the fruit: Unlike raspberries or strawberries, apricots and peaches need to be cooked before being puréed or they will oxidize and discolour very rapidly.

COULIS DE FRAMBOISES
Raspberry coulis

This refreshing and colourful sauce can accompany many sweets, especially rich, sumptuous desserts, where it will provide a welcome note of freshness.

Makes 300 ml/½ pt
Difficulty: 🎩
Total recipe time: 10 minutes

——— INGREDIENTS ———
300 g/11 oz ripe raspberries

100 g/3½ oz caster sugar

juice of ¼ lemon

Planning ahead
The sauce can be made up to 3 days in advance and kept covered in the fridge.

First check the raspberries, removing any discoloured or bad ones, then hull and briefly wash them and drain on a tea towel.
Purée the fruit with the sugar, then force through a fine nylon sieve (to prevent discoloration), using a ladle. Taste and enliven with lemon juice. Store in a covered container in the fridge.

——— VARIATIONS ———
Strawberries, wild strawberries, loganberries or redcurrants can also be done this way; the sugar content will vary depending on the type of fruit and its ripeness.
The *coulis* is also delicious served hot; add an extra 50 g/2 oz sugar.

Chef's note
Sugar: The quantity given is for *ripe* raspberries. If slightly unripe, increase the sugar and omit the lemon juice.

SIROP A SORBET
Sorbet syrup

This syrup can be made well in advance and kept in a sealed container in the fridge. It is used in many desserts, for moistening sponges and especially for making sorbet.

——— INGREDIENTS ———
400 g/14 oz caster sugar

325 ml/11 fl oz water

50 ml/2 fl oz liquid glucose

Combine all the ingredients in a small saucepan and boil for 1 minute, skimming off any impurities. Cool and store.

SAUCE AU CHOCOLAT
Chocolate sauce

Makes 200 ml/7 fl oz (6–8 servings)
Difficulty: 🎩
Total recipe time: 10 minutes.

——— INGREDIENTS ———
100 g/3½ oz best dark dessert chocolate

150 ml/5 fl oz water

20 g/¾ oz unsalted butter

Planning ahead
You can make this sauce a few hours in advance and keep it covered in a bain-marie or in the fridge. Reheat over a gentle heat, stirring constantly.

Break the chocolate into small pieces and melt it in a small saucepan over low heat, stirring occasionally. Add the water, bring to the boil, stirring constantly and finally whisk in the butter.

The sauce can be served tepid or cold (in which case, loosen it with a little more water).

Chef's note

Choose the best quality chocolate; it will determine the quality of the sauce. If you cannot find unsweetened chocolate, add 1 tablespoon cocoa powder when melting the chocolate.

SAUCE CARAMEL ARMAGNAC

Caramel sauce with Armagnac

Makes 300 ml/½ pt (6–8 servings)
Difficulty: 🍳
Total recipe time: 15 minutes
Special equipment: 1 small, deep, straight-sided saucepan

──── INGREDIENTS ────

250 g/9 oz caster sugar

50 ml/2 fl oz cold water

150 ml/5 fl oz hot water, to thin down the caramel

2 tablespoons Armagnac

Planning ahead

The sauce can be made a few days in advance and kept refrigerated.

1. Making the caramel
(10 minutes)

Put the cold water in a small straight-sided saucepan and add the caster sugar in a mound in the centre of the pan. Bring to the boil and cook over medium heat to a rich, dark caramel, brushing the sides of the pan with water to prevent it from burning.

2. Completing the sauce
(5 minutes)

When the caramel is dark, with a slightly acrid scent, draw the pan off the heat, tilt it away from you and add the hot water. Take care, as the caramel will spit. Swirl the pan to incorporate the water thoroughly and simmer for 1 minute. Draw off the heat and add 2 tablespoons Armagnac (the older the better), taste and add a little more Armagnac if necessary, stirring it in with a wooden spoon.

Storing

Cool then transfer to a small bowl, seal with clingfilm and refrigerate.

Chef's notes

Cooking the caramel: If cooking on gas, make sure the flames do not wrap around the sides of the saucepan or the caramel will catch and crystallize. Brush the sides of the pan with water during cooking to prevent this.

The colour of the caramel will determine the taste of the sauce: if it is too dark, the sauce will be bitter – if too light, the sauce will be too sweet and will have no caramel taste. The colour of the caramel in the pan can be deceptive; check by spooning a little onto a white plate.

SAUCE CARAMEL AU GINGEMBRE ET CITRON VERT

Butterscotch sauce flavoured with ginger and lime

Makes 400 ml/14 fl oz
Difficulty: 🍳
Total recipe time: 20 minutes
Special equipment: Sugar pan, pastry brush

──── INGREDIENTS ────

50 ml/2 fl oz water

200 g/7 oz caster sugar

100 ml/3½ fl oz liquid glucose

juice of 1 lime

500 ml/18 fl oz double cream

25 g/1 oz root ginger, unpeeled, washed and finely chopped

Planning ahead

The sauce can be made up to 4 days in advance and kept covered in the fridge.

Pour the water into a sugar pan, put the sugar in a mound in the centre of the pan and add the liquid glucose. Bring to the boil and cook over medium heat to a rich, dark caramel. Brush the inside of the pan with water from time to time during the cooking to prevent crystallization.

Tilt the pan away from you and add the lime juice, then the cream and finally the peeled ginger. Bring back to the boil for 1 minute until well blended and the sauce has a deep glaze. Strain through a fine sieve into a bowl or storage container and leave to cool. Cover with clingfilm and refrigerate.

Chef's note

See *Sauce caramel armagnac* (left) for more information.

CREME ANGLAISE
Vanilla custard

It is not often that the French borrow a recipe from England but *crème anglaise,* as its name implies, is an exception, although it bears little resemblance to the original English recipe! *Crème anglaise* is used as a base for ice creams and mousses and as an accompaniment to many sweets.

Makes 500 ml/18 fl oz
Difficulty: ♙
Total recipe time: 10 minutes

— INGREDIENTS —

6 egg yolks

65 g/2½ oz caster sugar

2 vanilla pods, split lengthways, scraped and finely chopped

500 ml/18 fl oz milk

Have ready a large china bowl and a sieve.
In a large mixing bowl, cream together the egg yolks and sugar until a pale straw colour.
Combine the milk and chopped vanilla pods in a heavy-bottomed saucepan, bring to the boil and simmer for about 5 minutes. Draw off the heat and cool for 30 seconds.
Pour the milk onto the eggs and sugar, whisking continuously, then return the mixture to the saucepan over medium heat and stir to bind the custard until it coats the back of a wooden spoon. Strain immediately into a china bowl, stir for a few minutes then keep in the fridge.

— VARIATIONS —

Lemon cream: Add 6 strips of lemon zest to the milk during simmering and proceed as above.
Orange cream: Add 8 strips of orange zest during simmering and a dash of Grand Marnier when cool.

Chocolate cream: Add 30 g/1 oz chocolate during simmering.
Coffee cream: Add 50 ml/2 fl oz coffee essence (see below) while simmering.
Vanilla ice cream: See below.

Chef's notes

Vanilla pods: See page 12.
Adding the milk to the eggs and sugar: Although this recipe is very simple, there are still a few difficulties. If the egg yolks are subjected to too strong a heat, the custard will curdle. The partial cooking of the yolk binds and thickens the custard. Stir constantly to distribute the heat and watch carefully – there is a precise moment when the custard will be ready.
Even when strained, the custard can still curdle, so continue stirring for 1 or 2 minutes until tepid.
A longer, but foolproof (well, almost!) method is to use a bain-marie. Stand the saucepan in 90°C/194°F water and follow the recipe.

GLACE A LA VANILLE
Vanilla ice cream

This rich, velvety ice cream lets you rediscover the taste of real vanilla!

Serves 4–6
Difficulty: ♙
Total recipe time: 15 minutes, plus 1 hour resting and 15–25 minutes churning.
Special equipment: ice cream maker

— INGREDIENTS —

6 egg yolks

100 g/3½ oz caster sugar

2 vanilla pods

250 ml/9 fl oz milk

250 ml/9 fl oz double cream

Planning ahead
Chill serving plates or glasses 1 hour in advance.

1. Making the vanilla custard
(10 minutes)
Follow the method for *Crème anglaise* left, substituting cream for half the milk to give the ice cream its rich, smooth texture. Leave to cool then refrigerate for 1 hour.

2. Churning (15–20 minutes)
Churn the sieved custard in the ice cream maker for 15 – 25 minutes, depending on your machine.

3. Serving
Serve in chilled glasses or plates with Chocolate sauce (page 31), a fruit *coulis* (page 31) or *Sauce caramel au gingembre et citron vert* (page 32).

— VARIATIONS —

These are endless; see Variations on *Crème anglaise.*
You can make this ice cream without an ice cream maker. Place in a container after Stage 1 and freeze for at least 6 hours.
The basic *crème anglaise* mixture also makes a good ice cream, although the texture will not be as smooth and rich.

ESSENCE DE CAFE
Coffee essence, for flavouring creams and sauces for desserts

Makes 100 ml/3½ fl oz (enough to flavour 1 L/1¾ pt *crème anglaise*)
Difficulty: ♙
Total recipe time: 15 minutes

— INGREDIENTS —

100 g/3½ oz caster sugar

2 level tablespoons instant coffee powder

50 ml/2 fl oz espresso coffee (optional)

175 ml/6 fl oz hot water

Dissolve the coffee powder in the hot water. Place the sugar in a sugar pan and cook to a dark, bitter caramel. Tilt the pan away from you, add the dissolved coffee and espresso, if using, and simmer, swirling the pan from time to time, until the caramel is diluted. Leave to cool, pour into a jar, cover and keep at room temperature.

Coffee cream

Make 1 L/1¾ pt *crème anglaise* (see page 33) and add 100 ml/3½ fl oz coffee essence and 50 ml/2 fl oz strong unsweetened espresso coffee to retain the flavour of fresh coffee.

Chef's note

It is extremely important to make a dark caramel or the sauce will be far too sweet.

CREME PATISSIERE
Pastry cream

Pastry cream has many uses – as a lining for fruit tartlets, as a filling for cakes and éclairs and as a base for soufflés (see page 35).

Makes 600 ml/1 pt
Difficulty: 🍳
Total recipe time: 20 minutes

──────── INGREDIENTS ────────
500 ml/18 fl oz milk

1 vanilla pod, split lengthways

6 egg yolks

100 g/3½ oz caster sugar

25 g/1 oz plain flour

20 g/¾ oz cornflour

1 teaspoon caster sugar, for dusting the surface of the cream

Planning ahead

This cream can be made up to 4 days in advance and kept, covered, in the fridge.

In a large heavy-bottomed saucepan, bring the milk to the boil, add the split vanilla pod and infuse at just below simmering point for about 5 minutes. Draw off the heat and remove the vanilla.
Cream together the egg yolks and sugar then whisk in the flour and cornflour. Pour 100 ml/3½ fl oz of the hot milk into the egg, sugar and flour mixture and whisk until well blended. Bring back to the boil, whisking until smooth. Add the remaining milk and boil for 1 minute, whisking continuously.

Storing

Transfer to a bowl or container and sprinkle the surface with caster sugar to prevent a skin from forming. Cool, seal with clingfilm and refrigerate.

Chef's notes

The constant whisking is very important to remove any small lumps.
The split vanilla pods can be re-used (see page 13). If you want a stronger flavour, scrape and chop the vanilla pod.

GANACHE
Chocolate cream

This cream is used in many chocolate desserts, such as mousses and truffles (see below) and *Pavé au chocolat* (page 261).

Makes 325 ml/11 fl oz
Difficulty: 🍳
Total recipe time: 15 minutes

──────── INGREDIENTS ────────
150 ml/5 fl oz double cream

115 g/4 oz plain dessert chocolate, (see chef's note on Sauce au chocolat page 32)

Planning ahead

This cream can be made in advance. Reheat it over a gentle heat, beating constantly.

Bring the cream to the boil, draw off the heat and add the chocolate, whisking constantly until well mixed. Keep the *ganache* in a cool place until it becomes firm and easy to handle.

──────── VARIATIONS ────────
Enrich the *ganache* with 65 g/2½ oz unsalted butter, or flavour it with your choice of liqueur or coffee essence.

CHOCOLATE TRUFFLES

──────── INGREDIENTS ────────
300 ml/½ pt ganache, plain or flavoured with a liqueur

200 g/7 oz best plain dessert chocolate, melted over a bain-marie

100 g/3½ oz cocoa powder

1. Moulding the truffles

Place the *ganache* in a piping bag fitted with a plain 1 cm/½ in round nozzle and pipe out chestnut-sized balls onto a sheet of greaseproof paper. Leave to cool then refrigerate for 2–3 hours until firm.

2. Dipping the truffles in chocolate

Hold each truffle with a fork and dip into melted chocolate, then roll in cocoa powder until completely coated. Place on a tray lined with greaseproof paper and refrigerate.
For extremely light truffles, place the *ganache* in a mixing bowl and whisk at high speed.

SOUFFLE
MAKING

I still remember my despair when I first attempted soufflés. Time and again they failed – such is the price of learning by yourself. Books were of little help; they merely described a succession of apparently simple operations, none of which helped me to understand where I was going wrong.

I hope that my explanation will help you to achieve a perfect soufflé every time.

SWEET SOUFFLES

The traditional method
There are many ways to make soufflés, but with this basic recipe, you can make almost any variety (eg: *Tartelette soufflée aux framboises*, page 157 and *Soufflé au caramel*, page 264).

Equipment
Mixing bowl for beating the egg white: Use scrupulously clean china or stainless steel. Copper bowls (traditionally used to obtain the best bulk) are now thought to release tiny particles of dangerous copper.

Whisk (for beating the whites by hand): Use a large supple balloon whisk to make beating easier and give more bulk. Alternatively, use an electric mixer with a whisk.

Supple spatula for folding the soufflé mixture into the pastry cream.

Soufflé dishes should be made of oven-proof china – the finer the better, for heat conduction. I prefer individual bowls to one large one, as they give you more control over the cooking. The heat permeates the soufflé mixture better and faster, leaving the soufflé just cooked outside and barely cooked inside. The presentation is better, too.

Oven: Always check the accuracy of the oven thermostat with a thermometer. Cook soufflés at the bottom of the oven; if cooked higher up, strong heat is reflected off the top of the oven onto the top of the soufflés, which impairs the rise and may cause the tops to burn.

GRAND MARNIER
SOUFFLE

For the soufflé dishes
1 teaspoon unsalted butter, at room temperature

2 tablespoons caster sugar, to line the soufflé dishes

Soufflé base
200 ml/7 fl oz warm Crème pâtissière (see page 34)

2 egg yolks

2 tablespoons Grand Marnier

8 egg whites

40 g/1½ oz caster sugar

1 teaspoon lemon juice

1. Preheat the oven to 190°C/375°F/gas 5.

2. Using your hands, evenly butter the inside of the soufflé dishes, then put 2 tablespoons sugar in the first bowl and rotate until completely coated. Tip the excess into the next bowl and repeat. This isolates the soufflé mixture from the dish, enabling the soufflé to rise without hindrance. Badly buttered bowls will produce an uneven rise or prevent it completely. Butter fixes the sugar in place and gives a delicious crust.

3. Put the warm pastry cream into a mixing bowl, add the egg yolk and Grand Marnier and whisk well together. Keep warm.
The pastry cream is the soufflé base and holds the flavour. Check the degree of moistness; if it is too wet, the egg whites will not be able to absorb and lift it. The cream should still be warm when incorporated into the egg whites; this helps to prevent lumps and gives better lifting power.
Egg yolks are added for richness, not binding power; in some soufflés (eg: raspberry and blackcurrant) they are not needed at all.
Flavouring: Many liqueurs can be substituted. Fruit *coulis* can also be used; some (eg: raspberry, blackcurrant and apricot) must be reduced beforehand to concentrate the flavour and keep the base firm. Strongly textured and flavoured *coulis*, such as lime, lemon and passion fruit, do not need reducing.

4. Beat the egg whites at medium speed to a soft peak, add the sugar and lemon juice, increase the speed and beat for a few more seconds until just firm but not too stiff. This will give the soufflé a wonderful melting texture. During the whisking, the egg white will expand to create millions of tiny air bubbles which will expand during baking and cause the soufflé to rise. If the whites are beaten too stiffly, the mixture will be too close-textured, making the soufflé too firm. One-week old eggs are best; very fresh egg whites have a high water content and are prone to graining.
The mixing bowl must be scrupulously clean, as any trace of fat or yolk will severely reduce the bulk obtained by beating.

5. Whisk in one-quarter of the beaten egg white into the warm pastry cream mixture for 2–3 seconds, until smooth. This brisk, brief whisking lightens the base mixture and eases the incorporation of the remaining egg white.
Using a spatula, delicately fold in the remaining egg whites with large circular movements until just incorporated. Do not overmix, or you will break down the air bubbles in the egg white and impair the rise.

6. Fill the soufflé dishes right to the top, smooth the surface with a spatula, then push the mixture about 2 mm/ $^{1}/_{12}$ in away from the edge of the bowls with your thumb; this prevents the soufflé from catching on the lip of the dish as it rises.

7. Space the dishes well apart in the bottom of the preheated oven, allowing the heat to circulate freely and bake for 12–13 minutes. After about 5 minutes, the soufflés will begin to rise. Check that they are rising evenly; if not, free the edges with a knife. Dust the tops with a thin layer of icing sugar once or twice; it will melt and produce a delicious caramelized glaze. Remove the cooked soufflés and serve.

Chef's notes

Soufflés are not as fragile as you may think. You *can* open the oven door for a few seconds without them disintegrating. Do not remove them as soon as they have risen, however, as the centres must also be cooked. If they are removed too soon, they will indeed collapse. Overcooking produces the same result, as the air bubbles will eventually burst open.

An ideal soufflé should have a melting texture, with a barely cooked and soft, creamy centre. It will stand for at least 2 or 3 minutes without deflating.

A soufflé should have enough flavour of its own and should not need a sauce poured into the centre. This is unsightly and immediately destroys the texture. I often serve a sorbet or slices of the same fruit used in the soufflé.

SAVOURY SOUFFLES

These are basically made in the same way as sweet soufflés.

Line the buttered dishes with fine breadcrumbs and add an extra squeeze of lemon to the egg whites instead of sugar during beating to improve the flavour and prevent graining.

MOUSSE
MAKING

Many people rightly regard mousses and *quenelles* as the ultimate culinary achievement – a feat worthy of respect and admiration. The basic method is actually quite simple but a really melting, tasty mousse requires a great deal of care at every stage.

Mousse and *quenelle* mixtures are basically the same, the main difference being that mousses are held together in a container (such as a ramekin or terrine) and cooked in a bain-marie, while *quenelles* are shaped with spoons and poached, unprotected, in lightly salted, trembling water or stock and therefore need less cream.

It is always difficult to make mousses in small quantities; they are never as light and delicate. Do not use less than 150 g/5 oz of the main ingredient.

1. Puréeing the flesh in a food processor

It is essential to purée the main ingredient properly in order to break down the fibres and tissues, or the mousse may turn out grainy. Rub the mixture between your fingers; it should be perfectly smooth. When processing, stop the motor at least twice and use a supple spatula to stir in any mixture trapped under the blade.

2. Adding salt and pepper

Salt and pepper added at this stage will be evenly distributed. The salt causes the proteins in fish and meat to swell; this firms up the consistency of the mousse mixture and helps the subsequent incorporation of cream.

3. Adding eggs or egg yolks

Eggs perform all kinds of miracles for the cook; here both yolks and whites provide the binding element (although meat and fish often contain enough natural proteins to bind the mixture on their own). I prefer to use egg yolks to enrich the mousse rather than whites, which need to be counterbalanced by more cream and thus dilute the mousse's essential flavour.

4. Chilling the mixture

The friction of the food processor blade causes the mousse mixture to heat up as it is puréed. It is then essential to chill it for about 30 minutes per 150 g/5 oz of basic ingredient; if cream is added to a tepid mixture, the liquids, fats and solids may separate.

5. Incorporating the cream

Chilled whipping cream gives the lightest results. Use a food processor (the easier method) or incorporate it by hand for ultimate lightness.

Using a food processor: With the motor running, add the cream to the chilled mixture in a steady trickle. Make sure it is absorbed steadily; if you add too much at once, you may whip the cream and the mixture will separate. If it is absorbed too slowly, the mixture will warm up and separate. Halfway through mixing, scrape out any mixture trapped under the blade, then continue; it takes about 2 minutes to incorporate 575 ml/1 pt cream.

By hand: This method is harder, but it does produce the lightest and fluffiest mousses and *quenelles*.

Put the prepared mixture in a stainless steel bowl and chill. Stand the bowl on ice and, using a wooden spatula, incorporate the cream little by little. Start by tracing small circles, then work and lift the mixture vigorously to trap as much air as possible. Don't worry – it will not separate. It is hard work, but the magical result will make it all worthwhile.

6. Sieving the mousse

This removes all the small fibres and nerves from the mixture.

Use a fine mesh circular sieve and a plastic scraper (you can make your own from a plastic ice cream carton) or a fine conical sieve and a ladle. Force through only a small amount of mixture at a time.

If you do this last, there is hardly any waste; the mixture is light and creamy and passes easily through the sieve. Traditionally, the mixture is sieved before adding the cream, but I find this wastes time and effort, not to mention good basic ingredients and expensive sieves which collapse under the pressure!

7. Testing the mousse

Cooking is an inexact science; the quantity of cream needed depends on the type and freshness of the meat, fish and eggs used for the mousse. Start by adding only four-fifths of the cream and reserve the rest until you have tested the mousse.

To test, quarter-fill a small buttered ramekin with mousse mixture. Cook in a bain-marie with the water at just below simmering point. Taste to check seasoning and texture; the mousse should have a melting texture but still hold its shape. Add the remaining cream to the main mixture and correct the seasoning if necessary.

8. Cooking the mousses

Great care must be taken when cooking mousses as their structure is so delicate.

Preparing the moulds: Butter the insides lightly; the fine film of butter makes unmoulding the mousses easier.

The bain-marie: Use a deep roasting pan lined with greaseproof paper to protect the mousse from the heat from underneath.

Pour in enough hot water to come at least three-quarters of the way up the sides of the moulds; this ensures that the temperature of the mousses is constant throughout.

Cover the bain-marie with pierced foil or buttered paper, which allows the steam to hover above the mousses before escaping and keeps the surface moist. If the foil or paper is sealed too tightly, the heat builds up and the mousses rise like tiny soufflés, then collapse miserably, especially when a high proportion of egg white is used.

Temperature: I prefer to cook my mousses at a relatively low 160°C/325°F/gas 3. This produces a delicate, trembling mousse, just bound together. A higher oven temperature will produce an overcooked and less delicate mousse. Most oven thermostats are inaccurate; check with an oven thermometer until you get to know the behaviour of your oven.

Timings may vary according to the thickness of the moulds, quantities being made etc., so always check whether the mousses are ready. The surface should be slightly convex and the centre should feel firm when pressed with your finger.

9. Serving the mousses

Hold the ramekin and shake it sideways; this should free the mousse. If not, slide a knife down to the bottom of the mould and, pressing the blade firmly against the side, make one continuous circle around the edge. Hold a plate firmly over the mould and invert.

Testing and cooking quenelles

If the mixture has been prepared and refrigerated a day in advance (which makes shaping easier), the cooked texture will be firmer. Test to see how much more cream should be added.

To test: Poach a spoonful of mixture directly in salted water at just below simmering point (85°C/185°F).

Shape the chilled *quenelles* with 2 spoons dipped in hot water (see diagram, page 142) and cook in lightly salted water at just below simmering point; boiling water will destroy their fragile texture.

(page 124) ... (page 143) ... (page 142)

— VARIATIONS —

You can enrich a mousse by adding softened butter before incorporating the cream. Work it with your fingertips until perfectly smooth; cold or lumpy butter cannot blend in properly and your cooked mousse will be dotted with little pockets of fat. Add the butter after the eggs, if using, then chill. You must use a food processor to incorporate the cream if you have added butter, as the high fat content will make the chilled mixture quite solid. Work the mixture with a spatula before cooking to lighten it.

Concentrate the flavour of a delicate mousse by adding some essence of the main ingredient. This is particularly worthwhile in shellfish mousses like *Raviolis de homard* (page 124). Add 2 tablespoons essence per 300 g/11 oz mixture before sieving.

Mousses can be transformed into delightful soufflés simply by adding beaten egg whites (eg: *Soufflé de sole et tourteau*, page 143).

Experiment with other fish mousses and *quenelles*: the chart below shows the quantities of cream needed for 300 g/11 oz fish, 2 egg yolks, 1 teaspoon salt and 2 large pinches of pepper.

Fish	Cream for mousse	Cream for quenelles
scallops	450 ml/16 fl oz	400 ml/14 fl oz
sea bass	500 ml/18 fl oz	420 ml/14½ fl oz
turbot	600 ml/1 pt	500 ml/18 fl oz
langoustines	650 ml/22 fl oz	550 ml/19 fl oz
brill	450 ml/16 fl oz	400 ml/14 fl oz
salmon	750 ml/1¼ pt	600 ml/1 pt

VEGETABLE MOUSSES

Vegetable mousses do not need as much care and attention since they contain no binding proteins and the cream can simply be poured in. Most often the vegetables are puréed and chilled, then the cream, eggs and salt are all added at once and the mixture is forced through a sieve.

Cooking: Vegetable mousses retain a lot of liquid. To reduce the risk of sticking, line the bottom of the moulds with buttered greaseproof paper, then pour in the mixture and cook gently.

PASTA FOR RAVIOLI OR FRESH — NOODLES —

Making fresh pasta is actually much simpler than you might imagine.

Serves 4
Difficulty: 🍳
Total recipe time: 5–20 minutes plus 1 hour resting
Special equipment: food processor – or 2 strong hands!

INGREDIENTS FOR THE —— BASIC DOUGHS ——

No. 1 (soft – ideal for ravioli)
250 g/9 oz medium strength plain white flour

5 egg yolks

2 pinches of salt

2 tablespoons olive oil

1–2 tablespoons water

a tiny pinch of saffron powder

No. 2 (hard–best for noodles, tagliatelle etc.)
250 g/9 oz plain white flour

2 whole eggs, plus 1 egg yolk

2 pinches of salt

4 tablespoons water

a tiny pinch of saffron powder

1. Using a food processor
(5 minutes)
Put all the ingredients in the given order into the food processor and mix for about 30 seconds until just blended. Knead the dough until perfectly smooth, wrap in clingfilm and leave to rest in the fridge for 1 hour before using.

2. By hand (20 minutes)
Place the flour in a mixing bowl and make a small well in the middle. Put in the eggs, egg yolk, salt, olive oil and water and mix with your fingertips, gradually drawing the flour into the centre. Work the dough until fairly homogenous, adding another tablespoon of water if necessary. Place the dough on a lightly floured surface and knead it thoroughly until perfectly smooth. Wrap in clingfilm and leave to rest in the fridge for 1 hour.

—— VARIATIONS ——
Spinach and herb pasta: Add 1 tablespoon Chlorophyll of spinach (see page 18) flavoured with your favourite herbs for a delicate green pasta.
Saffron pasta: Dilute 3 sachets of saffron powder in 2 tablespoons boiling water, cool then mix with the pasta ingredients instead of water.
Red pepper pasta: Add 1 tablespoon Chlorophyll of red peppers (see page 18).
Black pasta: Use 2 tablespoons squid ink and 1 teaspoon soy sauce instead of water.

Chef's notes
Flour: The flour must not be too strong in gluten or it will be far more difficult to work and will produce a less smooth pasta. Depending on the strength of the flour, you will need more or less water.
Saffron powder is added to enhance the colour, not for flavouring.
If you can find really fresh farm eggs with their deep yellow yolks (almost impossible nowadays), omit the saffron.
Clingfilm: It is vital to wrap the pasta while resting to prevent a crust from forming.

Rolling pasta by hand
This is no easy matter, and you cannot really produce as fine a result by hand as you can by using a pasta machine. However it is worth a try!
Cut the rested dough into 4 or 5 pieces. Place on a lightly floured surface, flatten, then roll out as thinly as possible. Roll the pasta sheets onto themselves and cut into strips.

Rolling pasta in a machine
Fix the machine onto the side of a table. Cut the dough into 4 and flatten slightly with a rolling pin. Roll the dough using the thickest setting, then fold each sheet on itself and repeat, thinning it each time on a finer setting until the pasta is about 0.25 mm/$1/50$ in thick. Place in the machine and cut to the desired width.

Drying
If you are not using the pasta immediately, drape it loosely on a tray to dry. Dried pasta can be stored in an airtight container for 3–4 weeks.

Freezing
Place the freshly cut pasta in a large container and seal. It will keep for up to 2 weeks.

Cooking

Bring to a fast boil 2 L/3½ pt water with 2 level tablespoons salt and cook the pasta for about 2 minutes, depending on thickness, stirring occasionally to prevent sticking (it is not necessary to add oil, as this simply floats to the surface and does not help). Taste after 1 minute; the pasta should be *al dente*. Drain under cold running water to remove excess starch.

Chef's notes

When rolling out the dough, use no flour, or as little as possible; if too much is absorbed, the pasta will become glutinous and slimy when cooked.

Since so many simple dishes can be made from fresh pasta, a pasta machine (which is not expensive) is a sound investment and will become a good friend.

RAVIOLI

Divide 350 g/12 oz pasta dough No. 1 in two. Flatten into rectangles 0.5 mm/¹⁄₂₄ in thick by hand or in a pasta machine. Stretch as thinly as possible and leave to rest for a few minutes.

Place teaspoons of your chosen filling (see recipes, pages 124 and 131) about 4 cm/1½ in apart on one rectangle and brush the other with water. Place the plain sheet on top of the filled sheet.

Seal the edges by pressing down with a pastry cutter then cut out the ravioli with a pastry cutter or pastry roller, depending on whether you need round or square ravioli. Of course there are many other shapes you can make; I enjoy fashioning these beautiful little tortellini: cut out a 6.5 cm/2½ in circle and stretch as thinly as possible. Brush the edges with water, place the filling in the middle, then fold it and draw back the extremities to produce a lovely flower shape (see right).

SHAPING FILLED PASTA

Roll the dough as thinly as possible in a pasta machine.

Cut it into rounds with a pastry cutter.

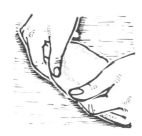

Stretch it even more thinly.

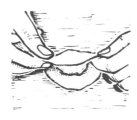

Brush the edges with water. Put the filling in the centre and fold the dough over. Press the edges together.

Shape by bringing the two corners together and pressing firmly.

Cooking

Cook in 2 L/3½ pt full-boiling water with 2 tablespoons salt for 1 minute, then simmer for 1–2 minutes depending on thickness.

Storing

Ravioli can be stored in an airtight container in the freezer for up to 1 week, or prepared 1 day in advance and kept in the fridge.

Chef's notes

I find it best to freeze ravioli before cooking when they are filled with a delicate mousse. Freezing solidifies the mousse and, during the initial fast boiling, allows the pasta to part-cook before the mousse has time to expand. Both will be ready at the same time after 2–3 minutes at just below simmering point.

PASTRY, DOUGH AND SWEETS

PATE SUCREE
Sweet short pastry

This pastry is used mainly for tarts and *petits fours*.

Makes two 27 cm/11 in tarts or sixty 4 cm/1½ in tartlets
Difficulty: 🍳
Total recipe time: 10 minutes, plus at least 2 hours chilling

— INGREDIENTS —

1 egg

1 egg yolk

85 g/3 oz icing sugar, sifted

a pinch of salt

finely grated zest of ½ lemon (optional)

125 g/4½ oz butter, softened

250 g/9 oz medium strength flour, sifted

Planning ahead
This pastry can be made up to 4 days in advance and kept in the fridge, wrapped in clingfilm.

In a large mixing bowl beat together the egg, egg yolk, icing sugar, salt and lemon zest (if used) for 1 minute. Add the softened butter and mix thoroughly. Sift in the flour and rub in with your fingertips until the dough has a rough sandy texture, then press it together. Wrap in clingfilm and refrigerate for at least 2 hours before using.

— VARIATIONS —
Add a dash of vanilla essence or finely grated orange zest, as appropriate. You could also add about 50 g/2 oz ground almonds, plus 1 tablespoon milk with the flour.

PATE SABLEE FINE
Shortbread pastry

Unashamedly rich, delicate, melting and crumbly.

Makes one 27 cm/11 in tart or sixty 4 cm/1½ in tartlets
Difficulty: 🍳
Total recipe time: 20 minutes

— INGREDIENTS —

250 g/9 oz medium-strength flour, sifted

a pinch of baking powder (optional)

2 egg yolks

2 tablespoons whipping cream

85 g/3 oz icing sugar, sifted

a pinch of salt

a dash of vanilla essence (optional)

175 g/6 oz unsalted butter, diced, at room temperature

Planning ahead
This pastry must be prepared in advance and refrigerated.

Thoroughly mix the flour and baking powder if using.
In a large mixing bowl, beat together the egg yolks, whipping cream, icing sugar, salt and vanilla essence (if using) then mix in the softened butter until well blended. Slowly sift in the flour, incorporating it with your fingertips until you obtain a crumbly, sandy dough. Do not overmix.
Place the dough on a lightly floured work surface and work it quickly with the palms of your hands, shaping it into a ball. Wrap in clingfilm and chill in the fridge for at least 2 hours before using.

Chef's notes
This pastry is particularly delicate, so handle it with care and do not overmix at any stage. See *Pâte brisée* (page 41) for cooking instructions.
With its high fat content, the pastry will be hard to work when first removed from the fridge, so remove it 30 minutes before use.
Baking powder: Used in small quantities, it will not affect the flavour and will lighten the pastry by releasing gases during the baking.

PATE A CHOUX
Choux pastry

Use for éclairs, profiteroles, small *choux* for *petits fours*. It can be piped into many different shapes (swans, small or large éclairs), filled with whipped cream or sorbets, dredged with icing sugar, set on different fruit *coulis*, to make a number of simple and attractive desserts.

Makes about 40 large éclairs or 100 small éclairs or *petits fours*
Difficulty: 🍳
Total recipe time: 30 minutes
Special equipment: piping bag with plain nozzle

— INGREDIENTS —

125 ml/4½ fl oz cold water

125 ml/4½ fl oz milk

½ teaspoon salt

1½ teaspoons caster sugar

115 g/4 oz unsalted butter, chilled and diced

200 g/7 oz strong flour, sifted

6 size 3 eggs, cracked into a jug

eggwash (1 egg yolk mixed with a pinch of salt and caster sugar and 2 teaspoons milk), to glaze (optional)

Planning ahead
This pastry can be prepared several hours in advance.

1. Cooking the paste (7–10 minutes)

Combine the water, milk, salt, sugar and diced butter in a thick-bottomed saucepan and boil for 1–2 minutes. Draw off the heat and add the sifted flour all at once, stirring and mixing until well blended.

Place over a strong heat and stir constantly for 5–7 minutes to evaporate as much liquid as possible – until the pastry leaves the sides of the pan. Draw off the heat and allow to cool for about 2 minutes, stirring occasionally, then add the eggs 2 at a time and mix thoroughly with a wooden spoon until you produce a smooth, rich-looking paste.

2. Piping and cooking choux buns and éclairs (20 minutes)

Preheat the oven to 190°C/375°F/ gas 5.

Lightly butter a baking tray.

Put the dough into a large piping bag fitted with a plain round nozzle (1 cm/½ in diameter for small *choux*, 1.5 cm/¾ in for large *choux* or éclairs) and pipe onto the baking tray. To give the *choux* an attractive shiny finish, brush with egg wash and mark with the back of a fork. Bake small *choux* in the preheated oven for about 15 minutes and large ones for 20 minutes, until they puff out and have turned an attractive golden brown.

Leave the oven door slightly ajar during the final 5 minutes of cooking so that the steam can escape. Cool on a pastry rack.

Storing

Pipe the *choux* pastry onto the baking tray and open freeze, then remove, store in an airtight container in the freezer and bake from frozen when needed. It will keep for about 2 weeks.

── VARIATIONS ──

Add a pinch of nutmeg and 60 g/2 oz grated Gruyère cheese to the dough to make delicious appetizers.

Chef's notes

After adding the flour, you must evaporate as much water as possible from the dough. It will sweat slightly, then come away from the sides of the pan. If not sufficiently dried, escaping steam will cause the pastry to crack during baking.

Cool the pastry slightly before adding the eggs, to ensure that the eggs do not cook.

PATE BRISEE
Shortcrust pastry

Recipe no. 1 (for savoury tartlets)

Since this recipe contains little butter, it has a crunchy texture and can hold a moist filling for a long time without becoming unpleasantly soggy.

Makes about 450 g/1 lb
Difficulty: 🍴
Total recipe time: 20 minutes

── INGREDIENTS ──

250 g/9 oz medium strength flour, sifted
···
½ teaspoon salt
···
½ teaspoon caster sugar
···
50 g/2 oz unsalted butter, diced, at room temperature
···
2 egg yolks
···
225 ml/8 fl oz water
···
1 teaspoon white wine vinegar
···

Planning ahead

Prepare the dough at least 4 hours in advance so that it can firm up and lose its elasticity.

---

1. Making the dough

Place the flour, salt, sugar and diced butter in a large mixing bowl and rub into a rough sandy texture with your fingertips. Make a well in the middle and add the egg yolks, water and vinegar. Gradually draw in the flour and blend until the ingredients are just mixed.

Place on the work surface, knead it for a few seconds, shape into a ball, then cut a deep cross in the dough to help remove elasticity, wrap it in clingfilm and refrigerate for at least 4 hours.

2. Lining a 27 cm/10½ in flan ring

On a lightly floured surface, roll the rested dough into a 30 cm/12 in circle, 2 mm/1/12 in thick. Place on a tray and refrigerate for 10 minutes.

Wrap the pastry round a rolling pin, then unroll it over the flan ring, carefully firm it in place and trim off the excess. Push up the edges with your thumb so they stand about 2 mm/ 1/12 in above the rim, pinch them and finally prick the bottom of the pastry case with a fork.

3. Baking blind

Sometimes large tarts need to be baked blind; line the pastry with foil, weight it with a layer of beans or rice (to minimize shrinkage), and bake for about 5 minutes in a preheated oven at 220°C/425°F/gas 7. Remove the foil and beans, then bake for a further 5 minutes.

4. Lining tiny tartlet tins

Take about 30 g/1 oz of the rested dough, roll it into a ball and wrap it in clingfilm, twisting the top. This will be used to press the pastry in place.

On a lightly floured work surface, roll the remaining pastry into a 30 x 25 cm/12 x 10 in rectangle, about 2 mm/ 1/12 in thick and refrigerate it on a tray. Arrange your tartlet tins closely together. Wrap the rested dough round a rolling pin then unroll it over your tartlet tins. Use the small ball of pastry to press the dough into the moulds, then cut off the excess by rolling over them with a rolling pin. Thumb up the pastry to come 2 mm/ 1/12 in above the sides.

Shape any remaining pastry back into a ball, wrap in clingfilm and keep for later use.

Refrigerate the lined tins for about 30 minutes before baking to minimize shrinkage.

For perfectly shaped tartlets, press another tartlet tin of the same size into each pastry-lined tin.

Recipe no. 2 (for a richer, more melting and flaky pastry)

─── INGREDIENTS ───

250 g/9 oz medium strength flour, sifted

1 ½ teaspoons caster sugar

1 teaspoon salt

175 g/6 oz unsalted butter

1 egg

1 tablespoon water

1 teaspoon vinegar

Make the dough as above or use a food processor. Depending on the type of flour used, you may need an additional tablespoon of water.

Chef's notes

Take care not to overwork the dough as this will make the cooked pastry hard. It is very important to rest the dough before use or it will shrink during cooking.

This dough can be kept for one week in the fridge, wrapped in clingfilm.

PATE FEUILLETE
Puff pastry

I will never forget the luncheon I cooked at a London hotel to celebrate the publication of the 1979 Egon Ronay guide. I had only two years' cooking experience and with true heroism I was determined to prepare every dish from scratch. Our team started work at 5am, while others had wisely prepared their dishes in advance in their own restaurants.

My puff pastry turned out to be a disaster. From the fourth turn, the butter started showing through in small, then larger patches. It was far too late to start again and pride prevented me from asking the hotel pâtissier to give me some of his puff pastry. I kept hoping that mine would turn out all right. It did not.

It was a nightmare – hard layers of pastry with butter leaking out all over the place.... I felt like ending it all there and then with a large kitchen knife.

Somehow I survived, as did the guests, but from then on I resolved never to leave things to chance, to find out precisely how and why.

Puff pastry is not easy to make. I hope this recipe will make it slightly simpler for you – the large quantity of water makes the dough easier to work with, the vinegar reduces elasticity and the egg yolks give the pastry an appetizing colour.

Makes 30–34 x 8 cm/3½ in rounds
Difficulty: 🎩 🎩 🎩
Total recipe time: 1 hour 20 minutes, plus 4 hours resting

─── INGREDIENTS ───

500 g/1 lb 2 oz medium strength flour, plus extra for turning the pastry

50 ml/2 fl oz vinegar

250 ml/9 fl oz cold water

2 teaspoons salt

2 egg yolks

100 g/3½ oz unsalted butter, creamed

400 g/14 oz unsalted butter, chilled

eggwash (1 egg yolk with 2 teaspoons milk and a pinch each of salt and caster sugar), to glaze

Planning ahead

Stage 1 can be completed 1 day in advance.

1. Making the dough (15 minutes)

In a small bowl, mix together the water, vinegar and egg yolks.

Put the flour in an electric mixer fitted with a dough hook.

Add the creamed butter to the flour and mix at slow speed for about 3 minutes, until well absorbed. Still at slow speed, gradually add the water/vinegar/egg mixture until well blended. Increase to high speed for the final 30 seconds. Do not overwork, or the dough will be too elastic. Place the dough on a lightly floured surface and roll into a ball. With a knife, make 4 or 5 deep incisions to help break down the elasticity. Wrap the dough in clingfilm, shape into a 16 cm/6 in square and chill for at least 3 hours.

2. Adding butter to the dough
(10 minutes) (see diagram, page 43)

Place the cold butter (straight from the fridge) between 2 sheets of paper and beat it into a 18 cm/7 in square with a rolling pin, until pliable.

Unwrap the dough, place on a lightly floured surface, square it up and roll into a 28 cm/11 in square.

Place the square of butter in the centre (see diagram), roll out the corners a little further if necessary, and fold them over, overlapping them slightly like the back of an envelope. Roll out to about 20 cm/8 in square. The butter will be completely enclosed and sandwiched between two layers of dough of equal thickness.

Chill for at least 30 minutes.

PREPARING PUFF PASTRY

Roll the dough away from you into a square about 1 cm/½ in thick, as described in Stage 2, and place the butter in the middle.

Fold the corners over the butter to make an 'envelope'. Roll out and chill (see Stage 2).

Stage 3: using light, even pressure, roll the dough gently away from you into a 70 x 40 cm/28 x 17 in rectangle. Do not roll too hard, or the butter will leak out.

Fold the pastry onto itself in 3 layers, folding one end to the middle and the other end over the first fold. Proceed with the second and following turns as described in Stage 3.

3. Folding the buttered dough
(30 minutes, plus 1 hour resting)
Lightly flour your work surface.
First turn: Roll the dough into a 70 x 40 cm/28 x 17 in rectangle (start rolling from the centre, with even pressure, turn the dough round and repeat), then fold into 3, stretching the corners and sides so they meet exactly. Gently flatten the edges to seal.
Second turn: Give the dough one quarter turn to the left and roll out once again into a 70 x 40 cm/28 x 17 in rectangle. Fold it in 3, stretch the corners and flatten to seal as above. Chill for 30 minutes.
Third and fourth turns: Repeat the process twice more. Chill the dough for 30 minutes minimum.
Fifth and sixth turns: Proceed as above, wrap the dough in clingfilm or polythene and chill for at least 2 hours. At this stage the dough can be kept refrigerated for up to 3 days.

4. Thinning the dough (5 minutes)
Lightly flour your work surface, roll the dough into an 80 x 35 cm/32 x 14 in rectangle, 5 mm/¼ in thick, and cut in half. Place both halves on a tray lined with greaseproof paper, cover with clingfilm and refrigerate for at least 30 minutes before use.

5. Cutting the dough (10 minutes)
Place a chilled sheet of puff pastry on a lightly floured surface, and cut into the required shapes with a knife or pastry cutter.
Place the pastry shapes on a baking sheet dampened with cold water, leaving at least 3 cm/1¼ in between them. Prepare the second sheet in the same way. Brush the tops with eggwash, taking care that it does not run onto the sides.

6. Baking the pastry (15 minutes)
Preheat the oven to 220°C/425°F/gas 7.
Bake the pastry shapes for about 15 minutes until well risen and golden. Enjoy this precious moment!

Transfer to a cooling rack for about 5 minutes. Using a sharp serrated knife, cut off the tops and, with a teaspoon, scrape out the uncooked, indigestible insides, leaving only a thin, flaky, weightless crust. The pastry cases are now ready for filling.

To use the trimmings
You will be left with a substantial quantity of trimmings, which can be used in many savoury or sweet tarts. Reshape into a ball and refrigerate for at least 2 hours.
Cheese straws: Roll the trimmings into a rectangle 3 mm/⅛ in thick, chill for 30 minutes, then brush with eggwash and sprinkle with finely grated Gruyère cheese. Press lightly with your hands and cut into 6 cm/2 in sticks 5 mm/¼ in thick. Twist each one, space well apart on a dampened pastry sheet and bake in a preheated oven at 220°C/450°F/gas 7.
Allumettes glacées: prepare as for cheese straws but spread the pastry sheet with royal icing. Cut into small rectangles using a knife dipped in hot water, then lift them onto the baking sheet and bake for about 10 minutes. Serve with coffee.
Apple tart: Use 400 g/14 oz trimmings, 8 russet or Granny Smith apples, sliced, 100 g/3½ oz butter, 100 g/3½ oz caster sugar.
Roll the pastry to 2 mm/¹⁄₁₀ in thick and refrigerate for 30 minutes. Cut into 4 x 17 cm/6 in rounds and score a circle 1 mm/¹⁄₂₄ in inside the edges (use a plate as a template). Place overlapping slices of apple in the inner circles, brush with melted butter, sprinkle with caster sugar and bake in a hot oven for about 30 minutes. Sprinkle with a little more sugar before serving.

Chef's notes
Flour must be medium strength. If too weak in gluten, the dough will not be pliable; if too high in gluten, it will be too elastic and prone to shrinkage.

Water must be cold so that the dough remains fairly firm.

Placing the butter in the dough: The butter must come straight from the fridge, then be flattened to soften it and give it the same texture as the dough. Check by touching. If too soft or too hard, the butter will spread unevenly and create pockets of fat which will leak through when the pastry is baked.

Rolling and folding the dough: Roll firmly but evenly away from you, always starting from the centre. Turn the dough and repeat. The repeated folding and rolling creates hundreds of fine uniform layers of butter and dough, which produce this small miracle during the baking.

Resting times: Constant chilling is needed to keep the layers of butter and dough even and at the same temperature and to allow the dough to firm up. If your kitchen is warm, chill after each turn.

Cutting the pastry: Chill the dough first; cutting soft dough will make the edges of those hard-earned fine layers stick together and reduce the rise.

Eggwash gives a glossy finish. Make sure it does not drip on the sides, or the layers will stick together and reduce the rise. A successful puff pastry should rise to at least 5 times its original thickness.

Storing
Cut out the pastry and freeze for up to 2 weeks. It will keep in the fridge for 3 days.

BISCUIT
Sponge biscuit

This very important multi-purpose light sponge is used as a base for many desserts.

Makes one 30 x 40 x 2 cm/12 x 16 x ¾ in sheet
Difficulty:
Total recipe time: 15 minutes
Special equipment: electric mixer with whisk, large baking tray, large piping bag with 1.5 cm/⅝ in round nozzle (for sponge fingers), sugar dredger, 20 x 4 cm/8 x 1½ in cake tin or charlotte mould

INGREDIENTS
4 egg yolks

4 tablespoons cold water

85 g/3 oz caster sugar

4 egg whites, plus 25 g/1 oz caster sugar

100 g/3½ oz medium strength plain white flour, sifted

icing sugar, for dredging

Planning ahead
Although this sponge can be wrapped in clingfilm and frozen, it is best eaten on the day it is made.

1. Mixing the egg yolks, sugar and water (5 minutes)
In an electric mixer, whisk together the egg yolks, sugar and water until aerated and light and quadrupled in volume. Place in a large bowl and keep aside.

2. Beating the egg white
(4 minutes)
Wash and dry the mixing bowl. At medium speed, beat the egg whites to a soft peak, then add the sugar, increase to full speed and beat until firm.

3. Mixing the white into the yolks; incorporating the flour (3 minutes)
Using a large slotted spoon, mix one-third of the beaten egg white into the yolks until well incorporated then, cutting and lifting, carefully fold in the remaining egg white. When the mixture is just mixed, sift in the flour and continue cutting and lifting until well blended. The mixture is now ready to be cooked.

VARIATIONS
20 g/¾ oz melted butter added after the flour will give the sponge a richer texture.
30 g/1 oz cocoa powder can be added to the flour to make a chocolate sponge biscuit.

Uses
Roulades and Swiss rolls: Line a baking tray with baking parchment, spread the mixture evenly with a palette knife to a thickness of about 5 mm/¼ in and bake in a preheated oven at 180°C/350°F/gas 4 for 7 – 8 minutes.
This will make two 23 x 30 cm/9 x 12 in sheets of sponge biscuit.
When cooked, turn out onto a wire cooling rack lined with a tea towel, peel off the baking parchment and leave to cool for about 10 minutes before using.
Cakes: Lightly butter and flour a 20 x 4 cm/8 x 1½ in cake tin, shake off excess flour, then fill with the mixture and bake in a preheated oven at 180°C/350°F/gas 4 for 20 minutes. Turn out onto a wire rack and leave to cool for 2 hours. Slice horizontally with a sharp serrated knife and fill with your chosen filling.
Lining charlottes, mousses etc. (see *Mousse légère aux fruits de la passion et mangue,* page 93): Cook as above, leave to cool for 20 minutes then slice horizontally into 5 mm/¼ in rounds with a sharp serrated knife.
Sponge fingers: Line a baking tray with baking parchment and pipe on 10 x 3 cm/4 x 1½ in fingers, using a 1.5 cm/⅝ in nozzle. Dust with a little

icing sugar, wait 2 or 3 minutes then dust them again and bake in a pre-eated oven at 200°C/400°F/gas 6 for about 8 minutes.

Remove, cool slightly, then lift off with a palette knife and leave to cool completely on a wire rack. Store in an airtight container. They are quite delicious dipped in Champagne – a delightful French habit!

Chef's notes

Beating the egg white: Make sure the mixing bowl is scrupulously clean and dry or the volume of egg white will be reduced considerably.

Mixing the egg white into the yolks: This is done in 2 stages; first, one-third of the white is beaten into the yolk mixture to lighten it and ease further incorporation of the remaining white. The second stage must be done with great care, cutting and lifting.

Adding the flour: Ask someone to help you, as the sifting and incorporation of the flour should be one continuous process. If the flour is added all at once, it will be unevenly distributed and may form lumps and thus spoil the biscuit. Do not overmix or the air trapped in the egg whites will escape and the biscuit will be heavy.

Icing sugar: This will form a lovely crust when cooked.

Baking: It is best to use non-stick baking parchment. Alternatively, use greaseproof paper brushed with a film of butter, or a baking tray brushed with butter and dusted with a little flour.

To check if the biscuit is cooked, touch it – it should be lightly springy. If you are making a large cake, insert a trussing needle into the centre; the needle should come out dry and hot.

MERINGUE ITALIENNE
Cooked meringue

Difficulty: 🍳
Total recipe time: 25 minutes
Special equipment: electric mixer, sugar pan, sugar thermometer

——— INGREDIENTS ———
3 egg whites
....
1 tablespoon lemon juice, strained
....
50 ml/2 fl oz water
....
175 g/6 oz caster sugar
....

Planning ahead

This meringue can be made up to 4 days in advance and stored in an airtight container in the fridge.

1. Cooking the sugar (10 minutes)

Put the water in a straight-sided sugar pan and add the sugar. Bring to the boil over a medium heat, stirring from time to time. When the syrup reaches 105°–110°C/220°–225°F, leave on the heat and start beating the egg whites.

2. Beating the egg whites
(5 minutes)

In a electric mixer on medium speed, beat the egg whites to a soft peak, then add the lemon juice and beat until firm.

3. Mixing the sugar syrup and egg whites (10 minutes)

When the temperature of the sugar syrup reaches 120°C/225°F, set your mixer onto its lowest speed and gradually add the boiling syrup, pouring it in between the sides of the mixing bowl and the whisks. Continue beating at low speed until the meringue is tepid.

Store in an airtight container until required.

Chef's notes

Temperature of the syrup: You can add the syrup at 110°/225°F but the meringue will be less firm. Watch the temperature carefully; it must not exceed 120°C/225°F. If you have no sugar thermometer but plenty of confidence, use the following method: dip your thumb and index finger into cold water, then immediately in hot syrup and immediately back into cold water, rubbing the sugar between your fingers. If it can be shaped into a ball, it is ready. Please do not attempt this unless you feel really confident or have a first aid kit!

Beating the egg whites: Lemon juice prevents graining and counterbalances the sweetness of the meringue.

NOUGATINE AND CRAQUELIN
Golden caramel mixed with flaked almonds

I vividly remember conceiving the delightful idea of presenting our after dinner *petits fours* and chocolates in beautifully moulded nougatine *bon-bonnières*. After 4 hours' hard work, we produced ten beautifully sculpted baskets complete with handles and lids; they looked quite magnificent. Happily we filled them with caramels and chocolates and sent them off to the guests.

I hid in a corner and watched. At first the guests just looked and admired the presentation, then curiosity led them to lift the lids and, naturally, they couldn't resist eating all the little sweets inside. Then – horrors! – one guest snapped off a *nougatine* handle and ate it! I was prepared to forgive this one lapse, but he told his companions how good it was and they, too, began to demolish all our pretty *nougatine* baskets.

And so, to my dismay, it continued. Of the ten *bonbonnières* delivered, only three returned – and they were minus handles and flowers. What a disaster! Then I had another bright idea; on each basket lid I placed a note saying "Please do not eat me!" Did it work? No chance. Confronted by such a challenge, they ate the lot. I persevered for about 2 weeks before adopting a new system: now I serve the *petits fours* and chocolates on a heavy silver tray – such a pity.

To make 250 g/9 oz *nougatine* (enough to line four 8 x 2 cm/3 x ¾ in moulds)
Difficulty: 🍳
Total recipe time: 15 minutes, plus 15 minutes to cut and shape
Special equipment: sugar pan or straight-sided thick-bottomed saucepan, palette knife, hardwood or steel rolling pin, pastry cutters or tartlet tins

—————— INGREDIENTS ——————
50 ml/2 fl oz water
....
200 g/7 oz caster sugar
....
100 g/3½ oz flaked almonds (the thinner the better)
....
1 teaspoon groundnut oil, for greasing
....

Planning ahead
The *nougatine* can be made in advance and stored in an airtight container. Reheat in a preheated oven at 150°C/300°F/gas 2.

1. Cooking the nougatine
(15 minutes)
Preheat the oven to 200°C/400°F/gas 6.
Scatter the almonds on a baking tray

and toast in the preheated oven until pale golden. Reduce oven temperature to 150°C/300°F/gas 2 for Stage 2. Meanwhile, put the water and sugar in a sugar pan and cook over medium heat to a light, pale caramel.
Add the toasted almonds and cook for 1 more minute, stirring with a wooden spoon.
Immediately pour the mixture into a lightly oiled baking tray, leave to cool for a few seconds then turn it over with a spatula (do not touch it with your hands).
Lightly oil the work surface.

2. Rolling, cutting and shaping the nougatine (15 minutes)
You need organization, speed and strong arms.
Roll the *nougatine* as thinly as possible then, when it becomes too hard to roll, put it back on the baking tray and return it to the oven, leaving the door ajar, for about 1 minute. Continue to roll and reheat the *nougatine* until it is about 2–3 mm/¹⁄₁₀ in thick.

3. Cutting the nougatine sheet
The *nougatine* must be warm when cutting, or it will be too brittle and will snap. Cut into appropriate shapes with a heavy knife or pastry cutters.

4. Moulding the nougatine
Cut the mixture into 4 pieces, roll them one at a time to a 2–3 mm/¹⁄₁₀ in thickness, then return them to the oven to become supple and push into the tartlet tins with your thumbs. Work as quickly as possible. Trim overhanging bits with scissors.
To make handles, melt the trimmings, roll very thinly and cut into 5 cm/2 in strips.

To make craquelin
Cool the trimmings, then grind to a fine powder in a food processor. Sprinkle over soufflés or use in ice cream and delicious desserts like *Feuillantines caramelisées aux pommes*, page 208.

Chef's notes
Cooking the nougatine: The almonds are lightly toasted to improve their flavour.
Caramel: Swirl the sugar pan from time to time so that the caramel cooks evenly. Do not colour it too much, or too much water will evaporate and the *nougatine* will be harder to cut and handle.
Rolling, cutting and shaping the nougatine: This is the hard part. It is vital to be fully prepared before rolling and cutting. Oil the baking tray and work surface and have all your equipment to hand.
Be sure to roll the *nougatine* as thinly as possible to appreciate its wonderfully snappy texture.

PRALINES AU KIRSCH
Caramelized almonds with kirsch

A delicious garnish for vanilla, chocolate or almond ice cream, or an accompaniment to coffee.

Makes 200 g/7 oz
Difficulty: 🍳
Total recipe time: 15 minutes

—————— INGREDIENTS ——————
150 g/5 oz whole shelled almonds, skinned or unskinned
....
150 g/5 oz icing sugar
....
100 ml/3½ fl oz kirsch or water
....
20 g/¾ oz unsalted butter
....

Planning ahead
The pralines can be made a few days in advance and kept in an airtight container.

Combine the almonds, icing sugar and kirsch in a heavy-bottomed saucepan. Cook over a strong heat until the kirsch has evaporated and the

sugar has a sandy texture.
Reduce the heat and cook for a further 5 minutes, stirring continuously, until lightly caramelized. Draw off the heat and stir in the butter. Cool on a lightly oiled tray and store in an airtight container.

--- VARIATIONS ---

Mix hazelnuts with the almonds or use them on their own.
Use water instead of kirsch.

GARNISHES

CHAPELURE PROVENÇALE

Breadcrumbs scented with olive oil, garlic and herbs

These breadcrumbs are delicious sprinkled onto a fricassee of mushrooms at the last moment.

Makes about 125 g/4 oz
Difficulty: 🍳
Total recipe time: 10 minutes

--- INGREDIENTS ---

100 g/3½ oz dried bread, without crusts

2 garlic cloves

3 tablespoons olive oil

1 sprig of thyme, finely chopped

15 g/½ oz parsley, finely chopped

a few basil, tarragon, or chervil leaves, finely chopped (optional)

salt and freshly ground white pepper

Grind the bread to crumbs in a food processor and turn out into a small bowl.
Crush the garlic, chop finely and mix with the olive oil.
Strain the oil through a fine sieve into the breadcrumbs and mix to obtain a fine, sandy texture. Season, then mix in the chopped herbs.

Storing

Store in a covered container in the refrigerator for 1 week or for up to 2 weeks in the freezer.

Chef's notes

The bread must be completely dry before you grind it, or the moisture combined with the olive oil will make the mixture lumpy.
Parsley: Pat dry only once, before chopping. Some people only press it in a tea towel afterwards, but this only weakens its vigorous taste and leaves you with tasteless pieces of green fibre.
Vary the herbs and add more to suit your taste; rosemary and basil are good additions.

LARDONS

Lardons are strips cut from the belly of pork where the layers of lean and fat meat are juxtaposed, giving them their succulent, melting mellowness. They can be cut from cured and smoked belly or from unsmoked 'green' belly.

Remove the rind and bone out any cartilage, then cut into slices about 5 mm/¼ in thick, 5 mm/¼ in wide and 3 cm/1¼ in long (the size can vary to suit the dish they accompany).
Blanch in unsalted boiling water for 2–3 minutes (smoked *lardons* need a little longer, due to the high salt content) then refresh and drain.
Use to garnish salads and meat dishes (eg: *Salade franche-comtoise*, page 224).

BRUNOISE DE LEGUMES AU PISTOU

Diced vegetables with the scents of Provence

A rich, colourful garnish made from finely diced mixed vegetables flavoured with olive oil, basil and garlic – the classic scents of Provence. It goes wonderfully well with any Provençal dish.

Serves 8
Difficulty: 🍳
Total recipe time: 40 minutes

--- INGREDIENTS ---

4 garlic cloves

8 basil leaves

1 tablespoon olive oil

¼ onion

100 g/3 ½ oz fennel

½ medium red pepper

1 medium courgette

100 g/3 ½ oz aubergine

4 medium tomatoes

50 ml/2 fl oz first press olive oil

1 sprig of thyme

salt and freshly ground white pepper

Planning ahead
The dish can be prepared and cooked 1 day in advance. Keep refrigerated.

1. Preparing the pistou (15 minutes)
Garlic: Peel, halve and remove the green germ. Blanch in at least 1 L/ 1¾ pt water, then simmer for 10 minutes until the garlic is soft and has lost its powerful taste and aggressive scent. Refresh in cold water.
Basil: Wash and purée with the flat of a large knife.
Crush and purée the garlic with the flat of a large knife and mix with the basil and 1 tablespoon olive oil.

2. Preparing the vegetables
(20 minutes)
Onion: Peel and cut into 3 mm/⅛ in dice.
Fennel, courgette and red pepper: Wash and cut into 3 mm/⅛ in dice.
Aubergine: Cut into 3 mm/⅛ in dice, leaving the skin on.
Tomatoes: Peel, halve, deseed with a teaspoon and dice finely.
Place all the diced vegetables separately on a tray. Add a pinch of salt and a few turns of pepper and set aside.

PREPARING VEGETABLE
BRUNOISE AND MIREPOIX

Above and below: Cut the peeled vegetables lengthways into 3 mm/ ⅛ in strips for bruniose and 1 cm/ ½ in strips for mirepoix.

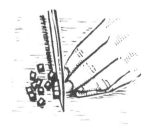

Cut across into small dice.

3. Cooking the dish (10 minutes)
In a large sauté pan, sweat the chopped onion and thyme in the olive oil for 10 minutes without colouring. Add the fennel and cook for a further 3 minutes. Increase the heat, then add the diced red pepper, aubergine and courgette and cook for 3 more minutes. finally add the *pistou* and diced tomatoes and cook for a final 2 minutes, stirring from time to time so that all the flavours infuse. allow to cool on a tray.

Storing
When cool, put in a covered container and refrigerate for up to 2 days.

——— VARIATIONS ———
A few diced, blanched olives would make a delicious addition.
You can turn this into a richly flavoured soup by adding 750 ml/1¼ pt water; simmer for 5 minutes and add a few more shredded basil leaves.

Chef's notes
Sweating the diced onions: Be careful not to brown them, or the *pistou* will taste quite different – more representative of Lyonnaise cuisine than Provençal!

———————————————

PUREE DE COINGS
Quince purée

A wonderful accompaniment for any game.

Serves 4
Difficulty: 🍳
Total recipe time: 25–30 minutes

——— INGREDIENTS ———
1 kg/2¼ lb very ripe quinces

2 L/3½ pt water acidulated with 2 tablespoons vinegar

500 ml/18 fl oz cold water

juice of ½ lemon

100 g/3½ oz caster sugar, plus a pinch (optional)

40 g/1½ oz unsalted butter

1. Preparing the quinces
(15 minutes)
Peel, core and quarter the quinces and cut them roughly into 2.5 cm/1 in squares, dropping them into a bowl with 2 L/3½ pt acidulated water as you go.

2. Cooking the quinces and puréeing (20 minutes)
In a large saucepan, bring to the boil 500 ml/18 fl oz cold water with the lemon juice and sugar.
Drain the quinces, put them in the boiling water, cover and simmer for about 15 minutes until soft. Remove with a slotted spoon, (the chilled cooking liquid makes a most pleasant drink) drain in a colander, then purée for about 3 minutes until completely smooth.

3. Finishing and serving
Pour the purée into a medium saucepan and if too liquid, stir over medium heat until it reaches a good consistency. Stir in the butter, taste and add a tiny pinch of caster sugar if necessary.

——— VARIATIONS ———
A tiny slice of root ginger can be added during simmering.
For an even smoother texture, force through a fine sieve after puréeing.

Chef's notes
Quinces: This recipe calls for very ripe quinces; they should be a deep yellow colour and have a strong scent. Less ripe quinces will need a longer cooking time and an extra pinch of sugar added at the end.

ZESTES CONFITS
Candied orange, lemon, lime or grapefruit zests

Use a garnish to add colour, taste and texture to a dessert.

Serves 6–8
Difficulty: 🎩
Total recipe time: 20 minutes

INGREDIENTS
4 oranges or *6 limes* or *lemons* or *3 grapefruit*

200 ml/7 fl oz Sorbet syrup (see page 31)

juice of ½ lemon

at least 1 L/1¾ pt boiling water

Planning ahead
The sorbet syrup must be made in advance.

Cut long strips of zest from the fruit then cut into fine *julienne* (see diagram). Blanch for 8–10 minutes in plenty of boiling water, put in a colander and refresh under cold running water.
Place in a small saucepan with the syrup acidulated with the lemon juice, bring to the boil and simmer for 3 minutes. Draw off the heat, taste to check the texture is right then transfer to a small bowl and leave to cool. Seal with clingfilm.

SEGMENTING CITRUS FRUIT

Cut off the ends of the fruit with a sharp knife. Cut off the peel in sections, cutting downwards, making sure to remove all the pith.

Cut down between the membrane to remove the segments.

ZEST JULIENNE
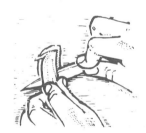

To julienne the zest, cut off the rind and cut away the pith.

Hold down the zest with your index finger and thumb and cut fine slices on the diagonal.

Storing
The candied zests will keep for up to 2 weeks in a covered container.

VARIATION
Lemon, lime, orange and grapefruit zests can all be cooked together.

Chef's notes
Blanching: This is done to remove excessive bitterness. It is important to blanch the zests in at least 1L/1¾ pt water to disperse the bitterness, which would be recycled into the zests in a smaller quantity of water.
Lemon juice is added to the syrup to counterbalance its sweetness.
Cooking time: This will vary slightly depending on the thickness of the *julienne*. Check by tasting after 3 minutes simmering. If undercooked, the zests will be unpleasantly bitter and hard; if overcooked, they will be mushy and too sweet.

Vegetables

Our guests at Le Manoir often gaze in wonder at the appearance, taste and texture of our vegetables. Frankly, I find their compliments puzzling, since our vegetables are cooked so simply. Vegetables are not merely an ornamental garnish. I regard them as a dish in their own right, which should complement perfectly the main course they accompany.

My only criterion for vegetables is simplicity; but for simplicity to triumph, several rules must be strictly observed.

Freshness

The vegetables must be absolutely fresh. I am lucky enough to have a large garden, so my harvest can be carefully planned. Nothing beats picking wonderful young vegetables still covered in morning dew, pulling tiny carrots from the ground, picking young courgettes crowned with their golden yellow flowers....

If you do not have a garden, you can find equally fresh vegetables at a 'Pick Your Own' farm (see page 274) or nearby vegetable market. Make the effort to buy the freshest possible vegetables you can. The results will speak for themselves on the plate.

When to pick

Vegetables are best eaten young – but not too young, as their flavour will not have developed and you will be sacrificing taste for looks. Older vegetables begin to lose their colour and often have a coarse taste and fibrous or woody texture.

Cooking

Vegetables should provide a clean taste to complement the more complex or richer taste of the dish they accompany. Most young vegetables

Peel the vegetables and cut into 5 cm/ 2 in lengths.
Stand each piece on end and slice lengthways into 4.

With a small, sharp knife, trim the pieces into barrel or olive shapes.

are delicate, so try to preserve or enhance their flavour, texture and colour when choosing your cooking method.

The most common (and most misunderstood) way to cook vegetables is boiling in water; under- and overcooking are the commonest mistakes. They should be boiled as follows; I use French beans as an example.

Haricots verts au beurre

Top and tail the beans, wash and drain. Boil 2 L/3½ pt water with 2 level tablespoons salt. Plunge the beans into galloping boiling water and cook, uncovered, for 2–3 minutes according to size, until cooked but still quite firm. Test by tasting. Lift out the beans with a slotted spoon and plunge

immediately into cold water until completely cold. Drain and refrigerate until needed.

Serving

Melt 20 g/¾ oz butter with 4 tablespoons water, a pinch of salt and 2 turns of white pepper. Add the beans, cover and boil for 1 minute. Remove the lid and cook for 1 minute, until the beans are coated with a fine film of butter. Taste and correct the seasoning.

If the vegetables differ in size, start cooking the larger ones a little earlier. Always use plenty of water and add the vegetables when it is at full boil.

Cook uncovered to allow the acids (which are present in most vegetables and can cause discoloration) to escape. In a domestic kitchen, you can cover the pan for the first minute to speed up the boiling.

It is important to use plenty of salt to fix the chlorophyll and preserve the colour. The cooking time is short, so the salt will not permeate the vegetables and make them too salty.

Refreshing

Plunging the vegetables into cold water arrests the cooking and preserves taste, colour and texture. It also saves time and effort when serving your complete dish. Just reheat them in a little butter and serve.

The emulsion of butter and *water* is important, since water creates steam which heats the vegetables quickly and thoroughly. The water must not evaporate totally or the vegetables will be too greasy; they should simply be coated with a fine film of butter and water emulsion.

The final seasoning should be light to allow the taste of the vegetables to come through.

CAROTTES GLACEES

Glazed baby carrots

Serves 4
Difficulty: 🎩
Total recipe time: 20 minutes

INGREDIENTS

20 baby carrots, with their ferny tops

2 teaspoons unsalted butter

a pinch of caster sugar (optional)

1 small sprig of tarragon, washed

salt and freshly ground white pepper

Trim the carrot tops, leaving on about 2 cm/1 in leaves, then wash and peel the carrots and place in cold water. Taste a little of the raw carrot, to assess its sweetness.
In a large sauté pan, melt the butter with a tiny pinch of salt and a pinch of caster sugar if desired. Add the carrots in a single layer, barely cover with cold water and bring to the boil. Cover with buttered greaseproof paper and simmer for about 10 minutes. Remove the paper, add the tarragon and reduce the liquid until the carrots are glazed. Season with a turn of pepper and serve.

Chef's notes

Tarragon: Blanch older tarragon in boiling water for a few seconds as it can easily overpower the taste of the carrots.
Reducing the cooking liquid: This will not only give the carrots an attractive glaze, but will also concentrate their flavour.

MANGE-TOUT AU CITRON

Mange-tout acidulated with lemon

Serves 4
Difficulty: 🎩
Total recipe time: 25 minutes

INGREDIENTS

450 g/1 lb small English mange-tout, topped and tailed, washed and drained

2 L/3½ pt water

40 g/1½ oz unsalted butter

juice of ½ lemon

salt and freshly ground white pepper

Boil the water with 2 tablespoons salt, put in the mange-tout and blanch for about 2 minutes. Taste, refresh in plenty of cold water and drain. In a medium saucepan heat the butter with 4 tablespoons water and season with 4 large pinches of salt and 4 turns of pepper. Bring to the boil, add the mange-tout, cover and cook for just a few seconds. Remove the lid and cook for 1 minute until the mange-tout are coated with a fine film of butter. Stir in the lemon juice, taste, correct the seasoning and serve immediately, as the lemon juice will quickly discolour the mange-tout.

FEVETTES A LA CREME ET PERSIL PLAT

Young broad beans cooked in cream and parsley

Serves 4
Difficulty: 🎩
Total recipe time: 30 minutes

INGREDIENTS

2.5 kg/5½ lb young broad beans

150 ml/5 fl oz whipping cream

¼ garlic clove, crushed

a small bunch of flat-leaved parsley

salt and freshly ground white pepper

Planning ahead

Stage 1 can be completed in advance.

1. Preparing the broad beans and parsley

Shell the beans, blanch in boiling water for 5 seconds, refresh, drain, make an incision in the skin and squeeze the beans out of their outer skin. Set aside.
Parsley: Wash, shake dry, pick off the leaves and blanch in boiling water for 30 seconds. Refresh, drain and reserve.

2. Cooking

Put the cream and garlic in a medium saucepan, season with a pinch of salt and 2 turns of pepper. Bring to the boil, add the broad beans and simmer for 1 minute. Add the parsley and simmer for a further 30 seconds. Taste and correct seasoning if necessary. Serve on hot side plates.

VARIATIONS

Young fresh haricot beans can also be cooked this way: increase the simmering time.

Chef's notes

The broad beans must be young. Older broad beans become too starchy and uninteresting.
Blanching the beans: Blanch for 5 seconds only – just enough to soften the outer skin. The outer skin must be removed as it is tough and unappetising. The tender emerald green beans inside will make all this work well worthwhile!

EPINARDS AU BEURRE

Spinach cooked in butter

Serves 4
Difficulty: 🎩
Total recipe time: 15 minutes

─────── INGREDIENTS ───────

675 g/1½ lb spinach
....
50 g/2 oz unsalted butter
....
salt and freshly ground white pepper
....

Planning ahead
Stage 1 can be completed well in advance. Keep the spinach covered, in the fridge.

1. Preparing the spinach
Remove all the large central veins and discard any blemished leaves. Fill the sink with water and soak the spinach for a few minutes, drain, wash in a change of water and drain again.

2. Cooking and serving
In a large saucepan, make a *beurre noisette* (see page 24) then add the spinach and stir with a wooden spoon. Season with a pinch of salt and 6 turns of pepper, stir, cover and cook for 1 minute. Remove the lid and cook for another 2 or 3 minutes, until tender. Taste, correct the seasoning if necessary and serve immediately.

─────── VARIATIONS ───────

Swiss chard is also delicious cooked this way.
Beurre noisette can be replaced by melted butter.

Chef's notes
Many varieties of spinach are rather tasteless; choose carefully. Often spinach is cooked in gallons of water (losing both taste and vitamins) and wrung dry to remove the excess water. This is criminal!
The cooking time is only approximate; check by tasting near the end.

MOUSSE D'EPINARDS

Spinach mousses

Serves 4
Difficulty: 🎩
Total recipe time: 55 minutes
Special equipment: four 4 cm/1½ in ramekins, blender or food processor

─────── INGREDIENTS ───────

550 g/1¼ lb spinach
....
1 garlic clove
....
250 ml/9 fl oz whipping cream
....
50 g/2 oz unsalted butter
....
3 eggs
....
1 teaspoon salt
....
freshly ground white pepper
....

Planning ahead
The mousses can be moulded up to 8 hours in advance. They can be cooked half an hour in advance and kept warm in a bain-marie.

1. Preparing the spinach and cream (10 minutes)
Preheat the oven to 160°C/325°F/gas 3 for Stage 3.
Trim the spinach stalks and wash the spinach in two changes of water. Drain and set aside.
Garlic: Peel and slice, then simmer in the cream for 5 minutes.

2. Making the mousse mixture
(10 minutes) (see Mousse making, page 36)
Make a *beurre noisette* (see page 24). Throw in the spinach, stir, cover and cook for 2 minutes.
Remove the garlic, then add the cream to the spinach and boil for a few seconds. Draw off the heat and leave to cool.
Finely purée the spinach and cream with the eggs, salt and 6 turns of pepper for 2 to 3 minutes. Place in a bowl,

taste, correct the seasoning and keep aside.
Brush the inside of the ramekins with a film of *beurre noisette* then fill with the mousse mixture.

3. Cooking the mousses
(35 minutes)
Line the bottom of a shallow roasting pan with greaseproof paper. Stand the moulds in the pan and add hot water to come three-quarters of the way up the sides of the ramekins.
Loosely cover the pan with pierced buttered foil and cook in the preheated oven for 35–40 minutes.

4. Serving
Warm 4 side plates.
Invert the ramekins onto the middle of the plates and shake them gently from side to side to release the mousses.

─────── VARIATIONS ───────

Swiss chard, lettuce, leeks and blanched parsley also make delicious mousses.

Chef's notes
Spinach: Some varieties of spinach have little or no flavour. Choose carefully to prevent your mousses from suffering the same fate. Coarse annual spinach is very good.

PETITS LEGUMES AU VINAIGRE DE MIEL

Pickled vegetables in honey vinegar

A delicious accompaniment for terrines, pâtés and cold meats.

Serves 4
Difficulty: 🎩
Total recipe time: 25 minutes, plus at least 2 days marinating.

INGREDIENTS

¼ cucumber

12 pickling onions

12 cauliflower florets

2 carrots

2 tablespoons acacia honey

1 tablespoon salt

Marinade

100 ml/3½ fl oz white wine vinegar

50 ml/2 fl oz dry white wine

50 ml/2 fl oz water

1 level teaspoon salt

8 turns of freshly ground white pepper

1. Preparing the vegetables

(15 minutes)

Cucumber: Peel, halve, deseed and cut lengthways into 2 mm/¹⁄₁₂ in ribbons.
Onions: Peel and remove the second fibrous layer of skin.
Cauliflower: Wash and trim the stalks.
Carrots: Wash, peel and cut lengthways into 2 mm/¹⁄₁₂ in strips on either side of the central core.

2. Blanching the vegetables

(8 minutes)

In a medium saucepan, boil 1 L/1¾ pt water with 1 tablespoon salt. Blanch the onions for 5 minutes. After 3 minutes, add the cauliflower and carrots. Drain the vegetables, refresh under cold running water and pat dry.

3. Preparing the marinade and marinating the vegetables (2 minutes, plus at least 2 days marinating)

Mix together all the marinade ingredients in the given order, then put in the vegetables, cover and leave to pickle for at least 2 days.

4. Serving

Drain the vegetables and serve.

Chef's notes

The ribbons of cucumber are marinated raw.

Do not keep the vegetables for more than a week, or the acid in the vinegar will affect their colour and texture and blemish the fragile ribbons of cucumber.

This garnish does not suit delicate pâtés, such as *foie gras,* but any strong-flavoured country pâté will welcome such friendly company. If you cannot find acacia honey, use any good quality honey.

PUREE DE MARRONS

Chestnut purée

Serves 4
Difficulty: 🍳
Total recipe time: 55 minutes

INGREDIENTS

400 g/14 oz fresh chestnuts (about 30)

1 L/1¾ pt oil for deep-frying

1 eating apple, peeled, cored and diced

20 g/¾ oz celeriac, peeled and diced

350 ml/12 fl oz Light chicken stock (see page 21) or water

1 teaspoon caster sugar

100 ml/3½ fl oz milk

4 tablespoons whipping cream

20 g/¾ oz unsalted butter

salt and freshly ground white pepper

Planning ahead

The chicken stock must be made in advance. The purée can be made 1 day in advance and kept covered in the fridge.

1. Shelling the chestnuts

Make a circular incision in the chestnut shells and deep-fry in batches of 10 for 10 seconds. Drain and use a small knife to remove the shells, which will now peel away quite easily.

2. Cooking the chestnuts

In a medium saucepan, combine the chicken stock with the diced apple and celeriac, caster sugar and the peeled chestnuts. Bring to the boil and cook, uncovered, at just below simmering point for 10 minutes. Taste to check if chestnuts are cooked.

3. Puréeing the chestnuts

In a small saucepan, bring the milk to the boil, draw off the heat and set aside.
Drain and discard the cooking juices from the chestnuts.
Purée the chestnuts in a food processor until smooth, stir in the milk and sieve into a small saucepan.

4. Finishing the dish and serving

Place the purée over a gentle heat and add the cream and butter to enrich it and create the right consistency. Taste and correct the seasoning with salt, pepper and a pinch of caster sugar if necessary. Serve in a warm serving bowl.

VARIATIONS

The chestnuts can be served whole; add 20 g/¾ oz butter to the chicken stock and cook them very slowly so they do not disintegrate. Strain the cooking liquid into a small saucepan and reduce to a syrupy consistency then put back the chestnuts and cook over a strong heat to glaze.

Chef's notes

Buy a few extra chestnuts in case any are bad.
Deep-fry the chestnuts for only a few seconds – any longer and they will discolour and harden. Alternatively, blanch them in boiling water for 4 minutes before peeling.

PETITS NAVETS GLACES

Glazed baby turnips

Serves 4
Difficulty: 🎩
Total recipe time: 40 minutes

─── INGREDIENTS ───

20 small turnips with their tops

40 g/1½ oz unsalted butter

1 level teaspoon caster sugar

salt

For cooking the tops

1 teaspoon unsalted butter

4 tablespoons water

salt and freshly ground white pepper

1. Preparing the turnips
Trim the tops, leaving on about 3 cm/ 1¼ in stalk, and reserve some of the most tender-looking leaves. Wash the turnips and selected leaves and keep them in separate bowls of water.

2. Cooking the turnips
Stand the turnips upright in a small sauté pan, packed close together. Add 40 g/1½ oz butter, 1 level teaspoon caster sugar and a pinch of salt. Cover with cold water just up to the base of the stalks and bring to the boil. Simmer for about 30 minutes, then check if they are cooked.

3. Glazing the turnips and cooking the leaves
Increase the heat and evaporate most of the water, rotating the pan to keep the turnips coated with a film of butter. Keep warm.
In a small saucepan melt 1 teaspoon butter with 4 tablespoons water and season with a pinch of salt and 2 turns of pepper. Bring to the boil, add the leaves, cover and cook for 2 minutes. Taste and correct the seasoning if necessary.

4. Serving
Arrange the turnips attractively on a flat serving dish and surround with the leaves. Serve immediately.

─── VARIATIONS ───
Many root vegetables, such as radishes, baby onions and shallots, can be cooked this way.

Chef's notes
Turnips are best when young; they have a pleasant, delicate bitterness. Older turnips can also be cooked this way but do not use the leaves. Halve or quarter the turnips, shape and blanch before cooking.

Assiette du jardinier

GRATIN DE NAVETS

Gratin of turnips

Serves 8
Difficulty: 🍳
Total recipe time: 40 minutes

— INGREDIENTS —

700 g/1½ lb turnips, peeled and thinly sliced

350 ml/12 fl oz whipping cream

½ bayleaf

1 sprig of thyme

3 white peppercorns, crushed

1 garlic clove

a dash of white wine vinegar

salt

Planning ahead
This dish can be prepared 1 hour in advance and kept warm.

Preheat the oven to 180°C/350°F/gas 5.
Boil the cream with the ½ bayleaf, thyme, peppercorns, garlic, vinegar and a pinch of salt for 3 minutes.
Arrange the sliced turnips overlapping in a 20 cm/8 in sauté pan. Strain the cream over them and press down. Cook in the preheated oven for 20 minutes and serve.

POMMES MAXIME

Potato galettes

Serves 4
Difficulty: 🍳
Total recipe time: 30 minutes
Special equipment: 4 non-stick tartlet tins (for use on a solid hob) or a large heavy non-stick frying pan

— INGREDIENTS —

2 250 g/9 oz King Edward potatoes

1 tablespoon melted butter, plus 2 teaspoons for greasing and brushing

1 teaspoon corn oil

salt and freshly ground white pepper

Planning ahead
The *galettes* can be cooked half an hour before the meal, then warmed in a hot oven just before serving.

1. Preparing the potatoes
(10 minutes)
Wash and peel, then shape into cylinders, 4 cm/1½ in diameter. Place in cold water.
Slice each cylinder into 2 mm/1/10 in rounds (you should have about 70 slices in all), place in a bowl and add 1 tablespoon melted butter and the corn oil, a pinch of salt and 2 pinches of pepper. Mix thoroughly, making sure all the potato rounds are well coated with fat.

2. Cooking the potatoes
(20 minutes)
Lightly butter the insides of the tartlet tins and arrange the potatoes first around the edges, overlapping them like petals of a flower and then in the centre. Cook on a solid hob at medium heat for 8 minutes per side, brushing with a little melted butter every 4 minutes. Alternatively brush the frying pan with butter, arrange the potatoes in 4 overlapping circles. Fry for 8 minutes, brushing with butter every 4 minutes, then carefully turn over the potato *galettes* and cook the other side for 8 minutes, until crisp and golden. Invert them onto warmed plates and serve.

Chef's notes
Do not wash the potatoes after slicing; their starch will hold the *galettes* together during cooking.
One pinch of salt is quite sufficient for seasoning since the water in the potato will evaporate during cooking.
The potato *galettes* should be golden brown, so watch carefully during cooking to see that they do not burn.

POMMES DE TERRE AUX PISTILS DE SAFRAN

Saffron potatoes

Serves 4
Difficulty: 🍳
Total recipe time: 35 minutes

— INGREDIENTS —

550 g/1¼ lb potatoes, peeled

2 shallots, peeled and finely chopped

20 g/¾ oz unsalted butter

a pinch of saffron threads or saffron powder

1 sprig of thyme

1 bayleaf

100 ml/3½ fl oz. Light chicken stock (see page 21) or water

salt and freshly ground white pepper

Planning ahead
If using saffron threads, rehydrate them in 2 tablespoons water for 1 hour beforehand.
The chicken stock (if used) must be made in advance.
The dish can be prepared 1 hour in advance, then warmed in a hot oven before serving.

1. Preparing the potatoes
(15 minutes)
Halve or quarter the larger potatoes. Trim them all into small barrel shapes and keep in cold water.

2. Cooking the potatoes
(20 minutes)
In a medium sauté pan sweat the potatoes in the butter for 1 or 2 minutes, then add the saffron, thyme and bayleaf and season with a pinch of salt and 4 turns of pepper. Shake the pan to make sure all the potatoes are well coated with saffron.
Add the chicken stock or water, cover the pan with buttered paper and

simmer for about 15 minutes. Remove the paper and reduce at full boil until the potatoes are glazed.

3. Serving
Remove the thyme and bayleaf, taste one potato, correct the seasoning if necessary and serve.

Chef's notes
Saffron threads are expensive. They have a concentrated but slightly bitter flavour, so must be rehydrated before using to regain their delicacy. *Potatoes:* Most varieties can be used, even new potatoes.

JULIENNE DE LEGUMES FRITES
Deep-fried vegetable sticks

Serves 4
Difficulty: 🎩
Total recipe time: 30 minutes

— INGREDIENTS —
3 medium turnips (200 g/7 oz)
2 small courgettes (100 g/3½ oz)
200 g/7 oz celeriac
1 L/1¾ pt sunflower oil

Planning ahead
These can be made in advance. See Chef's notes on *Chips de céleri-rave frits,* page 57.

Wash and peel all the vegetables, then cut into very fine sticks (1 mm/¹⁄₁₆ in thick). Keep the different types separately.
Heat the oil to about 180°C/360°F and deep-fry each vegetable for about 2 minutes until they turn a rich golden brown. Remove, shake off excess oil then drain on absorbent paper and keep warm until ready to serve.

PUREE D'AUBERGINES
A rustic purée of aubergines

Serves 4
Difficulty: 🎩
Total recipe time: 1 hour 25 minutes

— INGREDIENTS —
2 large aubergines
1 garlic clove, peeled and halved
¼ lemon
1 tablespoon olive oil
100 ml/3½ fl oz double cream
1 teaspoon salt
freshly ground white pepper

Planning ahead
This purée can be made 1 day in advance and kept covered in the fridge.

1. Preparing and cooking the aubergines (1 hour 10 minutes)
Preheat the oven to 190°C/375°F/gas 5.
Trim the stalks, halve the aubergines lengthways and rub the surface first with a face of garlic (reserve the garlic for Stage 2), then with a face of lemon, to prevent discoloration.
Make a few deep incisions in the flesh, sprinkle with olive oil and place the aubergines flesh side up on a baking tray. Cover loosely with foil and cook in the preheated oven for 1 hour, or a little longer, depending on size.
Remove and leave to cool for a few minutes.

2. Making the purée (15 minutes)
Chop the garlic.
In a small saucepan bring to the boil the cream, garlic, 1 level teaspoon salt and 4 turns of pepper and leave to infuse for about 1 minute.
Scoop out the flesh of the aubergines and purée in a food processor. Turn out into a small bowl and stir in the flavoured cream. Taste and correct seasoning if necessary. Serve.

ECHALOTES CARAMELISEES
Caramelized shallots

Serves 4
Difficulty: 🎩
Total recipe time: 50 minutes

— INGREDIENTS —
30 shallots (about 350 g/12 oz), peeled
20 g/¾ oz unsalted butter
salt and freshly ground white pepper

Planning ahead
This dish can be cooked in advance and kept warm.

Melt the butter in a sauté pan, put in the shallots, closely packed together, add a pinch of salt and 2 turns of pepper and cook uncovered over a moderate heat for about 10 minutes. Partially cover with a lid and cook over moderate heat for about 30 minutes, stirring occasionally, until the shallots are melting and brown. Taste, correct the seasoning and serve.

— VARIATIONS —
Button onions can also be cooked this way.

Chef's notes
When peeling the shallots, remove the tough second layer of skin and cut them just above the roots so they remain whole once cooked.
They can also be baked in a fairly hot oven (200°C/400°F/gas 6); the cooking time will vary depending on the size of the shallots.

CHIPS DE CELERI-RAVE FRITS

Golden brown, crispy celeriac chips

A wonderful accompaniment for roast game.

Serves 4
Difficulty: 🍳
Total recipe time: 20 minutes
Special equipment: deep-fryer

——— INGREDIENTS ———
750 g/1¾ lb celeriac

1 L/1¾ pt sunflower or corn oil, for frying

Wash the celeriac, cut off the tops and peel. Quarter, then cut into the thinnest possible slices. Deep-fry 4 at a time, until they turn a rich golden brown, keeping them well separated with a kitchen fork. Lift out the frying basket, shake off excess oil then drain the celeriac chips on absorbent paper and keep warm until ready to serve.

——— VARIATIONS ———
Deep-fried turnips are also delicious (see *Bécassines rôties au vieux Madère*, page 206).

Chef's notes
Slice the celeriac as finely and evenly as possible. Thick or uneven slices will burn.
Do not cook all the slices at once; this will lower the temperature of the oil, causing the chips to soak it up and stick together.
The edges will darken first, but do not worry; the chips must be cooked through to the middle. Remove them when the oil stops sizzling, indicating that no moisture is left.
Do not season the chips – frying concentrates the already spicy flavour of the celeriac.

SALSIFIS GLACES

Glazed salsify

Serves 4
Difficulty: 🍳
Total recipe time: 40 minutes

——— INGREDIENTS ———
12 salsify roots

2 tablespoons white wine vinegar

25 g/1 oz unsalted butter

a squeeze of lemon

300 ml/½ pt Light chicken stock (see page 21) or water

salt and freshly ground white pepper

Plannning ahead
The salsify can be cooked 1 hour in advance.

1. Preparing the salsify
Wash and scrub with a hard brush to remove any dirt. Peel and place in 2 L/ 3½ pt cold water acidulated with 2 tablespoons vinegar to prevent discoloration. Cut into 4 cm/1½ in sticks.

2. Cooking the salsify
In a medium saucepan, sweat the salsify in the butter and a squeeze of lemon for 2 minutes. Add the chicken stock or water and season with a tiny pinch of salt and 4 turns of pepper. Bring to the boil, cover and simmer for about 15 minutes. Remove the lid, and reduce at full boil until the salsify is glazed. Taste and correct seasoning.

——— VARIATIONS ———
Add a spoonful of whipping cream and some chopped parsley.

Chef's notes
Wear rubber gloves when handling the salsify or it will stain your fingers.

RIZ SAUVAGE AU NATUREL

Wild rice

Serves 4
Difficulty: 🍳
Total recipe time: 1 hour 10 minutes

——— INGREDIENTS ———
150 g/5 oz wild rice, washed and drained

1 tablespoon unsalted butter

1 shallot, peeled and finely chopped

200 ml/7 fl oz Light chicken stock (see page 21) or water

Planning ahead
The rice can be cooked several hours in advance.
The chicken stock (if used) must be made in advance.

Preheat the oven to 180°C/350°F/ gas 4.
In a medium saucepan, sweat the chopped shallot in 2 teaspoons butter for 2 minutes without colouring. Stir in the rice and season with a pinch of salt and 4 turns of pepper. Add the stock or water, bring to the boil, cover with buttered greaseproof paper and cook in the preheated oven for about 1 hour. Taste and correct the seasoning. Make a *beurre noisette* with the remaining butter (see page 24), stir it into the rice and serve.

Chef's notes
Wild rice (actually a dried grass) is expensive but it has a far better flavour than refined, processed rice. The cooking time may vary from type to type so check by tasting towards the end. Do not expect the soft texture of white rice; wild rice should remain firm. Do not cook at a higher temperature as excess heat will make the rice burst open.

Spring

***

Time to wake up — after the uniformity and peace of Winter, Spring brings a burst of change. There is excitement everywhere; farmers and people from all walks of life begin to plan and re-emerge. It is the most hopeful of all seasons, with the first shoots heralding the arrival of warmth and sunshine.

A chef's imagination is fired by the sight of delicate, fresh leaves struggling to burst out. The colours, too, are delicate, all shades of pastel, with barely a hint of the fruits to come. The tastes are subtle and suggestive rather than deliberate statements. After the dreary monotony of winter, what a relief to cook the first baby courgettes, still crowned with their flowers, marry tender spears of asparagus with the first morels, carve a juicy slice of Spring lamb and prepare the fresh salmon from the fast-flowing Scottish rivers.

POTAGE LEGER AUX QUAT' SAISONS

Light vegetable soup

"This delicious, simple soup filled with all the flavours of the garden was on our menu when we opened our first small bistro in Oxford. I still enjoy its simplicity and unsophisticated goodness."

Serves 4
Difficulty:
Total recipe time: 30 minutes

INGREDIENTS

1 shallot, peeled and diced

1 medium carrot, peeled and diced

1 tablespoon unsalted butter

a small handful of French beans, chopped

1 small leek, washed, trimmed and chopped

1 medium courgette, washed and diced

4 tarragon leaves, finely chopped

1 sprig of chervil, finely chopped

4 basil leaves, finely chopped

6 sorrel leaves, finely shredded

1 medium tomato, peeled, deseeded and diced

750 ml/1¼ pt hot water or Light chicken stock (see page 21)

100 ml/3½ fl oz whipping cream

salt and freshly ground white pepper

lemon juice

Planning ahead
The vegetables and herbs can be prepared in advance.

1. Making the soup (10 minutes)
In a large saucepan, sweat the diced shallot and carrot in the butter for 5 minutes. Add the chopped French beans, leek and courgette and sweat for 1 more minute. Add 750 ml/1¼ pt hot water or stock, bring to the boil, skim and simmer for 5 minutes, then add the chopped herbs. At the last moment, toss in the shredded sorrel and diced tomato. Taste, season with salt and pepper, add a dash of lemon juice and finally stir in the cream.

2. Serving
Serve in a warmed china soup tureen or in 4 warmed soup bowls.

VARIATIONS
Use any garden vegetables for this soup.
For an even lighter clear soup, omit the whipping cream.
Purée in a blender to make a delicious cream of vegetable soup.

Chef's notes
Preparing the vegetables: Be careful not to dice the vegetables too finely; they should have a good texture.
Sorrel and tomato are added at the last moment as they only need a few seconds to cook.
The whole idea of the soup is to capture the freshness of the vegetables so 10 minutes cooking is quite sufficient. Add the herbs right at the end to retain their freshness and liveliness.
Many other vegatables may be used.

TARTARE DE SAUMON SAUVAGE A LA CROQUE DE CONCOMBRES

Tartare of marinated wild salmon with cucumber salad

"Without doubt, the salmon is the king of all fish. Every Spring, these remarkable creatures return from the sea to their birthplace, high upstream in the fast-flowing rivers of England, Wales, Scotland and Ireland and here they spawn; it is an extraordinary and mysterious journey, during which they fight the impetuous currents, shooting rapids and scaling waterfalls as if triggered by some powerful hidden mechanism, thrusting their bodies into magical curves. These fascinating fish are at their most succulent in the Spring. This recipe is a small tribute to a magnificent creature; it mirrors the two main colours of Spring – delicate pink and fragile green."

Serves 8
Difficulty: ♟♟
Total recipe time: 1 hour, plus 13 hours marinating and resting
Special equipment: tweezers, 6 cm/ 2½ in pastry cutter, clingfilm

————— INGREDIENTS —————
450 g/1 lb wild salmon fillet
1 tablespoon fresh dill, chopped
zest of ⅛ lemon, finely sliced
1 tablespoon caster sugar
½ teaspoon Dijon mustard
2 teaspoons soured cream
lemon juice
salt and freshly ground white pepper

Cucumber salad
½ medium cucumber
1 teaspoon salt
1 teaspoon white wine vinegar
2 tablespoons non-scented oil

Garnish
½ lemon
4 tablespoons soured cream
1 tablespoon caviar, salmon eggs or lumpfish roe, chilled
a small bunch of fresh dill

Planning ahead
Prepare the salmon at least 12 hours (even 2–3 days) in advance, but do not leave in the marinade for more than 12 hours; after this time, wash and dry the fish and keep refrigerated, wrapped in clingfilm.
The cucumber salad can be prepared 2 or 3 hours in advance.
The garnish can be prepared and the dish dressed 1 hour in advance; keep in a cool place.

1. Marinating the salmon
(20 minutes, plus 1 hour resting and 12 hours marinating)
Remove the skin and gently tweeze out any stray bones. Place the salmon on a piece of clingfilm large enough to enclose it completely.
In a bowl, mix together 1 tablespoon salt, the sugar, sliced lemon zest and dill and gently rub the mixture into both sides of the salmon. Seal the clingfilm like a parcel and place in the bottom of the fridge for 12 hours.
At least 30 minutes before serving,

unwrap the salmon, rinse under cold running water and pat dry with a paper towel. Cut the salmon into 3 mm/⅛ in cubes and place in a bowl. In a separate bowl, mix together the mustard, soured cream, lemon juice and 4 turns of pepper, then mix in the salmon cubes. Correct the seasoning and leave in a cool place for 1 hour. Meanwhile make the cucumber salad.

2. The cucumber salad
(5 minutes, plus 30 minutes resting)
Peel the cucumber, halve lengthways and scoop out the seeds with a teaspoon. Slice finely, place in a colander, sprinkle with salt and leave for 30 minutes to remove the indigestible acids. Rinse under cold running water, pat dry and place in a small bowl. Add the wine vinegar, oil and 2 turns of pepper and mix thoroughly.

3. The garnish (5 minutes)
Remove the skin and pith of the lemon and cut out the segments, slicing them into wafer-thin triangles. Put the dill in cold water to prevent wilting and cut off the tiny fronds.

*Tartare de saumon sauvage à la
croque de concombres*

4. Serving (20 minutes)
Have ready 8 small white plates and a pastry cutter. Place the pastry cutter in the centre of a plate and fill it nine-tenths full with salmon. Press down gently with the back of a teaspoon. Top with a teaspoon of soured cream and smooth over with a metal spatula. Carefully lift off the pastry cutter.
Surround the salmon with overlapping slivers of cucumber and arrange a circle of lemon triangles on the top; arrange a little mound of caviar in the centre. Finally arrange the fronds of dill around the edge like a royal garland – highly appropriate!

──────── WINE ────────
Avoid a powerful wine, which would interfere with the delicate build-up of flavours. Try a young dry white from Burgundy, like a Montagny or St Véran, or a white Bandol from Provence or Bergeron from Savoie. Pink Champagne would be ideal!

Chef's notes
Use only wild or the best farmed salmon for this dish.
Do not cut up the marinated salmon too finely, or it will be like eating mince; too large and it will look unattractive. Serve the *tartares* with *brioche* or hot toast, but prepare the toast at the last moment, or it will be horribly soggy. Remember British Rail!

MOUSSETTE DE SAUMON FUME

Smoked salmon mousse

Serves 4
Difficulty: 🍳
Total recipe time: 25 minutes, plus at least 2 hours chilling
Special equipment: 2 stainless steel bowls, food processor

──────── INGREDIENTS ────────
200 g/7 oz wood-smoked salmon, sliced and trimmed
....
2 pinches of cayenne pepper
....
¼ lemon
....
300 ml/½ pt whipping cream, chilled
....
a pinch of salt
....

Planning ahead
The mousse must be made at least 2 hours (and up to 12 hours) in advance. Keep refrigerated, covered with clingfilm.
It can be arranged on the serving plates 1 hour before the meal.

1. Making the mousse
(20 minutes, plus 2 hours chilling)
Combine the smoked salmon, salt, cayenne and lemon juice in a food processor and purée for 2 minutes only. With the food processor on the lowest speed, slowly add half the chilled whipping cream. Force the purée through a fine sieve into a stainless steel bowl and refrigerate for 10 minutes.
In a large mixing bowl whip the remaining 150 ml/5 fl oz chilled cream to a light peak and fold into the salmon purée, cutting and lifting with a spatula. Refrigerate for at least 2 hours.

2. Serving (5 minutes)
Using two dessert spoons dipped in warm water, shape the mousse into *quenelles*, arranging 3 attractively on each plate. Serve to your guests.

──────── VARIATIONS ────────
Smoked trout or mackerel are also delicious done this way.
For a more complex dish, line the bottom of 4 ramekins with a fish jelly and the insides with smoked salmon. Fill with the mousse, reinforced with 2 leaves or sachets of gelatine leaves and refrigerate. Turn out onto the middle of the plates and decorate with a sprig of dill.

Chef's notes
Smoked salmon: Whenever possible try to buy home-cured salmon smoked over wood.
Puréeing the salmon: Do not process for more than 2 minutes or the friction of the blade will heat the mixture and cause the salmon to sweat.
The cream: This must be cold and is added in 2 stages. First add the unwhipped cream to loosen the purée, then carefully fold in the whipped cream to ensure that the mousse turns out light and delicate. Take care not to overmix or it will granulate and subsequently separate.
Setting the mousse: Since the mousse contains no gelatine, it needs at least 2 hours chilling to set.

EMINCE D'AVOCAT AU CRABE, GINGEMBRE ET PAMPLEMOUSSE ROSE

Avocado with crab, ginger and pink grapefruit

"Quite daring, I thought in 1978! To me, this dish symbolizes the first taste of freedom that *nouvelle cuisine* brought; it captures the excitement and feeling of adventure to come as the era of avocado and prawns and all that it stood for came to a close."

Serves 4
Difficulty: ♙
Total recipe time: 1 hour 35 minutes, plus 1 hour cooling
Special equipment: 1 large saucepan, mallet

————— INGREDIENTS —————

1 675 g/1½ lb live crab

30 g/1 oz fresh ginger root

salt and freshly ground white pepper

Mayonnaise
2 egg yolks

½ teaspoon Dijon mustard

300 ml/10 fl oz grapeseed oil

juice of ½ lemon

Mustard vinaigrette
1 teaspoon Dijon mustard

100 ml/3½ fl oz groundnut oil

1 tablespoon white wine vinegar

2 tablespoons warm water

Garnish
2 ripe but firm avocados

1 fresh garden lettuce, trimmed

1 pink grapefruit

Planning ahead
The crab can be cooked and dressed, the ginger cooked and the mayonnaise prepared 1 day ahead. It is essential to cook the crab at least 2 hours in advance.
The vinaigrette and salad can be made several hours in advance.

1. Cooking the crab
(20 minutes, plus 1 hour cooling)
Bring to the boil 2 L/3½ pt water with 1 tablespoon salt. Peel the ginger and reserve. Add the peelings to the water and simmer for a few minutes to release the flavour.
Now you will need courage, especially if the crab is still quite lively. Wash it under cold running water and scrub with a brush. Plunge into the fast-boiling water and simmer for 10 minutes. Take off the heat and leave for another 10 minutes. Remove the crab from the water and place on a tray to cool for 1 hour.

2. Dressing the crab (20 minutes)
On a chopping board covered with a tea towel, dismember the crab and crack the legs and claws with a mallet. Ease out the flesh with a tablespoon, discarding any pieces of shell.
Insert the blade of a heavy knife in between the stomach and top shell and lever off the shell. Discard the stomach and 'dead man's fingers'. Scrape out all the meat and the brown creamy parts from inside the outer part of the shell. Place the brown meat

in a small bowl and crush with a fork. Mix 2 tablespoons into the white meat and keep in a cool place. (Keep the shells and remaining brown meat for a light crab soup.)

3. The ginger (20 minutes)
Finely slice the root and cut into fine sticks. Poach in at least 2 L/3½ pt boiling water for 15 minutes, taste to check that the flavour is not too fierce and the ginger is tender, then refresh and drain.

4. The mayonnaise (10 minutes)
(see page 26)
Using a wire whisk, mix the egg yolks with the mustard, a pinch of salt and 2 pinches of pepper. Gradually pour on the oil in a constant trickle, whisking all the time until completely absorbed. Add the lemon juice, taste and correct the seasoning.
Mix 2 tablespoons mayonnaise and the ginger sticks into the crab meat, season and set aside. Keep the remaining mayonnaise for another use.

5. The vinaigrette (5 minutes)
(see page 29)
Put the mustard in a small bowl and very slowly add the oil in a continuous trickle, whisking all the time. Add half the vinegar and continue whisking until the oil is completely absorbed. Add the remaining vinegar and 2 tablespoons warm water to obtain a smooth consistency. Season to taste.

6. The salad and grapefruit
(15 minutes)
Avocados: Halve lengthways and re-move the stones. With a point of a knife, trace a line down the centre of the skins and peel the avocados. Place face down on a chopping board and cut into 5 mm/¼ in slices.
Lettuce: Wash and pat dry. Lay 2 or 3 leaves on top of each other, roll up and shred with a sharp knife. Shred all the lettuce in this way.
Grapefruit: Remove the peel and pith and halve each segment lengthways.

7. Dressing and serving (5 minutes)
Toss the shredded lettuce in 2 table-spoons vinaigrette. Place a little mound in the centre of 4 plates and en-circle with overlapping slices of avo-cado. In the centre, place a generous mound of crab salad and arrange the segments of pink grapefruit around the edge.
Spoon a ribbon of vinaigrette over the avocado and finish with 2 or 3 turns of pepper.

Chef's notes
If you cannot face the ordeal of having to kill a crab, buy one ready-boiled. It may be less moist and probably less tasty – certainly less dangerous!
Although you only need 2 table-spoons of mayonnaise for this recipe, it is impossible to prepare such a small quantity. The remainder will keep, covered, at room temperature for up to 2 days. Make the mayonnaise with grapeseed oil, which can be refriger-ated without separating.

GELEE DE SAUMON SAUVAGE EN AIGRE-DOUX

A melting jelly of wild salmon, topped with a film of sour cream and diced cucumber

"Salmon bones are of little use when it comes to making a full-flavoured fish stock, but I was brought up to throw nothing away – so I devised this delicious Spring or Summer starter!"

Serves 4
Difficulty:
Total recipe time: 50 minutes, plus 4 hours chilling
Special equipment: muslin cloth, 4 china serving bowls

——— INGREDIENTS ———
800 g/1¾ lb salmon bones and heads
½ medium onion, finely chopped
½ small leek, washed, trimmed and finely chopped
65 g/2½ oz fennel bulb or trimmings
25 g/1 oz celery, finely chopped
2 sprigs of parsley and 1 sprig of thyme, tied together
1 garlic clove, unpeeled and crushed
250 g/9 oz tomatoes, deseeded and chopped
6 white peppercorns, crushed

½ star anise
50 ml/2 fl oz Noilly Prat
50 ml/2 fl oz dry white wine
600 ml/1 pt Light fish stock (see page 20) or water
1–2 leaves of gelatine or 1–2 sachets of powdered gelatine
100 g/3½ oz salmon fillet, washed and finely chopped
salt and freshly ground white pepper
a pinch of cayenne pepper
juice of ½ lemon

Garnish
¼ medium cucumber
lemon juice
4 tablespoons sour cream
paprika

Planning ahead
The jelly must be prepared and left to set in serving bowls at least 4 hours (and up to 2 days) in advance. Keep re-frigerated, sealed with clingfilm.
The dish can be completed 2–3 hours in advance. Remove from the fridge 15 minutes before serving.

1. Preparing the fish bones and vegetables (20 minutes)
Cut off the gills from the salmon head with scissors. Chop the bones into 5–7 cm/2–3 in pieces and put in a bowl with the head under running water for 10 minutes to remove all traces of blood. Drain.

2. Cooking the jelly (30 minutes plus 4 hours setting)
In a large saucepan combine all the fish bones, chopped vegetables, tomatoes, herbs and spices. Add the Noilly Prat, white wine and fish stock, quickly

Gelée de saumon sauvage en aigre-doux

bring to the boil, skim, season with 2 large pinches of salt and simmer gently for 20 minutes.

Gelatine: Soak in cold water until supple. If using powdered gelatine, dissolve in 1–2 teaspoons hot water.

Salmon fillet: Add to the stock after 20 minutes and simmer for a further 10 minutes, then add the gelatine.

Pass the stock through a fine conical sieve lined with a damp muslin cloth, pressing lightly on the bones with a ladle. You should obtain 400 ml/ 14 fl oz of clear stock.

Testing the jelly: Put 2 tablespoons stock in a small bowl in the freezer for about 5 minutes until it sets. Taste to check texture and seasoning and correct with salt, cayenne pepper and lemon juice.

Leave the stock to cool until tepid, then pour into 4 china bowls, cover with clingfilm and refrigerate for at least 4 hours until set.

3. The garnish (30 minutes plus 30 minutes freezing)

Cucumber: Peel, halve lengthways and dice finely. Sprinkle with salt, marinate for 15 minutes then place in the freezer for at least 30 minutes. Defrost under running water, drain and pat dry. Taste and correct the seasoning as necessary.

Put 4 tablespoons sour cream in a small bowl and stir in a pinch of salt, 4 turns of pepper and a squeeze of lemon.

Take the jelly out of the fridge 15 minutes before serving.

4. Serving

Mask each salmon jelly with a film of sour cream. Season with a pinch of paprika and scatter the diced cucumber on top.

—————— VARIATIONS ——————

Cut a small salmon fillet into 1 cm/ ½ in dice, poach in a *bouillon* for 1 minute, cool and nestle in the bottom of each bowl before pouring over the stock.

Scatter a generous teaspoon of caviar or salmon eggs on top of the sour cream and cucumber.

PARFAIT DE FOIE DE VOLAILLES
A L'ENRUBANEE DE PETITS
LEGUMES EN AIGRE-DOUX

Chicken liver pâté garnished with baby vegetables pickled in honey vinegar

"This very easy dish makes an ideal starter for a dinner party, since both the pâté and vegetables must be prepared at least one day in advance."

Serves 4
Difficulty: ♙

Total recipe time: 1 hour 35 minutes, plus 1 day resting
Special equipment: 20 x 16 cm/8 x 6 in terrine, food processor

---
INGREDIENTS
---

400 g/14 oz plump fresh chicken livers

8 shallots

1 garlic clove

1 sprig of thyme

50 ml/2 fl oz Cognac

100 ml/3½ fl oz dry Madeira

100 ml/3½ fl oz port

400 g/14 oz unsalted butter, plus 1 teaspoon

5 eggs

melted dripping or cooking fat, to seal

salt and freshly ground white pepper

Pickled vegetables (see page 52), to serve

Planning ahead
Order fresh chicken livers well in advance and ask your butcher to remove the gall. If the livers are dark, soak them in milk for 1 day to remove all traces of blood. Wash, drain and pat dry before using.
The pâté and pickled vegetables must be made at least 1 day in advance.

---

1. Preparing the pâté (10 minutes)
Preheat the oven to 150°C/300°F/ gas 2.

In a medium saucepan, sweat the chopped shallots and garlic in 1 teaspoon butter without colouring. Add the Cognac, Madeira and port, bring to the boil and reduce the liquid by four-fifths. Set aside.
Butter: Melt slowly in a small saucepan.
Chicken livers: If the galls are still attached, cut the flesh away from them. If any of the bitter liquid from the gall touches the liver, wash thoroughly. Purée the livers in a food processor for 1 minute, then add the cooked shallot and alcohol mixture. Add the eggs, 1 tablespoon salt, 1 teaspoon pepper and lastly the melted butter. Blend for a few seconds until the mixture is thoroughly amalgamated. Using the back of a ladle, force the mixture through a fine conical sieve into the terrine. Cover with buttered greaseproof paper.

2. Cooking the pâté (1 hour 20 minutes, plus 1 day resting)
Line a deep roasting pan with foil. Put in the terrine and pour in enough hot water to come three-quarters of the way up the sides of the terrine. Cook in the oven for 1 hour and 20 minutes. Check the oven temperature with a thermometer (do not trust the thermostat); if it rises above 300°C/150°F/ gas 2, the pâté will become overcooked and grey.
To check if the pâté is cooked, insert a trussing needle into the centre for 2 seconds, then withdraw it; it should be hot and dry. Remove the cooked pâté from the oven and leave to cool

at room temperature for 1–2 hours. Seal with a little melted fat to prevent discoloration and allow to rest for 1 day.

3. Serving (5 minutes)
Remove the fat from the surface of the pâté. If the top is still slightly grey, scrape off a fine layer with a teaspoon and smooth over. Dip the terrine into a bowl of hot water for a few seconds and turn out the pâté onto a chopping board. Dip the blade of a sharp knife into hot water and carve generous slices. Arrange on individual plates or a serving dish, scatter ribbons of pickled vegetables around the edge and serve.

VARIATIONS

Replace the chicken livers with duck or calves' livers. For a superb, truly luxurious pâté, replace one-third of the quantity of livers with *foie gras*. If you have time to spare, add a really special finishing touch; freeze the unmoulded pâté for 20 minutes. Warm a little *foie gras* or duck fat just to melting point and brush a fine film over the pâté. Freeze for a few minutes and repeat the process until the pâté is finely coated with fat.

WINE

Alsace wine is often overlooked, but a spicy Pinot Gris (Tokay d'Alsace) has plenty of depth and would be perfect.

Chef's note
Liver is prone to oxidization, so do not keep the pâté for more than 4 days.

SALADE DE CAILLE RUSTIQUE

A salad of quail prepared in the old-fashioned way

Serves 4
Difficulty:
Total recipe time: 55 minutes
Special equipment: boning knife,
2 cm/¾ in round pastry cutter

—————— INGREDIENTS ——————

4 quail, with their livers

1 teaspoon unsalted butter

1 teaspoon non-scented oil

50 g/2 oz mixed salad leaves (eg: curly endive, batavia, radicchio)

salt and freshly ground white pepper

Walnut vinaigrette

1½ tablespoons walnut oil

2 tablespoons non-scented oil

1 tablespoon white wine vinegar

Garnish

3 slices white bread

1 tablespoon melted butter

1 garlic clove (optional)

60 g/2 oz smoked belly of pork

4 quail's eggs

1 sprig of chervil

Planning ahead
The salads and vinaigrettes can be prepared several hours in advance. The quail can be roasted 30 minutes beforehand.

1. The salads and vinaigrette
(15 minutes)
Preheat the oven to 230°C/450°F/gas 8.
Salads: Combine the salad leaves in a bowl.
Walnut vinaigrette: Mix together all the ingredients, adding a large pinch of salt and 4 turns of pepper.

2. The quail (10 minutes, plus 5 minutes resting)
Singe over a naked flame to remove stubble. Season. In a hot sauté pan, heat the butter and oil, put in the quail and brown on all sides for 1 – 2 minutes. Turn the birds onto their backs and roast in the oven for 7–10 minutes depending on their size.
Pour off the cooking fat and reserve it. Cover the quail with buttered paper and leave to rest for 5 minutes. Leave the oven switched on. Meanwhile, prepare the garnish.

3. The garnish (15 minutes)
Croûtons: Using the pastry cutter, cut the bread into rounds, brush lightly with melted butter, place on a baking sheet and toast in the hot oven until

crisp and golden. If you like, rub the toasted *croûtons* with a cut garlic clove. Set aside.
Lardons: Remove the rind from the pork belly and slice the meat into 2 cm x 3 mm/¾ x ⅛ in strips. Blanch in unsalted boiling water for 1–2 minutes, refresh, drain and sauté in 1 teaspoon butter for a few seconds.
Quail's eggs: Using a small paring knife, make an incision in the shells to cut through the tough inner layer, but be careful not to puncture the yolks. Crack the eggs into a small bowl.

4. Boning the quail: (5 minutes)
Pull the legs away from the breast, cut, then section at the joint to produce 2 separate pieces from each leg. Carve out the breasts and halve lengthways. Lightly season the inside of the breasts with salt and a little pepper and return all the boned quail to the sauté pan. Carefully coat each piece with the cooking juices as you put it in the pan. Keep the carcasses for making stock or sauces.

5. The quail's livers and eggs
(5 minutes)
Season the livers and fry for 30 seconds in the reserved cooking fat. Remove, put in the eggs and fry for just 20 seconds. At the last moment, season lightly and add a dash of vinegar.

6. Serving (5 minutes)
In separate dishes, reheat the quail, *lardons* and *croûtons* in a warm oven for 2 minutes.
Strain the remaining cooking juices from the quail into the vinaigrette. Toss the salad in the vinaigrette and sprinkle with *croûtons* and *lardons*, mixing them in lightly.

Place a generous mound of salad on each plate and arrange a breast and leg of quail around the edge. Top each mound of salad with a quail's liver and egg, season with pepper, decorate with a sprig of chervil and serve tepid.

VARIATIONS

Sliced artichoke hearts, French beans or a few wild mushrooms tossed in butter make lovely additions to this salad as do slivers of pan-fried *foie gras* added to the garnish – in this case, omit the *lardons*.

For a simpler, but still delicious traditional dish, increase the quantity of salad and top with 3 or 4 fried quail's eggs, omitting the quail altogether.

WINE

Normally I would suggest a really fine red wine to complement roast quail, but the vinegar in the dish would impair its flavour. Serve a lively young wine – Beaujolais, a red Sancerre or a good Provençal wine such as Château Vignelaure, served slightly chilled.

Chef's notes

For a totally successful dish, you should use fresh quail which have been hung for about a week to enhance their flavour. Unfortunately quail farming has become so industrialized that nowadays you will probably only find frozen quail, already drawn. It really is worth making the effort to shop around for fresh birds – only then will you understand and taste the simple magic that this dish has to offer.

CHARTREUSE AUX POINTES D'ASPERGES ET POIREAUX A L'INFUSION DE CERFEUIL

Chartreuse of asparagus spears and leeks served with an emulsion of chervil and lemon

"In France the leek is called 'poor man's asparagus'. The combination of the asparagus of rich and poor has proved most successful – food for thought, I think.
Swathed in emerald ribbons, the asparagus mousse has a deliciously concentrated flavour and makes a feast for both eye and tastebuds; surely the very essence of Spring."

Serves 8
Difficulty: 🍳🍳
Total recipe time: 1 hour 45 minutes
Special equipment: 8 x 7 cm/3 in ramekins

INGREDIENTS
3 young leeks

Mousse
400 g/14 oz asparagus
150 g/5 oz chicken breast
4 sprigs of chervil
1 whole egg
1 egg yolk
200 ml/7 fl oz milk
150 ml/5 fl oz whipping cream
salt and freshly ground white pepper

Sauce
4 – 6 sprigs of chervil, chopped
200 ml/7 fl oz Fumet de légumes (see page 22)
2 tablespoons whipping cream
40 g/1½ oz unsalted butter, chilled and diced
juice of ¼ lemon

Garnish
1 leek
12 asparagus spears
8 sprigs of chervil
1 teaspoon unsalted butter
½ truffle (optional)
15 wild mushrooms (girolles, morels or oyster mushrooms) (optional)

Planning ahead
The leek-lined *chartreuses* can be prepared half a day in advance. Cover tightly with clingfilm and refrigerate until ready to cook.
The vegetable stock must be prepared in advance.
The sauce must be finished and the garnish cooked at the last moment.

1. Cooking the leeks and lining the ramekins (40 minutes)
In a large saucepan, boil 2 L/3½ pt water with 2 tablespoons salt.
Leeks: Using a paring knife, trim just above the roots then make an incision 3 mm/⅛ in deep down the entire length and peel away 2 or 3 layers of leaves. Discard the green tops, root and coarse outer leaves. Perhaps your rabbit will enjoy them!
Make another incision lengthways to

*Chartreuse aux
pointes d'asperges
et poireaux à
l'infusion de cerfeuil*

free the tender leaves and cut into 5 x 2 cm/2 x ¾ in ribbons. Wash in cold water, then blanch in boiling water for 1 minute.

Reserve the water for the mousse. Lift out the leek ribbons and refresh in iced water. Drain and gently pat dry with a tea towel. Separate white and green ribbons onto 2 plates.

Lightly butter the ramekins and, mustering all your patience with thoughts of the beautiful end result, line them with ribbons of leek: leaving a very small circle unlined in the centre of each ramekin, start by placing one end of each ribbon near the centre and drape the ribbon over the edge, leaving a 2 cm/¾ in overhang. Alternate white and green ribbons, overlapping them slightly.

2. Preparing the mousse mixture (20 minutes) (see Mousse making, page 36)

Asparagus for the mousse and garnish: Peel, trim and discard the lower third which will be bitter. Keep about 250 g/9 oz spears for the mousse. Plunge all the spears into the reserved boiling water from the leeks for about 3 minutes. Refresh in iced water, drain and pat dry. Set aside the 12 spears for the garnish and roughly chop the rest.

Chicken breast: Dice. Place the chicken and chervil in a blender with the egg, egg yolk, milk, the chopped asparagus, 1½ teaspoons salt and a generous pinch of pepper, purée finely, then add four-fifths of the cream. Test the mixture in a small ramekin for taste and texture, add the remaining cream if necessary and correct the seasoning. Using a ladle, force the mixture through a fine conical sieve into a small bowl.

3. Cooking the mousses
(25 minutes)

Preheat the oven to 170°C/325°F gas 3.

Pour the mousse mixture into the lined ramekins and seal with the overhanging ribbons of leek. Place the ramekins in a roasting pan lined with a double thickness of greaseproof paper and pour in enough hot water to reach two-thirds of the way up the sides of the ramekins. Cover loosely with pierced foil and bake in the preheated oven for 20–25 minutes, checking after 20 minutes to see if the mousses are cooked. Keep warm in the bain-marie. Meanwhile make the sauce.

4. The sauce (5 minutes) (see Savoury sauces, page 26)

Bring the vegetable stock to the boil in a small saucepan. Add the cream and chopped chervil and reduce the heat. Gradually whisk in the cold diced butter.

Season with salt, pepper and lemon juice to 'lift' the sauce. Pass through a fine conical sieve into a small saucepan and keep warm.

5. The garnish (10 minutes)
Leek: Remove the coarse outer leaves and finely slice the white part diagonally. Wash under tepid running water.

Asparagus spears: Halve lengthways.

Truffle (if using): Remove the rough skin (keep it for flavouring other recipes) and slice off thin rounds. Cut into fine *julienne*. Make an emulsion with 1 teaspoon butter, 6 tablespoons water and a pinch of salt. Put in the leek, boil for 3 minutes then add the asparagus spears and truffle *julienne* to warm. Taste and correct seasoning.

6. Serving (5 minutes)
Warm 8 plates.

Turn out the *chartreuses* onto the middle of each plate and arrange the sliced leek, 3 asparagus spears and the truffle *julienne* around the edge. Remove the ramekins and top the *chartreuses* with sprigs of chervil. Pour the sauce around.

———— VARIATIONS ————

Use other vegetables for the mousse – courgettes, spinach, broccoli or leeks.

For vegetarians, here is a simple alternative mousse which omits the chicken breast: 2 eggs, 2 egg yolks, 250 g/9 oz cooked asparagus spears, 200 ml/7 fl oz milk, 200 ml/7 fl oz cream, salt, pepper and a small bunch of chervil. Purée, force through a fine conical sieve, then continue as above.

If you are in a hurry, omit the ribbons of leek. Simply make the mousse and scatter some wild mushrooms around for a generous-looking garnish.

Chef's notes
Leeks: Britain prides herself on growing enormous vegetables, leeks in particular. Impressive, yes, but their leaves are often too thick for lining the ramekins in this recipe. You may have to split the cooked ribbons into two layers. This is surprisingly easy to do, since the knife will run with the fibres. At all costs, avoid leeks which have seeded; they are woody and useless.

The cooked mousses should not be left standing in a warm temperature for too long, or the colour of the leeks will deteriorate into a dull grey.

POINTES D'ASPERGES ET FLEURS DE PETITS POIS, SAUCE HOLLANDAISE

Asparagus tips and pea flowers served with the lightest hollandaise sauce

Serves 4
Difficulty: 🎩
Total recipe time: 45 minutes
Special equipment: balloon whisk, *sabayon* or stainless steel bowl

INGREDIENTS

28 asparagus spears

24 pea shoots with their flowers

4 teaspoons unsalted butter

lemon juice

salt and freshly ground white pepper

Hollandaise sauce (see page 28)

125 g/4½ oz best unsalted butter

3 egg yolks

100 ml/3½ fl oz cold water

a tiny pinch of salt

6 turns of pepper

a pinch of cayenne pepper

a squeeze of lemon

Planning ahead
The asparagus tips can be blanched and refreshed in cold water in advance, then warmed through just before serving, but cook the pea shoots at the last moment.
The hollandaise sauce can be made half an hour before the meal and kept warm in a bain-marie.

1. Preparing the asparagus and pea shoots (15 minutes)
Asparagus: Discard the bitter, inedible base, peel the stalks and cut into 12 cm/5 in lengths. Wash the tips in cold water and reserve. Keep the middle part of the stalks for making sauces or soups.
Pea shoots: Cut off the thicker part of the stalks and carefully wash the tops in cold water. Place in a medium saucepan with 4 tablespoons cold water, 2 teaspoons butter, a pinch of salt and 4 turns of pepper. Set aside.

2. The hollandaise sauce
(20 minutes)
Follow the method on page 28. Cover with buttered paper and keep warm in a bain-marie until needed.

3. Cooking the asparagus tips and pea shoots (5 minutes)
Cook the asparagus tips in 3 L/5½ pt fast-boiling water for 4–5 minutes. Taste to check if cooked. Using a slotted spoon, place the tips on a tea towel.
Pea shoots: Put in the same water, cover and cook over high heat for 1 minute only.

4. Finishing the dish and serving
(5 minutes)
Warm 4 plates.
In a small saucepan, melt 1 teaspoon butter with a dash of lemon juice. Line each plate with 2 tablespoons hollandaise sauce, arrange the asparagus tips attractively on top and surround with pea shoots and flowers. Brush the asparagus tips with the melted butter and season with a turn of pepper.

VARIATIONS
To enhance the presentation, tie individual bundles of asparagus with fine ribbons of leek.
Broad bean shoots can be used instead of pea shoots and are equally delicious.

WINE
Asparagus tends to nullify the taste of wine. If you must drink some, choose a light dry white.

Chef's notes
Pea shoots are not only very decorative but also very delicious. Pick them when the peas are flowering and use only the youngest shoots, as older ones will be fibrous.
Hollandaise sauce: The success of this dish depends so much on the lightness of the sauce, which must be the lightest possible foam, just bound together. The serving plates must be just warm; if they are too hot, the fragile sauce will cook and separate.

COQUILLES ST-JACQUES EN FEUILLETE

Scallops baked in their shells, topped with a golden pastry lid

Serves 4
Difficulty: 🍳
Total recipe time: 1 hour 5 minutes

INGREDIENTS

250 g/9 oz Puff pastry, chilled (see page 42)

flour, for dusting the work surface

4 large or 8 small scallops

1 tablespoon unsalted butter

lemon juice

eggwash (1 egg yolk beaten with 1 teaspoon milk)

salt and freshly ground white pepper

200 g/7 oz rock salt, for baking

450 g/1 lb rock salt or 1 large handful blanched fresh seaweed for serving

Vegetable julienne

1 small carrot, cut into julienne

1 small leek, washed, trimmed and cut into julienne

1 small courgette, cut into julienne

4 large firm button mushrooms, peeled and cut into julienne

2 tablespoons unsalted butter

4 young tarragon leaves, washed

a small bunch of chervil, washed and trimmed

1 tablespoon dry white wine

Planning ahead

Make the puff pastry well in advance, or use best quality bought pastry made with butter.

Order the scallops and seaweed from the fishmonger and ask him to open and clean the scallops for you. If he won't, change your fishmonger! You will need both the top and bottom scallop shells.

The dish can be prepared several hours in advance and kept refrigerated ready for baking.

1. The pastry lids (10 minutes)

Lightly flour the work surface and roll out the puff pastry into a 35 cm/14 in square, 2 mm/¹⁄₁₀ in thick. Place on a lightly floured tray and refrigerate for a few minutes to firm up.

Using a top scallop shell as a template, cut out 4 lids about 1 cm/½ in wider all round than the shell. Refrigerate the lids and keep the pastry trimmings for use in another recipe.

2. Preparing the scallops (20 minutes)

Wash in plenty of cold running water to remove all traces of sand, then cut each scallop into 2 rounds. In a small saucepan, melt 1 tablespoon butter with a pinch of salt, a little pepper and a squeeze of lemon. Liberally brush the scallops with this mixture, then place in the fridge so that the butter solidifies on the scallops.

Scrub and wash the shells, wipe dry and reserve.

3. The vegetable julienne (15 minutes)

Preheat the oven to 240°C/475°F/ gas 9.

In a small saucepan, bring to the boil 6 tablespoons water with 1 tablespoon butter, a pinch of salt, 3 turns of pepper and the tarragon and chervil leaves. Add the carrot *julienne,* cover and cook for 1 minute. Add the *julienne* of leek, cover, cook for 1 more minute, then add the *julienne* of courgette. Cook for 30 seconds only, then strain the juices into another pan, place all the vegetables on a plate and leave to cool.

Add the wine to the juices and boil for 1–2 minutes to remove the alcohol. You should be left with 4 tablespoons liquid. Whisk in the remaining butter and keep at room temperature.

4. Assembling and baking the dish (20 minutes)

Divide the vegetable *juliennes,* including the mushrooms, between the 4 bottom scallop shells. Top each with the scallops and 1 tablespoon vegetable juice.

Pastry lids: Brush the outside edges of the scallops with water. Cover the scallops with the lids and tuck under the overhanging edges, pressing them firmly so that they stick to the shells. Mix the egg yolk with the milk and a pinch of salt and brush over the lids. With a small knife, score lines radiating out from the base of the lids to look like real scallop shells. Pierce the lids in 2 or 3 places with the point of a knife so that the steam can escape. Heap 4 mounds of rock salt onto a flat baking tray and settle in the scallop shells, nestling them down firmly. Bake for 8 minutes at the top of the hot oven so that the heat is reflected onto the pastry first; it should be light and flaky and the scallops barely cooked.

5. Serving

Pile the rock salt or blanched seaweed onto 4 plates or a serving dish and settle in the pastry-topped scallop shells. Serve and let your guests have the fun of opening them!

VARIATIONS

Replace the scallops with queen scallops or small fillets of turbot,

brill or salmon.
Use any herbs you like and add a *julienne* of fennel or young spinach.
Use both top and bottom scallop shells, seal with a thin band of puff pastry and bake in a hot oven for 6 minutes. Didier Oudill, Michel Guérard's chef, serves the dish this way.

——— WINE ———

Scallops have a delicate flavour, so do not overpower the dish with too rich a wine. Serve a fresh wine from the Loire – Sancerre or a young Savennières, 'Clos de Papillon'. If you prefer a drier wine, serve a lively young Montagny or Macon-Lugny.

Chef's note
Tarragon: Unless the leaves are very young, blanch them for 5–10 seconds in unsalted boiling water and refresh to remove any coarseness.

PANACHE DE POINTES D'ASPERGES ET MORILLES FRAICHES AU MARC DE GEWÜRZTRAMINER

The first asparagus spears and fresh morels, their juices scented with wine and marc de Gewürztraminer

"After a long winter it is always a great joy to welcome these two wonderful ingredients."

Serves 4
Difficulty:
Total recipe time: 25 minutes

——— INGREDIENTS ———
32 fresh morels
16 young green asparagus spears
400 ml/14 fl oz Light chicken stock (see page 21)
1 tablespoon marc de Gewürztraminer
1 tablespoon whipping cream
50 g/2 oz unsalted butter, chilled and diced
lemon juice
salt and freshly ground white pepper

Planning ahead
The chicken stock must be made in advance.

1. Preparing the morels and asparagus (10 minutes)
Morels: Carefully trim the stalks, cut in half and wash briefly in two changes of tepid water to evict any small insects which have made their homes inside the caps. Gently pat dry, taking care not to damage the morels.

Asparagus: Cut off and discard the bottom to leave an 8 cm/3 in spear.

2. Cooking the morels and asparagus spears (10 minutes)
Asparagus: In a medium saucepan, bring the chicken stock to the boil and season with a pinch of salt and 4 turns of pepper. Boil the asparagus spears for 3–4 minutes, lift out, refresh in cold water and reserve on a small plate.
Morels: Add the *marc de Gewürztraminer* to the chicken stock, bring back to just below simmering point and gently poach the morels for 3–4 minutes. Lift out with a slotted spoon and put with the asparagus spears. Reserve the cooking liquid.

3. Finishing the sauce (5 minutes)
Strain the cooking juices into another saucepan, bring to the boil and reduce by half. Add the cream, then whisk in the cold diced butter. Taste, correct the seasoning and enliven the sauce with a squeeze of lemon. Return the morels and asparagus to the sauce and leave them to infuse for 1–2 minutes before serving.

4. Serving
Warm 4 soup plates or serving dishes. Arrange the morels and asparagus attractively in the centre and pour the light sauce around the edge.

——— VARIATIONS ———
If you cannot find the delicately scented *marc de Gewürztraminer*, use *marc d'Arbois* instead.
Fill the morels with chicken mousse, poach and slice in half.

——— WINE ———
The obvious choice is Gewürztraminer or Arbois wine.

Chef's notes
Morels: You can use dried morels, but the dish will not be quite as delicate. Soak them in plenty of cold water for 20 minutes before using.
The morels must be cooked at just below simmering point in order to preserve their texture.

TOP

Filet de turbot et saumon sauvage en paupiette de choux aux grain de caviar

BOTTOM

Panache de pointes d'asperges et morilles fraîches au marc de Gewürztraminer (page 74)

FILETS DE TURBOT ET SAUMON SAUVAGE EN PAUPIETTE DE CHOUX AUX GRAIN DE CAVIAR

Fillets of turbot and wild salmon wrapped in cabbage leaves and served with a delicate juice spiked with caviar

FILETS DE TURBOT ET SAUMON SAUVAGE EN PAUPIETTE (CONT.)

Serves 4
Difficulty: 🍲 🍲
Total recipe time: 45 minutes
Special equipment: steamer

INGREDIENTS

300 g/11 oz fillet of turbot, skinned

150 g/5 oz middle cut fillet of wild salmon, skinned

20 g/¾ oz unsalted butter

juice of ½ lemon

4 tiny sprigs of dill

salt and freshly ground white pepper

Paupiettes

1 fat white cabbage

1 teaspoon unsalted butter

Sauce

100 ml/3½ fl oz Nage de légumes (see page 22)

1 tablespoon vodka

1 tablespoon whipping cream

40 g/1½ oz unsalted butter, chilled and diced

1 tablespoon large grain caviar (preferably Beluga)

lemon juice

Planning ahead

Prepare the *nage* 1 or 2 days in advance and keep covered in the fridge.

The *paupiettes* can be assembled several hours in advance, but should be steamed at the last moment.

1. Preparing the turbot and salmon (10 minutes)

Turbot: Cut into eight 6 cm/2¼ in squares, 1 cm/½ in thick. Keep the trimmings for another use.

Salmon: Cut into four 6 cm/2¼ in squares, 1 cm/½ in thick.

In a small saucepan, melt the butter with a good pinch of salt, 6 turns of pepper and a squeeze of lemon and brush all over the turbot and salmon. Place a sprig of dill on each square of salmon and sandwich the salmon between the squares of turbot. Place on a large plate and refrigerate.

2. Preparing the cabbage (10 minutes)

In a large saucepan boil 5 L/9 pt water with 3 tablespoons salt. Make a deep incision around the core and slide the cabbage into the water. Cover with a heavy lid to keep it totally immersed and boil for 6 minutes. Peel off 4 outer leaves; they should come away quite easily. Taste to check the texture; if it seems too crunchy, boil for a further 2 minutes, until supple. Refresh, drain and pat dry. Keep the rest of the cabbage for another use.

3. Assembling the paupiettes (10 minutes)

Cut out the core of the cabbage leaves and cut each leaf into two 16 x 6 cm/6 x 2½ in rectangles. Butter them lightly and season. Lay one over another to form a cross; make 4 crosses.

Lay a parcel of turbot and salmon in the centre of each cross and fold over the leaves to enclose the fish completely. Brush with a little melted butter and wrap tightly in clingfilm or tie up with string. Refrigerate.

3. Steaming and resting the paupiettes (10 minutes)

Line a steaming rack with buttered greaseproof paper and pierce the paper all over. Put in the *paupiettes*, cover and steam for exactly 7 minutes. The timing is crucial. Take off the heat and leave to finish cooking for 3–4 minutes. Meanwhile, make the sauce.

5. The sauce (5 minutes)

Boil the *nage de légumes* with the vodka, add the cream then whisk in the cold diced butter. Correct the seasoning and add a squeeze of lemon. Take off the heat, cool until just warm, then stir in the caviar.

6. Serving

Warm 4 plates or a serving dish. Remove the clingfilm or string from the *paupiettes* and sprinkle with a tiny pinch of pepper. Using a very sharp knife, cut the *paupiettes* across the middle without cutting through the bottom layer of cabbage and part the edges to reveal the colours inside.

Place an opened parcel in the centre of each plate and pour the sauce around the edge. It would not be a sin to nestle a final teaspoon of caviar in the middle of each parcel!

VARIATIONS

Substitute brill for the turbot and salmon trout for the wild salmon.

Cabbage: Although the texture and wild flavour of white cabbage is more pleasant, the dish is easier to prepare with Savoy cabbage: blanch the leaves individually for 3 minutes.

A little diced or turned cucumber (see page 50) gently warmed in the *nage* makes a delicious addition.

WINE

A *brut* Champagne is the ideal partner for the caviar, but a light white Burgundy would also be suitable: Montagny, perhaps or one of the more distinguished Maconnais wines such as Macon-Lugny or Château de Vire.

Chef's notes

Caviar is an acquired taste, but once acquired – well, you will find that you need at least 1 tablespoon for this recipe. There is no substitute for caviar. If you can't find or afford it, omit it altogether. Do not use lumpfish roe. As a last resort, you could use salmon eggs, but personally I find them rather less interesting.

Be careful to cool the sauce before stirring in the caviar; if the sauce is too hot, the caviar will become hardboiled. There are few sacrilegious acts in cooking, but this is definitely one of them. The idea is simply to warm the caviar and allow the taste to diffuse into the sauce.

COURGETTES EN FLEUR FARCIES
AU COULIS DE TOMATES CRUES

*Baby courgettes and their flowers filled with diced
vegetables, on a bed of raw tomato coulis*

"I am lucky enough to have a large, well-stocked garden where I can pick emerald green baby courgettes, crowned with their bright yellow flowers. If you are not so fortunate, you can find these baby courgettes at a 'Pick Your Own' farm (see page 274) – offering you a breath of fresh air as well as a basket of wonderfully fresh vegetables!
Never feel guilty about picking these vegetables so young. Not only do you catch them at their most succulent and tasty, but you also promote new growth."

Serves 4
Difficulty:
Total recipe time: 1 hour
Special equipment: food processor or blender

INGREDIENTS

*8 small courgettes (about 40 g/1½ oz
each), with their flowers*

1 sprig of thyme

1 tiny sprig of marjoram

2 tablespoons olive oil

salt and freshly ground white pepper

Vegetable brunoise

*1 small courgette, washed, drained and
finely diced*

*3 medium tomatoes, peeled, deseeded
and diced*

4 basil leaves, washed and shredded

1 garlic clove, peeled and halved

2 tablespoons olive oil

Raw tomato coulis

6 ripe medium tomatoes

*garlic clove from the courgette flower
filling*

*20 g/¾ oz unsalted butter, chilled and
diced*

3 tablespoons olive oil

a pinch of caster sugar (optional)

Planning ahead
Stages 1–3 inclusive can be completed in advance.

1. Preparing and blanching the courgettes and flowers
(10 minutes)
Detach the flowers from the courgettes by hand, then neatly cut off the ends of the stalks.
Courgettes: rub with a damp cloth to remove the tiny hairs and wash briefly.
Flowers: Many small insects choose these magnificent flowers as their home, so open them carefully and run some water inside.
Blanch the courgettes in 3 L/5½ pt boiling salted water for 3 minutes, refresh in plenty of cold water, drain and place on a tray lined with absorbent paper. Keep the cooking water.
Slide the flowers into the same boiling water for 5 seconds only, strain, gently shake out excess water and put them with the courgettes.

2. Cooking the brunoise and filling the flowers (20 minutes)
Preheat the oven to 230°C/450°F/ gas 8.
In a medium frying pan, heat 2 tablespoons olive oil until hot then throw in the diced courgette and garlic and cook for 2 minutes. Add the diced tomatoes and shredded basil, season with salt and 6 turns of pepper and cook for 1 minute. Taste and correct seasoning if necessary. Remove the garlic, slice it finely and reserve it for the tomato *coulis* (Stage 3).
Put the mixture into a small container and leave to cool.
Now comes the filling of the flowers – a delicate operation. Open them up and, using a teaspoon, fill them with the diced courgette and tomatoes, twisting each end of the flowers to hold in the filling. Place the filled flowers on a large tray.

3. The raw tomato coulis

(10 minutes)

Tomatoes: Wash, halve then purée with the sliced garlic reserved from Stage 2. Force this purée through a fine conical sieve into a saucepan, warm over a low heat and whisk in first the cold diced butter then, gradually, the olive oil. Taste and season with salt, a few turns of pepper and, if it is a little acidic, a pinch of sugar.

4. Pan-frying the courgettes and flowers (10 minutes)

Fan out the courgettes and season them and the flowers with salt and pepper.

In a large non-stick frying pan heat 2 tablespoons olive oil with a sprig of thyme and marjoram until very hot. Fry the courgettes for 20 seconds then turn them over and cook for a further 20 seconds. Add the flowers and fry for 5 seconds on each side.

Place the frying pan in the preheated oven for about 3 minutes then remove and keep warm. Taste and correct seasoning if necessary.

5. Serving

Have ready 4 hot plates.

Spoon the warm tomato *coulis* onto each plate then arrange the fanned courgettes topped by their flowers. Give each courgette and flower a final turn of pepper and serve to your guests.

--- VARIATIONS ---

This dish can be varied and adapted in so many ways; one of the most brilliant is from Jacques Maximin. Poach the courgettes and flowers, fill the flowers with a courgette mousse and serve on a truffle-scented *sabayon*. Develop your own ideas from this basic concept, which should certainly tease your imagination!

--- WINE ---

A Tavel rosé or any good quality Provençal rosé makes a perfect partner for this dish.

Chef's notes

Tomatoes: The riper they are, the better the *coulis* will be. Truly ripe sun-soaked tomatoes do not need de-seeding.

Poaching the flowers: Observe the timings given, otherwise the flowers will become slimy and too fragile to handle.

Raw tomato coulis: Do not boil, or the tomatoes will lose their freshness and fragrance and the raw pulp will cook through and granulate. If this should happen, add 2 more chopped tomatoes, purée and force through the sieve again.

ESCALOPE DE SAUMON SAUVAGE AUX HERBES A SOUPE ET BEURRE DE TOMATES

Escalope of wild salmon on a bed of watercress, lettuce, sorrel and baby spinach, served with raw tomato butter

"In this simple, attractive dish, the fillets of barely-cooked salmon contrast with the lively, peppery taste of watercress, the tender sorrel and spinach and the freshness of the uncooked purée made from the first tomatoes of Provence."

Escalope de Saumon sauvage aux herbes à soupe et beurre de tomates

ESCALOPE DE SAUMON
SAUVAGE (CONT.)

Serves 4
Difficulty: 🍳
Total recipe time: 30 minutes

────────── INGREDIENTS ──────────

*450 g/1 lb middle cut fillet of wild
salmon, skinned*

*300 g/11 oz Tomato butter (see
page 25)*

2 teaspoons unsalted butter

juice of ¼ lemon

1 teaspoon rock salt

salt and freshly ground white pepper

Vegetables

8 young lettuce leaves

50 g/2 oz young spinach, trimmed

1 bunch watercress, trimmed

1 small bunch of chives, snipped

24 young sorrel leaves, trimmed

20 g/¾ oz unsalted butter

1 tablespoon whipping cream

2 teaspoons butter, chilled

a dash of white wine vinegar

Planning ahead
The salmon and vegetables can be prepared in advance, as can the tomato
butter, but add the butter to the sauce
at the last moment.

1. Preparing the salmon fillet
(15 minutes)
Carefully tweeze out any small bones
running down the middle of the fillet.
Slice off the greyish vein from the skin
side, using a very sharp vegetable
knife.
Cut the fillet into 4 equal squares. Slice
down the middle of each square
almost but not right through, then
run the knife towards the thickest
edge and open up the fillet like 'but-
terfly wings' to obtain a rectangular
fillet about 12 x 7.5 cm/4½ x 3 in and
1 cm/½ in thick. Refrigerate.

**2. Cooking the vegetables and
herbs** (8 minutes)
In a medium saucepan, bring to the
boil 6 tablespoons water with a large
pinch of salt, 2 turns of pepper and
20 g/¾ oz butter. Throw in the watercress, cover and cook for 4 minutes.
Add the spinach and lettuce and cook
for a further 2 minutes. Lastly, put in
the chives and sorrel for a few seconds
only. Do not overcook, or the sorrel
will lose its texture. Stir in the cream
and the chilled butter, taste, correct
the seasoning and add a dash of wine
vinegar. Set aside.

3. Cooking the salmon
(30 seconds)
Heat the grill. Warm 4 plates or a serving dish. In a small saucepan, melt
1 tablespoon butter with a dash of
lemon juice.

Season the salmon fillets. Lightly butter a non-stick frying pan, heat then
put in the salmon fillets and fry for
5 seconds on each side to seal but
not colour. Brush them with the
melted butter then place under the
grill for 20 seconds only. The salmon
should be barely cooked through; do
not overcook it or you will ruin the
texture and flavour. Gently press a
fillet with the back of your index
finger, taste and adjust the seasoning,
adding a squeeze of lemon.

4. Serving (3 minutes)
Gently warm the tomato butter without boiling, or it will separate.
Arrange the watercress, sorrel and
spinach in the centre of the plates and
coat with 1 tablespoon cooking juice.
Place the salmon fillets on top,
sprinkle with a few grains of rock salt
and spoon the warm tomato butter
around. Serve at once.

────────── VARIATIONS ──────────
Fillet of salmon trout would be
equally delicious.

────────── WINE ──────────
This lovely dish is full of sharp refreshing flavours. Choose a wine with
the same characteristics – a white from
the Rhône, such as Hermitage or St
Joseph.

Fish

RAGOUT DE POISSONS ET COQUILLES ST-JACQUES AUX LEGUMES PRIMEURS ET FINES HERBES DU POTAGER

Fillets of lightly poached fish and scallops, served with young spring vegetables scented with garden herbs

Serves 4
Difficulty
Total recipe time: 1 hour 5 minutes

INGREDIENTS

175 g/6 oz fillet of turbot

175 g/6 oz fillet of John Dory

4 fillets from a 350g/10 oz Dover sole

150 g/5 oz fillet of wild salmon

4 large scallops or 8 small scallops, with their coral

salt and freshly ground white pepper

Sauce

a small bunch of chervil

8 tarragon leaves

200 ml/7 fl oz Fumet de sole (see page 20)

50 ml/2 fl oz Gewürztraminer

1 tablespoon whipping cream

65 g/2½ oz unsalted butter, chilled and diced

lemon juice

Vegetables

a small handful each of baby carrots, shelled peas and spinach

2 tarragon leaves

4 broccoli spears

2 small courgettes

1 leek

6 sprigs of chervil

3 tablespoons unsalted butter

a pinch of caster sugar

Planning ahead
Order all fish well in advance. Ask your fishmonger to skin and trim the fillets and to open and clean the scallops. Keep the fish bones to make the stock.
The fish stock must be made in advance.
Stages 1–3 inclusive can be completed several hours in advance.

1. Preparing the fish (10 minutes)
Turbot, John Dory and salmon: Cut the fillets into 4.
Dover sole: Cut each fillet in half widthways.
Scallops: Wash under cold running water to remove all traces of sand. Cut in half.
Coral: Poach for about 2 minutes in boiling salted water. Refresh, drain and cut into fine strips. Set aside for the sauce.

2. Preparing the vegetables and herbs (15 minutes)
Preheat the oven to 175°C/350°F/gas 3.
Carrots: Leave on 2 cm/¾ in of the tops, wash and peel.
Spinach: Wash carefully in two changes of water and drain.
Courgettes: Wash, trim and cut diagonally into 3 mm/⅛ in slices.
Leek: Trim green top and root and remove weathered leaves. Halve lengthways, then cut each leaf into small ribbons.
Chervil: Wash, pick a few sprigs for decoration and finely chop the remainder.

3. Cooking the vegetables
(10 minutes) (see page 50)
Bring to the boil 2 L/3½ pt water with 2 level tablespoons salt.
Carrots and tarragon: Cook in a small saucepan with 200 ml/7 fl oz water, ½ tablespoon butter and a pinch of caster sugar for 5 – 7 minutes. Glaze the carrots in their juices (see page 51) and set aside.
Broccoli spears and courgettes: Throw into the fast-boiling water for 3 minutes, refresh and set aside.
Spinach and ribbons of leek: Throw into the fast-boiling water for 1 minute, refresh and put with the broccoli spears and courgettes. Combine all the vegetables except the carrots in a small saucepan with 1 tablespoon butter, 2 tablespoons cold water, a pinch of salt and 3 turns of pepper.

4. Poaching the fish (15 minutes)
Place all the fish except the salmon in a large sauté pan. Pour in the wine and fish *fumet* and season with salt and pepper. Bring almost to simmering point, partially cover, leaving a small gap for the steam to escape, and poach in the preheated oven for about 8 minutes. Add the salmon fillets after 6 minutes. Remove from the heat, put the lid on tightly, and leave to rest for 5 minutes in a warm place (16°C/60°F).

5. The sauce (10 minutes)
Strain the cooking juices from the fish into a small saucepan, add the chopped chervil and tarragon and bring to the boil. Add the cream, whisk in the cold diced butter and finally toss in the poached coral. Taste and season with salt, pepper and a squeeze of lemon.

6. Finishing the dish and serving
(5 minutes)
Warm 4 plates.
Gently warm the carrots and other vegetables. Arrange the vegetables and fish in the centre of each plate, pour the sauce around and decorate with sprigs of chervil. Serve at once.

––––––– VARIATIONS –––––––
Many other varieties of fish can be used – monkfish, sea bass, lemon sole or sea trout. Queen scallops can be used instead of scallops.
Any vegetables are suitable, but they must be very young and tender.

––––––– WINE –––––––
This dish merits a fine dry white wine: a Burgundy such as Rully or St Véran, or a top-quality white Graves would go nicely with it.

Chef's notes
Tarragon: Use young leaves. Older ones must be blanched first to remove coarseness.
Poaching the fish: Do not put the lid on tightly when poaching or the heat will build up and spoil the taste and texture of the fish.
Wild salmon is the most delicate of fish which requires only the residual heat during the resting time to cook it.

FILET D'AGNEAU DE LAIT ROTI, FLAN DE CRABE AU SABAYON DE CURRY

Roast fillet of a new season's lamb served with a crab flan masked with a curry sabayon

"The sweetness of new season's lamb matches the flavour of the crab perfectly; the curry acts as the link."

Serves 4
Difficulty: 🎩 🎩 🎩
Total recipe time: 1 hour 40 minutes
Special equipment: 1 cm/½ in fluted pastry cutter, *sabayon* bowl, four 5 x 3 cm/2 x 1¼ in dariole moulds, 4 x 5 cm/2 in circles of buttered grease-proof paper

––––––– INGREDIENTS –––––––
1 whole loin new season's lamb, boned weight 700–800 g/about 1¾ lb
2 tablespoons non-scented oil
salt and freshly ground white pepper

For the crab flan
150 g/5 oz white crab meat, plus 1 tablespoon brown crab meat
2 egg yolks
¼ teaspoon curry powder
a pinch of salt and cayenne pepper
100 ml/3½ fl oz milk
butter for greasing the moulds

Curry sabayon
¼ teaspoon curry powder, plus
1 teaspoon unsalted butter
2 egg yolks
4 tablespoons water
85 g/3 oz unsalted butter
2 tablespoons whipping cream
a pinch of salt and cayenne pepper

Basil juice
100 ml/3½ fl oz Fumet de légumes (see page 22)
½ garlic clove, peeled
4 basil leaves, washed and finely shredded
1 tablespoon whipping cream
25 g/1 oz unsalted butter, chilled and diced
lemon juice

Garnish
¼ small courgette
1 medium red pepper
butter

Planning ahead
Order a milk-fed lamb well in advance; it should be hung for 8–10 days so that the flavour develops and the meat becomes tender. Ask your butcher to bone it and cut four thin 10 x 7.5 cm/4 x 3 in rectangles of fat from the flaps. These will be used for wrapping the fillets.
Order a 900 g/2 lb crab; ask the fishmonger to cook it and extract the meat, keeping white and dark meat separate.
The vegetable stock must be made in advance.
Stages 1 and 2 can be completed in advance.
The curry *sabayon* can be made 1 hour in advance. Keep warm in a bain-marie.

TOP LEFT
Filet d'agneau de lait rôti, flan de crabe au sabayon de curry

TOP RIGHT
Gelée de saumon sauvage en aigre-doux (page 65)

BOTTOM
Terrine d'agrumes au coulis de fruits de la passion (page 98)

The basil juice can be prepared 15 minutes before the meal. Add the lemon juice at the last moment.

1. Preparing the fillets of lamb and garnish (20 minutes)

Trim off any nerves from the boned loin of lamb. Divide the fillet into 4 portions, season each with 2 turns of pepper then wrap in a rectangle of fat and tie up into a neat shape with string.

Courgette: Cut into fine *julienne*, blanch for 30 seconds in salted boiling water, refresh, drain and place in a small saucepan.

Red pepper: Halve, spoon out the core and seeds and blanch in boiling water for 3 minutes. Refresh, drain and peel. Cut out 24 rounds with the pastry cutter and place with the courgette *julienne*, 4 tablespoons water, 1 tablespoon butter, a pinch of salt and 2 turns of pepper.

2. Preparing and cooking the crab flans (45 minutes)

Preheat the oven to 180°C/350°F/gas 4.

Make sure the crab meat contains no small pieces of shell. Mix together the white and brown meat, egg yolks, a large pinch of curry powder and a pinch of salt and cayenne pepper, then mix in the milk and taste.

Butter the insides of the dariole moulds and line each with a circle of buttered greaseproof paper. Fill with the crab mixture.

Place the moulds in a small roasting tin lined with greaseproof paper and pour in hot water to come three-quarters of the way up the moulds. Cover loosely with greaseproof paper and cook in the preheated oven for 40 minutes. Leave in a warm place.

3. Curry sabayon (10 minutes)
(see page 228)

Combine the curry powder and 1 teaspoon butter in a *sabayon* bowl and cook gently for 2–3 minutes. Cool then add 4 tablespoons cold water and 2 egg yolks. Whisk with a balloon whisk for about 5 minutes, until bulky.

Place the bowl over a bain-marie and continue whisking until the mixture is partly cooked, then draw off the heat. Melt 30 g/1 oz butter then whisk into the *sabayon*.

In a stainless steel bowl, whip 2 tablespoons cream to a light peak. Mix into the *sabayon*, taste, season with a pinch of salt and cayenne pepper, and sharpen with a squeeze of lemon.

Leave the bowl in the bain-marie but take it off the heat. Cover with buttered greaseproof paper to prevent a skin from forming.

4. Cooking the fillets of lamb
(10 minutes plus 15 minutes resting)

Increase the oven temperature to 200°C/400°F/gas 6.

In a large frying pan, sear the lamb fillets all over in 2 tablespoons hot oil for 30 seconds. Discard the oil then roast in the preheated oven for 10 – 12 minutes. Remove, cover with foil and leave to rest in a warm place for about 15 minutes.

Meanwhile, prepare the basil juice and garnish.

5. The basil juice and garnish
(5 minutes)

Basil juice: In a small saucepan, boil the *fumet de légumes* with the garlic and reduce by half. Draw off the heat. Add the finely shredded basil, remove the garlic and whisk in 1 tablespoon cream and the cold diced butter. Season with a pinch of salt and 3 turns of pepper, then sharpen the sauce with a squeeze of lemon. Keep warm.

Garnish: Simmer the garnish in its butter and water emulsion for 2 minutes.

6. Arranging the dish and serving
(5 minutes)

Heat the grill until very hot.

By now the lamb fillets will be beautifully pink, tender and tasty; return them to the oven for 3 minutes to warm through.

Loosen the crab flans by tracing one continuous circle around the insides of the dariole moulds with a small knife. Turn out onto the plates, remove the paper lining and arrange 2 courgette sticks and 3 red pepper rounds. Mask the mousses with a large tablespoon of curry *sabayon* and brown under the grill for 30 seconds, if you like.

Take the lamb fillets from the oven, cut off the string and remove the protective layer of fat. Roll the fillets in the juices they released during resting. Slice each fillet into four medallions, arrange attractively on the plates and season with a few grains of salt and pepper. Spoon 2 tablespoons basil juice and 1 teaspoon lamb juices around the medallions and serve.

—— WINE ——

Serve a slightly chilled red Loire wine; a St Nicholas de Bourgueil, Chinon Rouge or Saumur-Champigny.

Chef's notes

Preparing the lamb fillets: The fillets are wrapped in a fine layer of fat to prevent drying or discoloration.

Basil juice: The lemon juice is added right at the end so that the citric acid does not spoil the flavour of the basil.

Serving: Since the plates are placed under the grill they do not need to be warmed beforehand. The grill must be red hot to brown the *sabayon* without cooking it. If you omit this stage, it will not affect the quality of the dish.

CARRE D'AGNEAU DE LAIT ROTI, SON JUS PARFUME A LA TAPENADE

Best end of new season's lamb, roasted with mustard and Provençal breadcrumbs, served with an olive and caper scented juice

Serves 4
Difficulty: 🍳
Total recipe time: 1 hour 10 minutes

――――― INGREDIENTS ―――――

2 800 g/1¾ lb best ends of milk-fed lamb (400 g/14 oz prepared and trimmed weight)

3 tablespoons olive oil

2 tablespoons Dijon mustard

100 g/3½ oz Provençal breadcrumbs (see page 47)

salt and freshly ground white pepper

Juice
100 ml/3½ fl oz olive oil

bones and trimmings from the lamb

1 onion, peeled and diced

200 ml/7 fl oz Veal stock (see page 18)

8 black peppercorns, crushed

1 sprig of thyme

6 needles of rosemary

Tapenade
12 stoned black olives

10 capers, rinsed

1 garlic clove, blanched for 5 minutes, refreshed and puréed

1 anchovy fillet, soaked in cold water for 5 minutes and drained

1 tablespoon olive oil

Garnish
20 mixed black and green unstoned olives

100 g/3½ oz Purée of aubergines (optional) (see page 56)

Planning ahead
The veal stock, Provençal breadcrumbs and aubergine purée must be made in advance.

Order the best ends well in advance. Ask the butcher to prepare them and make sure all tiny chine bones have been removed or the lamb will be difficult to carve. Ask him to chop the bones into small pieces and to cut off excess fat from the trimmings. Reserve 4 small bones to place under the best ends during cooking.

Stages 1–3 inclusive can be completed 1 day in advance.

1. The lamb juices (40 minutes)
(see Savoury sauces, page 26)
Preheat the oven to 230°C/450°F/gas 8.

In a medium roasting pan, heat the olive oil until smoking, then sear the lamb bones to colour lightly. Add the chopped onion and sweat for 2–3 minutes. Roast in the preheated oven for about 30 minutes. Skim off and spoon out the fat, pour in the veal stock and 100 ml/3½ fl oz water and scrape up the caramelized juices from the bottom of the pan. Pour the juices into a saucepan, bring to the boil, skim, then add the crushed peppercorns, thyme and rosemary and simmer for about 20 minutes. Strain

through a fine sieve back into the saucepan and reduce to about 250 ml/9 fl oz. Set aside.

2. Preparing the olives and tapenade (10 minutes)
Olives: Taste one; if it is too strong, blanch them all for a few minutes in boiling water, refresh and drain. Put the unstoned olives in a small bowl. Purée the 12 stoned black olives, capers, garlic and anchovy fillet in a blender with 1 tablespoon olive oil. Place in a small bowl and set aside.

3. Roasting the lamb (20 minutes plus 10 minutes resting)
In a large sauté pan, heat the 2 tablespoons oil reserved from Stage 1 and sear the best ends all over, to colour lightly. Rest them on a few of the chopped bones so that they are not in direct contact with the strong heat from the bottom of the pan (this is especially important for the fillet). Season and roast in the oven for 10 minutes.

Remove, coat the lamb with the mustard then with the Provençal breadcrumbs. Arrange the best ends back on the bones and roast for a further 10 minutes so that the breadcrumbs form a scented crust. Leave to rest in a warm place for 10 minutes. Meanwhile, complete the juices.

4. Completing the lamb juices (5 minutes)
Bring the juices back to the boil, stir in the *tapenade* and cook for 2 minutes for all the flavours to infuse. Force

through a fine sieve, pressing the juices through with a small ladle. Taste and season with a few grains of black pepper. You should not need salt. Keep warm.

5. Assembling the dish and serving
(10 minutes)

Warm 4 plates and have a carving board ready.

If using aubergine purée, reheat it and put in a serving dish.

Return the best ends to the oven for 3–4 minutes.

Warm the reserved olives in 2 tablespoons lamb juices.

Carve the lamb in front of your guests, allowing 4 cutlets per person.

Shape the aubergine purée into small *quenelles* using 2 dessert spoons and place on either side. Sprinkle the lamb with a few grains of salt and black pepper, spoon out the juice and divide the olives between the plates.

--- VARIATIONS ---

To simplify the dish, omit the coating of mustard and breadcrumbs and serve the lamb with a simple juice.

--- WINE ---

Any fine red wine will complement this dish. Try a Château la Borderie from Bergerac or a Domaine de la Bernarde or Bandol from Provence. Serve cool.

Chef's notes

Lamb: In Great Britain we are fortunate to have the most wonderful quality new season's lamb for about 8 months of the year – February to April from Cornwall; in the spring and summer from Wales; by the late summer or early autumn from Scotland. I always ask my butcher to hang the lamb for about 8 days to tenderise it and allow the delicate flavour to come through.

Roasting the lamb: The best ends are cooked in 2 stages; if they were coated with breadcrumbs from the start, these would overcook and burn.

The juice: No salt is needed, since both the olives and anchovies are salty.

ROGNON DE VEAU A LA FRICASSEE D'ESCARGOTS

Fricassee of veal kidneys and snails served with herb butter

Serves 4
Difficulty: ♟
Total recipe time: 40 minutes

--- INGREDIENTS ---

2 veal kidneys, still wrapped in their fat

24 snails (see page 12)

85 g/3 oz chanterelles, or any other wild mushrooms (optional)

¼ garlic clove

1 tablespoon unsalted butter

a dash of lemon juice

200 ml/7 fl oz Light chicken stock (see page 21), reduced to 2 tablespoons glace

1 teaspoon whipping cream

a small bunch of chives, washed and finely chopped

salt and freshly ground white pepper

Herb butter

1 shallot, peeled and finely chopped

1 small frond of dill

1 small sprig of mint

1–2 coriander leaves

1 tiny sprig of flat-leaved parsley

1 small bunch of chives

¼ teaspoon Dijon mustard

a dash of white wine vinegar

65 g/2½ oz unsalted butter, softened

salt and freshly ground white pepper

Planning ahead

The herb butter can be made a few days in advance and kept in the freezer.

Order the veal kidneys well in advance (see page 248).

The chicken stock must be made in advance.

1. Making the herb butter
(10 minutes)

Wash and finely chop all the herbs. Mix them in a bowl with the mustard, a dash of vinegar and the softened butter until thoroughly blended. Taste and season with a little salt and pepper. Cover with clingfilm and refrigerate.

2. Preparing the kidneys and snails
(15 minutes)

Preheat the oven to 200°C/400°F/gas 6 for Stage 3.

Kidney: Peel away the white fat wrapping the kidney and cut off most of the nerves inside. Chop the kidney into pieces following the natural lines, and keep in the fridge.

Snails: Strain the liquid from the snails and rinse them under cold running water. Pat dry and reserve.

Chanterelles: Cut into equal-sized pieces.

3. Cooking the kidneys, snails and chanterelles (10 minutes)
In a small frying pan, sear the kidney pieces in 2 teaspoons hot butter for 30 seconds, without browning. Season and place in the preheated oven for 5 minutes. Remove and leave to rest in a warm place for 5 minutes, loosely covered with buttered foil.
Season the snails with salt and pepper. Rub the bottom of a small sauté pan with a face of garlic, then heat 2 teaspoons butter until hot and pan-fry the snails for 1 minute.
If using, season the chanterelles with salt and pepper and sauté in 2 teaspoons hot butter for 30 seconds, then add a dash of lemon juice. Keep covered, away from the heat.

4. Making the sauce (5 minutes)
In a small saucepan, bring the 2 tablespoons reduced chicken stock to the boil, add the cream and whisk in the diced chilled herb butter. Add the snails, chanterelles and the cooking juices and keep warm. Slice the kidney pieces, add them to the sauce and boil for 2 or 3 seconds. Draw off the heat, taste and correct seasoning.

5. Serving
Heat 4 plates or a serving dish.
Arrange the fricassee of kidneys, snails and chanterelles on the plates, sprinkle with chopped chives and serve to your guests.

— WINE —
A fine dry white from the Rhône will suit the dish very well; try a Crozes-Hermitage 'Mule Blanche', or a white Châteauneuf du Pape from Château Rayas.

Chef's note
Snails: Although fresh snails would be ideal, you can find some very good quality ready-prepared snails. Use only the best.

MEDAILLON DE VEAU ET SES BEATILLES

Pan-fried medallions of veal served with a Madeira sauce, garnished with sweetbread, brains and veal marrow

Médaillon de veau et ses béatilles

"Unfortunately, when it comes to food, the English language is sadly deficient, lacking the descriptive subtleties of French. This dish is actually far better than it sounds! It took me twelve years of cooking in Britain before I dared include it on my menu; it has now become an extremely popular and much appreciated dish."

MEDAILLONS DE VEAU (CONT.)

Serves 4
Difficulty: 🍲🍲
Total recipe time: 1 hour, plus 3 hours soaking
Special equipment: 4 small frying pans

—————— INGREDIENTS ——————

550 g/1¼ lb middle cut veal fillet

1 veal brain (about 300 g/11 oz)

1 veal sweetbread (about 300 g/ 11 oz)

100 g/3½ oz veal marrow, from the spinal cord

salt and freshly ground white pepper

For poaching the brain and marrow

500 ml/18 fl oz cold water

50 ml/2 fl oz white wine vinegar

1 level teaspoon salt

Garnish

12 small green asparagus spears

1 L/1¾ pt boiling water

20 g/¾ oz unsalted butter

1 level teaspoon chopped chervil

Madeira sauce

20 g/¾ oz button mushrooms, finely chopped

1 teaspoon unsalted butter

1 tablespoon ruby port

50 ml/2 fl oz dry Madeira

100 ml/3½ fl oz Veal stock (see page 18)

20 g/¾ oz white truffle, diced (optional)

For pan-frying the meats

4 teaspoons unsalted butter

3 teaspoons groundnut oil

To complete the juices
Brain:

40 g/1½ oz unsalted butter

a dash of white wine vinegar

1 teaspoon lemon juice

20 tiny capers (or 10 larger) washed, drained and chopped

2 lemon segments cut into tiny triangles (see page 49)

1 small sprig of parsley, finely chopped

Veal:

cooking juices

2 tablespoons water

Sweetbread:

cooking juices

20 g/¾ oz unsalted butter, chilled and diced

a squeeze of lemon

Planning ahead

Order veal – which must be from a milk-fed calf – sweetbread, spinal cord (marrow) and brain well in advance.

Soak the brain, sweetbread and marrow for at least 3 hours before using to remove all traces of blood.

Stages 1–3 inclusive can be completed 1 day in advance.

1. Preparing the meats

(25 minutes, plus 3 hours soaking for the offal)

Put the brain, sweetbread and spinal marrow in a large saucepan and leave to soak under cold running water for at least 3 hours, then:

Brain: Drain, remove the membrane and any blood filaments wrapping the brain and rinse in cold water. Drain and set aside.

Marrow: With a small knife, peel off the membrane, taking care not to crush the marrow and cut it into 2 cm/ ¾ in segments.

In a medium saucepan, combine 500 ml/18 fl oz cold water, the vinegar and 1 level teaspoon salt. Add marrow segments, bring to the boil, skim and simmer for 5 minutes. Remove the marrow with a straining spoon, refresh in cold water, drain and reserve in a bowl lined with absorbent paper. Simmer the brain for 15 minutes in the same stock, then leave it to cool in the stock.

Sweetbread: Drain and scald in fast-boiling water for 5 seconds, then refresh, drain and place on a tea towel. With a small knife, peel away the cartilage, fats and fibres, taking care not to damage its shape. Pat dry, cover with clingfilm and set aside.

Veal fillet: Trim off all the nerves then cut into 4 medallions. (If not using immediately, brush them all over with melted butter, seal with clingfilm to minimize oxidization and refrigerate on a small plate.)

2. Preparing and blanching the asparagus (5 minutes)

Preheat the oven to 230°C/450°F/gas 8 for Stage 4.

Trim the asparagus to 10 cm/4 in lengths then poach in 1 L/1¾ pt boiling salted water for 3–4 minutes. Refresh, drain and cut each spear in half diagonally. Place on a plate, seal with clingfilm and refrigerate.

3. Making the Madeira sauce
(5 minutes)

In a medium saucepan, sweat the chopped mushrooms in 1 teaspoon butter for 1 minute, then deglaze with the port and Madeira. Bring to the boil and reduce by half. Add the veal stock and simmer for a further 2 minutes. Loosen with 2 tablespoons cold water then strain through a fine sieve into a small saucepan and infuse the diced truffles, if you are using them.

4. Cooking the veal medallions, sweetbread, brain and marrow
(20 minutes, plus 10 minutes resting)

You will need 4 separate frying pans as the meats should be cooked simultaneously. Cook the veal medallions, sweetbread and brain in 1 teaspoon

each hot butter and groundnut oil.

Veal medallions: Sear and brown them for 1 minute on each side, then place in the preheated oven for 10 minutes. Remove, spoon out all the cooking fat and leave the medallions to rest (still in their pan) in a warm place for 5–10 minutes, loosely covered.

Sweetbread: Season with a pinch of salt and pepper and sear for 1 minute, then cook in the preheated oven for 15 minutes. Remove, spoon out all the cooking fat and leave to rest in a warm place, loosely covered with buttered paper.

Brain: Remove from its cooking liquid, drain, pat dry and season with salt and pepper. Sear for 1 minute and cook for 10 minutes in the preheated oven. Remove, discard the cooking

fat and keep warm, loosely covered with buttered paper.

Marrow: Season, sear for 1 minute in 1 teaspoon hot butter, then discard the cooking fat and keep warm, loosely covered with buttered paper.

5. Making the juices and garnish
(5 minutes)

These stages must also be done simultaneously.

Place all the meats in a large roasting pan and warm in the oven for 5 minutes. Keep the frying pans used for the veal and sweetbread.

Over a medium heat, deglaze the veal pan with 2 tablespoons water, scraping up all the caramelized juices with a wooden spoon. Whisking the juices, reduce to a rich, glazed, syrupy consistency and reserve.

Over a medium heat, add 2 tablespoons water to the sweetbread pan, bring to the boil and whisk in 20 g/ ¾ oz cold diced butter. Taste, season with salt and pepper and 'lift' the sauce with a dash of lemon juice. Keep warm.

In a small saucepan, make a *beurre noisette* (see page 24) with 40 g/1½ oz butter, a dash of vinegar and a squeeze of lemon, then add the capers and lemon triangles. Draw off the heat, taste, and season with a few grains of salt.

In a small frying pan make a *beurre noisette* with 20 g/¾ oz butter and pan-fry the asparagus for a few seconds. Add the chopped chervil, season with a pinch of salt and keep warm.

5. Assembling the dish and serving
(5 minutes)

Heat 4 plates.

Roll the medallions in their reduced cooking juices, place one in the centre of each plate and spoon over the Madeira sauce.

Slice the sweetbread into 4, arrange on the plates and spoon over its juices.

Slice the brain into 4, arrange on the plates, then add the chopped parsley to the *beurre noisette* and pour a little over each slice. Top the veal medallions with the marrow segments, decorate with the asparagus and serve to your guests.

——————— VARIATIONS ———————

If brain is a stumbling block, replace it with veal kidney.

A few wild mushrooms could be tossed into this dish. The diced truffle can be replaced by tiny diced button mushrooms.

To simplify the dish, omit the Madeira sauce; simply serve the veal cooking juices with 1 tablespoon water.

——————— WINE ———————

Serve a lightly chilled red wine from the Loire valley – a Bourgueil or Chinon.

Chef's note

Juice for the brain: Due to the presence of lemon and vinegar in the butter, you must add the parsley only at the last moment, or it will denaturate and discolour.

FRICASSEE DE POULET DE BRESSE AU VIN JAUNE D'ARBOIS ET MORILLES FRAICHES

Fricassee of Bresse chicken with Arbois wine and morels

"This classic dish, a small tribute to my native Franche-Comté, reflects the region's attitude to gastronomy – unashamedly rich and delicious!"

Serves 4
Difficulty: 🍳
Total recipe time: 40 minutes

—— INGREDIENTS ——

1.5 kg/3 – 3½ lb poulet de Bresse

25 g/1 oz unsalted butter

salt and freshly ground white pepper

Sauce
100 g/3½ oz fresh morels, or 20 g/ ¾ oz dried morels, prepared (see page 17)

2 tablespoons marc d'Arbois

300 ml/½ pt vin jaune

400 ml/14 fl oz double cream

Planning ahead
Order a *poulet de Bresse* well in advance. Ask your butcher to joint it and cut the breasts lengthways into 3 pieces.
The dish can be completed 30 minutes before the meal and kept warm in a bain-marie.

1. Cooking the chicken
(25 minutes)
Preheat the oven to 200°C/400°F/ gas 6.
Season the jointed chicken with salt and pepper.
In a thick-bottomed saucepan large enough to hold all the chicken pieces in one layer, heat the butter until hot and sear the chicken for about 5 minutes, without browning. Tilt the pan and spoon out the fat then cover and place in the oven for 10 minutes.
Remove the breasts and keep in a warm place in a dish covered with foil.
Return the remaining chicken pieces to the oven for a further 15 minutes.
Remove the wings and legs with a slotted spoon and place with the breasts.

2. Making the sauce (15 minutes)
Skim off most of the fat on the surface of the juices, then place the cooking pan over strong heat and deglaze with the *marc d'Arbois* and *vin jaune*. Reduce by three-quarters then add the morels and cream. Boil for 1 minute. Add the chicken pieces, plus any juices they have released and cook for 5 minutes at just below simmering point. Taste and correct the seasoning.

3. Serving
Warm 4 plates.
Divide the chicken between the plates and spoon over the sauce and morels.

—— VARIATIONS ——
Use guinea fowl instead of chicken.
Dry sherry can be used instead of marc d'Arbois, if you prefer.
This is really a different dish, not a variation, but forgive me – I would love you to taste this second speciality from Franche-Comté. Cut 4 slices white bread 4 cm/1½ in thick into rectangles, dry in a low oven (120°C/ 250°F/gas ½) for 5 minutes, then hollow out the centres with a spoon, without piercing the bottom. Brush all over with butter and toast in a hot oven for about 10 minutes until golden.
Meanwhile sweat 100 g/3½ oz fresh morels in 20 g/¾ oz butter for a few minutes and add 500 ml/18 fl oz double cream! Simmer for 15 minutes and season. Spoon the cream and morel sauce into the hollowed-out centres of the golden toast. God will surely understand and forgive this most delectable sin of gourmandise.

—— WINE ——
In France each region takes special pride in matching local food with local wine; this dish is no exception. Try to find one of the best 'yellow' wines from the Jura, such as Château Chalon or l'Etoile.

Chef's notes
Chicken: See page 274 for where to buy Bresse poultry. If you cannot find one, use a Landes chicken instead.
Vin jaune is made from the savagnin grape. The special vinification process (6 to 7 years in the cask) ensures that the best Arbois wines are almost immortal. They are deep yellow and reminiscent of fino sherry.
Marc d'Arbois: If you cannot find this, replace with a *marc* from Burgundy. (*Marc* is a spirit distilled from the grape pulp after the grapes have been pressed.)

CANETON ROTI AUX SAVEURS DU PRINTEMPS

Roast duckling served with its juices and Spring vegetables

Serves 4
Difficulty: ♟
Total recipe time: 1 hour 10 minutes

INGREDIENTS

2 1.5 kg/3–3½ lb ducklings, preferably canetons croisés (see Chef's notes)

salt and freshly ground white pepper

Juices
wings and necks from the ducks

1 teaspoon caster sugar

2–3 tablespoons red wine vinegar

200 ml/7 fl oz Brown chicken stock (see page 21)

4 young tarragon leaves

Vegetables
12 tiny turnips, washed and peeled, leaving on 3 cm/1 in stalk

8 baby carrots, washed and peeled, leaving on 3 cm/1 in stalk

12 baby onions

a handful of young broad beans, shelled

a handful of young peas, shelled

a few pea shoots and flowers

12 young lettuce leaves

50 g/2 oz mixed lardons (smoked and unsmoked) (see page 47)

1 tablespoon butter

4 sprigs of chervil, washed and chopped

Planning ahead
Order the ducklings well in advance and ask the butcher to cut the wings short, to remove the wishbones and to give you the necks and livers. (Use the livers for *Petit pain de foies de volailles*, page 232.)

Make the brown chicken stock in advance.
The vegetables must all be prepared in advance.

1. Preparing the ducklings
(10 minutes)
Preheat the oven to 230°C/450°F/gas 8 for Stage 2.
Chop the wings and necks and trim off most of the fat from around the insides of the ducklings, reserving about 20 g/¾ oz for Stage 2. Cut off the legs at the joints and pull out most of the nerves and tendons. Singe the ducks over an open flame to remove any stubble. Score criss-cross lines over the breasts; this will help to melt the fat.

2. Roasting the ducklings
(25 minutes plus 20 minutes resting)
Melt the reserved duck fat in a large deep roasting pan, heat until hot then sear the ducks for 3 minutes on each side and 1 minute on each breast. Add the necks and wings, turn the ducks onto their backs and roast in the preheated oven for about 30 minutes.
Place the cooked ducks on a small tray and leave to rest in a warm place. Tilt the roasting pan and spoon out the fat, leaving the necks and wings in the pan.
Meanwhile, complete Stage 3.

3. Blanching the vegetables and lardons (10 minutes)
Put the *lardons* in 400 ml/14 fl oz cold unsalted water, boil for 2 minutes then refresh and set aside.
In a large saucepan bring to full boil 2 L/3½ pt water with 2 level tablespoons salt. Blanch the turnips, carrots, and baby onions for about 5 minutes then refresh, drain, and place in a large sauté pan with 1 small table-

spoon butter and 6 tablespoons cold water. Add the broad beans, pea shoots and flowers, lettuce leaves, *lardons*, and chopped chervil. Season with a pinch of salt and 2 turns of pepper. Reserve for Stage 5.

4. Making the juice (15 minutes) (see Savoury sauces, page 26)
Add 1 level teaspoon caster sugar to the roasting pan and caramelize over medium heat. Add 2 tablespoons red wine vinegar and reduce until almost evaporated then add the chicken stock and 100 ml/3½ fl oz cold water. Bring to the boil, scraping up all the caramelized juices from the bottom of the pan.
Transfer to a medium saucepan and add just enough cold water to cover the bones. Bring to the boil, skim and simmer for about 10 minutes. Add the tarragon during the last 5 minutes.
Strain the juices into a small saucepan, taste, correct the seasoning and 'lift' with a dash of red wine vinegar, if necessary.

5. Finishing the vegetables
(2 minutes)
Cover the sauté pan, bring to the boil and cook for about 2 minutes.

6. Assembling the dish and serving
(8 minutes)
Warm 4 plates.
Return the ducklings to the oven for 5 minutes and bring the juice back to the boil. Either serve the vegetables separately and carve the ducks in front of your guests, or in the privacy of your kitchen, arrange a breast, leg and thigh on each plate, surround with the mixed Spring vegetables and spoon the duck juices around.

——— VARIATIONS ———

Substitute or add other vegetables, such as baby courgettes, baby beetroot or parsley roots.
Guinea fowl, squab or chicken can also be served this way.

Chef's notes
Vegetables: The success of this dish depends entirely upon the quality of the vegetables, which must be perfectly tender and fresh. They should be cooked *al dente*, so check by tasting towards the end of the cooking time.
Ducklings: Canetons croisés are beautiful cross-bred wild/domestic ducks. You will probably only find them at high quality specialist butchers and poulterers but they are well worth seeking out.

GRANITE DE PAMPLEMOUSSE ROSE ET SAUTERNES

Iced flakes of grapefruit juice sweetened with Sauternes

"To serve a sorbet in the middle of a three-course meal is pure affectation and, in fact, quite unpleasant. However, during a long 'gourmet' meal, light iced flakes such as these can be wonderfully refreshing. They also make a delicious dessert."

Serves 12
Difficulty: ♟
Total recipe time: 10 minutes, plus 3 hours freezing

——— INGREDIENTS ———

juice of 2 pink grapefruit
....
2 teaspoons caster sugar
....
200 ml/7 fl oz Sauternes
....
juice of ¼ lemon
....

In a medium saucepan, bring to the boil the grapefruit juice and sugar.

Skim, draw off the heat and cool for about 3 minutes, then add the Sauternes and lemon juice. Leave to cool completely, then taste and sweeten with a little more caster sugar if necessary. Pour into a large deep container and freeze for at least 3 hours.

Serving
Chill dessert glasses in the freezer for about 15 minutes.
Remove the *granité* and chip off large iced flakes with a teaspoon. Arrange them in the chilled glasses and serve immediately.

——— VARIATIONS ———

Many fruit water ices can be made by the same basic method.
Beaumes-de-Venise can be used instead of Sauternes.

Chef's notes
Pink grapefruit: Their gentle bitterness provides just the right balance of acidity and sweetness, although you may need to add a little more sugar if the grapefruit are slightly unripe. Add as little as possible, since a high sugar content will prevent the *granité* from freezing.

MOUSSE LEGERE AUX FRUITS DE LA PASSION ET MANGUE

A light passion fruit and mango mousse served with its own coulis

Serves 4–6
Difficulty: 🎩🎩
Total recipe time: 1 hour 10 minutes, plus 4 hours chilling
Special equipment: 20 x 4 cm/8 x 1½ in stainless steel flan ring, 20 cm/ 8 in round cake board, electric mixer, food processor or blender

---
INGREDIENTS

Base

20 cm/8 in round of Sponge biscuit, 5 cm/2 in thick (see page 44)

juice of 4 passion fruit

Mousse

17 passion fruit (to make 250 ml/ 9 fl oz juice)

½ medium mango (about 100 g/ 3½ oz)

2½ leaves of gelatine

Meringue

3 egg whites

65 g/2½ oz caster sugar

juice of ¼ lemon

200 ml/7 fl oz chilled whipping cream

Jelly

½ leaf of gelatine

50 ml/2 fl oz passion fruit juice

3 tablespoons water

1 level teaspoon caster sugar

uncooked pulp of 1 passion fruit

Passion fruit coulis (see page 30) and candied zests from 2 oranges (see page 49), for serving

Planning ahead
The sponge biscuit, *coulis* and candied orange zests must be made in advance. This dessert can be completed 1 day in advance.
Chill plates for 1 hour before serving.

---

1. Preparing the fruit
(20 minutes)
Passion fruit: Halve, remove the pulp with a teaspoon (reserving one for garnishing the jelly) and purée in a food processor for 1 minute until the black pips have separated from the flesh. Force the pulp through a fine sieve into a small saucepan, pressing the juice through with a ladle. You should obtain about 350 ml/12 fl oz juice. Reserve 50 ml/2 fl oz for moistening the biscuit and another 50 ml/2 fl oz for the jelly.
Mango: Peel and chop the flesh. Set aside.

2. Lining the flan ring
(5 minutes)
Trim the sponge biscuit to 19 cm/ 7½ in diameter. Stand the cake board in the centre of an upturned tray.
Carefully place the sponge biscuit on the cake board and fit the flan ring around (there should be a small gap between sponge and ring). With a pastry brush, moisten the sponge with 50 ml/2 fl oz passion fruit juice.

3. Making the mousse
(25 minutes, plus 4 hours chilling)
Soften the gelatine in cold water for a few minutes.
In a small saucepan, bring to the boil 200 ml/7 fl oz of the passion fruit juice, skim and reduce to about 100 ml/ 3½ fl oz. Add the softened gelatine, stir until completely melted then draw off the heat and leave to cool. Add the

remaining 50 ml/2 fl oz uncooked passion fruit juice and the chopped mango, purée and keep at room temperature.
In an electric mixer, beat the egg whites to a soft peak, then add the caster sugar and beat until firm, finally adding the lemon juice.
In a separate bowl, lightly whip the chilled cream by hand, then fold in the egg whites. Carefully fold in the puréed passion fruit and mango until just blended, then pour the mousse mixture into the lined flan ring and smooth over the top with a long palette knife until perfectly flat. Place in the coldest part of the fridge for at least 4 hours, until the mousse has set.
Meanwhile, make the jelly.

4. Making the jelly (15 minutes)
Soften the ½ gelatine leaf in lukewarm water for a few minutes.
In a small saucepan, bring to the boil the 50 ml/2 fl oz passion fruit juice reserved from Stage 1 with 3 tablespoons water and 1 level teaspoon sugar. Skim to clarify the juice, then add the softened gelatine. Transfer to a small bowl, leave at room temperature for about 10 minutes, then add the reserved passion fruit pulp and whisk lightly to disperse the pips. Cool to almost setting point.

5. Glazing the mousse
(5 minutes, plus 10 minutes chilling)
When the mousse is set, pour the jelly over, spreading it evenly across the surface with a palette knife. Refrigerate for 10 minutes for the jelly to set. Run a knife dipped in hot water in one complete circle between the mousse and the flan ring to free the sides, then carefully lift off the flan ring.

6. Serving

Prepare yourself at the table with the chilled plates, a jug of warm water and a cake slice.

Drain the orange zests from their syrup, add them to the passion fruit *coulis* and pour into a sauceboat.

Dip the cake slice into the warm water and cut the mousse into slices. Surround each with 2 tablespoons *coulis* laced with orange zests.

──────── WINE ────────

A full-flavoured *brut* Champagne, like Louis Roederer or Veuve Clicquot, would be the ideal companion for this dessert.

──────── VARIATIONS ────────

Many other fruits can be used for this dessert:

Oranges: Reduce the juice to 100 ml/ 3½ fl oz, allow to cool and flavour with 2 tablespoons Grand Marnier.

Pears: Poach 3 medium-sized pears in a sorbet syrup, purée, reduce to 100 ml/ 3½ fl oz and flavour with Poire William liqueur (the jelly can be made with some of the cooking liquid).

Raspberries: Purée 300 g/11 oz raspberries, reduce to 100 ml/3½ fl oz, cool and flavour with fresh raspberry purée; stud the mousse with fresh raspberries.

Apricots: Poach 350 g/12 oz apricots with 2 tablespoons water and 1 teaspoon lemon juice for 5 minutes, purée and reduce to 150 ml/5 fl oz.

If you are short of time, omit the sponge biscuit and jelly and simply mould the mousse in small ramekins.

Chef's notes

Passion fruit: The best are firm and smooth. If crinkled, the taste will be still good but they will yield less juice. Negotiate a good price with the greengrocer and buy a few more!

Juice: If using a blender, purée for only a few seconds or the black pips will be pulverized and spoil the mousse.

Gelatine: this recipe needs only a small amount, to keep the mousse light and melting. In warm weather, you may need an extra leaf.

Cream for the mousse must be chilled and only lightly whipped, to avoid separation.

Making the mousse: Beating the egg white is the most important part, to ensure the mousse is light and fluffy. The egg whites should be quite stiff and the cream beaten only lightly so that it does not granulate. Do not overmix when adding the egg whites and purée. Cut and lift in large movements, to obtain the lightest texture.

───────────────────────

SORBET DE CHAMPAGNE

Champagne sorbet

"This refreshing sorbet can be served in the middle of a multi-course meal, or as a dessert."

Serves 4–6
Difficulty: 🍳
Total recipe time: 20–30 minutes
Special equipment: *sorbetière*

──────── INGREDIENTS ────────

½ bottle brut Champagne

200 ml/7 fl oz Sorbet syrup (see page 31)

1 teaspoon marc de Champagne

1 tablespoon lemon juice, strained

Planning ahead

The sorbet can be made up to 4 hours before the meal and kept in the freezer. The sorbet syrup must be made in advance.

Chill 4 glasses in the freezer 30 minutes before serving.

Mix together all the ingredients, put in the sorbetière and churn for 15–25 minutes. Spoon the sorbet into the chilled glasses and serve immediately.

If you are serving the sorbet as a dessert, garnish it with wild strawberries macerated in a tiny quantity of caster sugar and orange juice, or with a finely sliced poached peach.

──────── VARIATIONS ────────

This sorbet can be made with many other wines, the best being a Gewürztraminer (plus *marc de Gewürztraminer*). You will need only 150 ml/5 fl oz sorbet syrup.

For a sorbet made with a sweet Sauternes, use only 100 ml/3½ fl oz sorbet syrup.

For a festive note, make the sorbet with pink Champagne.

Chef's notes

See notes on Sorbet making, page 102.

PAQUET SURPRISE DU MANOIR

*A delicate lemon mousse encased in a crisp marzipan pastry
parcel, served with cherries cooked in their own juices and kirsch*

Serves 4
Difficulty: 🍳🍳
Total recipe time: 1 hour 45 minutes,
plus 1 hour chilling
Special equipment: electric mixer
with whisk, food processor, 20 cm/
8 in flan ring, 2 cm/1 in deep template made from a plastic container
(see diagram, page 96), cherry stoner.

— INGREDIENTS —
Lemon vanilla cream
200 ml/7 fl oz milk

1 vanilla pod, split lengthways

peel of ½ lemon

4 egg yolks

40 g/1½ oz caster sugar

65 ml/2½ fl oz lemon juice

finely grated zest of 1 lemon

To finish the mousse
3½ leaves of gelatine

200 ml/7 fl oz whipping cream, chilled

*3 egg whites, plus 20 g/¾ oz caster
sugar, plus 1 tablespoon lemon juice*

For the parcels
*200 g/7 oz white marzipan, at room
temperature*

1 egg white

1 teaspoon plain flour

butter, for greasing the pastry sheet

Sauce
500 g/1 lb 2 oz fresh black cherries

100 g/3½ oz caster sugar

2 tablespoons water

1 teaspoon lemon juice

1 tablespoon kirsch

Garnish
4 small sprigs of mint, washed

8 fresh or glacé cherries, halved

Planning ahead
Make the template in advance.
Stages 1–5 inclusive can be completed
1 day in advance.
The mousse must be wrapped 1 hour
before the meal.

*Paquet surprise
du Manoir*

1. Lemon vanilla cream

(20 minutes plus 10 minutes cooling) (see *Crème anglaise,* page 33).

Soften the leaves of gelatine in cold water.

In a medium saucepan, combine the milk, split vanilla pod and lemon peel. Bring to the boil and infuse at just below boiling point for 5 minutes.

In a mixing bowl, cream together the egg yolks and sugar until pale yellow, then add the milk, whisking continuously. Return to the saucepan and place over a medium heat, stirring with a wooden spoon to bind the custard. When it begins to coat the back of the spoon, draw off the heat and stir in the softened gelatine.

Strain immediately into a bowl and continue stirring for 1 or 2 minutes. Add the lemon juice and grated zest and cool for 10 minutes.

2. Making the mousse (10 minutes)

(see Mousse making, page 36)

Lightly whip the chilled cream and return it to the fridge.

Using an electric mixer, beat the egg whites to a light peak, then add the caster sugar and lemon juice and beat until firm.

Delicately fold the egg white into the lightly whipped cream. Mix one-quarter of this mixture into the lemon cream, then carefully fold in the remainder.

3. Moulding the mousse (5 minutes)

Line the base of a large tray with greaseproof paper. Place the flan ring on the tray and line with a thin band of greaseproof paper. Fill the ring with mousse mixture, smooth the surface with a palette knife and refrigerate for at least 4 hours.

Cut the chilled mousse into four 6 cm/ 2¼ in squares using a knife dipped in hot water, and refrigerate on a plate lined with greaseproof paper. You will have some mousse left over; cover with clingfilm and freeze it for another use.

4. Preparing the marzipan pastry mixture (5 minutes)

Grind the marzipan in a food processor for a few seconds, add the egg white and flour and process to a smooth paste. Reserve in a small bowl.

5. Preparing and cooking the cherry sauce (30 minutes)

Preheat the oven to 190°C/375°F/gas 5 for Stage 6.

Wash the cherries, drain and remove stems and stones over a bowl with a cherry stoner.

Purée 150 g/5 oz of the cherries in a blender. Strain the juices through a fine sieve into a medium saucepan and add the sugar, water, lemon juice and the remaining cherries. Bring to the boil, reduce the heat, cover and cook for 5 minutes at just below simmering point.

Place the cherries in a bowl, strain the juice into a small saucepan and reduce to 100 ml/3½ fl oz concentrated sauce. Mix in the kirsch, cover with clingfilm and refrigerate.

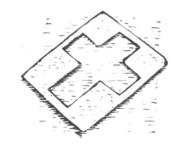

Cross-shaped template for making the marzipan pastry parcels. For further information, see page 270.

6. Pre-cooking the marzipan mixture (20 minutes) (see template diagram below)

First place the 4 square lemon mousses in the freezer for 20 minutes to harden, so they do not melt when wrapped in the warm marzipan pastry in Stage 7. Place the cross-shaped template on a lightly buttered non-stick baking sheet and, holding it firmly with one hand, spread the marzipan mixture evenly over the template (it should be about 1 mm/¹⁄₂₄ in thick). Lift off the template and cook the marzipan cross in the preheated over for 5 minutes until golden brown.

Place the baking sheet on your work surface, cool for 1 minute, then carefully slide a spatula under the cross and place upside down on another sheet. Wipe the baking sheet clean and repeat the entire process to make 4 marzipan crosses.

7. Wrapping the mousse in marzipan pastry (15 minutes, plus 1 hour chilling)

Remove the lemon mousses from the fridge and keep them handy, as you must work fast in order to wrap the hot pastry around the cold mousses. Reheat 1 marzipan pastry cross (smooth side down) in the oven for 3 minutes until pliable. Put a lemon mousse in the centre of the cross and quickly wrap the sides of the cross around the mousse so it is totally enclosed. Transfer immediately to a tray and place in the coldest part of the fridge. Repeat with the 3 remaining crosses and mousses. Chill for 1 hour before serving.

8. Assembling the dish and serving
Divide the cherries and sauce between 4 plates, place a parcel of lemon mousse in the centre and top with 2 half cherries and a mint leaf. Serve to your guests.

———— VARIATIONS ————

Lemon mousse can be replaced by different flavoured mousses; change the accompanying sauce accordingly. The mousse can also be replaced by a rich ice cream. Slide a crunchy mandarin nougat into the ice cream and serve with Chocolate sauce (see page 31). The ice cream must be frozen at -18°C/-4°F.
For a really impressive presentation, pipe a ribbon of melted chocolate onto each parcel.

———————— WINE ————————

A sweet wine from the southern Rhône valley such as Muscat de Beaumes-de-Venise would be ideal.

Chef's notes
Cherries: Juicy black cherries are the best for this dish. Cook them gently so that they keep their shape and texture. The liquid must not boil.
Making the mousse: Each stage must be carried out precisely – first the mixing then the folding. Take care not to overmix or the light texture of the mousse will suffer.
Moulding the mousse: The flan ring must be lined to prevent the mousse from discolouring.
Wrapping the mousses in the pastry: Wrap the mousses one at a time on the hot pastry tray, as the marzipan pastry will re-harden quickly and become impossible to fold.

GLACE AUX PRUNEAUX D'AGEN
A L'ARMAGNAC

Vanilla ice cream studded with prunes marinated in Armagnac

Serves 4–6
Difficulty: ♙
Total recipe time: 15 minutes plus 12 hours macerating and 15–25 minutes churning
Special equipment: ice cream maker (optional)

———— INGREDIENTS ————

150 g/5 oz Agen prunes

100 ml/3 ½ fl oz Armagnac

Vanilla ice cream

6 egg yolks

100 g/3½ oz caster sugar

½ vanilla pod

250 ml/9 fl oz milk

250 ml/9 fl oz double cream

Planning ahead
The vanilla custard can be made 1 day in advance (see page 33 for method). Chill glasses for serving.

1. Preparing and macerating the prunes
(5 minutes plus 12 hours macerating)
Halve and stone the prunes. Put them in a small bowl or jar with the Armagnac, seal with a lid or clingfilm and leave to macerate for 12 hours. By this time most of the Armagnac will have been absorbed. Chop each prune half in two and keep any remaining Armagnac for Stage 3.

2. Making the vanilla custard
(10 minutes)
Follow the method on page 33.

3. Churning the ice cream and adding the prunes
(15–25 minutes)
Strain any excess Armagnac into the vanilla custard.
Churn the cold custard in the ice cream maker. When it starts to firm up, add the prunes and continue churning until the ice cream has a firm, rich consistency. Store in the freezer until ready to serve. Serve in chilled glasses.

Chef's notes
Prunes: The best come from Agen; they are beautifully moist and scented. If they are too shrunken and dried out, soak them in 300 ml/½ pt tepid water with 2 tablespoons caster sugar for 15–30 minutes before using.
If you do not have an ice cream maker, simply mix the vanilla cream with the macerated prunes, place in a container and freeze. When the mixture starts to set, stir with a wooden spoon to distribute the prunes evenly through the ice cream.

TERRINE D'AGRUMES AU COULIS DE FRUITS DE LA PASSION

Refreshing segments of bittersweet pink grapefruit and orange embedded in an orange jelly, served with a coulis of passion fruit

Serves 10–12
Difficulty: ♟
Total recipe time: 1 hour, plus 6 hours setting
Special equipment: 24 x 8 x 10 cm/ 10 x 3½ x 5 in china terrine, food processor

―――― INGREDIENTS ――――

8 large oranges (675 g/1½ lb segments)

8 medium pink grapefruit (350 g/ 12 oz segments)

Jelly
3 leaves of gelatine

200 ml/7 fl oz fresh orange juice (squeezed from the cores)

50 g/2 oz caster sugar

1 teaspoon Grand Marnier (optional)

candied zests of 3 oranges and 2 pink grapefruit (see page 49)

400 ml/14 fl oz Passion fruit coulis (see page 30)

Planning ahead
The terrine can be made 1 day in advance and kept refrigerated, sealed with clingfilm.
Place the china terrine in the refrigerator as you start the recipe.
Chill the plates 1 hour before serving.

1. Preparing the fruits (25 minutes)
Peel 4 pink grapefruit and 3 oranges with a potato peeler. Cut the peel into fine *julienne* and candy following the method on page 49. Reserve in the syrup.
Peel the remaining oranges and grapefruit, segment all the fruit, keeping the oranges and grapefruit separate and keep all the cores. Purée the orange cores in a food processor and strain the juices into a bowl, pressing the pulp with a ladle. You should obtain about 300 ml/½ pt juice. Reserve 200 ml/7 fl oz for the jelly. (Keep and candy any peel not needed in this recipe and purée the grapefruit cores and keep the juice for another recipe, for example *Granité de pamplemousse rose,* page 92.)
Drain the grapefruit and orange segments in separate colanders and reserve on separate trays lined with 3 layers of kitchen paper.

2. The orange jelly (15 minutes)
Soften the gelatine in cold water for a few minutes.
In a small saucepan boil the orange juice for 1 minute, skim and stir in the softened gelatine until melted. Draw off the heat, strain and allow to cool, then add the Grand Marnier (optional).

3. Moulding the terrine
(10 minutes, plus 6 hours chilling)
Remove the china terrine from the refrigerator and line with a 3 mm/1/10 in layer of orange jelly (about 100 ml/ 3½ fl oz). Chill until set. Arrange alternating layers of orange and grapefruit segments on the jelly along the length of the terrine and slightly overlapping. Continue to build up layers of orange and grapefruit segments. Press the segments lightly, pour over the jelly to cover all the fruit, then seal the terrine with clingfilm and place in the coldest part of the fridge for at least 6 hours.

4. Turning out the terrine, slicing and serving (10 minutes)
Fill a deep roasting pan with about 4 cm/1½ in hot water. Cover an inverted tray with a fine tea towel. Remove the clingfilm, then stand the terrine in the hot water for 5 seconds and free the sides with a knife dipped in hot water, keeping the blade pressed against the sides. Turn the terrine out onto the tea towel.
Cut off the ends of the terrine, then carve into 1.5 cm/½ in slices, using a sharp serrated knife dipped in hot water. Do not apply any pressure; let the knife do the work. Use a large spatula to transfer the slices carefully onto the chilled plates, spoon the passion fruit *coulis* over and around and lace the sauce with candied orange and grapefruit zests. Serve to your guests.

―――― VARIATIONS ――――

Place slices of mango in the middle of the terrine, or use only orange slices or add colourful red fruit like strawberries and raspberries. You can also make individual terrines in small ramekins, or make a beautiful arrangement of fruit on the plate and coat with jelly and mint leaves.

―――― WINE ――――

Try one of the delicious dessert wines from the Coteaux du Layon in the Loire valley such as Quarts des Chaumes or Bonnezeaux.

Chef's notes
Choose sweet oranges or, if you can find them in winter, blood oranges.
Turning out the terrine: Dip the china terrine in hot water for only 4–5 seconds, just enough to free the jelly.

CREPE SOUFFLEE AU GRAND MARNIER "FAÇON SUZETTE"

Pan-fried Grand Marnier soufflé, served on a crêpe basted with orange butter

Crêpe soufflée au Grand Marnier "façon Suzette"

Serves 4
Difficulty: 🎩 🎩 🎩
Total recipe time: 55 minutes
Special equipment: electric mixer, *sabayon* bowl, 16 cm/6 in crêpe pan, 4 non-stick frying pans (16 cm/6 in diameter, 3 cm/1½ in deep)

―――――― INGREDIENTS ――――――

Crêpes
1 egg

4 teaspoons caster sugar

175 ml/5 fl oz milk

50 g/2 oz flour

a pinch of salt

4 teaspoons butter, plus 1 teaspoon melted butter for cooking the crêpes

Garnish
3 oranges

200 ml/7 fl oz water

85 g/3 oz caster sugar

Sauce
400 ml/14 fl oz orange juice (from 2 oranges, plus oranges in garnish)

1 teaspoon unsalted butter

40 g/1½ oz caster sugar

1 tablespoon Grand Marnier

Soufflé mixture
2 egg yolks

2 tablespoons water

3 teaspoons caster sugar

4 egg whites

1 teaspoon lemon juice

1 tablespoon Grand Marnier

1 teaspoon unsalted butter

icing sugar for dredging

Planning ahead
Prepare the crêpe batter several hours in advance.
Stages 1 and 2 can be completed 1 day in advance.
Stage 3 can be completed 1 hour before serving.

1. Making the crêpe batter

(5 minutes, plus 30 minutes resting)
Crack the eggs into a mixing bowl and cream them with the sugar. Whisk in the milk. Sieve the flour into another bowl with the salt, then gradually whisk in the egg mixture until the batter is smooth. Pass it through a fine conical sieve.
Heat 4 teaspoons butter until foaming and golden, whisk into the batter and leave to rest at room temperature for 30 minutes.

2. Preparing and candying the orange zests and segments for garnish (15 minutes) (see page 49)

In a small straight-sided saucepan, boil the water and sugar.
Peel 3 oranges in long strips with a potato peeler. Cut the zests into fine *julienne* and blanch in 1 L/1¾ pt boiling water for about 8 minutes. Drain, refresh, then simmer for 3 minutes in the syrup. Leave to cool.
Remove the pith, then segment the oranges, halving the larger segments. Place in a large bowl. Squeeze the juice from the cores.

3. Orange butter sauce (15 minutes)

Sieve all the squeezed juices from the cores in Stage 1 and the juice from 2 oranges into a small bowl. You will need about 400 ml/14 fl oz juice in all.
In a small saucepan, melt 1 teaspoon butter. Add the sugar and cook over medium heat to a pale golden caramel. Add the orange juice, bring to the boil and reduce to about 200 ml/7 fl oz sauce, skimming constantly. Add ½ tablespoon Grand Marnier.
Drain the cooled candied orange zests and stir in the remaining Grand Marnier. Put in a shallow ovenproof dish.

4. Cooking the crêpes, dipping them in orange butter (10 minutes)

Brush a crêpe pan with the melted butter and heat until very hot. Pour in a small ladleful of batter and rotate the pan to make a thin pancacke. Cook for 30–40 seconds, then turn over

with a spatula and cook the other side for 30–40 seconds. Make 5 or 6 crêpes in this way, choose the 4 best and dip both sides into the warm orange sauce. Place in the ovenproof dish with the candied orange zest and reserve.

5. Making the soufflé mixture

(10 minutes) (see Sabayon making, page 27 and Soufflé making, page 35)
Heat the grill for Stage 5.
Pour about 5 cm/2 in water into a large shallow saucepan and set over low heat to make a bain-marie.
In a *sabayon* bowl, whisk 2 tablespoons cold water with the egg yolks and sugar until the light foam is almost 5 times its original volume. Place the bowl over the bain-marie and continue whisking until the foam thickens slightly and looks homogenous. Remove, add 1 tablespoon Grand Marnier and continue whisking off the heat until cooled. Set aside.
In an electric mixer on medium speed, beat the egg whites to a light peak, then add the sugar and lemon juice, increase to full speed and beat until firm. Carefully fold the beaten egg white into the *sabayon* base until well incorporated.

6. Pan-frying the soufflés

(3 minutes, plus 3–5 minutes under the switched-off grill)
Lightly butter the bottom and sides of 4 small frying pans. Set over medium heat until the butter is hot then dust each with a little icing sugar. Put in the soufflé mixture, leaving the edges of the frying pans free, smooth the tops into slight dome shapes with the back of a spatula and cook for 1 minute. Dust the surfaces with icing sugar and glaze under the hot grill for 1 minute. Turn off the grill and leave the soufflés under for a further 3–5 minutes.

7. Assembling the dessert and serving (3–4 minutes)

Now you must work as quickly as possible. Have ready 4 warm plates.

Reheat the crêpes and sauce.
Lay 1 crêpe flat in the middle of each plate, arrange the orange segments around the edge and spoon on the sauce and candied zests. Using a small palette knife, free the edges of the soufflés stuck to the sides of the pans and turn them out onto the orange-lined crêpes. Serve immediately.

—————— VARIATIONS ——————
Replace the Grand Marnier with lemon, chocolate (10 g/⅓ oz cocoa powder and 10 g/⅓ oz chocolate), or 1 tablespoon raspberries, blackcurrants or apricots, reduced to the consistency of jam. Serve the fruits with their own *coulis*.
To simplify the dish, replace the *sabayon* with ½ egg yolk mixed with 1 tablespoon Grand Marnier.

—————— WINE ——————
Serve a dry Blanc de Blancs or *méthode champenoise*.

Chef's notes

The *sabayon* base makes the soufflés wonderfully light, but it is the trickiest part of the recipe. It is difficult to judge precisely when the *sabayon* is cooked; and it is vitally important for it to be cooked perfectly. If undercooked, the egg white will not support all the moisture and the soufflés will collapse when cooked.
Pan-frying the soufflés: For a uniform heat, solid tops are better than gas. The timing is crucial; after 1 minute on the stove, the soufflés will be one-third cooked, with a delicious caramelized crust underneath. Under the hot grill, the top third will cook and when you turn off the grill, residual heat will cook the middle. Too strong a heat or longer cooking times will make the soufflés expand beautifully – and then deflate. To test whether the soufflés are cooked, touch the tops in the centre; they should be firm and lightly springy. If they are properly cooked, they will remain risen for about 5 minutes.

ILES FLOTTANTES "FAÇON MAMAN BLANC"

'Floating islands' – my mother's way

"A dessert from my childhood – specially for the children . . . and all the grown-ups. Sponge biscuits soaked in kirsch and real vanilla custard, topped with an island of poached meringue masked with caramel; this is a variation of one of the most celebrated desserts of France, found in small brasseries and great restaurants alike."

Serves 4
Difficulty:
Total recipe time: 50 minutes, plus 4 hours chilling
Special equipment: electric mixer or mixing bowl and a large balloon whisk, 20 cm/8 in shallow saucepan, straight-sided sugar pan

─────── INGREDIENTS ───────

12 sponge fingers (see Biscuit, page 44)

50 ml/2 fl oz water

25 g/1 oz caster sugar

1 tablespoon kirsch

Meringue
6 egg whites

250 g/12 oz caster sugar

For poaching the meringue
1 L/1¾ pt milk

4 vanilla pods, split lengthways

Custard
85 g/3 oz caster sugar

10 egg yolks

the milk used for poaching

Caramel
50 ml/2 fl oz water

100 g/3½ oz caster sugar

Planning ahead
The sponge fingers must be made in advance. You will have to make more than you need for this recipe; freeze the remainder on a pastry sheet.
Stages 1–5 can be completed in advance. You can add the caramel 1 hour before serving.

1. Making the syrup (5 minutes)
Put the water and sugar in a small saucepan and bring to the boil. Draw off the heat, allow to cool then add the kirsch.

2. Preparing the meringue (10 minutes)
In an electric mixer on medium speed, beat the egg whites to a light peak, then add the sugar, increase to full speed and beat until firm.

3. Poaching the meringue (15 minutes)
Put the milk and split vanilla pods in a large shallow pan and bring to the boil. Reduce heat to just below simmering point and infuse the vanilla pods for about 5 minutes.
Using 2 tablespoons dipped in hot water, scoop out 12 *quenelles* of meringue and poach 6 at a time in the simmering milk for 2 minutes. Turn them over and poach for 2 more minutes. Remove with a straining spoon and leave to drain on a small tray. Poach 6 more meringues in this way, cool and refrigerate. Remove the vanilla pods and reserve the milk.

4. Making the custard
(5 minutes) (see Vanilla custard, page 33 for more information)
In a mixing bowl, cream the egg yolks and sugar until pale yellow. Stirring constantly, pour over the hot milk from Stage 3, pour back into the saucepan and place over medium heat. Stir continuously with a wooden spoon until the custard begins to thicken and coats the back of your spoon. Strain immediately into a large serving bowl.

5. Assembling the dish
(5 minutes, plus 4 hours chilling)
Lightly dip the sponge fingers into the syrup and slide them into the warm custard. Add the 12 poached meringues in a mound on top, then chill the dessert for at least 4 hours.

6. Making the caramel and serving
(10 minutes) (see page 32 for more information)
Pour the water into a straight-sided sugar pan, then add the sugar in a mound in the centre of the pan. Over medium heat, cook to a rich caramel then, tilting the pan away from you, loosen with 1 dessert spoon warm water and swirl the pan to incorporate it. Pour a fine coating of caramel onto the poached meringue and serve immediately.

— WINE —
In my region it is the custom to serve Champagne with this sweet. Since food is one of our last surviving traditions, let us observe it!

Chef's notes
Egg whites: Make sure they are free from any trace of yolk, shell or fat. Your mixing bowl must be scrupulously clean. Any egg yolk will impair coagulation and reduce the volume of beaten egg white by as much as half.
Preparing the meringue: The egg whites must be beaten continuously. Never stop, especially at the beginning when the foam is most unstable. Do not add the sugar until soft peaks form; if added too early, it will reduce the final volume considerably and lengthen the beating time. Be careful not to over-beat, or the mixture will granulate and separate.
Poaching the meringue: Do not boil the milk, or the egg whites will expand, then deflate miserably. The poached meringues should be cooked through and firm to the touch.
Assembling the dish: Add the biscuits to the custard while it is still warm so that they can soak it up.
Equipment: If you do not have an electric mixer, use a stainless steel bowl and a large supple balloon whisk.

— VARIATIONS —
You can make the simpler classic *îles flottantes* without the sponge fingers. Sprinkle over some toasted flaked almonds before adding the caramel. The caramel can be replaced by Raspberry *coulis* (see page 31).

SORBET A LA RHUBARBE
Rhubarb sorbet

Serves 4–6 (makes about 500 ml/ 18 fl oz sorbet)
Difficulty: 🍳
Total recipe time: 25 minutes, plus 15–25 minutes churning
Special equipment: *sorbetière*, blender

— INGREDIENTS —
450 g/1 lb rhubarb

85 g/3 oz caster sugar

50 ml/2 fl oz water

lemon juice (optional)

Planning ahead
You can prepare this sorbet a few hours before the meal and keep it in the freezer.
Chill plates or glasses for serving 30 minutes in advance.

1. Preparing the rhubarb
(10 minutes)
Trim and partly peel the rhubarb (the skin will tint the sorbet a delicate pink), chop it into small segments, wash and drain.

2. Cooking the rhubarb
(7 minutes)
Put the cold water in a large saucepan, add the rhubarb and sugar, cover with a lid and boil for 2 minutes. Remove the lid and simmer, uncovered, for about 5 minutes until the rhubarb is cooked, then draw off heat and allow to cool.

3. Liquidizing and straining
(8–10 minutes)
Liquidize the rhubarb then force the purée through a fine sieve. Taste and correct with a little more sugar or lemon juice as necessary.

4. Churning (15–25 minutes)
Churn in a *sorbetière* for 15–25 minutes, according to your machine, then store in the freezer until needed.

5. Serving
Mould the sorbet into oval shapes using 2 tablespoons dipped in hot water and place 3 in the centre of each chilled plate.

Chef's notes
Nowadays, you can buy excellent and cheap ice cream makers or *sorbetières* for domestic use. It is well worth investing in one; you can whip up such a huge variety of ice creams and sorbets in a very short time.
Tasting: When making a sorbet, never taste the mixture hot, as you will get a false impression of the sugar/acidity content. Allow the mixture to cool first, then taste and correct.
Storing: It is not advisable to store the sorbet in the freezer for more than 6 hours or it will harden. If this happens, melt it and churn once again.

CASSOLETTE DE SOUFFLE GLACE AU GRAND MARNIER, SAUCE AU CHOCOLAT

The lightest iced Grand Marnier soufflé, set in a thin nougatine 'saucepan', served with chocolate sauce

Cassolette de Soufflé glacé au Grand Marnier, sauce au chocolat

Serves 4
Difficulty: 😋 😋 😋
Total recipe time: 1 hour 5 minutes, plus 6 hours freezing
Special equipment: four 8 cm/3½ in ramekins, four 8 cm/3½ in straight-sided tartlet tins, electric mixer

—————— INGREDIENTS ——————

4 nougatine 'saucepans', moulded in straight-sided tartlet tins (see Nougatine, page 45)

4 'handles' and 4 'lids' (optional)

candied zests of 2 oranges (see page 49)

Iced soufflé mixture
juice of 2 oranges

40 g/1½ oz caster sugar

100 ml/3½ fl oz cooking syrup from the candied zests

3 egg yolks

2 tablespoons water

3 egg whites, with 30 g/1 oz caster sugar and the juice of ¼ lemon, for the meringue

200 ml/7 fl oz whipping cream, chilled

150 ml/5 fl oz Grand Marnier

Garnish
2 oranges

1 teaspoon Grand Marnier

1 teaspoon caster sugar

4 small kumquats, with 50 g/2 oz caster sugar and 150 ml/5 fl oz water (optional)

Planning ahead
The *nougatine* 'saucepans', iced soufflés and chocolate sauce must be made in advance. Chill a small tray for unmoulding the soufflés.

1. Preparing the orange juice

(15 minutes)

Finely chop the candied zests and reserve 100 ml/3½ fl oz cooking syrup. Squeeze the oranges and strain the juices into a small saucepan; you should have about 200 ml/7 fl oz juice. Add the sugar, the reserved syrup from the zests and the chopped zests. Boil for about 3 minutes, skim and keep warm over a very low heat. Meanwhile, make the iced soufflés.

2. The sabayon (17 minutes) (see

Sweet *sabayon,* page 30)

Combine 2 tablespoons cold water and the egg yolks in the bowl of an electric mixer and whisk at medium speed for about 5 minutes, until 4 or 5 times their original volume. Gradually pour in the hot orange syrup and beat at high speed for 2 minutes, then cool the *sabayon* by beating at slow speed for another 10 minutes, until cold. Beat in the Grand Marnier at the end.

3. The meringue (5 minutes) (see

page 45)

Whip the egg whites to soft peaks, sprinkle in the sugar and add the lemon juice. Beat until firm and set aside.

Lightly whip the cream.

4. Mixing the ingredients and filling the ramekins (6 minutes)

Fold the *sabayon* into the egg white with a large slotted spoon, then fold in the whipped cream until just blended; do not overmix – this operation will only take 1 minute.

Fill the ramekins with mousse mixture and smooth over with a spatula. Freeze for at least 4 hours.

Dip the ramekins in warm water for a few seconds. Run the blade of a knife dipped in hot water between the mousse and the ramekin in one continuous circle and invert the soufflés onto the chilled tray. Place in the freezer again.

5. Preparing the garnish

(15 minutes) (see page 49).

Oranges: segment, cut each segment into tiny triangles and place in a small bowl, sprinkled with 1 teaspoon caster sugar and 1 teaspoon Grand Marnier.

Kumquats: Blanch for 8 minutes in plenty of boiling water, then candy them in a syrup made with 150 ml/5 fl oz water and 50 g/2 oz caster sugar. Leave to cool in the syrup.

6. Assembling and serving

(5 minutes)

Have ready 4 chilled dessert plates.

Spoon 3 tablespoons chocolate sauce (see page 31) into the middle of each plate, spread it into a circle and place a *nougatine* 'saucepan' in the middle of each plate. Arrange 5 orange segments around the edge.

Place an iced soufflé in each *nougatine* 'saucepan', decorate with the kumquats and orange triangles and serve at once.

VARIATIONS

Make the soufflés with any fruits or liqueur you like.

To simplify the dish, make iced soufflés in small ramekins. Make bands of greaseproof paper double the height of the ramekins, wrap round the ramekins and fasten with sellotape. Fill with mousse to within 2 cm/¾ in of the top, freeze for at least 4 hours, remove the paper and serve the iced soufflés in the ramekins.

WINE

We have recently discovered a very interesting wine from California, 'Essensia', made from a novel hybrid grape, the 'muscat orange flower'. It is not too sweet and has a delicate faint orange flavour which perfectly suits chocolate and orange desserts.

Chef's notes

Whipped cream: This must be cold; if tepid, it may separate. Do not whip it too stiff, or it could granulate.

Mixing the sabayon, whipped cream and meringue: Do this as quickly as possible, lifting, folding and blending delicately; overmixing will reduce the volume and lightness.

Freezing: The ideal temperature is –10°C to –12°C/14°F to 10.4°F so that the mousse mixture remains mellow and soft; if kept at a lower temperature, the texture of the iced mousse will be much firmer.

TERRINE DE CANARD CONFIT
A LA PRESSE A LA FRICASSEE
DE CEPES

FILET DE BARBUE BRAISE AUX
FEVETTES "FACON DUGLERE"

POMME SOUFFLEE AU
SABAYON DE CIDRE

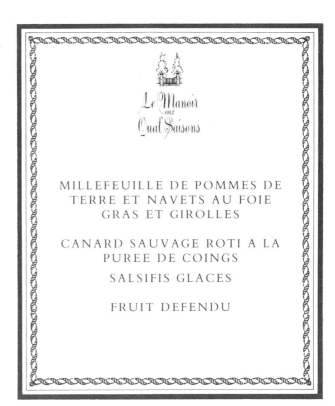

MILLEFEUILLE DE POMMES DE
TERRE ET NAVETS AU FOIE
GRAS ET GIROLLES

CANARD SAUVAGE ROTI A LA
PUREE DE COINGS

SALSIFIS GLACES

FRUIT DEFENDU

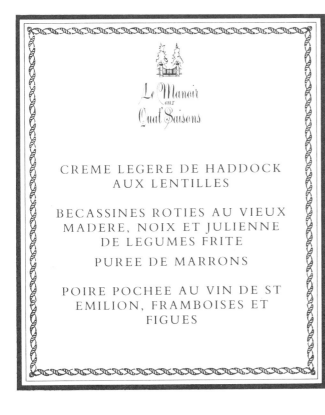

CREME LEGERE DE HADDOCK
AUX LENTILLES

BECASSINES ROTIES AU VIEUX
MADERE, NOIX ET JULIENNE
DE LEGUMES FRITE

PUREE DE MARRONS

POIRE POCHEE AU VIN DE ST
EMILION, FRAMBOISES ET
FIGUES

SALADE DE COQUILLES
ST-JACQUES ET
TOPINAMBOURS A LA
VINAIGRETTE PARFUMEE A
L'HUILE DE NOISETTE

ROGNON DE VEAU ROTI A
LA PUREE D'ECHALOTES AU
FUMET D'HERMITAGE

RIZ SAUVAGE AU NATUREL

FEUILLETE DE POIRE AU
CARAMEL PARFUME AU
GINGEMBRE, CREME VANILLE
AU CITRON VERT

Summer

◆

Season of warmth and full display of colours and ripening; there is no shyness left. Nature proudly displays all its richness. The colours are vivid now — there is a definite statement, a clear taste from matured, ripe fruit and vegetables. Nature smiles and provides an elegant display of plenty. There is an overwhelming choice and abundance of vegetables, bursting with full flavour — sun-ripe tomatoes, the finest soft fruits with their glowing colours. The flavours are triumphant, and one is spoilt for choice in this richest and most explosive season of the year.

BISQUE LEGERE DE LANGOUSTINES

A light langoustine soup

"A most useful and delicious light soup made with the carcasses of shellfish used in other recipes."

Serves 4
Difficulty: 🍳
Total recipe time: 1 hour

──────── INGREDIENTS ────────

800 g/1¾ lb langoustine, lobster or crayfish carcasses (claws, heads and shells)

100 ml/3½ fl oz olive oil

1 small onion, peeled and diced

1 small carrot, washed, peeled and diced

½ celery stalk, washed and diced

3 outer leaves of fennel, washed and diced

1 garlic clove, lightly crushed

1 star anise

1 sprig of thyme

1 sprig of young tarragon, washed

6 ripe tomatoes, washed and finely chopped

1 teaspoon tomato purée

100 ml/3½ fl oz Cognac, plus 1 teaspoon

200 ml/7 fl oz dry white wine

1½ L/2½ pt Light fish stock (see page 20) or water

100 ml/3½ fl oz whipping cream

salt and freshly ground white pepper

Garnish

150 ml/5 fl oz whipping cream

a squeeze of lemon

a dash of Pernod

12 young tarragon leaves, washed and finely chopped

Planning ahead

Stages 1–3 inclusive can be completed 1 day in advance.

1. Preparing the vegetables and herbs (10 minutes)

Mix together all the diced vegetables, thyme and star anise. Peel and chop the tomatoes but do not deseed them. Set aside.

2. Preparing the langoustines (10 minutes)

Scrape inside the langoustine heads with a teaspoon handle to remove the intestines, liver and stomach, then roughly chop the carcasses.

3. Cooking the bisque and sieving (30 minutes)

In a large sauté pan heat the olive oil until smoking then sear the langoustine carcasses for 1 minute. Add the diced vegetables, herbs (except the tarragon) and spices and sweat over low heat for a few minutes.

Tilt the pan and spoon out excess oil then deglaze with 100 ml/3½ fl oz Cognac and the wine and reduce to a quarter of its volume.

Add the chopped tomatoes and tomato purée, then the fish stock or water. Bring back to the boil, skim and simmer for 20 minutes, adding the sprig of tarragon towards the end.

Force the stock through a hard sieve into a medium saucepan, pressing down hard to extract as much juice and flavour as possible. Bring to the boil, skim until totally free of fat, and reduce to about 1 L/1¾ pt. Stir in 100 ml/3½ fl oz whipping cream and 1 teaspoon Cognac, taste and correct the seasoning with salt and pepper. Keep warm.

4. Preparing the garnish (10 minutes)

Whip the cream to a light peak and add a pinch of salt, 2 turns of pepper, a squeeze of lemon, and a dash of Pernod and the chopped tarragon. Chill until needed.

5. Serving

Serve from a large china tureen into warmed soup bowls then spoon the cold tarragon cream on top.

──────── VARIATIONS ────────

Glaze the bisque under a hot grill.
Add a few shelled langoustine tails to the bisque at the last moment.

Chef's notes

Tomatoes: Truly ripe tomatoes contain enough acidity to counterbalance the sweetness of the langoustines. If the tomatoes are not quite ripe, deseed them as the seeds will be too acidic.

Tarragon: Blanch older tarragon for a few seconds to remove coarseness then refresh before using.

Searing the langoustines: The oil must be very hot or the langoustine carcasses will simply stew in their juices, making a characterless bisque. Stop searing at the precise moment when the carcasses give off a strong scent, just before they colour, or the bisque will be overpoweringly strong.

Sieving: Grinding the carcasses in a food processor before sieving will greatly improve the taste and colour of the bisque. If you do this, first pass the bisque through a sieve then strain it through two layers of damp muslin.

Adding lemon to the cream: Add only a tiny squeeze of lemon and fold it in carefully so that the cream does not separate.

POTAGE DE ROUGET AU FUMET DE VIN ROUGE

A full-flavoured red mullet soup

Serves 4
Difficulty: ♟♟
Total recipe time: 1 hour 10 minutes
Special equipment: hard sieve or food processor, muslin cloth, 2 cm/¾ in round pastry cutter

──── INGREDIENTS ────

800 g/1¾ lb red rock mullet

½ onion, finely chopped

100 g/3½ oz fennel trimmings, finely chopped

1 carrot, finely chopped

4 tablespoons olive oil

1 star anise

5 strips of dried orange zest

3 garlic cloves, crushed

700 ml/1¼ pt red wine

1 tablespoon soy sauce

Fondue de tomates, made with 500 g/ 1 lb 2 oz tomatoes and 1 tablespoon tomato purée (see Beurre de langoustines, page 25)

500 ml/18 fl oz Light fish stock (see page 20)

4 basil leaves, shredded

4 coriander leaves, shredded

salt and freshly ground white pepper

Garnish

2 slices of white bread

1 garlic clove

8 coriander leaves

1. The red mullet (15 minutes)
2. Wash and pat dry. Chop roughly, including the heads, tails and guts.

2. The soup (45 minutes)
Combine all the vegetables, olive oil, star anise, orange zests and crushed garlic in a large saucepan and sweat for 5 minutes without colouring. Pour in the red wine and bring to a fast boil. Skim the surface. Reduce the liquid by one-third, then add the *fondue de tomates,* cold fish stock, soy sauce and finally the chopped red mullet. Boil for 2–3 minutes, skim and simmer for a further 15 minutes.
Rub through a metal sieve, pounding the fish with a wooden spoon to extract all the juices or purée in a food processor, then pass through a very fine conical sieve back into the saucepan. Reduce, skimming occasionally, until the soup has a beautiful dark red sheen and an intense flavour. Season and add the chopped basil and coriander leaves. Simmer for 5 minutes, then strain through a damp muslin cloth and keep warm.

3. The garnish (10 minutes)
Preheat the oven to 230°C/450°F/ gas 8.
Croûtons: Cut the bread into rounds with the pastry cutter and toast in the oven until golden. Rub with a cut face of garlic.
Coriander: Finely shred the leaves.

4. Serving
Warm 4 bowls or a tureen and pour in the hot soup. Scatter over the shredded coriander. Serve the *croûtons* separately.

──── VARIATIONS ────
For a cheaper version of this dish, use just the red mullet bones. It will still be very good.

Chef's notes
Buy Mediterranean rock mullet if you can find them; they have a most powerful yet sophisticated flavour. Otherwise fresh Cornish mullet are available from May to late September. Use frozen mullet only as a last resort. Ask your fishmonger to scale but not gut the mullet.

CREME GLACEE DE CONCOMBRES A L'INFUSION DE CERFEUIL

Iced chervil and cucumber soup

Serves 4
Difficulty: 🎩
Total recipe time: 55 minutes, plus chilling

———— INGREDIENTS ————

800 ml/27 fl oz Light chicken stock (see page 21) or water

25 g/1 oz chervil

½ garlic clove

100 ml/3½ fl oz whipping cream

100 ml/3½ fl oz sour cream

1 small cucumber

a pinch of cayenne pepper

salt and freshly ground white pepper

1. Infusing the chervil (10 minutes)
In a medium saucepan, bring the chicken stock to the boil.
Chervil: Wash, reserve 4 sprigs for garnish and finely chop the remainder, leaving the stalk on.
Garlic: Remove the green germ.
Add the chopped chervil and the garlic to the chicken stock and cook at full boil for 5 minutes. Pass through a fine sieve and leave to cool.

2. Preparing and marinating the cucumber (35 minutes)
Peel and halve lengthways. Reserve 2 strips of peel for the soup. Scoop out the seeds with a teaspoon and finely slice the cucumber. Spread out the slices on a tray and sprinkle with 1 teaspoon salt. Marinate for 30 minutes, then rinse thoroughly under cold running water. Reserve one-third for garnish.

3. Completing the soup
(5 minutes, plus chilling)
Combine two-thirds of the cucumber with the reserved peel and the infusion of chervil and liquidize for about 2 minutes until smooth. Pass through a fine sieve, stir in the whipping and sour cream and season with salt, pepper and a little cayenne. Chill.

4. Serving
Divide the cucumber garnish between 4 bowls. Pour over the chilled soup and top with a sprig of chervil.

SALADE CROQUANTE AUX PETITS LEGUMES ET FLEURS DU POTAGER

Tender vegetables and thyme flowers soused in lemon vinaigrette

Serves 4
Difficulty: 🎩
Total recipe time: 1½ hours

———— INGREDIENTS ————

10 sprigs of flowering thyme

1 prepared artichoke heart (see page 18)

4 baby beetroot

12 baby onions

12 chanterelles or firm white button mushrooms

2 young fennel bulbs

a large handful each of French beans, mange-tout, broad beans, young pea pods

4 baby courgettes

2 medium tomatoes or 12 cherry tomatoes

shoots and flowers from the peas or mange-tout

½ teaspoon flour

salt

caster sugar

juice of ¼ lemon

Vinaigrette
¼ onion, finely sliced

½ garlic clove, unpeeled and crushed

3 tablespoons olive oil

3 tablespoons dry white wine

1 strip of orange zest

1 strip of lemon zest

2 coriander leaves, finely chopped

2 basil leaves, finely chopped

6 tarragon leaves, finely chopped

2 sprigs of thyme, finely chopped

juice of ¼ lemon

a large pinch of caster sugar

salt and freshly ground white pepper

1. The vinaigrette (20 minutes)

In a medium saucepan, sweat the onion and garlic in 1 tablespoon olive oil for 5 minutes without colouring. Add the wine and boil to reduce the alcohol. Add 4 tablespoons water, the orange and lemon zests and all the chopped herbs and simmer for 5 minutes to allow all the complex scents and flavours to mingle.

Strain, cool, then whisk in 2 tablespoons olive oil. Taste and season with ¼ teaspoon salt, 5 turns of pepper, a pinch of caster sugar and the lemon juice. If too acid, add another pinch of caster sugar. Taste, correct seasoning and set aside.

2. Preparing the thyme
(15 minutes)

Cut off the flowers and simmer for 10–15 minutes in lightly salted water until tender. Refresh and set aside (the remaining thyme can be kept for another use). Meanwhile, prepare the vegetables.

3. Preparing the vegetables
(35 minutes)

Beetroot: Wash, remove fine root and cut stalk 2.5 cm/1 in above bulb.
Onions: Peel.
Chanterelles: Trim and scrape base of stalks, wash quickly in plenty of water. Pat dry. If using *button mushrooms,* trim the stalks and peel the caps.
Fennel: Wash and peel off the fibrous outer layer. Depending on size, halve or quarter the bulb.
French beans: Top and tail.

Mange-tout: Top and tail unless they are extremely young.
Broad beans: Shell.
Peas: Shell. If very young, do not cook them.
Shoots and flowers: Wash, taking care not to damage flowers.
Courgettes: Cut off base of stem, gently rub with a cloth to remove hairs.
Tomatoes: Peel, halve and deseed with a teaspoon. Cut each half into 3. If using cherry tomatoes, simply wash them.

4. Cooking the vegetables
(20 minutes)

Artichoke: Cook in 200 ml/7 fl oz boiling water with a pinch of salt and the juice of ¼ lemon. Simmer for 15 minutes, draw off the heat and when cool cut into 8 triangles.
Onions and chanterelles: In a small saucepan bring the vinaigrette to the boil and simmer the baby onions for 10 minutes, adding the chanterelles after 9 minutes. Draw off the heat and leave to cool.
Remaining vegetables: Bring to the boil 2 L/3½ pt water with 2 tablespoons salt. Add the vegetables in the following order and cook for the time indicated: fennel 4 minutes; French beans 3 minutes; mange-tout 2 minutes; broad beans 1 minute; peas, pea shoots and flowers 30 seconds. All the vegetables should be ready at the same time.

Drain in a colander and plunge into iced water for a few seconds. Drain again.

Broad beans: Remove outer layer of skin.

5. Dressing and serving

Put all the drained vegetables and tomatoes in a large mixing bowl, except the pea shoots and flowers. Add all but 1 tablespoon vinaigrette, then the onions and mushrooms and mix together. Taste and season. Mix the pea shoots and flowers and the thyme flowers with the remaining vinaigrette and arrange attractively on the salad. Finish with 2 or 3 turns of pepper. Serve the salad in the old-fashioned way, in a beautiful china bowl or on individual plates.

Chef's notes

Pea flowers may not always be available – the salad will still be lovely without them.
Thyme flowers grow from May to August, the ideal time being mid-June. If you do not grow thyme in your garden, you will certainly find it at one of the many herb farms throughout Britain.
Fennel: If you can find fennel complete with its fern, use the fern for a delicious sorbet (see page 124).
Cooking the vegetables: The timings may vary according to size and age.
The vinaigrette: 5 minutes is the optimum cooking time. Beyond this, the flavours will alter and deteriorate. Try to preserve the natural, unspoilt taste of the herbs which complement the freshness of the vegetables.

SALADE DE COQUILLES ST-JACQUES ET THON AU JUS A LA CORIANDRE

A salad topped with warmed scallops poached in a coriander-scented juice garnished with slivers of tuna fish

Serves 4
Difficulty: ☖
Total recipe time: 50 minutes

―――――― INGREDIENTS ――――――

16 medium scallops with their coral

100 ml/3½ fl oz Nage de légumes (see page 22)

¼ coffee spoon Dijon mustard

1 tablespoon whipping cream

8 coriander leaves, washed and finely chopped

150 g/5 oz fresh tuna fillet

lemon juice

salt and freshly ground white pepper

Garnish

2 strips of lemon zest, cut into fine julienne

coral from the scallops

1 tablespoon olive oil

2 sprigs of coriander, washed and finely chopped

Brunoise of vegetables

2 shallots, peeled and finely diced

¼ celery stalk, peeled and finely diced

1 small carrot, peeled and finely diced

1 small fennel bulb, finely diced

1 small courgette, finely diced

1 small ripe tomato, peeled, deseeded and finely diced

1 tablespoon olive oil

1 coffee spoon white wine vinegar

Salad and vinaigrette

a handful of mixed salads (radicchio, curly endive, lettuce), washed and trimmed (see page 17)

1 tablespoon olive oil

1 coffee spoon white wine vinegar

Planning ahead

Order the scallops and tuna fillet well in advance. Ask the fishmonger to open and clean the scallops, and keep the coral. Ask for the shells too.

Stages 1–3 inclusive can be completed in advance, but only add the vinaigrette to the salads at the last moment.

1. Preparing the scallops and tuna
(10 minutes)

Scallops: Separate the coral. Carefully pull any fibres from around the scallops and wash the scallops and coral under cold running water to remove any trace of sand. Keep coral aside for stage 2.

Slice each scallop into 4 or 5 rounds, about 3 mm/¹⁄₁₀ in thick.

In a large sauté pan, whisk the mustard into the vegetable stock and mix in the cream. Throw in the chopped coriander and season. Finally add the scallops, loosening the rounds so they do not stick when they are warmed in Stage 4. Cover the pan and keep aside.

Tuna fish: Using a very sharp knife, slice into 12 fine slivers. Set aside.

1. Preparing the garnish
(30 minutes)

Lemon zest julienne: Blanch in plenty of simmering water for 15 minutes, refresh and set aside.

Coral: Poach in barely simmering water for 3 minutes, refresh, pat dry and slice into fine slivers. Season and pan-fry in hot olive oil for a few seconds. Place in a small container lined with kitchen paper.

Vegetable brunoise: Mix all the diced vegetables with 1 tablespoon olive oil and the white wine vinegar. Season and set aside.

3. The salads and vinaigrette
(5 minutes)

In a small container mix together 1 tablespoon olive oil and 1 coffee spoon white wine vinegar and season with salt and pepper. Toss in the salad leaves.

4. Cooking the scallops
(6 minutes)

Bring juice with the scallops almost to simmering point, keeping the pan covered. Turn off the heat and leave to rest for about 5 minutes. Taste, correct seasoning then enliven the juice with a squeeze of lemon.

5. Serving (4 minutes)

Lightly warm 4 plates.

Around the edge of each plate shape the finely diced vegetables into 3 oval

mounds and arrange 3 slivers of tuna between them. Arrange a little dressed salad in the centre of the plates and cover completely with scallop rounds. Pour 1 tablespoon juice over the scallops and scatter over the corals and lemon *julienne*.

Serve to your guests.

—————— VARIATIONS ——————

Replace the tuna with fine slivers of salmon.

If you do not like raw fish, you can cure the tuna (see page 123) or omit it.

—————————— WINE ——————————

The vinaigrette will spoil a fine wine. Far better to serve a light, dry regional white wine; I suggest a Chignin Bergeron blanc from Savoie or young Alsace Sylvaner.

Chef's notes

Tuna and scallops must be fresh; do not

substitute frozen.

Coral: poached coral is pretty tasteless, but if you pan-fry it after poaching, you will bring out its most enjoyable flavour.

Lemon zest: If overcooked it will be tasteless – undercooked, bitter, so check by tasting from time to time during blanching.

Cooking the scallops: The idea is barely to cook them so that their taste comes through.

—————————————————————————————

SALADE "TERRE ET MER"

A salad from the earth and sea

Serves 4
Difficulty: 🎩🎩
Total recipe time: 1 hour 10 minutes
Special equipment: 1 large saucepan for cooking the lobsters

—————— INGREDIENTS ——————

2 450 g/1 lb live lobsters

4 baby monkfish tails, filleted (total weight 300 g/11 oz)

4 tablespoons olive oil

1 small garlic clove, peeled and halved

1 sprig of thyme

salt and freshly ground white pepper

For finishing the juices

2 tablespoons olive oil

a squeeze of lemon

Salads

a handful each of rocket, cornsalad or radicchio, washed and trimmed

a handful of French beans

8 sprigs of mint

2 fronds of dill

2 teaspoons white wine vinegar

2 tablespoons olive oil

Planning ahead

Order live lobsters well in advance. Order monkfish tails and have them filleted.

Stages 1 and 2 can be completed up to 6 hours in advance.

Stage 3 can be completed 1 hour before the meal; keep lobsters and monkfish tails in a warm place.

1. Blanching and shelling the lobsters/preparing the monkfish
(30 minutes)

In a large saucepan bring to the boil 3 L/5 pt unsalted water.

The most humane way to kill the lobsters is to take a heavy implement and apply a sharp blow to the base of the head.

Using a large knife cut off the tails (at the base of the head) and twist off legs and claws. Blanch tails and claws for 3 minutes, refresh under cold running water, drain and shell (see *Homard braisé*, page 133). If you find any eggs beneath the tails, collect them with a teaspoon. Keep heads to make a light lobster sauce or bisque (see *Bisque légère de langoustines*, page 108).

Monkfish tails: Cut each fillet in two and tie with 8 turns of string to retain the shape. Put on a small tray with the lobster and refrigerate.

2. Preparing the salads and vinaigrette (20 minutes)

French beans: Wash and blanch in plenty of boiling water for 3 minutes. Refresh, drain, halve lengthways and place on a tray lined with a tea towel, together with the prepared salad leaves.

Mint: Pick off the leaves, wash, drain and shred.

Dill: Wash, shake dry, chop roughly.

Vinaigrette: In a small bowl mix the vinegar with the olive oil, a pinch of salt and 4 turns of pepper. Add the chopped mint and dill and set aside.

3. Cooking the lobster and monkfish (10 minutes)

Preheat the oven to 400°F/200°C/ gas 6.

Season the lobster and monkfish with 2 pinches of salt and 4 turns of pepper. In a large sauté pan heat 4 tablespoons olive oil with the split garlic clove and thyme. Sear the lobster tails and monkfish fillets for 1 minute without colouring.

Add 4 tablespoons water, cover and place in the preheated oven for 5 minutes, then put in the meat from the lobster claws and cook for a further 5 minutes. Remove from the oven, cover loosely with foil and leave to

TOP

Salade de coquilles St-Jacques et thon au jus de coriandre
(page 112)

BOTTOM

Coquilles St-Jacques et champignons poêlés au jus de veau blond
(page 132)

rest away from the heat for 5 minutes. Strain the juices into a small saucepan and add 2 tablespoons olive oil. Taste, season and finally lift the juices with a squeeze of lemon. Keep warm.
Cut off the string from the monkfish fillets and return them to the lobster. Keep in a warm place, covered loosely with foil.

4. Finishing and serving the dish
(10 minutes)
Warm 4 plates.
Toss the salads in the vinaigrette and arrange attractively around each plate.
Monkfish: Slice each fillet into 5 rounds and arrange them in a circle in the centre of the plates. Season lightly with a tiny pinch of salt and ½ turn of pepper. Sprinkle each medallion with a drop of lemon juice.
Lobster: Halve the tails lengthways and remove the black thread-like in-

testine running down the centre. Top the monkfish medallions with a half tail and 1 claw. Pour the juices over and serve.

VARIATIONS

Substitute tiny whole rock red mullet, turbot or brill for the monkfish and langoustines for the lobsters.
Substitute other vegetables for the French beans – young pea shoots with their flowers, artichoke hearts or broad beans.

Chef's notes

Lobsters must be bought alive. Once dead, the serum escapes from the flesh and the texture will become like cotton wool and unusable.
Rocket: Its peppery taste is very important; do not use a substitute, although other salads can replace the cornsalad or radicchio.
Blanching the lobsters: Blanching only part-cooks the lobsters and allows the shells to be removed easily. Observe the timing strictly. If you find it difficult to shell the lobsters, leave the claws unshelled and provide your guests with lobster picks and lobster crackers.
Finishing the dish: Only toss the salads in vinaigrette at the last moment as the vinegar will quickly destroy their lovely texture.

CHARLOTTE DE LEGUMES AUX SAVEURS DE PROVENCE ET MIGNONS D'AGNEAU AU ROMARIN, VINAIGRETTE AUX HERBES

Charlotte of Provençal vegetables and rosemary-scented lamb, served with a herb vinaigrette

"The table laid in the shadow of an olive tree under a deep blue sky, the lazy, monotonous chirping of crickets – sunny Provence would be the ideal setting for this dish. But no matter where you are – under your own trees on a fine summer's day, this refreshing herb-scented charlotte will bring the sun to your table and transport you to wherever your imagination leads."

Charlotte de légumes aux saveurs de Provence et mignons d'agneau au romarin, vinaigrette aux herbes

CHARLOTTE DE LEGUMES
(CONT.)

Serves 12–15
Difficulty: 🎩 🎩
Total recipe time: 1 hour 50 minutes,
plus 1 day resting
Special equipment: 24 x 10cm/10 x
4 in terrine, wooden board to fit inside, 300 g/12 oz weight, kitchen
string, clingfilm

────── INGREDIENTS ──────

Charlotte

*6 lamb tenderloins or 1 350 g/12 oz
lamb fillet*

*6 10 x 8 cm/4 x 3 in thin slices pork or
lamb back fat*

10 large spinach leaves

6 sprigs of rosemary

6 sprigs of thyme

125 ml/4 fl oz olive oil

2 artichoke hearts (see page 17)

1 large or 2 small firm ripe aubergines

1 large red pepper

1 large yellow pepper

3 medium or 8 small courgettes

1 large fennel bulb

3 ripe tomatoes

salt and freshly ground white pepper

Tomato coulis

1.5 kg/3½ lb ripe tomatoes, chopped

1 tablespoon tomato purée (optional)

a large pinch of caster sugar (optional)

*5 leaves of gelatine or 1 sachet of
powdered gelatine*

1 onion, finely chopped

4 garlic cloves, finely chopped

1 fresh bayleaf or ½ dried bayleaf

1 sage leaf

2 sprigs of thyme

1 tablespoon tomato purée (optional)

a large pinch of caster sugar (optional)

8 basil leaves, chopped

Garnish

1 fennel bulb

20 French beans

*24 coriander leaves, washed and finely
chopped*

*Herb vinaigrette, to serve (see
page 29)*

Planning ahead
The terrine must be made at least 1
day ahead and can even be made 2 or 3
days in advance, to allow the flavours
to mingle and develop.
The vinaigrette must also be prepared
a day in advance.
The dish can be dressed 1 hour before
serving and kept at room temperature.

1. Lining the terrine (10 minutes)
Spinach: Cut off the stems and wash
the leaves in cold water. Blanch in 2 L/
3½ pt boiling water and 2 tablespoons
salt for 30 seconds, until cooked but
still firm. Refresh, drain and pat dry.
Season, then remove the central veins.
Reserve the cooking water for the
courgettes.
Line the terrine first with clingfilm,
then with overlapping spinach leaves,
leaving enough overhang of both to
enclose the completed terrine completely. Set aside.

*Lamb fillet will need to be sliced: cut it
lengthways into triangular sections (see
Stage 2).*

2. The lamb tenderloins
(15 minutes)
Preheat the oven to 200°C/400°F/
gas 6.
Remove any nerves or fibres. If using
a fillet, cut lengthways into 6 triangular slices (see diagram). Season. Place a
tenderloin on each rectangle of back
fat and top with a sprig of rosemary
and thyme. Wrap the lamb completely in the fat and tie in 2 places with
string.
Heat 1 tablespoon olive oil in a frying
pan, put in the lamb parcels and roast
in the oven for 4 minutes, then transfer to a stainless steel dish and leave to
cool. (The oil can be used for a delicious vinaigrette.)
Remove the back fat, turn the lamb in
the cooking oil, taste and correct the
seasoning. Leave the oven switched
on for the aubergine and peppers.

3. The vegetables (30 minutes)
Aubergine: Remove stem and slice into
5 x 3 cm/1¼ in rounds. Season. Heat 3
tablespoons olive oil until smoking
and fry the aubergine until the underside is lightly coloured. Add another
tablespoon oil, turn over the aubergine and fry to colour the other side.
Cook in the hot oven for 8 minutes,
then drain on absorbent paper. Correct the seasoning if necessary and set
aside.
Red and yellow peppers: Core, halve
lengthways and remove seeds. Lightly season the inside, score the skin

with the point of a knife and place face down in the pan used for cooking the aubergine. Brush with olive oil and place in the oven for 20–25 minutes, until the skins blister. Cool and peel. Season and set aside.

Courgettes: Trim and plunge into the fast-boiling water from the spinach for 5–6 minutes. Refresh, drain and slice lengthways. Set aside.

Fennel: Separate the layers and plunge into fast-boiling water for 3–4 minutes, refresh, drain and pat dry. Set aside.

Tomatoes: Remove stem, slit the skin and plunge into boiling water for 3 seconds. Refresh, drain and peel. Halve, remove seeds with a teaspoon, then cut each half into 3 pieces and set aside.

4. The tomato coulis (25 minutes)

Gelatine: Soften in cold water until supple.

Tomatoes: Chop roughly and squeeze out the seeds if not perfectly ripe. In a large sauté pan, sweat the onion, garlic and herbs in 85 ml/3 fl oz olive oil for 6–8 minutes, until soft but not coloured. Add the chopped tomatoes, tomato purée and sugar if necessary, cover and boil briskly for 2 minutes. Remove the lid and simmer gently, stirring occasionally, for about 15 minutes until scented and pulpy. Add the chopped basil during the last 5 minutes. You should have exactly 350 ml/12 fl oz pulp.

Season with salt, pepper and sugar if necessary. Stir in the softened gelatine until completely dissolved, then, with the back of a ladle, force through a fine conical sieve into a small bowl and cool until just tepid.

5. Assembling the charlotte
(10 minutes)

Spread 1 cm/½ in layer of tomato *coulis* over the bottom of the terrine. Layer the vegetables into the terrine in the following order, coating each layer with a film of *coulis* to bind: aubergine, yellow pepper, red pepper,

courgettes, fennel, artichokes, tomatoes. Arrange the sliced tenderloins on top and coat with tomato *coulis*.

Fold over the overhanging spinach leaves, then wrap with the clingfilm. To settle the terrine, pick it up and tap the bottom on your work surface. Place the wooden board on top of the clingfilm and finally the 300 g/12 oz weight. Refrigerate for at least 24 hours.

6. The garnish (10 minutes)

Fennel: Trim off the root and cut into *julienne*. Wash and drain.

French beans: Top and tail and blanch in boiling salted water for 3–4 minutes. Refresh, drain and halve lengthways.

Stir 1 tablespoon vinaigrette into both the beans and fennel.

7. Dressing and serving
(10 minutes)

Remove the weight and wood, open the clingfilm and invert the terrine onto a chopping board. Remove the clingfilm. With a sharp serrated knife, applying no pressure, cut off and discard the rather unattractive end slice. Carefully cut 1 cm/½ in slices and, using a fish slice, transfer a slice to the middle of each plate.

Stir the vinaigrette and spoon it around the terrine. Scatter over the fennel, French beans and coriander.

Brush the slices of terrine with a film of olive oil to make them shine and finish with a half turn of pepper.

———— VARIATIONS ————

Replace the lamb with fillets of monkfish fried in olive oil and saffron, or omit the lamb and use more aubergine or courgette. For a simpler, but delicious dish, use only aubergines.

You could spike the charlotte with black olives, blanched for 1 minute and halved.

For 6 servings, halve the ingredients and assemble the charlotte in 6 individual ramekins. Dice all the vegetables and slice the lamb.

———— WINE ————

A spicy refreshing rosé from Provence is ideal: try one from the Domaine Ott or Domaine de la Bernarde.

Chef's notes

Spinach: This not only looks attractive, but also holds the fragile charlotte together. Do not overcook it or it will lose its strength and fresh colour.

Back fat: This seals the herbs in with the lamb, allowing the flavours to infuse. It also protects the delicate meat from discolouring and drying out.

Aubergines soak up oil like blotting paper. Do not worry – they will release most of it while cooking in the oven. Colour them only lightly.

Wood and weight: These compress and reinforce the delicate structure of the charlotte.

TERRINE DE BOUILLABAISSE
A LA VINAIGRETTE DE SAFRAN

Layers of fish and shellfish served with saffron vinaigrette

"My favourite fish terrine – the textures of the highly seasoned fish and the crunchiness of
the vegetables give this dish so much character."

*Terrine de bouillabaisse à la
vinaigrette de safran*

Serves 12
Difficulty: ♟ ♟
Total recipe time: about 3 hours, plus 1 day resting
Special equipment: tweezers, food processor, 23 x 9 x 8 cm/9 x 3½ x 3 in china terrine, wooden board to fit inside, 1 kg/2¼lb weight

─── INGREDIENTS ───

12 langoustines

4 tablespoons olive oil

2 200 g/7 oz red mullet

300 g/11 oz monkfish fillet

300 g/11 oz John Dory fillet

300 g/11 oz scorpion fish

salt and freshly ground white pepper

Marinade
2 tablespoons olive oil

4 sprigs of rosemary

4 basil leaves

freshly ground white pepper

Stock
1 medium onion, finely diced

trimmings from the fennel

1 small carrot, washed, peeled and finely diced

white of 1 medium leek, washed, trimmed and finely diced

4 medium tomatoes, peeled, deseeded and finely chopped

12 coriander leaves, washed and finely chopped

½ garlic clove, unpeeled and crushed

bones from the fish, roughly chopped

4 tablespoons olive oil

2 sachets of powdered saffron

a large pinch of cayenne pepper

750 ml/1¼ pt Light fish stock (see page 20) or water

For completing the jelly
4 leaves of gelatine

100 g/3½ oz monkfish fillet and ½ egg white, to clarify (see page 23)

Vegetables and herbs for the terrine
8 baby or 2 large fennel bulbs, cut into strips

1 medium onion, cut into 1 cm/½ in strips

1 tablespoon olive oil

1 sprig of thyme

½ bayleaf

1 tablespoon white wine vinegar

8 basil leaves

1 small bunch of coriander

Saffron vinaigrette
1 pinch of saffron threads or 1 sachet of powdered saffron

1 garlic clove

100 ml/3½ fl oz olive oil

6 tablespoons water

a large pinch of salt

a large pinch of cayenne pepper

½ tablespoon white wine vinegar

a pinch of caster sugar

Planning ahead
Order all fish well in advance. If any are not available see Variations. Ask your fishmonger to scale, gut and fillet the fish, and to give you the bones for the stock. The langoustines must be bought alive.
The marinade must be made in advance.
The fish must be marinaded the day beforehand.
The light fish stock must be made in advance.
The terrine must be made 1 day in advance to allow all the flavours to infuse.

1. Preparing the fish and marinating (20 minutes, plus 1 day marinating)
Langoustines: Pull apart the bodies and tails. Twist the middle of the tail fins and pull gently to remove the black thread-like intestine. Keep the shells and claws for Stage 2. Blanch the tails for 3 minutes in boiling salted water. Peel off the shells, cover and set aside.
Red mullet: Run the blade of a knife along the skin against the lie of the scales to remove any which are left. Gently tweeze out any small bones from the centre of the fillet.
Monkfish: Cut into 1 cm/½ in slices.
Scorpion fish: Halve lengthways and remove any bones from the middle. Place all the fish in a roasting dish and coat with the marinade. Cover with clingfilm and refrigerate for 1 day.

2. Simmering the stock (40 minutes)
In a large saucepan, sweat all the vegetables, garlic, tomatoes, saffron and cayenne in olive oil for 5 minutes. Add the langoustine heads and claws and cook for 1 minute. Add the fish bones and stock or water, bring to the boil and simmer for 15 minutes. Throw in the chopped herbs and cook for 5 minutes more, skimming occasionally. Pass through a fine conical sieve into a saucepan.

3. Cooking the fish and shellfish (15 minutes)
Remove the fish from the marinade and season with salt and pepper.
In a large saucepan, heat 4 tablespoons olive oil with a large pinch of saffron until hot. Sear the red mullet on the flesh side for 30 seconds, remove with a fish slice and keep aside.
Add the fish stock from Stage 2, bring to just below simmering point and add all the fish. After 5 minutes, remove the John Dory; after 7–8 minutes, remove the monkfish and scorpion fish. Cool the stock and skim off as much fat as possible.
Gelatine: Soften in cold water.

4. Clarification (30 minutes) (see page 23)

Purée the monkfish and ½ egg white in a blender and whisk into the tepid stock. Bring to the boil and simmer for 10 minutes, adding the softened gelatine towards the end. Pass the now clear, saffron-scented stock through a fine conical sieve lined with a damp muslin cloth into a medium saucepan and reduce to 350 ml/ 12 fl oz. Taste and correct the seasoning with salt, pepper and cayenne. Cool until almost set.

Meanwhile, cook the fennel and onion.

5. Cooking the fennel and onion (25 minutes)

Fennel: Cut into strips. Blanch in boiling salted water for 3–4 minutes, refresh, drain and pat dry. Taste and season with salt and pepper.

Onion: Cut into 1 cm/½ in strips, season lightly then sweat in 1 tablespoon olive oil with ½ bayleaf and sprig of thyme for 2 minutes. Add the white wine vinegar and cook over a gentle heat for about 15 minutes, without colouring. Draw off the heat and allow to cool.

6. Building the terrine (15 minutes)

Basil and coriander: Wash, pat dry.

Cover the bottom of the terrine with a 5 mm/¼ in coating (about 50 ml/ 2 fl oz) of saffron-scented jelly and refrigerate until set.

Put in the red mullet, skin side down, coat with a little saffron jelly and top with the basil and coriander. Make a layer of fennel, a layer of onion, then another layer of fennel. Build up the terrine with the fillets of monkfish, John Dory, langoustine tails and finally the scorpion fish, interspersing each layer with strips of onion and fennel and coating with a film of saffron jelly. Press each layer down gently and season with a little salt and pepper.

Seal the terrine with clingfilm, put in the wooden board and weight and refrigerate for 1 day.

7. The saffron vinaigrette (40 minutes)

Garlic: Peel, halve and remove the green germ.

In a small saucepan, sweat the saffron and garlic in the olive oil for 2 minutes. Add 6 tablespoons cold water, a large pinch of salt, a pinch of cayenne pepper, the vinegar and a pinch of sugar. Draw off the heat and infuse for at least 30 minutes. Remove the garlic, taste and correct the seasoning if necessary.

8. Serving the dish

Chill 12 serving plates.

Remove weight, wood and clingfilm. Dip the terrine in hot water for 3 seconds, turn out onto a large flat serving dish and present it to your guests. With a very sharp serrated knife dipped in hot water, cut 1.5 cm/ ⅝ in slices, using little or no pressure so as not to disturb the layers, and place on the chilled plates. Spoon the saffron vinaigrette around the edge.

———— VARIATIONS ————

Langoustines can be replaced by a 450 g/1 lb lobster; see pages 13, 127 for how to prepare and cook.

Although a wide variety of fish can be used, red mullet and scorpion fish provide the dish with its essential flavour. If necessary, scorpion fish can be replaced by sea bream.

Baby squid would make a nice addition.

Layers of red peppers, roasted in the oven and peeled, add another vivid colour and flavour.

If using garden fennel, keep the fern for a fennel sorbet (see page 124).

———————— WINE ————————

A dry white from Provence will suit the dish very well; try a Domaine de la Bernarde or Bandol.

Chef's notes

Cooking the red mullet: This needs little cooking as the fillets are so fragile. Remove them with a fish slice.

As this dish is served cold, the flavours must be spicy and quite fiery.

If using water instead of fish stock, you will need 5 leaves of gelatine to set the terrine.

MOUSSETTE DE POIVRONS ROUGES

Mousse of red peppers

"This fresh and tangy mousse is delicious served with a Tomato vinaigrette (page 29) or Tomato sorbet (page 122)."

Serves 12
Difficulty: 🎩
Total recipe time: 40 minutes, plus 3 hours chilling
Special equipment: 24 x 10 cm/10 x 4 in terrine or a china bowl, food processor

INGREDIENTS

¼ onion, finely chopped

2 tomatoes, deseeded and chopped

3 red peppers, cored, deseeded and chopped

1½ leaves of gelatine, or ½ teaspoon powdered gelatine

2 tablespoons olive oil

½ teaspoon cayenne pepper

2 tablespoons white wine vinegar

1 teaspoon raspberry vinegar

400 ml/14 fl oz whipping cream, chilled

salt and freshly ground white pepper

Planning ahead
As the mousse needs to set, prepare it at least 3 hours in advance and chill.
You can shape the mousse into *quenelles* half an hour before serving, arrange on the plates and keep in a cool place.

1. Preparing the mousse base
(20 minutes)
Soak the gelatine leaves in cold water for a few minutes until supple. In a large saucepan, sweat the chopped onion in the olive oil for 1 minute without colouring. Add the chopped tomatoes and red peppers, 1 teaspoon salt and ½ teaspoon cayenne pepper. Cook for a further 6–7 minutes over a strong heat, stirring to prevent sticking.

Purée, then return the mixture to the saucepan and reduce for about 5 minutes, stirring constantly, to obtain about 200 ml/7 fl oz purée. Add the soaked gelatine and stir until completely dissolved. Force the purée through a sieve into a small bowl and allow to cool slightly.

Meanwhile mix together the white wine and raspberry vinegar and reduce by two-thirds over high heat. Stir into the purée and leave to cool in the fridge.

2. Making the mousse
(10 minutes, plus 3 hours chilling)
Cream: Whip to soft peaks. Using a wooden spoon, mix one-quarter of the whipped cream into the mousse mixture, incorporating it in fast circular movements. Gently fold in the remaining cream with a wooden spatula. Taste and correct seasoning. Transfer the mousse to a terrine or china bowl, smooth the surface with a palette knife, cover with cling-film and refrigerate for at least 3 hours until set.

3. Serving (10 minutes)
Chill 12 plates.
Using two dessertspoons dipped in hot water, shape the mousse into *quenelles* and place 3 on each plate.

Storing
The mousse can be kept for 2 or 3 days in a covered container in the fridge.

VARIATIONS
You can turn this recipe into a *bavarois* of red peppers simply by adding 3 more gelatine leaves to the mousse mixture and chilling the mousse in a 2–3 cm/1 in deep china flan dish. Dip the dish into hot water to unmould the mousse and turn out onto a serving plate. Refrigerate again and mask the surface with a little jelly made with 100 ml/3½ fl oz water, half a finely diced red pepper and 1 gelatine leaf.

Chef's notes
Whipping cream: The cream must not be whipped solid or it will separate when incorporated into the red pepper purée. It should be light and fluffy but still hold together. One-quarter of the whipped cream is mixed in briskly at first to lighten the mixture and make it easier to incorporate the remaining cream. Make sure that the first step is done fast and the second slowly and gently, lifting and folding to maintain the light delicate texture. The cream must be chilled; butter fats are more likely to separate if they are tepid or at room temperature. Make sure that the red pepper purée is cold before incorporating the cream!

SORBET AUX TOMATES

Tomato sorbet

"A refreshing summer sorbet which can be served as a starter or appetizer, or in the middle of a multi-course meal."

Serves 12
Difficulty: 👨‍🍳
Total recipe time: 50 minutes
Special equipment: blender, *sorbetière*

INGREDIENTS

1.5 kg/3¼ lb ripe tomatoes
(Marmande, Roma or cherry)

85 g/3 oz caster sugar

8 basil or *tarragon leaves, finely shredded*

1 small onion, finely chopped

3 tablespoons olive oil

1 sprig of thyme

2 strips of orange zest

1½ level teaspoons salt

a large pinch of cayenne pepper

1 teaspoon white wine vinegar

Planning ahead
The sorbet can be prepared half a day in advance and churned in the *sorbetière* 1 hour before serving.
Place 12 plates or serving glasses in the freezer 1 hour before the meal.

1. Making the sorbet syrup
(5 minutes)
In a small saucepan, boil 100 ml/ 3½ fl oz water with the sugar until you obtain a clear syrup. Cool.

2. Preparing and cooking the tomatoes (25 minutes)
Tomatoes: Wash, halve, deseed with a teaspoon and chop finely. Divide into one-third and two-thirds and keep separately.
In a medium frying pan sweat the onion, thyme and orange zests in the olive oil for 5 minutes without colouring. Add the one-third chopped tomatoes, bring to the boil, cover and simmer for 5 minutes, stirring occasionally to prevent sticking.
Remove the lid and continue simmering until most of the water has evaporated and the mixture becomes pulpy. Draw off the heat and leave to cool.

3. Puréeing and churning
(15 minutes)
Purée the cooled mixture with the uncooked tomatoes, salt, cayenne pepper and most of the syrup. Taste. If it is a little acidic, add the remaining syrup.
Using a ladle, force through a fine conical sieve into a *sorbetière* and churn for 6–10 minutes until the sorbet holds together. Place in a container, cover and put in the freezer.

4. Serving (5 minutes)
Using 2 dessert spoons dipped in hot water, shape the tomato sorbet into *quenelles* (see page 142) and place on the chilled plates or glasses. Serve immediately.

Storing
Once churned, the sorbet must be served within 2–3 hours; due to its low sugar content, it will soon crystallize and harden.

Chef's notes
Tomatoes: The success of this dish depends upon using best quality, ripe tomatoes.
The sorbet is made with both cooked and raw tomatoes. The cooked tomatoes will lose their acidity and water content and the reduction will concentrate their flavour. The uncooked tomatoes provide the freshness and liveliness.
A savoury sorbet will never be quite as smooth as a sweet one because of the small quantity of sugar used.

FILETS DE THON MARINES A LA CORIANDRE ET BRUNOISE DE LEGUMES

Cured fillets of tuna scented with coriander, served with a vegetable brunoise

Serves 4
Difficulty: 🎩
Total recipe time: 30 minutes, plus 10–12 hours curing
Special equipment: filleting knife

INGREDIENTS

900 g/2 lb tuna steak, or 600 g/1 lb 6 oz trimmed tuna fillets

50 g/2 oz fresh coriander, washed and chopped

20 g/³⁄4 oz salt

15 g/¹⁄2 oz caster sugar

1 teaspoon freshly ground white pepper

lemon juice, for serving

Vegetable brunoise

1 shallot, peeled and finely chopped

1 small celery stalk, finely diced

1 small carrot, peeled and finely diced

1 small courgette, finely diced

2 fennel leaves, finely diced

1 large firm ripe tomato, peeled, deseeded and finely diced

Vinaigrette

4 strips of lemon zest, cut into julienne

20 coriander leaves, washed and chopped

100 ml/3¹⁄2 fl oz olive oil

1 tablespoon white wine vinegar

4 tablespoons cold water

salt and freshly ground white pepper

Planning ahead

Order the tuna steak well in advance. Ask the fishmonger to fillet and skin it. The tuna must be cured at least 12 hours before the meal. Stages 1–3 inclusive can be completed up to 2 days in advance.

1. Preparing and curing the tuna

(10 minutes)

Tweeze out any small bones running down the centre of the fillets. Line a tray with a large sheet of clingfilm and lay the tuna fillets in the middle.

In a small bowl, mix the chopped coriander with the salt, sugar and 1 level teaspoon pepper. Scatter the mixture evenly over both sides of the tuna fillets, wrap tightly in the clingfilm and place in the bottom of the fridge (the least cold area) for at least 12 hours.

Unwrap the cured tuna, rinse under cold running water, pat dry and refrigerate until needed.

2. Vegetable brunoise

(5 minutes)

Mix all the diced vegetables in a bowl, cover with clingfilm and refrigerate.

3. Preparing the vinaigrette

(15 minutes)

Lemon julienne: Blanch in plenty of boiling water for 8–10 minutes, refresh under cold running water, drain and put in a small bowl with the chopped coriander. Add the olive oil, vinegar and cold water and season with a pinch of salt and 8 turns of pepper.

Add the vinaigrette to the diced vegetables, taste and correct seasoning if necessary. Keep at room temperature.

4. Serving

Have ready 4 large serving plates. Halve each tuna fillet lengthways, then carve into 28 3 mm/¹⁄10 in slices. Arrange 7 tiny steaks like a flower on each plate. Stir the vinaigrette into the vegetable *brunoise* and spoon out around the tuna.

Season the fish with 2 or 3 turns of pepper and enliven each serving with a squeeze of lemon. Serve to your guests.

VARIATIONS

If you enjoy raw fish, reduce the curing time or omit it altogether.

Salmon, sea bass, monkfish and halibut can all be prepared this way.

Make a lovely palette of colours and flavours by alternating the tuna with slices of cured salmon with dill (see *Tartare de saumon sauvage,* page 61).

Chef's notes

Tuna: I cannot overstress the importance of using the very freshest fish if this dish is to be successful.

Curing (see *Tartare de saumon sauvage,* page 61): The curing time is very important: after 12 hours the salt and flavour of coriander will have penetrated about halfway through the flesh. The fish will be then half-raw, half-cured and will still retain plenty of its own taste. The balance of flavours will be just right.

Blanching the lemon zest removes bitterness. Use at least 1 L/1³⁄4 pt water, or the bitterness will simply be recycled.

SORBET AU FENOUIL

Fennel sorbet

"This aromatic and refreshing sorbet is equally delicious served at the start of a meal or in the middle of a *menu dégustation*."

Serves 8
Difficulty: 🍳
Total recipe time: 40 minutes
Special equipment: blender, *sorbetière*

INGREDIENTS
300 g/11 oz fresh fennel fern or stalks

85 g/3 oz caster sugar

salt and freshly ground white pepper

lemon juice

Planning ahead
The sorbet mixture can be prepared 1 day in advance, then churned 3 or 4 hours before the meal.
Chill the serving glasses 30 minutes in advance.

1. Preparing the fennel fern
(15 minutes)
Wash, drain and chop finely.

2. Infusing the fennel, and liquidizing (15 minutes)
Boil 1 L/1¾ pt water with a pinch of salt, 6 turns of pepper and the caster sugar. Add the chopped fennel fern and cook at a fast boil for 3 minutes. Turn off the heat and leave the fennel to infuse in the liquid for a further 5 minutes. Place on ice to cool.
Purée in a blender for 1 minute. Strain the liquid through a fine sieve, pressing the fennel gently with a small ladle. Taste, correct seasoning if necessary with a little more salt and 2 or 3 turns of pepper, then sharpen the flavour with a squeeze of lemon.

3. Churning the sorbet
(10 minutes)
Pour the liquid fennel mixture into the *sorbetière* and churn until firm with a good texture.

4. Serving
Scoop the sorbet into 8 chilled glasses and serve immediately.

Chef's notes
Fennel fern: If you cannot find fresh fennel complete with fern, use 500 g/ 1 lb 2 oz chopped fennel bulb instead.
Infusing the fennel: Do not infuse for more than 5 minutes or the sorbet will turn an unappetizing grey-green.
Liquidizing: Do not process the fern for too long, or the colour will be too intense. The ideal colour is a soft, pale green.
Since the sorbet has a low sugar content, its texture will not be as velvety as that of a sweet sorbet. Do not churn it more than 3 or 4 hours in advance; if it remains frozen for too long, the sorbet will turn to ice and become far too hard.

RAVIOLIS DE HOMARD ET SON JUS AUX TAGLIATELLES DE LEGUMES

Lobster ravioli served with a vegetable julienne

Serves 4
Difficulty: 🍳🍳🍳
Total recipe time: 2 hours 20 minutes, plus 1 hour freezing
Special equipment: food processor, 6.5 cm/2½ in pastry cutters, pasta machine

INGREDIENTS
1 675 g/1½ lb live lobster

Mousse
150 g/5 oz lobster flesh

1 level teaspoon salt

a large pinch of cayenne pepper

1 egg white

200 ml/7 fl oz whipping cream

1 tablespoon essence of lobster (from Stage 3)

Juice
4 medium tomatoes, finely chopped, with their seeds

1 garlic clove, finely chopped

100 g/3½ oz onion, finely chopped

¼ celery stalk, finely chopped

outer leaves of fennel, finely chopped

1 sprig of tarragon, finely shredded

2 tablespoons olive oil

1 sprig of thyme

lobster shell

2 tablespoons Cognac

100 ml/3½ fl oz dry white wine

700 ml/1¼ pt water

2 tablespoons whipping cream

40 g/1½ oz Beurre de langoustines (page 25) or plain unsalted butter, chilled and diced

Ravioli

150 g/5 oz ravioli dough (see Pasta, page 38)

1 tablespoon melted butter, for serving

Vegetable julienne

1 large fennel bulb, washed and cut into julienne, outer leaves reserved

3 medium courgettes, washed and cut into fine julienne

1 medium carrot, washed, peeled and cut into fine julienne

1 tablespoon unsalted butter

4 tarragon leaves

salt and freshly ground white pepper

Planning ahead

Order the lobster well in advance – preferably a female, with a lovely cluster of eggs beneath the tail. It must be bought alive. (Lobsters with a missing or broken claw are always sold cheaper.)

The ravioli dough must be made in advance.

The lobster juice can be prepared in advance.

The ravioli can be filled with the lobster mousse 2 days in advance and kept in a sealed container in the freezer, ready to be poached at the last moment.

The vegetable *julienne* can be prepared in advance, kept covered, then cooked at the last moment.

The shellfish butter (if used) must be prepared in advance.

1. Preparing the lobster

(15 minutes)

Preheat the oven to 180°C/350°F/gas 4.

In a large saucepan, bring to the boil 3 L/5½ pt cold water with 3 level tablespoons salt. The most humane way to kill the lobster is to apply a sharp blow to the base of the head with a heavy implement. Plunge it into fast-boiling water for 4 seconds – no more – then refresh in cold water, drain and place on a large tray.

See page 14 for how to shell and prepare. Scoop out the dark green coral and keep it to bind the sauce (Stage 8). Finally scrape the inside of the head with a teaspoon to remove the film of coagulated blood and keep this for colouring the mousse (Stage 3).

Chop the claws, legs and shell with a cleaver and keep aside.

2. The lobster mousse

(35 minutes) (see Mousse making, page 36)

Dice about 65 g/2½ oz of the lobster tail, season lightly and pan-fry in hot olive oil for 1 minute. Keep for the mousse mixture.

In a food processor, purée the remaining lobster flesh (about 150 g/5 oz) with the coagulated blood from the shells, adding 1 level teaspoon salt, a large pinch of cayenne pepper and the egg white.

Put the mixture into a stainless steel bowl, refrigerate for 20 minutes, then stand the bowl on ice. Incorporate four-fifths of the cream little by little, first tracing small circles with a wooden spoon, then beating the mixture vigorously, lifting it to trap as much air as possible. Do a test to check the taste and texture and correct with the remaining cream as necessary.

Force the mixture through a fine sieve and mix with the diced, pan-fried lobster. Refrigerate.

3. Making the lobster juice and essence (45 minutes)

In a medium frying pan, sweat the chopped onion, celery, fennel and garlic in 2 tablespoons olive oil for 5 minutes, then add chopped tomatoes and thyme. Cook for a further 5 minutes.

Meanwhile, in a saucepan sear the chopped lobster shells in hot olive oil for 2–3 minutes, then pour off the oil (which can be used for dressing salads) and deglaze with 2 tablespoons Cognac. Add the wine, boil for 1 or 2 seconds, then add the sweated vegetables. Pour in 700 ml/1¼ pt cold water, bring back to the boil, skim and simmer for about 20 minutes, skimming occasionally. After about 15 minutes, toss in the shredded tarragon and boil for 1 more minute.

Force the lobster juice through a fine sieve, pressing down hard with a wooden spoon to extract as much juice from the shell and vegetables as possible. Reserve half the juices and reduce the rest to about 2 tablespoons *glace* or essence of lobster. Allow to cool, then mix with the mousse mixture.

4. Assembling the ravioli

(15 minutes, plus 1 hour freezing)

On a lightly floured work surface, roll out the dough and cut out twenty 6.5 cm/2½ in rounds with a pastry cutter. Stretch the rounds as thinly as possible and brush the edges with a little cold water.

Place 1 teaspoon lobster mousse in the lower third of the circles and close them up into half moons. Fold over the moistened ends and press them down firmly to seal. Place the ravioli on a large tray and freeze for at least 1 hour.

5. Cooking the julienne of vegetables (5 minutes)

In a medium saucepan, bring to the boil 50 ml/2 fl oz cold water with 1 tablespoon butter. Toss in the tarragon leaves, 2 pinches of salt, 6 turns of

LEFT

Nage de homard au cumin

RIGHT

Raviolis de homard et son jus aux tagliatelles de légumes

pepper, then the *julienne* of fennel and carrot. Cook for 2 minutes, then add the *julienne* of courgette and cook for 1 more minute. Taste and correct seasoning as necessary.

6. Completing the lobster juice
(10 minutes)
In a small saucepan, reduce the reserved lobster juice by one-third. Stir in the cream and whisk in the cold, diced shellfish butter. Taste, correct seasoning and keep warm.

7. Cooking the ravioli
(10 minutes)
In a large saucepan, boil 2 L/3½ pt water with 2 tablespoons salt. Poach the ravioli at full boil for 1 minute, then cook for 5 minutes at just below simmering point.

8. Serving (10 minutes)
Warm 4 plates or a large serving dish. Lift the ravioli out of the boiling water and place on a tea towel to absorb excess water. Brush lightly with melted butter. Arrange the *julienne* of vegetables attractively in the middle of the plates with a teaspoon of their cooking juices and set the ravioli on top. Pour the lobster juice around and spice each ravioli with a final turn of pepper if you like.
If there are any lobster eggs, poach them in a little salted water for a few seconds, and scatter them around the ravioli.

——— VARIATIONS ———
Lobster can be replaced by crayfish or langoustines.
A few diced tomatoes scattered

around add a note of freshness.
This dish can be served tepid with a vinaigrette made with the strained olive oil used for cooking the lobster, plus 2 tablespoons olive oil, 2 tablespoons water, a tiny dash of vinegar, finely shredded fresh basil, salt and white pepper.

Chef's notes
Blanching the lobster: The lobster is plunged into boiling water for a few seconds not to cook it, but so that the flesh can be removed easily. Refresh under cold water immediately after blanching to arrest cooking.
Shelling the lobster: When you remove the flesh, some of the juices will escape. Discard these as they contain acids and enzymes which will destroy the mousse if mixed in.

NAGE DE HOMARD AU CUMIN

Roasted lobster in a caraway-scented juice

Serves 4
Difficulty: ♟
Total recipe time: 1 hour 5 minutes
Special equipment: fish scissors

INGREDIENTS

*2 live lobsters, 675 g/1½ lb each, or
1 1.5 kg/3 lb lobster*

1 fennel bulb

1 carrot, finely chopped

¼ onion, finely chopped

1 tomato, deseeded and chopped

4 tablespoons olive oil

*600 ml/1 pt Nage de légumes (see page
22) or water*

salt and freshly ground white pepper

Garnish

2 small courgettes

2 leaves of fennel (from the stock)

1 teaspoon unsalted butter

1 basil leaf

Juice

*1 teaspoon caraway seeds, soaked in
2–3 tablespoons water*

8 coriander leaves, finely chopped

1 tablespoon whipping cream

*20 g/¾ oz unsalted butter, chilled and
diced*

lemon juice

Planning ahead

Order female lobsters if possible, with
a lovely cluster of eggs beneath the
tail. You must buy live lobsters –
those with broken or missing claws
are always a good bargain.
Soak the caraway seeds 1 day in advance to soften them, or they will be

inedible. The lobsters, stock and garnish can be prepared several hours in
advance; cook the garnish at the last
moment, while you are roasting the
lobsters.

**1. Blanching and preparing the
lobsters** (20 minutes)
In a large saucepan, bring to the boil
3 L/5 pt unsalted water. The most
humane way to kill the lobsters is to
apply a sharp blow to the base of the
head with a heavy instrument. Plunge
them into the fast-boiling water for
exactly 3 minutes, refresh in cold
water, drain and place on a tray.
First twist off the legs and tail from the
body. Using fish scissors, cut round
the inside of the shell, peel it back and
pull out the meat, starting from the
tail end.
With a large heavy knife, pierce the
'cross' on the lobster heads and cut in
half lengthways. Remove the stomach and creamy parts.
Claws: Cut through the joints and
open up each section by cracking the
ends. Ease out the meat. Reserve all
the meat and any eggs and chop up all
the shell.

2. The lobster stock (30 minutes)
Peel off 100 g/3½ oz outside layers of
fennel and chop finely. Reserve the remainder for the garnish.
In a large saucepan, heat 3 tablespoons
olive oil and sear the chopped lobster
carcasses until they turn a beautiful
bright red. Toss in all the chopped
vegetables and sweat for 2–3 minutes.
Add the *nage de légumes* or water,
bring to the boil, skim, then simmer
for about 20 minutes, skimming occasionally. Using the back of a ladle,
force the stock through a fine conical
sieve into a small saucepan. Reduce
to about 300 ml/½ pt. Set aside until
Stage 5.

3. Roasting the lobster (5 minutes,
plus 8 minutes resting)
Preheat the oven to 180°C/350°F/
gas 4.
Heat the remaining olive oil in a small
saucepan and sear the lobster meat
with a pinch of salt. Partially cover the
pan and place in the oven for 5 minutes. Pour off the oil (which you can
use to dress salads) and leave the lobster to rest for 5–8 minutes so that it
becomes tender and succulent.
Meanwhile, prepare the garnish.

4. The garnish (10 minutes)
Courgettes: Wash, cut diagonally into
5 mm/¼ in slices. In a saucepan, combine 6 tablespoons water with 1 tablespoon butter and a basil leaf, bring to
full boil, put in the sliced courgettes
and cook for 2 minutes. Season
lightly.
Fennel: Peel away 2 layers, cut into
small triangles and blanch for 2 minutes in fast-boiling salted water. Refresh, drain and add to the courgettes.
Taste and correct the seasoning.

5. Finishing the juice (5 minutes)
In a small saucepan, bring to the boil
the 300 ml/½ pt lobster stock plus any
juices released by the lobsters during
the resting time. Add the soaked caraway seeds, chopped coriander and
the cream and finally whisk in the cold
diced butter. Season with salt, pepper
and a squeeze of lemon. If you have
any lobster eggs, toss them in at the
last moment just until they turn from
black to red; do not overcook, or they
will become hard and unpalatable.

6. Serving (5 minutes)
Warm 4 soup plates or a serving dish.
Slice the lobster tails into 4 and divide
equally between the plates, together
with the meat from the claws. Encircle with courgettes and fennel

triangles and pour the caraway-scented lobster juice around the edge.

This is a perfect occasion for a fine young white Burgundy from Puligny-Montrachet, Meursault or Auxey-Duresses. A substantial buttery Californian Chardonnay from one of the leading wineries – Alexander Valley, Chalone, Clos du Val or Simi – would also be most enjoyable.

Chef's note
Do not infuse the caraway seeds in the sauce for too long or their intense flavour will overpower the delicate lobster. There should only be a hint of caraway flavour.

QUEUES DE LANGOUSTINES A LA JULIENNE DE COURGETTES ET SES RAVIOLIS

Pan-fried Dublin bay prawns served tepid on a julienne of courgettes, garnished with ravioli

"The langoustines we receive directly from Scotland are creel-caught rather than dredged, so no damage is done to these delicate creatures. They arrive lively, elegant and fragile, dressed in translucent pink. They are my favourite shellfish."

Serves 4
Difficulty:
Total recipe time: 1 hour 5 minutes

————— INGREDIENTS —————
20 medium langoustines
100 ml/3½ fl oz olive oil
salt and freshly ground white pepper

Courgette julienne
2 medium courgettes
2 basil leaves, washed and shredded
¼ garlic clove
50 ml/2 fl oz olive oil

Vinaigrette
cooking oil from the langoustines
cooking juices from the courgettes
2 basil leaves, shredded
lemon juice
a pinch of caster sugar

Garnish
2 medium tomatoes, peeled, deseeded and finely diced
8 Ravioli of langoustines made with half quantities (see page 131)
2 orange segments, cut into small triangles

Planning ahead
Order langoustines well in advance. They must be bought alive as they are extremely delicate and will deteriorate rapidly once dead and lose their firm texture. Order 30 to give you enough for the ravioli and a few extra. The ravioli must be prepared in advance but poached only at the last moment. Stages 1, 2 and 3 can be done in advance.

1. Preparing and first cooking of langoustines (see page 13)
(40 minutes)
Wash in plenty of cold water to remove any traces of dirt.
Pull the tails from the bodies. Twist the middle of the tail fins and carefully remove the black intestinal thread. Keep the heads and claws for other

recipes (see Chef's notes).
Blanch the langoustine tails in plenty of boiling water for 1 minute. Refresh, cool, peel off the shells and replace the peeled tails in the pan.

2. Preparing the courgette julienne (10 minutes)
Courgettes: Wash, trim and cut lengthways into 3 mm/⅛ in strips. Place in a small saucepan with the garlic, 4 tablespoons water and the olive oil.
Bring to the boil 1 L/1¾ pt lightly salted water for poaching the ravioli.

the ravioli into the vinaigrette for 1–2 minutes before serving and cover.

3. Second cooking of langoustines; poaching the ravioli

(5 minutes plus 5 minutes resting)
Season the langoustine tails and sear in the olive oil over a strong heat for 30 seconds. Turn off the heat, cover and leave to rest for 3–4 minutes.
Meanwhile, poach the ravioli in the boiling water for 2 minutes, drain, place on a large plate and cover with a wet tea towel to prevent them from discolouring or drying out.

4. Cooking the courgette julienne
(2 minutes)
Cover, boil for 1 minute until *al dente,* then take off the lid and leave to cool. Remove the garlic.

5. The vinaigrette (3 minutes)
Strain all the juices from the courgettes and langoustines into a small bowl and season. Toss in the shredded basil and orange triangles. Taste and enliven with a squeeze of lemon and a pinch of caster sugar if necessary. Put

6. Serving (5 minutes)
Warm 4 plates or a large serving dish. Warm the diced tomatoes in 1 table-spoon vinaigrette for 2–3 seconds. Warm the langoustine tails.
Make a nest of courgette *julienne* in the centre of each plate and top each with 5 langoustine tails. On either side place a little mound of diced tomatoes and top with the ravioli. Pour the vinaigrette around the edge and serve tepid, not hot.

──────── VARIATIONS ────────

Langoustines can be replaced by lobster, langouste or crayfish.
Lobster: Blanch the claws and tails for 4 minutes. Remove the shell and pan-fry in olive oil for 1 minute then rest, covered, for a further 10 minutes.
Freshwater crayfish: Pan-fry whole in hot olive oil for 30 seconds. Cool, peel off the shells, then cook in olive oil for a further 2–3 minutes.
To simplify the dish omit the ravioli, or make it with ready-made sheets of won-ton dough (available in most Chinese supermarkets).

──────── WINE ────────

A dry white Graves will suit this dish very well. Try a Château Carbon-nieux or Caillou Blanc Sec de Château Talbot.

Chef's notes
The langoustine claws and heads can be used to make a bisque (see page 108) or *Beurre de langoustines* (page 25).
Langoustines, first cooking: At this stage, they will only be cooked rare to allow the shells to be removed more easily.
Second cooking: is done in two stages – pan-frying, then resting in the pan. The oil used must be hot (about 90°C/ 194°F) but not boiling, as excessive heat will damage the delicate texture of the langoustines. The resting time is very important since it allows the flesh to relax and residual heat to complete the cooking. The langoustines will have a firm texture and remain perfectly moist. They will release some of their wonderful juices into the olive oil, which then forms the basis of the vinaigrette.
Ravioli: Do not leave the cooked ravioli in the water; they will soak it up and the flavour will be diluted. Drain immediately, cover and keep on a plate.

TOP
Papillotte en croûte aux fruits d'été,
aux graines de sésame et d'oiseaux
(page 160)

CENTRE
Ris de veau rôti aux amandes,
pistaches et pignons de pin (page 147)

BOTTOM
Queues de langoustines à la julienne
de courgettes et ses raviolis (page 128)

RAVIOLIS DE LANGOUSTINES A LA FONDUE DE TOMATES ET COURGETTES, VINAIGRETTE AUX HERBES

Ravioli of langoustines filled with diced tomatoes and courgettes, served with a herb-scented vinaigrette

Serves 4
Difficulty: 🎩🎩
Total recipe time: 1 hour 5 minutes
Special equipment: 6 cm/2½ in pastry cutter, pasta machine

──── INGREDIENTS ────
150 g/5 oz ravioli dough (see Pasta, page 38)

8 langoustine tails and claws, blanched and shelled (see pages 13, 128)

2 tablespoons olive oil

20 young spinach leaves

salt and freshly ground white pepper

a pinch of flour

Filling
50 g/2 oz onion, finely chopped

1 small courgette, washed, trimmed and finely diced

2 small ripe tomatoes, peeled, deseeded and diced

2 basil leaves, washed and shredded

6 coriander leaves, washed and shredded

2 tablespoons olive oil

Herb vinaigrette
heads and shells from the langoustines

4 tablespoons olive oil

½ garlic clove

a pinch of caster sugar

4 coriander leaves, washed and shredded

2 basil leaves, washed and shredded

lemon juice

salt and freshly ground white pepper

Garnish
4 ripe tomatoes, peeled, deseeded and diced

1 tablespoon olive oil

Planning ahead
Order the langoustines (which must be live) well in advance.
The ravioli dough must be made in advance. Roll out very thinly then cut into 20 rounds and stretch them as thin as possible.
Stages 1–3 inclusive can be completed in advance. Poach the ravioli only at the last moment.

1. Preparing the vegetables
(5 minutes)
Spinach: Trim stalks, wash leaves in plenty of cold water, then blanch in boiling salted water for 10 seconds. Refresh, pat dry (keeping them flat), season and keep aside for Stage 5.

2. Cooking the vegetables
(10 minutes)
In a medium frying pan, sweat the diced onion in 1 tablespoon olive oil for 5 minutes. Add the courgettes and sweat for 1 minute, then finally add the diced tomatoes, coriander and basil. Season and transfer to a tray to cool.

3. Preparing the langoustines
(5 minutes)
Finely dice the tail and claw meat and

season with salt and 4 turns of pepper. Sweat in the frying pan used for the vegetables. Cool then keep with the diced vegetables. Reserve the cooking oil and shells.

4. The vinaigrette (10 minutes)
Remove the intestines and stomachs from the langoustine heads. Sear them in 4 tablespoons hot olive oil for 10 seconds then add the shells from the tails and claws, garlic, a pinch of salt and caster sugar, 2 turns of pepper and 6 tablespoons cold water. Draw off the heat and leave to infuse for 5 minutes.
Strain through a fine sieve, taste and correct the seasoning. Add the shredded basil and coriander and enliven the vinaigrette with a squeeze of lemon. Set aside.

5. Assembling the ravioli
(30 minutes)
Lay the blanched spinach leaves flat on your work surface and place 1 teaspoon of the vegetable/langoustine filling in each. Wrap them up tightly to make 20 little parcels.
Lay out the 20 rounds of ravioli dough on a dry surface and stretch as thinly as possible. Brush the edges with cold water. Sit the spinach parcels in the lower third of each pasta round, then close up the raviolis into a half moon shape and press the edges together tightly. Take hold of both pointed ends, fold back and press together (see diagram, page 39).
Poach the ravioli in a large saucepan of boiling salted water for 2 minutes, drain and set aside.

6. The garnish (2 minutes)
Season the diced tomatoes with a pinch of salt and a few turns of pepper and warm in 1 tablespoon olive oil over a gentle heat for 30 seconds.

7. Serving (3 minutes)
Warm 4 plates.
Add the ravioli to the tepid vinaigrette, cover and leave for 1 minute.
Place a little mound of diced tomatoes in the centre of each plate, encircle with the ravioli and pour the tepid vinaigrette around.

Storing
The ravioli can be stored in the fridge for up to 12 hours. Rest them on kitchen paper (which absorbs the moisture released by the vegetables and prevents sticking) and cover.
They can also be frozen for later use. Store in an airtight container.

————— VARIATIONS —————
Ravioli of lobster or crayfish can be made the same way; replace the coriander with tarragon.

Chef's notes
Langoustine claws: It is not easy to extract meat from the claws. Make a small incision just above the joints before cooking, which will make it easier to extract the meat after cooking.
Blanching the spinach leaves: This makes the spinach supple. It is cooked when the ravioli are poached.
The vinaigrette: The oil must be hot for searing the langoustine heads or they will stew. Do not let them colour, however, or the vinaigrette will be too strong.

COQUILLES ST-JACQUES ET CHAMPIGNONS POELES AU JUS DE VEAU BLOND

Pan-fried scallops and mushrooms, served with a light veal stock scented with thyme and rosemary

Serves 4
Difficulty: ♟
Total recipe time: 25 minutes
Special equipment: non-stick frying pan, deep-fryer

————— INGREDIENTS —————
4 fat scallops, with their corals

1 tablespoon olive oil

lemon juice

salt and freshly ground white pepper

Garnish
12 celery leaves

12 tiny sprigs of parsley

12 firm white button mushrooms, finely sliced

500 ml/18 fl oz cooking oil for deep-frying

2 tablespoons olive oil

Sauce
1 tablespoon unsalted butter

100 ml/3½ fl oz Veal stock (see page 18)

1 sprig of thyme

4 needles of rosemary

1 strip of dried orange zest

Planning ahead
Order fresh scallops well in advance; frozen ones simply will not do. Ask your fishmonger to open and clean them for you.
Pan-fry the scallops 10 minutes before the meal and keep covered in a warm place.
The mushrooms can be pan-fried in advance, arranged on the plate and re-heated at the last moment.
The celery and parsley can be deep-fried 1 hour in advance.
The sauce must be finished only at the last moment.

1. Deep-frying the parsley and celery leaves (5 minutes)
Heat the cooking oil in a deep-fryer and fry the celery leaves and parsley sprigs for 1½ minutes, until they turn crisp and deep rusty gold. Drain on absorbent paper and keep warm.

2. Pan-frying the mushrooms (2 minutes)
Season with salt and pepper. Heat 1 tablespoon olive oil until smoking, then flash-fry the mushrooms for about 30 seconds, until lightly coloured. Drain on kitchen paper and set aside.

3. Pan-frying the scallops and coral (10 minutes)
Coral: Poach in barely simmering salted water for 3 minutes. Refresh, then slice lengthways into fine strips. Season with a pinch of salt and 2 turns of pepper and fry in 1 tablespoon hot olive oil until lightly coloured. Set aside.

Scallops: Brush a large non-stick frying pan with olive oil and heat until smoking. Fry the scallops for 1 minute on each side, until lightly browned, then season with salt and pepper. Place in a small stainless steel bowl with a squeeze of lemon, cover loosely with buttered greaseproof paper and keep warm.

4. The sauce (8 minutes)

In a small saucepan, heat 1 tablespoon butter until golden, then whisk in the veal stock and boil with the thyme, rosemary and dried orange zest. Reduce by one-third, add the juices released by the scallops then pass the sauce through a fine conical sieve into another small saucepan. Season with a tiny pinch of salt, 2 turns of pepper and a squeeze of lemon. Warm the scallops and coral in the sauce for 1–2 minutes, without allowing it to boil.

5. Serving

Warm 4 plates or a large serving dish. Place the scallops in the centre of the plates and encircle with overlapping slices of mushroom. Pour over the sauce and decorate with deep-fried parsley, celery leaves and the strips of coral. Season the scallops with a final half turn of pepper and serve immediately.

—————— VARIATIONS ——————

This recipe is intended as a starter. For a main course, increase the number of scallops.

—————— WINE ——————

Scallops always have a hint of sweetness and need a dry white wine to counteract this. Since pan-frying the scallops gives this dish a full flavour, a fine white Burgundy (Puligny-Montrachet or Meursault Premier Cru), or Grand Cru Chablis would not go amiss.

Chef's notes

Parsley and celery leaves: It is important to shake off any excess water before deep-frying as it causes the hot oil to sizzle and spit dangerously. When the sizzling stops, all the water has evaporated and the parsley and celery leaves are cooked.

Scallops: The direct heat of pan-frying is just enough to cook the scallops medium rare and form a lovely golden crust. Residual heat will complete the cooking and allow the scallops to remain moist. At this stage they will release some of their luscious juices which are used to complete the sauce.

Mushrooms: Sauté very briefly in hot olive oil so that they are lightly coloured but retain their moisture and texture.

HOMARD BRAISE AU JUS A LA BASILIC ET AUX PETITS LEGUMES D'ETE

Braised lobster tails in basil-scented juices, served with young summer vegetables

Serves 4
Difficulty: ♟♟
Total recipe time: 1 hour 20 minutes
Special equipment: 6 L/10 pt saucepan

—————— INGREDIENTS ——————

4   450 g/1 lb live lobsters

Juices

4 teaspoons unsalted butter

1 tablespoon olive oil

shells from lobster tails and claws

1 large tomato, washed and roughly chopped

½ garlic clove

4 basil leaves

600 ml/1 pt water

1 teaspoon whipping cream

freshly ground white pepper

a squeeze of lemon

Garnish

8 baby beetroot, plus a pinch of caster sugar

8 baby turnips

8 baby carrots, plus a pinch of caster sugar and 4 tarragon leaves

4 tiny fennel bulbs

4 baby courgettes with their flowers

1 large tomato

a handful of French beans

a handful of mange-tout

8 broad beans, shelled

a handful of young peas, shelled

12 pea flowers

4 sprigs of chervil

4 sprigs of flat-leaved parsley

2 tablespoons unsalted butter

4 purple basil leaves (optional)

salt and freshly ground white pepper

Homard braisé au jus à la basilic et aux petits légumes d'été

Planning ahead
Order lobsters (which must be live) well in advance. Try to get one female which will hold a lovely cluster of eggs under the tail.
Stages 1–4 inclusive can be completed in advance.

1. Preparing, blanching and shelling the lobsters (20 minutes)
Blanch in 6 L/10 pt water and shell (see *Nage de homard*, page 127 for method). Wrap the heads in clingfilm and freeze for use in another recipe (see Variations in *Bisque legère de langoustines*, page 108).

2. Preparing the lobster juices
(20 minutes)
In a large saucepan, heat 2 teaspoons butter and 1 tablespoon olive oil until hot, then sear the shells from the tails and claws for 2 minutes without col-

ouring. Add the garlic, basil and chopped tomato and cover with 600 ml/ 1 pt cold water. Bring to the boil, skim and simmer for 15 minutes. Force through a hard sieve into a small saucepan, pressing down on the shells with a ladle to extract as much juice and flavour as possible. Keep aside.

3. Preparing the vegetables
(30 minutes)
Preheat the oven to 200°C/400°F/ gas 6.
In a large saucepan, boil 3.5 L/6 pt water with 2 level tablespoons salt.
Baby beetroot: Trim the tops to about 2 cm/1 in above the bulb, cut off the roots, wash, drain and wrap in foil with 1 teaspoon butter, a large pinch of sugar, a pinch of salt and 2 turns of pepper. Place in a small casserole and cook for 15 minutes in the preheated oven. Peel and rewrap in foil.

Baby turnips: Trim as for beetroot, peel and cook in the oven for about 5 minutes with 1 teaspoon butter, a pinch of salt and 2 turns of pepper, barely covered with cold water.
Carrots: Trim tops to about 2 cm/1 in, peel and cook for about 4 minutes with 1 teaspoon butter, 4 tarragon leaves, a pinch each of sugar and salt and 2 turns of pepper, barely covered with cold water.
Courgettes: Detach the flowers, trim stalks and rub courgettes with a tea towel to remove the tiny hairs. Wash and cook the courgettes for 2–3 minutes in lightly salted boiling water, refresh, drain and keep in the saucepan with 1 tablespoon butter and 4 tablespoons cold water. Rinse the insides of the courgette flowers and blanch in boiling water for 10 seconds. Refresh, drain and place on a small plate.
Tomato: Peel, halve, deseed and dice

finely. Season with salt and pepper, spoon into the courgette flowers and seal by twisting the tops. Put the filled flowers in a large frying pan with 1 teaspoon olive oil.

Fennel: Cut off the fern and roots, then blanch for 3–4 minutes in lightly salted boiling water. Refresh, drain and put with the courgettes.

French beans and mange-tout: Top and tail, then blanch the beans for 3–4 minutes and the mange-tout for 2 minutes in fast-boiling water. Refresh, drain and put with the courgettes and fennel.

Broad beans and peas: Mix the uncooked broad beans and peas with the courgettes and fennel.

Pea flowers: Wash, shake dry and mix with the above.

Chervil and parsley: Wash, shake dry, pick the leaves and mix with the above.

4. Braising the lobster tails; finishing the juices (10 minutes)
Place the lobster tails in the juices from Stage 2, bring to simmering point,

partially cover and cook in the oven for 5 minutes. Add the claws and cook for 5 more minutes.

Strain the juices into a small saucepan, bring to the boil and whisk in 1 teaspoon cream and 20 g/¾ oz butter. Season with a pinch of salt, a few turns of pepper and a squeeze of lemon. Keep the juices and lobster warm.

5. Finishing the dish and serving
(10 minutes)
Warm 4 plates.

Return the beetroot to the oven for 5 minutes. Bring the turnips and carrots to the boil and place in the oven for 2 minutes. Season the mixed vegetables, add the parsley and chervil, cover and simmer for 3 minutes. Taste and correct seasoning. Divide the vegetables between the plates.

Slice open the lobster tails and remove the black thread-like intestine. Place 2 half tails in the centre of each plate, top with the claws and pour the juices over and around. Rest the purple basil leaves on top of the lobster and serve at once.

— VARIATIONS —
If you have found any lobster eggs, heat them in the juice at the last moment until they turn red.
Langoustines can also be cooked this way.

— WINE —
Serve a fine white Burgundy, Puligny-Montrachet or Meursault, or perhaps a Premier Cru Chablis (Bougros, Montée de Tonnerre, or Fourchaume).

Chef's notes
Lobsters: If they are not bought alive, the serum which holds the flesh together will be lost and they will be like cotton wool.
Vegetables: It may not be easy to find all the young vegetables listed in this recipe. Older vegetables should be sliced. The given cooking times are for very young, tender vegetables, so taste to check the texture is right.
Blanching the lobsters: This makes it easier to extract the meat from the shell.

BLANCS DE ROUGET AU PISTOU DE LEGUMES ET FUMET DE VINROUGE

Roast fillets of red mullet filled with pistou of vegetables, served with a red wine sauce

Serves 4
Difficulty: ⊔ ⊔ ⊔
Total recipe time: 1 hour 5 minutes

— INGREDIENTS —
8 red mullet, 125 g/4½ oz each

3 tablespoons olive oil

salt and freshly ground white pepper

½ quantity Pistou (see page 47)

Sauce
2 tablespoons olive oil

¼ onion, finely diced

½ celery stalk, finely diced

50 g/2 oz fennel trimmings, finely diced

1 garlic clove, unpeeled and crushed

6 tomatoes, washed, deseeded and finely chopped

4 basil leaves, finely shredded

½ star anise

1 sprig of thyme

2 strips of dried orange zest

500 ml/18 fl oz red wine

bones and heads from the red mullet, chopped

8 livers from the red mullet (see Chef's notes)

100 ml/3½ fl oz Veal stock (see page 18) (optional)

1 tablespoon unsalted butter, chilled and diced

lemon juice

Planning ahead

Order the red mullet well in advance. Ask the fishmonger to scale, gut and fillet the fish and to give you the bones and livers. If you cannot buy prepared red mullet, see page 14.

The mullet can be marinated and the *pistou* must be made 1 day in advance. You can prepare and fill the fillets early in the day and keep them, covered, in the fridge.

You can also make the sauce a few hours ahead, but add the butter only at the last moment.

1. Preparing the fillets of red mullet (20 minutes)

Ensure they are completely de-scaled by running the blade of a knife along the skin against the lie of the scales to remove any which are left. Gently tweeze out any small bones from the middle of the fillets. Coat well with olive oil and season both sides with salt and pepper.

2. Filling the fillets with pistou (10 minutes)

Roll up the fillets, leaving a space in the middle for the *pistou* and secure with a cocktail stick. Fill each fillet with 1 teaspoon *pistou,* firming it down gently with a teaspoon.

Line a roasting tin with greaseproof paper, brush with olive oil and carefully put in the prepared fillets. Set aside.

Preheat the oven to 200°C/400°F/ gas 6.

3. The sauce (25 minutes)
(see Savoury sauces, page 26)

Heat the oil in a large heavy-bottomed saucepan, and sweat the onion, celery, fennel, crushed garlic, star anise, thyme, and dried orange zest for 5 minutes, without colouring.

Add the chopped tomatoes and simmer until soft and pulpy.

Pour in the red wine, bring to the boil, skim, then reduce by one-third.

Throw in the chopped fish heads and bones, cover with 200 ml/7 fl oz cold water and bring back to the boil. Skim, then simmer for 15 minutes. Meanwhile purée the red mullet livers and mix with the shredded basil. Add the veal stock, if using, and the puréed livers and basil and simmer for a further 2 minutes. Force the mixture though a fine conical sieve into a medium saucepan, gently pressing the bones and vegetables with a ladle to extract all the juices.

Bring back to the boil, skim, reduce slightly, then whisk in 1 tablespoon cold diced butter. Taste, and correct the seasoning with salt, pepper and a squeeze of lemon juice.

4. Cooking the red mullet
(8 minutes)

Roast the stuffed fillets, still on the lined roasting tin, in the preheated oven for 7–8 minutes. Remove the cocktail sticks.

5. Serving

Heat 4 plates or a large serving dish. Pour the sauce into the middle of the plates and rest the fillets of red mullet in the centre.

VARIATIONS

A few melting slices of poached veal marrowbone topped with breadcrumbs and toasted under the grill would make a delicious accompaniment to this dish; it can also be served with a tomato *coulis* enriched with olive oil.

Coriander or rosemary can be used instead of basil.

WINE

A Provençal red would be ideal for this dish. Try one from the Domaine de la Bernarde, or a Bandol. Almost any other medium to light red would do – Bergerac or Château de la Bouderie.

Chef's notes

Red mullet: Ideally, you should use Mediterranean red rock mullet. If you cannot find this smaller variety, larger Cornish or Indian Ocean red mullet will do.

Livers: As small Mediterranean mullet have such an intense flavour, do not add the livers to the sauce; it would be too strong. Only add the puréed livers if you are using the milder Cornish or Indian Ocean variety.

Vegetables: You can dice these in a food processor, but do not overprocess or you will end up with a purée!

Cooking the red mullet: The best way to tell if they are cooked is to press them between your index finger and thumb; they should feel firm – neither flaky (overcooked) nor too supple (undercooked).

DOS DE LOUP DE MER FARCI, AU JUS D'ESTRAGON ET A LA FONDUE DE FENOUIL

Steamed fillet of sea bass filled with its mousse, served with a light tarragon juice on a bed of fennel

Serves 4:
Difficulty: 🎩🎩
Total recipe time: 1 hour 30 minutes
Special equipment: Food processor, tweezers, clingfilm, steamer

INGREDIENTS

4 140 g/4½ oz fillets from a 1.4 kg/ 3 lb sea bass

1 tablespoon unsalted butter

lemon juice

8 young tarragon leaves

salt and freshly ground white pepper

Light fish stock (see page 20)
bones and head from the sea bass

trimmings from 2 fennel bulbs, from the garnish

½ onion

1 tablespoon unsalted butter

2 tablespoons tarragon vinegar

100 ml/3½ fl oz dry white wine

Mousse
150 g/5 oz tail from the sea bass

a pinch of cayenne pepper

1 egg yolk

a dash of Pernod

250 ml/9 fl oz whipping cream

Garnish
2 fennel bulbs, cut into julienne

2 teaspoons unsalted butter

4 ripe tomatoes, peeled, deseeded and diced

1 teaspoon olive oil

Sauce
1 tablespoon whipping cream

10 tarragon leaves, finely chopped

2 tablespoons unsalted butter, chilled and diced

Planning ahead
Order a 1.4 kg/3 lb sea bass well in advance. Ask your fishmonger to scale, gut and fillet it, leaving the skin on. You will need four 140 g/4½ oz unskinned fillets, plus 150 g/5 oz skinned tail fillet. Keep the bones, head and gills.
Stages 1–4 can be completed half a day in advance.
The garnish can be prepared half a day in advance, but cooked only at the last moment.

---

1. Light fish stock (20 minutes plus soaking time)
Follow the method on page 20. Meanwhile, prepare the fish.

2. The sea bass and its mousse
(30 minutes) (see Mousse making, page 36)
Gently tweeze out the central bones from the fillets.
Using a very sharp knife, make an incision almost through the entire width of the fillets and open them up like a small book to make space for the mousse. Refrigerate.
The mousse: Purée the skinned tail in a food processor. Add ½ teaspoon salt, a pinch of cayenne, the egg yolk and a dash of Pernod and process until smooth.

Transfer to a small stainless steel bowl and chill for 15 minutes. Stand the chilled bowl on ice and trickle in the cream, beating the mixture vigorously until completely incorporated. Force the mixture through a fine sieve into a small bowl and refrigerate.

3. Filling the sea bass with mousse
(15 minutes)
In a small saucepan, melt 1 tablespoon butter with a pinch of salt and pepper and a dash of lemon juice.
Cut out four 20 cm/8 in squares of clingfilm, spread on a chopping board and butter lightly. Place a fillet skin-side down on each square. Open up the fillets, season lightly and fill each with 1 tablespoon mousse. Fold back the flaps and brush all over with the melted butter.
Put 2 tarragon leaves on top of each parcel and enclose completely in the clingfilm.

4. The garnish (10 minutes)
Fennel: Put in a pan with 2 teaspoons butter and 6 tablespoons lightly salted water and simmer until tender.
Diced tomatoes: Place in a small bowl with a teaspoon of olive oil, a tiny pinch of salt and a few grains of pepper and keep warm.

5. Steaming the bass
(10 minutes)
Prepare a steamer, put in the sea bass parcels, still wrapped in the clingfilm, skin-side up, cover and steam for 8 minutes. Draw off the heat, remove the lid and leave the bass to rest in the steamer for 3–4 minutes.

Dos de loup de mer farci, au jus d'estragon et à la fondue de fenouil

6. Finishing the sauce (5 minutes)
Reduce the fish stock by one-third, to about 200 ml/7 fl oz concentrated juices. Add the cream and chopped tarragon and finally whisk in the cold diced butter. Taste and correct the seasoning with salt, pepper and lemon juice and add the diced tomatoes at the last moment.

7. Serving
Warm 4 plates or a serving dish.
Place the parcels of sea bass on a tray and remove the clingfilm. Brush with any remaining lemon butter so that the skin glistens. Build a small mound of fennel *julienne* in the middle of each plate and rest the sea bass on top. Pour the sauce around the edge.

—— VARIATIONS ——
Add a few pan-fried Scottish langoustine tails for the ultimate garnish, or fill the bass with a delicious langoustine or lobster mousse.
Basil, coriander and dill all complement sea bass well and can be used instead of tarragon.
The sauce can be made with 200 ml/ 7 fl oz *nage de légumes* (see page 22) instead of the fish stock.
Fillets of turbot, John Dory or brill can be cooked the same way, but will need a slightly longer cooking time.

—— WINE ——
Try a white Rhône like a Crozes-Hermitage 'Mule Blanche' or St Joseph Blanc.

Chef's notes
Sea bass: The skin is left on to hold the delicate flesh firmly in place. It also provides a wonderful flash of steely silver.
Tarragon: Blanch older leaves before cooking to prevent coarseness.
Steaming the sea bass: As the fillets are sealed in clingfilm, the heat will accumulate quickly; 8 minutes steaming is enough for 140 g/4 ½ oz fillets. The subsequent resting time is vital, as it allows the heat slowly to penetrate the mousse inside and complete the cooking.

FILETS D'OMBRE CHEVALIER A LA DUXELLE DE CHAMPIGNONS SAUVAGES, SAUCE CHAMPAGNE

Fillets of char filled with wild mushroom duxelles, served with Champagne sauce

Serves 4
Difficulty: 🍳
Total recipe time: 50 minutes
Special equipment: filleting and paring knives, tweezers, kitchen string

INGREDIENTS

4 250 g/9 oz char, trout or sea trout

2 teaspoons unsalted butter

lemon juice

salt and freshly ground white pepper

Sauce

4 shallots, finely chopped

1 small leek

50 g/2 oz button mushroom stalks, from the duxelles

bones from the fish, roughly chopped

2 teaspoons unsalted butter

3 sprigs of parsley

¼ bay leaf

1 sprig of thyme

300 ml/½ pt Champagne

300 ml/½ pt whipping cream

20 g/¾ oz unsalted butter, chilled and diced

Mushroom duxelles

400 g/14 oz firm white button mushrooms

50 g/2 oz wild mushrooms (optional)

⅛ onion, finely chopped

1 tablespoon unsalted butter

a small bunch of parsley, finely chopped

Garnish

20 g/¾ oz trumpets of death

1 teaspoon unsalted butter

Planning ahead
Order the char well in advance. Ask your fishmonger to cut off the fins, to gut, scale and fillet the fish, leaving the skin on and to give you the bones.
The fish can be prepared and the sauce and *duxelles* made in advance. Keep the sauce warm in a bain-marie.

1. Preparing the char fillets (10 minutes)
See page14 if your fishmonger has not filleted them.
Gently tweeze out the small bones running down the middle of the fillets. Leave the skin on.

2. Champagne sauce (25 minutes)
Leek: Trim off the root and green tops and halve lengthways. Reserve 2 or 3 outer leaves and finely chop the heart.
Mushrooms: Wash briefly and pat dry. Cut off the stalks and chop finely. Reserve the caps for the *duxelles*.
Herbs: Wash the parsley and shake dry. Form the reserved leek leaves into a cross, place the herbs inside, wrap into a small parcel and tie with string.
In a medium saucepan, sweat the shallots and leek in 2 teaspoons butter for 2 minutes without colouring. Add the mushroom stalks and fish bones and sweat for a further minute. Pour in the Champagne, bring to the boil, skim, reduce by half then add the parcel of herbs and the cream and simmer for 15 minutes.

Strain the sauce through a fine conical sieve into a medium saucepan, pressing it through with a small ladle, and reduce until smooth and creamy. Whisk in the cold diced butter, taste and season with salt, pepper and a squeeze of lemon. Keep in a warm place.
Meanwhile, prepare the mushroom *duxelles*.

3. The mushroom duxelles and the garnish (20 minutes)
Preheat the oven to 200°C/400°F/gas 6.
Mushrooms: Dice the caps into 3 mm/⅛ in cubes or chop roughly, then process for only a few seconds in a food processor. Place in a small container, squeeze over a few drops of lemon juice and mix well.
Wild mushrooms (if using): Trim base of stalks, scrape the skin, wash briefly and pat dry. Dice finely and mix with the button mushrooms. In a small sauté pan, sweat the chopped onion in 1 tablespoon butter for 4–5 minutes without colouring. Add the chopped mushrooms, season and cook over high heat until most of the moisture has evaporated. Taste, correct seasoning and allow to cool before adding the chopped parsley.
Trumpets of death: Trim the stalks, halve lengthways and remove anything reminiscent of the forest; wash them only briefly.
Melt the butter in a small pan, add the mushrooms, mix well and season with a pinch of salt and a turn of pepper. Set aside.

4. Cooking the char fillets
(7 minutes)

Season with salt and a turn of pepper. In a large non-stick frying pan, heat 2 teaspoons butter until it sizzles, then sear the fillets without colouring for 15 seconds on the flesh side. Turn them over onto the skin side and cook in the preheated oven for 4–5 minutes. Press the fish with the back of your index finger to check if it is cooked; if it feels too supple, it is undercooked – if flaky, overcooked. Taste, correct the seasoning if necessary and 'lift' with a squeeze of lemon. Very carefully peel off the skin and keep the fillets warm.

5. Serving (5 minutes)
Heat the grill.
Warm 4 plates or a large serving dish. Reheat the mushroom *duxelles*.
Place 4 char fillets on a buttered baking tray, spoon over the *duxelles* and then cover with the remaining 4 fillets. Heat in the oven for 2–3 minutes. Place the trumpets of death under the hot grill during the final minute.
Bring the Champagne sauce back to the boil.
Lay the parcels of char on the plates, spoon the sauce around and scatter over the trumpets of death. Serve at once.

—— VARIATIONS ——
If char prove difficult to find, trout or sea trout are equally delicious.
A few sorrel leaves added to the sauce at the last moment give an extra touch of freshness.

—— WINE ——
The most obvious wine to serve with this would be full-flavoured *brut* Champagne (Bollinger) – vintage if possible.

Chef's notes
Cooking the char fillets: Leave the skin on; it will retract and make the fillets curve into a natural 'valley' to hold the mushroom *duxelles*.

ESCALOPE DE TURBOT AU JUS
A LA CIBOULETTE

Fillet of turbot served with chive-scented juices

"Give your imagination free rein with this recipe, which is one of the simplest ways to enjoy the taste and texture of this fabulous fish. By varying or adding to the ingredients, you can create a wealth of new dishes with seed mustard, tarragon, basil, diced tomatoes, asparagus, wild mushrooms, *julienne* of vegetables – the possibilities are endless for those in a creative mood."

Serves 4
Difficulty: ♟
Total recipe time: 25 minutes.

—— INGREDIENTS ——
4 150 g/5 oz fillets of turbot

2 teaspoons unsalted butter

lemon juice

salt and freshly ground white pepper

Juice
4 shallots, roughly chopped

8 button mushrooms, finely sliced

a small bunch of chives, finely snipped

20 g/¾ oz unsalted butter, chilled and diced

6 tablespoons dry white wine

4 tablespoons water

1 tablespoon whipping cream

40 g/1½ oz unsalted butter, chilled and diced

lemon juice

1 teaspoon seed mustard (optional)

Planning ahead
Order a large turbot (which will have a better flavour) well in advance; ask the fishmonger to fillet and skin it and divide it into 150 g/5 oz portions.
You can prepare and part-cook the vegetables in advance, up to the addition of the wine. Finish cooking the turbot 20 minutes before serving.

1. Preparing the turbot (5 minutes)
Place the fillets on a large plate. In a small pan, melt the butter and add a squeeze of lemon, a pinch of salt and a little pepper. Brush generously over the fillets and refrigerate.

2. Cooking the vegetables and turbot fillets (10 minutes, plus 5 minutes resting)
Preheat the oven to 180°C/350°F/ gas 4.
In a sauté pan, sweat the shallots in 20 g/¾ oz butter for 3–4 minutes, until soft but not coloured. Add the sliced mushrooms and sweat for 1 minute. Pour in the wine and boil for a few seconds to remove the alcohol and some of the acidity. Finally add 2 tablespoons water.

Arrange the turbot fillets on the bed of shallots and mushrooms and bring to simmering point. Partially cover the pan, leaving a small gap for the steam to escape, and cook in the oven for 6–8 minutes, depending on the thickness of the fillets. Do not overcook, or you will ruin the texture of the fish. Remove from the oven, put the lid on firmly and leave to rest for 5 minutes so that the fillets continue to cook and remain moist and tender.

3. Finishing the sauce (5 minutes)
Strain all the cooking juices through a fine conical sieve into a small saucepan. Bring to the boil, throw in the snipped chives, stir in the cream and finally whisk in the cold diced butter. Season with salt, pepper and lemon juice. If you are using seed mustard, add it just before serving.

4. Serving
Warm 4 plates or a serving dish. Using a fish slice, place a turbot fillet in the centre of each plate, pour the sauce around the edge and serve.

―――――― VARIATIONS ――――――
Many types of fish can be prepared in this way – brill, John Dory, halibut, sole, cod and plaice are all suitable.

―――――――― WINE ――――――――
A fine white Burgundy is the ideal choice for this dish. If the cost of a Puligny-Montrachet is too daunting, try a less exalted wine such as a St Véran or Pouilly-Vinzelles or a fragrant Sancerre.

QUENELLE DE BROCHET SOUFFLEE AUX ECREVISSES DU WINDRUSH

Quenelles of pike from the Windrush, simmered in a freshwater crayfish sauce

"One of the many advantages of living in Oxfordshire is the abundance of superb river fish. Local fisherman often bring me their catch of freshwater fish – perch, zander and magnificent pike caught in the chalky tributaries of the Thames. This dish has sentimental value, since it was the very first I cooked professionally – with less than professional results!"

Serves 4
Difficulty: ♙♙
Total recipe time: 1 hour 15 minutes, plus 30 minutes chilling for the mousse
Special equipment: tweezers, food processor, large sauté pan, large oven-to-table casserole

―――――― INGREDIENTS ――――――
Quenelles
175 g/6 oz fillet of pike

1 teaspoon salt

2 pinches of cayenne pepper

3 eggs

150 g/5 oz unsalted butter, softened

150 ml/5 fl oz whipping cream

Garnish
tails from the freshwater crayfish

2 tablespoons non-scented oil

2 tablespoons Cognac

4 tarragon leaves

4 tablespoons cold water

Sauce
heads and claws of 32 medium freshwater crayfish (about 450 g/1lb)

100 ml/3½ fl oz non-scented oil

1 garlic clove, lightly crushed

1 sprig of thyme

¼ bayleaf

8 tarragon leaves

2 sprigs of parsley

200 g/7 oz Fondue de tomates (see Beurre de langoustines, page 25) or 1 tablespoon tomato purée

1 small carrot, washed, peeled and finely diced

2 fennel leaves, washed and finely diced

½ celery stalk, washed and finely diced

1 small onion, peeled and finely diced

4 tablespoons Cognac

200 ml/7 fl oz dry white wine

500 ml/18 fl oz cold water

200 ml/7 fl oz whipping cream

salt and freshly ground white pepper

Planning ahead

For fisherman – first catch your pike and don't throw it back! For others, order 175 g/6 oz fillet of young 'jack' pike well in advance. Ask your fishmonger to scale and bone the fish for you.

The *fondue de tomates* must be prepared in advance.

---

1. Preparing the quenelle mixture

(10 minutes, plus 30 minutes chilling) (see Mousse making, page 36)

Cream the softened butter with your fingertips until smooth and free of lumps.

Pike: Tweeze out any small bones running down the middle of the fillet, then roughly chop the fish and purée in a food processor with the salt and cayenne pepper. With the motor running, add the eggs one by one, finally adding the creamed butter until the mixture is completely smooth. Turn out into a mixing bowl and refrigerate for 30 minutes.

Place the bowl on ice and slowly incorporate most of the cream. Taste, correct seasoning, then force the mixture through a fine sieve. Test the mixture (see page 37) by shaping a tiny *quenelle* with 2 teaspoons (see below) and poach in water just below boiling point for 4 minutes. Taste and correct seasoning, adding the remaining cream if necessary. Cover with clingfilm and place in the fridge.

2. Preparing the crayfish

(20 minutes)

Wash under cold running water for a few minutes then drain in a colander. Twist off the tails and reserve the heads and claws for the sauce.

Pinch the middle of the tails and pull out the black intestines, then pan-fry the tails for 30 seconds in hot olive oil. Season with 2 pinches of salt and 4 turns of pepper, then add the Cognac, tarragon and 4 tablespoons cold water, cover and leave to stand for 30 seconds. Strain the juices into a small container and leave the tails to cool be-

fore shelling. Add the tails to the juices, cover with clingfilm and refrigerate. Keep the shells for the sauce.

3. The sauce (30 minutes)

In a large sauté pan, heat the oil until smoking hot, then sear the crayfish heads and claws for about 2 minutes until they turn bright red. Reduce the heat, add the tail shells and diced vegetables, garlic and herbs and sweat for 5 minutes, stirring from time to time.

Deglaze with the Cognac and wine and boil for 1 minute. Add the *fondue de tomates* or tomato purée and 500 ml/ 18 fl oz cold water, bring back to the boil, skim and simmer for about 20 minutes.

Force the stock through a hard sieve, pressing with a wooden spoon to extract as much juice as possible, then pass through a fine sieve into a small saucepan. Bring to the boil, skim and reduce to about 100 ml/3 ½ fl oz. Finally add the cream and boil for 2 minutes.

Preheat the oven to 190°C/375°F/gas 5 for Stage 5.

4. Shaping and poaching the quenelles (10 minutes) (see page 37)

Have ready 2 tablespoons in a jug of warm water.

Three-quarters fill a large saucepan with lightly salted water, bring to the boil and reduce heat to just below simmering point. Using a warm tablespoon, scoop out a large spoonful of mousse and use the second spoon to mould an egg shape or *quenelle* (see diagram). Form all the mousse mixture into *quenelles* and poach for about 4 minutes.

Use 2 warm tablespoons to shape quenelles.

5. Simmering the quenelles and crayfish tails in the sauce

(15 minutes)

Lightly brush an ovenproof dish with a film of butter.

Remove the poached *quenelles* and drain on absorbent paper, then arrange in the dish, leaving some space between them for expansion. Pour the sauce over and around. Bring to simmering point, cover and cook in the preheated oven for 15 minutes. Add the crayfish tails during the final 5 minutes.

6. Serving

Warm 4 plates.

Serve the *quenelles* and crayfish tails in front of your guests, lifting them carefully onto the plates. Spoon the sauce over and around.

--- VARIATIONS ---

Zander, though milder than pike, can also be used. It is quite delicious.

The sauce can be made with lobster or langoustines instead of freshwater crayfish.

--- WINE ---

A spicy, dry white wine with a clean finish such as Pouilly Fuissé or a better value Pouilly Vinzelles or Pouilly Loché would be ideal.

Chef's notes

Freshwater crayfish: They must be bought alive or the serum holding the flesh together will leak out and they will lose their texture once cooked.

Searing the tails: This simply part-cooks the tails, making them easier to shell. They will finish cooking in the sauce.

The searing in hot oil is vital to the flavour of the sauce. During this stage there will be a specific moment when the scent is obvious and pleasant; at this point, reduce the heat and put in the diced vegetables and herbs to sweat.

Sauce: To give the sauce a better colour and flavour, grind the crayfish carcasses in a food processor or large pestle and mortar.

Poaching the quenelles: The water must not boil, or it will destroy the delicacy of the *quenelles,* which must be barely cooked at this stage, since they will be simmered in the sauce for 15 minutes during Stage 5. At this stage, an exchange of flavours will take place between the pike and the sauce, producing a wonderful aroma; the light sauce will reduce to a luscious, velvety texture, and the *quenelles* will expand, becoming extremely light, delicate and fluffy. Take care not to tear them during serving.

SOUFFLE DE SOLE ET TOURTEAU A LA CITRONELLE ET GINGEMBRE

Soufflé of Dover sole and crab with lemon grass and ginger

Soufflé de sole et tourteau à la citronelle et gingembre

SOUFFLE DE SOLE (CONT.)

Serves 6
Difficulty: ♙♙

Total recipe time: 1 hour 15 minutes,
plus 30 minutes chilling
Special equipment: food processor,
six stainless steel rings 7.5 x 4 cm/
3 x 1½ in

INGREDIENTS

6 80 g/3 oz fillets of Dover sole

1 tablespoon unsalted butter

juice of ¼ lemon

3 large tablespoons white crab meat

1 tablespoon brown crab meat

30 g/1 oz root ginger

a pinch of cayenne pepper

salt and freshly ground white pepper

Soufflé mixture

150 g/5 oz fillets of Dover sole

1 egg yolk

150 ml/5 fl oz whipping cream

3 egg whites

juice of ¼ lemon

Sauce

*2 lemon grass leaves or 15 g/½ oz
dried lemon grass stalks*

5 g/⅙ oz ginger peelings (see Stage 1)

2 tablespoons brown crab meat

*250 ml/9 fl oz Nage de légumes (see
page 22)*

1 tablespoon whipping cream

*60 g/2 ½ oz unsalted butter, chilled
and diced*

a squeeze of lemon

Garnish

20 g/¾ oz root ginger (see Stage 1)

3 pink grapefruit segments

a pinch of caster sugar

Planning ahead

Order two 400 g/14 oz Dover sole in
advance. Ask your fishmonger to skin
and fillet them into 8 fillets – 6 for
lining the rings and 2 for the soufflé.
Keep the bones to make a fish stock.

Have the crab cooked and separated
into white and brown meat.

The *nage de légumes* must be made in
advance.

The soufflé mixture can be prepared
12 hours in advance and kept covered
with clingfilm ready to be cooked.

The garnish can be prepared in advance.

The sauce base can be made in advance. Incorporate the cream and cold
diced butter at the last moment, while
you are cooking the soufflés.

1. Preparing and blanching the ginger (35 minutes)

Wash and peel, keeping half the peelings for the sauce.

Cut the peeled root into fine *julienne*
and blanch for a total of 15 minutes in
2 changes of boiling water, (acidulate
the second water with lemon juice).
Refresh, drain and dice about 5 g/⅙ oz
for Stage 2. Set the rest aside.

2. Preparing the crab meat and grapefruit (5 minutes)

In a small bowl, mix together the
white and brown crab meat and diced
ginger. Taste and season with salt and
a pinch of cayenne pepper.

Cut the pink grapefruit segments into
tiny triangles and put in a small bowl
with a pinch of caster sugar.

3. Preparing the soufflé base and sole fillets (15 minutes, plus 30 mi-nutes) (see Mousse making, page 36)

Soufflé base: In a food processor, purée
150 g/5 oz sole fillets with 1 level teaspoon salt and the egg yolk until
smooth, transfer to a stainless steel
bowl and refrigerate for 30 minutes.
Meanwhile, prepare the 6 fillets for
the moulds. With a sharp knife, score
the skin side and lay the fillets side by
side on a sheet of clingfilm or

polythene. Cover with another sheet
of clingfilm and flatten the fillets gently with a heavy knife to the height of
the metal rings (about 4 cm/1 ½ in).

Cut out six 15 cm/6 in squares of
clingfilm.

Place each ring on a square of
clingfilm and wrap it around the base
to make a false bottom. Butter the inside of the rings.

In a small saucepan, melt 1 tablespoon
butter with the juice of ¼ lemon, a
pinch of salt and 4 turns of pepper.
Brush onto both sides of the fillets.
Press the fillets around the inside of
the rings, (unscored side against the
rings) making sure that the ends
overlap.

Remove the soufflé mixture from the
fridge and stand the bowl on ice. Add
the cream, a little at a time, incorporating it first by tracing small circles,
then by beating the mixture vigorously, lifting it to trap as much air as
possible. Force through a sieve into
another bowl and season with 6 turns
of pepper.

Egg whites: Whisk with a generous
pinch of salt until soft peaks form.
Add the juice of ¼ lemon and beat until smooth and firm.

Using a wooden spoon, incorporate
one-quarter of the beaten egg white
into the soufflé mixture in fast circular
motions, then fold in the rest, cutting
and lifting until smooth.

One-quarter fill the sole-lined rings
with soufflé mixture and cover with 1
tablespoon prepared crab meat and
ginger. Top with the remaining
soufflé mixture, smoothing over the
surface.

4. The sauce (10 minutes)

Preheat the oven to 230°C/450°F/gas 8
for Stage 5.

In a medium saucepan, simmer the
nage de légumes with the lemon grass,
ginger peelings and 2 tablespoons
brown crab meat for 2–3 minutes to
infuse the flavours. Force through a
fine conical sieve into a small saucepan, pressing with a ladle to extract as

much juice as possible.

Bring back to the boil and stir in 1 tablespoon cream. Add the ginger *julienne* and finally whisk in the cold diced butter. Taste, season with salt and pepper and enliven with a squeeze of lemon. Mix in the grapefruit triangles.

5. Cooking the soufflés

(12 minutes)

Place the filled rings in a deep roasting pan, leaving plenty of space between them, and pour in hot water to about 1 cm/½ in depth. Cook in the preheated oven for 12 minutes.

6. Serving

Warm 6 plates.

Sit the cooked soufflés on a large tray, remove the clingfilm from the base, then lift off the rings and place a soufflé in the centre of each plate. Strain the juices remaining on the tray into the sauce and pour the sauce over and around the soufflés.

You have just accomplished a great feat! Serve to your guests.

Chef's notes

The mousse can be made with scallops; in this case you will need only 120 ml/4 fl oz cream.

Lemon grass is easy to find in season (May–September). Out of season you can buy dried sticks of lemon grass from Chinese supermarkets.

Blanching the ginger: 15 minutes blanching tenderizes the fibrous texture and tempers its fierce flavour. Use plenty of water to disperse the flavour; if you use too little, the fieriness will be reabsorbed.

CARRE DE COCHON DE LAIT AU JUS A LA MARJOLAINE

Roast best end of sucking pig, served with a marjoram-scented juice

"To me, sucking pig is the most refined, tender and delicately scented meat — a simple dish fit for a king!"

Serves 4
Difficulty:
Total recipe time: 1 hour

INGREDIENTS

2 400 g/14 oz best ends of sucking pig, prepared

1 tablespoon groundnut oil

salt and freshly ground white pepper

Juice

chine bones and trimmings from the pig (about 300 g/11 oz), cut in small pieces

1 tablespoon groundnut oil

1 medium onion, peeled and diced

½ celery stalk, washed and diced

1 small carrot, washed, peeled and diced

1 garlic clove, unpeeled and lightly crushed

100 ml/3½ fl oz dry white wine

100 ml/3½ fl oz Veal stock (see page 18)

4 sprigs of fresh marjoram

a dash of white wine vinegar

Garnish

24 fresh or canned mirabelle plums

1 teaspoon caster sugar (optional)

4 tablespoons water or syrup from the canned plums

Planning ahead

You will need to order a whole sucking pig at least a week in advance, as butchers do not sell separate cuts of this delicacy. Ask your butcher to joint the pig into legs, shoulders and saddle, which can be frozen for later use. Ask for the head and belly too, to make a delicious brawn.

The best ends should be prepared leaving 12 bones, trimmed, with the chine removed. You will need all the offcut bones and trimmings for the juice.

The veal stock must be made in advance.

1. Making the juice (40 minutes) (see Savoury sauces, page 26)

Preheat the oven to 230°C/450°F/gas 8.

In a non-stick roasting pan heat 1 tablespoon oil until hot and sear the offcut bones to colour lightly. Sweat the diced vegetables and garlic for a few minutes then cook in the preheated oven for 20 minutes until the bones and vegetables are well browned.

*Carré de cochon
de lait au jus
à la marjolaine*

Tilt the pan and discard the fat, then deglaze with the wine. Bring to the boil and scrape up all the caramelized juices at the bottom of the pan with a wooden spoon. Add the veal stock and 200–300 ml/7–10 fl oz cold water, pour into a medium saucepan and boil for 1 or 2 minutes skimming occasionally. Add the marjoram and simmer for about 15 minutes.

Strain the stock through a fine sieve into a small saucepan and reduce to a deliciously scented juice. Taste and season with a tiny pinch of salt (if needed) a pinch of pepper and enliven with a dash of white wine vinegar. Set aside.

Increase the oven temperature to 240°C/475°F/gas 9 for Stage 3.

2. Preparing and cooking the garnish (5 minutes)

Mirabelles: If fresh, remove the stones and taste to test how ripe they are. Cook them at just under simmering point with 4 tablespoons water and 1 teaspoon sugar (more if necessary) for 5 minutes. Keep aside.

If using canned mirabelles, simply place them in a bowl with 4 tablespoons of their juice.

3. Cooking the best ends of sucking pig (25 minutes plus 15 minutes resting)

With the point of a sharp knife score the skin 3 mm/⅛ in deep in between the ribs.

Wrap the rib ends in foil so they do not burn during cooking.

In a large roasting pan sear the fillet sides of the best ends in 1 tablespoon oil to colour lightly, then season all over with salt and pepper. Rest the best ends on a few offcut bones, so that the flesh does not come directly in contact with the strong heat at the bottom of the pan, and roast at the top of the oven (where the heat can reflect onto the skin to produce the delicious crackling) for about 25 minutes.

Transfer to a wire cooling rack placed over a tray and leave to rest in a warm place for 10–15 minutes.

Discard the fat from the roasting tin, add a few tablespoons of water and scrape up all the caramelized juices. Mix these into the juice from Stage 1.

4. Carving and serving the dish
(10 minutes)

Heat 4 plates.

Return the best ends to the oven for 2–3 minutes and warm the mirabelles.

Bring the juice back to the boil and serve in a sauceboat.

Place the best ends on a carving board and present the dish to your guests.

Insert the blade of your carving knife in between the golden crackling and the meat and cut the crackling into diamond shapes. Carve the small cutlets, sprinkle with a few grains of salt and pepper and arrange them in the centre of the plates. Scatter over the mirabelles and pour the juice around. Serve to your guests.

——— VARIATIONS ———
Saddle, leg or shoulder of sucking pig can be done the same way.
Other varieties of plum can replace the mirabelles; prunes are delicious.

——— WINE ———
Serve a delicate dry white wine from Burgundy such as white Mercurey or Santenay blanc 'Clos Rousseau' or Montagny.

Chef's note
Cooking the best ends: Roast at the highest possible temperature to achieve a golden crust with moist and tender meat.

RIS DE VEAU ROTI AUX AMANDES, PISTACHES ET PIGNONS DE PIN

Veal sweetbread served with a hazelnut juice, studded with almonds, pistachios and pine kernels

"I remember being most disappointed when I first saw and cooked sweetbreads; they looked rather pathetic and off-putting. I had heard so much about this gastronomic delight that it was a total anticlimax.
Later I came to understand that success of this dish depends so much on the type and freshness of the sweetbread. There are two types, the long, dangly ones from the throat, and the oval or round ones from the heart; always use the latter. They should be firm and white with no bruising and no scent. I realize that the cooking of all offal is anathema to some of you, but do try this recipe . . . ."

Serves 4
Difficulty: ♟
Total recipe time: 40 minutes, plus 1 hour soaking
Special equipment: food processor or pestle and mortar

——— INGREDIENTS ———
1 veal sweetbread (from the heart)

1 tablespoon clarified butter

salt and freshly ground white pepper

Sauce
1 tablespoon flaked almonds

6 hazelnuts

1 shallot, finely chopped

1 teaspoon unsalted butter

100 ml/3½ fl oz Light chicken stock (see page 21)

1 tablespoon whipping cream

30 g/1 oz unsalted butter, chilled and diced

lemon juice

Garnish
2 tablespoons flaked almonds

1 tablespoon pine kernels

1 tablespoon pistachio nuts

1. Preparing the sweetbread
(10 minutes plus 1 hour soaking)
Soak the sweetbread in cold running water for at least 1 hour. Scald in boiling water for 5 seconds, then peel away the cartilage, fat and fibres, taking care not to tear or damage the shape of the sweetbread. Pat dry and season. Reserve the trimmings.

2. Cooking the sweetbread
(4 minutes, plus 15 minutes resting)

Preheat the oven to 200°C/400°F/gas 6.
Heat the clarified butter in a non-stick frying pan and fry the sweetbread for 2 minutes on each side, until golden. Discard the fat and season the sweetbread with salt and pepper. Line a frying pan with buttered greaseproof paper, put in the sweetbread and cook in the oven for 10 minutes.
Cover the pan with another sheet of buttered greaseproof paper and leave to rest for 15 minutes.

3. Preparing the garnish
(10 minutes)
Heat the grill and toast all the almonds until golden brown, including those for the sauce. Keep warm. Toast the pine kernels for 1–2 minutes. Toast the hazelnuts until golden, then rub off the skins in a tea towel.
Plunge the pistachios into boiling

water and remove the skins to reveal the bright green nuts beneath.

4. The sauce (10 minutes)
Crush 1 tablespoon toasted almonds and the hazelnuts, using the flat of a heavy knife, pestle and mortar or food processor.
Sweat the shallot in 1 teaspoon butter until soft, then add the reserved

sweetbread trimmings, crushed almonds and hazelnuts, chicken stock and any cooking juices from the sweetbread. Bring to the boil, skim and simmer for 5 minutes to allow the flavours to blend. Strain into a small saucepan and return to the boil. Add the cream then, over low heat, whisk in the cold diced butter. Season and add a squeeze of lemon. Keep warm.

5. Serving (5 minutes)
Warm 5 plates.
Warm the pistachios in the sauce. Cut the sweetbread into 4 equal slices and place one on each plate. Pour over the sauce and delicately sprinkle the remaining almonds and pine kernels around the sweetbread.

CANARD CROISE AU SIROP DE MAIS, CROUSTILLANT AUX OIGNONS CONFITS

Roast duckling with corn syrup, served with a garnish of sliced onions and coriander in filo pastry

Serves 4
Difficulty: 🍳
Total recipe time: 1 hour 20 minutes

—— INGREDIENTS ——
2 ducklings

4 teaspoons non-scented oil

salt and freshly ground white pepper

Sauce
wings and necks from the ducklings, chopped

1 tablespoon groundnut oil or duck fat

50 ml/2 fl oz white wine vinegar

2 tablespoons soy sauce

2 tablespoons corn syrup

300 ml/½ pt Brown chicken stock (see page 21)

1 tablespoon Cognac

1 tablespoon whipping cream

1 tablespoon chopped coriander

10 g/⅓ oz lemon grass, chopped (optional)

1 teaspoon ginger root peelings (from the garnish)

Garnish
4 10 cm/4 in squares of filo pastry

12 cocktail onions (about 100 g/4 oz), finely sliced

2 teaspoons unsalted butter

a large pinch of caster sugar

1 teaspoon white wine vinegar

1 level tablespoon chopped coriander

4 chives or outside leaves of spring onions, cut into ribbons, blanched for a few seconds and refreshed

10 g/⅓ oz blanched ginger julienne (see page 144)

Planning ahead
Order the ducklings well in advance. Ask your butcher to cut the wings short, to cut off the necks, remove the wishbones and the nerves and tendons from the legs.

The filo pastry must be made in advance, if you are making your own. Stages 1–3 inclusive can be completed a few hours in advance.

1. Preparing the ducklings
(10 minutes)
Preheat the oven to 240°C/475°F/gas 9 for Stage 2.
Singe the birds over an open flame to remove any stubble (or remove with a small sharp knife). With the point of a knife score lines 5 mm/¼ in deep across the skin to allow the fat to run out easily. Season to taste.

2. Making the sauce (40 minutes)
(see Savoury sauces, page 26)
In a large frying pan, sear the duck wings in hot oil to colour lightly, then roast in the preheated oven for 20 minutes.
Meanwhile, in a small saucepan, caramelize 1 tablespoon of corn syrup, then add the vinegar and reduce to about 1 tablespoon. Add the soy sauce, the remaining corn syrup, chicken stock, Cognac and cream, and bring to the boil.
Skim, add the remaining duck trimmings and simmer for 10 minutes, then add the chopped coriander,

lemon grass and ginger peelings and simmer for another 2 minutes. Taste, season with 1 or 2 turns of pepper and correct with a dash of vinegar if the sauce is a little too sweet. Reduce the oven temperature to 230°C/450 °F/ gas 8.

3. Preparing the garnish
(15 minutes)

Put the sliced onions in a small frying pan with the butter, a pinch of salt, sugar and pepper and sweat for 3–4 minutes. Pour in the vinegar and reduce it completely. Add the chopped coriander, then taste, correct the seasoning, draw off the heat and allow to cool.

Lay the 4 squares of filo pastry flat on your work surface, place a little onion mixture in the centre of each and wrap into small parcels. Tie with ribbons made from chives or spring onion tops and refrigerate on a small lightly-oiled baking tray.

4. Roasting the ducklings
(25 minutes plus 10 minutes resting)

Heat the oil in a large frying pan, put in the ducklings and sear for 2 minutes on each side, then for a further 2 minutes on each breast, until browned. Season, then turn the birds on their backs and roast in the preheated oven for 25 minutes.

Remove, cover loosely with foil and leave to rest for about 10 minutes in a warm place. Leave the oven on for Stage 5.

5. Cooking the garnish; assembling the dish and serving
(15 minutes)

Warm 4 plates or a large serving dish. Bake the onion parcels in the preheated oven for 6 minutes.

Carve off the duck legs, then separate them at the joint between leg and thigh. Carve out the breasts and season the insides of all the duck pieces.

Return the legs and thighs to the oven for 10 minutes and the breasts for 3 minutes; skin side down.

Warm the sauce, spoon it onto the plates and arrange the duck pieces in the centre of the plates. Scatter over the ginger *julienne* and place an onion parcel on the side.

— VARIATIONS —

The skin from the duck breasts can be peeled off, sliced, crisped under the grill and added to the onion parcels.

Guinea fowl can also be prepared this way.

Add small spring onions, lightly blanched and warmed in melted butter to the garnish.

Serve the duck with coriander pancakes filled with a *julienne* of black radishes – definitely a Chinese influence!

— WINE —

Since this dish is highly flavoured and quite spicy, a clean, fresh dry white wine suits it best – try a light young Burgundy such as Montagny or St Véran. If you prefer a red wine, choose a 4- or 5-year-old claret, perhaps one of the excellent 'second wines' from one of the classed growth châteaux such as Château de Marbuzet from Clos d'Estournel.

Chef's note
Please read Chef's notes in *Caneton rôti au saveurs du printemps,* page 91.

*Canard croisé au sirop de maïs,
Croustillant aux oignons confits*

PINTADEAU ROTI AU CITRON VERT

Roast guinea fowl with lime

"Guinea fowl is often underrated, despite its most distinctive character. It is well worth shopping around to find corn-fed farm birds."

*Pintadeau rôti
au citron vert*

Serves 4
Difficulty: ♔♔
Total recipe time: 1 hour 20 minutes

—— INGREDIENTS ——

2 1 kg/2¼ lb guinea fowl

2 teaspoons groundnut oil

2 teaspoons unsalted butter

salt and freshly ground white pepper

Sauce

bones from the guinea fowl

2 teaspoons groundnut oil

2 teaspoons unsalted butter

2 large shallots, peeled and chopped

juice of ½ lime

100 ml/3 ½ fl oz ruby port

100 ml/3 ½ fl oz dry Madeira

2 sprigs of lemon thyme

200 ml/7 fl oz Brown chicken stock (see page 21)

Garnish

32 redcurrants

3 teaspoons caster sugar

zest of 1 lime, cut into fine julienne (see page 49)

segments from ½ lime, cut into small triangles

Planning ahead

Order the guinea fowl well in advance and ask the butcher to hang them for 4–6 days to develop the flavour. Ask him to pluck and draw the birds, to section the legs at the knee joints and to remove the wishbones. Ask for the livers too; they can be used for *Petit pain de foies de volaille* (page 232.)

The brown chicken stock must be made in advance.

Stages 1 and 2 can be completed in advance.

Stages 3 must be started 1 hour before the meal to allow time for making the sauce, which requires the guinea fowl wings and carcasses.

1. Preparing the guinea fowl
(10 minutes)

Singe the birds over an open flame to remove stubble, or remove with a small sharp knife.

2. Preparing the garnish
(5 minutes)

Preheat the oven to 220°C/425°F/gas 7 for Stage 3.

Redcurrants: Mix with 1 teaspoon sugar and keep in a small container.

Julienne of lime zest: Blanch for 10 minutes in plenty of boiling water, refresh and place in a small saucepan with 1 teaspoon sugar and 1 tablespoon cold water.

Lime segments: Sprinkle with 1 teaspoon caster sugar and keep in a small container.

3. Cooking the guinea fowl
(30 minutes)

In a large heavy sauté pan, heat the groundnut oil and butter until hot, then brown the guinea fowl for 2 minutes on each leg and 30 seconds on each breast. Season with salt and pepper.

Add the wings and necks, turn the birds onto their backs and roast in the preheated oven for 20 minutes, basting occasionally.

Remove, leave to rest for 10 minutes then carve out the breasts, cut off the legs and season the insides. Keep in a warm place loosely covered with foil.

4. Making the sauce (20 minutes)
(see Savoury sauces, page 26)

Chop the guinea fowl carcasses into small pieces.

In a large sauté pan, heat the oil and butter until hot then sear the carcasses lightly. Add the chopped shallots and sweat for 2 minutes. Tilt the pan and remove excess fat, then add the lime juice and boil until evaporated. Add the port and Madeira, bring to the boil and reduce by half. Add the lemon thyme, chicken stock and 300 ml/½ pt cold water, bring back to the boil, skim and simmer for 15 minutes.

Strain through a fine sieve into a small saucepan and reduce to about 200 ml/7 fl oz, skimming off all the impurities. Taste and season with a few grains of salt and a pinch of pepper. Keep warm.

5. Assembling the dish and serving
(15 minutes)

Heat 4 plates and turn on the grill.

Strain the cooking juices released by the guinea fowl into the sauce and return the thighs to the oven for 6–8 minutes and the breasts for 3 minutes. Heat the redcurrants under the grill for 3 minutes. Separately warm the lime triangles and zests.

Arrange the redcurrants and lime triangles around the inside of each plate and place the guinea fowl breasts in the centre, flanked by a thigh and topped by a leg. Scatter the lime zests and spoon the sauce over and around. Serve at once.

--- VARIATIONS ---

Quail are delicious prepared this way.

--- WINE ---

The sauce is light but quite tangy and lively. A well rounded, flowery, scented white wine from Alsace is best – Tokay d'Alsace or Riesling.

Chef's notes

Guinea fowl: It really is worth looking for the real thing rather than those industrially produced, tasteless birds. Hanging will enhance the flavour of the birds.

The sauce: If it lacks sharpness, add a further dash of lime juice; if it is too acid, soften with a coffee spoon of redcurrant jelly.

GROUSE AUX MURES

Roast grouse, served with a blackberry sauce

Serves 4
Difficulty 🎩
Total recipe time: 1 hour 5 minutes
Special equipment: trussing needle, string, blender or food processor

INGREDIENTS

4 350 g/12 oz young grouse

2 teaspoons unsalted butter

2 teaspoons non-scented oil

salt and freshly ground white pepper

Sauce
100 g/3 ½ oz ripe blackberries

breast bones from the grouse

1 teaspoon unsalted butter

1 tablespoon red wine vinegar

100 ml/3 ½ fl oz ruby port

50 ml/2 fl oz red wine

*200 ml/7 fl oz Brown chicken stock
(see page 21)*

a pinch of caster sugar (optional)

Garnish
20 ripe blackberries

a pinch of caster sugar (optional)

Planning ahead
Order the grouse well in advance. They must be fresh and should not have been hung for more than 2 days. Ask the poulterer to pluck and draw them and to remove the wishbones.

1. Preparing the grouse
(5 minutes)
Preheat the oven to 200°C/400°F/gas 6 for Stage 2.
Cut off the feet at the joints then singe the birds over an open flame to remove any stubble. Truss them (see page 16).

2. The sauce (30 minutes)
Purée the blackberries in a blender and set aside.
Chop out and discard the backbones from carcasses. Roughly chop the breast bones. In a large sauté pan sear the chopped breast bones in ½ tablespoon each of butter and non-scented oil, until lightly coloured. Pour off the excess fat then deglaze with the vinegar, allowing it to evaporate completely. Add the port, bring to the boil then add the veal stock and 200 ml/ 7 fl oz cold water. Bring back to the boil, skim and simmer for about 5 minutes. Finally add the puréed blackberries and simmer for a further 5 minutes.
Strain through a fine sieve into a small saucepan, using a small ladle to press through as much juice and flavour as you can. Reduce the sauce to about 200 ml/7 fl oz, taste and season with salt and pepper.

3. Cooking, resting and carving the grouse (15 minutes plus 5 minutes resting)
Season the birds inside and out with salt and pepper.

In a large frying pan, heat the butter and oil until hot, put in the birds on their thighs and sear for 30 seconds each side. Lay them on their backs and cook in the preheated oven for 10–12 minutes.
Season the breasts and legs and leave to rest for 5 minutes before carving (keep the carcasses to make the sauce).

4. Serving (5 minutes)
Warm 4 plates or a large serving dish. Add the whole blackberries to the sauce and simmer for 1 minute.
Slice the breasts in two, cut the legs at the thigh joints, arrange attractively around the plates and pour the sauce over. Serve to your guests.

VARIATIONS
Replace the blackberries with blueberries.

WINE
Serve the best available mature red, either Bordeaux or Burgundy.

Chef's notes
Grouse have a powerful and majestic flavour. Hanging them for too long distorts this natural richness into an overpowering strength.
Sear the birds directly on the thighs, not on the breasts where the skin is too delicate.
Blackberries must be ripe; taste before using. The acidity of under-ripe berries is accentuated when they are heated. If the berries are too sour, add a little sugar.

Biscuit glacé aux framboises "façon
Maman Blanc"

BISCUIT GLACE AUX FRAMBOISES "FAÇON MAMAN BLANC"

Iced biscuit filled with warm raspberries, served with raspberry coulis

"I took the basic idea for this dish from one of my mother's recipes (*Iles flottantes*, page 101). She has tested it and approves!"

Serves 4
Difficulty: 👨‍🍳 👨‍🍳
Total recipe time: 1 hour 15 minutes
Special equipment: four 8 cm/3 in *savarin* moulds, electric mixer, piping bag with 1 cm/½ in nozzle, blender

—————— INGREDIENTS ——————
Biscuits (for more information see page 44)
4 egg yolks
....
4 tablespoons cold water
....
85 g/3 oz caster sugar
....
4 egg whites
....
25 g/1 oz caster sugar
....
100 g/3½ oz plain white flour, sifted
....
butter and flour to line the moulds
....

Syrup
100 ml/3½ fl oz water
....
65 g/2½ oz caster sugar
....
1 tablespoon kirsch
....

Meringue (see Chef's notes, *Iles flottantes*, page 101)
3 egg whites
....
125 g/4 oz caster sugar
....

For poaching the meringue and making the vanilla custard
500 ml/18 fl oz milk
....
1 vanilla pod, split
....
4 egg yolks
....
25 g/1 oz caster sugar
....

Raspberry coulis
300 g/11 oz ripe raspberries, washed, drained and hulled
....
150 g/5 oz caster sugar
....
1 tablespoon raspberry liqueur (optional)
....

Garnish
200 g/7 oz freshly-picked raspberries
....
4 tablespoons Raspberry sorbet (see page 159) (optional)
....

Planning ahead
Stages 1–4 inclusive can be completed up to 1 day in advance.
Raspberry sorbet, if used, must be made in advance.

1. Preparing, cooking and moistening the biscuits
(30 minutes)
Preheat the oven to 190°C/375°F/ gas 5.
Brush the insides of 4 *savarin* moulds with melted butter then coat with a very thin film of flour, shaking off the excess. Set aside.
In an electric mixer, whisk together the egg yolks, 4 tablespoons cold water and the caster sugar until the mixture is light and aerated and has quadrupled in volume.
In a separate mixing bowl, beat 4 egg whites to a soft peak, then add 25 g/ 1 oz caster sugar and beat until firm.
Fold the egg white into the yolk mixture then carefully fold in the sifted flour. Spoon the mixture into a piping bag fitted with a 1 cm/½ in nozzle and pipe it into the prepared moulds. The

excess biscuit mixture can be used in another recipe.
Bake in the preheated oven for 10 minutes, allow to cool for a few seconds then turn out onto a small tray. In a small saucepan, bring to the boil 50 ml/2 fl oz water with 30 g/1 oz caster sugar, allow to cool, then add the kirsch and brush the syrup over the biscuits. Arrange the biscuits quite close together in a single layer in a shallow saucepan.

2. Preparing and poaching the meringues (25 minutes)
In an electric mixer on medium speed, beat 3 egg whites to a soft peak, then add 125 g/4 oz sugar. Increase to full speed and continue beating until firm.
In a large saucepan, boil the milk with the sliced vanilla pod and simmer for about 2 minutes.
Reduce the heat to just below simmering point.
Using 2 dessert spoons dipped in warm water, shape the meringue into 20 *quenelles* (see page 142) and slide them one at a time into the milk.
Cover the pan, leaving the lid slightly ajar, and poach the meringues for about 5 minutes. Remove with a slotted spoon and drain on a small tray lined with a tea towel. Keep the milk for Stage 3.

3. Preparing the vanilla custard; soaking the biscuits (7 minutes)
(see Vanilla custard, page 33)
In a large mixing bowl, cream together 4 egg yolks with 2 tablespoons sugar. Pour the hot milk from Stage 2 over the mixture and, stirring

continuously with a wooden spoon, cook over medium heat until the custard begins to thicken. Strain it over the biscuits, allow to cool then cover with clingfilm and refrigerate.

4. The raspberry coulis
(5 minutes)
Purée the raspberries with the sugar and raspberry liqueur. Use a ladle to force the pulp through a fine sieve into a small saucepan.

5. Warming the raspberries in the coulis (3 minutes)
Wash the raspberries briefly, drain, hull and add to the *coulis*. Warm over a

gentle heat for 2–3 minutes, taking care that it does not boil. Taste, and add more sugar if necessary.

6. Serving (5 minutes)
Arrange one soaked biscuit in the middle of each serving plate and place the warmed raspberries inside the hollow and around the edge. Top with the tiny *quenelles* of meringue (and sorbet, if used) and pour the warm *coulis* around. Serve to your guests.
For this dish to be completely successful, the biscuit and meringues must be ice-cold and the raspberries and *coulis* just warm – a cocktail of different tastes, textures and temperatures.

———— VARIATIONS ————
The dish can also be made using wild strawberries or blackberries, with their own *coulis*.
Serve the remaining vanilla custard separately in a sauceboat.

Chef's notes
Poaching the meringue: Do not let the milk boil while poaching the meringues; they will expand, then deflate.
Vanilla custard: The custard must be thin enough to permeate the biscuits. Make sure that it does not thicken too much.

SOUPE DE FRUITS D'ETE

Summer fruits steeped in raspberry sauce

Serves 4–6
Difficulty:
Total recipe time: 45 minutes, plus 6 hours marinating

———— INGREDIENTS ————

2 peaches

200 ml/7 fl oz dry white wine

240 g/8 ½ oz caster sugar

1 orange slice

100 g/3 ½ oz black cherries, stoned

juice of ¼ lemon

100 g/3 ½ oz raspberries, hulled

100 g/3 ½ oz strawberries, hulled

100 g/3 ½ oz blackberries

segments from 2 oranges

Sauce

200 g/7 oz raspberries, hulled

200 g/7 oz strawberries, hulled

80–100 g/3–3 ½ oz caster sugar

cooking liquid from the peaches

Planning ahead
This dessert must be prepared 6 hours in advance.

1. Preparing the fruits
(40 minutes)
Peaches: Place in a small saucepan with 700 ml/1 ¼ pt water, the wine, 150 g/5 oz sugar and the orange slice, bring to the boil and skim. Reduce the heat to just below simmering point, cover with pierced foil and cook for about 30 minutes. Leave to cool in the cooking liquid. Peel, remove the stones and quarter the peaches.

Cherries: Place in a small saucepan with 20 g/¾ oz sugar, the lemon juice and 4 tablespoons water, bring to the boil, cover and cook for 1 minute. Leave the cherries to cool in their cooking liquid.
Raspberries and blackcurrants: Place on separate plates, sprinkle each with 20 g/¾ oz sugar and leave to marinate for 30 minutes.
Strawberries: Quarter the large ones and halve the medium ones. Place on a plate, sprinkle with 20 g/¾ oz sugar and leave to marinate for 30 minutes.
Orange segments: Depending on the sweetness, sprinkle with about 2 teaspoons sugar and leave to marinate for 30 minutes.
Meanwhile, make the sauce.

2. Preparing the sauce
(10 minutes)
Purée the raspberries and strawberries in a blender with the sugar and 200 ml/7 fl oz cooking liquid from the peaches. Taste; if the sauce is a little acidic, add more sugar. Strain through a fine sieve into a large mixing bowl and reserve.

3. Mixing the fruit with the sauce
(2 minutes)
Add all the fruits and any juices they have released to the sauce, stir, cover with clingfilm and refrigerate for at least 6 hours so that all the flavours mingle and infuse.

4. Serving
Pour the fruits and sauce into a serving bowl or serve in individual glasses or bowls.

— VARIATIONS —
Many other fruits can be used instead of those suggested.

Serve the dish with a blackcurrant or raspberry sorbet, or present it in small scooped-out Cavaillon melon shells, adding the scooped-out flesh to the dessert.

Chef's note
All the fruits must be perfectly ripe.

TARTELETTE SOUFFLEE AUX FRAMBOISES

The lightest soufflé baked in a melting sweet shortcrust case

Serves 4
Difficulty: ♟♟
Total recipe time: 1 hour 10 minutes, plus 1 hour resting for the pastry
Special equipment: electric mixer, food processor, 4 flan rings, 7.5 cm/3 in diameter, 4 cm/1½ in deep, four 25 x 4 cm/10 x 1½ in bands of double thickness foil, four 30 x 9 cm 12 x 3½ in bands of greaseproof paper, 8 cm/3 in pastry cutter, piping bag with 1.5 cm/8 in nozzle

— INGREDIENTS —
250 g/9 oz Pâte sucrée (see page 40)

a handful of flour, for dusting

1 egg yolk mixed with 1 teaspoon milk

1 teaspoon melted butter with 2 tablespoons caster sugar, for lining the pastry cases

Soufflé mixture
1 tablespoon Crème pâtissière (see page 34)

400 g/14 oz raspberries, hulled

100 g/3½ oz caster sugar

1 tablespoon lemon juice

4 egg whites

1 teaspoon lemon juice

Garnish
24 freshly picked raspberries, hulled

1 teaspoon caster sugar

1 tablespoon raspberry liqueur (optional)

1 teaspoon butter and 1 tablespoon caster sugar, for the greaseproof paper

Sauce
200 g/7 oz raspberries, hulled

50 g/2 oz caster sugar

lemon juice (optional)

icing sugar for dusting

Planning ahead
Please read Soufflé making (page 35) before embarking on this recipe. The pastry cream and pastry must be made in advance.
Stages 1–4 inclusive can be completed 1 day in advance.

1. Rolling the pastry; lining the rings (20 minutes, plus 1 hour chilling)
On a lightly floured work surface, roll out the pastry into a 30 cm/12 in square, 2 mm/¹⁄₁₂ in thick. Cut out four 24 x 4 cm/10 x 1½ in bands, then cut out 4 rounds with the pastry cutter. Place the rounds on a lightly buttered baking sheet and brush the edges with a little beaten egg yolk and milk. Lightly butter the inside of the flan rings.
Line the sides of the flan rings with the bands of pastry (roll them up loosely, then unroll against the insides).
Sit the lined rings on the pastry rounds and press down to trim any excess. Make sure the bottom edges of the pastry are well stuck together. Prick the bases with a fork and cover the inside with a band of double thickness foil, to prevent shrinkage during cooking; refrigerate for about 1 hour. Preheat the oven to 200°C/400°F/gas 6 for Stage 5.

2. Preparing the garnish
(2 minutes)
Place 24 raspberries in a small bowl and sprinkle with sugar and raspberry liqueur, if using. Seal with clingfilm and refrigerate.

3. Preparing the cooked raspberry purée for the soufflé base
(15 minutes)
Purée the raspberries with the sugar and lemon juice. Force through a fine sieve into a thick-bottomed saucepan (you should obtain about 250 ml/9 fl oz purée) and reduce over a strong heat to a thick jammy consistency (about 3 tablespoons), stirring continuously. Add the *crème pâtissière* and

whisk until smooth. Place in a mixing bowl over a warm bain-marie.

4. Preparing the raspberry coulis
(5 minutes)

Purée the raspberries with the sugar, then force through a fine sieve into a small bowl, pressing the pulp with a ladle to extract as much juice as possible. Taste and correct with a little more sugar or lemon juice as necessary.

5. Baking the pastry cases blind; preparing them for the soufflés
(20 minutes)

Bake the pastry-lined rings in the pre-heated oven for about 4 minutes, then quickly remove the foil bands and return the rings to the oven for a further 3–4 minutes, until the pastry is cooked. Remove, cool for a few minutes then lift off the rings.

Liberally butter the insides of the pastry cases, put 1 tablespoon sugar in one case, rotate to distribute the sugar evenly, then pour the excess sugar into the next case. Repeat until all are finely coated.

Brush the 4 bands of greaseproof paper with melted butter and dust with caster sugar.

Wrap the bands of greaseproof paper, sugared side inwards, around the outsides of the pastry cases. Place 6 marinated raspberries from Stage 2 in each case and leave on a baking sheet.

Reduce the oven temperature to 190°C/375°F/gas 5.

6. Making the soufflé mixture
(5 minutes)

In an electric mixer on medium speed, beat the egg whites to a light peak, then add 1 teaspoon lemon juice, increase to full speed and beat until firm. Briskly whisk one-quarter of the egg white into the warm raspberry purée from Stage 3, then carefully fold in the rest with a spatula until just mixed.

Spoon the soufflé mixture into a large piping bag fitted with a 1.5 cm/⅝ in nozzle and pipe into the pastry cases; the mixture should come about 5 mm/¼ in above the top of the cases. Bake in the preheated oven for 8–10 minutes.

7. Serving (3 minutes)

Spoon 2 tablespoons raspberry *coulis* into the middle of each serving plate and spread it out in a circle using the back of a spoon. Carefully remove the greaseproof paper from the soufflés, dust the tops with icing sugar and serve at once.

--- VARIATIONS ---

To simplify the dish, omit the pastry cases and bake the soufflés in small ramekins. Once you are confident about this, do try baking them in the pastry cases; the contrasting textures and flavours are excellent.

The *crème pâtissière* can be omitted but the taste will be less interesting and the texture firmer.

The soufflés can be made with many fruits; try lemon soufflé served with warm or cold cherries (see *Petit paquet surprise du Manoir,* page 95), or line the pastry case with sliced poached pears for a chocolate soufflé, or serve an apricot soufflé with its own *coulis;* blanch the kernels for 15 minutes then cook to a pale caramel with icing sugar and a teaspoon of kirsch. Add to the tops of the soufflés.

Chef's notes

Baking the pastry cases blind: Let the pastry rest for at least 1 hour before baking to minimize shrinkage. The foil also helps to prevent this. Remove it halfway through to ensure uniform cooking of the pastry.

Reducing the raspberry purée: Always use a wide, thick-bottomed saucepan for this type of operation to ensure fast and even evaporation of the liquid. Whisk constantly to prevent it from catching. It is important to reduce it to a jammy consistency (this does not impair the taste of the raspberries), otherwise the soufflés will be too wet, giving rise to all sorts of problems.

The cooked soufflés will hold their shape for at least 4 or 5 minutes, so you have plenty of time to remove the greaseproof paper before serving.

Desserts

SORBET AUX ABRICOTS

Apricot sorbet

Serves 4
Difficulty: 🍳
Total recipe time: 25-50 minutes.
Special equipment: food processor, *sorbetière*

———— INGREDIENTS ————

500 g/1 lb 2 oz ripe apricots, washed, halved and stoned

250 ml/9 fl oz Sorbet syrup (see page 31)

juice of 1/2 lemon

Garnish (optional)
kernels from the apricot stones

icing sugar

1 tablespoon kirsch

Planning ahead
The sorbet and garnish can be prepared a few hours in advance. Chill 4 plates in the freezer 30 minutes before serving.

1. Cooking the apricots
(10 minutes)
Place the apricots in a thick-bottomed saucepan with the sorbet syrup and lemon juice. Cover and boil for 1 minute, then remove the lid and cook for 5–10 minutes, until pulpy, according to the ripeness of the fruit.

2. Puréeing and sieving (5 minutes)
Liquidize the pulp to a smooth purée then force through a fine sieve and leave to cool. Taste when cool and add a little more lemon juice or sugar as necessary.

3. Churning the sorbet
(10–25 minutes)
Churn until smooth and firm. Store in the freezer.

4. The garnish (25 minutes) (optional)
Preheat the oven to 230°C/450°F/gas 8.
Crack the apricot stones, remove the kernels and blanch in 1 L/1¾ pt simmering water for about 15 minutes. Drain, halve and place on a small ovenproof dish with the kirsch. Dredge generously with icing sugar then toast in the preheated oven for about 5 minutes until golden.

5. Serving
Dip 2 tablespoons in hot water and scoop out the sorbet, arranging it on the chilled plates. Sprinkle over the toasted kernels.

———— VARIATIONS ————
Peach or nectarine sorbets can be made in the same way.

Chef's notes
Apricots: They must be ripe and firm. If slightly under- or over-ripe, the cooking time and quantities of lemon juice or sugar will vary. Cook covered for the first minute so that the fruit softens and releases its juices, then uncover and cook until the apricots are pulpy. Taste to check the texture.

SORBET AUX FRAMBOISES

Raspberry sorbet

Serves 4–6
Difficulty: 🍳
Total recipe time: 20–30 minutes
Special equipment: *sorbetière,* food processor

———— INGREDIENTS ————

750 g/1¾ lb ripe raspberries, hulled and washed

200 g/7 oz caster sugar

lemon juice (optional)

Planning ahead
Place the washed, hulled raspberries in a stainless steel bowl, sprinkle with the sugar and leave for 2–3 hours for the sugar to dissolve.
Chill 4 plates in the freezer 30 minutes before serving.

1. Puréeing the raspberries
(5 minutes)
Purée in a food processor then force the pulp through a fine sieve. Taste and correct with a tiny drop of lemon juice or caster sugar, depending on the ripeness of the fruit.

2. Churning the sorbet
(15–25 minutes)
Churn in a *sorbetière* until smooth and firm.

3. Serving
Using 2 dessert spoons dipped in hot water, place the sorbet in the middle of the chilled plates and serve immediately.

PAPILLOTTE EN CROUTE AUX FRUITS D'ETE, AUX GRAINES DE SESAME ET D'OISEAUX

Summer fruits baked in a parcel of strudel pastry sprinkled with sesame and poppy seeds

Serves 4
Difficulty: ♟
Total recipe time: 50 minutes, plus 2–4 hours marinating the fruits

INGREDIENTS

2 29 x 24 cm/11½ x 9½ in sheets of strudel or filo pastry

eggwash (1 egg yolk, beaten with 1 teaspoon milk)

icing sugar for dredging

2 teaspoons each sesame and poppy seeds

4 rounds of Sponge biscuit (see page 44), 10 cm/4 in diameter, 5 mm/¼ in thick (optional)

1 teaspoon butter and 2 tablespoons caster sugar, for the baking trays

The fruits
1 ripe peach

4 red Victoria plums

2 apricots

150 g/5 oz mango

150 g/5 oz pineapple

1 large orange

20 raspberries

4 mint leaves

Marinade
200 ml/7 fl oz Sorbet syrup (see page 31)

½ teaspoon lemon juice

1 tablespoon kirsch

Planning ahead
The sponge biscuit and sorbet syrup must be made in advance.
Stages 1–3 inclusive can be completed 2 hours in advance. Keep at room temperature, ready to be baked.

1. Preparing for fruits (15 minutes, plus 2–4 hours marinating)
Combine the cold syrup, lemon juice and kirsch in a large china bowl. Boil a saucepan of water for blanching.
Peach, plums and apricots: Blanch in the boiling water for 30 seconds, refresh, peel and remove the stones.
Cut the peach into 8 segments and halve the apricots and plums.
Orange: Peel, remove the segments and squeeze the juice from the core into the sorbet syrup.
Mango: Peel, remove the stone and cut the flesh into 8 segments.
Pineapple slice: Peel, core and cut the flesh into 8 segments.
Raspberries: Wash, drain and hull. Place all the fruits in the syrup, seal with clingfilm and marinate for 2–4 hours.

2. Preparing the pastry (5 minutes)
Peel off 4 layers and cut into 27 x 21 cm/10½ x 8½ in rectangles. Using scissors, cut out four 19 cm/7½ in rounds (for the bottom layer) and four 21 cm/8½ in rounds for the top layer. Put them separately on 2 flat plates and seal with clingfilm.

3. Assembling the papillottes
(15 minutes)
Preheat the oven to 230°C/450°F/gas 8 for Stage 4.
Lightly butter 2 baking trays, sprinkle with sugar and shake off the excess.

Drain the fruits in a colander over a saucepan.
Place 2 smaller rounds of pastry side by side on each baking tray, place a round of sponge biscuit (if using) in the centre and brush lightly with syrup. Arrange the fruits in a mound on the sponge biscuit or pastry and top with a mint leaf. Brush the edges of the pastry with eggwash, then cover with the larger pastry 'lids' and firm down so that they stick together. Fold over the edges and press firmly; the parcels must be completely airtight.

4. Baking the papillottes
(5–7 minutes)
Brush the tops with eggwash, sprinkle with sesame and poppy seeds and dredge liberally with icing sugar. Bake in the bottom of the preheated oven for 5–7 minutes.

5. Serving
Prepare 4 large serving plates.
Using a large spatula, lift the puffed-up, browned and glazed *papillottes* onto the plates and serve immediately.

WINE
A spicy Gewürztraminer or Riesling *vendage tardive* has the perfect balance of fruit and freshness for this dessert.

Chef's notes
The warmth of cooking will accentuate the fruits' acidity, which is why they are marinated in the syrup.
Strudel or filo pastry can be bought in most delicatessens. Handle with care; the layers can easily tear. They also dry out easily, so work fast, especially in Stage 2. Seal them with clingfilm immediately after cutting into rounds.

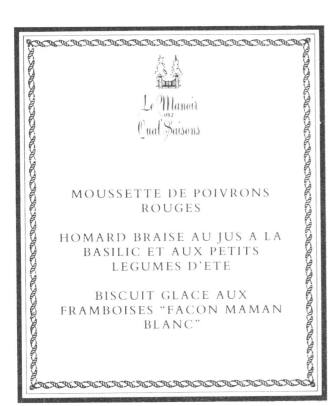

MOUSSETTE DE POIVRONS
ROUGES

HOMARD BRAISE AU JUS A LA
BASILIC ET AUX PETITS
LEGUMES D'ETE

BISCUIT GLACE AUX
FRAMBOISES "FACON MAMAN
BLANC"

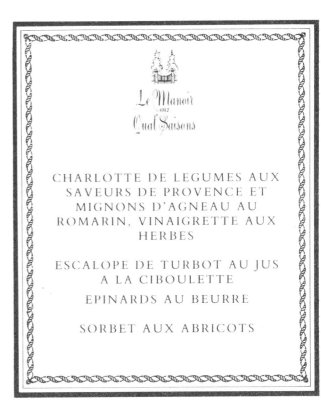

CHARLOTTE DE LEGUMES AUX
SAVEURS DE PROVENCE ET
MIGNONS D'AGNEAU AU
ROMARIN, VINAIGRETTE AUX
HERBES

ESCALOPE DE TURBOT AU JUS
A LA CIBOULETTE
EPINARDS AU BEURRE

SORBET AUX ABRICOTS

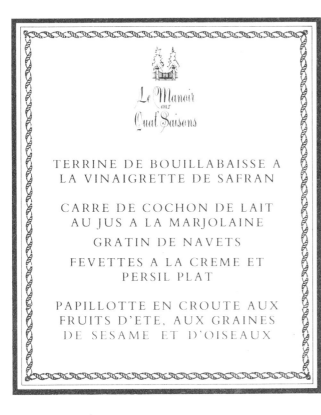

TERRINE DE BOUILLABAISSE A
LA VINAIGRETTE DE SAFRAN

CARRE DE COCHON DE LAIT
AU JUS A LA MARJOLAINE
GRATIN DE NAVETS
FEVETTES A LA CREME ET
PERSIL PLAT

PAPILLOTTE EN CROUTE AUX
FRUITS D'ETE, AUX GRAINES
DE SESAME ET D'OISEAUX

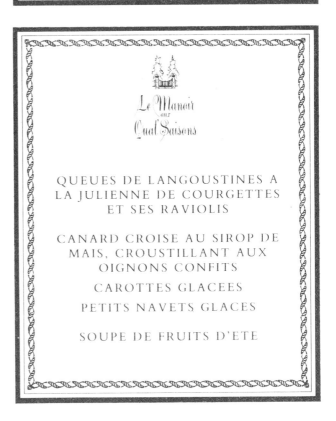

QUEUES DE LANGOUSTINES A
LA JULIENNE DE COURGETTES
ET SES RAVIOLIS

CANARD CROISE AU SIROP DE
MAIS, CROUSTILLANT AUX
OIGNONS CONFITS
CAROTTES GLACEES
PETITS NAVETS GLACES

SOUPE DE FRUITS D'ETE

Autumn

◆

Harvest time — golden colours take over the vivid display of Summer. The fruits are fully developed and ripened. Now is the time for gathering and collecting, putting aside for the scarcities of Winter. Jam making, wine making, bottling — all take full advantage of the offerings of this magnificent season. Game appears in the markets; rich, deep flavours tempt the palate.

Cooking takes on a different character too, with more powerful and rustic tastes, sauces with a hint of richness and deeper colours and flavours. Wild mushrooms and ceps accompany delicious wild partridges; deep amber vinous sauces complement the flavour of woodcock; root vegetables accompany gently simmered dishes; all in all, there is frenzied activity in the kitchen.

POTAGE DE CRESSON AU CITRON VERT

A peppery watercress soup with lime, which can be served hot or cold

Serves 4
Difficulty: 🎩
Total recipe time: 45 minutes

INGREDIENTS

400 g/14 oz watercress

3 shallots or ¼ onion, finely chopped

1 small potato

1 small leek

1 tablespoon unsalted butter

600 ml/1 pt Light chicken stock (see page 21) or water

2 tablespoons whipping cream

salt

Garnish

1 bunch of watercress

½ lime

a large pinch of caster sugar

4 tablespoons whipping cream

Planning ahead
The garnish can be prepared and the soup cooked 2 hours in advance, but only add the cream to the soup at the last moment. Cool the cooked soup on ice to preserve its vivid green colour and lively taste. To serve the soup hot, reheat it without boiling.

1. Preparing the vegetables for the soup (10 minutes)
Watercress: Trim off the bottom half of the stalks and discard, together with any weathered leaves. Wash the remainder under cold running water, drain and chop finely.
Potato: Cut into 5 mm/¼ in cubes.
Leek: Trim off the root and green top. Slice the heart lengthways, wash well and chop finely.

2. The garnish (10 minutes)
Watercress: Pick off the leaves and blanch in plenty of boiling salted water for 20 seconds. Refresh, drain and set aside.
Lime: Peel off the rind and pith with a sharp knife. Divide into segments and cut each segment into tiny triangles. Place in a bowl with a pinch of sugar. Reserve 1 teaspoon lime juice.
Cream: Whip lightly with a tiny pinch of salt. Gently fold in the reserved lime juice.

3. Cooking the soup (20 minutes)
In a medium saucepan, sweat the vegetables in the butter for 3–4 minutes. If the potato sticks, stir in 2 tablespoons water. Add the chicken stock, bring to the boil and season with a pinch of salt. When the soup is at full boil, throw in the watercress and boil for not more than 7–8 minutes.
Purée the soup in a blender until perfectly smooth. Using a ladle, force the soup through a fine conical sieve back into the pan and stir in the cream. Correct the seasoning; keep warm.

4. Serving (5 minutes)
Warm 4 soup bowls.
Warm the lime segments in a small saucepan. In another pan, warm the watercress leaves with 1 teaspoon butter, a pinch of salt and 1 tablespoon water. Pour the soup into the bowls and top with the whipped cream. Decorate with watercress leaves and lime segments and serve.

Chef's notes
Do not leave the hot soup standing for more than 10 minutes, or it will lose its colour and taste.

CREME LEGERE DE HADDOCK AUX LENTILLES

Smoked haddock soup garnished with lentils and croûtons

"It takes a Scotsman to put whisky in his soup (and a Frenchman to put red wine in his!)
Based on an old Highland recipe, this soup is just the thing for a chilly evening, even though
I have reduced the amount of whisky by a factor of 5!"

Serves 4–6
Difficulty: ♙
Total recipe time: 45 minutes
Special equipment: 2 cm/¾ in round pastry cutter

INGREDIENTS

900 g/2 lb smoked haddock fillet (preferably oak-smoked), skinned and cut into 2 cm/¾ in dice

1 small onion, chopped

2 celery stalks, chopped

1 garlic clove, crushed

20 button mushrooms, finely chopped

a large pinch of curry powder

a pinch of saffron threads or 2 sachets of saffron powder

2 tablespoons unsalted butter

150 ml/5 fl oz whisky

600 ml/1 pt milk

600 ml/1 pt Light fish stock (see page 20) or water

3 egg yolks

200 ml/7 fl oz whipping cream

lemon juice

salt and freshly ground white pepper

Garnish

100 g/3½ oz green lentils

10 g/¼ oz smoked bacon rind

3 slices of white bread

1 tablespoon of butter, melted

100 g/3½ oz smoked haddock fillet

Planning ahead

The soup and garnish can be made the day before; add the egg yolks and cream at the last moment.

If you are using saffron threads, soak them in 3 tablespoons water for at least 2 hours before using.

Pick over the lentils to remove any tiny stones and soak for at least 2 hours before using. Soaking and cooking times will vary according to the type of lentils.

1. The garnish (30 minutes)

Preheat the oven to 200°C/400°F/gas 6.

Lentils: Place in a small saucepan with 300 ml/½ pt water and the bacon rind and simmer for 30 minutes on the stove or, covered, in the oven.

Croûtons: Cut the bread into rounds, brush with melted butter, place on a baking tray and toast in the oven until golden and crisp.

Haddock: Cut into 16 cubes.

Meanwhile, make the soup.

2. The soup (15 minutes)

In a large saucepan, sweat all the chopped vegetables in the butter for 5 minutes. Add the curry powder, saffron and diced haddock and cook for a further 3 minutes, stirring from time to time. Pour in the whisky and quickly bring to the boil to reduce the alcohol. Add the milk and fish stock, bring back to the boil, skim and simmer gently for 10 minutes.

3. Completing the soup and serving (15 minutes)

Warm 4 soup plates or a tureen.

Purée the soup in a blender or food processor, then force through a fine conical sieve back into the saucepan and bring back to simmering point.

In a small saucepan, warm the cubed haddock for the garnish in 200 ml/7 fl oz soup for 3–4 minutes.

In separate bowls, whisk the egg yolks and cream, then combine them. Gently whisk in a little soup, then stir the mixture back into the saucepan of soup to enrich it. Do not let the soup boil, or the eggs will solidify. Season with pepper and a squeeze of lemon; you will need very little salt, since the haddock is already salty.

Place the lentils and haddock cubes in the bottom of the soup plates or tureen and fill up with soup. Serve the *croûtons* separately.

VARIATIONS

Replace the lentils with a *julienne* of red peppers cooked in an emulsion of butter and water.

For a lighter soup, omit the egg yolks and use only 100 ml/3½ fl oz whipping cream.

Chef's notes

If you are a Scotsman, you may prefer to use at least 3 times the given quantity of whisky; add it right at the end so that the alcohol does not evaporate!

The soup will actually serve more than 4 people, but it is best to make plenty so that you can offer a second helping.

JAMBON DE CANARD

Duck ham

Serves 4
Difficulty:
Total recipe time: 15 minutes, plus 24 hours marinating and 5–6 days drying

INGREDIENTS

2 duck breasts (total weight 250 g/ 9 oz), boned but with the skin on or 2 magrets de canard

Marinade
20 whole black peppercorns, crushed

1 teaspoon coarse salt

1 sprig of thyme

¼ bay leaf

1 small garlic clove, peeled and sliced

1 coffee spoon Cognac

a dash of red wine vinegar

Planning ahead
Once dried, the duck ham can be kept in the refrigerator for up to 15 days, wrapped in clingfilm.

1. Marinating the duck breasts
(5 minutes, plus 24 hours chilling)
Place the duck breasts, skin side down, on a small plate and sprinkle over the Cognac and a dash of red wine vinegar. Scatter over the coarse salt, crushed peppercorns and garlic slices. Place a sprig of thyme and ¼ bayleaf on top and seal with clingfilm. Refrigerate for 24 hours.

2. Drying the duck breasts
(10 minutes, plus 5–6 days drying)
Uncover and discard the thyme, bayleaf and garlic.
Wrap each duck breast in 2 layers of muslin and tie with string. Hang the duck breasts in a dry place for 10–14 days (depending on their weight and the drying conditions).

3. Slicing the duck ham and serving
Have ready 4 plates.
Unwrap the duck breasts, place them on a carving board and trim off any dried flesh and excess fat under the skin. Carve fine slices and arrange them attractively on the plates.

VARIATION
Scatter fine shavings of this ham over a dressed salad – delicious.

WINE
A light red wine – a Cru Beaujolais, eg: Côte de Brouilly, Juliénas – will make a good match.

Chef's notes
Boned duck breasts can be found in most supermarkets. Choose large ones, since there will be a substantial weight loss during drying. *Magrets de canard* are the breasts from ducks fattened for producing *foie gras*. They are very large and ideal for this duck ham.
Drying: The time will vary according to humidity, air circulation and temperature. To check if the ham is ready, pinch the middle of the breasts: they should be supple but firm.
Room conditions should be very dry, with an ambient temperature of about 16°C/60°F.
Avoid a draughty room, or the flesh will dry out completely and become crusty. If there is too much humidity, the duck breasts will turn mouldy.

SALADE DE COQUILLES ST-JACQUES ET TOPINAMBOURS A LA VINAIGRETTE PARFUMEE A L'HUILE DE NOISETTE

Scallop and Jerusalem artichoke salad dressed with a hazelnut vinaigrette

"A sound and harmonious marriage of two delicate, well-matched flavours from the sea and from the earth."

Salade de coquilles St-Jacques et topinambours à la vinaigrette parfumée à l'huile de noisette

SALADE DE COQUILLES
ST-JACQUES ET
TOPINAMBOURS (CONT.)

Serves 4
Difficulty: 🍳
Total recipe time: 50 minutes
Special equipment: steamer

─────── INGREDIENTS ───────

Scallop and artichoke salad

1 handful of mixed salad leaves (curly endive, batavia, cornsalad)

12 small radicchio leaves

8 fat Jerusalem artichokes

8 large or 12 medium scallops with their coral

1 tablespoon hazelnut oil

1 tablespoon olive oil

juice of ½ lemon

100 g/3½ oz flaked almonds

salt and freshly ground white pepper

Vinaigrette

1 tablespoon olive oil

1 teaspoon white wine vinegar

Planning ahead

Order the scallops in advance from your fishmonger.

The salads, Jerusalem artichokes and scallops can be prepared several hours in advance. You can also cook the scallops and artichokes 10 minutes before the meal; place on a small tray and cover. Heat the dressed plates just before serving.

The vinaigrette can be made 1 hour before serving; add the scallop juices at the last moment.

1. The salads (10 minutes) (see page 17)
Wash in plenty of cold water, pat dry and place in a salad bowl.
Almonds: toast under the grill.

2. Jerusalem artichokes

(15 minutes)
Fill the bottom of a steamer with salted water and put in the rack.
Peel the artichokes into smooth barrel shapes (see diagram, page 50). Cut each into 3 or 4 5 mm/¼ in rounds. Place on the steaming rack, salt lightly, cover and steam with the water at full boil for 5–8 minutes. Do not overcook, or the artichokes will become unpleasantly mushy. Place on a small tray, cover and set aside.

3. The scallops (15 minutes)

Wash the scallops, corals and shells in cold water to remove all traces of sand. Pat dry. Keep the shells for another recipe (eg: *Coquilles St-Jacques en feuilleté*, page 73).
Pierce the corals with the point of a knife so that they do not burst during cooking. Steam for 2 minutes, leave to cool, then cut into thin strips and season. Heat 1 tablespoon olive oil in a heavy-based pan, put in the corals and flash fry for a few seconds. Place on a small tray.
Cut the scallops into 5 mm/¼ in rounds and salt lightly. Heat the remaining oil in the pan you used for the corals and when it begins to smoke, toss in the scallop rounds and cook on one side only for 1 minute, until golden. Place on a tray, uncooked side down and sprinkle with lemon juice. Leave to rest for 5 minutes.

4. The vinaigrette (5 minutes)
Pour the juices released by the scallops into a bowl, add the hazelnut and olive oils and the wine vinegar. Season, adding a dash of lemon juice if necessary and mix well.

5. Serving (5 minutes)
Preheat the oven to 200°C/400°F/gas 6.
Add two-thirds of the vinaigrette to the salad, toss and season to taste. In the middle of each plate, place a small attractive mound of salad and encircle with alternating and overlapping rows of scallop (golden side up) and artichoke. Scatter over the almonds and coral and pour the remaining dressing over the artichokes and scallops. Warm the dressed plates in the oven for 15 seconds and serve tepid.

─────── WINE ───────

Don't serve a fine wine with this dish; neither the Jerusalem artichokes nor the highly flavoured vinaigrette will do a good wine any favours. However, a Gewürztraminer, itself scented and spicy, would make a lively sparring partner.

Chef's notes

Salt the scallops just before cooking, as salt draws out the juices. Leave them to rest uncooked side down, because some juices will flow out and become discoloured if they come into contact with the golden side. The corals are usually pretty tasteless when steamed, but frying gives them a delicious nutty flavour and a striking orange colour.

TERRINE DE CANARD CONFIT A LA PRESSE A LA FRICASSEE DE CEPES

Confit of duck legs and livers cooked in duck fat then pressed, served with a fricassee of ceps

Serves 8–12
Difficulty: ♟♟
Total recipe time: 4 hours, plus 12 hours marinating and 12 hours resting
Special equipment: 24 x 10 cm/10 x 4 in terrine, wooden board to fit inside, 2 kg/4½ lb weight.

INGREDIENTS

10 duck legs and thighs

1.5 L/2½ pt duck or goose fat

250 g/9 oz duck livers, galls removed

salt and freshly ground white pepper

Marinade

2 garlic cloves, peeled and crushed

2 sprigs of thyme

4 bay leaves

4 tablespoons freshly ground black pepper

100 g/3½ oz coarse salt

Garnish (optional)
300 g/11 oz ceps, shiitake or button mushrooms

1 teaspoon duck fat

1 coffee spoon walnut oil

1 teaspoon lemon juice

Planning ahead
Order duck legs and livers well in advance.
Wash and soak livers in milk for 2 hours before using.
The dish must be prepared at least 1 day in advance to allow for 12 hours marinating, plus 12 hours resting.
The terrine can be carved 1 hour before the meal.

1. Preparing the duck legs
(10 minutes plus 12 hours marinating)
Singe over an open flame to remove any stubble, rub with a cloth and arrange, closely packed, on a small stainless steel dish.
Mix the coarse salt with 2 tablespoons black pepper and scatter over the duck legs. Crumble over the thyme and bay leaves, seal the dish with clingfilm and refrigerate for at least 12 hours (but not more than 24 hours).

2. Cooking and boning the duck legs (2¼ hours cooking; 4 hours resting; 35 minutes boning)
In a large saucepan, bring the duck fat to the boil. Wipe off excess salt from the duck legs then gently simmer them in the fat for about 2 hours. Draw off the heat and leave to cool at room temperature.
Remove the duck legs, drain in a colander, peel off the skin, then detach the meat in the largest possible pieces. Taste, correct seasoning and keep the meat on a small dish. Strain the fat into another saucepan for Stage 3.

3. Preparing and cooking the livers (15 minutes)
Rinse and pat dry. Bring the duck fat just to simmering point then draw off the heat. Immerse the livers in the fat for 3 minutes then drain on absorbent paper. Season with 1 turn of black pepper and leave to rest for about 2 minutes.

4. Building the terrine
(35 minutes plus 12 hours resting)
Line the terrine mould with foil or clingfilm, leaving a 10 cm/4 in overhang all round. One-third fill with the duck meat, add all the livers and top with the remaining meat, packing

each layer down firmly as you go. Fold over the foil and compress the terrine with the wooden board and 2 kg/4½ lb weight. Refrigerate for at least 12 hours.

5. Preparing the garnish
(10 minutes)
Ceps: Trim the base, peel the stalks and gently rub off any dirt on the caps with a damp cloth. Slice finely, season with a pinch of salt and a few turns of white pepper then sauté in a little duck fat for 1 minute. Draw off the heat, add the walnut oil and lemon juice and keep warm.

6. Carving the terrine and serving
(5 minutes)
Remove the weight and wood, tap the bottom of the terrine to loosen it, then ease it out and peel off the foil. Carve 1 cm/½ in slices with a sharp serrated knife, using little or no pressure so as not to disturb the fragile layers.
Arrange a slice in the middle of each plate, scatter over the mushrooms (which should be tepid) and serve.

WINE
A spicy Tokay d'Alsace (Pinot Gris) Réserve will complement this full-flavoured terrine perfectly.

Chef's notes
Duck fat can be collected whenever you cook a duck; store it in the freezer. You can also buy it from specialized gourmet shops (see page 274).
Cooking the livers: In order for the livers to remain moist and pink they must not be cooked in boiling fat.
Building the terrine: It is very important to pack each layer down firmly, as there is no binding element in the terrine.

MOSAIQUE DE GIBIERS AUX NOISETTES ET CHAMPIGNONS SAUVAGES

Terrine of fillets of venison, teal, pigeon and pheasant, wrapped in a mousse of their own livers, studded with wild mushrooms and hazelnuts

Serves 10–12
Difficulty: 🎩 🎩 🎩
Total recipe time: 2 hours, plus 12 hours marinating the game and 24 hours resting the terrine
Special equipment: 24 x 10 cm/10 x 4 in terrine, wooden board to fit inside, 1 kg/2¼ lb weight, food processor

INGREDIENTS

1 young pheasant (1 kg/2¼ lb) or 2 boned pheasant breasts (175 g/6 oz each)

2 teal or 1 mallard

2 wood pigeons

175 g/6 oz fillet of venison

8 thin slices of pork back fat (25 g/1 oz each)

Marinade

100 ml/3½ fl oz ruby port

2 tablespoons Cognac

1 sprig of thyme

½ bayleaf

1 teaspoon freshly ground white pepper

7 juniper berries, finely crushed

5 x 2 cm/1 x ½ in strip of dried orange zest (see page 49), ground

Mousse

3 medium shallots

1 garlic clove

a pinch of dried thyme

50 ml/2 fl oz ruby port

2 fl oz dry Madeira

2 tablespoons Cognac

85 g/3 oz chicken livers

40 g/1½ oz each teal and pheasant livers

125 g/4½ oz unsalted butter

2 small eggs

salt and freshly ground white pepper

For studding the terrine

125 g/4½ oz wild mushrooms (ceps, girolles, trumpets of death)

1 teaspoon sunflower oil

25 g/1 oz hazelnuts (about 30)

20 g/¾ oz flaked almonds

Garnish

2 apples

a little icing sugar

1 tablespoon unsalted butter

100 g/3½ oz fresh cranberries

2 tablespoons caster sugar

toasted bread or pain brioche, to serve

Planning ahead
Order fresh chicken livers and all the game well in advance. Ask your butcher to pluck and draw the game birds, to give you the livers (gall removed) and to bone out the breasts. You will not need the carcasses and legs in this recipe but keep them for another use (soups, stocks, sauces).
The terrine must be made 1–3 days before serving.

1. Preparing and marinating the game (15 minutes, plus 12 hours marinating)
Mix together all the marinade ingredients in a small casserole. Skin the pheasant, teal and pigeon breasts.
Venison: Using a sharp paring knife, remove the sinews.

Place all the meats in the marinade, turning them over, cover with clingfilm and refrigerate for about 12 hours. Turn once again during the marinating.
Meanwhile, prepare the mousse.

2. Preparing the mousse
(40 minutes)
All livers: Place under running water for 30 minutes, drain and pat dry.
Shallots: Peel and chop finely.
Garlic: Peel, halve, finely chop one half and reserve the other half for sautéeing the mushrooms (Stage 3).
In a small saucepan, slowly melt the butter.
Place the shallots and chopped garlic in another small saucepan with a pinch of thyme, the Madeira, port, Cognac, a large pinch of salt and 4 turns of pepper. Bring to the boil, reduce by half then sieve and cool.
Purée, add the livers and process until the mixture is completely smooth, then add the eggs. Force the mousse mixture through a conical sieve then whisk in the reduced alcohol and melted butter and refrigerate.

3. Preparing and cooking the wild mushrooms; toasting the hazelnuts and almonds (20 minutes)
Wild mushrooms: Trim the bases, scrape the stalks, wipe caps clean with a damp cloth and slice thickly. Rub the bottom of a non-stick sauté pan with a face of garlic, heat the oil and fry the mushrooms for 30 seconds, seasoned with a pinch of salt and pepper.
Hazelnuts: Toast under the grill for 3–4 minutes, place in a tea towel and rub off the skins.
Almonds: Toast under the grill for 1 minute until pale golden.

4. Building the terrine
(15 minutes)
Preheat the oven to 150°C/300°F/gas 2.
Pheasant breasts: Cut into 3 lengthways.

Teal and pigeon breasts: Halve lengthways.
Venison: Cut lengthways into 4 strips.
Wrap the strips of teal, pigeon and venison in the back fat.
Line the terrine first with clingfilm then with back fat, leaving enough overhanging to wrap the terrine once assembled.
Line the base of the terrine with a layer of mousse mixture, then build up layers of game fillets, mousse, wild mushrooms, hazelnuts and almonds. Fold back the overhanging back fat and seal with clingfilm.

5. Cooking the terrine and resting
(1 hour 20 minutes cooking;
2 hours resting; 24 hours to settle)
Place the terrine in a deep roasting pan lined with greaseproof paper, half-fill with hot water and cook in the pre-heated oven for 1 hour 20 minutes.
Remove and leave the terrine to rest for 2 hours at room temperature. Settle the wooden board inside the terrine, weight it with a 1 kg/2¼ lb weight and refrigerate for at least 24 hours.

6. Preparing and cooking the garnish (10 minutes)
Apples: Peel, quarter and slice finely. Place on a lightly buttered baking tray, brush with 1 tablespoon melted butter, dust with a little icing sugar and place under the grill for a few minutes to caramelize.
Cranberries: In small saucepan, bring to the boil 1 tablespoon water with 2 tablespoons caster sugar, then reduce heat to just below simmering point. Gently cook the cranberries for about 5 minutes, cool and set aside.

7. Carving the terrine and serving
(5 minutes)
Tap the bottom of the terrine on your work surface to loosen it, then turn out onto a carving board. With a sharp serrated knife, using little or no pressure, carve into 1 cm/½ in slices and arrange one slice in the middle of each

plate. Top each with 2 caramelized apple 'leaves' and put 2 or 3 cranberries in the middle to resemble a sprig of holly.
Serve with toasted bread or *pain brioche*.

—————— VARIATIONS ——————
Other game (eg: woodcock or partridge) can be used.
Scatter cooked cranberries in the terrine to provide some additional colour and acidity.
Line the bottom of the terrine with a Sauternes jelly (see page 23).
This dish will be even better if allowed to rest for 2 days before serving.

—————— WINE ——————
Try a white Rhône wine, like Condrieu – a complex, spicy and flowery wine with a long aftertaste.

Chef's notes
Pheasant must have been hung for about 1 week for its flavour to develop. For other game, 1–3 days hanging will be quite sufficient.
Cooking the terrine: After 1 hour 20 minutes, check if the terrine is cooked: insert a trussing needle into the centre, wait 3 seconds then withdraw and test with your tongue. The needle should be warm and dry.

TERRINE DE FOIE GRAS

Fattened duck or goose liver

"*Foie gras* is one of the jewels in the crown of French cuisine. I thought that Le Manoir's grounds would be the perfect setting for producing this magical delicacy.
However, I discovered that the practice of fattening ducks and geese is forbidden in England – something of a hypocrisy, since the authorities seem to have no qualms about battery farming, or rearing pigs under ultra-violet light in crowded conditions.
Still, at least we can continue to import *foie gras*, and savour it made into that dramatic pink marbled paté, or simply cut into slivers and quickly pan-fried, served with *brioche* or a salad."

Foie gras is produced in many countries – Czechoslovakia, Hungary, Israel, France . . . and of course, every country claims that theirs is the best!
The best season for French *foie gras* is from October to March. See page 274 for where to buy it in England.
Raw *foie gras* should be off-white or delicate pink in colour and there should be no greying or yellowing.
Duck livers should weigh 600–800 g/ 1 ¼ – 1 ¾ lb. A good test of quality is to take hold of the top of one of the lobes (at room temperature) and pull apart: the *foie gras* should stretch slightly, with little resistance, then crack open. Unfortunately, few suppliers are likely to let you do this! I'm afraid the next assessment must take place during the cooking and eating.
Goose liver: traditionally the most commonly used in France, but recently somewhat out of favour. The ideal weight is 1.2–2 kg/2½–4 lb.

Serves 12
Difficulty: 🎩
Total recipe time: 1 hour 50 minutes, plus 2–3 days resting
Special equipment: 23 x 9 x 8 cm/ 9 x 3½ x 3 in terrine, wooden board to fit inside, 1 kg/2¼ lb weight, thermometer

—————— INGREDIENTS ——————
2 575 g/1½ lb raw duck foie gras

Marinade
2 teaspoons salt
1 coffee spoon ground white pepper
a pinch of mace
a large pinch of caster sugar
½ tablespoon each ruby port, aged dry Madeira and Cognac

Madeira or Sauternes jelly, to garnish (see page 23) (optional)

Planning ahead
Order the *foie gras* well in advance and ensure it is at room temperature before cleaning.
Madeira or Sauternes jelly, if used, must be made 1 day in advance.
The terrine must be prepared and cooked at least 2 days before serving for the flavours to mature.

1. Preparing the foie gras
(20 minutes, plus 6 hours soaking)
Place the *foie gras* on a chopping board lined with a tea towel and separate the lobes. With a sharp paring knife, cut off all traces of green left by the gall bladder and peel off the thin membrane wrapping the livers.
Slice the 4 lobes widthways to reveal all the tiny nerves and veins which must be removed. With the point of your knife, loosen them from the top and, working downwards, pull them away (you will have to cut quite deep

into the livers to remove this network of veins).

Plunge the livers into a large bowl with 2 L/3½ pt iced water (with plenty of ice) and 1 tablespoon salt and refrigerate for 3–4 hours.

2. Marinating the foie gras; building the terrine (10 minutes, plus 1 hour resting)

Drain the livers and pat dry. Place on a tray and open up the lobes.

In a small bowl, mix together the salt, pepper, mace and sugar. Sprinkle the mixture over the livers, inside and out.

Mix together the Madeira, port and Cognac, and drizzle over the livers. Close the livers back into shape. Place one large lobe in the bottom of the terrine, press it down, cover with the two smaller lobes and top with the second large lobe. Press down again. The livers should come about 1 cm/½ in above the top of the terrine; they will subside during cooking. Seal with clingfilm and leave to marinate in the fridge for 1 hour.

3. Cooking the terrine (1 hour 20 minutes, plus 2–3 days resting)

Preheat the oven to 110°C/225°F/gas ¼.

Line the bottom of a deep roasting pan with 3 or 4 sheets of newspaper. Fill with water to a depth of 5 cm/2 in. Place over medium heat and heat to exactly 70°C/158°F (you will need a thermometer). Put in the terrine, leaving on the clingfilm and cook in the preheated oven for 1 hour 20 minutes.

Remove and leave to cool at room temperature for 30 minutes.

Press the board onto the terrine, pour the excess fat and liquid into a bowl and refrigerate it for about 1 hour.

Place a 1 kg/2¼ lb weight on the board and refrigerate the terrine for 6 hours.

Remove the weight and board. Melt the reserved clarified fat and pour over the terrine to seal. Refrigerate for at least 16 hours.

4. Serving

Have ready 12 plates.

Dip the terrine into hot water for a few seconds then invert onto a chopping board. Cut into 12 equal slices, using a sharp serrated knife dipped in hot water. Place one slice in the middle of each plate and scatter around diced cubes of Madeira or Sauternes jelly, if you like.

— VARIATIONS —

Slide a few fresh ceps or shiitake mushrooms into the middle of the terrine; cut into 3 mm/⅛ in slices, lightly pan-fry, season, pat dry and cool slightly before using.

— WINE —

Each French region will recommend its own wine to accompany *foie gras*! Try a Tokay from Alsace, a Sauternes or a Jurançon *doux*.

Chef's notes

Foie gras: The quality of the liver determines the quality of the dish. See page 172 for more information.

Removing the nerves: This will be easier if the livers are soaked in iced water to dilute and remove any traces of blood. Remaining *foie gras* fat can be used for frying, in vinaigrettes or for *Terrine de foie gras aux truffes et jeunes poireaux confits* (page 225).

Cooking the terrine: Follow the cooking instructions precisely. If the temperature is too low, the terrine will not cook through; if too hot, the *foie gras* will overcook, shrink and discolour. Check the temperatures of your oven and the bain-marie with a thermometer.

Leave the terrine for at least 2 or 3 days so that the flavours can develop and mature.

MILLEFEUILLE DE POMMES DE TERRE ET NAVETS AU FOIE GRAS ET GIROLLES

Slivers of foie gras sandwiched between layers of crispy potatoes and turnips, garnished with wild mushrooms

"A dish rich with many flavours and textures, whose charm is heightened by the contrasting backgrounds of the main ingredients – the rustic potato and turnip and the noble *foie gras*. A great dish for a chilly Autumn night. If it looks too daunting, come and enjoy it at Le Manoir!"

Millefeuille de pommes de terre et navets au foie gras et girolles

Serves 4
Difficulty: 👨‍🍳 👨‍🍳 👨‍🍳
Total recipe time: 1 hour 5 minutes
Special equipment: grater or mandoline, fine conical sieve, colander, 7.5 cm/3 in pastry cutter, large heavy-bottomed frying pan.

────── INGREDIENTS ──────

Sauce
120 g/4 oz button mushrooms

1 tablespoon non-scented oil

6 shallots

1 teaspoon unsalted butter

50 ml/2 fl oz sherry vinegar

50 ml/2 fl oz ruby port

50 ml/2 fl oz dry Madeira

1 teaspoon old Amontillado sherry (optional)

a pinch of dried cep powder (optional)

200 ml/7 fl oz Veal stock (see page 18)

100 ml/3½ fl oz Light chicken stock (see page 21) or water

2 tablespoons whipping cream (optional)

1 sprig of thyme

1 strip of orange peel

Millefeuilles
500 g/1 lb 2 oz potatoes

120 g/4 oz small turnips

80 g/3 oz unsalted butter, melted

200 g/7 oz fresh foie gras

salt and freshly ground white pepper

Garnish
12 shallots

20 g/¾ oz unsalted butter

3 tablespoons water

caster sugar

a handful of chanterelles, ceps, morels, oyster or button mushrooms

a squeeze of lemon

4 or 5 tarragon leaves

a small bunch of chervil, washed

¼ truffle, sliced (optional)

Planning ahead
Stages 1 – 3 inclusive can be completed 1 hour in advance.
The *foie gras* can be cooked 15 minutes in advance and kept warm.
The chanterelles, tarragon and chervil for the garnish can be prepared in advance, but must be cooked only at the last moment.

1. The sauce (20 minutes) (see Savoury sauces, page 26)
Mushrooms: Wash, pat dry and chop finely. Sauté in 1 tablespoon hot oil to colour lightly. Keep aside.
6 shallots: Peel and chop finely. In another sauté pan, sweat in 1 teaspoon butter until they turn an attractive rusty colour. Deglaze with the sherry vinegar and allow it to evaporate completely before adding the port, Madeira, sherry and cep powder, if using, and finally the sautéed mushrooms. Reduce by two-thirds, skimming from time to time. Add the veal and chicken stock and stir in the cream, if using. Throw in the thyme and orange peel and bring to the boil. Skim and force through a fine conical sieve into a small saucepan. You should be left with about 200 ml/7 fl oz sauce. Taste and season as necessary; if too sharp whisk in 2 teaspoons cold diced butter and a pinch of caster sugar. If too bland, add a dash of vinegar. Stir in 2 tablespoons water to prevent a skin from forming and set aside.

2. Preparing and cooking the shallots (25 minutes)
Preheat the oven to 180°C/350°F/gas 4.
Peel the 12 shallots, put them in a small saucepan with 6 tablespoons water, 1 teaspoon butter and a pinch of salt and caster sugar, cover and cook in the preheated oven for 20 minutes, until soft and melting. Place the pan over a strong heat and reduce the cooking juices until the shallots colour and caramelize. Set aside.
Meanwhile, prepare the *galettes*.

3. The galettes (40 minutes)
Lower the oven temperature to 150°C/300°F/gas 2.
Potatoes: Wash, peel and grate finely. Place in a colander and rinse under cold running water. Drain, wrap in a tea towel and squeeze out as much water as you can. Put them in a mixing bowl.
Turnips: Wash, peel and grate. Mix in with the grated potato and season with a large pinch of salt and 3 pinches of pepper. Pour over 60 g/2 ½ oz melted butter and stir thoroughly so that the vegetables are well coated with butter to prevent sticking during cooking.
Brush the bottom of a large non-stick frying pan with melted butter, sit the pastry cutter inside and drop in a small amount of potato and turnip mixture, firming it down gently with your fingertips. Cook for about 1 minute until crisp, then lift off the pastry cutter, carefully turn over the *galette* and cook until crisp and golden. Make 12 *galettes* in this way. Place on a wire cooling rack and dry in the oven for 5 minutes to remove excess fat. The *galettes* can now be stored for up to 2 hours. Keep at room temperature.

4. Preparing and cooking the foie gras (2 minutes, plus resting time)
Using a sharp knife dipped in hot water, cut the *foie gras* into four small slices and season lightly. Place a heavy-bottomed sauté pan over strong heat (with no fat – the *foie gras* has plenty of its own) and when really hot toss in the *foie gras* and fry for 10 seconds. It will puff up, sizzle and smoke – don't panic; this is normal! Turn over the slices and cook for another 10 seconds, until golden

brown. Place on a small tray and leave to rest in a warm place.

5. Completing the garnish
(10 minutes)

Mushrooms: Using a paring knife, gently scrape off the skin and trim the stalks. Dip briefly into cold water to remove all traces of dirt and carefully pat dry with a tea towel. Cut the larger mushrooms so that they are all the same size.

Fry in 1 teaspoon of warm butter for 1 minute with a pinch of salt, a squeeze of lemon and the chopped tarragon. Taste, correct seasoning and set aside.

6. Dressing and serving the dish
(10 minutes)

Heat 4 plates.

Separately warm the *foie gras, galettes,* shallots and wild mushrooms in the oven for 1 minute.

Place the *foie gras* on absorbent paper to remove excess fat. Cut each slice into 4 slivers. Arrange a *galette* in the centre of each plate, top with 2 slivers of *foie gras,* then another *galette,* 2 more slivers of *foie gras* and finish with a crispy *galette* to complete the *millefeuilles.* Pour the sauce over the caramelized shallots and bring to the boil. If you are using sliced truffle, add it now. Pour the sauce around the *millefeuilles,* allowing 3 shallots for each guest. Garnish with the wild mushrooms and place a sprig of chervil on the top of the *millefeuilles.* Serve immediately.

---VARIATIONS---

To enhance the garnish, soak some small turnips in cooked port and soy sauce for 3 or 4 hours, then bring to the boil in 1 teaspoon butter and reduce until they turn a deep glossy red. You can use dried ceps or morels; cut in half and soak in cold water for 3 hours, changing the water 2 or 3 times. As a last resort, use button mushrooms instead of wild mushrooms.

Calves', duck or chicken livers can replace the *foie gras;* garnish the dish with *lardons* (see page 47).

---WINE---

Claret lovers can try a mature, mellow Bordeaux from St Julien, Margaux or St Estèphe. For the Burgundy enthusiast, an equally round, but lighter style of wine from the Côte de Beaune will do well. A more original partner for this dish might be a young Sauternes, Barsac or Montbazillac – but make sure your guests are also adventurous!

Chef's notes

Shallots: Remove the tough, fibrous second layer of skin.

Potatoes: The variety you choose will greatly affect the quality of the dish. Old potatoes such as Bintje, King Edward and Desirée are the best. Do not wash new potatoes after grating, since they contain just enough starch to bind the trellis of potatoes; squeeze out excess water in a tea towel.

Foie gras: If you have any left over, sprinkle with port and brandy (to prevent oxidization and fermentation) and wrap tightly in clingfilm. It will keep for 1 – 2 days.

Resting the foie gras: The *foie gras* will still be very rare at this stage; resting in a warm place allows it to cook very gently to medium rare. Be careful not to overcook it, or the wonderful silky texture will be lost and you will end up with nasty thick greyish pieces of liver.

Tarragon: Blanch older tarragon in boiling water for 3 seconds, then refresh to remove coarseness.

The millefeuille: If 1 large pinch of salt seems too little for the quantity of potatoes, remember that 90% of their weight is water which will evaporate during cooking, so too much salt will ruin the dish. The wafer-thin layers of potato and turnip must become very crisp in order to highlight the contrast between these and the soft, mellow *foie gras.*

CEPES FARCIS AUX ESCARGOTS ET FUMET DE VIN ROUGE

*Ceps filled with snails and chicken mousse, served with a
red wine sauce*

"We always hear about the ceps from Périgord and other parts of France – but what about those from Oxfordshire, the New Forest and Scotland? They do exist, and are just as meaty and tasty, but for some reason only visiting Hungarians or Germans bother to pick them! Apart from the canny Scots, who have walked over these mushrooms for years, we in Britain have not yet realized the gastronomic potential of this freely available local produce. By placing advertisements in the local paper, I find that keen-eyed neighbouring ramblers often bring me baskets full of fat, healthy ceps nestled on a bed of autumn leaves and deep green bracken. What an offering!"

Serves 4
Difficulty: 🎩 🎩 🎩
Total recipe time: 1 hour 30 minutes, plus 30 minutes freezing
Special equipment: fine conical sieve, piping bag with a 1 cm/½ in nozzle (optional), apple corer

INGREDIENTS

8 medium or 12 small ceps or 12 large firm button mushrooms

½ clove garlic

2 tablespoons olive oil

eggwash (1 egg yolk, beaten with 1 tablespoon water)

Mousse

125 g/4 oz cooked chicken breast

1 egg yolk

100 g/3½ oz unsalted butter, softened

1 shallot, finely chopped

½ medium fennel bulb, peeled and finely diced

12 snails, prepared

250 ml/9 fl oz whipping cream, well chilled

1–2 drops Pernod

salt and freshly ground white pepper

Breadcrumbs

50 g/2 oz dried breadcrumbs

15 g/½ oz parsley, finely chopped

10 flaked almonds, toasted and ground

½ clove garlic, finely chopped

1 teaspoon hazelnut oil

Sauce

4 shallots, finely chopped

1 teaspoon unsalted butter

250 ml/9 fl oz good red Rhône wine

100 ml/3½ fl oz Veal stock (see page 18)

1 sprig of thyme

¼ garlic clove

6 tarragon leaves, chopped

20 g/¾ oz unsalted butter, chilled and diced

Planning ahead

The mousse and breadcrumbs can be prepared several hours in advance.
You can prepare the sauce about 1 hour ahead, but only whisk in the butter at the last moment.

1. The Mousse (30 minutes)
(see Mousse making, page 36)
Chicken breast: Purée in a food processor until smooth. Add 1 level teaspoon salt, the egg yolk and 80 g/3 oz softened butter and process until the butter is completely amalgamated. Place in the freezer for 15 minutes, or refrigerate for 30 minutes.
Shallot and fennel: Sweat in the remaining butter for 1 minute. Set aside.
Snails: Wash in a colander under cold running water. Pat dry and season. Heat 1 tablespoon butter until foaming, then add the snails and sauté for not more than 1–2 minutes. Leave to cool.
Slice 9 snails lengthways and reserve for garnish. Cut the remaining 3 snails into small dice and add to the shallot and fennel.
Take the mousse mixture from the freezer, return the bowl to the food processor and, with the motor running, add the chilled cream in a steady trickle. Add a drop or two of Pernod (not too much) and season to taste. Rub through a fine sieve into a separate mixing bowl and, with a wooden spoon, mix in the shallot, fennel and diced snails. Place in the fridge.

TOP LEFT

Poire pochée au vin de St Émilion, framboises et figues (page 209)

TOP RIGHT

Perdreau rôti au jus à l'embeurrée de jeunes choux (page 203)

BOTTOM

Cèpes farcis aux escargots et fumet de vin rouge (page 177)

2. The breadcrumbs (10 minutes)
Mix together the breadcrumbs, parsley, ground almonds and garlic, then add the hazelnut oil and mix until the texture is sandy. Set aside.

3. The ceps (30 minutes, plus 30 minutes freezing)
Rub with a damp cloth to remove dirt or small leaves. Remove the stalks and chop these roughly, reserving one-quarter for the sauce. If you are using button mushrooms, reserve all the stalks. With an apple corer, gouge out a little flesh from inside the cap of the ceps to make a space for the mousse.
Rub a medium sauté pan with the garlic. Heat the olive oil until almost smoking, then throw in the cep caps, season and sauté for 1 minute only – just enough to seal them. Place upside down on kitchen paper and leave until cold. Fill the caps generously with mousse, using a teaspoon or the piping bag. Place in the freezer to harden for 30 minutes.

4. The sauce (10 minutes) (see Savoury sauces, page 26)
In a medium saucepan, sweat the

shallots in the butter until soft but not coloured. Throw in the chopped cep or mushroom stalks, then pour in the wine and reduce by two-thirds. Add the veal stock, thyme, garlic and chopped tarragon and bring back to the boil. Reduce until the sauce is shiny and well textured. Strain through a fine conical sieve into a small pan and, just before serving, whisk in the cold diced butter and adjust the seasoning.

5. Cooking and serving (20 minutes)
Preheat the oven to 190°C/375°F/gas 5.
Take the ceps from the freezer and brush the exposed mousse with the eggwash. Roll in the breadcrumbs and place in a buttered roasting pan. Cook for 10–15 minutes, depending on the size of the ceps.
Warm the snails and 4 plates. Place the ceps in the centre of the plates, pour the sauce around them and garnish with snails. Serve immediately.

——— VARIATIONS ———
If you do not like snails, omit them and garnish the dish with *lardons* (see page 47) and/or roast shallots.

——— WINE ———
The choice is quite open, provided it is red. The dish can withstand a robust wine, such as a 6- or 7-year-old Cahors or Madiran, but if you prefer something lighter, a younger Bergerac would be less dominating and most appropriate, since it comes from the Périgord – the 'cep capital' of France.

Chef's notes
Keep the fennel peelings and spare cep stalks and dry them to use in other sauces.
Do not use cheap plonk for the sauce, or it will retain these characteristics. Use a good table wine or, better still, some of the wine you have chosen for the meal.

COQUILLES ST-JACQUES AU BEURRE DE GINGEMBRE

Scallops poached in a ginger-scented juice

Serves 4
Difficulty 🎩🎩
Total recipe time: 1 hour 15 minutes

——— INGREDIENTS ———
16 large scallops

Garnish
¼ medium cucumber

1 medium courgette

1 tablespoon unsalted butter

salt

Sauce
2 shallots, peeled and finely chopped

6 coriander leaves, washed and finely shredded

25 g/1 oz ginger root

juice of ½ lemon

1 tablespoon unsalted butter

100 ml/3½ fl oz Noilly Prat

200 ml/7 fl oz Nage de légumes (see page 22)

2 teaspoons whipping cream

60 g/2½ oz unsalted butter, chilled and diced

a squeeze of lemon

a pinch of caster sugar

salt and freshly ground white pepper

Planning ahead
Order the scallops well in advance and ask your fishmonger to open them for you. Keep the shells to use in other recipes.
The *nage de légumes* must be prepared in advance.
Stages 1–3 can be prepared in advance, but the scallops, sauce and garnish must be cooked only at the last moment.

1. Preparing the scallops
(5 minutes)
Wash under plenty of cold running water to remove any traces of sand. Drain in a colander, then cut each scallop into 2 or 3 rounds. Chill.

2. Preparing the garnish
(10 minutes)
Cucumber: Wash, peel, halve and deseed with a teaspoon. Cut each half lengthways into 3, then cut into small sticks and shape with a sharp paring knife (see page 50). Place on a large freezer-proof plate, salt lightly and place in the freezer for 1 hour.
Courgette: Wash, trim and slice diagonally or cut into small sticks and shape with a sharp paring knife.

3. Preparing the ginger for the sauce (25 minutes)
Peel with a sharp knife and reserve the peelings for the sauce. Cut the root into fine sticks and blanch for 5 minutes in 1 L/1¾ pt boiling water

acidulated with lemon juice. Change the water and repeat, blanching the ginger for 15 minutes in all. Refresh and set aside.

4. Cooking the garnish
(5 minutes)
Cucumber: Remove from the freezer and place in a colander. Run under cold water to defrost and remove excess salt.
Courgettes: In a small saucepan bring to the boil 4 tablespoons water with 1 tablespoon butter, a pinch of salt and 2 turns of pepper. Cook the courgettes for 2–3 minutes until nicely glazed. Throw in the cucumber at the last moment to warm through.

5. Poaching the scallops and
making the sauce (30 minutes)
In a large sauté pan, sweat the shallots in 1 tablespoon butter for 2–3 minutes without colouring. Deglaze with the Noilly Prat and reduce by half. Add the vegetable *nage*, throw in the ginger peelings and simmer for 2 minutes.
Strain the ginger-scented stock into another saucepan, put in the scallops and poach gently for 2 minutes without boiling. Cover and leave to rest for a further 2 minutes.
To complete the sauce, strain the juices into a small saucepan and reduce by one-third. Stir in the cream, add the shredded coriander, then whisk in the cold diced butter. Towards the end, add the ginger *julienne*. Taste, season with salt, pepper and a pinch of sugar and enliven the sauce with a squeeze of lemon.

Serving
Warm 4 soup plates.
Place a mound of scallops in the centre of the plates, scatter with the warmed courgette and cucumber and pour the sauce over. Serve at once.

--- VARIATIONS ---

Small fillets of sole, turbot or salmon can be used instead of or in addition to the scallops for an even more colourful and lively dish.
Queen scallops can replace the scallops.
Blanched lemon zests would make a nice addition to the sauce.
Use basil instead of coriander.

--- WINE ---

Serve a clean, light, refreshing dry white. Try one of the lesser-known wines from the Loire – Reuilly blanc, or its neighbour Quincy.

Chef's notes
Scallops: The success of this dish depends upon the quality and freshness of the scallops. If you cannot find fresh ones, do not attempt this recipe. As poached coral has a rather uninteresting flavour, I do not use it in this dish. It can, however, be used as a garnish; blanch, cut into small strips and pan-fry in hot olive oil.
Ginger must be blanched twice for two reasons: to tenderize the fibrous texture and to temper its fierce flavour. Check by tasting. The large quantity of water is necessary to disperse the flavour. If only a small amount of water is used, the excess flavour cannot escape and will be reabsorbed.
Poaching the scallops: Boiling will shrink and toughen the scallops; just bring the stock to simmering point, then turn off the heat and allow residual heat to complete the cooking.

SOUFFLE AU FROMAGE DE CHEVRE, SALADE A L'HUILE DE NOISETTES

Twice-baked soufflés of goat's cheese served with hazelnut-scented vinaigrette

Serves 4
Difficulty: 🎩🎩
Total recipe time: 55 minutes
Special equipment: four 10 x 5 cm/ 4 x 2 in ramekins, food processor

--- INGREDIENTS ---

Béchamel
10 g/⅓ oz plain white flour

10 g/⅓ oz unsalted butter

65 ml/2½ fl oz milk

1 egg yolk

40 g/1½ oz goat's cheese, (St Estèphe, Cabecou) puréed or creamed

For lining the ramekins
1 tablespoon unsalted butter, creamed, at room temperature

50 g/2 oz dried white bread, without crusts

20 hazelnuts

For completing the soufflés
4 egg whites

a pinch of salt

1 coffee spoon lemon juice

40 g/1½ oz goat's cheese, chilled and diced

salt and freshly ground white pepper

Garnish

2 handfuls of mixed salads (eg: curly endive, cornsalad), washed and trimmed (see page 18)

3 tablespoons Hazelnut vinaigrette (see page 29)

1 teaspoon non-scented oil, for greasing

Planning ahead

Stages 1–3 inclusive can be completed up to 1 day in advance.

Refrigerate the soufflés on a lightly oiled stainless steel tray and seal with clingfilm. Keep at room temperature for 1 hour before their second cooking.

1. Preparing the breadcrumbs; lining the ramekins (15 minutes)

Preheat the oven to 230°C/450°F/gas 8 or turn on the grill.

Hazelnuts: Toast in the hot oven or under the grill for 5 minutes, turning occasionally. Rub in a cloth to remove the skins and cool.

Dried bread: Grind in a food processor with the hazelnuts. Liberally butter the bottom and sides of the ramekins and coat with a generous layer of hazelnut breadcrumbs.

Reduce the oven temperature to 180°C/350°F/gas 4 for Stage 3.

2. Preparing the soufflé mixture (10 minutes)

Béchamel sauce: In a small saucepan, bring the milk to the boil then immediately draw off the heat.

In another saucepan, slowly melt the butter then stir in the flour and cook for about 5 minutes until blonde. Slowly add the milk, stirring constantly to prevent lumps, then bring to the boil and simmer for 1 minute, stirring all the time. Draw off the heat and mix in the egg yolk and creamed goat's cheese. Set aside.

In a large mixing bowl beat, the egg whites to a light peak with a pinch of salt, then add the lemon juice and continue whisking until the mixture is smooth and stiff.

Thoroughly mix one-fifth of the beaten egg white into the base mixture to lighten it and ease the incorporation of the remaining egg white. Delicately fold in the remaining egg white until well blended, taste and correct seasoning (remember that when cooked, the flavours will be intensified).

Half-fill the ramekins with the soufflé mixture, sprinkle the diced goat's cheese in the middle, then cover with the remaining mixture and smooth the surface with a spatula. Run your thumb around the inside edge of the ramekins so that the soufflés can rise slightly without spilling over.

3. First baking of the soufflés

(7–8 minutes plus 20 minutes resting) Place the ramekins in a shallow roasting tin, pour in 1 cm/½ in hot water and bake in the preheated oven for 7–8 minutes. Leave to cool for about 10 minutes, then shake the ramekins sideways to loosen the soufflés and turn them out carefully onto a lightly oiled pastry tray. Leave to cool for at least 10 more minutes.

4. Second baking of the soufflés

(5 minutes) Return the soufflés to the hot oven or place under the grill for 5 minutes to give them a delicious crust.

5. Assembling the dish and serving

During the second cooking of the soufflés, toss the salads in the hazelnut vinaigrette, taste, correct seasoning then arrange in a circle on the plates. Place the little soufflés in the centre of the plates and serve warm.

VARIATIONS

The dish can be made with any cheese which has a strong, distinctive flavour.

For a simpler dish, serve the soufflés in the ramekins after their first cooking and omit the salads.

WINE

A Loire wine suits this dish perfectly. Try a Savennières 'Clos du Papillon', Reuilly or Muscadet *sur lie*.

Chef's notes

Goat's cheese: It is now possible to find many varieties of home-produced goat's cheese in England. You must use a mature cheese with a strong scent rather than a fresh one.

Béchamel: Cook the *roux* until blonde to to give it a lovely nutty taste. Add the milk a little at a time, whisking continuously to prevent lumps from forming.

Beating the egg white: The lemon juice will help coagulation and prevent the egg white from graining and will intensify the flavour.

Unlike most soufflés, here the egg white is beaten stiffly to minimize the rise.

Adding the diced goat's cheese: Chill before using to make dicing easier. Place the cheese in the centre of the soufflés, or they will burst open during the second cooking.

First cooking of the soufflés: A little hot water is poured into the roasting tin to protect the soufflés from the direct strong heat coming up from the bottom and prevent them from rising too much. They are cooked at a relatively low temperature for the same reason and should be barely cooked after the first baking.

BOUDIN DE FAISAN AU RIZ SAUVAGE, SAUCE CREME AUX GIROLLES

Pheasant 'sausage' on a bed of wild rice, served with a cream of wild mushrooms

Serves 8
Difficulty: 🎩🎩
Total recipe time: 1 hour 35 minutes
Special equipment: food processor, stainless steel bowl, piping bag with 1 cm/½ in nozzle, 1 small ramekin

―――――― INGREDIENTS ――――――

Wild rice

100 g/3½ oz wild rice (see page 57)

1 shallot, finely chopped

2 teaspoons unsalted butter

1 sprig of thyme

½ bayleaf

200 ml/7 fl oz Light chicken stock (see page 21) or water

salt and freshly ground white pepper

Mousse

25 g/1 oz fresh white breadcrumbs, soaked in a little milk

1 medium onion, finely chopped

1 teaspoon unsalted butter

1 pheasant liver, washed and dried

½ clove, crushed

200 g/7 oz pheasant breast, diced

125 g/4½ oz pork back fat

1 egg

a large pinch of nutmeg or mace

1 tablespoon Cognac

350 ml/12 fl oz whipping cream

160 cm/63 in sausage casing

salt and freshly ground white pepper

Sauce

250 g/9 oz wild mushrooms (eg: chanterelles)

4 shallots, finely chopped

2 teaspoons unsalted butter

400 ml/14 fl oz whipping cream

lemon juice

Almond and breadcrumb coating

6 whole hazelnuts, shelled

50 g/2 oz ground almonds

50 g/2 oz dried white breadcrumbs

2 tablespoons unsalted butter

Garnish

100 g/3½ oz wild mushrooms

1 teaspoon unsalted butter

lemon juice

Planning ahead

Prepare the pheasant liver in advance; remove the gall bladder and soak the liver in 100 ml/3½ fl oz each milk and water for 6 hours to dilute the blood.

The fresh white breadcrumbs for the mousse must be soaked in milk 2 hours in advance.

The wild rice must be soaked in cold water for 1 hour before use.

Stages 1 – 3 inclusive can be prepared in advance; leave the *boudin* coated in breadcrumbs ready for pan-frying.

The wild mushrooms can be prepared in advance but must be cooked only at the last moment.

―――――

1. Cooking the wild rice (1 hour 10 minutes)

Preheat the oven to 160°C/325°F/gas 4.

Drain the rice.

In a medium saucepan, sweat the shallot in the butter for 2–3 minutes. Stir in the rice (making sure each grain is coated with the melted butter) then add a large pinch of salt, 6 turns of pepper, thyme and ½ bayleaf and cover with the chicken stock. Bring to simmering point, partially cover and cook in the preheated oven for 1 hour. Taste, correct the seasoning, remove the bayleaf and thyme, cover the pan and set aside.

Meanwhile, prepare the mousse.

2. Preparing and cooking the mousse (35 minutes plus 30 minutes chilling) (see Mousse making, page 36)

Squeeze out some of the milk from the breadcrumbs.

In a medium saucepan, cook the chopped onion in the butter and 3–4 tablespoons water for 10 minutes, until the water has completely evaporated.

In a food processor, first grind the back fat to a paste, then add the diced

pheasant breast, 1½ teaspoons salt, 6 turns of pepper, the egg, Cognac, pheasant liver, breadcrumbs, softened onion, nutmeg and clove and process until smooth.

Transfer the mixture to a stainless steel bowl and refrigerate for 30 minutes.

Place the bowl on ice and slowly incorporate four-fifths of the cream, beating the mixture vigorously to lighten it.

Test the mixture in a small ramekin and correct with cream and seasoning as necessary.

Sausage casing: Wash inside and out with plenty of running water, drain and cut into 20 cm/8 in lengths, tying a knot at the end of each piece. Fill the piping bag with mousse mixture and, wrapping the skin around the nozzle, pipe in the mixture, leaving enough loose skin to tie in a knot. Repeat with all the skins.

Poach in 2 L/3½ pt almost-simmering water for 20 minutes, then refresh. When cold, cut open the ends with scissors and, using a sharp knife, free the *boudins* by cutting through the skin. Chill.

3. The breadcrumbs
(10 minutes)
Hazelnuts: Toast under the grill for 5 minutes until golden. Crush to a paste. Put in a small bowl with the ground almonds and breadcrumbs and season with a pinch of salt and 2 turns of pepper.

In a small saucepan melt 2 tablespoons butter, coat the *boudins* all over and roll them in the breadcrumbs. Set aside.

4. Cream of wild mushrooms
(15 minutes)
Mushrooms: Trim the stalks, wash briefly in plenty of cold water and pat dry. Scrape off any sediment, dirt or rough skin. Reserve about 100 g/ 3½ oz of the smallest for the garnish and chop the rest very finely.

In a medium saucepan, sweat the chopped mushrooms and shallots in the butter for 5 minutes. Pour in the cream, bring to the boil and reduce by half. Purée in a blender, then, using a ladle, force through a fine conical sieve into a small saucepan, pressing the purée to extract as much juice as possible. Taste, season with a pinch of salt and a few turns of pepper and 'lift' the sauce with a squeeze of lemon.

5. Pan-frying the boudins and garnish (10 minutes)
Preheat the oven to 160°C/325°F/ gas 3.

In a large non-stick frying pan heat 2 teaspoons butter and pan-fry the *boudins* until golden. Place in the preheated oven for 5 minutes. Return the wild rice from Stage 1 to the oven to reheat.

Season the whole mushrooms and pan-fry in 1 teaspoon butter, taste and enliven with a squeeze of lemon.

6. Serving
Warm a large flat dish or 4 plates.

Place a large spoonful of wild rice in the middle of each plate, set the *boudins* in the centre and pour the sauce around. Scatter with wild mushrooms.

— VARIATIONS —

Any game bird is suitable for this dish, but if you use grouse omit the liver which has too strong a flavour. Chicken and chicken liver can also be used – or substitute *foie gras* and half a diced truffle for the chicken liver.

Serve a delicate pheasant juice instead of the cream of wild mushrooms.

Almost any wild mushrooms can be used for garnish. Trumpets of death

enhance the flavour and add a dramatic note.

Simplify the dish by cooking the mousse in ramekins in a bain-marie.

— WINE —

A spicy young Gewürztraminer would be ideal.

Chef's notes
Pheasant: the breast should come from a bird which has been hung for about 10 days so that it lends enough character to the dish.

Sausage casing: This skin (taken from a pig's intestine) is salted to preserve it and must be washed thoroughly before use. Natural casings can sometimes be obtained from butchers, although many now use synthetic skins. Natural skin is supple and will curve attractively as the mousse expands during cooking, while synthetic skin will not change shape.

Pheasant liver: Cut out the gall bladder before soaking, making sure that no liquid escapes onto the liver itself. Any trace of this greenish liquid will ruin the taste of the dish.

Poaching the boudins: Do not let the water boil or the mousse will expand and burst out of the skin.

Removing the boudins from the skins: Be very careful here. Slide the blade of a small knife under the skin to cut it and not the mousse. If the mousse is damaged it will burst open when reheated.

BALLOTINE DE SAUMON A L'EFFEUILLE DE JEUNES CHOUX ET LARDONS, SAUCE BEURRE BLANC

Ballotine of salmon wrapped in Savoy cabbage leaves, served with beurre blanc

"The melting mousse, the smoky taste of the salmon and the rustic crunchiness of the young cabbage all combine to make this a really special introduction to a sumptuous Autumn dinner."

Serves 12
Difficulty: ♟♟
Total recipe time: 1 hour 55 minutes
Special equipment: clingfilm, fish kettle or large saucepan, muslin cloth, trussing needle, long sharp serrated knife

─── INGREDIENTS ───

Mousse

400 g/14 oz middle cut salmon fillet, skinned

100 g/3½ oz unsalted butter

20 g/¾ oz smoked salmon

1 egg white

1 teaspoon salt

a generous pinch of cayenne pepper

450 ml/¾ pt whipping cream, chilled

Salmon roulade and garnish

2 slices from the salmon fillet

1 young Savoy cabbage

180 g/6 oz smoked belly of pork, for lardons (see page 47)

1 tablespoon unsalted butter

Beurre blanc, for serving (see page 24)

Planning ahead
Order 400 g/14 oz middle cut salmon fillet in advance. The *ballotine* can be prepared and assembled 1 day in advance and kept in the fridge ready to be poached.

The *beurre blanc* can be made 1 hour in advance and kept warm in a bain-marie; whisk it from time to time.

───────────────

1. The mousse (15 minutes, plus 30 minutes resting) (see Mousse making, page 36)
Cream the butter with your fingertips until free from lumps. Keep at room temperature.

Using a sharp knife, cut 2 long slices from the salmon fillet; they should be about 3 mm/⅛ in thick and as wide as possible. Set aside for the *roulade*.

You should be left with about 250 g/ 9 oz salmon. Cut into cubes and process in a food processor with the smoked salmon, egg white, salt and cayenne, until smooth. Add the creamed butter and blend until thoroughly amalgamated. Leave in the bowl and chill for 30 minutes.

Return the bowl to the food processor and pour in 350 ml/12 fl oz chilled cream in a steady trickle. Test a little mousse in a small ramekin to check the flavour and texture. Taste and adjust the seasoning and add more cream if necessary. Rub the mousse through a fine sieve into a bowl, cover with clingfilm and refrigerate.

2. The roulade (20 minutes)
Cabbage: Cut off the coarse outer leaves and core. Reserve 8 leaves for the garnish. Blanch the remaining leaves in boiling salted water for 1 minute, until supple and still firm but not crunchy.
Lardons: Follow the method on page 47. Reserve two-thirds of the *lardons* for garnish.

Lay the reserved salmon slices on a sheet of clingfilm so that they overlap. Place another sheet of film on top and, with a heavy knife, gently flatten the salmon into a 20 x 15 cm/8 x 6 in rectangle. Remove the top sheet of clingfilm and lightly season the fish.

Using a supple spatula, coat the salmon with a fine layer of mousse. Arrange a layer of blanched cabbage leaves on top, overlapping slightly and cover with another thin layer of mousse. Lay one-third of the *lardons* down the centre. Roll the *roulade* lengthways into a sausage shape and twist the clingfilm at both ends to secure it tightly.

3. Assembling the ballotine
(10 minutes)
Spoon out two-thirds of the remaining mousse onto a sheet of clingfilm and mould it into a loaf shape about 20 x 8 x 8 cm/8 x 3¼ x 3¼ in. Use a teaspoon dipped in hot water to run a 3 cm/1¼ in deep groove down the centre of the loaf to hold the *roulade*.
Remove the clingfilm from the *roulade* and press the *roulade* snugly into the groove. Place the remaining mousse

on top of the *roulade* and, using a spatula dipped in hot water, shape the *ballotine* into a cylinder. Fold over the clingfilm, twist both ends to seal, then wrap the *ballotine* in a damp muslin cloth or tea towel. Fasten securely with string at both ends and tie it twice in the middle.

4. Poaching the ballotine
(30–35 minutes)
Fill a fish kettle or large saucepan with water and bring to the boil. Reduce the heat to just below simmering point and carefully lower in the *ballotine*. Cover with a cloth to keep it submerged and ensure even cooking. Poach for 30–35 minutes. To check whether the *ballotine* is cooked through, insert a trussing needle into the centre for exactly 3 seconds, then remove and quickly feel the lower part of the needle with your tongue; it should be warm and dry – if not, poach the *ballotine* for a little longer.

5. The garnish (5 minutes)
Roll up the reserved raw cabbage leaves and shred finely.
In a medium saucepan, boil 100 ml/3½ fl oz water with 1 tablespoon butter and a pinch of salt. Put in the shredded cabbage and cook for 2 minutes. Toss in the reserved *lardons* at the last minute to warm through.

6. Serving (5 minutes)
Warm 12 plates.
Carefully lift the *ballotine* from the pan and place on a tea towel. Remove the muslin cloth and cut both ends of the clingfilm with scissors. Role the *ballotine* over the tea towel to soak up the running juices.
Using a sharp serrated knife, carefully cut the *ballotine* into 1 cm/½ in slices; it is extremely delicate, so apply little or no pressure. Place a slice in the centre of each plate, arrange the shredded cabbage and *lardons* around the edge and finish with a swirl of *beurre blanc*.

VARIATIONS
Wrap the *ballotine* in blanched spinach or cabbage leaves; this adds a colourful note and helps to keep the mousse in shape as you cut it. Line a sheet of clingfilm with the leaves and assemble the *ballotine* on the leaves.
For a quicker starter, which only takes 1 hour and is still a real treat, make the salmon mousse and bake it in ramekins in a bain-marie for 15–20 minutes at 160°C/325°F/gas 3. Serve with *beurre blanc* and the garnish of cabbage and *lardons*.

WINE
Serve a Pouilly Fumé – its name and taste are most appropriate!

Chef's notes
Smoked salmon: Although the quantity may seem insignificant, do not be tempted to use more as the smoky taste will overpower and unbalance the combination of flavours.
If the *ballotine* is ready before you want to serve it, lift it out of the pan and leave it still wrapped in the muslin. It will keep hot for at least 25 minutes.

GIGOTIN DE LOTTE BRAISE EN MOUCLADE

Monkfish tails braised in mussel juice and scented with saffron

Serves 4
Difficulty: 🍳
Total recipe time: 50 minutes
Special equipment: muslin cloth, deep non-stick roasting pan

INGREDIENTS
4 250 g/9 oz monkfish tails, skinned

3 tablespoons olive oil

salt and freshly ground white pepper

Sauce
8 shallots, finely chopped

1 sprig of parsley

8 coriander leaves or 4 crushed seeds

1 garlic clove, lightly crushed

400 g/14 oz mussels, preferably Bouchot (see Chef's notes)

100 ml/3½ fl oz dry white wine

a pinch of saffron threads or powder

1 tablespoon whipping cream

1 tablespoon Chlorophyll of red pepper (optional) (see page 18)

40 g/1½ oz unsalted butter, chilled and diced

Planning ahead
Soak the saffron threads in 2 tablespoons water 1 day in advance.
The Chlorophyll of red pepper must be made in advance.

1. Cooking the mussels
(10 minutes)
Using a small knife, scrape the shells, pull out the beards, wash the mussels in plenty of cold water and drain.
In a large saucepan, combine half the chopped shallots, the wine, parsley, coriander and crushed garlic. Boil briskly for 1 or 2 seconds, then throw in the mussels. Cover the pan and keep at full boil for 3–4 minutes, until

the mussels have just opened. Do not overcook, or they will become rubbery and discoloured. Take the pan off the heat, strain the juices through muslin and add 2–3 tablespoons cold water. Remove the mussels from their shells, return to the juices and set aside.

2. Cooking the monkfish (15 mintes, plus 15 minutes resting)
Preheat the oven to 180°C/375°F/gas 4.
Dry the monkfish tails in a tea towel and sprinkle with a little salt and pepper.
Heat the olive oil in a deep non-stick roasting pan, put in the monkfish and sear all over for 2 minutes. Add the remaining chopped shallots and cook for a further 2 minutes. Pour in 150 ml/5 fl oz of the mussel juice, cover the pan with buttered greaseproof paper and braise in the oven for 10–12 minutes.
Remove from the oven, strain off the cooking juices, cover and leave the

fish to rest in a warm place for about 10 minutes. The residual heat will complete the cooking, keeping the fish moist and firm.

3. Finishing the sauce (10 minutes)
Using a fine conical sieve, strain the juices from the braised monkfish into a small saucepan and add the soaked saffron. Bring to the boil and add the cream and chlorophyll, if using. Finally, whisk in the cold diced butter and put the mussels back into the sauce. Add a few turns of pepper if necessary but no salt, since the mussels already contain enough.
Meanwhile, reheat the monkfish tails for 5 minutes in the oven, then fillet them and cut into medallions.

4. Serving
Warm 4 plates or a large serving dish. Arrange the medallions of monkfish in the middle of each plate and spoon the mussel-studded sauce over and around them.

Any firm white fish, such as turbot, brill or John Dory, can be prepared in this way.
Cockles or winkles make an attractive addition to the garnish and a *julienne* of red peppers would provide a rich splash of colour. For extra texture and taste, add a few poached mussels in their shells at the last moment.

WINE
A dry white wine is best. Try an elegant Premier Cru Chablis like 'Mont de Milieu' or 'Montée de Tonnerre' or a lighter Montagny from the Côte Chalonnaise.

Chef's notes
Monkfish: For ease of service, the tails can be served whole on the bone. They have only a central backbone, so there are no sharp bones to worry about.
Mussels: Try to use Bouchot mussels as they do not contain sand.

FILET DE DORADE FUME AU CHARBON DE BOIS, AU COULIS DE TOMATES CRUES ET A L'HUILE D'ANCHOIS

Wood-smoked fillet of royal sea bream served with a raw tomato coulis and anchovy vinaigrette

Serves 4
Difficulty:
Total recipe time: 1 hour 10 minutes
Special equipment: filleting knife, tweezers, small smoker, blender

INGREDIENTS
4 150 g/5 oz fillets of royal sea bream, from 2 450 g/1 lb fish
1 tablespoon olive oil
lemon juice
salt and freshly ground white pepper

Garnish
1 small onion, finely sliced
1 tablespoon olive oil
1 sprig of thyme
½ bayleaf
2 5 x 1 cm/2 x ½ in strips of dried orange zest (see page 49)
a pinch of caster sugar
1 tablespoon white wine vinegar
1 small courgette, finely diced

2 fennel leaves, finely diced
1 firm ripe tomato

Tomato coulis
4 ripe tomatoes
20 g/¾ oz unsalted butter, chilled and diced
2 tablespoons olive oil
a pinch of caster sugar (optional)

Filet de dorade fumé au charbon de bois, au coulis de tomates crues et à l'huile d'anchois

Anchovy vinaigrette

3 tablespoons olive oil

1 tablespoon anchovy oil

2 strips of dried orange zest

1 sprig of thyme

½ bayleaf

lemon juice

Planning ahead

Order two 450 g/1 lb sea bream well in advance. Ask the fishmonger to de-scale them, cut off the fins, gut and fillet them.

Stages 1–4 inclusive can be completed 1 hour in advance.

1. Preparing and smoking the sea bream (10 minutes)

Preheat the oven to 180°C/350°F/gas 4.

If the sea bream has not been filleted by the fishmonger, follow the instructions on page 14.

Run a large knife blade down the whole length of the fillets, against the lie of the scales, to remove any which are left. Gently tweeze out the small bones running down the centre. Score the skin side.

Smoke the fillets for 30 seconds on each side and set aside.

2. Preparing the garnish (20 minutes)

Onion: In a medium sauté pan, combine the sliced onion, olive oil, thyme, ½ bayleaf, dried orange zest, a pinch of salt, 3 or 4 turns of pepper, the sugar and vinegar. Cover and bring to the boil. Cook in the preheated oven for 30 minutes. Taste, correct the seasoning and set aside.

Vegetable brunoise: Mix together all the diced vegetables and keep in a small container.

3. The raw tomato coulis (15 minutes)

Tomatoes: Wash, halve, leaving the seeds in and purée. Force through a fine sieve into a small saucepan and warm gently. Whisk in first the cold diced butter then the olive oil. Taste, season and add a pinch of sugar if necessary. Keep warm.

4. The anchovy vinaigrette
(15 minutes)

Increase the oven temperature to 200°C/400°F/gas 6 for Stage 5.

In a small saucepan mix the olive and anchovy oils with 2 tablespoons cold water. Add the dried orange zest, thyme, ½ bayleaf, a pinch of salt and a few turns of pepper. Boil for 30 seconds, take off the heat and infuse the oils for about 10 minutes. Strain through a fine sieve, taste, correct the seasoning and acidulate with a squeeze of lemon. Finally add the vegetable *brunoise*. Keep warm.

5. Cooking the sea bream
(5 minutes)

Season each fillet with a pinch of salt and 2 turns of pepper.

In a large non-stick frying pan, fry the fillets in 1 tablespoon hot olive oil for 40 seconds on the flesh side without colouring, then turn them over onto the skin side and cook in the preheated oven for 5 minutes.

6. Serving (5 minutes)

Warm 4 plates.

Reheat the candied onions, warm the tomato *coulis* and anchovy vinaigrette. Spoon 2 tablespoons tomato *coulis* into the centre of each plate and surround with anchovy vinaigrette spiked with the vegetable *brunoise*. Scatter the onions over the tomato *coulis* and rest the sea bream on top. Enliven the fillets with a squeeze of lemon and a turn of pepper. Serve immediately.

VARIATIONS

Almost any fish can be prepared this way.

Intensify the flavour by searing the skin side with a red hot skewer.

WINE

A refreshing Provençal rosé (Bandol, Domaine de la Bernarde) will match this dish perfectly, or try one of the modern, crisp dry white wines from Bordeaux (Graves).

Chef's notes

Sea bream: There are many varieties of this fish. The best are pink Mediterranean or royal sea bream. Other good varieties include red or grey sea bream from the English Channel.

Smoking the fish: Observe the smoking time precisely; there should be only a delicate aftertaste. If the idea of smoking is too daunting, the sea bream will still be delicious *au naturel*.

Vegetable brunoise: Dicing the vegetables by hand is time consuming; for ease and speed, cut the courgette and fennel into roughly equal chunks and process quickly in a food processor. The tomato must be diced by hand. The *brunoise* should not be cooked, simply warmed in the anchovy oil.

Tomato coulis: Do not allow it to boil or the raw pulp will cook through and become grainy. Boiling will also destroy the refreshing taste of the tomatoes. Should this happen, add 2 more chopped tomatoes, purée and sieve again.

FILET DE BARBUE BRAISE
AUX FEVETTES "FACON DUGLERE"

Braised fillet of brill with young broad beans, tomatoes and flat-leaved parsley

Serves 4
Difficulty:
Total recipe time: 1 hour

INGREDIENTS

4 150 g/5 oz fillets of brill

2 teaspoons melted butter, with a dash of lemon juice

salt and freshly ground white pepper

1 kg/2¼ lb broad beans in their pods

For cooking the fish and sauce

20 g/¾ oz unsalted butter

1 small onion, finely chopped

65 g/2½ oz button mushrooms, washed and sliced

200 ml/7 fl oz dry white wine

100 ml/3½ fl oz water

4 medium tomatoes, peeled, deseeded and chopped

For finishing the sauce

2 tablespoons whipping cream

25 g/1 oz butter, chilled and diced

lemon juice

Garnish

50 g/2 oz flat-leaved parsley

2 medium tomatoes, peeled, deseeded and diced

a few leaves of chervil, washed

Planning ahead
Stages 1, 2 and 4 can be completed in advance.

1. Preparing the fillets of brill
(5 minutes)
Place the fillets on a large plate. Melt 2 teaspoons butter with a dash of lemon juice and a pinch of salt and pepper. Brush all over the fillets, cover the plate with clingfilm and set aside.

2. Preparing the broad beans
(25 minutes)
Preheat the oven to 180°C/360°F/gas 4 for Stage 3.
Shell the broad beans, blanch for 15 seconds in fast-boiling water, refresh and drain. Slit the ends of the beans and squeeze them out of their first skin. Keep the beans covered with a damp tea towel until Stage 5.

3. Cooking the fillets of brill
(15 minutes, plus 10 minutes resting)
In a medium sauté pan sweat the chopped onion for 2–3 minutes in 20 g/¾ oz butter. Add the sliced mushrooms and sweat for a further 2 minutes without colouring. Deglaze with the wine, boil for 30 seconds to reduce acidity then add the chopped tomatoes and 100 ml/3½ fl oz water. Lay the fillets of brill on top and cover the pan with buttered greaseproof paper. Cook in the preheated oven for about 10 minutes.
Remove, place the fillets on a plate and season each with a few grains of salt. Cover with foil and keep in a warm place.
Meanwhile, blanch the parsley.

4. Blanching the parsley
(2 minutes)
Blanch in fast-boiling salted water for 15–20 seconds, refresh and drain.

5. Making the sauce (10 minutes)
Strain the cooking juices from the fish through a fine sieve into a small saucepan, pressing down onto the tomatoes and onion with a ladle to extract as much flavour and juice as possible. Bring to simmering point, add the beans and cook for 1 minute then whisk in the cream and cold diced butter. Add the blanched parsley and chopped chervil and leave to infuse in the sauce for about 1 minute. Taste, correct the seasoning with salt and pepper and 'lift' the sauce with a squeeze of lemon. Finally add the diced tomatoes and strain any remaining juices from the brill into the sauce.

6. Assembling the dish and serving
Heat 4 plates.
Warm the fillets for 2 minutes in the oven if necessary.
Place 1 fillet in the centre of each plate and pour the sauce over and around. Add the broad beans and serve.

────── VARIATIONS ──────
Fillets of most fish (turbot, John Dory, sole and plaice) can be prepared this way.

────── WINE ──────
Serve a wine from the Loire valley, such as Reuilly, Savennières or Muscadet *sur lie*.

Chef's notes
Broad beans must be young. Large broad beans are starchy and unpleasant.
Parsley: Flat-leaved parsley has a better taste and texture than the common curly variety.
Blanching the broad beans: This does not cook them but simply eases the removal of their coarse outer skin. They only require a minute or so in the hot sauce to cook.
Cooking the fillets of brill: The cooking time will vary according to the thickness of the fillets.
Making the sauce: Do not infuse the parsley for too long or it will overpower the sauce.

PAPILLOTTE DE ROUGET ET DORADE AUX PETITS LEGUMES

Fillets of red mullet and sea bream with vegetables, scented with Provençal herbs, baked in a paper parcel

Papillote de rouget et dorade aux petits légumes

Serves 4
Difficulty: ♙♙

Total recipe time: 1 hour 35 minutes,
plus 1 hour marinating

INGREDIENTS

4 fillets from a 180g/6 oz red mullet

4 fillets from a 450 g/1 lb sea bream

1 egg white, to seal the papillottes

Marinade

2 tablespoons olive oil

4 sprigs of rosemary

4 basil leaves

freshly ground white pepper

Juice

4 tomatoes, deseeded and chopped

30 g/1 oz fennel trimmings (from the garnish)

2 shallots, peeled and chopped

1 garlic clove, crushed

bones and heads from the red mullet and sea bream, washed and chopped

6 basil leaves, finely shredded

50 ml/2 fl oz dry white wine

½ bayleaf

2 tablespoons olive oil

lemon juice

a pinch of caster sugar (optional)

salt and freshly ground white pepper

Vegetable garnish

2 Saffron potatoes (see page 55)

1 tablespoon olive oil

1 sprig of thyme

a pinch of saffron threads

½ bayleaf

1 fennel bulb

2 courgettes

2 tomatoes

8 black olives

1 cooked artichoke heart (see page 18)

4 basil leaves

4 sprigs of rosemary

Planning ahead

Order the red mullet and sea bream well in advance. Ask the fishmonger to scale, gut, and fillet them and to give you the bones.

The whole dish can be prepared a few hours in advance, but cook the *papillottes* only at the last moment.

Rehydrate the saffron threads in 2 tablespoons water at least 1 hour before using.

1. Preparing and marinating the fish (10 minutes, plus 1 hour marinating)

Check there are no scales remaining on the fish. Gently tweeze out any remaining bones from the middle of each fillet. Halve the fillets diagonally and place in a dish.

Sprinkle over the marinade ingredients and season with 8 turns of pepper. Cover and leave to marinate for 1 hour at room temperature.

2. The juices (25 minutes)

In a large saucepan, combine all the chopped vegetables, fish, thyme and ½ bayleaf, pour in the white wine and 400 ml/14 fl oz cold water and bring to the boil. Skim, add the shredded basil and simmer gently for about 10 minutes. Pass the juices through a fine conical sieve, return to the pan and reduce to 150 ml/5 fl oz.

Whisk in the olive oil, taste and season with salt, pepper and a squeeze of lemon. If the juice is a little sharp, balance with a pinch of caster sugar. Leave to cool.

3. The garnish (30 minutes)

Fennel: Cut off the root to free the remaining leaves. Cut each leaf into small triangles.

Courgettes: Wash, trim and cut diagonally into 5 mm/¼ in slices. In a large suacepan, bring to the boil 1 L/1¾ pt water with 1 tablespoon salt. Cook the fennel triangles in full-boiling water for 3 minutes. Add the courgettes and cook both for 1 more minute. Refresh and drain.

Tomatoes: Peel, halve and deseed with a teaspoon. Cut each half into 3.

Black olives: Blanch in unsalted boiling water for 5 minutes, refresh and drain.

Artichoke heart: Cut into small triangles.

4. Assembling the papillottes
(20 minutes)

Preheat the oven to 230°C/450°F/gas 8.

Lightly salt the inside of the red mullet and sea bream fillets.

Lightly break the egg white with a fork. Cut out four 35 cm/14 in circles of greaseproof paper and brush a little egg white around the edges. Arrange a layer of vegetables on the lower half, keeping aside a few slices of courgette and fennel. Coat with 2 tablespoons juice and rest the fish fillets on the bed of vegetables. Add the saffron potatoes and the remaining courgette and fennel slices. Top with basil and a small sprig of rosemary and season with 2 turns of pepper. Finally decorate each one with 2 black olives. Fold over the greaseproof paper and fold over the edges to seal in the juices.

5. Cooking the papillottes
(10 minutes)

Bake on a large, lightly oiled baking tray for 8 minutes.

6. Serving

Warm 4 plates and a serving dish.
Present the *papillottes* to your guests on the dish, open them up then serve on the plates, still wrapped in a parcel.

VARIATIONS

Many other fish can be cooked this way, including salmon, sea bass and turbot. Cooking times will vary; allow 6 minutes for salmon and

8 minutes for turbot. Scallops or langoustines can be used in addition to the red mullet and sea bream.

Vary the vegetables as you like, but make sure that they will retain that Provençal touch.

If you can find tiny Mediterranean red mullet, cook them whole in the *papillottes*, on their own.

When cooking two types of fish in a *papillotte* (where you cannot monitor cooking) remember that each has a different texture and therefore needs a different cooking time. Make sure that the fish which need longer cooking are smaller than the others so that they will be ready at the same time.

--- WINE ---

A rosé or white wine from Provence will heighten the character of this dish. Try a Domaine de la Bernarde or Domaine Ott, or perhaps a delicious Tavel rosé from the Rhône.

Chef's notes

Tomatoes: If you can find some of those beautifully ripe, sun-soaked tomatoes you need not remove the seeds.

Cooking *en papillotte* is a wonderful technique; as flavours cannot escape from the paper parcel, they intensify. The fish inside the parcel is rested on the bed of vegetables to avoid direct contact with the heat which rises in the oven. It is cooked by the steam from the vegetables and juices.

Seal the *papillottes* tightly to prevent heat loss. The egg white solidifies in the heat and maintains a tight seal.

It is very important to observe the cooking time precisely, as there is a strong build-up of heat, especially in the final minute.

RIS DE VEAU CRESSONNIERE

Roast veal sweetbreads served with a dry sherry sauce and watercress

Serves 4
Difficulty: ♙
Total recipe time: 55 minutes

--- INGREDIENTS ---

4 200 g/7 oz veal heart sweetbreads, soaked under running water for 1–2 hours (see Chef's notes in Ris de veau aux amandes, page 147)

2 teaspoons unsalted butter

salt and freshly ground white pepper

Sauce

leaves from 100 g/3½ oz watercress, washed and drained

3 medium shallots, peeled and chopped

1 teaspoon unsalted butter

100 ml/3½ fl oz dry sherry

100 ml/3½ fl oz Light chicken stock (see page 21) or cold water

1 tablespoon whipping cream

1 egg yolk

40 g/1½ oz unsalted butter, chilled and diced

cooking juices from the sweetbreads

Diced vegetable garnish

1 medium carrot, washed, peeled and finely diced

1 small courgette, washed and finely diced

1 small celery stalk, washed and diced

1 large firm white mushroom cap, wiped and finely diced

1 teaspoon unsalted butter

6 tablespoons cold water

Planning ahead

Order heart sweetbreads well in advance. They should be firm, white and well rounded.

The chicken stock must be made in advance if used.

The diced vegetables can be prepared in advance.

1. Preparing and blanching the sweetbreads (10 minutes)

Drain the sweetbreads then scald in boiling water for 5 seconds. Refresh in cold water and pat dry. Peel away any cartilage, fats and fibres, taking care not to tear them or damage the shape. Pat dry and set aside.

2. The sauce (first stage)
(10 minutes)

Preheat the oven to 220°C/425°F/gas 7.

In a medium saucepan, sweat the chopped shallots in 1 teaspoon butter for 3 minutes without colouring. Deglaze with the sherry and reduce by half. Add the chicken stock or water and bring to the boil. Strain and keep for Stage 5.

3. Cooking the sweetbreads
(20 minutes)

In a medium non-stick sauté pan, sear the sweetbreads in 1 teaspoon *beurre noisette* (see page 24) for about 2 minutes on each side. Season with salt and pepper, then pour off the cooking fat, brush the remaining teaspoon butter over the sweetbreads and roast in the preheated oven for 15 minutes. Remove and leave to rest in the pan for 10 minutes, loosely covered with foil.

4. Cooking the diced vegetable garnish (5 minutes)

In a medium saucepan, boil 6 tablespoons water with 1 teaspoon butter and a pinch of salt. First add the diced carrot and cook for 1 minute. Add the celery and cook for 1 minute, then add the courgette and cook for 2 minutes; finally add the mushroom and cook for 1 minute. Taste, correct seasoning and keep aside.

5. Finishing the sauce

(5 minutes)
Bring the stock from Stage 2 back to the boil and add the watercress leaves. Cover, cook for 2 minutes then draw off the heat.
In a small bowl, mix together the cream and egg yolk and stir into the sauce to bind it. Finally whisk in the cold diced butter.
Add all the diced vegetables and the cooking juices released by the sweetbreads, taste and correct the seasoning.

6. Serving the dish (5 minutes)

Warm 4 plates or a large serving dish. Warm the sweetbreads in the oven for 5 minutes, then arrange them in the centre of the plates and pour the watercress sauce around.

VARIATIONS

A few leaves of sorrel and young spinach would make a good addition.
Lamb sweetbreads can also be cooked this way.
The binding of egg yolk and cream can be omitted.

WINE

Since sweetbreads have such a rich texture, a light dry white Burgundy will suit this dish very well; try Macon Chaintre, Montagny or St Véran.

Chef's notes

Sweetbreads (see page 147): You may not be able to find beautifully proportioned sweetbreads weighing 200 g/ 7 oz each; they are usually reserved for restaurants like Le Manoir – sorry! If so, ask for 2 larger sweetbreads (400 g/ 14 oz each) and more than double the cooking time. Slice them just before serving and season each slice, as the seasoning will not have penetrated the whole sweetbreads.
Watercress can be very peppery or mild, depending on the variety. Taste it raw; if it is too strong, blanch for 20 seconds before using.
Blanching the sweetbreads: This is not to cook them but simply to solidify the fibres and cartilages so that they can be peeled away easily.
Binding the sauce: At this stage the sauce must not be allowed to boil or it will cook the egg yolk. After adding the cream and egg yolk mixture, place the pan over a gentle heat and stir slowly until the sauce coats the back of a spoon.

COTE DE BOEUF FUMEE AU BOIS ROTIE SAUCE BORDELAISE

Roast wood-smoked ribs of beef, served with a shallot and red wine sauce

Serves 4–6
Difficulty: 🍳
Total recipe time: 1 hour
Special equipment: smoker or barbecue

INGREDIENTS
---

2 1.15 kg/2½ lb wing ribs of beef, trimmed

4 teaspoons unsalted butter

2 teaspoons groundnut oil

offcut bones and trimmings from the ribs, chopped

salt and freshly ground black pepper

Bordelaise sauce

6 shallots, peeled and finely chopped

20 g/¾ oz unsalted butter

1 tablespoon red wine vinegar

500 ml/18 fl oz St Emilion red wine

1 sprig of thyme

20 g/¾ oz smoked bacon

200 ml/7 fl oz Veal stock (see page 18)

8 young tarragon leaves

1 small teaspoon Dijon mustard

1 teaspoon unsalted butter (optional)

salt and freshly ground black pepper

For smoking

oak or cherrywood chips

a few bayleaves

2 sprigs of rosemary

2 or 3 juniper berries, crushed

Garnish

20 g/¾ oz veal marrow

salt and freshly ground white pepper

a pinch of coarse sea salt

Planning ahead

Order the wing ribs well in advance (see Chef's notes). Ask your butcher to trim the fat leaving a small layer around the meat, and to bone out the chine, leaving the meat attached only to the rib. Ask him to tie the eye of the ribs with 2 turns of string to retain its shape during cooking and to give you all the trimmings and bones.

Order the veal marrow bones (cracked open) well in advance. Extract the marrow and soak in water for 12 hours to remove any blood.

The veal stock must be made in advance.

Stages 1 and 2 can be completed 1 day in advance. Keep refrigerated covered with clingfilm.

1. Smoking the ribs

(1 minute)

Place the ribs on the griddle and smoke for 30 seconds per side. Place on a small tray, cover with clingfilm and set aside.

2. Making the sauce (35 minutes)

(see Savoury sauces, page 26)

Preheat the oven to 220°C/425°F/ gas 7.

In a large saucepan, sweat the chopped shallots in 1 tablespoon butter for 5 minutes without colouring. Deglaze with the red wine vinegar and reduce until completely evaporated. Add 450 ml/¾ pt St Emilion (reserving 50 ml/2 fl oz) and reduce by half, skimming occasionally. Add the thyme, bacon and veal stock and reduce by half, then add the remaining red wine and the tarragon. Boil for about 1 minute until you obtain a light textured, deep-coloured sauce, then whisk in the Dijon mustard.

Strain the sauce into a small saucepan, taste and season with a pinch of salt and 4 turns of black pepper. Stir in the reserved wine, loosen with 2 tablespoons cold water to prevent a skin from forming and set aside.

Meanwhile, roast the beef.

3. Roasting the ribs of beef

(40 minutes plus 15 minutes resting)

In a large roasting pan heat 2 teaspoons each of butter and groundnut oil until hot. Sear the ribs for 2 minutes per side, to brown. Place the chopped offcut bones under the ribs to isolate them from the strong heat at the bottom of the pan, season the ribs with salt and black pepper, rub a little butter on each rib then roast in the preheated oven for about 30 minutes, basting occasionally.

Remove, place the offcut bones on a small tray, rest the ribs on top and leave to rest for 15 minutes in a warm place, loosely covered with foil.

Tilt the roasting tray and spoon out the cooking fat, then add 4 tablespoons cold water and scrape the bottom of the pan to dilute the caramelized juices. Strain the juices into the sauce.

Cook the veal marrow while the beef is resting.

4. Preparing and cooking the marrow (10 minutes)

Slice the soaked marrow into 5 mm/ ¼ in rounds using a sharp knife dipped in hot water. Place in a saucepan with 500 ml/18 fl oz salted cold water and bring to the boil. Reduce heat to just below simmering point and cook for 7–8 minutes. Remove the marrow with a slotted spoon, season with a few grains of coarse sea salt and keep warm in a serving dish.

5. Carving the ribs of beef and serving (5 minutes)

Heat 4 plates.

Add the juices released by the ribs during resting to the sauce, then place the ribs on a carving board and present them to your guests. Carve them in front of your guests, seasoning each slice with a few grains of salt and a few turns of black pepper. Fan out the slices in the centre of each plate and pour the sauce around. Serve the marrow separately.

———— VARIATIONS ————

The ribs can be replaced by other cuts of beef such as sirloin, fillet or rump. Many garnishes can accompany this dish: the marrow can be masked with Provençal breadcrumbs (see page 47) and Caramelized shallots (see page 57) would also be delicious.

———— WINE ————

A fine St Emilion (particularly from a château close to the Pomerol border) is the obvious choice, and of course Château Petrus from Pomerol itself immediately springs to mind. But many less renowned châteaux such as La Tour du-Pin-Figeac or Croque Michotte are quite superb and represent outstanding value for money.

Chef's notes

Ribs of beef: The fore rib (the first 4 ribs close to the shoulder) is a delicious cut but not quite as tender as the wing rib. The wing ribs hold the sirloin, are extremely tender and have much less waste. Not surprisingly this cut is quite expensive.

Whatever your choice try to buy ribs from a Charolais/Angus cross or a pure-bred Aberdeen Angus which has been hung for 2–3 weeks. The meat should be a deep red, marbled with thin veins of fat and a soft, fairly dry looking texture.

St Emilion: If you don't use a St Emilion, at least use a good full-flavoured red table wine – the quality of the sauce depends largely upon the quality of the wine. 50 ml/2 fl oz wine is added at the end to reintroduce the vitality and colour of the wine to the sauce. If the sauce is a little acidic add a tiny pinch of caster sugar and whisk in 1 teaspoon butter.

Tarragon: If you can't find really young tarragon, blanch it in boiling water for a few seconds, drain, refresh then chop before adding to the sauce.

Resting the beef: This is very important. The fibres of the meat tense up during cooking and a period of resting allows

the meat to relax and become tender.
The sauce: I prefer to add the tarragon at the end so it does not denaturate or overpower the flavour of the sauce.
Smoking the beef adds a wonderful scent which mingles with the taste of the meat. 30 seconds per side is quite sufficient or the smoky taste will become overpowering. I do not advise doing this in the kitchen as your extractor fan is unlikely to cope! If you do not have a smoker, use a barbecue instead – or simply omit this stage. Use dry wood, (cherry, pine and oak are best) light it and when the flames die down, throw the bayleaves, rosemary and juniper berries into the embers and briefly smoke the beef.

RABLE DE LAPIN ROTI AUX GRAINES DE MOUTARDE ET SES CUISSES BRAISEES AU JUS D'ESTRAGON

Roast saddle of rabbit served with a seed mustard sauce, its legs braised in a tarragon-scented juice

"The marriage of two techniques – the traditional long, slow braising of the legs and the short roasting of the saddles."

Serves 4
Difficulty: 🎩 🎩 🎩
Total recipe time: 1 hour 50 minutes

INGREDIENTS

2 small rabbits

salt and freshly ground white pepper

For braising the legs
Mirepoix:

1 small carrot, washed, peeled and diced

¼ celery stalk, washed and diced

2 field mushrooms, wiped clean and diced

4 shallots or *1 small onion, peeled and diced*

3 tablespoons non-scented oil

1 garlic clove, unpeeled

2 sprigs of parsley

2 sprigs of thyme

½ bayleaf

1 sprig of tarragon

4 tablespoons white wine

300 ml/½ pt cold water

2 dashes of soy sauce

a dash of red wine vinegar

chopped bones from the rabbits

1 teaspoon Dijon mustard

1 tablespoon flour

For the saddles
4 tarragon leaves

1 sage leaf

2 pigs' cauls (optional)

2 tablespoons non-scented oil

Garnish
1 lettuce

2 teaspoons unsalted butter

4 tablespoons cold water

100 g/3½ oz smoked streaky bacon for lardons (see page 47)

100 g/3½ oz fresh tagliatelle (see Pasta, page 38) (optional)

1 tablespoon whipping cream

kidneys from the rabbit

1 teaspoon unsalted butter

Sauce for the saddles
1 shallot, peeled and chopped

1 teaspoon unsalted butter

4 tablespoons dry white wine

4 tablespoons Light chicken stock (see page 21) or water

1 tablespoon whipping cream

¼ teaspoon Dijon mustard

1 sprig of tarragon, blanched, refreshed and chopped

1 level tablespoon seed mustard

20 g/¾ oz unsalted butter

a squeeze of lemon

Planning ahead
Order the rabbits well in advance. Have them jointed into legs and saddles and ask for the bones, livers and kidneys.
Fresh tagliatelle, if used, must be made in advance.
Chicken stock, if used, must also be made in advance.
Stages 1 – 3 inclusive can be completed 1 day in advance.

1. Preparing the legs and saddles
(15 minutes)

Preheat the oven to 150°C/300°F/gas 2.

Hind legs: Chop them off neatly just above the hip bones. (The front legs are only used for flavouring the braising juices.)

Saddles: Remove the kidneys and keep them aside for Stage 5, covered with a film of oil. Lay the saddles on their backs, trim off the loose skin then trim all the nerves and fibres from the fillet. Place 2 tarragon leaves and ½ sage leaf on each saddle then wrap them individually in a pig's caul and fasten with 3 turns of kitchen string. Keep aside.

2. Preparing the mirepoix; braising the legs (55 minutes)

In a small saucepan, sweat the diced vegetables in 1 tablespoon oil for 5 minutes to colour lightly. Add the garlic and herbs and draw off the heat.

Rabbit legs: Season with 4 pinches of salt and 8 turns of pepper, coat with a little mustard, then dip into a bowl of flour and shake off the excess.

In a heavy casserole, heat 2 tablespoons oil until hot, then brown the legs and chopped bones all over. Drain excess oil, then add the diced vegetables and herbs, white wine, cold water, soy sauce and vinegar. Bring to the boil, cover and cook in the preheated oven for 45 minutes. Lift out the legs with a straining spoon, cover loosely with buttered greaseproof paper and keep warm. Discard the front legs and all chopped bones.

Strain the juices into a small saucepan, pressing down onto the vegetables with a ladle to extract as much juice and flavour as possible. Bring to the boil, skim and reduce to a light, highly aromatic juice. Taste and correct seasoning with salt and pepper. Meanwhile, prepare the garnish.

3. Preparing the garnish
(25 minutes)

Lettuce: Cut off most of the root and peel off weathered leaves. Quarter the lettuce, wash in 2 changes of water, drain and put in a medium saucepan with 2 teaspoons butter, 4 tablespoons cold water, 2 pinches of salt and 4 turns of pepper.

Streaky bacon: Cut into *lardons* and blanch, then add to the lettuce.

Tagliatelle: Cook in plenty of lightly salted boiling water for about 2 minutes, refresh under cold running water and place in a small saucepan with the cream. Season and set aside.

Increase the oven temperature to 200°C/400°F/gas 6 for Stage 4.

4. Roasting the saddles; making the sauce (25 minutes)

In a roasting pan, heat 2 tablespoons oil until hot, sear the saddles all over then roast in the preheated oven for 15 minutes. Remove, spoon off the fat and leave to rest for 5 minutes.

Peel off the caul protecting the saddles and leave them in the roasting pan, covered with greaseproof paper.

In a medium saucepan, sweat the chopped shallots in 1 teaspoon butter for a few minutes without colouring, then deglaze with the wine and boil for a few seconds to remove alcohol. Add the chicken stock or water and reduce by half. Stir in the cream, draw off the heat and whisk in the mustards, chopped tarragon and butter. Taste, season with a pinch of salt and 4 turns of pepper and 'lift' with a squeeze of lemon. Keep warm.

5. Cooking the garnish (6 minutes)

Flash-fry the rabbit kidneys in 1 teaspoon butter, then place in the oven for 5 minutes. Keep warm.

Cook the lettuce and *lardons*, covered, for 2–3 minutes and gently bring the noodles and cream to simmering point.

6. Finishing the dish and serving
(10 minutes)

Heat 4 plates.

Legs: Warm them in their braising juices for 5 minutes.

Saddles: Return to the oven for 5 minutes then carve into fine slivers.

Kidneys: Slice finely and season with a few grains of salt and pepper.

At the top of each plate, place one rabbit leg and a single lettuce leaf. Scatter the *lardons* and, on the lower half of the plate, arrange a little mound of tagliatelle. Surround with slivers of saddle topped by a few slices of kidney. Spoon the brown juice over the legs and the mustard sauce over the saddles. Serve to your guests.

VARIATIONS
This dish is really two dishes in one. To simplify, make one or the other!

WINE
A spicy Alsace wine (Gewürztraminer or Riesling) will be perfect. Try to find wines from the best Alsace growers such as Trimbach, Dopff or Hügel.

Chef's notes
Mushrooms: Try to use open field mushrooms as they have a better flavour and will lend more colour to the sauce.

Wrapping the saddles in pigs' cauls prevents them from drying out, which they are prone to do. You could wrap the saddles in the layer of rabbit skin that you peel off.

Braising the legs: Browning the legs is very important; they must turn a dark nutty brown, or the juices will lack flavour and colour. At no stage during braising must the stock be allowed to boil; this will cloud the juices and toughen the meat.

Meat

ROGNON DE VEAU ROTI A LA PUREE D'ECHALOTES AU FUMET D'HERMITAGE

Veal kidneys roasted in their jackets, served on a purée of shallots with an Hermitage red wine sauce

Serves 4
Difficulty: 🎩
Total recipe time: 2 hours 10 minutes

──── INGREDIENTS ────
2 veal kidneys wrapped in their fat

2 teaspoons unsalted butter

salt and freshly ground white pepper

Purée of shallots
1 garlic clove, peeled

625 g/1 lb 6 oz shallots

60 g/2½ oz unsalted butter

lemon juice

a large pinch of caster sugar

1 sprig of thyme

Garnish
16 shallots

2 teaspoons unsalted butter

4 tarragon leaves

Sauce
8 shallots (reserved from the purée)

2 teaspoons unsalted butter

1 garlic clove, lightly crushed

¼ bayleaf

1 sprig of thyme

100 ml/3½ fl oz ruby port

500 ml/18 fl oz Hermitage red wine

200 ml/7 fl oz Veal stock (see page 18)

2 tablespoons whipping cream

a sprig of tarragon

a pinch of caster sugar

Planning ahead
Order the veal kidneys well in advance and specify that they must still be wrapped in their own fat (see Chef's notes).
The veal stock must be made in advance.
The sauce can be prepared and cooked in advance.

1. Preparing the kidneys
(20 minutes)
Preheat the oven to 200°C/400°F/gas 6.
Trim the excess fat from around the kidneys, leaving a layer about 1 cm/½ in thick. Using a sharp knife, halve the kidneys lengthways and cut out the nerves exposed in the middle. Tie up each half with 2 turns of string and refrigerate.

2. The purée of shallots (40 minutes)
The shallots: Peel and reserve 8 for the sauce.
In a small saucepan, melt 2 teaspoons butter. Add a squeeze of lemon, a large pinch of sugar, a pinch of salt, 4 turns of pepper, the peeled garlic clove, thyme and 4 tablespoons cold water. Add the peeled shallots in a single layer, cover and cook in the preheated oven for 30 minutes, adding a little water from time to time.
Remove the thyme, then purée the shallots and cooking juices in a blender until smooth. Add the remaining butter and blend for another 30 seconds.
Return the purée to the saucepan, taste and correct the seasoning. Cover with buttered greaseproof paper to prevent any discoloration or skin from forming. Keep in a warm place.

3. Roasting and resting the kidneys
(1 hour)
In a small saucepan, melt 2 teaspoons butter. Place the 4 kidney halves, cut side up, in a large sauté pan, brush with the melted butter and season with salt and pepper. Cover loosely with buttered greaseproof paper and cook in the preheated oven for about 30 minutes.
Resting: Wrap each kidney half individually in foil and leave in a warm place for 30 minutes.
Meanwhile leave the oven switched on and prepare the sauce and the garnish.

4. The sauce (20 minutes)
Chop the reserved peeled shallots, place in a small saucepan with 2 teaspoons butter, the lightly crushed garlic clove, bayleaf and thyme and sweat for 5 minutes without colouring. Deglaze with the port and wine, bring to the boil, skim and reduce by two-thirds.
Add the veal stock, cream and tarragon. Simmer, skimming occasionally, until the sauce has acquired a lovely sheen. You should have about 200 ml/7 fl oz sauce. Season with salt, 4 or 5 turns of pepper and finally a pinch of

*Rognon de veau
Rôti à la purée
d'echalotes au fumet
d'Hermitage*

sugar. If the sauce is still too sharp, whisk in 2 teaspoons butter and another pinch of sugar. Pass the sauce through a fine conical sieve back into the saucepan, stir in 4 tablespoons cold water and set aside.

5. The garnish (35 minutes)

Shallots: Trim the roots but do not peel. Wrap in foil with the butter and tarragon leaves and bake in the pre-heated oven for 30 minutes. Remove from the oven, cut in half and keep warm.

6. Serving (10 minutes)

Return the foil-wrapped kidneys to the oven for about 5 minutes.
Warm 4 plates.
Bring the sauce back to the boil, and reheat the purée of shallots.
Unwrap the kidneys on a chopping board. Cut the string and use a table-spoon to free the kidneys from their layer of fat. Cut each kidney into 5 mm/¼ in slices, taste and correct the seasoning. Spoon 2 teaspoons purée of shallots into the centre of each plate and smooth into a 5 x 1 cm/2 x ½ in rectangle running across the width of the plate. Lay the slices of kidney on top, pour the sauce around and place 2 unpeeled halved shallots on each side.

VARIATIONS

A sprinkling of Provençal bread-crumbs (see page 47) makes an attrac-tive final touch.
Substitute an onion purée for the shal-lot purée.

WINE

The natural choice for this dish must be the same wine as you used for the sauce – Hermitage – or try a mature Côte Rôtie from the northern Rhône or a Châteauneuf du Pape.

Chef's notes

Veal kidneys are too often sold bruised, tired and ageing. A fresh kidney should be bought still wrapped in its fat (which should be white and dry). The kidney itself should be pink or creamy white. Do not accept any-thing else.
Preparing the kidneys: The kidneys are halved to allow better heat penetra-tion. The covering of fat preserves their beautiful colour and prevents them from drying out.
Purée of shallots: Make sure that there is always some liquid in the pan during cooking to prevent caramelization and ensure that the purée remains a beauti-ful creamy white.
The sauce: Depending on the wine you

use, the sauce will be more or less acid; adjust the sharpness to your taste with another tablespoon of cream or a pinch of sugar. The sauce will initially turn cloudy when you add the cream, but after a few minutes simmering it will regain its deep purple sheen. If it is ready a little in advance, stir in 2 or 3 tablespoons cold water to prevent a skin from forming. Reduce it back to the correct consistency just before serving.

Wine: If you cannot find an Hermitage, use any deep, powerful red wine instead.

Roasting the kidneys: Nothing tastes more disagreeable than undercooked veal kidneys. This is why the cooking is carried out in two stages – first roasting in the oven to medium rare, and then a period of resting away from the heat, still wrapped in foil. At this stage, the heat travels slowly through to the centre of the kidneys and completes the cooking. The kidneys remain a delicate pink, relax and become tender.

SARCELLE ROTIE AU FUMET DE VIN ROUGE A L'EMBEURREE D'ENDIVES

Roast teal served with a red wine sauce on a bed of chicory

"I find teal the most interesting variety of wild duck; it is much smaller than mallard but has a far superior, stronger yet more refined flavour. Those fine gourmets the Romans appreciated the difference centuries ago when they domesticated these wild birds in order to consume them regularly at their lavish and wonderfully decadent feasts."

Serves 4
Difficulty: 👨‍🍳
Total recipe time: 55 minutes
Special equipment: trussing needle, kitchen string, boning knife

INGREDIENTS

4 teal, unhung

1 teaspoon unsalted butter

1 teaspoon sunflower, corn or groundnut oil

Sauce

2 shallots, finely chopped

¼ celery stalk, finely diced

1 small carrot, finely diced

100 g/3½ oz field or button mushrooms, finely sliced

1 sprig of thyme

¼ bay leaf

2 teaspoons unsalted butter

carcasses from the teal

1 tablespoon red wine vinegar

200 ml/7 fl oz strong red wine (Rhône or Bergerac)

200 ml/7 fl oz Veal stock (see page 18)

2 tablespoons whipping cream

1 coffee spoon redcurrant jelly (optional)

salt and freshly ground white pepper

Garnish

1 head of chicory

1 teaspoon unsalted butter

1 teaspoon whipping cream

a pinch of caster sugar

lemon juice

Planning ahead

Order the teal well in advance; they must not have been hung for more than 2 or 3 days. Ask the butcher to pluck and draw them and to give you the neck and wings.

The teal, *mirepoix* and garnish can be prepared 3 or 4 hours in advance.

The teal can be cooked 1 hour in advance; cook them medium rare and keep covered away from the heat. Warm in the oven for 3 minutes before serving.

1. Preparing the teal (10 minutes)

Singe the birds over an open flame to remove stubble. Cut off the feet just below the knee joints and, with a boning knife, cut out the wishbones. Truss the birds (see page 16) and set aside.

Preheat the oven to 200°C/400°F/gas 6 for Stage 4.

2. The mirepoix (10 minutes)

Mix all the diced vegetables with the thyme and bayleaf. Set aside.

3. Preparing the garnish (5 minutes)

Chicory: Cut off the base, wash, drain and halve lengthways. Slice finely and place in a small saucepan with 2 tablespoons cold water, the butter, cream, a tiny pinch of salt, 2 turns of pepper and a small squeeze of lemon. Set aside.

4. The sauce (20 minutes)

Sear the teal necks and wings in 2 teaspoons butter for 5 minutes, add the *mirepoix* and colour lightly. Deglaze with the vinegar, letting it evaporate completely. Add the wine and reduce by half to remove alcohol and excess acidity, then pour in 100 ml/3½ fl oz cold water and the veal juice. Bring to the boil, skim and stir in the cream. Simmer for 10 minutes.

Strain through a fine sieve into a small saucepan and reduce until you have a richly-coloured sauce with a good texture. Taste; if it is too acidic, add the redcurrant jelly, then season with a pinch of salt and a few turns of pepper. Loosen with 2 tablespoons cold water and keep warm.

5. Cooking the teal, carving and finishing the sauce (10 minutes, plus 10 minutes resting)

In a large frying pan, heat the butter and oil until hot, put in the birds on their thighs and sear for 2 minutes on each side. Cook in the preheated oven (still on their thighs) for 4 minutes, then turn over and cook for a further 4 minutes.

Pour off the cooking fat and leave the birds to rest for 5 minutes, covered loosely with foil. Carve.

Season the insides of the breasts with a pinch of salt and a turn of pepper and leave the carved teal to rest in the pan in a warm place (60°C/140°F), covered with foil. Chop all the carcasses and add them to the sauce. Simmer for another 5 minutes, then strain into a saucepan, pressing on the carcasses to extract as much flavour as possible.

6. Cooking the garnish (2 minutes)

Place the pan of chicory over a strong heat, cover and boil for 30 seconds. Draw off the heat, taste and correct the seasoning with salt and pepper.

7. Serving (5 minutes)

Warm 4 plates.

Warm the breasts and thighs of teal in the oven for 3–4 minutes. Slice the breasts into fine escalopes and arrange in an attractive mound in the middle of each plate. Rest the thighs and legs on top and surround with the finely sliced chicory. Spoon the sauce around and serve immediately.

VARIATIONS

Widgeon, mallard, woodcock or snipe are also delicious served this way.

WINE

This is an ideal occasion on which to serve a really fine mature red wine – a classic Burgundy such as Bonnes Mares or Chambolle Musigny, any mature classed growth claret or an old Hermitage or Châteauneuf from the Rhône.

Chef's notes

Teal have a deliciously delicate flavour. They are at their best 2 or 3 days after being shot. Contrary to popular belief, few game birds benefit from being hung for at least a week, when they often become unpleasant and overpoweringly strong. As teal are not large, allow one bird per guest for a 4 course menu; you may need 2 each for a 3 course menu.

Mushrooms: Open field mushrooms are best as their flavour is stronger and they add colour to the sauce.

The sauce: A sauce can be ruined by too much acidity. Make sure you reduce the vinegar completely so that it becomes only a background flavour. The wine, however, should only be reduced enough to remove the alcohol and some of the acidity. Taste from time to time during the reduction process; there will come a point when the sauce loses its sharpness and takes on a pleasantly vinous character.

Wine: Use a powerful wine for the sauce; a light wine will not provide enough character and the sauce will lack that rich, vinous appeal.

COFFRE DE VOLAILLE DE BRESSE EN VESSIE, AUX TRUFFES ET MOUSSERONS

Breast of Bresse chicken cooked in a pig's bladder, scented with truffles and mousserons

"A variation on a great French classic."

Serves 4
Difficulty: ☗☗
Total recipe time: 1 hour 20 minutes
Special equipment: steamer or large pan with a lid

──────── INGREDIENTS ────────

2 chicken breasts on the bone, from a corn-fed Bresse or Landes chicken

2 dried pigs' bladders

20 g/¾ oz fresh truffles or 2 tablespoons truffle juice

65 g/2½ oz fresh foie gras

50 g/2 oz mousserons

1 tablespoon Armagnac

1 tablespoon dry sherry

2 tablespoons port

150 ml/5 fl oz Light chicken stock (see page 21)

salt and freshly ground white pepper

For completing the sauce
4 tablespoons whipping cream

30 g/1 oz unsalted butter, chilled and diced

a squeeze of lemon

Garnish
150 g/5 oz each of turnips, swede, parsnips and carrots

a handful of French beans, washed, topped and tailed

1 tablespoon unsalted butter

Planning ahead
Order a corn-fed chicken and the dried pigs' bladders well in advance. Stages 1–3 inclusive can be completed in advance.
If using a whole chicken, trim the wings close to the body, remove the wishbone, turn it onto its breast and cut out the backbone. Keep the bones for the chicken stock, which must be made in advance.

1. Preparing the chicken breasts, bladders and mushrooms
(15 minutes)
Cut thin rounds from the fresh truffles.
Slide your fingers under the skin on the chicken breasts to make room for the truffles and insert them between the skin and flesh. Season with a few grains of salt and pepper.
Mousserons: Discard the stems, wash the caps briefly in cold water, drain and pat dry.
Pigs' bladders: Rehydrate them in plenty of cold water for about 10 minutes, then drain and cut the opening large enough to take the chicken breasts.

2. Filling the bladders (15 minutes)
Halve the *foie gras*. Hold the chicken breasts with the wings tucked close in to the body and slide them into the bladders. Taking hold of each bladder in turn, fill each with half the *foie gras*, mushrooms, Armagnac, sherry, port and chicken stock and a large pinch of salt (you will need an assistant for this operation!). Tie the openings tightly

with about 10 turns of string, fold back the loose skin and tie with 5 more turns of string.

3. Cooking the dish (40 minutes)
Prepare a steamer with the water just at simmering point. Place the filled bladders on the steaming rack, leaving a little space between them, cover and steam for 40 minutes.

4. Preparing the garnish
(15 minutes)
Wash and peel all the root vegetables, cut into small pieces then trim into attractive barrel shapes. Keep each vegetable separate, covered with a damp cloth.

5. Cooking the vegetables
(10 minutes)
In a large sauté pan, heat the butter with a pinch of salt and 2 turns of pepper. Add 200 ml/7 fl oz cold water and bring to the boil. Put in the turnips and cook for 1 minute, then add the swedes, parsnips and carrots and cook for a further 5 minutes, allowing the water to evaporate until the vegetables are coated with a fine film of butter and water emulsion. Cook the French beans in boiling salted water for 2 – 3 minutes, then add them to the root vegetables.

6. Preparing the sauce; boning the breasts and serving (10 minutes)
Again, you will need two people for this – one to carve, the other to make the sauce. First lift the balloon-like bladders out of the steamer and place

them on a serving dish. Arrange the vegetables on the dish and present these dramatic-looking parcels to your guests.

If you feel brave enough, open them at the table. Cut a large opening with scissors, remove the chicken breasts, lift the meat off the bone and carve. Sprinkle the insides of the breasts with salt. Divide the *foie gras,* mushrooms and vegetables between the serving plates.

Meanwhile your partner will prepare the sauce; pour the juices from inside the bladders into a small saucepan, bring to the boil and skim off all the fat. Add the cream then whisk in the cold diced butter. Taste, correct seasoning and enliven with a squeeze of lemon. Serve the sauce separately in a sauceboat.

VARIATIONS

Guinea fowl can also be prepared this way.

The classic recipe calls for a whole chicken, but the difficulty lies in cooking the legs without overcooking the breasts.

The pigs' bladders can be replaced by roasting bags, but the dish will not be quite the same!

WINE

With this highly aromatic dish, serve one of the great chardonnays – Puligny-Montrachet les Folatières, Combettes or Pucelles, or a Meursault Charmes. Less expensive but very pleasant would be a white Santenay 'Clos Rousseau' or Pernand-Vergelesses.

Chef's notes

Mousserons: Their particular flavour suits this dish best, though other varieties of fresh or dried wild mushrooms can be used. Rehydrate dried mushrooms in water for 15 minutes before use.

The foie gras can be omitted – a shame, but the dish will still be most delicious.

Coffre de volaille de Bresse en vessie, aux truffes et mousserons

Fresh truffles can be difficult to find and are inevitably expensive. If you must substitute tinned truffles, use only those labelled 'first cooking', or use truffle juice with a little port and Armagnac.

Chicken (see Where to buy, page 274): The choice is vitally important; Bresse chickens are without doubt the best. They are fed only on corn and the natural foods they peck from the ground and their taste and texture are unsurpassed. If you cannot find these, use maize-fed Landes or the best quality free-range birds you can find. *Pigs' bladders* may sound and look pretty awful. Would it help to tell you they are sold treated and washed thoroughly? The exchange of flavours which takes place during the cooking process is so wonderful that it is well worth conquering any misgivings you may have!

PERDREAU ROTI AU JUS A L'EMBEUREE DE JEUNES CHOUX

Roast young partridge served on a bed of cabbage leaves

"We are still privileged in England to find real grey leg English partridge; as soon as the season starts, these birds are the first to honour our table."

Serves 4
Difficulty: 🍳
Total recipe time: 1 hour 20 minutes
Special equipment: trussing needle, kitchen string

INGREDIENTS

4 young partridges (about 250 g/9 oz each, dressed weight), with their livers

2 teaspoons unsalted butter

2 teaspoons groundnut oil

salt and freshly ground white pepper

Juice
wings and necks of partridges

2 shallots, chopped

2 teaspoons unsalted butter

2 teaspoons non-scented oil

1 sprig of thyme

1 tablespoon red wine vinegar

1 small garlic clove, lightly crushed

1 juniper berry, crushed

4 tablespoons white wine

150 ml/5 fl oz Brown chicken stock (see page 21)

Garnish
1 small green cabbage

1 tablespoon unsalted butter

50 g/2 oz each smoked and unsmoked streaky bacon for lardons (see page 47)

Planning ahead
Order 4 young wild partridges well in advance; they should be hung for 4–6 days to develop their delicate flavour. Ask the butcher to pluck and draw the birds, to remove the wishbones and give you the livers, necks and wings. Stages 1–3 can be prepared in advance.

1. Preparing the partridges
(10 minutes)
Singe any stubble over an open flame or remove with a small sharp knife, truss the birds (see page 16) and season inside and out.
Livers: Remove the gall, soak under running water for a few minutes, pat dry, season and pan-fry for a few minutes in 1 teaspoon butter. Chop finely.

2. Preparing the juice (20 minutes)
In a medium sauté pan, heat the butter and oil until hot then sear the partridge wings and necks until lightly coloured. Add the shallots and sweat gently for 2–3 minutes. Pour off the fat, add the vinegar and allow to evaporate completely. Add the wine, boil for 30 seconds then add 100 ml/3½ fl oz cold water, the chicken stock, thyme and garlic. Bring to the boil, skim, and simmer for 10 minutes. Add the livers and simmer for 1 more minute. Strain through a fine sieve and reserve for Stage 5.

3. Preparing and blanching the cabbage and lardons (25 minutes)
Preheat the oven to 190°C/375°F/gas 5 for Stage 4.
Cabbage: Quarter and remove the core. Wash and drain. Blanch the leaves in plenty of boiling salted water for 1 minute, refresh in cold water and drain. Place in a saucepan with 1 tablespoon butter and season. Set aside.
Lardons: Follow the method on page 47. Mix with the cabbage.

4. Roasting the partridges
(12 minutes plus 10 minutes resting)
In a large frying pan, heat the butter and oil and brown the partridges for 2 minutes on each thigh and 30 seconds on each breast. Turn them on their backs and roast in the preheated oven for 12 minutes. Pour off the fat and leave to rest for a few minutes in a warm place, covered with grease-proof paper.

5. Finishing the juice (5 minutes)
Add the reserved juices to the frying pan and scrape up the caramelized bits from the bottom. Bring to the boil, skin and reduce until the juice is light-textured and well coloured. Taste and correct seasoning.

6. Assembling the dish and serving (10 minutes)
Warm 4 plates.
Return the partridges to the oven for 5 minutes.
Meanwhile cook the cabbage, covered, for a further 2–3 minutes. Arrange the cabbage leaves in a circle in the centre of the plates, leaving some space around the edge for the gravy. Sit the partridges in the middle, pour the gravy around and scatter over the *lardons*. Serve the dish at once.

--- VARIATIONS ---
Squabs or wild pigeon are also delicious cooked this way.
For a more substantial sauce, bone the partridges after roasting, add the chopped bones to the juices, infuse for a further 5 minutes then strain into a saucepan and cook as above.

--- WINE ---
The choice is open provided that the wine has sufficient character to match the wide range of flavours in the dish. A white wine must be distinctive – a spicy Gewürztraminer or Riesling would be delicious – or try a mature but mellow red wine, like a Beaune.

Chef's notes
Partridge: The quality of this dish depends on the type of partridge you choose. French red leg partridges are often said to be the best; this is no longer true, as the wild red leg is practically extinct and only cross-breeds are now available – large, white-fleshed, tasteless birds resistant to all known diseases. They have no place in a good cook's kitchen.
The English grey leg is the best. Choose young birds between 2 and 5 months old. They should be small (about 250 g/9 oz dressed weight) with good rounded breasts and a deeper pink colour beneath the skin. They should smell pleasant but not gamey. The given roasting time is for 250 g/9 oz birds. Adjust as necessary.
Cabbage: If you can find small delicate-tasting young Autumn cabbage, do not blanch the leaves. Simply cook at the last moment for 3–4 minutes in 100 ml/3½ fl oz water with 1 tablespoon butter, salt and pepper.

CANARD SAUVAGE ROTI A LA PUREE DE COINGS

Wild duck served with its juices and a quince purée

Serves 4
Difficulty: 👨‍🍳 👨‍🍳
Total recipe time: 1 hour 20 minutes
Special equipment: piping bag with 5 mm/¼ in star nozzle

--- INGREDIENTS ---
2 wild duck (mallard)
20 g/¾ oz unsalted butter
25 ml/1 fl oz non-scented oil
salt and freshly ground white pepper

Juices
carcasses from the ducks
cooking fat from searing the ducks
4 tablespoons Cognac
400 ml/14 fl oz cold water

200 ml/7 fl oz Brown chicken stock (see page 21)
a pinch of ground cinnamon

Garnish
1 orange
1 coffee spoon unsalted butter
1 teaspoon caster sugar
400 g/14 oz Quince purée (see page 48)

Planning ahead
Order the wild ducks well in advance; they should be hung for no more than 3 days. Ask your butcher to pluck and draw the birds, to remove sinews from the legs and the wishbones and to truss them. Ask for the necks and wings to use for the sauce.
The chicken stock must be prepared 1 day in advance.
The quince purée must be made in advance.
Stage 2 can be completed several hours in advance.

1. Preparing and roasting the wild ducks (35 minutes)

Preheat the oven to 230°C/450°F/gas 8.

Singe the ducks over an open flame to remove stubble.

In a large sauté pan, heat the butter and oil, put in the birds and sear the breasts and thighs for 2–3 minutes. Season with salt and pepper, turn them on their backs and roast in the preheated oven for 20 minutes. Transfer to a small tray, cover with foil and leave to rest for 5 minutes. Reserve the cooking fat for Stage 4.

Meanwhile, prepare the garnish.

2. Preparing the garnish (20 minutes)

Orange: Using a potato peeler, peel off large strips of zest and cut them into fine *julienne* (see page 49). Blanch in 1 L/1¾ pt boiling water for about 10 minutes, drain and refresh. Put the zests in a small saucepan with 1 coffee spoon butter, 1 teaspoon sugar and the juice of half the orange, bring to the boil and reduce until glazed.

Quince purée: Warm the purée in a small saucepan, then place half in the piping bag and keep in a warm place. Cover the remaining purée with buttered paper and keep warm.

3. Carving the ducks and preparing the sauce (35 minutes)

Reserving all the juices remaining in the tray, transfer the ducks to a chopping board and, with a sharp boning knife, cut off the legs and section at the joint between drumstick and thigh. Cut out the breasts, season the insides, peel off the skin, and reserve the breasts, legs and thighs on a small tray. Cover with foil and keep warm.

Skin: Roll the skin, cut into fine strips and place in a baking dish in a hot oven to crisp for about 5 minutes.

Carcasses: With a heavy knife, chop the carcasses, wings and necks into small pieces, place in the sauté pan used for searing the ducks and brown them over a strong heat for about 6 minutes. Tilt the pan to skim off as much fat as possible, then deglaze with Cognac. Pour in 400 ml/14 fl oz cold water and the chicken stock, bring to the boil, skim and simmer for 10 minutes.

Strain the juices into a small saucepan, pressing on the bones with a ladle to extract as much juice and flavour as possible. Add a pinch of cinnamon, bring to the boil and reduce to about 200 ml/7 fl oz. Taste and season with a tiny pinch of salt and 3 or 4 turns of pepper. Keep warm.

4. Assembling the dish and serving (10 minutes)

Warm 4 plates.

With a sharp knife, slice the duck breasts into fine slivers (keeping the overall shape of the breasts intact), then return the sliced breasts, legs, thighs and crisped skin to the oven for 2–3 minutes.

Pipe a ribbon of quince purée around the inside of each plate, place a duck thigh in the centre, fan the breast over, top with the leg and scatter over the crisped duck skin. Place the orange zests on top and spoon the juices over and around. Serve immediately.

Serve the remaining quince purée separately in a sauceboat.

--- VARIATIONS ---

Any variety of wild duck can be done this way.

Diced quinces can be added to the sauce.

--- WINE ---

One of the lighter red wines from the Côte de Beaune will suit this dish perfectly; a Volnay Caillerets, Champans or les Brouillards.

Chef's notes

Assembling the dish: To simplify, arrange the breasts, legs and thighs on a hot serving dish, pour the sauce around and scatter over the orange zests. Serve the quince purée separately.

*Canard sauvage
rôti à la purée
de coings (page 204)*

BECASSINES ROTIES AU VIEUX MADERE, NOIX ET JULIENNE DE LEGUMES FRITE

*Roast snipe in a sauce of old Madeira and walnuts,
garnished with deep-fried turnips and celeriac*

"Thank God man has not yet found a way to farm these tiny game birds, which are fit for a feast; their flesh is particularly delicate and their flavour quite unsurpassed."

Serves 4
Difficulty: 🍳🍳
Total recipe time: 1 hour 5 minutes
Special equipment: deep-fryer

─────── INGREDIENTS ───────
8 snipe, drawn and trussed, with their livers

2 teaspoons sunflower or corn oil

2 teaspoons unsalted butter

salt and freshly ground white pepper

Sauce
100 g/3½ oz button mushrooms, trimmed and finely sliced

3 shelled walnuts, crushed to a paste

50 ml/2 fl oz port

100 ml/3½ fl oz vintage Madeira

150 ml/5 fl oz Brown chicken stock (see page 21)

livers from the snipe

Garnish
12 fresh walnuts

2 medium turnips, washed, peeled and cut into julienne

200 g/7 oz celeriac, washed, peeled and cut into julienne

oil for deep-frying

Planning ahead

Order the snipe well in advance. They should have been hung for no more than 3 days. Ask the butcher to pluck, draw and truss the birds (but not to remove the feet) and to keep the livers, wings and necks.

The veal stock must be made in advance.

Stages 1 and 2 can be completed several hours in advance.

1. Preparing the snipe
(10 minutes)

Preheat the oven to 230°C/450°F/gas 8.

Singe the snipe over an open flame to remove stubble (or remove it with a sharp knife).

Remove the gall bladder from the livers, season and put the livers back into the birds. It is not necessary to bard them, since the cooking time is short.

2. Preparing the vegetables and walnuts for the garnish
(20 minutes)

Fresh walnuts: Crack them open carefully, halve and blanch in simmering water for 1 minute. Drain, refresh and peel. Set aside.

Turnip and celeriac julienne: Deep-fry in hot oil, 4 at a time, until a deep golden brown, keeping the strips separated with a kitchen fork. Lift out, shake off excess oil and drain on absorbent paper.

3. Searing and roasting the snipe
(7 minutes)

In a roasting pan, heat 2 teaspoons each of oil and butter, then sear the birds all over for 2 minutes. Pour off excess fat and season the birds with salt and pepper. Turn them onto their backs and roast in the preheated oven for 5 minutes.

Transfer the roast snipe to a chopping board and reserve the cooking fat in the pan. Using a teaspoon, remove the livers from inside the birds and crush to a purée. Reserve the puréed livers for the sauce.

Divide the legs and thighs. Cut out the backbones, leaving the breasts on the bone. Loosely cover the legs and breasts with foil and keep warm. Chop the backbones and reserve for the sauce.

4. The sauce (20 minutes)

Heat the reserved oil and butter in the sauté pan and sauté the snipe necks and wings for 1 minute until lightly coloured. Add the sliced mushrooms and sear over a strong heat for 2 minutes. Tilt the pan to pour off excess fat then deglaze with the port and Madeira. Reduce by half, then add 200 ml/7 fl oz cold water, the chicken

Bécassines rôties au vieux Madère, noix et julienne de légumes frite

stock and finally the walnut paste. Add the chopped backbones and simmer for 5 minutes, then whisk in the puréed livers and simmer for a further 3 minutes.

Force first through a hard sieve, pressing on the bones with a ladle to extract all the juices and flavour, then pass through a fine sieve into a small pan. Bring to the boil and reduce to a light consistency mid-way between a sauce and a juice before adding the blanched walnuts. Taste and season with a tiny pinch of salt and 4 turns of pepper.

5. Assembling and serving the dish
(10 minutes)
Warm 4 plates.

Return the snipe and turnip and celeriac *julienne* to the oven for 2–3 minutes.

Place 2 snipe in the centre of each plate, arranging the legs next to the breasts to reconstitute their original shape and arrange a mound of deep-fried turnip and celeriac on either side. Spoon the sauce over and around, add the whole walnuts and serve.

─── VARIATIONS ───

Woodcock, partridge and pheasant can all be cooked this way.
Finely sliced apples, sprinkled with caster sugar and glazed under the grill would add a suitably Autumnal note to the dish.

─── WINE ───

Serve the best mature claret or Burgundy you can afford.

Chef's notes
Vintage Madeira can be replaced by any good quality dry Madeira.
Walnuts: Fresh walnuts are used for the garnish as they have a more delicate flavour. Ready-shelled walnuts have a stronger flavour which is better suited to the sauce.
Roasting the snipe: Use a sauté pan large enough to leave sufficient space between the birds for the heat to circulate freely. If they are too tightly packed, the legs will not be cooked. Observe the cooking time rigorously.

───────────

FEUILLANTINES CARAMELISEES AUX POMMES, CREME AUX GOUSSES DE VANILLE

Leaves of caramelized craquelin and acidulated apples served with vanilla custard

Serves 4
Difficulty: ♟
Total recipe time: 25 minutes
Special equipment: sugar pan, round 7 cm/3 in pastry cutter

─── INGREDIENTS ───
4 medium Granny Smith apples
1 teaspoon unsalted butter
1 tablespoon caster sugar
2 tablespoons water
juice of ⅛ lemon
a dash of Calvados (optional)
400 ml/14 fl oz Vanilla custard (see page 33)
icing sugar for dusting

Craquelin *(see pages 45–6)*
50 ml/2 fl oz water

200 g/7 oz caster sugar
100 g/3½ oz flaked almonds

Apple sorbet, to garnish (see page 212) (optional)

Planning ahead
The apple sorbet, if used, must be made in advance.
The vanilla custard must be made in advance.
The *craquelin* can be made a few days in advance.
The apple segments can be cut and soaked 3 hours in advance and kept at room temperature.

1. Making the leaves of craquelin
(10 minutes)
Preheat the oven to 200°C/400°F/gas 6.
Lightly oil a baking tray. Sprinkle the

finely ground *craquelin* powder in a very fine, even layer. Place in the oven for about 5 minutes until completely melted. Allow to cool for 1 minute, then cut 14 or 15 rounds with a pastry cutter. Transfer to a cooling tray using a spatula. You will only need 12 rounds, but make extra in case some get damaged.

2. Preparing and cooking the apples (8 minutes)
Peel, quarter and core. Cut into 3 mm/⅛ in slices and set aside.
In a large saucepan, melt the butter and sugar and cook for 2 minutes over medium heat. Add the lemon juice, water and apple slices, cover and cook for 1 minute.
Remove the lid, add a dash of Calvados if you like and cook for a further 2 minutes. Taste to check consistency – the apples should be cooked through,

but still firm. The juices should have produced a lovely syrup.

Put the apple slices on a tray to cool and, when cool, cover them with clingfilm.

3. Assembling the dish (5 minutes)

Have ready 4 plates.

Place a caramelized *craquelin* leaf in the centre of each plate, top with 2 layers of sliced apple, add another *craquelin*

leaf and repeat twice. Dust the tops with icing sugar, pour the vanilla cream around and, if you like, arrange a dessert spoon of apple sorbet on either side.

Chef's notes

Apples must be ripe, firm and slightly sharp in order to achieve the right balance between them and the snappy leaves of *craquelin*.

They are cooked in two stages, first covered to soften them, then uncovered to complete the cooking and reduce the juices to a syrup.

Craquelin: This must be completely cold before grinding. Be careful not to grind it to a paste or it will be difficult to handle.

In order to preserve the crisp texture, do not assemble the dish until you are ready to serve.

POIRE POCHÉE AU VIN DE ST EMILION, FRAMBOISES ET FIGUES

William pear poached in St Emilion, served with Autumn raspberries and figs

Serves 4

Difficulty: ♟

Total recipe time: 1 hour 15 minutes, plus 12 hours marinating

Special equipment: blender or food processor, apple corer

--- INGREDIENTS ---

4 small ripe William or Conference pears (125 g/4½ oz each)

100 g/3½ oz raspberries

400 ml/14 fl oz St Emilion red wine

300 ml/9 fl oz water

85 g/3 oz caster sugar

Garnish

200 g/7 oz ripe raspberries

4 large ripe figs

For finishing the sauce

2 tablespoons St Emilion wine

2 tablespoons puréed raspberries (from Stage 1)

For masking the pears

100 ml/3½ fl oz whipping cream

2 tablespoons blackcurrant liqueur

Planning ahead

Stages 1 to 3 inclusive must be completed 1 day in advance.

Stage 4 can be completed 3 hours in advance.

---

1. Preparing the fruits

(15 minutes)

Pears: Leaving the stalks on, peel, trim the bases so they can stand firmly and core. Wash.

100 g/3½ oz Raspberries: Hull, wash briefly, drain, purée and force through a fine sieve with a ladle. Reserve 2 tablespoons purée for Stage 4.

2. Poaching the pears (30 minutes)

In a medium saucepan mix the wine and cold water with the sugar and 100 g/3½ oz raspberry purée and boil for about 1 minute. Skim then strain into another medium saucepan.

Stand the pears upright in the pan and simmer for about 20 minutes. Leave to cool until tepid.

3. Steeping the raspberries and figs

(10 minutes plus 12 hours marinating)

200 g/7 oz Raspberries: Wash briefly, drain and hull.

Figs: Wash briefly, drain and make a

few incisions in the flesh.

Put the raspberries and figs in the tepid wine sauce, cover and marinate for 12 hours in the fridge.

4. Completing the sauce

(15 minutes)

Using a slotted spoon, transfer the pears to one small plate and the raspberries and figs to another.

Strain the sauce into a medium saucepan and reduce over a strong heat until it acquires a rich, dark sheen and has a semi-fluid consistency. Add 2 tablespoons wine and taste. Add 1 or 2 tablespoons reserved raspberry purée if too sweet. You should obtain about 150 ml/5 fl oz sauce.

5. Masking the pears (5 minutes)

Lightly whip the cream, stir in the blackcurrant liqueur and spoon over the pears.

6. Serving

Place a pear in the middle of each plate. Cut each fig into 6 segments and arrange attractively around. Scatter over the raspberries and spoon out the red wine sauce. Serve the dish immediately.

Chef's notes
William pears are only available in September. These plump yellow, delectably melting pears are undoubtedly the best variety to use in this recipe. Choose them ripe but still firm.
St Emilion can be replaced by a less expensive table wine.
Poaching the pears: Poach the pears gently at just below simmering point.

Too strong a boil will damage the fruit.
Steeping the fruits: The figs are pierced to allow the flavour of the marinade to come through.
The raspberries and figs are added to a tepid sauce to maximize the exchange of flavours between the fruits and the red wine. Make sure the sauce is just warm; if it is too hot, the fruits will

cook and become mushy.
Completing the sauce: The addition of 2 tablespoons red wine at this stage brings back the vinous character of the sauce and counterbalances the sweetness of the sugar. The quantity of wine needed will vary according to the strength of the wine; the more powerful the wine, the less you will need.

POMME SOUFFLEE AU SABAYON DE CIDRE

Calvados soufflé nestled in an apple, served with a cider sabayon

Serves 4
Difficulty: 🍳🍳
Total recipe time: 55 minutes
Special equipment: melon baller, electric mixer with whisk

—— INGREDIENTS ——
4 large eating apples (Juna Gold or Golden Delicious)

1 teaspoon unsalted butter

1 teaspoon caster sugar

a squeeze of lemon

a dash of Calvados

butter, for greasing the baking sheet

Garnish
2 eating apples

1 teaspoon unsalted butter

1 tablespoon caster sugar

100 ml/3½ fl oz Apple sorbet (see page 212) (optional)

Sabayon sauce
4 egg yolks

1 tablespoon caster sugar

200 ml/7 fl oz medium dry cider

1 tablespoon Calvados

Soufflé mixture
2 egg yolks plus 25 g/1 oz caster sugar plus 1 tablespoon Calvados

4 egg whites plus 25 g/1 oz caster sugar plus a squeeze of lemon

icing sugar, for dusting the soufflés

Planning ahead
Stages 1 to 3 inclusive can be completed in advance.
The apple sorbet, if used, must be made a few hours in advance and shaped into tiny *quenelles,* which can be stored on a plate in the freezer.

1. Preparing the apples
(10 minutes)
Slice off the top third of the 4 apples then trim the bases so that the apples can stand up straight. Using a dessert spoon, scoop out the flesh leaving an outer shell 5–7 mm/about ¼ in thick.
In a small saucepan, melt 1 teaspoon butter with 1 teaspoon sugar and add a

dash of Calvados and lemon juice. Brush onto the insides of the apples then wrap the apples in clingfilm and refrigerate.

2. Preparing the garnish
(10 minutes)
Peel 2 apples and scoop out 16 balls with a melon baller. In a small saucepan, melt 1 teaspoon butter with 1 tablespoon sugar, add the apple balls and cook over a strong heat for about 5 minutes until caramelized. Place in a small container and seal with clingfilm.

3. Making the cider sabayon
(15 minutes) (see Sweet sabayon, page 30)
In a mixing bowl, whisk together the egg yolks and sugar until pale yellow, then whisk in the cider and stand the bowl in a bain-marie at just below simmering point. Continue whisking for about 10 minutes until the mixture has a light but firm texture like whipped cream. Check the temperature with a thermometer – when it reaches 21°–26°C/70°-80°F, the *sabayon* will be ready. Draw off the heat and continue whisking for about 5 minutes until cooled. Cover with clingfilm and refrigerate.

4. Making the soufflé; filling the apples (10 minutes)

Preheat the oven to 190°C/375°F/gas 5.

In a mixing bowl cream together 2 egg yolks and 25 g/1 oz sugar until a pale straw colour. Set aside.

In an electric mixer, beat the egg whites to a light peak, then add 25 g/1 oz sugar and a squeeze of lemon and beat until very firm. Add 1 tablespoon Calvados to the egg yolk mixture then briskly whisk in a quarter of the egg whites. Fold in the remainder.

Remove the clingfilm from the prepared apples and fill with the soufflé mixture. Recreate the original shape of the apples by over-filling and smoothing the tops into dome shapes. Dust with icing sugar.

5. Baking the soufflés

(12 minutes)

Stand the apples on a lightly buttered baking sheet and bake in the preheated oven for 10 – 12 minutes.

6. Assembling the dish and serving

While the soufflés are cooking, place 3 tablespoons cider *sabayon* in the centre of your dessert plates, spreading it in a circle with the back of a spoon. Arrange 4 caramelized apple balls on each plate.

When the soufflés are ready, place 1 in the centre of each plate and arrange a *quenelle* of apple sorbet (if using) on either side. Serve the remaining sauce in a sauceboat.

VARIATIONS

Replace the *sabayon* with an apricot *coulis* (see page 31) and the apple sorbet with a rich vanilla ice cream (page 33). Use the apple trimmings to make an apple purée.

WINE

Why not try a good dry or medium dry farm cider with this dessert?

Chef's notes

Apples: You must use only the suggested varieties, which should be perfectly ripe but still firm, or they could burst open during cooking.

Be careful not to tear the sides when scooping out the flesh, as they are the moulds which will hold the soufflé.

This dessert is designed to make the most of the combination of apple-based textures and flavours and the contrast between the barely-cooked apple shell and the melting soufflé. If the shell is too thick it will be under-cooked; too thin and it will collapse during cooking.

Making the soufflé: Unlike other soufflé mixtures, the egg whites must be beaten very firm to minimize the effects of steam on the soufflé caused by water evaporation from the apple skin.

Making the sabayon: The whisking is quite a performance and really needs two people to do it.

Pomme soufflée au sabayon de cidre

SORBET AUX POMMES

Apple sorbet

Makes 800 ml/1¼–1½ pt (enough to serve 12)
Difficulty: 🍳
Total recipe time: 45 minutes
Special equipment: blender, *sorbetière*

───── INGREDIENTS─────
1 kg/2¼ lb Granny Smith apples

150 g/5 oz caster sugar

juice of ½ lemon

Peel, halve, core and finely slice the apples.
In a large saucepan, boil 4 tablespoons water with the lemon juice and sugar. Add the sliced apples, cover, and boil gently for 5 minutes until softened. Remove the lid and cook for a further 5 minutes until the apples are almost cooked to a pulp. Purée, then pass through a sieve and leave to cool. Taste, then churn in a *sorbetière* for 12–25 minutes and freeze.

Chef's notes
Apples: When choosing fruit, always taste it first; the quality of the fruit will determine the quality of the sorbet. Ideally the apples should be sweet with just a hint of acidity.
Always allow the mixture to cool before tasting and churning. If tasted hot, you will get a false impression of the sweetness/acidity balance. You may need to add a little more caster sugar or lemon juice at this stage.

GLACE AU CARAMEL

Caramel ice cream

Serves 4–6
Difficulty: 🍳
Total recipe time: 40–50 minutes, plus 1 hour cooling.
Special equipment: sugar pan or high-sided, heavy-bottomed saucepan, ice-cream maker.

───── INGREDIENTS ─────
Vanilla custard
6 egg yolks

25 g/1 oz caster sugar

½ vanilla pod, split lengthways and scraped

250 ml/9 fl oz milk

250 ml/9 fl oz double cream

Caramel
100 ml/3½ fl oz water

150 g/5 oz caster sugar

Planning ahead
The caramel-flavoured vanilla custard must be cooled for about 1 hour

before churning.
Chill serving plates or glasses 1–2 hours before serving.

1. Making the vanilla custard
(10 minutes) (see page 33)
In a large mixing bowl, cream together the egg yolks and sugar until they turn a pale straw colour.
Combine the milk, cream and split vanilla pod in a large heavy-bottomed saucepan. Bring to the boil and simmer for about 5 minutes. Draw off the heat for 30 seconds and remove the vanilla pod.
Pour the milk onto the egg mixture and, whisking continuously, return the mixture to the saucepan set over medium heat. Stir until the custard coats the back of your spoon. Strain into a mixing bowl and stir for a few minutes.

2. Making the caramel
(10 minutes) (see page 32)
Pour the water into a sugar pan and add the sugar in a mound in the centre of the pan. Set over medium heat and cook to a rich, dark caramel.

3. Mixing the vanilla cream and caramel (3 minutes)
Pour the hot caramel into the warm vanilla cream, whisking until it is well incorporated. Cool for about 1 hour.

4. Churning (15 to 25 minutes)
Churn the cooled custard in an ice-cream maker for 15 – 25 minutes, depending on the machine.

5. Serving
Shape the ice cream into *quenelles* with 2 tablespoons dipped in hot water and arrange on the chilled plates. Serve with Chocolate sauce (page 31) or Caramel sauce with Armagnac (page 32) garnished with Caramelized almonds (page 46).

Chef's notes
The degree of browning of the caramel is very important. If it is too pale, the ice cream will be sweet and the caramel flavour will not come through. Brown the caramel as much as possible without burning; this will kill the sweetness and enhance the colour and caramel taste of the ice cream.

Desserts

FEUILLETE DE POIRE AU CARAMEL PARFUME AU GINGEMBRE, CREME VANILLE AU CITRON VERT

William pear in a melting puff pastry case, masked with a warm ginger butterscotch sauce and a cold lime custard

"One of my oldest desserts – and still one of my favourites."

Serves 4
Difficulty: ♟ ♟ ♟
Total recipe time: 1 hour 15 minutes
Special equipment: pastry sheet, sugar pan or heavy-bottomed straight-sided saucepan, pear-shaped pastry cutter (optional)

—— INGREDIENTS ——
2 William pears

600 ml/1 pt water

50 g/2 oz caster sugar

¼ vanilla pod, split lengthways

1 tablespoon lemon juice

Pastry cases
200 g/7 oz Puff pastry (see page 42)

a handful of flour, to dust the work surface

1 egg yolk mixed with 2 teaspoons milk, to glaze

Lime custard
3 egg yolks

1 tablespoon caster sugar

250 ml/9 fl oz milk

2 strips each of lemon and lime zest, finely chopped

¼ vanilla pod, split lengthways and chopped

Butterscotch sauce flavoured with ginger and lime (see page 32)
50 ml/2 fl oz water

50 ml/2 fl oz liquid glucose

15 g/½ oz root ginger, finely chopped

juice of ½ lime

250 ml/9 fl oz double cream

Garnish
4 small sprigs of mint

Lime sorbet (see page 266) (optional)

icing sugar for dredging

Planning ahead
The puff pastry must be made in advance (see page 42 for recipe).
Stages 1–4 inclusive can be completed 1 day in advance.
Stage 5 can be completed 1 hour in advance.

1. Rolling, chilling and cutting the puff pastry (15 minutes)
On a lightly floured surface, roll out the puff pastry to a 5 mm/¼ in thickness. Place on a lightly floured tray, cover with clingfilm and chill in the fridge for 20 minutes, or in the freezer for 10 minutes, to harden and lose some of its elasticity.
Cut into 4 pear shapes using a small knife or pastry cutters. Place in the fridge until Stage 5.

2. Poaching the pears
(20 minutes, plus cooling)
In a small saucepan, bring to the boil the water, sugar, vanilla pod and lemon juice. Reduce heat to just below simmering point.
Peel and halve the pears, remove the cores and stringy fibres, then wash briefly in cold water. Put them into the syrup, cover with pierced foil and poach gently for about 20 minutes. Leave the pears to cool in their cooking liquid.

3. Making the lime custard
(10 minutes) (see Vanilla custard, page 33)
Prepare yourself with a china bowl and a fine sieve.
Cream together the egg yolks and sugar until pale and straw-coloured. Combine the milk, lime and lemon zests and ¼ vanilla pod in a medium saucepan, bring to the boil and simmer for a few minutes to infuse all the flavours. Draw off the heat, allow to cool slightly then pour onto the egg and sugar mixture, whisking constantly. Return to the saucepan and, over medium heat, stir with a wooden spoon to bind the custard. When it coats the back of your spoon, strain immediately into the bowl and continue stirring until cooled. Refrigerate until needed.

4. Butterscotch sauce flavoured with ginger and lime (15 minutes)
(see page 32)
Combine the water, ginger, lime juice and glucose in a sugar pan and bring to the boil over a strong heat. Cook to a dark caramel. Add the cream, bring back to the boil and simmer for about 1 minute until the sauce is a rich dark brown.

5. Cooking the puff pastry cases
(10 minutes) (see page 42)
Preheat the oven to 220°C/425°F/gas 7.

Space the pastry cases well apart on a pastry sheet brushed with water. Glaze the tops with a little beaten egg yolk and milk and bake in the preheated oven for about 10 minutes.

Remove, leave to cool for a few minutes then slice off the tops with a sharp serrated knife. Scoop out the insides of the cases with a teaspoon to make 4 thin cases and 4 lids. Keep on a small tray.

6. Finishing and assembling the dish (5 minutes)

Prepare 4 large dessert plates.

Simmer the 4 pear halves in the butterscotch sauce for about 3 minutes, until hot. Warm the 4 pastry cases and lids in the oven for 1 minute. Dust the lids with icing sugar.

Place a pastry case in the middle of each plate, fill with a pear half, spoon over the lime butterscotch sauce. Top with a lid. Surround with 2 or 3 table-spoons lime custard and decorate with mint leaves. Place a *quenelle* of lime sorbet, if using, on either side and serve at once.

--- VARIATIONS ---

To simplify the dish, omit the puff pastry cases. It will still be delectable. You can also use apples, but do not poach them; bake halved apples in the oven for 10 minutes with 1 teaspoon butter, 2 tablespoons caster sugar and juice of ¼ lemon. Add the lime butterscotch sauce, cook a further 5 minutes and serve the same way.

--- WINE ---

Why not serve a lightly chilled aromatic Alsace Riesling, if possible a *vendange tardive*? Rieslings from Alsace are not as sweet as those from neighbouring Germany, but have a delicate and unique floweriness.

Chef's notes

Pears: It is well worth looking for William pears which have the heaviest scent and most melting texture. They are in full season in September.

Chilling the puff pastry: The pastry must be chilled after rolling; if cut immediately after rolling, it will shrink. Chilling also hardens it and makes it easier to handle. When you cut the firm pastry, it will not compress and stick the layers so they rise unevenly.

Cooking the pears: Taste one before cooking; do not rely on their pretty appearance. If slightly sharp, add an extra 50 g/2 oz caster sugar to the cooking liquid.

Removing the insides of the pastry cases: It is important to scrape out the heavy, indigestible uncooked dough to obtain crisp, melting cases. They must still be warm at this stage; do not attempt it when cold. The pastry is very delicate, so work with great care.

FRUIT DEFENDU

Forbidden fruit – a poached white peach set on an iced parfait, imprisoned in a cage of blonde caramel

Fruit defendu

Serves 4
Difficulty: 👨‍🍳👨‍🍳
Total recipe time: 1 hour 25 minutes plus 4 hours freezing
Special equipment: ice cream maker (optional), 4 round *savarin* moulds or ramekins, sugar pan, palette knife

—— INGREDIENTS ——
4 white peaches

300 ml/½ pt dry white wine

150 g/5 oz caster sugar

1 vanilla pod (optional)

2 slices each of orange and lemon

Kirsch ice cream
250 ml/9 fl oz milk

250 ml/9 fl oz double cream

6 egg yolks

65 g/2½ oz caster sugar

2 vanilla pods, split lengthways and scraped

50 ml/2 fl oz kirsch

Caramel cages
100 ml/3½ fl oz water

200 g/7 oz caster sugar

sunflower or grapeseed oil, for greasing the moulds

Sauce
200 ml/7 fl oz cooking juices from the peaches

2 white peaches

1 apricot

1 teaspoon caster sugar

a squeeze of lemon

4 small sprigs of mint, to garnish

Planning ahead

Stages 1–3 inclusive can be completed 1 day in advance.

Stage 4 can be completed a few hours before the meal.

Chill 4 large dessert plates for serving.

---

1. Making the kirsch ice cream

(30 minutes plus 4 hours freezing) (for more information see Vanilla ice cream, page 33)

In a heavy-bottomed saucepan bring the milk and double cream to the boil with the split vanilla pods.

Meanwhile, in a mixing bowl, cream the egg yolks and sugar to a pale straw colour. Draw the milk off the heat, remove the vanilla pods and whisk into the creamed eggs and sugar.

Return the mixture to the saucepan, place over medium heat and stir constantly until it thickens. Cool then add the kirsch. If using an ice-cream maker, churn the mixture, fill the *savarin* moulds or half-fill the ramekins and freeze for 1 hour until firm; otherwise, simply pour the mixture into the moulds and freeze for at least 4 hours.

2. Poaching the fruit (35 minutes plus cooling time)

Put the 4 peaches in a medium saucepan and cover with 750 ml/1¼ pt water and the white wine. Add the sugar, vanilla pod and orange and lemon slices. Boil for a few seconds and skim. Cover the pan with pierced greaseproof paper, reduce the heat to just below simmering point and cook for about 30 minutes.

Allow the peaches to cool in the cooking liquid.

3. Making the sauce (10 minutes)

Stone the raw peaches and apricot. Chop the flesh into small pieces and place in a small saucepan with 200 ml/ 7 fl oz of the cooking liquid from Stage 1. Bring to the boil and simmer for about 5 minutes. Cool then purée finely and strain through a fine sieve. Taste and correct with a little more sugar or a squeeze of lemon.

4. Making the caramel cages

(20 minutes) (see diagram, below) (see page 32 for how to make caramel)

With your hand spread a thin film of oil over the back of a large ladle. Have a fork or spoon ready.

Make a blonde caramel with the water and sugar, draw off the heat and cool for about 1 minute, until it begins to harden. Dip your fork or spoon into the caramel and pull the threads into a fine trellis over the back of the ladle. Very carefully twist the cage free and place on a small tray. By now the caramel in the pan will have hardened, so return it to the heat until softened and repeat the process until you have made 4 cages. Keep them at room temperature in a dry place.

Dip a spoon or fork into the caramel. Thread the caramel over the back of a lightly oiled ladle.

Make a second layer of caramel threads criss-crossing the first layer.

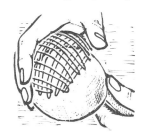

Carefully lift off the caramel cage.

5. Assembling the dish (15 minutes)

Dip the moulds in warm water for 1 or 2 seconds and turn out the ice creams onto a chilled plate. Place in the freezer for about 10 minutes.

Drain the peaches from their cooking liquid, remove the stems and peel, then slit the peaches down the middle and carefully extract the stones without damaging the shape of the fruit. Reshape the peaches.

Place an ice cream in the centre of each chilled dessert plate. Sit a peach on top, decorate with a tiny sprig of mint, spoon the sauce around and finally imprison each fruit in its caramel cage. Serve at once.

--- VARIATION ---

For a simple and refreshing sweet, serve the poached peaches just as they are in their own cooking liquid.

--- WINE ---

A chilled dessert wine like Beaumes de Venise, or a sweet Barsac such as Château Coutet would be delicious.

Chef's notes

Peaches: Use perfectly ripe peaches; white ones are delectable.

Ice-cream: You will have some left over. Keep it to use in another recipe.

Cooking the peaches: This must be done with great care. Do not allow the liquid to boil or even simmer, as this will impair the texture. Depending on the size of the fruit, the cooking time will vary a little. The peaches are ready when bubbles of air escape from the base of the stems.

Making the caramel cages: The ladle must be completely covered with a film of oil to prevent the caramel from sticking. This technique may take a little practice, but you will have great fun perfecting it. Dip the tip of your fork 1 cm/½ in into the caramel, hold it about 10 cm/4 in above the ladle and allow the threads of caramel to fall downwards. Stretch each thread as finely as possible to construct your latticed cage.

EMINCE D'AVOCAT AU CRABE,
GINGEMBRE ET
PAMPLEMOUSSE ROSE

FRICASSEE DE POULET DE
BRESSE AU VIN JAUNE
D'ARBOIS ET MORILLES
FRAICHES

ASSIETTE DU JARDINIER

MOUSSE LEGERE AUX FRUITS
DE LA PASSION ET MANGUE

CHARTREUSE AUX POINTES
D'ASPERGES ET POIREAUX A
L'INFUSION DE CERFEUIL

ESCALOPE DE SAUMON
SAUVAGE AUX HERBES A
SOUPE ET BEURRE DE
TOMATES

MOUSSE D'EPINARDS

HARICOTS VERTS AU BEURRE

CREPE SOUFFLEE AU GRAND
MARNIER "FACON SUZETTE"

POTAGE LEGER AUX QUAT'
SAISONS

CARRE D'AGNEAU DE LAIT
ROTI, SON JUS PARFUME A LA
TAPENADE

PUREE D'AUBERGINES

FEVETTES A LA CREME ET
PERSIL PLAT

PAQUET SURPRISE DU
MANOIR

FILETS DE TURBOT ET
SAUMON SAUVAGE EN
PAUPIETTE DE CHOUX AUX
GRAINES DE CAVIAR

CANETON ROTI AUX SAVEURS
DU PRINTEMPS

ILES FLOTTANTES "FACON
MAMAN BLANC"

Winter

Winter is the least generous season — the great leveller. Outside, nature is harsh and barren but indoors there is comfort and welcoming warmth. Winter is a festive season offering entertaining and gathering of friends and family in the cosiness of home. The ease and speed of much modern transport brings all sorts of vegetables and exotic fruits from other countries to your table to break the monotony of Winter. Game is plentiful, the *foie gras* is at its best and magical, fresh truffles allow the chef to enjoy this otherwise lean time of the year. While nature sleeps, preparing itself for the new Spring, we gather and enjoy and do the giving ourselves.

BOUILLON DE POULE ET LEGUMES AUX PETITS FARCIS

*A chicken bouillon garnished with wild mushroom ravioli
and foie gras wrapped in young cabbage leaves*

Serves 4
Difficulty:
Total recipe time: 40 minutes preparation, plus 2 hours 40 minutes simmering
Special equipment: pestle and mortar, muslin cloth

————— INGREDIENTS —————

*1.75 kg/4–4½ lb boiling fowl,
cleaned and cut into 8 pieces*

300 g/11 oz blade or *shin of beef, cut
into 6 pieces*

1 teaspoon soy sauce

1 large onion, chopped

¼ celery stalk, chopped

*50 g/2 oz celeriac, finely diced
(optional)*

2 turnips, finely diced

1 small leek, cleaned and chopped

3 tomatoes, deseeded and chopped

*100 g/3½ oz button mushrooms,
finely chopped*

1 garlic clove, crushed

10 black peppercorns, crushed

¼ bayleaf

½ clove

1 sprig of thyme

Foie gras parcels

*100 g/3½ oz cooked foie gras (see
page 172)*

2 leek leaves

2 turnips

2 cabbage leaves

freshly ground white pepper

Wild mushroom ravioli

*125 g/4½ oz ravioli dough (see Pasta,
page 38)*

*100 g/3½ oz wild mushrooms,
washed, trimmed and finely diced*

1 shallot, finely chopped

2 teaspoons unsalted butter

2 tablespoons whipping cream

salt and freshly ground white pepper

Planning ahead

The *bouillon* can be prepared 2 days in advance and kept, covered, in the fridge.

The ravioli can be made 2 days in advance and kept in the freezer.

The *foie gras* parcels can be prepared several hours in advance.

1. The bouillon (2 hours 40 minutes)

Bouquet garni: Tie the crushed peppercorns, garlic, ¼ bayleaf, ½ clove and thyme in a square of damp muslin.

Place all the prepared vegetables and the *bouquet garni* in a large pan.

Place the chicken and beef on the bed of vegetables and cover with 3 L/ 5½ pt cold water. Bring to the boil and skim. Add the soy sauce and simmer gently for about 2 hours, skimming occasionally.

Remove the chicken and beef and strain the *bouillon* first through a fine conical sieve, then through a damp muslin cloth into a large saucepan.

Bring back to the boil and skim off all traces of fat.

Meanwhile, make the ravioli, *foie gras* parcels and vegetable garnish.

2. Wild mushroom ravioli

(30 minutes)

Sweat the shallots in the butter without colouring, add the mushrooms and sweat until all the moisture has evaporated. Stir in the cream and cook until very thick and creamy. Cool, then make 8 small ravioli according to the method on page 39.

Cook for 5 minutes in a little *bouillon*.

3. Foie gras parcels and vegetable garnish (20 minutes)

Foie gras: Cut into twelve 2 cm/¾ in cubes and refrigerate.

Cabbage and leek leaves: Blanch in plenty of boiling salted water for 2–3 minutes. Refresh in cold water and pat dry. Set the leek aside.

Remove central vein from cabbage leaves and cut into twenty-four 6 x 1 cm/2½ x ½ in strips. Take 2 strips and form into a cross. Make 12 crosses and place a cube of *foie gras* in each. Season with a few grains of salt and ½ turn of pepper and fold up the cabbage strips to make little parcels.

Leek leaves: Cut into 2 mm/¹⁄₁₀ in ribbons and use to tie up the cabbage parcels.

Turnips: Wash, peel and cut into fine sticks or small barrel shapes. Cook in the *bouillon* for 5–7 minutes.

Gently warm the *foie gras* parcels in the *bouillon* for 2–3 minutes, taking care not to boil.

4. Serving

Warm 4 soup bowls or a soup tureen.

Using a slotted spoon, divide the turnips, *foie gras* parcels and ravioli between the soup bowls. Pour over the *bouillon* and serve immediately.

Use duck or turkey instead of chicken; turkey is particularly delicious.
For a simpler garnish, add some fresh vegetables, a few wild mushrooms, or a little vermicelli. If you are feeling extravagant, toss in a little fresh truffle. Old-fashioned Frenchmen tip a little red wine into their *bouillon*. Definitely an acquired taste!

Chef's notes

It may seem wasteful to use a whole boiling fowl as well as the shin of beef, but you do need it for a concentrated flavour. Keep the cooked chicken meat for curries or chicken *à la crème;* the shin of beef can be minced, mixed with 1 egg, chopped parsley and garlic and used to stuff whole plump tomatoes. Bake in the oven and serve with a tomato *coulis* (see page 30) or cream flavoured with chives and tarragon.
The bouillon: In order to produce a clear *bouillon,* use cold water and bring to the boil. The gradual heat will coagulate the proteins and albumens and carry them to the surface. Skim and simmer very gently to keep the *bouillon* clear; a strong boil will turn it cloudy. It will not become as clear as a consommé, but the flavour is more concentrated. For a completely clear consommé, clarify with egg white (see page 23) – but some flavour will be lost.
Serving: Do not put the *foie gras* parcels into boiling *bouillon* as the *foie gras* will melt.

POTAGE DE MOULES

Mussel soup

Serves 4
Difficulty: ♟
Total recipe time: 1 hour 5 minutes
Special equipment: 1 very large saucepan for cooking the mussels, food processor or blender

INGREDIENTS

1.75 kg/4–4½ lb Bouchot mussels

1 tablespoon unsalted butter

½ celery stalk, washed and finely chopped

1 small onion, finely chopped

1 teaspoon curry powder

1 large pinch of saffron threads or 1 sachet of saffron powder

a pinch of cayenne pepper

1 sprig of thyme

300 ml/1 pt dry white wine

100 ml/3½ fl oz Light fish stock (see page 20) or water

150 ml/5 fl oz whipping cream

Garnish

croûtons, made with 6 slices of white bread (see page 109)

20 coriander leaves

Planning ahead

Order Bouchot mussels well in advance. They must be heavy with sea water and tightly closed. Reject any which remain open.
The fish stock, if used, must be made in advance.
Rehydrate saffron threads in warm water for at least 20 minutes before using.
The soup can be made 1–2 hours in advance.

1. Cleaning the mussels
(20 minutes)
Scrub the mussels, remove the beards and wash in plenty of cold water. Drain and set aside.

2. Cooking the mussels (20 minutes)
In a large saucepan, melt the butter and sweat the chopped onion and celery, curry powder, saffron, cayenne pepper and thyme, for 5 minutes without colouring. Pour in the wine, boil for 1 minute to remove alcohol and acidity then add the fish stock or water.
Throw in the mussels, cover and cook for 5–6 minutes until all the shells have opened. Draw off the heat and allow to cool.

3. Puréeing and straining the soup
(20 minutes)
Remove the mussels from their shells and pull out any beards. Reserve 20 mussels in some of the stock for garnish. Discard the sprig of thyme. Purée the mussels, juices and chopped vegetables for 2 minutes until smooth, then pass the soup first through a fine sieve then through a damp muslin cloth. Stir in the cream and warm the soup over a gentle heat (on no account must it boil).

4. Serving (5 minutes)
Warm 4 soup bowls.
Chop the coriander leaves.
Warm the reserved mussels and divide them between the warmed bowls. Ladle in the soup, sprinkle with chopped coriander and serve the *croûtons* separately.

VARIATIONS

The soup is also delicious served cold; in this case omit the *croûtons*.

Chef's notes

Bouchot mussels: This method of mussel culture is said to have been discovered by a quick-witted Irishman, who had stretched nets between wooden poles in the sea in order to catch birds. He observed that the poles were soon covered with mussel spawn. Since the mussels then hatched well above the sea bed, they contained no sand and thus were not gritty.

Salt: None should be needed, since the mussels are already salty.

SALADE D'AILE DE RAIE, POMMES DE TERRE PERSILLÉES AU VIN BLANC

Boned skate wings on a bed of parsleyed potatoes cooked in white wine

Serves 4
Difficulty: 🎩
Total recipe time: 1 hour 5 minutes

INGREDIENTS

1.5 kg/3½ lb skate wings, cut into 4

Court bouillon

1 medium onion, diced

white of 1 medium leek, cleaned and finely chopped

1 small carrot, peeled and diced

½ celery stalk

1 garlic clove

10 coriander seeds

1 bayleaf

1 sprig of thyme

1 teaspoon freshly ground white pepper

50 ml/2 fl oz white wine vinegar

1 level tablespoon salt

1 L/1¾ pt water

Mayonnaise

1 teaspoon Dijon mustard

1 egg yolk

2 tablespoons anchovy oil

4 tablespoons groundnut oil

lemon juice

salt and freshly ground white pepper

Potato salad

a small bunch of parsley, washed, trimmed and finely chopped

4 shallots, finely chopped

450 g/1 lb King Edward potatoes, peeled and cut into 1 cm/½ in dice

1 tablespoon herring or anchovy oil

4 tablespoons white wine vinegar

100 ml/3½ fl oz dry white wine

salt and freshly ground white pepper

Garnish

24 capers, drained

a handful of croûtons, rubbed with ½ garlic clove (see page 109)

1 lemon

a small bunch of parsley

oil for deep-frying

Planning ahead

Order the skate well in advance. Ask the fishmonger to section the main bone to make boning easier.

Stages 1–5 inclusive can be completed in advance.

The skate can be poached 1 hour in advance then boned and kept in a little *court bouillon*.

1. Preparing the skate (5 minutes)
Wash in plenty of cold water, pat dry, wrap in clingfilm and refrigerate.

2. The court bouillon
(20 minutes, plus 1 hour resting)
Put all the ingredients for the *court bouillon* in a medium saucepan and simmer for 30 minutes. Draw off the heat and leave to rest for 1 hour.

3. The light mayonnaise
(10 minutes)
In a small mixing bowl, combine the mustard and egg yolk, gradually whisk in the anchovy and groundnut oils, then loosen with 2 tablespoons of the *court bouillon*. Taste, season with salt and pepper and 'lift' with a squeeze of lemon. Keep at room temperature.

4. The potato salad (30 minutes)
Preheat the oven to 150°C/300°F/gas 2.
Wash the diced potato in plenty of

TOP

Salade d'aile de raie, pommes de terre persillées au vin blanc

BOTTOM

Balloline de saumon à l'effeuille de jeunes choux et lardons, sauce beurre blanc (page 184)

water, then place in a saucepan, cover with cold water, bring to simmering point and cook gently for about 8 minutes.

Drain in a colander, place in a small roasting pan and dry in the preheated oven for 5–6 minutes.

Transfer to a medium saucepan, add the finely chopped shallots and wine vinegar and reduce until the vinegar has evaporated. Add the white wine, bring to the boil and finally add the herring or anchovy oil. Draw off the heat, leave to cool then add the chopped parsley and set aside.

5. Cooking the skate (20 minutes)

Bring the *court bouillon* to the boil in a large saucepan, slide in the skate wings, skim, then draw off the heat, cover the pan and leave for about 15 minutes.

Remove the skate, scrape off the skin and drain on absorbent paper. Bone by sliding a flexible knife between the bone and flesh. Place the flesh in a small casserole with 200 ml/7 fl oz of the tepid *court bouillon* and set aside.

6. Preparing the garnish

(15 minutes)

Lemon: Peel off the rind and pith and cut the segments into tiny triangles. Set aside.

Parsley: Trim stalks, wash, pat dry and deep-fry in hot oil for a few seconds. Remove with a slotted spoon and drain on absorbent paper.

7. Finishing the dish and serving
Warm 4 plates.

Make a small mound of potatoes in the centre of each plate, surround with the boned skate wings, (which should be tepid) season with 2 turns of pepper, spoon the sauce around and scatter over the *croûtons,* lemon triangles, capers and deep-fried parsley. Serve to your guests.

——— VARIATIONS ———
Cod or haddock can also be served this way.

——— WINE ———
A 2- or 3-year-old spicy Pouilly Fumé (de Ladoucette) would be lovely; or try the even more aromatic and powerful Savennières, 'Coulée de Serrant'.

Chef's notes
Skate: Do not buy very small wings as their flavour is somewhat insipid. Fresh skate should be firm to the touch and have no fishy or ammoniac smell whatsoever.

Anchovy oil: Use the oil from tinned anchovies.

Cooking the potatoes: Do not cook them at full boil – they will become mushy on the outside and still not be cooked inside. Cooking time will vary according to the variety used. Check by tasting.

Cooking the skate: If the fish is overcooked, it will lose it firmness and become like cotton wool. Draw the *court bouillon* off the heat as soon as it comes to the boil then slide in the skate, which will cook by residual heat.

SALADE FRANCHE-COMTOISE

"A simple, traditional salad from Franche-Comté, dressed with a creamy vinaigrette, with Gruyère cheese, ham, button mushrooms and croûtons."

Serves 4
Difficulty: 🎩
Total recipe time: 15 minutes

——— INGREDIENTS ———
1 curly endive

Vinaigrette
1 teaspoon Dijon mustard

2 tablespoons sunflower oil

3 tablespoons whipping cream

1 teaspoon white wine vinegar

salt and freshly ground white pepper

Garnish
125 g/4½ oz lightly smoked ham, cut into small strips

125 g/4½ oz Gruyère cheese, diced

croûtons, made with 2 slices of white bread (see page 109)

100 g/3½ oz firm white button mushrooms, washed and finely sliced

a tiny bunch of chives, washed and finely chopped

whole chives, for serving

Planning ahead
Stages 1 and 2 can be completed several hours in advance.

1. Preparing the salads and vinaigrette (10 minutes)
Curly endive: Remove weathered and dark green leaves and cut off the root. Wash the pale leaves in two changes of water, shake dry and chop roughly.
Vinaigrette: Put the mustard in a small mixing bowl and whisk in the oil in a steady trickle until completely absorbed. Whisk in the cream and wine vinegar, season with a pinch of salt and 4 turns of pepper and set aside.

2. Assembling the salad and serving (5 minutes)
Mix the garnishes into the vinaigrette, add the chopped endive and toss until all the ingredients are well blended. Sprinkle with chopped chives and arrange the whole chives in a criss-cross pattern over the top.

——— VARIATIONS ———
Lentils, cooked with smoked bacon and cooled, make a nice addition.
Gruyère can be replaced by Emmenthal, which is slightly less salty.

——— WINE ———
The vinaigrette will spoil a fine wine, so choose a simple, light white regional wine from Macon, Provence or Savoie.

TERRINE DE FOIE GRAS AUX TRUFFES ET JEUNES POIREAUX CONFITS

A terrine of foie gras and leeks scented with truffles

Serves 10
Difficulty:
Total recipe time: 1 hour 10 minutes, plus 12 hours chilling
Special equipment: 23 x 9 x 8 cm/ 9 x 3½ x 3 in terrine, plus a piece of cardboard wrapped in clingfilm to fit inside, 2 kg/4½ lb weight, wire cooling rack

INGREDIENTS

675 g/1½ lb Terrine de foie gras (see page 172)

30 small leeks

200 ml/7 fl oz foie gras fat (from the terrine)

1 teaspoon white wine vinegar

65 g/2½ oz fresh truffles

salt and freshly ground white pepper

1 teaspoon white wine vinegar and 1 tablespoon grape seed oil, to serve

Planning ahead

The terrine of *foie gras* must be made at least 3 days in advance (see page 172 for recipe).
The *foie gras* and leek terrine must be made 6 hours in advance.

1. Slicing the foie gras (5 minutes)

Cut into six 2 cm/¾ in slices, place on a tray and leave at room temperature to soften.
Line the terrine mould with a sheet of clingfilm, leaving enough overhang to wrap the completed terrine in Stage 5.

2. Preparing the truffles and infusing them in foie gras fat

(20 minutes)
Clean the truffles with a soft brush under cold running water. Do not peel them. Slice finely and season with salt and pepper.
Put the *foie gras* fat and 1 teaspoon wine vinegar in a deep roasting pan. Add the truffles, bring just to simmering point, then draw off the heat and leave the truffles to infuse for about 15 minutes. Remove the sliced truffles and keep on a small plate. Reserve the fat for stage 4.

3. Preparing and cooking the leeks

(20 minutes)
In a large saucepan, boil 4 L/7 pt water with 4 tablespoons salt.
Cut off the roots of the leeks and trim them to the length of the terrine.
Remove weathered and coarse leaves and wash the leeks in 2 changes of water. Boil them for 4–6 minutes according to size (taste to check) then refresh, drain and squeeze out excess water in a folded tea towel, 3 at a time. Taste and correct seasoning if necessary.

4. Dipping the leeks in foie gras fat

(5 minutes)
Stand a wire rack over a tray. Dip the leeks into the reserved *foie gras* fat and drain to remove excess.

5. Building the terrine

(10 minutes)
Line the terrine first with 2 layers of leeks, (6 leeks in each layer), alternating them top to tail to give a green and white striped effect.
Add a layer of about half the truffle slices, then a layer of 3 *foie gras* slices. Firm down the layers. Add another layer of leeks, then one of *foie gras*, scatter over the remaining truffle slices and finish with 2 layers of leeks. The last layer will stand slightly proud of the terrine.

Wrap the terrine with the overhanging clingfilm, place the clingfilm-wrapped cardboard on top and press down firmly to compress the leeks and foie gras. Put in the 2 kg/4½ lb weight and refrigerate for at least 6 hours before serving.

6. Slicing the terrine and serving

(10 minutes)
Remove weight and cardboard and peel back the clingfilm. Invert the terrine onto a carving board and slice with a sharp serrated knife, letting the blade do all the work so as not to disturb the fragile layers. Leave at room temperature for about 10 minutes before serving.
Mix 1 teaspoon wine vinegar with 1 teaspoon grape seed oil, season with a few grains of salt and pepper and brush over each slice. Serve to your guests.

WINE

Serve not too dry a white wine; Tokay d'Alsace or Riesling will be fine.

Chef's notes

Leeks must be young and very fresh.
Truffles must also be fresh so that they lend their flavour to the *foie gras* fat and leeks.
Cooking the leeks: All the water must be wrung out, or they will not bind together. Coat them liberally in the fat, which will help to hold the terrine together.
Building the terrine: The layers of leeks and *foie gras* must be well pressed together for the terrine to hold its shape.
The terrine must be eaten within 1 day, as the water in the leeks will start to permeate the *foie gras*.

SALADE D'AIGUILLETTES DE CANARD SAUVAGE AUX CELERI-RAVE ET POMMES

Salad of wild duck served with its juices, apples and celeriac

Serves 4
Difficulty: 🍞🍞
Total recipe time: 1½ hours
Special equipment: deep-fryer, muslin cloth

INGREDIENTS

2 wild ducks

1 teaspoon non-scented oil

Juice

50 ml/2 fl oz non-scented oil

50 ml/2 fl oz white wine vinegar

50 ml/2 fl oz Cognac

100 ml/3½ fl oz cold water

1 tablespoon Brown chicken stock (see page 21) (optional)

a dash of soy sauce

freshly ground white pepper

Garnish

400 g/14 oz chicory

2 tablespoons Walnut vinaigrette (see page 30)

2 Granny Smith apples

350 g/12 oz celeriac

500 ml/18 fl oz oil for deep-frying

salt and freshly ground white pepper

Planning ahead

Order the wild ducks well in advance. Ask your butcher to draw them, to cut off the legs and thighs and to cut out the backbones and wishbones. Keep all these trimmings; although the legs and livers are not used in this recipe, they can be used for another dish.

Stages 1 and 2 can be completed in advance.

Stage 3 and 4 can be completed 1 hour before the meal; keep the duck breasts in a warm place (60°C/140°F) loosely covered with foil.

The walnut vinaigrette must be made in advance.

1. Preparing the duck breasts
(5 minutes)

Preheat the oven to 230°C/450°F/ gas 8.

Singe the ducks over an open flame to remove any stubble (or remove with a small sharp knife). Set aside.

2. The juice (45 minutes)
(see Savoury sauces, page 26)

Chop the carcasses and sear them in 50 ml/2 fl oz hot oil for 3–4 minutes, then place on a roasting tray and cook in the preheated oven for about 20 minutes until well-coloured.

Remove from the oven, tilt the roasting tray and spoon out excess fat.

Deglaze the pan with the vinegar, letting it boil away completely, then add the Cognac and boil for a few seconds. Add 100 ml/3½ fl oz cold water, then transfer the carcasses and juices to a medium saucepan, cover with cold water, bring to the boil, skim and simmer for about 15 minutes.

Strain through a sieve lined with a damp muslin cloth into a small saucepan and reduce until you obtain a richly-coloured, scented juice.

Taste and season with a few turns of pepper. Add the chicken stock, if using, and a dash of soy sauce. Set aside. Reduce the oven temperature to 200°C/400°F/gas 6.

3. Preparing the chicory salad, apples and celeriac (20 minutes)

Chicory: Cut off the base and discard any weathered leaves. Halve the young leaves lengthways, wash briefly, drain and cut into 5 mm/¼ in slices. Mix in with the walnut vinaigrette, season with a pinch of salt and a few turns of pepper and set aside.

Apples: Peel, core and cut into 5 mm/ ¼ in dice.

Celeriac: Wash, peel and cut into 5 mm/¼ in dice.

In separate batches, deep-fry the diced apple and celeriac in hot oil for about 2 minutes until pale golden, then drain and place on absorbent paper. Season the celeriac with a tiny pinch of salt and a few turns of pepper. Set aside.

4. Cooking the duck breasts
(15 minutes, plus 10 minutes resting)

Rub 1 teaspoon butter onto the skin side of the breasts and season with salt and a little pepper. Brush a small roasting pan with a film of non-scented oil, place the breasts skin-side up in the pan and roast in the preheated oven for about 15 minutes.

Spoon out any fat, cover the breasts loosely with foil and leave to rest for 10 minutes in a warm place (about 60°C/140°F). Meanwhile, complete Stage 5.

5. Completing the dish and serving (5 minutes)

Have ready 4 plates.

Place a mound of chicory salad in the middle of each plate, warm the deep-fried apples and celeriac in the oven for 1 minute and gently warm the juices.

Lift the duck breasts off the bone, peel off the skin, dip them in their cooking juices and slice them diagonally as finely as possible. Top the chicory salad with slivers of wild duck, pour the juices around and scatter over the apples and celeriac. Serve to your guests.

VARIATIONS

Garnish the dish with a few deep-fried celeriac or celery leaves and a handful of pan-fried wild mushrooms.

You can also use the duck skin for garnish; roll, cut into fine ribbons and crisp under the grill for about 5 minutes, then drain on absorbent paper. Scatter over the dish.

WINE

Serve this dish with a light Burgundy from the Côte de Beaune, such as Aloxe-Corton or Monthélie, or a first growth Beaujolais – Moulin à Vent, Chénas or Fleurie.

Chef's notes

Wild duck: Any variety can be used – mallard, widgeon, teal or tufted duck. They should not be hung for more than 3 days – just enough to tenderize the flesh.

Making the juices: The coloration of the bones in the oven will determine the quality of the juice. If they are too light, they will produce pale, insipid juices; if too dark, the sauce will be excessively strong and bitter. Watch them carefully during their final 10 minutes in the oven.

Serving: The duck breasts should be served tepid, neither cold nor hot. If after their resting time the breasts are not warm enough, return them to the oven for a few minutes.

HUITRES A LA MANGUE
AU SABAYON DE CURRY

*Oysters lightly poached in their juices, served with diced
mango and a curry sabayon*

"Oysters eaten *au naturel* with just a squeeze of lemon juice and thinly sliced, lightly buttered
rye bread are delicious, of course, and purists may disapprove of this recipe.
In its defence, I find this dish not only sophisticated and interesting, but genuinely
good – and so do many of our guests. Give it a try."

Serves 4
Difficulty: ☺
Total recipe time: 1 hour
Special equipment: oyster knife,
muslin cloth, *sabayon* bowl

—————— INGREDIENTS ——————

24 no. 2 Colchester or *Belon oysters*

1 teaspoon curry powder

1 firm, just ripe mango

juice of ½ lemon

2 kg/4½ lb rock salt or *2 good handfuls
of fresh seaweed, for serving*

Curry sabayon

1 teaspoon curry powder

1 teaspoon unsalted butter

6 tablespoons oyster juice

3 egg yolks

65 g/2½ oz unsalted butter, melted

pinch of cayenne pepper

4 tablespoons whipping cream

Planning ahead
Order oysters and seaweed well in
advance. The oyster shells must be
tightly closed; do not accept any
which are already open.
The oysters, mango and plates can be
prepared several hours in advance.
The *sabayon* can be completed ½ hour
before the meal.

**1. Preparing and opening the
oysters** (15 minutes) (see page 14)
With a hard scrubbing brush, scrub
the oysters under cold running water
to remove all traces of dirt. Open
them over a strainer lined with a damp
muslin cloth and strain the juices into a
small bowl. Remove any grit which is
still attached to the oyster, but leave
the muscle, which has a lovely texture. Put the oysters back into their
juice and keep in a cool place.
Discard the flat top shells. Wash the
hollow shells and set aside.

2. Preparing the plates (5 minutes)
Seaweed: Wash, blanch for 1 minute,
refresh in iced water and drain.
Arrange attractively on 4 plates. Place
the hollow oyster shells on the bed of
seaweed, or, if you are using rock salt,
pour a generous mound onto each
plate and settle in the oyster shells.

3. The mango (10 minutes)
Peel and cut the flesh into 3 mm/⅛ in
cubes. Taste; if it is a little too sweet,
sharpen with a squeeze of lemon.
Refrigerate.

4. Cooking the curry powder
(5 minutes)
Gently cook both spoonsful gently in
1 teaspoon butter for 5 minutes. Keep
half for frying the oysters and half for
the *sabayon*.

5. The sabayon (15 minutes) (see
page 27)
Place the reserved curry powder in a

bowl, add 6 tablespoons strained oyster juice and the egg yolks and whisk
until the mixture has tripled in
volume. Stand the bowl in a hot bain-
marie and continue whisking until the
sauce is smooth and has the consistency of lightly whipped cream, then
whisk in the warm melted butter. If it
seems too thick, thin with 1 tablespoon oyster juice. Season with a
pinch of cayenne pepper and lemon
juice to taste. You should not need
salt, since the oysters are already salty.
Draw off the heat and leave the bowl
in the warm bain-marie.
Cream: Whip to a soft peak then
whisk into the *sabayon* just before
serving.

6. Pan-frying the oysters
(5 minutes)
Oysters: Drain off the remaining juice
and reserve.
Cooked curry powder: Place over high
heat in a non-stick frying pan until hot.
Flash-fry the oysters for 3 or 4 seconds
to firm up. Take off the heat and add a
squeeze of lemon. Leave for 1 minute
so that the heat permeates the oysters.

7. Dressing and serving (5 minutes)
Garnish each oyster shell with 1 teaspoon diced mango, top with an
oyster and mask with curry *sabayon*.
If you like, place the dressed plates
under a hot grill for 30 seconds to
brown the *sabayon* lightly and intensify the evocative seaside aroma of the
seaweed.
Serve immediately.

Try a white Loire wine; a lively Muscadet *sur lie* or Savennières 'Clos du Papillon'.

Chef's notes

Mango: If it is over-ripe, the flesh will be too sweet and the texture too soft. If under-ripe, the flesh will be crunchy and the flavour will not have developed.

Pan-frying the oysters: If the oysters are cooked during drying, they will become rubbery and dish will be a total failure. The frying should only seal them; the heat then permeates through while they are standing and the flavour is intensified.

Seaweed: Blanching turns it a deep sea-green; placing it under the grill brings out the wonderful scent of the sea.

HUITRES "CRESSONNIERE" A LA JULIENNE DE CONCOMBRES ET BEURRE DE CITRON

Oysters on a bed of peppery watercress with a julienne of cucumber, served with lemon-scented butter

"It is often said that to cook an oyster is an act of barbarism. Quite true – when oysters have been stewed or deep fried, they become flavourless and leathery. In this recipe the oysters are just warmed gently in their juices before serving; far from impairing the flavour, this actually intensifies it. Warming the oysters also firms up their slimy texture (the stumbling block for many), so that almost everyone can enjoy this dish, not only those oyster lovers who relish them *au naturel*."

Serves 4
Difficulty: 🎩
Total recipe time: 40 minutes
Special equipment: oyster knife, scrubbing brush, muslin cloth

—————— INGREDIENTS ——————

24 no. 1 or 2 oysters

Lemon butter

3 shallots, finely chopped

50 ml/2 fl oz white wine

200 g/7 oz unsalted butter, diced and chilled

juice of ½ lemon

1 tablespoon whipping cream (optional)

salt and freshly ground white pepper

Garnish

½ cucumber

3 bunches watercress, trimmed

1 teaspoon unsalted butter

2 kg/4½ lb rock salt or *2 large hand-fuls seaweed, for presentation*

Planning ahead

Order oysters and seaweed in advance. They can be opened several hours ahead; keep them refrigerated in their sea water or store in their shells on ice in an insulated container.

The cucumber must be prepared 2 hours in advance.

You can make the lemon butter 30 minutes before the meal; keep it warm in a bain-marie and whisk from time to time.

1. The oysters (15 minutes)
(see page 14)
Hold under cold running water and scrub with a hard brush to remove any traces of dirt. Open them over a strainer lined with a damp muslin cloth and strain the juices into a small saucepan.

Remove any grit which may still be attached to the oysters, but leave the muscle, which has a lovely texture. Place the oysters in their juices and keep in a cool place. Discard the flat top shells. Wash the hollow shells and reserve.

2. Preparing the plates (5 minutes)
Seaweed: Wash, blanch in plenty of boiling salted water, so that it turns a rich sea-green, then refresh. Arrange on 4 plates and place the hollow oyster shells on the bed of seaweed.

If you are using rock salt, pour a generous mound onto each plate and settle in the oyster shells.

3. The garnish (10 minutes, plus 30 minutes freezing)
Cucumber: Peel, halve lengthways and deseeded with a teaspoon. Cut into four 5 cm/2 in lengths, then into

2 mm/¹⁄₁₂ in *julienne*. Place on a tray, salt lightly and freeze for 30 minutes.
Watercress: Blanch for 1 minute in boiling salted water, refresh, drain and reserve.

4. The lemon butter (15 minutes)
(see *Sauce beurre blanc*, page 24)
Shallots: Put in a saucepan with the white wine, place over medium heat and reduce by three-quarters. Add 3 tablespoons juice from the oysters and gradually whisk in the cold diced butter, making sure that the temperature of the sauce remains consistently warm. Whisk until well emulsified. Season with pepper and most of the lemon juice; no salt will be needed as the oyster juice is already salty enough. If the sauce is too sharp, whisk in 1 tablespoon cream. Keep warm in a bain-marie.

5. The garnish (5 minutes)
Cucumber julienne: Run under cold water to remove excess salt. Warm through for a few seconds in 2 tablespoons oyster juice and 2 turns of pepper. The freezing should have turned the cucumber a deep emerald green.
Watercress: Warm through in a saucepan with 1 tablespoon water and 1 teaspoon butter. Season to taste.
Oysters: In a medium saucepan, warm the oysters in their juices for 1 minute over low heat. Do not boil. The outer frills should just begin to curl up.

6. Serving (5 minutes)
Warm the prepared plates in the oven for 1 minute to release the tantalising sea aroma. Fill the oyster shells with a small bed of watercress, top with the oysters and scatter over the cucumber *julienne*. Mask with the lemon butter and serve immediately.

—— VARIATIONS ——

Replace the watercress with spinach and the cucumber with sea asparagus (samphire).

—— WINE ——

Of course, the classic companion to oysters is Chablis and if you can stretch to a *premier* or *grand cru*, so much the better. An invigorating Muscadet (*sur lie* if possible) will make a refreshing and lively partner too.

CROUSTADE D'OEUFS DE CAILLE AU FUMET DE VIN ROUGE ET QUENELLES DE VOLAILLES FUMEES

Quail's eggs in a shortcrust tartlet, served with a red wine sauce garnished with smoky chicken quenelles

Serves 4
Difficulty: 🍳 🍳 🍳
Total recipe time: 1 hour 35 minutes
Special equipment: food processor, 8 small *brioche* moulds

—— INGREDIENTS ——

100 g/3½ oz Shortcrust pastry (see page 41)

Chicken quenelles
125 g/4½ oz chicken breast

25 g/1 oz lean smoked bacon or raw smoked ham

50 g/2 oz unsalted butter, creamed

250 ml/9 fl oz whipping cream

salt and freshly ground white pepper

Mushroom duxelles
100 g/3½ oz wild mushrooms (eg: pleurottes, girolles, pieds de mouton)

50 g/2 oz button mushrooms

3 dried morels, soaked

2 teaspoons unsalted butter

lemon juice

Sauce
4 shallots

1 tablespoon unsalted butter

400 ml/14 fl oz red wine

200 ml/7 fl oz Veal stock (see page 18)

3 tarragon leaves, finely chopped

1 sprig of thyme, finely chopped

1 tablespoon whipping cream

20 g/¾ oz unsalted butter, chilled and diced

¼ bayleaf

Garnish
16 shallots

2 tablespoons unsalted butter

pinch of caster sugar

60 g/2½ oz smoked belly of pork for lardons (see page 47)

8 young spinach leaves

100 ml/3½ fl oz white wine vinegar

16 quail's eggs

2 tablespoons whipping cream

Planning ahead

Make the pastry in advance.
Rehydrate the dried morels in cold water for 2–3 hours before using.
The entire dish can be completed 1–2 hours in advance; whisk the butter into the sauce just before serving.

1. The chicken quenelles

(20 minutes, plus 30 minutes chilling)
(see Mousse making, page 36)
Preheat the oven to 200°C/400°F/gas 6 for the tartlets.
Purée the chicken breast and smoked bacon in a food processor until perfectly smooth. Add 2 large pinches of salt, 4 or 5 turns of pepper and the creamed butter. Turn the mixture into a stainless steel bowl and chill for 30 minutes.
Incorporate four-fifths of the cream by beating and lifting, to produce as light a mixture as possible. Test and correct with the remaining cream and salt and pepper. Chill.

2. The tartlets (15 minutes)

Roll out the pastry as thinly as possible, then use it to line four of the *brioche* moulds and prick the bottom with a fork. Tightly fit a second mould over the top to prevent the pastry from shrinking during baking. Bake for 3 minutes in the preheated oven, then remove the top moulds. Return the tartlets to the oven for a further 2–3 minutes, until golden. Turn out onto a wire cooling rack.

3. The mushroom duxelles

(10 minutes)
Individually wash and pat dry all the mushrooms and dice finely. Season and sweat in a large sauté pan with the butter for not more than 2–3 minutes. Taste and season with salt, pepper and a squeeze of lemon.

4. The sauce (15 minutes)

Shallots: Peel all 20 and reserve 16 for the garnish. Finely chop 4 shallots and sweat in 1 tablespoon butter for 3–4 minutes until lightly coloured.

Deglaze the pan with the red wine and reduce by three-quarters, skimming the rising impurities. Add the veal stock and 200 ml/7 fl oz water, bring to the boil and reduce by half. Put in the herbs and simmer for 1 minute. Strain into a small saucepan and whisk in the cold diced butter. Taste and correct the seasoning.

5. The garnish *(20 minutes)*

Shallots: Put in a small saucepan with 6 tablespoons water, 1 tablespoon butter, a tiny pinch of caster sugar, a pinch of salt and 3 or 4 turns of pepper. Cover and cook at just below simmering point for 15 minutes, then remove the lid and allow the shallots to caramelize in their juices.
Lardons: Remove the pork rind and slice the meat into 2 cm x 3 mm/¾ x ⅛ in strips. Blanch in unsalted boiling water for 1–2 minutes. Drain, refresh under cold running water and set aside.
Chicken quenelles (see page 36): Using 2 teaspoons dipped in hot water, shape the chilled mixture into *quenelles*. Poach for about 5 minutes in lightly salted simmering water then drain on absorbent paper. Heat the butter until foaming and golden brown, put in the *quenelles* and fry for 30 seconds. Keep warm.

6. The quail's eggs (15 minutes)

In a large saucepan, boil 600 ml/1 pt water with the vinegar and 2 large pinches of salt, then reduce the heat to just below simmering point. Make a small incision in the middle of the egg shell with the point of a sharp knife and crack them open into a soup plate. Poach gently for 1 minute, refresh in cold water, drain and trim off any ragged edges. Place the eggs in a small saucepan with 2 tablespoons cream, a pinch of salt and 3 or 4 turns of pepper.

7. The spinach (3 minutes)

Remove the stalks and wash the leaves in 2 or 3 changes of cold water. Put in

a medium saucepan with ½ tablespoon butter and season with a pinch of salt. Cook over high heat for 2 minutes, then draw off the heat and set aside.

8. Completing the dish and serving (5 minutes)

Warm 4 plates or a large serving dish. Throw the *lardons* and caramelized shallots into the sauce and boil for 1 minute. Separately reheat the mushroom *duxelles,* spinach and quail's eggs without boiling.
Arrange a tartlet in the middle of each plate and line with 1 teaspoon *duxelles.* Top with 4 quail's eggs and interlace them with spinach leaves. Pour the sauce studded with *lardons* and shallots around the tartlets and decorate with the pan-fried *quenelles*.

VARIATIONS

Poached hens' eggs are equally delicious if you cannot find quail's eggs.
To simplify the dish, omit the tartlets and *quenelles* and simply nestle the eggs in spinach leaves.

WINE

A simple, light but fruity Beaujolais would be very pleasant; for something a little more refined, try a red Loire such as a young Chinon or Bourgueil from Touraine.

Chef's notes

Quail's eggs have a tough membrane beneath the shell, which makes them difficult to crack open. Cut through this second skin with the point of a sharp knife, taking care not to puncture the yolk.
Mushroom duxelles: Cook only briefly in order to seal in the moisture.

PETIT PAIN DE FOIES DE VOLAILLES, SAUCE PORTO AU LAURIER

A melting mousse of chicken livers, served with a port and tomato sauce scented with bay leaves

"I remember my mother making *petit pain de viandes* – assorted meats blended together and baked in ramekins. I have called this dish *Petit pain* as a small tribute – a nostalgic look back to my childhood. This variation on a classic dish was one of the first we served at Les Quat' Saisons when it was a small bistro. Delicious – and so easy to make."

Serves 8
Difficulty:
Total recipe time: 1 hour
Special equipment: eight 7 cm/3 in ramekins

―――― INGREDIENTS ――――
50 g/2 oz foie gras, raw or *cooked (optional)*

250 g/9 oz fresh chicken livers

3 eggs

3 egg yolks

300 ml/½ pt milk

300 ml/½ pt whipping cream

salt and freshly ground white pepper

melted butter, for greasing

Fondue de tomates (see *Beurre de langoustines*, page 25)
½ onion

½ garlic clove

8 ripe tomatoes

2 teaspoons unsalted butter

1 sprig of thyme

2 fresh bay leaves or *1 dried*

Sauce
3 tablespoons dry Madeira or *truffle juice*

6 tablespoons ruby port

300 ml/10 fl oz Brown chicken stock (see page 21) or *water*

80 g/3 oz unsalted butter, chilled and diced

Garnish
2 tomatoes, peeled, deseeded and diced

4 sprigs of chervil

Planning ahead
The *fondue de tomates* can be made 1 day in advance. The mousse mixture can be prepared half a day in advance and kept covered in the fridge. Cook at the last moment.
The sauce and garnish can be completed several hours in advance.
If the chicken livers are deep red, soak in milk overnight.

1. Fondue de tomates (25 minutes)
Follow the method on page 25.
Meanwhile, prepare the mousse.

2. Preparing and cooking the mousses (10 minutes preparation, 35 minutes chilling, 20–25 minutes cooking)
Preheat the oven to 160°C/325°F/gas 3.
Chicken livers: Remove the gall carefully, wash, pat dry, and chop roughly. In a blender, purée with the eggs, yolks and milk. Add the cream and season with salt and pepper. Blend for 1–2 minutes until smooth. Using a ladle, force the mixture through a fine conical sieve into a small bowl and refrigerate for 30 minutes.
Brush the insides of the ramekins with butter, refrigerate for a few minutes to harden the butter then fill with mousse mixture.
Line a roasting pan with greaseproof paper and half-fill with hot water. Put in the ramekins, cover with a sheet of buttered, pierced greaseproof paper and cook in the preheated oven for 20–25 minutes, until firm.
Remove from the oven and leave the mousses in the warm bain-marie, still covered, to prevent drying out.

3. Completing the sauce
(10 minutes) (see Savoury sauces, page 26)
Madeira or truffle juice and port: Bring to the boil in a medium saucepan and reduce by half. Add the chicken stock then the *fondue de tomates* and simmer for 5 minutes.
Pass through a fine conical sieve and return to the pan. Simmer, skim and finally whisk in the cold, diced butter. Taste and correct the seasoning.

4. The garnish (5 minutes)
Diced tomatoes: Warm through in a sauté pan with a knob of butter. Taste and add a pinch of caster sugar if necessary.
Chervil: Wash and remove stalks.

5. Serving (5 minutes)

Have ready 8 hot plates.

To turn out the mousses onto the plates, take hold of each ramekin and shake it sideways. This should free the mousse. If not, slide a knife blade down to the bottom of each ramekin and, pressing it firmly against the side, make one continuous circle. Turn out onto the middle of each plate. Lift off the ramekins and arrange a little diced tomato attractively on top of each mousse. Top with a sprig of chervil. Ladle the sauce around the edge and serve immediately.

VARIATIONS

The sauce can be replaced by Tomato butter (see page 25), which is equally delicious and far less time-consuming. A *brunoise* of wild mushrooms makes a lovely addition to the garnish; shape into *quenelles* and arrange beside the mousse.

The chicken livers can be replaced by rabbit, goose, duck, squab or calves' liver.

WINE

Serve a light, young, fruity Beaujolais or a red Sancerre.

Chef's notes

Bay leaves: Dried bay leaves are twice as strong as fresh ones so use only one, or you will upset the balance of flavours.

Cream: This can be replaced with 300 ml/½ pt milk; less mellow, perhaps, but equally delicious.

Madeira: If you use truffle juice instead, a sliver of truffle on top of the mousses will make the dish look even more special.

GATEAU DE TOPINAMBOURS AU COULIS D'ASPERGES

Jerusalem artichoke mousse with asparagus sauce

"This is one of my oldest and most popular recipes. The Jerusalem artichoke is the 'ugly duckling' of the vegetable family – knobbly, awkward to peel and difficult to cook evenly. I found it a real challenge.

If the quantity of artichokes in this recipe seems large, it is because so much of their weight is water which evaporates during cooking, leaving a wonderfully fragrant purée which gives the mousse its delicate and distinctive flavour."

Serves 4

Difficulty: ♟ ♟

Total recipe time: 1 hour 20 minutes

Special equipment: deep roasting pan, ten 7 x 4 cm/3 x 1½ in ramekins, 4 sheets of greaseproof paper

INGREDIENTS

Jerusalem artichoke mousse

1.5 kg/3½ lb Jerusalem artichokes, washed

juice of 1 lemon

4 eggs

4 egg yolks

400 ml/14 fl oz whipping cream

1 teaspoon melted butter, for greasing

salt and freshly ground white pepper

Asparagus sauce

2 shallots, chopped

1 small leek, trimmed and roughly chopped

350 g/12 oz green asparagus

80 g/3 oz unsalted butter, diced and chilled

50 ml/12 fl oz Light chicken stock (see page 21) or water

a small bunch of chervil

4 tablespoons whipping cream

salt and freshly ground white pepper

lemon juice

Planning ahead

The artichoke mousse can be prepared the day before.

The sauce can be partly prepared 1 hour in advance, but add the cream and butter at the last moment.

1. Preparing the mousse

(20 minutes, plus 10 minutes chilling) (see Mousse making, page 36)

Jerusalem artichokes: Wash, then peel with a small knife, slicing off the knobbly bits. Drop the artichokes into cold water as you finish peeling, then cut into 1 cm/½ in slices and steam or boil for about 20 minutes, until soft to the touch.

Place the artichokes and lemon juice in a blender and purée until smooth. Turn out the purée into a sauté pan and place over high heat, whisking continuously, until about two-thirds of the water has evaporated and you have about 500 ml/18 fl oz purée.

Cool down for about 10 minutes. The worst part is now over!

Combine the eggs and egg yolks in a bowl. Pour in the eggs and cream and whisk until smooth. Season to taste, adding a little more lemon juice if necessary. Rub the mixture through a fine sieve into a bowl.

2. Cooking the mousse
(30–40 minutes)

Preheat the oven to 160°C/325°F/gas 3.

Brush the ramekins evenly with melted butter. Cut 10 circles of greaseproof paper the same diameter as the ramekins, butter both sides and place a circle in each ramekin. Fill the ramekins with mousse and place in the roasting pan. Pour in enough hot water to come two-thirds of the way up the sides of the ramekins. Cover with a sheet of buttered greaseproof paper, making a few holes for the steam to escape. Bake for 30–40 minutes, until firm.

Leave the mousses in the bain-marie, still covered with the paper; they will stay hot for up to an hour. Meanwhile, make the sauce.

3. Asparagus sauce (20 minutes)

Asparagus: Peel and trim, discarding the bitter lower parts. Reserve the tips for garnish. Finely slice the stalks; you should have about 200 g/7 oz sliced asparagus.

Chervil: Remove the stalks, roughly chop half the leaves and reserve the remaining whole leaves for garnish.

In a medium saucepan, sweat the shallots, leeks and asparagus in 1 tablespoon butter for 1 minute. Pour in the chicken stock, bring to the boil, skim and simmer for 5 minutes, adding the chopped chervil during the final minute. Do not overcook, or the sauce will spoil. Purée in a blender for 2 minutes, then pass through a fine sieve back into the saucepan.

Whisk in the cream and bring the sauce to the boil. Draw the pan off the heat and whisk in the cold diced butter. Season with salt, pepper and a squeeze of lemon.

4. The garnish (10 minutes)

Boil the asparagus tips in salted water for 2–3 minutes, drain, season and toss gently in butter.

5. Serving (5 minutes)

Heat 10 plates.

Holding the ramekins, shake them sideways; this should free the edges of the mousses and allow you to turn them out onto the plates. If not, slide a knife blade down to the bottom of the ramekins and trace one continuous circle, pressing the blade firmly against the edge of the ramekin.

Place a plate over the ramekin and invert. Remove the greaseproof paper and slip the ramekins back over the mousses to keep them warm.

Pour a swirl of sauce around each mousse and decorate with asparagus tips. Remove the ramekins, top the mousses with a sprig or two of chervil and serve immediately.

——————— VARIATION ———————

Watercress sauce would also be delicious.

Chef's notes

Since peeling the artichokes is such an awful job, try to inveigle someone else (perhaps your unsuspecting child) into doing it for you!

Lemon juice prevents the artichokes from discolouring and counterbalances the sweetness of the artichokes.

TAGLIATELLES AU ROMARIN, TRUFFES BLANCHES DU PIEDMONT ET FRICASSEE DE CEPES

Tagliatelle scented with white truffles and rosemary, served with ceps from the New Forest

"This recipe is a successful combination of two powerful and robust flavours – rosemary and white truffles."

Serves 4
Difficulty: 🍳
Total recipe time: 30 minutes

INGREDIENTS

half quantity tagliatelle (see Pasta, page 38)

Sauce

250 ml/9 fl oz whipping cream

1 sprig of rosemary

10 g/⅓ oz fresh white truffle

salt and freshly ground white pepper

Garnish

20 g/¾ oz fresh white truffle

1 tablespoon olive oil

150 g/5 oz ceps or button mushrooms

lemon juice

1 ripe tomato, peeled, deseeded and diced (optional)

Planning ahead

The tagliatelle must be made in advance.
Stages 1–4 inclusive can be completed 1 hour in advance

1. Preparing the truffles and ceps
(10 minutes)

Truffles (for sauce and garnish): Using a soft brush, clean under cold running water and cut one-third into fine *julienne*. Place in separate small containers.
Ceps: Trim and scrape the stalks, clean the ceps with a damp cloth and cut into 3 mm/⅛ in slices. Place in a small container.

2. Cooking the tagliatelle
(10 minutes)

In a medium saucepan, boil 1 L/1¾ pt salted water, slide in the tagliatelle, stir to prevent sticking and cook for 5 minutes. Refresh in a colander under cold running water to remove excess starch and set aside.

3. Cooking the ceps (2 minutes)

Season with a pinch of salt and a few turns of pepper, then fry in 1 tablespoon hot olive oil for about 30 seconds. Sprinkle with a squeeze of lemon, taste, correct seasoning and place in a small container.

4. The sauce (6 minutes)

In a medium saucepan, simmer the cream with a sprig of rosemary for about 2 minutes. Strain into another saucepan and add the truffle *julienne*. Simmer gently for 2 minutes to infuse the flavours, then taste and correct the seasoning with salt and a few turns of pepper.

5. Serving

Warm 4 plates.
Separately warm the ceps and diced tomatoes. Add the tagliatelle to the sauce, mix delicately with a kitchen fork, cover and simmer gently for 2 minutes. Taste and correct the seasoning.
Twist the tagliatelle round a kitchen fork and place a little mound on each plate. Divide the remaining sauce equally, top with the warmed diced tomatoes and scatter over the sliced ceps. Finally grate 20 g/¾ oz white truffle over the tagliatelle and serve to your guests.

VARIATIONS

The highly perfumed white truffle is the jewel of Italian cuisine. It is rare and extremely expensive (about £1200 per kilo!). You can use Périgord black truffles; these are less scented, so infuse the rosemary for 30 seconds only to preserve the balance of flavours.

WINE

Drink a good Italian white wine such as a young dry DOC Frascati Superiore or Soave Classico.

Chef's notes

Truffles: Do not use tinned truffles unless the label specifies that they are 'first cooking'.
The sauce: This dish should achieve a perfect blend of two strong, characterful flavours. If the rosemary is infused in the cream for too long, its scent will completely overpower the more delicate truffle and ruin the dish. Do not boil the cream or it will reduce and thicken. It must stay light and thin.

TURBOTIN ROTI AU FENOUIL ET HUILE D'ANCHOIS

Baby turbot roasted on a bed of dried fennel moistened with anchovy oil

"This is a variation of one of the great regional classics of French cuisine: a handsome dish with wonderfully heady flavours – and very simple to make."

Turbotin rôti au fenouil et huile d'anchois

Serves 4
Difficulty: ♟
Total recipe time: 45 minutes

INGREDIENTS

2 450 g/1 lb baby turbot

300 ml/½ pt olive oil

20 dried sticks of fennel

4 dried strips of orange zest

2 sprigs of thyme

½ bayleaf

2 star anise

50 ml/2 fl oz anchovy oil

a dash of Pernod

salt and freshly ground white pepper

Beurre blanc (see page 24)

3 shallots

50 ml/2 fl oz white wine vinegar

50 ml/2 fl oz dry white wine

200 g/7 oz unsalted butter, chilled and diced

lemon juice

parsley sprigs and 2 lemons, to garnish

Planning ahead
Order the turbot well in advance. Ask your fishmonger to gut them and cut off the fins and gills.
Cut four 5 cm/2 in strips of orange zest and leave to dry in a warm place 1 day in advance.
The turbot and bed of fennel can be prepared in advance.
The *beurre blanc* can be made half an hour in advance and kept warm in a bain-marie.

1. Preparing the turbot (15 minutes)
Preheat the oven to 180°C/350°F/gas 4.
Wash the turbot thoroughly, pat dry and brush the white skin with a little olive oil. Set aside.

Combine the dried fennel, orange zests, thyme, bay leaf and star anise in a large roasting pan and add the olive and anchovy oils and a dash of Pernod.
Make sure that the herbs are well coated with oil to prevent them from burning during cooking.

2. Roasting the turbot (20 minutes)
Season the fish lightly and place them, white side up, on the bed of fennel and herbs. Roast in the preheated oven for 15 minutes, basting frequently. Switch off the oven and leave the fish to rest for 5 minutes before serving. Meanwhile make the *beurre blanc* following the method on page 24.

3. Finishing and serving the dish (10 minutes)
Warm a large, flat serving dish and 4 plates.
Halve the lemons and remove the pips.
Using two fish slices or spatulas, lift the turbot onto the serving dish and garnish with the lemons and parsley sprigs. If you have enough confidence, bone the fish in front of your guests, allowing 2 fillets per person. If this sounds like a nightmare, present the whole fish to your guests, then retreat to the kitchen to do the filleting in private. Complete each serving with a squeeze of lemon, a tiny pinch of salt and 1 turn of pepper. Serve the *beurre blanc* separately in a sauceboat.

VARIATIONS
Sea bass, brill or red mullet are also delicious served this way; naturally the cooking times will vary.
Serve a thyme and rosemary scented red wine sauce in addition to the *beurre blanc* for the ultimate accompaniment.
To enhance the appearance of the fish, criss-cross the white skin with a red hot skewer before roasting.
If you have a charcoal grill, use it to mark the white skin of the turbot for 2 minutes before roasting. This introduces a wonderful smoky flavour and improves the appearance of the dish.

WINE
White wines from Savoie strike an interesting balance between lightness and flavour, which suits this dish perfectly: try Chignin Bergeron, Apremont or the slightly richer Roussette de Savoie.

Chef's notes
Turbot: If baby fish are not available, substitute a 900 g/2 lb turbot and increase the cooking time to 20 minutes plus 5 minutes resting.
Olive oil: The herb-scented oil can be saved and used for frying other fish.
Fennel: If you have some garden fennel, cut off the fronds, tie into a bundle and fill the bellies of the fish before roasting.
Anchovy oil can be taken from tinned anchovies.
Roasting the turbot: Do not be tempted to roast at a higher temperature as the delicate flesh will shrink and flake in a stronger heat. It is important to baste the fish frequently, to moisten it and reintroduce the flavours of the oils, herbs and spices.
The resting time is also extremely important. At this stage residual heat will gently complete the cooking, leaving the flesh still moist and firm.
Seasoning: When roasting a whole fish, salt does not permeate the flesh. Season the inside of fillets before serving.
Serving: Turbot is one of the easiest fish to bone: leaving the delicious white skin on, make an incision down the centre of the fish, cut across, following the line of the central bones and remove each fillet by sliding your knife underneath. Turn the fish over, discard the black skin and remove the fillets.

BLANC DE LOUP DE MER PERSILLE AU JUS DE VEAU BLOND AUX FLEURS DE THYM, FEUILLES DE CELERI FRITES

Pan-fried fillets of sea bass coated with parsley breadcrumbs, served with a light veal juice and thyme flowers

Serves 4
Difficulty:
Total recipe time: 40 minutes

INGREDIENTS

450 g/1 lb fillets of sea bass

1 tablespoon olive oil

lemon juice

1 egg yolk

4 tablespoons Provençal breadcrumbs (see page 47)

salt and freshly ground white pepper

Sauce

200 ml/7 fl oz Veal stock (see page 18)

1 sprig of thyme

40 g/1½ oz unsalted butter

a dash of Pernod

lemon juice

Garnish

500 ml/18 fl oz oil, for frying

skin from the sea bass

leaves and tops of 2 celery stalks

12 thyme flowers (optional) (see page 275)

Planning ahead
Order a 1.5 kg/3–3½ lb sea bass well in advance and ask the fishmonger to scale, gut and fillet it. You should obtain 450 g/1 lb fillet (there is a lot of waste). Ask for the bones; although you do not need them for this dish, you can use them to make a fish stock. The veal stock and Provençal breadcrumbs must be made in advance.

1. Preparing the sea bass
(10 minutes)
Gently tweeze out all the bones running down the middle of the fillets, then remove the skin (see page 15) and reserve it for the garnish.
Cut the fillets neatly into 4 portions, brush with egg yolk, season with salt and pepper and coat generously with Provençal breadcrumbs.
Line a small roasting pan with greaseproof paper brushed with a film of olive oil, put in the fillets and refrigerate.

2. Preparing and cooking the garnish (10 minutes)
In a large deep saucepan, heat the frying oil until hot.
Sea bass skin: Roll tightly, cut into fine ribbons and deep-fry for about 2 minutes until golden and crisp. Drain on absorbent paper and season with a little pepper.
Celery leaves and tops: Wash, pat dry and deep-fry for about 1 minute until golden. Drain on absorbent paper.
Thyme flowers: Blanch for 30 seconds in salted boiling water, refresh, drain and set aside.

3. The sauce (10 minutes)
Preheat the oven to 200°C/400°F/gas 6 for Stage 4.
In a small saucepan bring to the boil the veal stock and thyme.
In a small frying pan, make a *beurre noisette* (see page 24) with the butter and whisk it into the veal stock. Add a dash of Pernod, taste and correct the seasoning with salt, pepper and a squeeze of lemon. Remove the sprig of thyme and toss in the thyme flowers.

4. Cooking the sea bass fillets
(7 minutes)
Cook in the preheated oven for 6–7 minutes.

5. Serving
Warm 4 plates or a large serving dish. Divide the sauce between the centre of the plates, rest the sea bass fillets in the middle and scatter the golden fried fish skin and celery leaves around. Serve immediately.

VARIATIONS
Fillets of turbot, brill, red mullet, skate, halibut or cod can be prepared in exactly the same way, but the cooking times will vary; learn how to feel the fish to test when they are cooked (see page 14).
The sauce can be replaced by a *beurre blanc* (see page 24).
Deep-fried celeriac or coriander leaves make an equally delicious garnish.

A light white Burgundy such as Montagny or Rully suits this dish best, although a fresh white Provençal wine like Bandol or Cassis also makes a good partner.

Chef's notes

Thyme flowers: If you cannot find these, infuse a few rosemary or marjoram leaves in the sauce instead and strain before serving.
Celery leaves and sea bass skin: Make sure they are quite dry before deep-frying, or they will sizzle and spit.
The vegetables are cooked when the oil stops 'singing'; all the moisture has been removed and the flavour is concentrated. You should not need salt.

DARNE DE CABILLAUD POELEE
A LA JULIENNE DE
COURGETTES ET CELERI FRITES

*Pan-fried cod steak served with parsley-scented veal stock,
garnished with deep-fried celery and courgettes*

"Because it is so readily available, this wonderful fish is seldom treated with reverence. With the veal stock acting as a perfect background to set off the flavours in the sauce, this recipe illustrates one of many ways an apparently unspectacular fish can be glorified."

Serves 4
Difficulty: 🎩
Total recipe time: 55 minutes
Special equipment: deep-fryer

—— INGREDIENTS ——
4 175 g/6 oz cod steaks

1 tablespoon unsalted butter

salt and freshly ground white pepper

Garnish
1 L/1¾ pt oil for deep-frying

2 medium courgettes

2 celery stalks

Sauce
2 shallots, peeled and finely chopped

a small bunch of parsley, washed and finely chopped

2 capers, finely chopped

1½ tablespoons unsalted butter

1 tablespoon white wine vinegar

200 ml/7 fl oz Veal stock (see page 18) or Brown chicken stock (see page 21)

a squeeze of lemon

Planning ahead
Order the cod steaks well in advance (the cod caught off the Cornish coast are excellent).
The veal stock must be made in advance.
The sauce can be prepared half an hour before the meal.
The garnish can be prepared 1–2 hours in advance.

1. Preparing and cooking the garnish (15–20 minutes)
Heat the cooking oil in the deep-fryer.
Courgettes: Wash, trim stalks and cut down the whole length into 2 mm/ ¹⁄₁₀ in *julienne* strips.
Celery: Wash, peel and halve lengthways. Cut into 2 mm/¹⁄₁₀ in *julienne* strips.
Test if the oil is hot enough by throwing in a stick of courgette: if it sizzles immediately, it is ready.
Pat dry the courgettes and celery and gently lower them into the deep-fryer. Fry until light golden.
Drain off excess oil and place on absorbent paper. Taste and season lightly. Keep at room temperature.

2. The sauce (15 minutes)
In a small saucepan, sweat the chopped shallots in 1 teaspoon butter for 1 minute without colouring. Add the vinegar and reduce completely. Add the chopped capers and parsley and finally the veal stock. Bring back to the boil and reduce until the sauce coats the back of a spoon. Pass through a fine conical sieve into another small saucepan.
Make a *beurre noisette* (see page 24) with 1 tablespoon butter and whisk into the sauce. Taste, season with a pinch of salt and a few turns of pepper and enliven the sauce with a squeeze of lemon. Keep warm.

3. Cooking and resting the cod steaks (20 minutes)
Preheat the oven to 180°C/350°F/ gas 4.
Season the cod steaks with salt and pepper. In a large non-stick frying pan, heat 1 tablespoon butter until pale golden. Gently fry the cod steaks for 2 minutes on each side.
Place the pan in the preheated oven for 5 minutes, basting the fish frequently. Remove and leave to rest for

Darne de cabillaud poêlée à la julienne de courgettes et céleri frits

5 minutes, covered with buttered greaseproof paper. Leave the oven switched on.

Strain the cooking juices through a fine conical sieve into the sauce.

4. Serving the dish (5 minutes)

Heat 4 plates or a large serving dish.

Enliven the cod steaks with a squeeze of lemon and return them to the oven for 2 minutes. At the same time, warm the deep-fried courgette and celery *julienne*.

Place a cod steak in the centre of each plate, pour the light sauce around and scatter with the courgettes and celery. Serve immediately.

--- VARIATIONS ---

A few deep-fried parsley sprigs make a delicious and colourful addition to the garnish.

Most fish can be cooked in this way.

--- WINE ---

Although a young Loire wine like a Muscadet *sur lie* or Savennières 'Clos du Papillon' would be most enjoyable, why not try one of the more distinctive white wines from Savoie such as Chignin Bergeron?

Chef's notes

Cooking the garnish: Deep-frying can be a dangerous business. If using gas, make sure that the flames do not lick around the top of the pan and that the pan is quite secure.

The courgettes and celery must be completely dry before deep-frying, as any moisture will make the oil spit, or worse still, boil over.

To tell if the vegetables are cooked: First they will turn a light rust colour, then, when all the moisture has evaporated, they will stop sizzling. The flavours will be more concentrated, so the vegetables should not need seasoning.

Making the sauce: The vinegar must be completely reduced or the sauce will be too sharp and the acidity will impair the taste of the parsley.

*Civet de poissons de rivière au fumet
de vin rouge (page 246)*

*Dos de loup de mer farci, au jus
d'estragon et à la fondue de fenouil (page 137)*

*Filet de dorade fumé au charbon de
bois, au coulis de tomates crues et à
l'huile d'anchois (page 186)*

*Escalope de turbot, coquilles St-
Jacques et blanc de poireaux au
saveurs des sous-bois (page 242)*

ESCALOPE DE TURBOT, COQUILLES ST-JACQUES ET BLANC DE POIREAUX AU SAVEURS DES SOUS-BOIS

Fillet of turbot with scallops, baby leeks and wild mushrooms

"This is one of my favourite fish dishes, delicate yet tasty, with an abundance of different textures and colours."

Serves 4
Difficulty: 🎩
Total recipe time: 1 hour
Special equipment: steamer with a lid, aluminium foil

––––––––– INGREDIENTS –––––––––
450 g/1 lb fillet of turbot, skinned

8 large scallops, with their corals

1 tablespoon unsalted butter, plus butter for greasing

lemon juice

2 teaspoons olive oil

salt and freshly ground white pepper

Sauce
4 shallots, finely chopped

90 g/3 oz button mushrooms, finely chopped

6 tablespoons dry white wine

2 tablespoons dry Madeira or truffle juice

40 g/1½ oz unsalted butter, chilled and diced

Garnish
2 small leeks

90 g/3 oz wild mushrooms (girolles, pieds de moutons or oyster mushrooms)

2 teaspoons unsalted butter

½ lemon

4 sprigs of chervil (optional)

Planning ahead
Order the fish well in advance; ask for a fillet from a large turbot, as it will have a better flavour and ask for the bones, too; these can be used for a fish *fumet* (page 20).
The turbot, scallops and vegetables can be prepared well in advance.

––––––––––––––––––––––––––––––––

1. The turbot and scallops
(20 minutes)
Turbot: Cut across into 4 equal portions and place on a plate.
Scallops: Cut out and butter four 10 cm/4 in squares of foil. Cut each scallop into 3 rounds and arrange in overlapping circles on the foil.
In a small saucepan, melt the butter with a pinch of salt and a squeeze of lemon. Brush this mixture all over the turbot pieces and over the top of the scallops and give each 1 turn of pepper. Refrigerate.
Coral: Blanch in simmering water for 5 minutes. Refresh, cut lengthways into fine slices and season lightly. Heat the olive oil, then fry the coral for a few seconds.

Preheat the oven to 180°C/350°F/gas 4.

2. Preparing the vegetables for the garnish (15 minutes)
Leeks: Using a sharp paring knife, trim off the roots and green tops. Make a small incision 3 mm/⅛ in deep down the whole length of the leeks, peel away 2 or 3 layers of coarse, weathered leaves and discard. Cut the hearts into 3 equal lengths, then shred into ribbons. Wash, drain and reserve.
Wild mushrooms: Wash briefly, pat dry and cut into 3 mm/⅛ in slices.

3. Cooking the turbot
(6–8 minutes, plus 5 minutes resting)
In a medium sauté pan, sweat the shallots in 1 tablespoon butter for 1–2 minutes, without colouring. Add the chopped button mushrooms and sweat for 1 minute. Pour in the wine and Madeira or truffle juice, boil briskly for 2–3 minutes to remove the alcohol and some of the acidity, then add 2 tablespoons water.
Draw the pan off the heat and place the turbot fillets on the bed of shallots and mushrooms. Partially cover the pan with a lid to let the excess steam escape and cook in the preheated oven for 6–8 minutes, depending on the thickness of the fillets. Remove the pan from the oven, put the lid on firmly and leave to rest away from the heat for 5–10 minutes, so that the turbot finishes cooking and releases some of its wonderful juices.

4. The garnish (5 minutes)
In a small saucepan, boil 4 tablespoons water with 1 teaspoon butter, a pinch of salt and 1 turn of pepper. Add the shredded leeks, cover and cook for 1 minute, then remove the lid and cook for a further 2–3 minutes. Season and set aside.

In another small saucepan, boil 2 tablespoons water with 1 teaspoon butter, a pinch of salt, 1 turn of pepper and a squeeze of lemon. Toss in the sliced wild mushrooms for 30 seconds, then set aside.

5. Steaming the scallops
(3 minutes)
Place the scallops (still on the foil) in a steamer, cover and steam for about 2 minutes. Draw off the heat and leave in the steamer, still covered.

6. Finishing the juice (3 minutes)
Strain the cooking juices from the turbot into a small saucepan, add the cooking juices from the wild mushrooms and bring to a fast boil before whisking in the cold diced butter. Whisk until well emulsifed, then season, adding a squeeze of lemon.

7. Serving (5 minutes)
Heat 4 plates or a serving dish until warm but not too hot, or the juice may separate.
Separately warm the turbot, scallops and sliced coral in the oven and correct the seasoning.
Arrange the turbot fillets on one side of the plates and slide the scallops off the foil onto the opposite side. Pour the sauce over and scatter the wild mushrooms and shredded leeks around the edge. For an attractive final touch, place a sprig of chervil in the middle of the scallop rounds. Serve.

——— VARIATIONS ———
Substitute or add finely sliced fresh truffles, button mushrooms or dried morels for the wild mushrooms and replace the leeks with tender spring onions or asparagus spears.
Fillets of brill or John Dory can also be cooked this way; for a simpler dish, omit the scallops.

——— WINE ———
A dry white *vin jaune* from the Arbois, with its smokey, walnut-like bouquet, would suit this dish perfectly. If you cannot find one, a Pouilly Fumé is always popular, especially one made by the Ladoucette family.

FILET DE BARBUE ET COQUILLAGES POCHES AUX ALGUES ET CITRON VERT

Fillet of brill and shellfish, poached with seaweed and lime

Filet de barbue et coquillages pochés aux algues et citron vert

Serves 4
Difficulty: ♔♔
Total recipe time: 1 hour 15 minutes

INGREDIENTS

4 150 g/5 oz fillets of brill

1 teaspoon butter

fresh lime juice

12 small clams

8 small oysters

12 Bouchot mussels

salt and freshly ground white pepper

Stock for poaching the shellfish
500 ml/18 fl oz water

½ small onion, chopped

1 medium carrot, washed and diced

2 sprigs of thyme

1 bayleaf

juice of ½ lemon, sieved

1 teaspoon salt

freshly ground white pepper

Sauce
2 shallots, peeled and chopped

1 teaspoon butter

200 ml/7 fl oz dry white wine

50 ml/2 fl oz shellfish poaching stock

juice from the oysters

100 g/3½ oz edible seaweed

1 tablespoon whipping cream

65 g/2½ oz unsalted butter, chilled and diced

juice of ½ lime, sieved

a tiny bunch of chives, washed and chopped

Planning ahead
Stages 1–4 inclusive can be completed several hours in advance.

1. Cooking the stock (35 minutes)
In a large saucepan, bring to the boil all the ingredients for the stock, skim and simmer for 20 minutes, then strain into another saucepan.

2. Preparing the shellfish
(15 minutes)
Clams: Brush under running cold water.
Mussels: With a small knife, scrape the shells and pull out the beards. Wash.
Oysters: Brush the shells under cold running water and open them over a bowl lined with a muslin cloth. Detach the oysters and reserve them in their own strained seawater.

3. Cooking the shellfish
(10 minutes, plus cooling)
Put the clams in the stock, bring to the boil, skim and simmer until the shells open. Turn off the heat and leave them to cool in the stock. Strain the stock, remove the clams from their shells and reserve in the strained stock. Put the mussels in a pan with 2 or 3 tablespoons stock, cover and cook for about 1 minute, until the shells just open. Remove from their shells and reserve in their stock.
The oysters will be warmed in the sauce at the last moment.

4. Preparing the sauce base
(10 minutes)
Preheat the oven to 180°C/350°F/gas 4 for Stage 5.
In a small saucepan, sweat the chopped shallots in 1 teaspoon butter, add the white wine and reduce by half. Add 50 ml/2 fl oz of the clam cooking stock, plus the strained oyster juices and 1 tablespoon mussel juice. Strain into a large sauté pan and add the seaweed.

5. Cooking the brill and finishing the sauce (20 minutes)
Melt 1 teaspoon butter with a large pinch of salt, a few grains of pepper and a dash of lime juice. Brush all over the brill.

Place the fillets on the bed of seaweed, cover, bring to the boil and cook in the preheated oven for 10 minutes. Put the brill fillets on a plate, season with a few grains of salt, cover with clingfilm and leave to rest in a warm place for 5 minutes.
Add the cream to the cooking juices and bring to the boil. Draw off the heat then whisk in the cold diced butter, taste and correct seasoning. Finally 'lift' the sauce with the lime juice.
Add the oysters and warm until they just begin to curl, then add the mussels and clams in their cooking juices.

6. Serving
Warm 4 plates or a serving dish.
Place one brill fillet on each plate, spoon out the sauce, evenly dividing the seaweed, oysters, mussels and clams. Sprinkle each serving with finely chopped chives and serve.

VARIATIONS
Substitute other types of fish or shellfish for those suggested (a handful of winkles makes an attractive addition).

WINE
Serve a Muscadet de Sèvres *sur lie*.

Chef's notes
Seaweed: Edible seaweed is available from most Chinese supermarkets, or substitute sea asparagus (samphire) which can be found on many British shores.
Clams: The smaller the better; smaller ones are more tender.
'Cooking' the oyster: The object is not to cook the oysters, but simply to warm them in the sauce and firm up their texture. This also intensifies their flavour.
Cooking the shellfish: Do not overcook or allow the stock to boil, or their flesh will become tough and rubbery.

CIVET DE POISSONS DE RIVIERE
AU FUMET DE VIN ROUGE

Freshwater fish from Oxfordshire streams and rivers,
cooked in a red wine sauce and served with baby vegetables

Serves 4
Difficulty: 🎩🎩
Total recipe time: 1 hour 40 minutes

——————— INGREDIENTS ———————

150 g/5 oz fillet of pike

200 g/7 oz fillet of perch

200 g/7 oz fillet of zander or grayling

200 g/7 oz fillet of carp

200 g/7 oz fillet of salmon

Fish stock
*bones from the fish (about 500 g/
1–1¼ lb)*

*200 g/7 oz button mushrooms,
trimmed, washed and sliced*

1 tablespoon olive oil

1 small onion, finely chopped

*2 small carrots, washed, peeled and
diced*

*100 g/3½ oz celeriac, washed, peeled
and diced*

30 g/1 oz unsalted butter

1 sprig of thyme

1 bayleaf

3 sprigs of parsley

2 cloves

*3 tomatoes, deseeded and finely
chopped*

700 ml/23 fl oz Hermitage red wine

200 ml/7 fl oz water

For completing the sauce
100 ml/3½ fl oz Hermitage red wine

*100 ml/3½ fl oz Brown chicken stock
(optional) (see page 21)*

*65 g/2½ oz unsalted butter, chilled
and diced*

a squeeze of lemon

salt and freshly ground white pepper

Garnish
*250 g/9 oz pickling onions or small
shallots*

50 g/2 oz unsalted butter

pinch of caster sugar

4 sprigs of flat-leaved parsley

4 small leeks

200 g/7 oz tiny button mushrooms

a squeeze of lemon

*250 g/9 oz unsmoked streaky bacon,
cut into lardons (see page 47)*

Planning ahead
Order all the fish well in advance. Ask for the skin to be left on, and keep the bones for the fish stock.
The chicken stock, if used, must be made in advance.
Stages 1–3 inclusive can be completed 1 day in advance.

1. Preparing and cooking the fish stock (30 minutes, plus 30 minutes soaking) (see page 20)
Wash all the fish bones under cold running water, then drain and keep aside.
In a small sauté pan, brown the mushrooms in 1 tablespoon hot olive oil.

In a large saucepan, sweat the diced vegetables in the butter for 5 minutes without colouring. Add the herbs, browned mushrooms, cloves and fish bones and sweat for a further 5 minutes, then add the chopped tomatoes. Deglaze with the wine and water, bring to the boil, skim and simmer for 20 minutes, skimming occasionally.
Strain the stock through a fine sieve, pressing on the bones and vegetables with a ladle to extract as much juice and flavour as possible.
Meanwhile, prepare the fish.

2. Preparing the fillets (5 minutes)
Tweeze out any small bones running down the centre of the fillets. Keeping each variety of fish separate, cut the fillets into 4 and keep on small plates.

3. Preparing the garnish
(30 minutes)
Onions: Peel and cut a cross on the bases.
Parsley: Wash, shake dry and pick the leaves.
Leeks: Trim the roots and green tops. Peel off the first two layers then slice the leeks diagonally into 2.5 cm/1 in segments, wash in plenty of cold water, drain and set aside.
Button mushrooms: Trim the stalks, wash briefly, pat dry, place in a bowl and sprinkle with a little lemon juice.

4. Cooking the garnish
(10 minutes)
Onions: Place in a small saucepan with 20 g/¾ oz butter, 6 tablespoons water, a pinch of salt and sugar and 2 turns of pepper and simmer for 8–10 minutes, until the water has completely evaporated, leaving the onions

— 246 —

coated with a film of butter. Taste to check texture and seasoning.

Parsley: Place in a small saucepan with 1 teaspoon butter, 4 tablespoons water, a pinch of salt and 2 turns of pepper and cook for 2 minutes.

Leeks: Place in a small saucepan with 1 teaspoon butter, 4 tablespoons water, a pinch of salt and 2 turns of pepper and cook for 3 minutes.

Button mushrooms: Place in a small saucepan with 20 g/¾ butter, a dash of lemon juice, a pinch of salt and 2 turns of pepper and cook at full boil for 2 minutes, to glaze.

Lardons: Blanch in boiling unsalted water for 3 minutes, then drain, and keep with the onions.

5. Cooking the fish and completing the sauce (20 minutes)

Season all the fillets lightly and have the fish stock ready in a large shallow sauté pan.

Place all the fish, except the salmon, side by side in the fish stock. Bring just to simmering point then reduce the heat so that no bubbles are breaking the surface. Cover and cook for 3 minutes. Add the salmon and cook for a further 2 minutes. Holding back the fish, strain the stock into a small saucepan. Leave the fish fillets in a warm place, covered.

Add another 100 ml/3½ fl oz red wine and the brown chicken stock, if using. Bring to the boil and reduce to about 400 ml/14 fl oz. Finally whisk in the cold diced butter, taste, season with salt and pepper and enliven with a squeeze of lemon.

6. Assembling the dish and serving

Warm 4 plates.

Separately warm all the garnishes.

Divide the fish equally between the plates, spoon the sauce over and scatter the garnishes. Serve at once.

VARIATIONS

Eel would make a nice addition. Vary the vegetables or fish as you wish.

WINE

A lightly chilled Grand Cru Beaujolais (Fleurie, Moulin à Vent or Chiroubles) or perhaps a red Sancerre, will suit this dish very well.

Chef's notes

Salmon is not an Oxfordshire fish at the moment, sad to say. However, it has returned to the Thames further downstream, so perhaps it will be again one day!

Cooking the fish: The texture of all these fish is delicate, so under no circumstances allow the poaching stock to boil, or the dish will be ruined.

Completing the sauce: 100 ml/3½ fl oz Hermitage is added at the end to reintroduce a fresh vinous character.

ASSIETTE AUX SAVEURS DE MON TERROIR "CLUB DES CENTS"

Pig's trotters filled with sweetbreads, garnished with veal tongue, kidneys and foie gras, served with the braising juices spiked with morels

"In my region of Franche-Comté the pig is regarded as a walking meal – and a much honoured one too. Every part is eaten – including of course the trotters. This recipe was inspired by Pierre Koffman's famed pig's trotters; I prepared it specially when the famous gastronomic circle from Paris *Le Club des Cents* came to visit Le Manoir. More of a recipe to enjoy at the restaurant than to attempt at home, it will certainly be a challenge."

Serves 4
Difficulty: 🍳 🍳 🍳
Total recipe time: 6 hours 40 minutes (including 1 hour soaking the sweetbread and 3 hours 10 minutes braising the trotters)
Special equipment: 20 cm/8 in cast iron casserole

INGREDIENTS

2 pig's trotters (hind legs), boned

1 cooked calf's tongue (see page 251)

½ veal kidney, wrapped in its fat (cut across)

4 20 g/¾ oz slices of foie gras (optional)

150 g/5 oz veal sweetbreads

20 small chanterelles or other wild mushrooms (optional)

lemon juice

25 g/1 oz unsalted butter

salt and freshly ground white pepper

For braising the trotters and making the sauce

1 small carrot, washed and diced

1 medium onion, diced

1 garlic clove, peeled and crushed

1 tablespoon unsalted butter

1 tablespoon brown sugar

2 tablespoons red wine vinegar

100 ml/3½ fl oz dry Madeira

300 ml/½ pt Light chicken stock (see page 21) or water

300 ml/½ pt Veal stock (see page 18)

½ bayleaf

1 sprig of thyme

200 ml/7 fl oz water

For filling the pig's trotters

150 g/5 oz chicken breast, diced

2 large pinches of salt

225 ml/8 fl oz whipping cream, chilled

1 small onion, roughly chopped

3 teaspoons unsalted butter

150 g/5 oz sweetbreads

1 teaspoon unsalted butter

50 g/2 oz fresh morels, trimmed, sliced into 3, washed in 3 changes of water, drained and patted dry

For completing the sauce

1 tablespoon whipping cream

85 g/3 oz fresh morels, as above

Planning ahead
Order the pig's trotters well in advance. Ask your butcher to bone them without piercing the skin, which will hold the filling.
The tongue must be cooked in advance and kept in its cooking juices.

1. Soaking the sweetbreads (see page 254); **preparing the trotters and kidney** (5 minutes, plus 1 hour soaking)
Preheat the oven to 180°C/350°F/gas 4 for Stage 2.
All sweetbreads (for filling and garnish): Soak under cold running water for at least 1 hour to remove all traces of blood.
Trotters: Shave off any hair (do not singe as the trotters will blister).
Kidney: With a sharp paring knife remove the nerves from the middle. Leave on the fat.
Meanwhile, braise the trotters.

2. Braising the trotters
(3 hours 10 minutes)
In a large heavy casserole, brown the diced onion, carrot and garlic in 1 tablespoon butter for 10 minutes. Add the brown sugar and caramelize, then pour in the vinegar and let it evaporate completely. Add the Madeira and trotters, then reduce the heat and turn the trotters over until they are well coated in the syrup.

*Assiette aux saveurs de mon terroir
"Club des Cents"*

Pour in the chicken and veal stock and finally add ½ bayleaf and a sprig of thyme. Bring back to the boil, skim and cover with pierced buttered paper. Cook in the preheated oven for 3 hours, carefully turning the trotters over every 20 minutes.

Remove from the oven, lift the trotters out onto two 30 cm/12 in squares of buttered foil, open them up and, with a spoon, scrape out the excess fat inside. Season lightly with salt and pepper and leave to cool at room temperature.

Add 200 ml/7 fl oz water to the reduced braising juices, then force through a fine conical sieve into a small casserole, pressing down onto the vegetables to extract as much flavour and juice as possible. Reserve for Stage 5.

Meanwhile, prepare the filling.

3. Preparing the filling (40 minutes)
(see Mousse making, page 36)

Purée the chicken breast in a food processor with 2 large pinches of salt, then refrigerate (still in the bowl) for 30 minutes. Return the bowl to the food processor and add the chilled cream in a steady trickle until well incorporated. Taste and correct seasoning. Force the mousse mixture through a fine sieve and refrigerate until needed.

In a small frying pan, sweat the chopped onion in 1 teaspoon butter for 5 minutes without colouring, then draw off the heat and set aside.

Sweetbreads: Scald in fast-boiling water for 5 seconds, then plunge into cold water, drain, place on a tea towel and peel away the cartilage and fibres, taking care not to damage the shape. Pat dry, halve and reserve half for Stage 5. Dice the other half into 1.5 cm/⅝ in cubes, season with salt and pepper, sear in 2 teaspoons hot butter for 1 minute then place in the preheated oven for 3 minutes. Remove and leave to cool.

Put one-third of the mousse in a bowl and mix in 50 g/2 oz sliced morels, the cooked onion and the cooked diced sweetbread. (This is all the mousse you will need; keep the remainder for a garnish or another dish.)

4. Filling the pig's trotters
(10 minutes)

Increase the oven temperature to 220°C/425°F/gas 7.

Open the trotters and spoon in the filling, pushing it up into the hoof cavity. Reshape the trotters and wrap them tightly in double-thickness buttered foil. Twist the ends to seal and refrigerate until needed.

5. Completing the sauce
(10 minutes) (see Savoury sauces, page 26)

Bring the braising juices to the boil, skim, then add 1 tablespoon cream. Reduce to about 250 ml/9 fl oz, add 85 g/3 oz sliced morels and simmer for 3 minutes. Taste and correct the seasoning; if it lacks sharpness, add a dash of red wine vinegar. Reserve.

6. Steaming the trotters; cooking the sweetbread, kidneys and wild mushrooms (25 minutes)

Trotters: Steam, still wrapped in their foil, for 20 minutes.

Reserved sweetbread: Season with salt and pepper and sear in 1 teaspoon *beurre noisette* (see page 24) for 3 minutes. Cook for 10 minutes in the preheated oven.

Kidney: Leave wrapped in its fat and cook in the preheated oven for 20 minutes.

Foie gras (optional): Season with salt and pepper and brown the slivers in a very hot non-stick pan without oil or butter for 30 seconds on each side. Keep in a warm place, on a small plate lined with absorbent paper.

Tongue: Reheat in its cooking stock, then peel and slice into 8 and reserve in the hot stock.

Chanterelles: Season with a pinch of salt and pepper, then pan-fry in 15 g/½ oz hot butter for 1–2 minutes. Add a squeeze of lemon and keep warm.

7. Assembling the dish and serving
(5 minutes)

Heat 4 plates.

Bring the sauce back to the boil.

Place the trotters on a carving board and carefully unwrap them. Halve horizontally.

Remove the kidney from its fat and carve into 4 slices. Season with salt and pepper.

Slice the sweetbread into 4 and season each slice with a few grains of salt and pepper.

Place one half trotter in the centre of each plate, arrange 1 slice of kidney, sweetbread and *foie gras* and 2 slices of tongue around, and spoon out the sauce spiked with morels. Scatter the chanterelles and serve to your guests.

─── VARIATIONS ───

A fine *julienne* of truffles is always welcome or, on a more rustic note, a few fat *lardons* (see page 47).

─── WINE ───

This is a wholesome dish with plenty of strong flavours. You should serve a mature, deep and powerful red wine, such as Côte Rôtie or Châteauneuf du Pape or a well-matured Burgundy.

Chef's notes

Kidney: It should be bought still encased in its white fat. The kidney itself should be a creamy pink colour.

Foie gras: See page 274 for where to buy.

Braising the pig's trotters: This first stage is very important as it will give the trotters their rich dark brown glaze. During the long cooking, the juices will reduce into an essence which will flavour and glaze the trotters. Be careful not to tear them when turning them over or the delicate filling will burst out.

Meat

QUEUE DE BOEUF ET LANGUE DE VEAU BRAISEES

Oxtail and calf's tongue braised in red wine

"A wholesome, robust winter dish."

Serves 4
Difficulty: 🎩 🎩
Total recipe time: 50 minutes preparation, plus 3 hours braising, plus 3 days marinating

———— INGREDIENTS ————

2 calves' tongues

2 1.25 kg/1½lb oxtails

Brine (to be made 3 days in advance)
500 ml/18 fl oz cold water

100 ml/3½ fl oz good red table wine

40 g/1½ oz salt

1 teaspoon caster sugar

1 sprig of thyme

½ bayleaf

4 black peppercorns, crushed

For cooking the tongues
1 medium onion, roughly chopped

2 medium carrots, washed, peeled and diced

8 black peppercorns, crushed

1 sprig of thyme

½ bayleaf

600 ml/1 pt Light chicken stock (see page 21) or water

For cooking the oxtails
5 tablespoons non-scented oil

1 large onion, roughly chopped

2 carrots, washed, peeled and diced

¼ celery stalk, washed and diced

2 garlic cloves, unpeeled and lightly crushed

10 black peppercorns, crushed

1 sprig of thyme

½ bayleaf

100 ml/3½ fl oz red wine vinegar

500 ml/18 fl oz good red table wine

1 L/1¾ pt Light chicken stock (see page 21) or water

300 ml/10 fl oz Veal stock (see page 18)

salt and freshly ground white pepper

Garnish
2 turnips

2 carrots

1 swede

1 parsnip

a pinch of caster sugar

a dash of white wine vinegar

3 teaspoons unsalted butter

Planning ahead
Order the oxtails and tongues well in advance. Ask your butcher to trim excess fat and sinew from oxtails and to joint them at the knuckles; you should obtain 12 pieces in all. Keep the trimmings for the sauce. Ask for the tongues to be trimmed.
Chicken and veal stock must be made in advance.
Soak the tongues 3 days in advance.
Stages 2–4 inclusive can be completed 1 or 2 days in advance. To serve the dish, simmer the meats for 15 minutes.

1. Preparing the brine, soaking the tongues (10 minutes, plus 3 days soaking)
Place all the ingredients for the brine in a large saucepan and boil for 2 minutes to infuse the flavours and dissolve the salt and sugar. Draw off the heat and allow to cool.
Trim and wash the tongues, then place them in the brine, cover the pan and leave to soak for 3 days in the fridge.

2. Preparing the vegetables for garnish (20 minutes)
All vegetables: Wash, peel and cut into barrel shapes (see page 50), fine *julienne* or large dice. Keep each separate and refrigerate on a small tray covered with a damp cloth.

3. Cooking the tongues (2½ hours)
Remove from the brine and wash thoroughly under cold running water. Put the vegetables, herbs and spices in a large saucepan, sit the tongues on top and cover with the chicken stock or water. Bring to the boil, cover the pan and cook at just below simmering point for 2½ hours. Allow to cool then lift out the tongues onto a chopping board lined with a tea towel and peel off the first layer of skin, using a small paring knife. Return tongues to the pan and set aside. While the tongues are cooking, cook the oxtail.

4. Cooking the oxtail (3 hours)
In a large saucepan, heat 3 tablespoons oil until smoking, then sear and brown half the oxtail pieces and the trimmings for about 7 minutes. Transfer to a small tray. Add another

tablespoon oil and repeat with the remaining oxtail. Remove and reserve.

To the same pan, add another tablespoon oil and sear all the diced vegetables, herbs and spices for 5 minutes. Tilt the pan and spoon off as much fat as you can, then deglaze with the vinegar and let it evaporate completely. Add the wine, bring to the boil and reduce by one-quarter.

Add the oxtail pieces and trimmings, pour in the chicken stock or water, bring to the boil and skim. Partially cover and cook gently at just below simmering point for 2¾ hours.

Remove oxtail pieces with a slotted spoon, place in a large bowl and cover. Force the cooking juices through a fine sieve into a medium saucepan, pressing the vegetables and trimmings with a ladle to extract as much juice and flavour as possible.

Bring to the boil and reduce to about 600 ml/1 pt rich but light-textured juices, skimming from time to time. Taste and season with salt and pepper. Put the oxtail pieces back into the pan, cover and keep warm.

5. Cooking the vegetables for garnish (10 minutes)

Turnips: Place in a small saucepan with a pinch of salt and caster sugar, a dash of white wine vinegar and 6 tablespoons water, bring to the boil, cover and cook slowly for 5–8 minutes, according to size. Cook the carrots, swedes and parsnips separately in the same way, omitting the sugar and vinegar, but adding 1 teaspoon butter. Taste and correct seasoning.

6. Assembling the dish and serving

Warm 4 plates or a large serving dish. Lift out the tongues and cut them into large slivers. Warm them in their cooking juices, then taste and correct seasoning if necessary.

Bring the oxtail back to the boil.

Place 3 pieces of oxtail on each plate, scatter over the slivers of veal tongue, pour the juices over and around and scatter on the vegetables. Serve.

— VARIATIONS —

Vary the vegetable garnish as you like. To simplify the dish, omit the tongues.

— WINE —

Try a lively red Provençal wine such as Château Vignelore or Bandol, or a Château de la Borderie from Bergerac.

Chef's notes

Soaking the calves' tongues in brine: The brine will penetrate the flesh, preserving the colour of the tongues during cooking.

Browning the oxtail: Brown well so that the pieces become flavourful in themselves and make a good richly-coloured juice.

Cooking the oxtail: The oxtail is cooked when you can tease away the flesh with a fork.

Seasoning: Season with care; the meats and stocks all contain a certain amount of salt, which will intensify as the juices are reduced, so you should need to add very little salt.

COTE DE VEAU ROTIE AUX MOUSSERONS

Roast veal cutlet served with its own juices spiked with wild mushrooms

"The concept of this dish should trigger your imagination – a simple roast whose caramelized juices are deglazed with water to produce a most delectable light, scented sauce."

Serves 4
Difficulty: ♟
Total recipe time: 50 minutes

INGREDIENTS

4 350g/12 oz veal cutlets, trimmed weight

2 teaspoons unsalted butter

2 teaspoons groundnut oil

salt and freshly ground white pepper

Sauce

300 ml/½ pt cold water

150 g/5 oz fresh mousserons or 20 g/ ¾ oz dried

20 g/¾ oz unsalted butter

a squeeze of lemon

Planning ahead
Order wing ribs of veal well in advance. The quality of the veal is of paramount importance: it must come from a milk-fed calf. The wing ribs (holding the loin) are the most tender and offer the least wastage. Ask your butcher to trim excess fat, cut off the chine, scrape the rib bones and tie up the cutlets. Ask for the offcut bones and trimmings to make a veal stock (see page 18).

1. Preparing the mushrooms
(15 minutes)
Preheat the oven to 230°C/450°F/gas 8 for Stage 2.
This is time-consuming: first remove all pieces of vegetation stuck to the mushrooms then cut off the stalk right under the cap. (The stalks are woody and inedible; dry them and keep for flavouring sauces.) Wash the mushrooms briefly in plenty of cold water, drain and wrap in a tea towel.

2. Cooking the veal (15 minutes plus 15 minutes resting)
Season the cutlets with salt and pepper.
Heat the butter and groundnut oil in a roasting pan until hot, then brown the cutlets for 2 minutes per side. Roast in the preheated oven for about 15 minutes, turning them over after 7 minutes. Stand the cutlets upright in another dish so that they do not soak in the juices they will release and leave in a warm place. Spoon off most of the fat in the roasting pan.

3. Making the sauce (10 minutes)
(see Savoury sauces, page 26)
Place the roasting pan over a medium heat and add 300 ml/½ pt cold water, scraping up all the tasty caramelized juices in the bottom of the pan. Strain into a small saucepan, bring to the boil, skim off any remaining fat and reduce to about 100 ml/3½ fl oz juices. Taste and correct seasoning with a pinch of salt and pepper. Set aside.

4. Cooking the mushrooms
(1 minute)
In a small saucepan, bring to the boil 3 tablespoons cold water and 20 g/¾ oz butter, with a large pinch of salt and 4 turns of pepper. Add the mushrooms, cover and cook for 1 minute, then add them to the juices.

5. Assembling the dish and serving
(10 minutes)
Heat 4 plates.
Return the veal cutlets to the oven for 5 minutes, seasoning each with a few grains of salt.
Strain the juices released by the cutlets into the sauce, taste and correct seasoning with a little salt and pepper. 'Lift' the juices with a squeeze of lemon.
Place a veal cutlet in the centre of each plate and spoon the sauce and mushrooms over and around.

VARIATIONS
Pork cutlets can be served this way.
Other varieties of wild mushrooms can replace the *mousserons*.
The juice can be scented with your favourite herbs, or studded with the first tiny peas or broad beans.

WINE
Serve a cool red wine from the Loire such as Bourgueil or Chinon.

Chef's notes
Mousserons: These tiny mushrooms have a wonderfully delicate aroma. Observe the cooking time precisely to preserve their taste and texture.
Cooking the veal: It is vital to sear the cutlets until well browned, as this determines the taste and colour of the juices.

BECASSE ROTIE AU FUMET DE ST EMILION, MOUSSE DE PAIN

Roast woodcock with a St Emilion sauce, garnished with bread mousse and cranberries

Serves 4
Difficulty: 👨‍🍳 👨‍🍳
Total recipe time: 1½ hours
Special equipment: four 5 x 3 cm/ 2 x 1½ in dariole moulds

————— INGREDIENTS —————

4 trussed woodcock, with their livers

2 teaspoons non-scented oil

2 teaspoons unsalted butter

salt and freshly ground white pepper

Sauce
2 shallots, peeled and finely chopped

50 g/2 oz celery, washed and finely chopped

65 g/2½ oz button mushrooms, finely sliced

1 juniper berry, crushed

1 sprig of thyme

wings and necks from woodcock

400 ml/14 fl oz St Emilion

200 ml/7 fl oz water

150 ml/5 fl oz Brown chicken stock (see page 21)

woodcock livers

1 coffee spoon redcurrant jelly

a squeeze of lemon

Bread mousse
300 ml/10 fl oz milk

65 g/2½ oz white bread, crusts removed

1 small onion, finely chopped

2 cloves

a pinch of ground nutmeg

½ egg

2 egg whites, plus a squeeze of lemon

butter for greasing the moulds

Cranberry garnish
2 tablespoons cranberries

2 teaspoons caster sugar

1 tablespoon water

Planning ahead
Order the woodcock well in advance; they should not have been hung for more than 3 days. Ask your butcher to pluck, draw and truss the birds and to give you the livers (gall removed), wings and necks.
The stock must be made in advance.
Stages 1–3 inclusive can be completed in advance, but cook the bread mousses only at the last moment.

1. Preparing the woodcock (10 minutes)
Preheat the oven to 180°C/350°F/ gas 4.
Singe the birds over an open flame to remove any stubble and replace the livers. Do not bard the birds, as they are covered with a thin layer of fat and the cooking time is short.

2. The vegetables and spices for the sauce (10 minutes)
Mix together all the prepared vegetables, spices and thyme and set aside.

3. Preparing and cooking the bread mousses (20 minutes) (see Mousse making, page 36)
In a small saucepan, bring the milk to the boil, draw off the heat and add the bread, spices, a pinch of salt and 4

turns of pepper. Allow to cool then whisk to a purée with the ½ egg.
Beat the egg whites until firm, adding a squeeze of lemon to prevent graining, then fold into the mousse mixture. Taste and correct the seasoning.
Butter the dariole moulds, line each with a small round of buttered greaseproof paper and fill with mousse mixture.
Stand the moulds in a deep roasting pan lined with greaseproof paper and two-thirds fill the tin with hot water. Cook in the preheated oven for 15 minutes, until the surface of the mousses is slightly convex. Remove from the oven and keep warm in the bain-marie.
Increase the oven temperature to 230°C/450°F/gas 8 for Stage 4.

4. Roasting and carving the woodcock (15–20 minutes)
Heat the oil and butter in a large sauté pan, put in the woodcock and sear on all sides for 2 minutes. Season with salt and pepper. Pour off and reserve the excess cooking fat. Turn the birds on their backs and roast in the preheated oven for 8–10 minutes.
Meanwhile, start making the sauce.
Leave the cooked woodcock to rest for a few minutes, then cut the trussing string and remove the livers with a teaspoon. Purée the livers with the flat of a knife and set aside.
Cut off the legs at the joint and carve out the breasts. Lightly season the insides of the breasts. Keep the breasts and legs in a warm place. Roughly chop the carcasses.

5. The sauce (20 minutes) (see Savoury sauces page 26)
In a small sauté pan, lightly brown the

woodcock wings and necks in the cooking fat reserved from Stage 4. Add the chopped vegetables and sear them for about 5 minutes over a strong heat. Deglaze with the wine, reduce by half, then add the cold water, veal stock and redcurrant jelly. After the woodcock have been carved, add the chopped carcasses to the stock, bring back to the boil and skim. Simmer for about 10 minutes then whisk in the puréed livers and simmer for a further 2 minutes. Force the stock through a hard sieve (pressing down on the bones and vegetables with a ladle to extract as much juice and flavour as possible), then strain the stock through a damp muslin cloth into a small saucepan. Reduce until the consistency is mid-way between a juice and a sauce. Taste, correct the seasoning with a pinch of salt and 4 turns of pepper and enliven the sauce with a squeeze of lemon.

6. Cooking the cranberries
(5 minutes)
Wash the cranberries and simmer in 1 tablespoon water and 2 teaspoons caster sugar for 3 minutes.

7. Assembling the dish and serving
(10 minutes)
Warm 4 plates.
Place the woodcock breasts and legs and the bread mousses in the oven for 2–3 minutes to warm. Bring the sauce back to the boil.
Separate the legs and thighs. Turn out the bread mousses onto the middle of the plates and surround with the woodcock breasts and legs.
Strain the juices released by the woodcock into the sauce, then spoon the sauce over and around. Scatter over the cranberries and serve.

— VARIATIONS —
Snipe would also be delicious served this way.

— WINE —
The most obvious choice is a fine red wine from St Emilion, such as the *premiers grands crus classés* Château Ausone or Château Magdelaine, or a *grand cru classé,* like Château l'Angelus. However any fine, mature red wine from Bordeaux, the Rhône (Côte Rôtie, Gigondas) or the Côtes de Nuit would suit this dish.

Chef's notes
Woodcock: If woodcock are hung for more than 3 days, their flavour becomes too strong.
Roasting the woodcock: Observe the cooking time carefully. Woodcock are best served medium rare so that they remain moist and tender.
Carving the woodcock: Salt will not permeate the flesh, so it is important to season the *insides* of the breasts after carving.

PIGEONNEAU DE GRAIN DE NORFOLK EN CROUTE DE SEL AU JUS DE TRUFFES

Norfolk squabs baked in a salt pastry crust, served with a light truffle juice

"Squabs are often confused with Trafalgar or wild pigeons. Although they come from the same family, gastronomically speaking, they are totally different.
During the 16th and 17th centuries squabs were often bred specially for the table in the great English manor houses (Le Manoir has a fine 17th-century dovecote in the grounds), but this practice fell into decline many years ago.
Now, however, the current interest in good food means that squabs are being bred in England once again and I find them as good as any from France. I think they are the most tender and flavourful of all poultry."

Serves 4
Difficulty: 🎩🎩
Total recipe time: 2 hours 20 minutes
Special equipment: trussing needle, kitchen string, boning knife, electric mixer with a dough hook, rolling pin, four 10 cm/4 in non-stick tartlet tins

— INGREDIENTS —

4 225 g/8 oz squabs, with their livers

8 slices of truffle (optional)

4 teaspoons unsalted butter

1 tablespoon groundnut or corn oil

Salt pastry
1 kg/2¼ lbs strong white flour, plus a handful for flouring

600 g/1 lb 5 oz fine table salt

7 egg whites

eggwash (2 egg yolks beaten with 1 tablespoon milk and a large pinch of caster sugar)

a handful of rock salt and 8 cloves, for decoration

Squab juice
neck and wings of squabs

2 teaspoons unsalted butter

4 shallots, finely chopped

100 g/3½ oz button mushrooms, finely sliced

3 tablespoons ruby port

4 tablespoons dry Madeira

4 tablespoons truffle juice (optional)

1 20 g/¾oz truffle, peeled and finely chopped (optional)

200 ml/7 fl oz Brown chicken stock (see page 21)

2 tablespoons whipping cream

salt and freshly ground white pepper

Garnish (optional)
Pommes Maxime (see page 55)

125 g/4½ oz raw foie gras

melted butter, for serving

Planning ahead
Order the squabs well in advance. Ask the butcher to hang them for 6 days to heighten the flavour before plucking and dressing. Ask him to cut off the feet, wings and necks, remove the wishbone (to make carving easier) and draw them, reserving the livers.
Stages 1–4 inclusive can be completed up to 4 hours in advance. The truffle juice can be made well in advance.

1. Preparing the squabs
(10 minutes)
Singe any stubble over an open flame. Truss the birds (see page 16) and, if you wish, slide a truffle slice under each breast, inserting it between the skin and flesh.
Sear the squabs in 1 tablespoon each hot butter and oil for 3 minutes on each thigh and 1 minute on each breast. Leave to cool.
Season the livers, pan-fry for a few seconds and place inside the squabs.
Chop the neck bones and wings and reserve them for Stage 4.

2. The salt pastry (10 minutes)
Combine 1 kg/2¼ lb flour and the salt in an electric mixer fitted with a dough hook. Mix at slow speed for 1–2 minutes, add the egg whites and increase to medium speed. Finally, slowly add 300 ml/9 fl oz cold water until the pastry just holds together. Shape into a ball.

3. Wrapping the squabs (40 minutes)
On a floured work surface, divide the pastry into 4 and flatten each piece into a circle. Roll to a thickness of 6–7 mm/¼ in and a diameter of about 28 cm/11 in. Using a small knife, cut out four 23 cm/9 in circles and set aside.

Pigeonneau de grain de Norfolk en croûte de sel au jus de truffes

Gather together all the pastry trimmings and roll again into a 5 mm/¼ in thickness. Cut out 8 'wings' and set aside. Mould the squab 'heads' from the pastry trimmings.

Lay a squab, breast down, in each circle of pastry and wrap it completely, making sure there are no holes or uncovered areas. Dampen the pastry 'wings' and attach to sides of squabs.

Lightly dampen the base of the pastry 'heads' and press firmly into place. Use the cloves for 'eyes'.

Brush the eggwash all over the pastry cases, except the bases. Sprinkle rock salt over the breast and wings. Place the squabs on a lightly oiled baking tray and refrigerate.

Preheat the oven to 240°C/475°F/gas 9 for Stage 5.

4. The sauce (25 minutes)

In a medium saucepan, sweat the shallots in the butter for 3–4 minutes without colouring, adding the mushrooms during the last minute.

In another saucepan, sear the squab necks and wings in the hot oil for 3–4 minutes to colour lightly. Deglaze with the port, scraping in all the caramelized juices from the bottom of the pan. Pour in the Madeira and boil for 30 seconds. Skim, then add to the shallots and mushrooms and reduce by half.

Pour in the chicken stock and stir in the cream and truffle juice, if using. Simmer for about 10 minutes, then force through a fine conical sieve, pressing hard with a wooden spatula to extract as much flavour as possible. If using a truffle, infuse it in the sauce for a few minutes. Taste, season and set aside.

5. Baking the squabs (30 minutes)
Bake for 25 minutes in the pre-heated oven, then leave to rest away from the heat for 5 minutes.

6. The garnish (3 minutes)
Foie gras: Cut into 4 slivers and season with salt and pepper. Heat an empty frying pan (with no fat) until hot then toss in the slivers of *foie gras*. They will smoke and sizzle. Turn them over after 30 seconds and cook for another 30 seconds. Keep warm on a plate lined with absorbent paper. Correct the seasoning.
Pommes Maxime: See page 55.

7. Serving (10 minutes)
Heat 4 oval fish plates and have ready a large carving board.
Sit these glorious squabs on a serving tray and brush with melted butter. Using a spatula, lift out the *pommes Maxime* from the tins and arrange them around the squabs. Top with a sliver of *foie gras*. Bring the sauce back to the boil and pour around. Present

this spectacle to your guests.
Unfortunately the work doesn't stop here, as the squabs must be freed from their inedible salt crust. If you feel confident, do this in front of your guests. First remove the pastry 'head' then slice open the crust. Place a fork inside the squab, lift it onto the carving board, cut off the trussing string and serve. If you are not too confident, you had better do this in the privacy of your kitchen.
Keep the carcasses as they will make an excellent sauce.

––––––– VARIATIONS –––––––
This technique can be used for a variety of dishes, eg: a whole sea bass, scented with tarragon, or lamb.

––––––– WINE –––––––
A light, well-rounded red wine from the Côte de Beaune would be ideal – perhaps a Volnay les Brouillards, or Pernand-Vergelesses.

Chef's notes
Preparing the squabs: Trim the wings as close to the breast as possible and truss the birds tightly so the bones cannot

pierce the salt crust. If the pastry does not completely enclose the squabs, the cooking time will be affected.
Searing the squabs: Do not salt the birds; the salt crust will do it for you. The object is not to cook the squabs but simply to crisp them up and colour the skin to enhance their taste and appearance. This stage does, however, partially cook the legs, which require a longer cooking time than breasts. It is important to allow the squabs to cool before wrapping them in the salt pastry.
Baking the squabs: The salt crust is not only for visual effect, but also greatly enhances the taste and texture; the juices and flavour are sealed in and the slow build-up of heat keeps the flesh moist and tender.
Observe the cooking time precisely. The heat builds up slowly at first, but since it cannot escape, it intensifies during the final 5 minutes. Even as little as 2 or 3 minutes less or more cooking time could grossly under- or overcook the squabs. Only adjust the cooking time if the dressed squabs weigh more or less than 225 g/8 oz.

NOISETTES DE CHEVREUIL AUX POMMES ET GRAINS DE CASSIS
Medallions of roe deer served with poivrade sauce, apples and blackcurrants

Serves 4
Difficulty: 🎩 🎩 🎩
Total recipe time: 1 hour 50 minutes, plus 24 hours marinating
Special equipment: muslin cloth, 5 mm/¼ in *parisienne* baller

––––––– INGREDIENTS –––––––
2 venison fillets, total weight 700 g/ 1¾ lb

1 tablespoon non-scented oil

salt and freshly ground black pepper

Marinade
600 ml/1 pt Hermitage red wine

bones from the best ends, chopped

1 large onion, chopped

1 carrot, peeled and diced

1 celery stalk, washed and diced

½ unpeeled clove garlic, crushed

1 sprig of thyme

1 bayleaf

5 juniper berries, crushed

1 teaspoon black peppercorns, crushed

Sauce poivrade
wine, bones and vegetables from the marinade

100 ml/3½ fl oz non-scented oil

100 ml/3½ fl oz red wine vinegar

400 ml/14 fl oz cold water

200 ml/7 fl oz Veal stock (see page 18)

2 tablespoons whipping cream

1 tablespoon Cognac

salt and freshly ground white pepper

For the garnish

1 Granny Smith apple

1 teaspoon unsalted butter

1 tablespoon blackcurrants

2 teaspoons caster sugar

Planning ahead

Order a best end of venison with 7 ribs per side (about 2.4 kg/5½ lb).

Ask the butcher to prepare the 2 fillets which together will weigh about 700 g/1¾ lb and to chop the bones.

The marinade must be made 1 day in advance.

Stages 2 – 4 inclusive can be completed 1 day in advance.

1. Making the marinade

(10 minutes)

In a medium saucepan, bring the Hermitage to the boil, skim and leave to cool.

Wrap the juniper berries, peppercorns, thyme and bayleaf in a small muslin cloth and tie with string.

Place the chopped bones in a large bowl, add the diced vegetables and parcel of herbs and spices.

Venison: Remove any sinews with a small sharp knife and add the fillets to the bones. Pour over the wine, cover with clingfilm and refrigerate for 24 hours.

2. Making the sauce

(1 hour 5 minutes)

Preheat the oven to 240°C/475°F/gas 9.

Strain the marinade through a colander into a mixing bowl and leave to stand for about 5 minutes. Separate the bones from the vegetables and pat both dry. Put the venison fillets on a plate and seal with clingfilm.

In a medium roasting pan, heat 100 ml/3½ fl oz oil until hot then sear the bones for about 10 minutes until browned. Add the vegetables and cook for 5 minutes to colour lightly. Roast in the preheated oven for 25 minutes until both bones and vegetables turn a rich dark brown. Pour off the fat then place pan over a strong heat, deglaze with the vinegar and reduce until it has almost completely evaporated. Add the strained marinade, bring to the boil and reduce by one-third. Taste (it should already be very pleasant) then add the cold water and veal stock, bring to the boil, skim and simmer for about 25 minutes. Strain through a fine sieve into a large saucepan, bring to the boil, skim, then stir in the cream and Cognac and reduce to about 200 ml/7 fl oz, until the sauce coats the back of a spoon. Taste and correct the seasoning with a pinch of salt and 4 turns of black pepper.

3. Preparing the garnish

(10 minutes)

Apple: Peel then, using a *parisienne* spoon, scoop out little balls and reserve in a small dish.

Blackcurrants: Place in a small container with the caster sugar and set aside.

4. Cooking the venison fillets

(15 minutes, plus 10 minutes resting)

Preheat the oven to 230°C/450°F/gas 8.

Pat the venison fillets dry and season with salt and black pepper. In a medium roasting pan, heat 1 tablespoon oil until hot and sear the fillets all over to colour lightly. Pour off the fat and roast in the preheated oven for about 10 minutes.

Remove, cover loosely with foil and leave to rest for a further 10 minutes so that the meat can relax.

5. Cooking the garnish (10 minutes)

Turn on the grill.

In a small frying pan, fry the apple balls in a teaspoon butter until golden. Place the blackcurrants under the grill for 5 minutes.

6. Assembling the dish and serving

(5 minutes)

Heat 4 plates or a large serving dish.

Add the juices released by the venison fillets to the sauce and return the fillets to the oven for 3 minutes.

To carve: Cut each fillet into 3 or 4 medallions and season each with a tiny pinch of salt and black pepper.

Arrange the medallions on the plates, spoon the sauce around and scatter over the apple balls and blackcurrants. Serve immediately.

--- WINE ---

Ideally you should serve a mature, powerful red wine with this dish – Chambertin, Bonnes Mares, or the more aromatic Musigny – all from the Côtes de Nuits.

Chef's notes

Venison should be hung for about 12 days to tenderize the meat and allow the taste to develop. Although you can use farmed venison, the best meat comes from the wild roe deer which can still be found in the wilder areas of England and Scotland.

Making the sauce: Since the bones, vegetables and venison will have absorbed some of the red wine, it is very important to remove excess moisture so that they will brown easily.

To correct the sauce: Depending on the wine used and the maturity of the venison the sauce may lack bite or be a little acid. If it is too acid, add ½ teaspoon redcurrant jelly, dark chocolate or a pinch of caster sugar; if too sweet, sharpen it with a dash of red wine or Cognac.

Blackcurrants: The amount of sugar needed will vary according to their ripeness. Taste before adding it.

Carving the venison: As salt cannot penetrate the whole fillets, season the carved venison with a few grains of salt and pepper.

SUPREMES DE PIGEON RAMIER AU JAMBON DE BAYONNE ET FUMET DE VIN ROUGE

*Pan-fried breasts of wood pigeon served on Bayonne ham
with a red wine sauce*

Serves 4
Difficulty: ☖☖
Total recipe time: 1 hour 10 minutes,
plus 1 day marinating

──── INGREDIENTS ────
*4 wood pigeons, drawn, with their livers
if possible*

½ tablespoon unsalted butter

½ tablespoon non-scented oil

8 slices of Bayonne ham

salt and freshly ground white pepper

Marinade
2 tablespoons red wine

1 tablespoon olive oil

1 sprig of thyme

2 juniper berries

a dash of Cognac

salt and freshly ground white pepper

Sauce
wood pigeon carcasses

6 shallots, finely chopped

1 carrot, finely diced

¼ celery stalk, finely diced

*100 g/3½ oz button mushrooms,
finely diced*

4 tablespoons non-scented oil

1 sprig of thyme

3 juniper berries, crushed

10 g/⅓ oz smoked bacon

¼ dried bayleaf

1 tablespoon red wine vinegar

2 tablespoons Cognac

100 ml/3½ fl oz ruby port

400 ml/14 fl oz red wine

*150 ml/5 fl oz Brown chicken stock
(see page 21)*

*2 tablespoons whipping cream
(optional)*

Garnish
12 shallots

a pinch of caster sugar

2 tablespoons unsalted butter

20 tiny button mushrooms

*50 g/2 oz each smoked and green belly
of pork*

wood pigeon livers (optional)

Planning ahead
Order the wood pigeons well in advance – if possible, have them hung for 2 or 3 days. Ask your butcher to draw the birds, but to keep the livers.
Bone the pigeons and marinate the breasts, with the skin on, in a covered dish in the fridge 1 day in advance. Keep the carcasses and legs for the sauce.
The sauce and garnish can be completed up to 1 day in advance.

1. The sauce (1 hour) (see Savoury sauces, page 26)
Preheat the oven to 230°C/450°F/gas 8.
Chop all the pigeon carcasses. In a large thick-bottomed saucepan, sear the carcasses and legs in 3 tablespoons hot oil for about 5 minutes, until lightly browned. Add the vegetables,

thyme, crushed juniper berries, smoked bacon and ¼ bayleaf and sweat gently for 2–3 minutes.
Cook in the preheated oven for 15 minutes until the carcasses and vegetables are cooked through and turn a rich golden brown.
Pour off the cooking fat, then deglaze the pan with the vinegar and let it evaporate completely over a strong heat. Add the Cognac, port and red wine and bring to the boil. Skim and simmer for 15 minutes until reduced by half.
Pour in 400 ml/14 fl oz cold water and the chicken stock and simmer for a further 20 minutes. Skim, then add the cream. Using a ladle, force the stock first through a hard sieve then through a fine conical sieve into another saucepan and reduce to about 200 ml/7 fl oz of concentrated juices. Taste and season.
Meanwhile prepare the garnish.

2. The garnish and Bayonne ham
(35 minutes)
Shallots: Put in a small saucepan with 6 tablespoons water, 2 teaspoons butter, a tiny pinch of sugar and a pinch of salt and pepper. Cover and cook at just below simmering point for 15 minutes. Remove the lid and allow the shallots to caramelize in their juices.
Mushrooms: Peel but do not wash. Sauté in 1 teaspoon butter until golden. Keep warm.
Smoked and green belly of pork: Cut into *lardons* (see page 47), blanch in boiling water and sauté in 1 teaspoon butter.
Pigeon livers: Pan-fry for 30 seconds in 1 teaspoon butter.
Bayonne ham: Soak in cold water for

2 minutes to remove excess salt, drain and set aside.

3. Cooking the pigeon breasts
(5 minutes, plus 5 minutes resting)
Preheat the oven to 230°C/450°F/gas 8.
Remove the pigeon breasts from the marinade and pat dry.
In a large non-stick frying pan, heat ½ tablespoon each of butter and oil until golden and foaming. Sear the breasts for 15 seconds on each side, then cook in the preheated oven for 3 minutes. Pour off the cooking fat, cover loosely with buttered foil and leave to rest away from the heat for 5 minutes. Strain the juices released during resting into the sauce.

4. Serving (5 minutes)
Warm 4 plates or a large serving dish. Warm the Bayonne ham in the oven or under the grill for a few seconds and place 2 slices in the centre of each plate. Arrange the pigeon breasts in the centre, pour the sauce over and around and scatter with shallots, *lardons* and button mushrooms. Serve immediately.

— VARIATIONS —
Deep-fried celery or celeriac leaves or *croûtons* make a delicious garnish.

— WINE —
Any mature fine red wine will complement this dish – a Burgundy from the Côtes de Nuits, a Rhône such as Côte Rôtie or Château Rayas, or a classed growth from the Medoc, St Emilion, Graves or Pomerol.

Chef's notes
Bayonne ham: The saltiness is intensified when the ham is warmed; it must be soaked in cold water for 2 minutes to remove just the right amount of salt.
The pigeon legs are used only in the sauce as they are so tough.
Wine: Use a vigorous red wine with plenty of colour for the sauce.
Cooking the pigeon breasts: Be careful not to overcook or they will become tough and inedible. They should be served rare to medium rare so that the flesh remains moist and tender.

PAVE AU CHOCOLAT, GRIOTTES
ET ANANAS, SAUCE CAFE

A rich chocolate dessert with pineapple and
kirsch-soaked cherries, with a coffee cream sauce

Serves 8
Difficulty: 🎩🎩
Total recipe time: 50 minutes, plus at least 2 hours chilling
Special equipment: eight 8 x 4 cm/3¼ x 1½ in stainless steel rings

— INGREDIENTS —

Ganache
150 ml/5 fl oz double cream
115 g/4 oz best plain dessert chocolate, chopped (see page 36)

Mousse
150 g/5 oz best plain dessert chocolate
3 egg yolks
7 egg whites
20 g/¾ oz caster sugar
a squeeze of lemon
85 g/3 oz fresh pineapple, chopped and drained on absorbent paper

9 maraschino cherries in kirsch, drained

cocoa powder for dredging

500 ml/18 fl oz Coffee cream (see page 33), for serving

Planning ahead
The coffee sauce must be made in advance.
The dessert can be prepared up to 2 days in advance and kept refrigerated, ready to assemble.

1. Making the ganache and lining the moulds (20 minutes)
In a small pan, bring the cream to the boil and draw off the heat. Add the chopped chocolate and whisk until thickened. Leave to cool.
Meanwhile, line a small tray with greaseproof paper. Using a small palette knife, line the inside of the stainless steel rings with a 3 mm/1/10 in layer of *ganache*. Place the rings on the tray and, holding them down firmly with one hand, spread 1 small teaspoon of *ganache* over the bottom to form a base. Refrigerate for at least 15 minutes so that the *ganache* hardens.

2. Making the chocolate mousse
(15 minutes)
Chop the chocolate and melt in a small bowl set over a pan of hot water. Whisk the egg whites to a light peak, add the caster sugar and a squeeze of lemon and continue whisking until firm.
Whisk the egg yolks into the melted chocolate until smooth, remove from the bain-marie and briskly beat in one-quarter of the beaten egg whites until well mixed. Sprinkle in the

chopped pineapple and cherries then carefully fold in the remaining egg whites to obtain the lightest possible mousse.

3. Filling the rings (5 minutes, plus 2 hours chilling)
Remove the lined rings from the fridge and fill with the mousse mixture, smoothing over the tops with a palette knife. Chill for at least 2 hours.

4. Turning out the mousses and serving (10 minutes)
Heat a baking tray, roll each ring on it for a few seconds, then ease out the mousses onto a cold tray and dust with cocoa powder. Using a palette knife, lift them onto the centre of the serving plates and surround with coffee sauce. Serve the remaining sauce separately in a sauceboat.

--- VARIATIONS ---

If you are pressed for time, omit the *ganache*, pineapple and cherries and just make a deliciously simple chocolate mousse.
Replace the coffee sauce with a rum-scented *Crème anglaise* (see page 33).
Garnish the mousse with some large chocolate flakes or petals made by scraping a block of chocolate (at room temperature) with a round pastry cutter. Arrange them like a flower on the top of the mousses.

Chef's notes
Cherries: Cherries steeped in kirsch or Cognac can usually be found in delicatessens. The process is rather lengthy if you do it yourself – about 2 months! Take 500 g/1 lb 2 oz ripe cherries. Wash, drain, trim the stalks to 3 cm/1½ in and place in a jar. Add 200 g/7 oz caster sugar, cover with kirsch or Cognac, seal and leave for about 2 months. Serve the cherries as an alcoholic sweet, with coffee, or in many desserts. The alcohol can be reused too.
Mousse: Do not let the chocolate and egg yolk mixture go cold or it will solidify before you can mix in the bulk of the egg white.

BROCHETTE DE FRUITS EXOTIQUES AU SABAYON, RIZ AU LAIT GLACE

Skewered, marinated exotic fruits, served on a bed of iced rice pudding glazed with a sabayon

Serves 4
Difficulty: 🍴🍴
Total recipe time: 2½ hours, plus 12–14 hours marinating
Special equipment: four 20 cm/8 in wooden or steel skewers, electric mixer

--- INGREDIENTS ---

20 green peppercorns

2 tamarillos

1 small mango (250 g/9 oz)

200 g/7 oz slice of pineapple, cut from the centre

4 guavas

2 figs

¼ banana

2 passion fruit

400 ml/14 fl oz cold Sorbet syrup (see page 31)

2 tablespoons lemon juice

Iced rice pudding
50 g/2 oz pudding rice

25 g/1 oz caster sugar

300 ml/½ pt milk

150 ml/5 fl oz whipping cream

½ vanilla pod, split lengthways

1 teaspoon unsalted butter

Sabayon
2 egg yolks

150 ml/5 fl oz syrup from the marinade

100 ml/3½ fl oz whipping cream

1 tablespoon Malibu liqueur

green peppercorns from the marinade

icing sugar for dredging

Planning ahead
Order the fruits well in advance. They must be top quality and perfectly ripe for their flavour to come through.
Marinate the fruit at least 12 hours in advance.
The rice pudding can be made 24 hours in advance and kept covered in the fridge.
The *sabayon* can be made 1 hour before the meal.

1. Preparing the fruit and peppercorns and marinating
(15 minutes, plus at least 12 hours marinating)
In a large mixing bowl, combine the sorbet syrup and lemon juice.
Green peppercorns: Wash in a sieve under cold running water for 20 minutes to remove excess fieriness.
Tamarillos: Peel and quarter.
Mango: Peel, slice either side of the

stone and dice the flesh into 1.5 cm/
½ in cubes.
Pineapple: Slice off the skin, remove
the core and cut the flesh into
triangles.
Guavas: Peel, halve, deseed with a
teaspoon and quarter.
Figs: Wash, trim the stalk and quarter.
Banana: Halve lengthways and cut
into small segments.
Place all the prepared fruit in the syrup
mixture.
Passion fruit: Halve with a serrated
knife and spoon the seeds and pulp
into the syrup.
Drain the peppercorns and add them
to the syrup.
Cover the bowl with clingfilm and
leave to marinate in the refrigerator
for at least 12 hours.

2. Preparing and cooking the rice pudding (1½ hours, plus cooling)
Preheat the oven to 150°C/300°F/
gas 2.
In a medium thick-bottomed saucepan, combine the milk, cream, sugar
and split vanilla pod, bring to the boil
and immediately draw off the heat.
Wash and drain the pudding rice then
add it to the milk, cover the pan with
buttered foil and cook in the preheated
oven for about 1¼ hours.
Leave to cool, still covered. Remove
the vanilla pod, then turn the pudding

into a bowl, seal with clingfilm and
refrigerate.

3. Skewering the marinated fruit (15 minutes)
Drain the syrup into a saucepan and
place the fruit on a small tray, separating each variety. Thread them alter-
nately onto the skewers and set aside.
Put the green peppercorns into a small
bowl and set aside.

4. Making the sabayon
(15 minutes) (see Sabayon making,
page 30)
In an electric mixer, beat the egg yolks
at high speed with 50 ml/2 fl oz of the
marinade for about 5 minutes until
it has become almost 5 times its original volume.
Meanwhile, bring to the boil 150 ml/
5 fl oz of the marinade.
With the mixer on its lowest speed,
gradually add the hot syrup to the
beaten egg yolks, pouring it in between the sides of the bowl and the
whisk. Increase to high speed and
continue beating for about 5 minutes,
until the mixture has cooled. Add the
Malibu liqueur.
Beat the cream to a light peak, then
carefully fold it into the *sabayon* base.
Add the peppercorns, transfer to a
china bowl and refrigerate until
needed.

5. Assembling the dish, glazing and serving (10 minutes)
Turn the grill full on.
Chill 4 large serving plates.
Spoon out the iced rice pudding in a
rectangular band 2 cm/¾ in deep,
3 cm/1 ¼ in wide and the same length
as the skewered fruits. Lightly embed
the fruits in the rice pudding and pull
out the skewers. Mask with *sabayon*,
dust with icing sugar and glaze under
the hot grill for a few seconds until
lightly browned. Serve at once.

———— VARIATIONS ————
If you prefer, simply moisten the
skewered fruits with the remaining
syrup and warm them in the oven.
Serve the *sabayon* cold, or serve a
Passion fruit *coulis* (see page 30).
In the height of summer, the fruits can
be replaced by cherries, strawberries,
raspberries, peaches and apricots.
For a simple dessert, serve the fruits as
an exotic fruit salad.

———— WINE ————
A sweet, intense, deep golden Montbazillac from Bergerac will match this
dish perfectly.

Chef's notes
Glazing the fruits: This process is not
designed to cook the fruits but to
warm them and glaze the *sabayon*.

SOUFFLE AU CARAMEL

Caramel soufflé

Serves 4

Difficulty:

Total recipe time: 55 minutes

Special equipment: sugar dredger, sugar pan, 4 soufflé dishes, 9 cm/3½in diameter x 6 cm/2¼ in deep

——— INGREDIENTS ———

Caramel pastry cream

Pastry Cream (for more information, see page 34):

3 egg yolks

10 g/⅓ oz caster sugar

15 g/½ oz flour

10 g/⅓ oz cornflour

250 ml/9 fl oz milk

Caramel (for more information, see page 32):

50 ml/2 fl oz water

100 g/3½ oz caster sugar

For the soufflé dishes

1 teaspoon unsalted butter, at room temperature

2 tablespoons caster sugar

Soufflé mixture

200 g/7 oz caramel pastry cream (see above)

8 egg whites

1 teaspoon lemon juice

Garnish

30 flaked almonds

icing sugar for dredging

Prune ice cream with Armagnac, to serve (see page 97) (optional)

Planning ahead

Before attempting this recipe please read Soufflé making (page 35).

The caramel pastry cream can be made 1 day in advance. Dust with icing sugar, cool, cover with clingfilm and refrigerate. Reheat before mixing in the beaten egg white.

The garnish of almonds can be prepared in advance. Store in a dry place.

The prune ice cream (if used) can be made 1 day in advance.

1. Preparing the caramel pastry cream (25 minutes)

Pastry cream: In a mixing bowl, cream the egg yolks with the sugar until they turn a pale straw colour, then whisk in the flour and cornflour. Bring the milk to the boil and pour one-third onto the egg and sugar mixture. Whisk until perfectly smooth, then whisk in the remaining milk. Return to the saucepan; place over medium heat and continue whisking until the custard thickens, then bring back to the boil for about 30 seconds. Transfer to a mixing bowl, sprinkle a little caster sugar on the surface to prevent a skin from forming and set aside.

Caramel: Pour the water into a sugar pan and add the caster sugar in a mound in the centre of the pan. Set over medium heat and cook to a rich, dark caramel.

Add the caramel to the warm pastry cream, stirring with a wooden spoon until well mixed. Keep 200 g/7 oz for the soufflé and use the rest for another recipe.

2. Preparing the soufflé dishes (5 minutes)

Preheat the oven to 190°C/375°F/gas 5.

Brush the inside of the dishes with butter and dredge with caster sugar.

3. Making and moulding the soufflés (10 minutes)

In a large mixing bowl, whisk the egg whites to a soft peak, then add the lemon juice and continue beating until firmer but still light.

Immediately whisk one-quarter of the egg white into the caramel pastry cream, then delicately fold in the remainder until just mixed.

Fill the soufflé dishes and smooth over the tops with a palette knife. With your thumb push away the soufflé mixture from around the edges.

4. Baking the soufflés (15 minutes)

Sprinkle the flaked almonds on top and bake in the preheated oven for about 12 minutes, dusting lightly with icing sugar after 5 minutes.

5. Serving

If using prune ice cream, spoon it onto small chilled plates and serve the soufflés on separate plates already prepared with fine folded napkins.

——— VARIATIONS ———

If you have any *craquelin,* grind it and sprinkle on the surface of the soufflés instead of icing sugar.

——— WINE ———

A brut Champagne would be delicious with this dessert.

Chef's notes

Caramel: Much depends on the degree of caramelization. It must almost burn for the true caramel taste to come through. If it is too pale, the soufflé will be tasteless and too sweet.

Adding the caramel: The pastry cream should still be warm when the caramel is added; if the caramel comes into contact with cold cream, it will solidify.

Soufflé au caramel

SORBET A LA BANANE

Banana sorbet

Serves 4
Difficulty: 🍳
Total recipe time: 20 – 35 minutes
Special equipment: blender or food processor, *sorbetière*

——— INGREDIENTS ———
400 g/14 oz ripe bananas
....
juice of 1½ lemons
....
150 ml/5 fl oz Sorbet syrup (see page 31)
....
200 ml/7 fl oz milk
....

Planning ahead
The sorbet can be prepared a few hours in advance and kept in the freezer.

The sorbet syrup must be made in advance.

1. Preparing the sorbet
(10 minutes)
Milk: Bring to the boil. Allow to cool.
Bananas: Peel and halve lengthways. With a small knife, remove the black thread in the middle which will discolour the sorbet. As you slice the bananas, place them in the lemon juice. Purée the bananas, lemon juice, stock syrup and cooled milk until smooth, then force the mixture through a fine sieve into a bowl.

2. Churning the sorbet
(10–25 minutes)
Churn in the sorbetière for 10–25 minutes, place in a sealed container and store in the freezer.

3. Serving
Dip a dessert spoon in hot water and spoon out the sorbet onto chilled plates or into large chilled glasses.

——— VARIATIONS ———
Add a teaspoon of rum and a dash of the best vanilla essence to the milk before boiling.
Serve with Caramel sauce (see page 32) studded with toasted almonds.

Chef's notes
Bananas are prone to oxidization so the sorbet must be prepared as quickly as possible.

SORBET AU CITRON VERT

Lime sorbet

Serves 4 – 6
Difficulty: 🍳
Total recipe time: 40 – 55 minutes
Special equipment: *sorbetière*

——— INGREDIENTS ———
juice of 8 limes
....
zest of 3 limes
....
300 ml/½ pt Sorbet syrup (see page 31)
....

Planning ahead
The sorbet can be made a few hours in advance and stored in the freezer.
The sorbet syrup must be made in advance.
Chill 4 plates or glasses in the freezer 30 minutes before serving.

1. Preparing the limes
(10 minutes)
Peel 3 limes with a potato peeler. Cut the peel into *julienne*, wash and drain. Squeeze 8 limes and strain the juice through a fine sieve.

2. Infusing the lime peel in sorbet syrup (15 minutes)
In a small saucepan, bring to the boil the syrup and *julienne* of lime peel. Draw off the heat and leave to infuse for about 5 minutes. Strain into the lime juice, cool, taste and add a little more lime juice or sugar as necessary.

3. Churning the sorbet
(15–25 minutes)
Churn in the *sorbetière* until smooth and firm.

4. Serving
Using 2 dessert spoons dipped in hot water, arrange the sorbet in the middle of the chilled plates or in the chilled glasses and serve immediately.

Chef's notes
Depending on the acidity of the limes, you may need a little more or less sugar.

MOUSSE PRALINEE A L'ARMAGNAC, SAUCE CARAMEL

Praliné and Armagnac mousses served with caramel sauce

Serves 8
Difficulty:
Total recipe time: 40 minutes, plus 4 hours freezing
Special equipment: electric mixer with whisk, eight 8 x 4 cm/3 x 1½ in ramekins

INGREDIENTS

Caramel
50 ml/2 fl oz hot water
125 g/4½ oz caster sugar

Sabayon base
4 egg yolks
50 ml/2 fl oz Sorbet syrup (see page 31)
25 g/1 oz Craquelin (optional) (see pages 45-6)
25 g/1 oz plain dessert chocolate
300 ml/½ pt whipping cream
1 tablespoon Armagnac or Cognac

300 ml/½ pt Sauce caramel Armagnac (see page 32)

Garnish
40 g/1½ oz flaked almonds
2 tablespoons icing sugar
2 teaspoons kirsch

Planning ahead
The caramel sauce and *craquelin*, if used, must be made in advance.
The whole dessert can be made 1 day in advance and kept in the freezer.
Chill 8 serving plates 1 hour before the meal.

1. Preparing the mousse mixture
(30 minutes)
Caramel: Pour 50 ml/2 fl oz water into a small thick-bottomed saucepan and add the caster sugar in a mound in the centre of the pan. Bring to the boil and cook over medium heat to a richly coloured caramel, brushing the sides of the pan with water from time to time to prevent it from burning. When the caramel is dark, with a slightly acrid scent, draw off the heat, tilt the pan away from you and add the hot water – be careful, the caramel will spit. Swirl the pan to incorporate the water thoroughly and simmer for 1 minute.
Sabayon base: In an electric mixer on high speed beat the egg yolks with the syrup until the mixture becomes bulky. Reduce to medium speed then add the hot caramel, pouring it between the sides of the mixing bowl and the whisk and continue whisking for about 10 minutes, until the mixture is cold. Stand the bowl on your work surface.
Melt the chocolate in a small bowl over a saucepan of hot water.
Whip the cream to a light peak.
First mix the chocolate with 2 tablespoons of the cream then add it to the main body of whipped cream.

Sprinkle over the *craquelin,* add 1 tablespoon Armagnac, then fold the cream into the egg yolk mixture until well blended.
Preheat the oven to 200°C/400°F/gas 6 for Stage 3.

2. Moulding the mousses and freezing (5 minutes plus 4 hours freezing)
Fill the ramekins with the mousse mixture, smoothing the surface with a spatula. Freeze for at least 4 hours.

3. Preparing the garnish
(5 minutes)
Mix all the ingredients in a small bowl, scatter onto a baking tray and toast in the preheated oven for 5 minutes until golden.

4. Serving
Dip the ramekins in hot water for 2–3 seconds then turn out the mousses onto a cold tray. Place a mousse in the centre of each plate, mask with caramel sauce and sprinkle over the toasted almonds.

VARIATIONS
Serve Caramelized almonds with kirsch (see page 46).

Chef's notes
Caramel: Thin with *hot* water to minimize the spitting.
Egg yolk mixture: The caramel must be added hot so that it partially cooks the egg yolk mixture; whisk until cool before adding the whipped cream.
Adding the chocolate: The melted chocolate must first be mixed with a little cream; if added directly to this quantity of cream it will resolidify and not mix in properly.

Mousse glacée à la noix de coco,
crème vanille au rhum

MOUSSE GLACEE A LA NOIX DE COCO, CREME VANILLE AU RHUM

Iced coconut mousse, served with rum-scented custard

"Guests often wonder what sparked off an idea for a recipe – visiting markets, bouts of deep thinking, simple spontaneity, curiosity? Yes all of these, but the origin of this recipe is somewhat different. I dreamt it up when I was on holiday on a tiny Caribbean island. Although most Caribbean food (especially that with an English influence) leaves much to be desired, I discovered many wonderful exotic fruits which set my imagination racing. As I sat on the warm sand in the shadow of a palm tree, listening to the gentle lapping of waves, two desserts were born – this coconut mousse and *Brochette de fruits exotiques* (page 262)."

Serves 4
Difficulty: ♟♟
Total recipe time: 1 hour 10 minutes, plus 6 hours freezing
Special equipment: four 7.5 cm/3 in ramekins, food processor, electric mixer with whisk

INGREDIENTS

1 ripe, firm mango (about 400 g/ 14 oz)

1 thick slice of pineapple cut from the centre (about 450 g/1 lb)

Iced mousse
2 tablespoons cold water

3 egg yolks

50 ml/2 fl oz water with 50 ml/2 fl oz coconut milk, 25 g/1 oz caster sugar and ¼ vanilla pod, split lengthways

1 tablespoon Malibu liqueur

150 ml/5 fl oz whipping cream

Garnish
1 tablespoon grated coconut, toasted until golden

diced trimmings of pineapple and mango

4 mint leaves

250 ml/9 fl oz Vanilla custard (see page 33), flavoured with 2 teaspoons rum, to serve

Tuile mixture (for the palm trees) (optional)
200 g/7 oz white marzipan

1 tablespoon white flour, sifted

2 egg whites

Caramel (for attaching the leaves and trunk to the base)
1 tablespoon water

50 g/2 oz caster sugar

Planning ahead
The mousse lined with mango and pineapple can be made several days in advance and kept in the freezer, sealed with clingfilm.
The rum-flavoured custard can be made 1 day in advance.
The garnish (if used) must be prepared several hours in advance (see diagram, page 270).
Remove the mousses from the freezer 1 hour before the meal and place in the fridge so that the fruit lining defrosts. Chill 4 plates for serving.

1. Preparing the fruits and lining the moulds (20 minutes)
Mango: Peel and cut either side of the stone to free the flesh. Cut the flesh as neatly as possible into strips approximately the height of your ramekins.
Pineapple: Slice off the skin, remove the core and cut into strips the same size as the mango.

Line all round the sides of the ramekins with alternating strips of fruit. Dice the remaining fruit and reserve for garnish.

2. Making the mousse (15 minutes) (see Sabayon making, page 30)
In an electric mixer on high speed, beat the egg yolks with 2 tablespoons water for 5 minutes, until about 5 times their original volume.
Meanwhile in a medium saucepan, boil 50 ml/2 fl oz water with the coconut milk, sugar and vanilla for 2 minutes.
Remove the vanilla pod, set the mixer on low speed and gradually pour the boiling syrup onto the egg yolk mixture, pouring it in between the sides of the bowl and the whisk. Increase to high speed and continue whisking until almost cold. Add the Malibu liqueur, then stand the mixing bowl on your work surface.
Meanwhile beat the cream to a light peak, then fold in the cooled egg yolk mixture. Spoon into the lined ramekins and smooth over the surfaces with a spatula. Place in the freezer for 6–8 hours to set.

3. Making the almond tuile mixture for palm trees (optional) (5 minutes)
Preheat the oven to 180°C/350°F/gas 4 for Stage 4.
In a food processor, blend the marzipan,

sifted flour and egg whites until smooth, put in a small bowl and reserve.

4. Cooking and shaping the palm trees (20 minutes)
See diagram and explanation below.

5. Assembling the dish and serving (10 minutes)
Remove the mousses from the freezer 1 hour before serving.

Have ready 4 chilled plates.

Turn out the mousses onto the middle of the plates, spoon the rum-scented vanilla custard around, sprinkle the base of the mousse with grated toasted coconut (to look like sand), and stand a palm tree close to the mousse 'island'. Scatter the diced mango and pineapple trimmings and top each mousse with a mint leaf. Serve.

VARIATIONS
The coconut can be replaced by 200 ml/7 fl oz passion fruit juice reduced to 100 ml/3½ fl oz; omit the Malibu liqueur.

To simplify the dish, omit the lining of mango and pineapple.

The palm tree is not as difficult to make as you might think and is fun to do. You could make other shapes, too – perhaps swans or butterflies.

WINE
A Sauternes would make a good companion for this dessert; try Château de Veyres, Suduiraut or la Tour Blanche.

Chef's notes
The mango must be firm, so that it can be cut easily; overripe flesh will be unmanageable.

Folding the whipped cream into the yolk mixture: Make sure the mixture has cooled completely before folding in the cream; if it is hot, or even warm, the results will be disastrous.

Storing
Do not keep the dessert frozen at below −12°C/10°F for too long; after 6 or 8 hours it will harden and lose its delicacy.

This recipe makes enough mousse for 6 servings. Put the extra mousse into small moulds and freeze for later use.

Use a sharp knife to cut out 6 leaf shapes from a plastic lid.

Cut out a rectangle for the trunk and make 4 trunks as the leaves.

Roll the trunks around a pencil to shape them.

Place this template on a buttered baking sheet and spread over a film of almond pastry.

Using a spatula, spread 4 circles on the baking sheet for the bases. Bake and cool for 1 minute.

Mould the bases into cones.

Lift off the template and repeat until you have 24 leaves.

While still warm, press 6 leaves together with your fingers. Mould them in a tartlet tin to shape them.

Dip both ends of the trunks in caramel. Stick one end to the leaves and the other onto the bases.

Desserts

SORBET AUX FRUITS DE LA PASSION

Passion fruit sorbet

Serves 4–6
Difficulty: 🍳
Total recipe time: 45 minutes – 1 hour
Special equipment: food processor, *sorbetière*

──────── INGREDIENTS ────────

17 passion fruit (for 400 g/14 oz pulp)

200 ml/7 fl oz Sorbet syrup (see page 31)

Planning ahead
The syrup must be made in advance. The sorbet can be made several hours ahead and kept in the freezer. Chill 4 or 6 plates or glasses in the freezer.

1. Preparing the passion fruit (15 minutes)
Cut in half with a serrated knife and scrape out all the pulp, seeds and pink skin with teaspoon.

2. Making and straining the sorbet mixture (15 minutes)
Mix the fruit pulp and seeds with the cold sorbet syrup. Purée in a food processor fitted with a plastic blade for about 2 minutes, then force the pulp and juices through a conical sieve, pressing with a small ladle.

3. Churning (15–25 minutes)
Churn in the sorbetière for 15–25 minutes, depending on your machine.

4. Serving
Using 2 tablespoons dipped in hot water, shape the sorbet into ovals and place 3 on each chilled plate or in a glass.

──────── VARIATIONS ────────

Add 100 g/3½ oz mango pulp. Keep some of the passion fruit shells and fill them with the sorbet, or serve in tulip-shaped *tuiles*.

Chef's notes
Puréeing the pulp: Do not use a blender, as the blades will grind the little black pips. Use the plastic blade of your food processor, which will detach the pulp from around the pips.

───────────────────────────────

NOUGAT GLACE A LA MANDARINE, SAUCE CHOCOLAT

The lightest iced dessert speckled with almonds and candied mandarin zest, served with a chocolate sauce

Serves 8–10
Difficulty: 🍳 🍳
Total recipe time: 1 hour, plus 12 hours freezing
Special equipment: electric mixer, food processor, sugar pan

──────── INGREDIENTS ────────

Nougat

20 g/¾ oz shelled walnuts

85 g/3 oz whole almonds, skinned

100 g/3½ oz caster sugar

50 ml/2 fl oz mandarin liqueur

20 g/¾ oz unsalted butter

zest from 5 mandarins

1 L/1¾ pt water

450 g/1 lb caster sugar

50 ml/2 fl oz mandarin liqueur

Cooked meringue

50 ml/2 fl oz water

50 g/2 oz caster sugar

2 tablespoons honey

3 egg whites

1 tablespoon lemon juice

300 ml/½ pt whipping cream

Garnish

segments from 5 mandarins

double quantity Chocolate sauce (see page 31)

Planning ahead

Stages 1–4 inclusive must be completed at least 12 hours in advance.

The chocolate sauce can be made a few hours in advance.

Chill serving plates beforehand.

1. Preparing the mandarins and candying the zests (20 minutes, plus 2 hours candying) (see page 49)

Score the mandarins with a sharp knife in 4 quarters just through the thickness of the skin and peel off.

Cut the zests into strips about 3 mm/⅛ in long and blanch in 2 L/3½ pt boiling water for about 8 minutes. Drain and refresh under cold running water.

Cover the mandarin segments with a damp cloth and refrigerate.

In a large saucepan, boil 1 L/1¾ pt water with the sugar and lemon juice. Skim, add the blanched strips of mandarin zest and cook for about 3 minutes at just below simmering point.

Drain the syrup and dice the zests. Put both in a bowl with the mandarin liqueur, seal with clingfilm and macerate for at least 2 hours.

2. Making the nougat (40 minutes)

Put the walnuts, almonds and sugar in a heavy-bottomed saucepan. Cook over medium heat until the sugar has a sandy texture, then add 50 ml/2 fl oz mandarin liqueur and cook to a blonde caramel. Draw off the heat and add the butter, then turn out onto a tray and leave to cool for 30 minutes. Chop or grind the nougat in a food processor to a coarse texture and reserve in a small bowl.

3. Making the cooked meringue (25 minutes) (see *Meringue italienne,* page 45)

Combine the water, sugar and honey in a sugar pan and boil over medium heat until the temperature reaches 110°C/225°F.

In an electric mixer on medium speed, beat the egg whites to a soft peak, then add the lemon juice and beat until firm.

With your mixer on its lowest speed, gradually add the hot syrup and continue beating until the mixture has cooled. Reserve. Beat the cream to a light peak.

4. Binding and moulding the nougat (2 minutes)

Using a spatula, fold the ground almonds and diced candied mandarin peel into the cooked meringue, then carefully fold in the whipped cream. Transfer the mixture to a large china bowl, seal with clingfilm and freeze for at least 12 hours.

5. Preparing the garnish (5 minutes)

Halve the reserved mandarin segments lengthways and remove any pips.

6. Assembling the dessert and serving

Place 2 spoons in a jug of warm water. Spoon a little chocolate sauce onto each plate. Use the spoons to shape the frozen nougat into *quenelles* and arrange 3 in the centre of each chilled serving plate. Arrange the mandarin segments around the edge and serve.

——— VARIATIONS ———

To simplify the dish, use bought candied mandarin or mixed peel. The flavouring can be changed; try Grand Marnier or kirsch.

If you have an ice cream maker, line the bottom and sides of a china bowl with mandarin sorbet. Spoon in the nougat mixture to within about 1 cm/½ in of the top, smooth over the surface, freeze for a few hours, then top the nougat with another 1 cm/½ in of mandarin sorbet. Freeze for 12 hours before serving. To serve, dip the bowl into warm water, invert onto a chilled tray and carve 1.5 cm/¾ in slices with a sharp serrated knife dipped in hot water. The sorbet will add a delicious note of freshness.

——— WINE ———

A Champagne or good *méthode champénoise* wine will be perfect.

Chef's notes

Mixing the ingredients: Do this as quickly as possible; overmixing will cause a loss of volume and lightness.

Freezing: If possible, freeze the dessert at -12°–-15°C/5°–10°F so that it remains smooth.

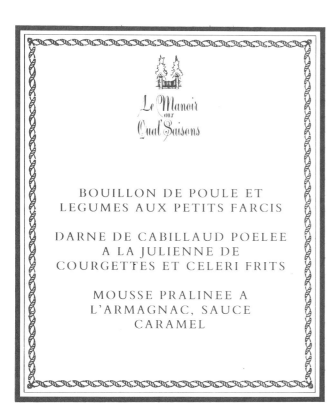

BOUILLON DE POULE ET
LEGUMES AUX PETITS FARCIS

DARNE DE CABILLAUD POELEE
A LA JULIENNE DE
COURGETTES ET CELERI FRITS

MOUSSE PRALINEE A
L'ARMAGNAC, SAUCE
CARAMEL

GATEAU DE TOPINAMBOURS
AU COULIS D'ASPERGES

BECASSE ROTIE AU FUMET DE
ST EMILION, MOUSSE DE PAIN

CHIPS DE CELERI-RAVE FRITS

BROCHETTE DE FRUITS
EXOTIQUES AU SABAYON, RIZ
AU LAIT GLACE

SALADE D'AILE DE RAIE,
POMMES DE TERRE PERSILLEES
AU VIN BLANC

QUEUE DE BOEUF ET LANGUE
DE VEAU BRAISEES

PAVE AU CHOCOLAT,
GRIOTTES ET ANANAS, SAUCE
CAFE

TERRINE DE FOIE GRAS AUX
TRUFFES ET JEUNES
POIREAUX CONFITS

BLANC DE LOUP DE MER
PERSILLE AU JUS DE VEAU
BLOND AUX FLEURS DE
THYM, FEUILLES DE CELERI
FRITES

EPINARDS AU BEURRE

POMMES SAFFRANEES

SOUFFLE AU CARAMEL

Too often when reading cookery books you realise the difficulty in finding the quality ingredients needed. We have therefore compiled a list of companies who deal in specialist produce (foie gras, truffles, Bresse chicken etc.). This list is not exhaustive and not every company or shop automatically stocks everything. They are however willing to assist you in every way possible (e.g. sending of produce direct to you by post or rail). Always ring for details on availability, season, prices etc.

Rouxel Ltd
Unit One
Chelsea Fields
278 Western Road
London SW19
Tel: 01 640 9928
This company imports every kind of specialist produce directly from France and distributes to agents in the North, the South, the Midlands, Scotland and Wales. Rouxel Ltd will be happy to supply you through one of their agents, but please place your order through the central office.

John Baily and Son Ltd
116 Mount Street
London W1Y 5HD
Tel: 01 499 1833

Boucherie Lamartine
229 Ebury Street
London SW1W 8UT
Tel: 01 730 3037

Food Hall
Brown, Thomas and Co. Ltd
Grafton Street
Dublin 2
Republic of Ireland
Tel: 0001 77 6861

George Campbell and Sons
18 Stafford Street
Edinburgh EH3 7BE
Tel: 031 225 7507

George Campbell and Sons
168 South Street
Perth PH2 8NY
Tel: 0738 38454

Hales Snails and Co.
Imperial House
Barton Dock Trading Estate
Barton Dock Road
Stretford
Manchester M32 0ZH
Tel: 061 864 1941

London Larder
Concorde House
4 Black Swan Yard
Bermondsey Street
London SE1 3XW
Tel: 01 403 6177

J.T. Morgan
44–46 Cardiff Central Market
Cardiff
Wales
Tel: 0222 388434

Alan Porter Provisions Ltd
Bar Lane
Roecliffe
Borough Bridge
North Yorkshire
Tel: 09012 2323

Mr Laurence Clore
Snipe and Grouse
Arch 18
Broughton Street
London SW8
Tel: 01 627 2327

Vin Sullivan of Abergavenny
Triley Mill
Abergavenny
Gwent NP7 8DE
Wales
Tel: 0873 2331

W.G. White Ltd
68 Churchfield Road
London W3 6DL
Tel: 01 992 8764

ASSOCIATIONS THAT CAN BE CONTACTED FOR INFORMATION ON SUPPLIERS

This list is not exhaustive. Addresses and telephone numbers are correct at date of printing.

—— SPECIALIST FOODS ——

The Delicatessen and Fine Food Association
6 The Broadway
Thatcham
Berks RG13 4JA
Tel: 0635 69033

—— MEAT ——

National Federation of Meat Traders
1 Belgrove
Tunbridge Wells
Kent TN1 1YW
Tel: 0892 41412

Scotch Quality Beef and Lamb Association
33 Melville Street
Edinburgh EH3 7JF
Scotland
Tel: 031 226 3797

Meat and Livestock Commission
Head Office
PO Box 44
Queensway House
Bletchley
Milton Keynes MK2 2EF
Tel: 0908 74941

Regional Offices

London
5 St John's Square
Smithfield
London EC1M 4DE
Tel: 01 251 2021

Northern
Copthall Tower House
Station Parade
Harrogate
North Yorkshire HG1 1TL
Tel: 0423 60361

Midlands
Anson House
Lammascote Road
Stafford ST16 3TB
Tel: 0785 52441

Eastern
St Andrew's House
St Andrew's Street North
Bury St Edmunds
Suffolk IP33 1TX
Tel: 0284 5755

South Eastern
55 Minster Street
Reading
Berks RG1 2JJ
Tel: 0734 581581

South Western
31 Trull Road
Taunton
Somerset TA1 4QQ
Tel: 0823 283161

Scotland
3 Atholl Place
Perth PH1 5ND
Tel: 0738 27401

Wales
21a North Parade
Aberystwyth
Dyfed SY23 2JL
Tel: 0970 612703

Specialist Suppliers

FISH

National Federation of Fishmongers Ltd
34 St Margaret's Road
Ruislip
Middlesex HA4 7NY
Tel: 0895 638114

Sea Fish Industries Authority
10 Young Street
Edinburgh EH2 4JQ
Scotland
Tel: 031 225 2515
Contact: Mr D. Harrison

British Trout Association
PO Box 189
London SW6 5LY

British Crayfish Marketing Association
Riversdale Farm
Stour Provost
Gillingham
Dorset
Tel: 074 785495

FRUIT, VEGETABLES ETC.

British Organic Farmers Association
86–88 Colston Street
Bristol BS1 5BB
Tel: 0272 299666

Organic Growers Association
86–88 Colston Street
Bristol BS1 5BB
Tel: 0272 299800

Soil Association
86–88 Colston Street
Bristol BS1 5BB
Tel: 0272 290661

Farm Shop and Pick Your Own
Association Limited
Agriculture House
London SW1X 7NJ
Tel: 01 235 5077

Scottish Grocers Federation
3 Loaning Road
Restalrig
Edinburgh EH7 6JE
Tel: 031 652 2482

Retail Fruit Trade Federation
108–110 Market Towers
1 Nine Elms Lane
London SW8 5NS
Tel: 01 720 9168

GENERAL

National Association of Shopkeepers
Lynch House
91 Mansfield Road
Nottingham NG1 3FN
Tel: 0602 410986

Guild of Conservation Food Producers
PO Box 157
Bedford MK42 9BY
Tel: 0234 61626

HERBS

The Herb Society
77 Great Peter Street
London SW1P 2EZ
Tel: 01 222 3634

WINE SUPPLIERS

These wine companies have been selected for inclusion in this book as they are regular suppliers of Le Manoir aux Quat' Saisons and we have found their service, knowledge and quality of wine to be of the highest standard. Should you wish to order from any of these companies, please mention to them that you obtained their address from this book.

Georges Barbier of London
267 Lee High Road
London SE12
Tel: 01 852 5801

Berkmann Wine Cellars
Le Nez Rouge Wine Club
12 Brewery Road
London N7 9NH
Tel: 01 609 4711

Marigold Bewicke
Wine & Cuisine
6 Grindstone Crescent
Knaphill
Woking
Surrey
Tel: 048 67 2732

The Curzon Wine Company
11 Curzon Street
Mayfair
London W1Y 7FJ
Tel: 01 499 3327

Domaine Direct
29 Wilmington Square
London WC1X 0EG
Tel: 01 837 1142 & 3521

Eldridge, Pope & Co. plc
Weymouth Avenue
Dorchester
Dorset DT1 1QT
Tel: 0305 251251

Heyman Brothers Ltd
130 Ebury Street
London SW1W 9QQ
Tel: 01 730 0324

The Hungerford Wine Company
128 High Street
Hungerford
Berkshire RG17 0DL
Tel: 0488 83238

Laytons Wine Merchants Ltd
20 Midland Road
London NW1 2AD
Tel: 01 388 5081

O. W. Loeb & Co. Ltd
64 Southwark Bridge Road
London SE1 0AS
Tel: 01 928 7750

Reid Wines
The Mill
Marsh Lane
Hallatrow
Bristol
BS18 5EB
Tel: 0761 52645

J.B. Reynier Ltd
16–18 Upper Tachbrook Street
London SW1V 1SL
Tel: 01 834 0242

Edward Sheldon Ltd
New Street
Shipston-on-Stour
Warwickshire CV36 4EN
Tel: 0608 61409, 61639 & 62210

BOOKS

A short list of quality books which are important for your interest and knowledge.

British Food Finds 1987, published by Rich & Green Ltd, 1 Moorhouse Road, London W2 5DH.

British Country Foods – Specialist Food Directory, published by British Country Foods, 4 St Mary's Place, Stamford, Lincs. PE9 2DN.

On Food and Cooking – The Science and Lore of the Kitchen by Harold McGee, published by George Allen & Unwin Ltd, 40 Museum Street, London WC1A 1LU. This book gives an amazing insight into the science of food and cooking.

The Triumph and the Shame by Richard Body.

The Food Scandal by Caroline Walker and Geoffrey Cannon.

North Atlantic Sea Food by Alan Davidson, published by Penguin. Revised edition 1986.

The World Atlas of Wine by Hugh Johnson, published by Mitchell Beazley Publishers.

Index

ACKNOWLEDGEMENTS

There are many people who helped me write this book. Among them I am indebted to Julian Colbeck, computer wizard and corrector of my English, who did not mind responding to phone calls around the clock. My thanks, too, to the editorial team of my publishers: Sarah Snape, Kate Whiteman, Cathy Rubinstein and everyone involved in the artwork.

My sympathy and thanks to the long-suffering testers, whose enthusiasm never flagged – Patricia Colbeck, Loraine Ferguson, Julie Fretwell, Ginette Gould, Julie Kavanagh and Mr Taylor of Bournemouth College.

My gratitude to my team, especially Clive Fretwell and Patrick Woodside, for their continuous co-operation and help; my secretaries Jane Foster and Monica Notarmarco; Alain Desenclos, Director of the restaurant, and his staff who put up with the intrusions of the photographic sessions, often during full service.

My credit and admiration to photographer Michael Boys, whose flair and brilliant professional skill so perfectly blended with my food, the *ambiance* of Le Manoir and the seasons, and with whom it was so easy and pleasurable to work; my thanks to his assistant Virginia Dehanes, for tolerating two difficult professionals!

My thanks also to Villeroi & Boch for their beautiful tableware.

Many thanks to Alan Davidson and Harold McGee for helping with queries on the chemistry of food; Hugh Johnson for contributing to the chapters and writing a preface on wine; Egon Ronay for writing the foreword and for his continued encouragement over the years; and to Felicity Bryan, my agent.

My special thanks to my fiancée, Kati Cottrell, who gave me help, moral support and love throughout the writing of this book.

RAYMOND BLANC

Bill Oddie
UNPLUCKED

Bill Oddie
UNPLUCKED
Columns, blogs and musings

Bill Oddie

BLOOMSBURY
LONDON · NEW DELHI · NEW YORK · SYDNEY

Bloomsbury Natural History
An imprint of Bloomsbury Publishing Plc

50 Bedford Square	1385 Broadway
London	New York
WC1B 3DP	NY 10018
UK	USA

www.bloomsbury.com

BLOOMSBURY and the Diana logo are trademarks of Bloomsbury Publishing Plc

First published 2015

A catalogue record for this book is available from the British Library.

Library of Congress Cataloguing-in-Publication data has been applied for.

ISBN (HB): 978-1-4729-1531-3
ISBN (ePub): 978-1-4729-1532-0

2 4 6 8 10 9 7 5 3 1

Typeset by Deanta Global Publishing Services, Chennai, India

Printed and bound in Great Britain by CPI Group (UK) Ltd, Croydon, CR0 4YY

Contents

OK, YOU CAN TAKE ONE BUT NO MORE...

Foreword

Nearly every day people smile at me in the street. A delightfully high percentage say something like 'Hi Bill' or 'How are you doing, Bill?' or even 'Thanks for all the pleasure you have given me over the years.' It doesn't come much more flattering than that. I love it. However, there are a few people – just a few – whose approach is not quite so sensitive. They tend to stare at me for a bit and then ask: 'Didn't you used to be Bill Oddie?' I usually mutter: 'I still am'. But such folk are immune to irony. They continue: 'I thought you were. You used to be on the telly!' As if I might have forgotten. I thank them for reminding me. 'Yeah, with those two other blokes, you used to ride a bike.' The memories come flooding back. 'Yeah, you, Tim Brooke something and... the other one.' As it happens Graeme Garden is used to being called 'the other one' and he wouldn't be bothered. But I am. By remembering me only for my part in *The Goodies* 40 years ago, this bloke has dismissed – or maybe just missed – the product of half my working career! I could ask him what he thought of my wildlife programmes, but I can anticipate the answer: 'My mum likes those.' He doesn't need to add: 'Can't stand 'em myself,' though he may imply that by asking me to autograph a bus ticket while informing me: 'It's not for me.' I sign: 'Goody wishes to mum,' which hopefully will keep them both happy.

Truthfully and fortunately, the public enquiry I get most often these days is: 'When are we going to see you on telly again?' When indeed?! My only possible – and truthful – response is: 'It's not up to me. Write to the BBC. Please!' They may well already have done, but nothing's happened yet. But – just for the record – I am still Bill Oddie.

So, the next question has to be: what have I been doing for the last three or four years? Well, one of them was largely spent in and out of bed and psychiatric hospital, suffering from what was eventually diagnosed as bipolar disorder. Looking back now, I can reassess periods and incidents throughout my life when my behaviour fitted the basic pattern of manic depression swinging between being miserable and grumpy, or hyperactive and extrovert. The deep depressions are easy to label as a mental illness, but the manic and belligerent episodes get labelled simply as 'character'. Sometimes productive and creative, and sometimes a pain in the arse. Yep, that's me. Or at least, that's what I used to be. These days, people who should know – like my family – say that I am a much more amiable person. I am also out of work.

I won't go into all the details of my departure from *Springwatch* and *Autumnwatch*, partly because I have never been fully able to work them out. Suffice it to say that I believe that a manic phase of the bipolar was the reason that I was eventually told: 'We won't be asking you to do the next series.' It almost sounds like a judge teasing a contestant on *The X Factor*. 'We won't be asking you… We'll be telling you!' At which point I hug the BBC Head of Natural History! (That'll be the day.) No such luck. The words I was hearing were a euphemism for 'You're fired!' I almost wish that was what they'd said. I imagine it is much easier to be indignant and defiant when you are curtly told: 'You're fired.' If they'd said that I would probably have stomped out. Instead, I cried.

Frankly, I never did get a detailed explanation, but I have to acknowledge that during my final *Autumnwatch* on Brownsea

Island and even more so during location filming for a series called
Inspired by Nature, I was ultra-critical, domineering, over-confident,
impatient, etc. These are all things I have been on and off all my
life, but in a state of bipolar-type mania, everything is heightened
and more overpowering for those you work and live with. I am
not saying that the BBC fired me because they realised that I was
bipolar. They didn't know. And neither did I until the last month
of the following year during which I was twice hospitalised for
my own safety (a euphemism I'll leave you to decipher) and had
to meet the crippling costs of private care, which didn't make me
feel any cheerier! Ironically, it was when I was admitted to an
NHS Crisis Centre that a doctor announced: 'I am putting you
on lithium.' Only a week or two later, I heard one of my daughters
ringing round with the glad tidings: 'He's back!'. Just in time for
Christmas! By the new year I felt fine and I have been that way
ever since. I can't claim that lithium is a guaranteed cure for
bipolar but it works for some people. It has worked for me.

Right then, that's got that stuff out of the way. But the question
remains: if I haven't been on the telly for a couple of years, what
have I been doing? Once I was optimistic enough to accept that
my recovery would be permanent, I made a decision to spend
much more of my time supporting the organisations I admire and
knew were contributing so much in the areas of nature
conservation and animal welfare. I am happy to say that most of
them (maybe all) were welcoming and appreciative. Over the past
two years, you may have been aware of my sporadic appearances
on the media on behalf of the Wildlife Trusts, the RSPB, RSPCA,
Compassion in World Farming, The Humane Society, the League
Against Cruel Sports, the International Fund for Animal Welfare
(IFAW), the World Land Trust, Global Witness and others. I have
tangled with ministers, appeared on *Newsnight* (though not with
Paxman) and have accumulated a fine collection of security passes
to the Commons and the Lords, though I have yet to appear on
Today in Parliament! In tune with the zeitgeist I have become an
ambassador (never without my Ferrero Rocher) for several NGOs
(non-governmental organisations). In this capacity, I have visited
Brazil, Argentina, South Carolina, Iceland, Guatemala, Zambia
and Borneo.

During this time I have seen quite a lot of wildlife – much of it endangered. Whales, orangutans, elephants, and a fair number of new birds for my world list. However, wonderful though these creatures be, undoubtedly the most satisfying, enlightening, inspiring and enjoyable aspect has been meeting some terrific human beings. I don't mean to be ungracious about lots of lovely people I have worked with in the past, but – put it this way – people involved in the world of NGOs tend to be, well, nicer than those in broadcasting, and a *lot* nicer than those in politics. Here's a catchphrase for life: 'Doing good, does you good.'

The other thing I have been doing a lot more of is writing: articles, essays, blogs, tweets and so on. In this book I have hopefully collected some of the most interesting, contentious, amusing, etc. For me, there are two major attractions about writing or compiling a book. One is that I am allowed to get on with it, at least till the editor reads the final version and insists on lots of changes and rewrites (note to ed: please don't). The other attraction is freedom from a word count. Most magazine articles have to fit one page and so musn't be much more than 600 words or, for two pages, 1,200 words, and so on. Whatever the word count, it is never enough. Non-writers may assume the shorter the easier, but if you have any enthusiasm or imagination you need space to indulge it. I can honestly say that every single article I have ever written has been too long and I or the editor have had to cut it down. Sometimes I weep as a gem of a sentence or a joke has to go. This book is my chance to reinstate some of them. Many of these pieces are first drafts, uncut, the length that nature – and I – intended. So even if you think: 'I am sure I read this one in *BBC Wildlife*,' keep going, 'cos I might have had to cut the best bit, and now I have the opportunity to put it back. I might even have added a bit more.

CLOSE TO HOME

OK, NOW ONE OF US IS A REFLECTION ...?!

CHAPTER ONE

How to Be a Ludicrous Gardener

'It's getting ludicrous,' my wife told me. She was referring to my garden. She meant it as a criticism. I took it as a compliment. I am not sure that 'ludicrous' is the appropriate word, but I admit my garden is not conventional. It is not meant to be.

It isn't big – about half a tennis court. I have divided it into clearly demarcated areas, some of them inspired by my international travels. For example, there is the 'magic tree' – actually a lilac – festooned with the kind of shiny, glittery, swivelling things you can buy at a 'New Age' shop, augmented with strips of coloured paper and a few fake insects. Roadside trees in India are often decorated thus. Then there are the 'Inca Ruins', created from a few crusty old house bricks, some fragments of clay pottery, and one of those plaques with a smiley sun's face on it, which looks Inca-ish, even though it is actually from Camden Town Garden Centre. There is also a thriving thicket of tropical jungle, with ferns, palm trees, bits of bamboo and a couple of Buddhas. This I originally called 'Vietnam', even though I had never been there. I have recently renamed it 'Borneo'.

I have also excavated five small ponds, divided by equally small rockeries, which look almost natural. The same can't be said of 'Gnome Corner', the home of an ever-increasing colony of nearly 100 gnomes, some pleasingly jolly, others morose, but most of them undeniably tasteless. The whole effect is – what is the word? Imaginative? Quirky? Unconventional? Oh, OK. Ludicrous!

But what about the wildlife? To be honest, at first glance, one could be forgiven for assuming that my garden has been specially designed to deter birds. For a start, it is not exactly quiet. When a breeze blows, windmills whirr and wind chimes of all sizes tinkle and clang, like an under-rehearsed Balinese gamelan orchestra. Then there are the plastic predators. Lots of them. Many gardens have one. Usually a plastic heron, posing by the pond to deter real herons from gobbling up the goldfish. Have you noticed that it doesn't work? For a very good reason. If a flying heron looks down and sees what appears to be another heron crouched immobile over the water, it assumes that there are fish to be caught, and is most likely to join its chum, real or plastic. Wildfowlers use the same technique to lure ducks. They put out decoys. The fact is that fake birds are, if anything, likely to attract others of the same species, not scare them away. I have three herons and two egrets in my garden. Admittedly, I have only ever had one real heron, but then I haven't got any fish.

I also have several of those model hawks and owls that are meant to frighten birds away from airfields and valuable crops. So, do they clear my garden too? I conducted an experiment. I put a very realistic plastic Peregrine Falcon on my shed roof. This is a bird feared by many others, especially pigeons, which make up the staple Peregrine diet. I returned to the back room and lurked by the open door with my camcorder. Within 10 minutes I had video of three Woodpigeons pottering round the Peregrine as if it were one of their own. It was almost as if they knew perfectly well it was a fake.

To confirm my conviction that birds are not daft, my garden is now guarded by the Peregrine, a Kestrel, an Eagle Owl, a Tawny Owl and no fewer than five Little Owls. I have pictures of them with Great Tits, Blue Tits and Robins perched on their heads! I even once – in the cause of science – put out a totally realistic model cat (not a stuffed real one). Barely a minute later, that too had a couple of Wrens hopping on its back, and a young rat gnawing at its tail!

Then there are my mirrors. The generally touted advice is that you should not put a mirror in a garden, because small birds will attack their own reflection, thinking it is a rival, and they could hurt themselves by pecking at the glass. I have indeed witnessed that kind of behaviour, but only by Dunnocks, and though there was a fair amount of fluttering, pecking and poking, I am pretty sure there was no beak-breaking or head-bruising. I even solicited a second opinion by placing a vanity mirror on the bird table. It got no reaction at all, although I reckon one particularly vain Robin did have a bit of a primp. Anyway, my noisy, garish, model-infested, ludicrous garden has five large mirrors and a number of little ones or even shards of mirror glass, suspended on fences, nestling in rockeries and wedged in bushes. Thus the many psychedelic features are reflected and multiplied, as if in a giant kaleidoscope. There is even a large mirrorball, which on sunny days sends showers of sunbeams dancing over the lawn, and even on the ceiling of the back room.

Despite all of this, I have 58 species on my garden list. Admittedly, this is over 20 years, and a fair proportion of them were flying or circling overhead, including eight birds of prey: Kestrel, Sparrowhawk, Hobby, Red Kite, Buzzard, Honey Buzzard, Osprey and (real) Peregrine. Most birdwatchers count 'flyovers' on their garden lists – 'species seen in, over or from your garden' – except the RSPB. The rules for the annual Big Garden Birdwatch clearly state: 'Please record the highest number of bird species seen in your garden (not flying over).' Sounds a bit

mean, doesn't it ? Well, no, it is all in the interest of facts, figures
and fun. Anyway, it doesn't mean you can't look at anything in
the air. Including the sunbeams. But one word of caution. If you
do have mirrors in your garden, make sure you don't count every
bird twice.

CHAPTER TWO

Not in my Backyard

My neighbours are not insensitive to nature. They think wildlife is fine. In its place. Its place, however, is 'somewhere else'. Not in, on or over their home.

We were recently gossiping in true neighbourly fashion, when we were distracted by a flypast of the 'Green Arrows', a small squadron of Ring-necked Parakeets. I smiled. My neighbour winced.

'You must agree, Bill, that really is a horrible noise?' I did not agree. 'They're going to cull them though,' enthused the lady of the house. I disillusioned her: 'No. They're culling Monk Parakeets. Ring-neckeds are definitely here to stay.' 'But that dreadful noise! It's like, it's like…'. She searched for an aptly offensive synonym. 'It's like a dentist's drill!' I was truly taken aback. Not by the vehemence of her outrage, but by the inappropriateness of the comparison. A dentist's drill? The call of the parakeet could perhaps be likened to the demonic screeching of a banshee, or maybe a

Jay with a loudhailer, but surely not a dentist's drill! I left them exaggeratedly covering their ears, so they didn't hear my parting mutter: 'Think yourself lucky you don't live in Australia.'

So my neighbours don't like nasty noises. Well, neither do I. Especially the most intrusive, ear-offending, teeth-tingling and unnecessary noise of modern times: the relentless roar of a leaf blower! And – here's an irony – from whose garden does this noise pollution emanate? My neighbour's!

It seems to me that there are people who don't mind watching a bit of nature, but are not so keen on living with it. The bloke on the other side loathes Woodpigeons. He once caused several panic calls to 999 by firing fusillades of gunshots from his garden terrace. When I enquired what the **** he was doing, he replied: 'It's the pigeons. They keep messing on the garden furniture. It's OK, they're blanks.' I know that Woodpigeons produce purple poo that quick-dries to the consistency of reinforced concrete, which can not only desecrate garden furniture, but also obliterate a windscreen, nevertheless, that is no excuse for sitting in your town-house garden blasting away with a shotgun, blanks or no blanks. As the police told him.

Of course, it is all a matter of attitude. Just as one man's weeds are another man's wildflowers, one man's pests are another man's 'pets'. Next door's wasps are likely to feel the fatal thwack of *The Sunday Telegraph*. Mine get coaxed into a wine glass with a postcard and are thrown to freedom. I found the velvet-furred family of baby rats that played hide and seek among my garden gnomes two years ago as cute as any mice. Next door started muttering about 'getting a man in'. I suspect he did. I haven't seen a rat since.

I am sure somebody did get a man in last year, when three fox cub corpses were found in various gardens, but I am certain that this slaughter was not perpetrated by the folks next door. They have become rather fond of our local fox, even though – or perhaps because – he is a bit of a scamp. One recent morning, I heard an incensed curse from over the garden fence: 'That bloody fox!'

'What's it done now?' I enquired with appropriate neighbourly concern.

'The damn thing's stolen my slippers!'

'He came in the house?'

'No. Yesterday evening, I left my slippers out on the patio, and he's had 'em!'

I had to chuckle. So did his wife. Eventually, so did he. 'Ah well,' he sighed philosophically, 'I'll just have to take it out on the leaf blower.'

'You do, and I'm going to get next door's shot gun!'

My threat was obliterated by the cacophony of the infernal machine. It also covered the startled squawking of half a dozen panicking parakeets that had been dangling on my peanuts.

As they swooped over my neighbour, he looked up, and I swear I read his lips: 'Mm. They are rather pretty. But what a horrible row!'

I should say so. He sounded worse than a dentist's drill.

CHAPTER THREE

Young People Today

Earlier this year the National Trust published a booklet called *Natural Childhood*, motivated by the assumption that most children these days don't have one! Indeed, the syndrome is so dire that it has been designated an adolescent illness: Nature Deficit Disorder, which – translated from the American – means 'not enough nature'.

The national newspapers were intrigued, especially by a list entitled: '50 things to do before you are 11¾', which could, I suspect, be retitled '50 things National Trust members used to do when they were kids'. No offence, but I can't imagine that many primary schoolchildren are National Trust members, or that they'd appreciate oblique Adrian Mole references. The list is clearly a nostalgia-fest, compiled by 'oldies', which could have been headed: 'What we used to do when we played out.' A phrase now long obsolete.

So what is on this pre-teen bucket list? Some suggestions are obvious enough. **Climb a tree. Make a mud pie. Bury someone in the sand.** That one worries me a bit, especially in the absence of **Dig them up again** or **Turn yourself in at the police station.** Nevertheless, as I perused further, I often nodded my approval, but I also noted the absence of any of the things that had connected *me* to nature when I was a little lad. Perhaps the National Trust decided not to condone them because they were illegal! Such as…

Scrumping apples. A euphemism indeed. *Stealing* apples more like. During 2011's riots people weren't saying: 'Hey, let's go and scrump some 42-inch TV sets!' Scrumping was fruit theft, but it lured the immature me into orchards and gardens, neither of which were familiar features of industrial Lancashire where I lived.

Bird egg collecting. Now illegal, and always reprehensible, but every schoolboy did it, and whenever I am asked how I got into birds and birding, songs, calls and habitats, I can only truthfully answer: 'By going egg collecting'.

Trespassing. When I were a lad, trespassing was unavoidable, simply because anywhere that was good for nature was also private. Notices told us that 'Trespassers Will Be Prosecuted'. Or to 'Keep Out'. Of course, we didn't, though getting in often involved danger or pain. Reservoirs were usually ringed by iron railings with spikes on top. Climbing them risked being skewered like a kebab. Sewage farms were fortified by high walls with broken glass on top. Farmland was more protected than a prison camp. The amount of barbed wire we had to climb over or under would have challenged Steve McQueen on his motorbike. Nor did we always make a Great Escape, and many's the time I felt the cuff of a farmer's horny hand, but it was a small price to pay to snaffle an egg from a Lapwing, Skylark or Yellowhammer, while honing nest-finding skills that Sherlock Holmes would have been proud of. So, I can't deny it, the thing that connected me to nature was crime!

But lurking behind my facetiousness, perhaps there is some deeper truth. A large part of 'playing out' was the thrill of dares and danger. The excited nervousness of possibly getting caught, or even prosecuted, whatever that was!

The fact is, we wanted to be naughty. All kids did, and all kids still do.

It is a fact that the National Trust booklet acknowledges. It could be subtitled 'How to let kids take acceptable risks'. However, will those risks be acceptable to health and safety? Or to paranoid parents? Or can they compete with the 'virtual' risks you can take in the latest version of Tomb Raider or whatever?

Changing the habits of children won't be easy, but there is an even tougher task. It is not just children who are suffering from Nature Deficit Disorder. We all are. So is the whole world.

WILD WORLD

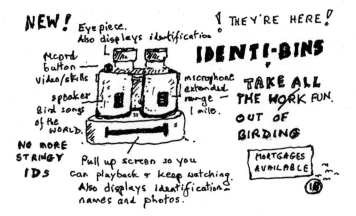

NEW! Eyepiece. Also displays identification

Record button
video/stills
speaker
Bird songs of the WORLD.

¡ THEY'RE HERE!

IDENTI-BINS

microphone extended range - 1 mile.

TAKE ALL THE WORK FUN. OUT OF BIRDING

NO MORE STRINGY IDs
Pull up screen so you can playback & keep watching. Also displays identification— names and photos.

MORTGAGES AVAILABLE

CHAPTER FOUR

New-fangled Birding

'When I were a lad, we didn't have binoculars. We had to make do with two toilet rolls and an elastic band.'

'And if you wanted a telescope, you carved one out of a marrow.'

'And there were no bird books. None at all. I tell a lie, there was one. Only it didn't have any birds in it. It didn't have anything in it. No pictures. No words. No point! We never saw anything. Nothing at all. But that didn't stop us going birdwatching. Every weekend, we'd ring our friends and tell them where we'd seen nothing, so they could come and see nothing with us. Things have changed since then.'

They certainly have. What's more, I am old enough to have witnessed – and benefited – from the many advances in birding equipment and techniques. I have seen telescopes turn from burnished brass into grey rubbery plastic stuff and shrink from the size of a blunderbuss to a small vacuum flask, thus evolving into 'spotting scopes'. Binoculars have basically retained their shape, and presumably always will – unless we evolve a third eye – but they are lighter, optically impeccable and bank-breakingly expensive. Bird books are arguably out of control, and indeed there may well now be more books than birds. In fact a cull may be necessary to make way for the proliferating DVDs, websites, apps and so on. The advances in communications have been entirely beneficial. Time was when birdwatchers rang each other and relied on 'the grapevine' for news. This became focused by Birdline's Rare Bird Alert, which could be consulted on a new-fangled 'mobile', which begat the 'pager', and has now evolved into the 'smartphone'. Don't you just hate that word 'smart'? It sounds so smug. Or is it me being intimidated by technology?

The truth is that, having been out of the loop (and into the 'loopy'?) for a year or two, I have only recently re-emerged into the current birding scene. I chose to dive in at the deep end by going on a trip to Guatemala, where the birds were almost totally unfamiliar, and the forests dauntingly dense. My first day out, I floundered.

'What's that?'

'Where?'

'There.'

'It's flown.'

'It's back.'

'Where?'

'There.'

'Gone again'.

'Lost it. Aaagh!'

I have rarely felt so inadequate. Nor so envious of my companions, who were mostly calmly and confidently calling out the sort of names you only get in South America: 'Scaly-throated Leaftosser.' (honestly!)

'Blue-crowned Chlorophonia.' (is that a bird or a disease?)

'Northern Bentbill!'

'Oh, come on! It can't be.' It is. Just flown out of the palm tree. And … 'What's *that*?' This time there was no 'call'. I realised that I was about to get my first demonstration of birding in the digital age. This is how it works.

The first requirement is physical. You need to be strong enough to carry binoculars, a telescope on a sturdy tripod, hooked over one shoulder, and a huge backpack, containing all manner of digital gear – soon to be revealed – and a laser pen. Yes, one of those things some twerp tried to blind Ronaldo with, or dazzle Andy Murray. I had regarded it as a weapon, until I went birding in Guatemala.

More than once I watched the routine spring into action. It went like this.

1: someone spots a little brown bird. But 2: no one knows what it is. While 3: I can't even see it. So 4: somebody points the laser pen, and a red or green dot flits up and down a huge tree until it hovers and stops. Pen man announces 5: 'The bird is 6 inches above the light.' Which, 6, it is. But what is it? Then 7: strong man steps forward, with digital camera fitted with a lens as big as a bazooka. The bird is tiny and nearly half a mile away, and yet the camera clicks and whirrs. Next 8: we all peer at the screen. A brown speck is just about visible, until 9: the digital zoom is activated, and the image magnifies so rapidly it is as if the bird is charging straight at us. Magnified to ultra-close-up, we can now see every stripe, streak and feather margin. The cameraman is even able to calculate the length of the wing! Until 10, an identification is mooted: 'Probably Yellow-bellied Flycatcher'. By now, at least three smartphone screens are touch-scrolling through Flycatchers of Central America, while a nearby iPod broadcasts a wispy snatch of virtual birdsong, at which the non-virtual bird flies closer and joins in, and 'probably' becomes 'definitely'.

Yellow-bellied Flycatcher. Tick.

So, is it progress? Or is it 'cheating'? Or do you miss the days of toilet rolls and marrow? I do.

HERE TODAY - GUAN TOMORROW.

CHAPTER FIVE

Climb Every Mountain

Any birdwatcher who keeps a world list is bound to have visited a few volcanoes. In order to see a Volcano Junco, you must go to Costa Rica and ascend to the edge of the crater of the Poás Volcano. It's not too arduous if you do it in a charabanc. The junco isn't spectacular: it looks rather like a smoked sparrow and is lava-coloured. So are a lot of lava-loving birds. On the volcanic Galapagos, the Lava Heron is black. So is the Lava Gull. (A seagull that isn't white! Doesn't seem right does it?)

Of course, these species are examples of a well-known natural law: that creatures are often the same colour as their surroundings. Mind you, by that token, rainforest birds should all be green, and wet. Some of them are. However, others are dazzlingly and almost luminously multicoloured, even some of those that live on volcanoes. But then not all volcanoes are covered in lava.

About a year ago, I joined a small party of British, American and Dutch journalists who had been invited to sample some of the birds of Guatemala. We were guests of Guatemala Nature Tours. We started with a couple of days of sociability and some gentle lowland birding, including a cruise across one of the calmest and bluest lakes I have ever seen, made all the more stunning by the reflections and backdrop of not just one but several volcanoes. Every now and then we were distracted by a distant rumbling. Thunder? Quarry blasting? It was coming from high in the mountains. Our binoculars revealed plumes of smoke and at least two of us swore we saw the earth move.

We were, however, assured that an eruption was not imminent. This was comforting news, since we had been told that our post-breakfast walk was going to be 'up the volcano trail'. It was at this point that I beckoned to our tour leader. I explained that I had spent a fair chunk of the past year in and out of hospital, and that the only walking I had done for several months was a casual stroll on Parliament Hill, which is quite steep but hardly competes with a volcano. Another member of our group sensed my trepidation and expressed concern about his 'dodgy knees', while a third asked that his advancing years be taken into account, at which I muttered that my years were further advanced than his. The tour lady assured us that we would all be fine. 'It is a good trail. Up through the forest. We will have a little rest at the lookout, then carry on to the crater if you want. Or we can just keep birding.'

'How long will it take us?' I asked. She hesitated. Was it because she didn't know or because she didn't want to tell us? 'About three hours I think.'

'There and back?'

'Three hours each way.'

'So six hours!'

'Maybe. Yes.'

It took us 12! Six up. Six down. Twelve hours! Well that's how long I took. The youngest and fittest took maybe about eight. Dodgy-knee man took nearer 10, while Mr Advancing Years apparently gave up at the lookout.

Oh yes, while we are at the lookout, what did we look out at? Trees. Miles and miles of trees. The same trees that grew alongside and over the trail so that the sun rarely broke through. The same trees whose tangled roots snaked upwards through and across the path and grabbed our ankles and tripped us up. The trees that hemmed us in on all sides and made sure the view from the lookout was the only one we got. That's the thing about volcanoes, once you are on 'em, you can't see 'em. Snow-capped peaks can only be viewed from a distance.

We trudged upwards and then downwards. I fell further and further behind the main party. A guide was assigned to stay with me, to catch me if I collapsed and, if necessary, to carry me. It wasn't necessary – quite – but, at least a dozen times coming down, my legs turned to jelly and gave way, so that I slid on my back for several yards, always yelling: 'It's OK! It's OK!' to reassure my sherpa that I hadn't had a heart attack.

Then it began to get dark. Any recognisable friendly voices had long since faded way ahead and below us. I had visions of my so-called friends piling into our minibus and driving off to quaff cold beers at a local bar. Meanwhile, somewhere on the mountain, there was me and my guide. Babes in the wood. We were enveloped in total blackness, apart from the feeble beam of a small torch, which cast shadows and made the forest even spookier. As I stopped for yet another rest, my wheezing and heavy breathing added to the soundtrack until it subsided into silence. If it had been a movie, there would have been a pause, then an ominous distant rumble, exploding into a mighty crash. And a panicked voice announcing: 'The volcano! It's erupting!' But it wasn't.

There was, however, a more incongruous sound approaching: Michael Jackson singing 'Thriller'! Then, a manly duo joined in the chorus in what I suspect were meant to be zombie voices. Not me and my guide. Two armed policemen who had been sent to make sure we came to no harm. I was relieved. Both by their presence and by the fact that it had only just struck me that – like most Central American countries – Guatemala has not long been free of bandits and guerrillas. Unfortunately, despite warnings, European birders are notorious for wandering off into the woods in pursuit of some local speciality.

Talking of which, you may be wondering what birds we saw up the volcano. In all honesty, not a lot. There were several species of wintering North American warblers, and the occasional glimpse of a woodcreeper, but frankly we'd had better views in the lowlands where the canopy wasn't quite as dense. There was, however, one specific reason we needed to get up to high altitude. To search for a quintessential ticking target, the Highland Guan, which sounds like a Scottish folk dance, but looks rather like a tree-dwelling turkey. It has red feet and a red wattle, but is otherwise, well, lava-coloured. It is also big. Worth a 12-hour hike?

I wouldn't know. I didn't see it. None of us did.

PS. It needn't happen to you!

Guatemala is a fascinating country, with stunning scenery and terrific wildlife. Just make sure you check the itinerary, and don't try and do too much. Mind you, if your main concern is the length of your checklist, choose a specialist travel company, and go for it.

ROOM FOR A LITTLE ONE ? NO!

CHAPTER SIX

Birds Online

In the olden days, nearly every year I would spend a week or so during the migration season on the tiny Shetland island of Out Skerries. There were no trees, no hedges and no electricity, which meant of course that there were no telegraph poles and no wires. Skerries was therefore in effect a perchless zone. Small birds had to make do with drystone walls and a few crofters' roofs. Then came a historic day. The generator chugged into silence, an underwater cable brought energy from the mainland, and up went the poles and the power lines. Most of the islanders were pleased, a few protested, but I was delighted. I was also excited, as I anticipated which species would be the first bird on the wire.

I predicted Wheatear, expected Meadow Pipit, but was thrilled when it was a Cuckoo, a bird we frequently hear but rarely see, unless it is perched out in the open – for instance, on telegraph wires. I am sure most birdwatchers have wondered:

'What would we do without wires?' More to the point: 'What would the birds do?'

Most 'accidental' man-made perches have their natural equivalent. A TV aerial is an iron treetop. A chimney stack is a brick tree stump. Both are ideal song perches. Likewise, drystone walls are rocky hedges, and dangling ropes could be lianas. But where in nature will you find a long length of highly strung horizontal cable, thin enough for a bird to grip, and with an unimpeded view, affording safety from predators and a lookout for prey, not to mention a symmetrical gathering point for the flock whose members like to line up together? Is there any image more iconic of migration than newly arrived or ready-to-depart Swallows dotted along the wires, like musical notes on the stave, or clothes-pegs on a washing line?

Poles and power lines are also much favoured by the 'perch and pounce' predators, principally birds of prey, such as shrikes and kestrels, with talons small enough to grip, and tails long enough to balance. Peregrines and buzzards pose on posts, often so still that they seem to be growing out of the top, or maybe carved like a totem, until they suddenly launch themselves either skywards, or downwards onto a rambling rodent. The most regal raptors claim the most majestic thrones. There is an area in Israel where a veritable forest of giant pylons undeniably constitutes one of the grossest blots on the landscape you will ever see, but it is arguably also the best place in the country for seeing a selection of large falcons and even larger eagles.

Poles and pylons also provide nest sites for a few species: Ospreys, storks, weavers and woodpeckers (as long as the pole is wooden, not steel!). Monk Parakeets build a ramshackle colonial nest the size of a small car and are capable of plunging a whole neighbourhood into blackout.

Talking of which, how come that the birds don't get electrocuted? Small birds are unlikely to touch two wires or the ground, and are therefore generally safe. However, the larger the wingspan the more the risk of double contact and electrocution, and many birds do die, especially raptors. Nevertheless, when power lines hit the headlines it is usually because of a bird strike, often by geese or swans. Sometimes the location of the pylons is criticised, but I admit I do have to question the steering competence of some Mute Swans, having recently watched a fully fledged free-flying bird flounder and flap across Hampstead Pond, take off and crash straight into a wooden fence!

So, poles and power lines, call them an eyesore or an obstacle, but I'm willing to bet most birds are grateful for them, and so are birdwatchers. Here are a couple of challenges: what is the least likely bird you have ever seen perching on a wire? (It has to hold steady for at least a minute, and no wing flapping.) Mine was a Curlew! And what's your 'most species line up' along a wire between two poles? My best was Portugal last August. Bee-eater, Woodchat Shrike, Southern Grey Shrike, Hoopoe, Roller, Red-rumped Swallow and Azure-winged Magpie, with a Little Owl on the post.

Electric!

Ave maria

Little old men in dinner jackets OK, but we do NOT look like NUNS!
and don't speak with your beak full....

CHAPTER SEVEN

It's an Ill Wind

Is weather wildlife? No, but weather is nature. And weather affects wildlife, especially wild weather. Not that we get really wild weather in Britain. We get rain, we get floods, we get cold spells and we are told we get droughts. Very occasionally, we get strong winds but, own up, you have to go back to the Great Storm (as history has recorded it) of 1987 to recall truly photogenic damage. I was filming an educational video at the Tower of London, but arrived to find the entrance blocked and continuity ruined, because what the previous day had been a grassy courtyard was completely obliterated by the massive tree that had stood proudly in the middle of it, but now lay sprawled and battered like a heavyweight boxer out cold on the canvas. These days, I would have snapped it with my iPhone and had it on Twitter in five seconds, where it would have joined thousands of posts depicting the aftermath of that uniquely stormy night, but back in that primitive era, we had to wait till the evening news before we could marvel or panic at the extent of the damage. Cars overturned, roofs blown away, whole woods flattened and wildlife – especially birds – compelled to go wherever the wind carried them.

Michael Fish may not have predicted the hurricane, but birdwatchers certainly anticipated its effect. The storm had gathered up its strength in the Bay of Biscay. The date was 18 October. So what seabirds would be in Biscay in October? Leach's Petrels, maybe shearwaters and surely Sabine's Gulls. The latter is a birders' favourite. Rather dainty and handsome (for a gull) and rare enough to be desired but not so rare that you don't stand a chance of ever seeing one, or even a handful, especially if you are on the west coast in a strong westerly which hampers the speed of their progress to wintering areas further south. On 18 October 1987, the wind in Biscay was so powerful it literally swept up fistfuls of Sabine's and hurled them north-east to the coast of Britain. Birders welcomed their arrival, and were doubly delighted when they started seeing birds – not down in Cornwall and Ireland – but in the middle of London and the Home Counties. All day, the mobiles and pagers trembled with new reports: Sabine's on the Thames, in parks, gravel pits and reservoirs. A record-breaking invasion never to be repeated, and it hasn't been. Yet.

However, in North America this sort of thing happens every year. Over there, extreme weather is accorded the status of an ancient god. It is to be feared and revered but it also has its fans and followers. There are clubs devoted to tracking down tornadoes and filming them at dangerously close range. Twister twitchers indeed. The TV weather channel – yes, showing non-stop weather and nothing else – mixes warnings, facts and forecasts with viewers' videos, which are viewed not with trepidation, but with almost childlike excitement. 'Oh boy, look at the tail on that! Wow, that is awesome! That's gotta be today's top twister. Filmed by Robert K. Cheeseburger, in Georgia. Way to go, Rob!'

Only once have I myself been close to a mighty wind. I was in New Jersey at Cape May, which is at the tip of a peninsula with the mouth of the Delaware River on one side and the Atlantic on the other. Hurricane Floyd had just finished battering the Bahamas and was now careering through the Carolinas towards Washington. It would then probably hit New Jersey. Hurricanes are unpre-dictable, but in the States they don't take any chances. As I drove down to Cape May I had already noticed permanent road signs indicating 'Evacuation Route'. They all pointed due north. Unsurprising, since the other three directions all led to the ocean! I was not aware of any panic on the streets of the rather sedate colonial-style resort of Cape May, despite the fact that the State Governor was on every TV screen declaring an official 'state of emergency'. It struck me that it was probably to avoid litigation. 'I can't force you to leave, but don't say I didn't warn you. And I hope your insurance companies have got that.'

The next morning was wet but not a deluge; the wind was strong but not lethal. Clearly the worst of Floyd had passed in the night. But what had he left behind? He'd been born not in Biscay but in the Bahamas. It was quite possible that he had scooped up some tropical birds and whisked them north up the east coast, even as far as Cape May, where binoculars would be palpitating with anticipation. A species that may be common in the Caribbean could be a celebrity in New Jersey. Somewhere a welcoming committee would be waiting, but where?

I rang the local birdline and was directed to a dilapidated beach café. I drove there immediately, leaving a splashy wake down the slightly flooded streets. Thanks to the admirable American style of having a numbered street sign on every intersection – why can't we do that? – I was soon skidding to a halt in the café car park. Clearly Floyd had been a bit rough with the café. What was probably an already flimsy building now looked on the brink of being totally blown away. Neverthless on the rickety forecourt were 20 or so blokes with binoculars and telescopes, staring out to sea and now and then yelling out adjectives. 'Sooty!' In the UK it would have been Sooty Shearwater, here it was Sooty Tern. Followed by 'Bridled', at home 'bridled' Guillemot, here Bridled Tern. Two species of 'tropical' terns abducted from the Caribbean. Both New Jersey rarities.

The locals were thrilled and I was pleased for them, but vicarious pleasure is not in a birder's nature. The truth was that I was getting more and more miffed because I couldn't see very well. Such is the penalty of being not much taller than a hobbit. These were nice guys, but nobody was about to let me push into the front row. However, just behind the café, was a grim grey building with a first-floor walkway, somewhat reminiscent of

Bates Motel in *Psycho*. 'Wouldn't it be better if we could get up there?' I asked. 'We'd be higher and drier. Can we get in there?' My words were greeted as if they were sacrilege, which indeed they were. 'That's a convent.'

'What? Like a convent school?'

'No, like a nunnery.'

'Oh. But are the nuns actually there?' I reasoned. 'They could've been evacuated. Or be away on a pilgrimage or something.'

'Lead us not into temptation,' somebody quipped. While someone else stuck his fingers in his ears to block out my wicked words. A third – continuing the frivolous blasphemy – raised his hands to the heavens and asked the Lord to give us a sign. At which moment, the café roof blew away, and one of the walls collapsed. It helped our decision. 'Aw, what the hell! Let's do it!'

Maybe the mention of hell unnerved me. Or the crucifixes or the Latin scriptures, not to mention the signs saying 'Strictly Private' and 'No Access'. At least two of us couldn't resist muttering 'forgive us our trespasses,' as we scurried up the iron staircase, our boots clanging like gongs on the metal steps. 'Are you sure the nuns aren't here?' I whispered. Even as I spoke, two black and white figures appeared in the courtyard. Identification was instant. Black and white Razorbill? Velvet Scoter? Black and white… Nuns! They didn't scream or yell at us, but neither did they ask if we had had any 'tropical overshoots'. Instead, they popped back out of sight. I for one was relieved. It was almost as if God had given us his blessing. He hadn't.

Ten minutes later three cops arrived. Proper US cops with gun belts and star-shaped badges and many-cornered caps, and – most unnerving of all – truncheons at the ready. 'What the hell are you guys up to?' drawled the chief officer, and then answered his own question. 'Goddam birders. Every time there is a storm I have to throw you guys out of here.' Oh my lord, I thought, they've got previous. I instantly decided to take the rap by playing the bemused Englishman. Which I was. 'It's my fault, officer. You see, this is my first hurricane. I suggested we came up here 'cos it's a much better view.'

'I am sure it is, but it freaks out the ladies. Do me a favour fellas, stay in the beach café, OK?'

'But it's nearly washed away,' I argued. The officer glared at me, just like my Latin teacher used to when he was about to say: 'Oddie, one more word out of you and you are in detention.' Only in this case it could be: 'You are in jail.' As we dolefully filed down the stairs, it struck me that if you are knowingly going to antagonise anyone you could hardly choose more intimidating foes than policemen and nuns!

We closed the iron gate with the big padlock and 'Keep Out' sign, with a line of nuns peeping over the balustrade like Puffins over a ledge. As the officer revved up his motorbike, he shouted over to us: 'Hey, fellas, one more thing.' We sighed a silent 'what now?' 'So, tell me, did Floyd blow in any good birds?' Recognising the opportunity for petty revenge, we collectively chorused. 'No!' In fact, in the brief time we'd been on the balcony we'd had 40 Sooties and 10 Bridleds, but we weren't going to tell him. Mind you, if any of the sisters were seawatchers, with a view like that, they must've seen even more. Gripped off by a nun! Well, there's a first.

IF THEY ONLY KNEW WHAT'S
GOING ON IN THE LADIES!

CHAPTER EIGHT

Birding in Transit

Most birdwatchers keep lists of how many species they have seen – on their local patch, in their garden, in the current year, in their life, in Britain, in Europe, in the world. If they travel abroad in search of ticks (new birds) they probably keep a trip list. They may well also keep 'transport' lists: a train list, a bus list, possibly a bike list (you are allowed to dismount but not to abandon your bike). The long-distance traveller may even keep an international airport list of birds seen in transit.

As soon as the pilot has announced: 'We shall be landing in a few minutes,' you should start peering through the windows to claim the cachet of spotting the first bird of the trip. Its identity will vary from country to country and continent to continent, but not perhaps as much as one might assume. Whatever the latitude or longitude it will probably be something white: a gull, a gannet or a tropicbird, if the descent is over the sea. If it is inland, it is quite likely to be Cattle Egrets. My best airport white bird was a Snowy Owl in Canada. And no, it wasn't one of those fake owls they put on airport roofs to scare other birds away. They are usually plastic Eagle Owls and, incidentally, they scare nothing. Birds aren't daft.

Birdwatching during landing is rarely productive. The plane is travelling too fast and bouncing too much, and even if you do glimpse something, you are strapped in and can't move, let alone hold your binoculars steady. Once the plane has landed and begun taxiing your chances improve. The majority of the world's airfields are indeed sited on fields, or at least have large grassy areas. A lot of it may be closely mown, but there are often rough patches perfect for birds that like grasslands. Larks and pipits aren't easily named when you are still strapped in your seat belt but you can have fun guessing and anticipating. There is always a chance of a harrier. If it is a male, you may be able to name the species before you are allowed to unfasten, stand up and try to elbow your way towards the exit. If you are in transit nowadays chances are you will have to disembark, be stuffed into a motorised cattle truck, and be chivvied into the terminal transit lounge, where the only windows look out on parked planes, luggage trollies and concrete. At least there is the consolation of a few species for your airport list. Almost wherever you are in the world, you can tick off Common Mynas, House Crows and House Sparrows, which are probably also thriving in the nearby city. Why, then, have House Sparrows almost gone from London? Is Regent's Park really less salubrious than an international airport? And how come the local swallows and swifts choose to nest under steel beams on concrete hangers, constantly deafened by jet engines and breathing in toxic fumes? At least they have the airport grassland just round the corner, where they can skim around feeding on bugs and butterflies and drinking from the ditches, where frustrated birders can't see them. It was not always thus.

Sadly, nowadays, high-level security means that birdwatching at airports is likely to be limited. Gone are those delightful days when we were offered the choice of spending transit time in the terminal or to stay on board and even be invited to stand at the top of the steps at the open exit door, where you could get a breath of fresh air, and brazenly scan across the grassland and sort out those larks and pipits. It was in such circumstances in Singapore that I spotted a small flock of Oriental Plovers, which I was able to point out to a rather attractive air hostess. I even erected my tripod and let her look through my scope. It wouldn't happen nowadays.

Mind you, I suppose I got a foretaste of the future tension we have to accept these days back in 1990, when I was returning from a trip to East Africa. It all seemed almost unreal. We had spent two nights camping in tiny tents at the bottom of Tanzania's Ngorongoro Crater, where a nocturnal excursion to the canvas-clad loo involved tiptoeing past African Buffaloes and dodging the Lions that were hopefully now satiated by dining on the antelope we had watched them chase down that very afternoon. A guard with a gun accompanied me, which was comforting, albeit a little inhibiting. Two days later, I was revelling in the luxury and privacy of an en-suite bathroom in a three-star lakeside hotel with an African moon rising above a backdrop of the giant snowy cone that is Mount Kilimanjaro. Almost unreal. So was what happened next.

It was the dead of night and I was deep in sleep. Suddenly, I was woken by the sound of engines revving, vehicles manoeuvring and someone hammering on every door in the corridor and yelling out words I have never heard before or since: 'Wake up! Your plane is going early!' Surely not. Planes don't go early. Nothing goes early. Someone insisted that the night porter phone the airport. He said he had but the phone was dead. So how did he know the plane was early? One of our group demanded to have a go. The night porter handed over the phone while muttering 'out of order'. It was. He muttered something else in Swahili, which probably translated as 'bloody suspicious tourists'. He repeated his original threat: 'Your coach is leaving,' plus more Swahili, no doubt 'or don't you believe that either?' He almost pushed us outside. 'Quickly. Hurry, quickly.' 'Is there any other way of hurrying?' I quipped, as we were herded out and onto our vehicle, not even being given time to snap the sunrise over Kilimanjaro. It was as if they couldn't wait to get rid of us. Bleary-eyed, unwashed and slightly trembly, I sensed a slight air of panic, or was it foreboding?

In fact, the next part of our journey home went calmly, except that I did wonder why we were returning to the UK via Addis Ababa in Ethiopia, a land wracked by widespread starvation and poverty but also, at that time, civil unrest and armed uprising. Being at an airport at such times is not relaxing, the only consolation being that with any luck it means that it won't be long before you can flee the country. Once again I and my fellow passengers were accompanied by a man with a gun, who frankly lacked the protective demeanour of the loo guard in the Ngorongoro. This man looked scared. He herded us into the main hall and left us to stare at the departures board. There were half a dozen international flights listed. On all five, passengers were requested to wait in the lounge. The uncomfortable feeling changed to concern, as the display changed to 'delayed', which disturbingly became 'delayed indefinitely'. And after an hour or so, a positively scary 'cancelled'. There was no explanation. No announcement about what was or wasn't happening. There was, however, a multilingual rumour going round that all planes had been commandeered by the Ethiopian military to transport troops to fight rebels in the north. It seemed that we could be in Ethiopia for some time.

Which wasn't such a bad thing since Ethiopia is a terrific country for birds, including several much-prized endemics. Three of us were clutching our binoculars and scopes − birders never check in their optics − and we had already noticed that the airport grounds were promisingly green with grass, bushes and trees. And there was even the occasional tantalising flick or flutter. There were birds. We needed to get at them. The only exit involved large glass doors through which a few people were coming and going. Some were armed, others were in uniform. Non-military personnel were having to show ID, tickets or passports. Most were being allowed through. Would we be? And if we were would we be allowed back in? Do we risk it? Of course. Most birders walk a thin line between determination and recklessness.

A passport, a ticket and a smile got us through. Within seconds we had scampered across a car park with a larger population of House Sparrows than London. Then we noticed one we didn't recognise. Some kind of thrush. We were soon engrossed in scribbling descriptions and sketches, leafing through a Tanzanian field guide, which the mystery species probably wouldn't be in, or taking photos. This was probably our big mistake. Not one, but two, and then three men with guns scampered towards us, yelling more menacingly than the night porter. I say 'men', but none of them looked more than 13 or 14. Their rifles looked older, but no doubt worked. The fact that the boys' fingers were trembling on the triggers, their foreheads sweating and their voices yelling almost hysterically was evidence that they considered us suspicious if not hostile. We couldn't blame them. Unfortunately, birding optics look like surveillance gear at best, at worst they could be mistaken for firearms. Wearing camouflaged jackets doesn't help. The time-honoured birdwatchers' defence tactic when under suspicion is to show the soldier, policeman or enraged landowner a field guide, show him a few pictures and mime flapping, while repeating 'birds', and maybe even doing a few bird impressions. This routine works best in countries where the concept of watching birds for pleasure is not totally unknown. It did not impress teenage Ethiopian soldiers, whose nerves were already in shreds. We allowed them to march us at bayonet point back into the terminal.

We were now burdened with a double whammy. The planes were still 'cancelled', and even worse we knew there were new birds out there – maybe even once-in-a-lifetime endemics – but we couldn't get at them. So near and yet so far. I decided to console myself with an unescorted visit to the loo. Within seconds, I came rushing out and beckoned my two comrades to follow me back into the cubicle. Perhaps, surprisingly, they willingly did so. What any onlookers thought I can't imagine. Well, I can, but I'd rather not. We closed the door and clicked on 'engaged'. Tim, the tallest by far, squeezed between us and examined the window. Yes, a window. Quite a small window, and quite high up. It had frosted glass but it had been left slightly open for ventilation. Tim pushed it fully open, thus creating a luxury birdwatching hide, complete with uninterrupted view and built-in conveniences.

The only design fault was that the window was so high that only very tall people like Tim could look through it. Small people like me could stand on tiptoe and still barely reach the sill. All I could see was a sliver of blue sky. I could, however, hear Tim's commentary. 'Pigeons. Er, White-collared Pigeon. Endemic, I think. And Brown-rumped Seedeaters. Oh, wait, yes, definitely Wattled Ibises. That is an endemic! Can you two see all right?'

Imagine the scene. A toilet cubicle made for one but accom-modating three. Three blokes crammed in like contortionists and lumbered with large backpacks, tripods, telescopes and cameras. There is a very tall man who is able to peer through the little window, a middle-sized one who can just see out if he stands on tiptoe, and a little one – me – with no choice but to clamber up to stand on the rim of the lidless toilet bowl, steadying myself by grabbing the cistern and risking pulling it off the wall and, on several occasions, when I lost balance, grasping at the chain, which saved me from slipping down the pan, but of course kept flushing. The scene reminded me of student days and 'How many people can you get into a mini?' or the Marx Brothers' routine with more and more people cramming into a cupboard. We were in there for maybe an hour. By the time we emerged, the 'cancelleds' had been replaced by boarding times and gate numbers, while the story about the military taking the planes had been dismissed as 'Chinese whispers'. Better still, I had added a dozen species to my international airport list.

That was 20 odd years ago. Nowadays, Ethiopia is a prime destination for birdwatchers. No doubt there are many books and websites advising 'where to watch birds in Ethiopia'. I do hope they include the gentlemen's toilet at Addis Ababa airport.

- MEET US - DON'T EAT US.

CHAPTER NINE

A Whale of a Time

I have now been on three whale-watching trips in – or should that be from? – Iceland. The first one was quite a few years ago, out of Húsavík in the north. We saw a couple of porpoises and a distant dolphin, but no whales whatsoever. This struck me as worryingly ironic. First, because the intention was to expand whale-watching as a tourist attraction. Second, because it was rumoured that the Icelandic whaling industry – dormant during a moratorium – had announced that it intended to resume its activities. It was a contradiction that to me seemed almost laughable, with only the small consolation that both whale-watching and whaling are a bit of an anti-climax if there are no whales!

In subsequent years, I have been on enough 'pelagics' in various parts of the world to realise that the fact that whales are not visible doesn't mean they aren't there. Any cetacean seeker will tell you there will be bad trips and there will be average ones, and now and again there will be a real mind-blower.

The second Icelandic trip, in August 2012, was not mind-blowing, but it was fascinating meeting and marvelling at the work of IFAW scientists monitoring the impact of the satisfyingly escalating whale-watching business, and meeting a splendidly cosmopolitan team of young volunteers who were intercepting tourists and appealing to them to 'Greet us. Don't eat us' – a plea on behalf of the whales, not the volunteers. A charmingly petite Polish girl had even disguised herself in a less than life-size whale costume, which was extremely hot, heavy and had no proper eyeholes. She could all too easily have toppled off the quayside and into the water, especially if 'helped' by anyone protesting about protesters, as it were. 'Try anything' tourists intent on sampling local specialities like whale steak can get belligerent if their dining plans – or even their morality – is challenged. IFAW's lobbying is peaceful, but the response may not be. Fortunately, on this trip I saw only civilised dialogue and this time I did see whales. Several Minkes, mainly some distance away and somewhat prone to diving and then surfacing somewhere you are not looking. The IFAW boat crew seemed reasonably happy with the survey so far, but they were extremely unhappy at another recent rumour that whaling was due to recommence.

And so to mid-March 2013. The weather was pretty awful. A raw easterly wind, a temperature below freezing and frequent blizzards of snow, hail or freezing rain. But that was in England! Iceland was much more clement. In Reykjavík, there was evidence that there had been a snowfall not long ago, with shovelled white piles at the roadside, and white caps on the distant hills, but the temperature was several degrees warmer than in London, the skies bluer, and sometimes even sunny, and, best of all, the sea was as flat and calm as the colloquial looking-glass. Off we sailed in search of Orcas.

I have been fortunate to previously have had two pretty memorable Orca experiences. One was in Canada, on Vancouver Island, where the local marine expert has rigged up a network of underwater microphones (hydrophones) out in the bay and quite some distance apart. I sat with him on a couch in his front room as if we were listening to music on his speakers. What we heard was the music of the whales somewhere out in the bay, but 'coming our way!' Of course, not even 'Free Willy' could have leapt through the bay window, but we were able to anticipate the Orcas' route, race to the jetty, leap into a speedboat and land – or rather be thrown out – on what we had been told was a small island, but turned out to be little more than a rock! The cameraman and I were almost swept into the water by the swell as a small pod of Orcas hurtled past us like glossy torpedoes, while the sound recordist was lost in his earphones, beaming with delight as he captured enough whale songs to release an album. Cetaceans really ought to get royalties from New Age relaxation records.

My next Orca experience showed the rather more ruthless side of Killer Whales and also why they deserve that name. We were filming on the Valdes Peninsula in Patagonia, Argentina. Most of the resident wildlife is not difficult to film. Penguins either snooze by their burrows or waddle off to the beach no faster than Charlie Chaplin. Elephant seals behave every bit as badly as they look as though they should. They either lie there farting very loudly, or every now and then a couple of massively misshapen bulls will try to bite each other's heads off. 'Normal' seals were much more pleasing to look at, and to smell. Generally, though, they were not much more active, largely lounging on the sand, occasionally nuzzling their cuddly little offspring, or even nudging them to go for a paddle in the shallows. Not always a wise idea.

The action that I and the film crew witnessed was unplanned and unexpected. We were literally packing the gear into our van, when someone – I think it was me – spotted a distant fin slicing through the water, parallel to the coast. I held my breath long enough to be sure I wasn't hallucinating. Then yelled 'Orcas! Coming this way!' The cameraman and sound recordist unpacked and set up their gear quicker than the gunners at the Edinburgh Tattoo. There were four or five fins proceeding with menace, in what was surely a hunting party. The animal that was about to be hunted seemed totally oblivious. Some of the larger seals were lolloping up the shingle to safety. But one didn't. A little one, a youngster, snuggled in the tideline foam, as cosy as in a duvet. The camera lens swung left. One of the larger whales had split from the group and was surging forward as if he had slipped into a higher gear. As he headed for the shore, he sank under the water. I whispered to the camera: 'I know what might happen, and I sort of want to see it, but then again, I don't. Maybe it'll escape.' At which moment, the cameraman panned onto the baby seal at the tideline. There were three seconds of nothing. Then the Orca leapt into the picture, grabbed the seal and started to shake it violently. Spray spurted everywhere. Soon there would be blood. Killer Whale indeed.

We expected the whale to slide back with its prey, as sleek and slick as it had come. But it didn't. Then we realised that it couldn't. It was probably an inexperienced male. Young and foolish, it had grounded itself on the sandbank and now it was panicking. It had no choice but to grant me my wish. With one last flourish it slung the seal pup back on the beach, and with a final flail and an ungainly lurch, it returned to the sea, and sank out of sight before the rest of the pod could start teasing it. Sometimes you get what you wish for!

All whales are special. Each species is different. Some barely or rarely break the surface. Others wave to you with their gigantic tails or leap into the air causing a cascade and a mighty splash. Some are still hunted. None should be.

Happily, Orcas are more suited to catching food than becoming it, though they have their problems, not least from ever-increasing noise pollution in the world's oceans. Drop a hydrophone into the water and listen on earphones. The first time I did that – in the Moray Firth in Scotland – I was half-deafened by a noise that sounded like Status Quo tuning up, or a race day at Brands Hatch. It was actually the engine of a single ship over half a mile away. Imagine the confusion and chaos this must cause to the subtle and complex communications of Orcas and other cetaceans.

And so to my most recent experience of Orcas, only (as I write) a couple of weeks ago. This time our boat sailed from somewhere I can neither remember, spell nor pronounce, but it wasn't a long way from Reykjavík. I have learnt to ration my optimism when setting out whale-watching, but folks around me showed no such restraint. In fact, I have never known such confidence. I was assured that 'the sea will not be rough' – and it wasn't. I was told 'we will see Orcas' – and we did! Just don't ask me where!

I do know that for the past two years huge shoals of herring have appeared so close to land that at one period thousands of them beached on the shore, at first providing great scavenging for gulls and White-tailed Eagles, then feed for domestic animals, and finally disintegrating into a pretty disgusting eye-and-nose-sore! Orcas would of course demand fresher fish. And for two years they have been getting them as the shoals of healthy herring have increased. And so too have the number of Orcas.

Whale-watching has never been easier. We simply sailed into the shelter of the bay, cut the engine and dropped a hydrophone to provide the live soundtrack of clicks, cries, howls, barks and no doubt all sorts of sounds that are beyond our frequencies. Are they just echolocation and contact calls? Or is it a language? Is it gossip? It was tempting to believe the latter. After all, there were quite a lot of them. Counting wasn't easy as they rose and dived, whacked fish with their tails, grabbed them in their teeth and finally swallowed them before popping up again, waving their dorsal fins. When several do that at the same time it looks like the bay has been invaded by a regatta of black sails. How many did we see? I'd say at least 30.

By the end of March, the Orcas will have refuelled with herring and there will come a day when the whale-watching boat will be disappointed. We don't know where the Orcas go. Surely not to Vancouver? Patagonia maybe? Or do they swim south-east, to South Africa, Sri Lanka or Malaysia? Orcas have an almost worldwide distribution. Just like us. We can't even be certain that they will return to Iceland later in the year. We hope they will. We hope that people will be able to enjoy them. And we hope that whaling will soon become a thing of the past.

IT'S NOT ONLY THE CORMORANTS THAT CAN'T FLY.....

CHAPTER TEN

Galapagoing

I first saw the Galápagos in black and white. When I was a lad, it seems that hardly a week went by without a new Darwin drama/documentary on telly, usually called something like 'The Voyage of the Beagle', or the 'Origin of Species', or maybe just 'Darwin'. They weren't what we now know as natural history programmes. They featured actors playing historical characters, wearing period costume and jotting in their journals while tiptoeing through the iguanas. Sort of *Life on Earth* meets *Downton Abbey*.

Thinking back, it is pretty amazing that these shows were filmed on the actual location. It wasn't the Scillies pretending to be the Galápagos. Nor was it possible to hire the wildlife from Animal Actors. A few sealions could have been procured from an aquarium, but I know of no pet shop in the world where you can buy a full set of Darwin's finches. These riveting programmes really were created out in the Pacific Ocean, 600 miles west of Ecuador and – especially with the advent of colour television – we could all see that the Galápagos archipelago was a truly extraordinary place. Not only were many of the species endemic and extremely rare, but they lived in a bizarre volcanic landscape. The Galápagos seemed to me to combine qualities that were intrinsic to maximum wildlife enjoyment: a context of characterful or impressive scenery, an abundance of creatures and a scarcity – or complete absence – of human beings.

The only people we saw on these TV 'reconstructions' were the actors portraying Mr Darwin, a few of his companions, and perhaps a misguided mariner who caught and cooked a Giant Tortoise for supper, and thus provoked a lecture from Mr D on the sacrosanct uniqueness of the island creatures. This scene would be followed by Darwin wandering pensively alone until his attention is drawn to a small flock of what look like female House Sparrows. He notes and sketches their variable beak sizes and emits a quizzical 'hmmmm'. An historic revelation is nigh! At which point, the soundtrack soars, the credits roll and we have to wait till next week's episode. For many years this was my vision of the Galápagos: a remote haven where wildlife could bask, swim, fly and multiply, and where a man could be alone.

That vision was still in my head, when in 1986 I accepted an invitation from a travel company to join a party of a dozen journalists on a small boat taking a short cruise round the Galápagos. Such a thing is known as 'a press trip'. Not to be confused with a press-gang, though in this case there were similarities. I had envisaged flying on a petite 'Island Hopper' plane, like the ones that have ferried me round Shetland or The Seychelles. Instead, we were herded onto a Boeing 727. Three hours later we were herded off at Baltra airstrip, not certain if we were guests or prisoners. We were lined up by a rather stern young woman in a bright yellow jacket and matching skirt who informed – or warned – us that once we had cleared passport control, we would be shouted at by men with megaphones. We must listen for our name and follow our man.

There were several men, but no megaphones. Instead, they all shouted names in the general direction of the tourists who had arrived on the 727. They were typical tourists. No recognisable scientists, no TV presenters – not even David Attenborough before he was a 'Sir' – and no actor in a frock coat giving us his Darwin. I was disappointed. I also had a feeling of foreboding. Over the following three and a half days, the disappointment increased and the feeling was fulfilled.

It started well enough. Within not much more than an hour, we were being encouraged to hop carefully from a gangplank onto the slippery rocks of a seabird island. It was not dissimilar from landing on Inner Farne, except that instead of Grey Seals bobbing around our boat, there were sealions. Black-headed Gulls were replaced by Lava Gulls (very rare) and Swallow-tailed Gulls (very beautiful), while lowering above us were massive frigatebirds, hooked beaks and jet black, like a cross between a vulture and a pterodactyl. Most of us stopped to gaze upwards and around, but our reverie was shattered by a voice that sounded like a female sergeant major. 'Attention! Keep up please. Keep up!' The lady in yellow who had met as at the airport was not only the tour company 'rep', she was also the tour guide. She shouted out a few names: 'Blue-footed Booby, Marine Iguana'. I ungraciously whispered to one of the journalists: 'A yellow twin set? Is she an air hostess or a chalet girl from *Hi-de-Hi!*?' 'She's certainly not a wildlife expert,' muttered another journalist, who had failed to extract any information from her that was any different from what was in the official guidebook. I sighed, found myself a comfy rock and crouched down to enjoy the company of a pair of Blue-footed Boobies, in the hope of photographing their high-stepping mating dance – surely the inspiration for John Cleese's silly walk – but no sooner had I adjusted my f-stop than I was summoned by 'teacher'. 'Hurry up, please! Get a move on!'

This I was not happy about. I was even less thrilled when the next day we sailed six hours to the Darwin Centre, where we barely had time to make Lonesome George feel less lonesome (sadly, of course, he is now an ex-Giant Tortoise) before we set sail for another four-hour journey to a beach where the number of iguanas was almost matched by the number of tourists, each group being herded and chivvied by lemon-suited guides. It wasn't crowded, but it certainly wasn't secluded.

Frankly, I was beginning to feel hassled. So were most of my fellow journalists. Murmurings of discontent evolved into words of protest when the next day's schedule was announced. 'We will sail north to the island of the Waved Albatross.'

'How long will it take?' came a nervous enquiry. Followed by: 'Will the sea be calmer? 'Cos it was very choppy today.' Someone else did the maths: 'So, that's 10, plus eight or nine… That's nearly 20 hours on the boat!' And about four hours on land.' It is not often that you get a mutiny on a wildlife cruise! We didn't get quite as far as ousting the skipper – or the guide – but we did refuse to sail further north.

The yellow lady protested: 'But you will miss the albatross.' Frankly, the only one who seemed to care was me, but I didn't care enough to endure another day retching or befuddled by Stugeron. Nevertheless, sensing that I may well have been the only 'heavy' birder in our group, she targeted me with temptation. 'Don't you want to see the Flightless Cormorant?'

'It's a cormorant and it can't fly. I'll imagine it.'

'OK, but what about Darwin's finches?' she pleaded, as if she was offering me the crown jewels. This, despite the fact that when I had requested elucidation on finch identification she had been totally bamboozled. Mind you, no great shame there. There are three ground finches: the Large Ground Finch, the Medium Ground Finch and – you guessed it – the Small Ground Finch. Straightforward enough you might think, except that according to the book: 'They are all identical in plumage, and each species varies in size'! I did enquire about the whereabouts of the Vegetarian Finch, the Vampire Finch and the Woodpecker Finch, but got no assurance that we'd see any of them if we sailed for nine days, let alone nine hours. I suspect she had never heard of them, but I am not making them up, honest.

And so the mutineers took over. We spent a leisurely day taking photos (there is nowhere easier in the world) and a delightful and genuinely calm evening moored in a blue bay with orange rocks, where journalists swam with the sealions, and I strolled along the strand listening to mockingbirds. For half an hour it was as if I had the Galápagos to myself.

That was in 1986; what is it like now? More hotels, more boats, more tourists? No doubt. More wildlife? Happily – thanks to the Ecuadorian Government and international designation – probably much the same. Problems with goats, cats, rats, etc? Same as it ever was. If you want to find out more there is masses on the internet. I am not the one to ask. I have never been back. Will I? Would I? Well, maybe if… Frock coats do rather suit me. And I've got the beard for it. My Darwin could have a new catchphrase: 'I want to be alone.' Or how about: 'We're gonna need a bigger boat!'

BIRDS ON THE BOX

I'm not sure I want to be on telly looking like this! ...

CHAPTER ELEVEN

They Couldn't Do That Now!

Picture this. A small suburban lawn. In the middle, there is half a tree. The trunk is riddled with cracks, crevices and holes. One hole is particularly conspicuous. It is only a couple of metres from the ground. If it were higher up, in a bigger tree – with branches – it would surely belong to a woodpecker. But not... At which point, we hear the impatient *tchek tchek* of an adult Great Spotted returning to the hole, and the frantic squeaking of fledglings inside it. What a set up! A photo or film opportunity if ever there was one. Only one problem, how do you get pictures from inside half a tree?

First, find a man with a steady hand and an electric saw. Slice a sliver of wood off the back of the tree trunk, thus exposing the nest chamber, and the fledglings. They can't fly yet, but they could fall out, so be ready to catch them. Now replace the sliver with a pane of clear glass. Next, rapidly erect a canvas hide at the back of the tree, so that a cameraman's lens will be able to observe and film whatever is happening through the glass. Now retire to the nearby kitchen and enjoy a nice cup of tea with Enid, the lady of the house. The kitchen window overlooks the lawn. Very soon Enid will call out: 'They're back. Woody and Winnie! Wood! Win! Yoohoo!' You might have thought that Enid's calling and waving might have unsettled the birds even more than the electric saw and the hide installation, but the fact is that once the eggs have hatched most parent birds exhibit extraordinary devotion, tolerance and bravery in caring for their offspring.

Nothing was going to deter Woody and Winnie from rearing their young, certainly not the sporadic rustling of a cameraman crawling into the hide, and setting up his enormous tripod, and focusing his lens through the little window and revealing three chicks that were so young they were not yet either 'great' nor 'spotted', or indeed even slightly feathered.

As days passed, they grew bigger, and turned from baby grey to adult black and white. The only colour in the scene was the yellowy glow of the cameraman's lamp through the glass, towards which the chicks duly directed their rumps. Birds that nest in the dark defecate towards the nearest light. This is usually the nest hole, but not in this case. The cameraman had to do a lot of wiping. Nevertheless, he got some fabulous footage, arguably verging on the historic.

But when – you may be wondering – was this? Was it the work of one of the great pioneers of wildlife filming? Cherry Kearton perhaps? Or maybe Heinz Sielmann – he definitely did woodpeckers. Probably using much the same techniques as we did. We? I mean, of course, the BBC Natural History Unit. Woody and Winnie Woodpecker featured on a series called *Bird in the Nest*, which was broadcast live in 1994, and again in 1995. The presenters, claustrophobically crammed into a small van – the 'Birdmobile' – were Peter Holden (from the RSPB) and myself. Among the ace cameramen/naturalists were Charlie Hamilton James and Simon King.

Contemporary equivalents of *Bird in the Nest* can now use astonishingly minuscule cameras that can easily be inserted into holes and burrows – or even the wildlife itself! – but they are also bound by strict rules and guidelines about what can and can't be done, not to mention the ubiquitous 'health and safety', for people and for wildlife.

Not so back in the mists of the mid-1990s. Nest set-ups were achieved by whatever disconcertingly ingenious means was necessary. Filming Kestrels involved erecting a precarious scaffolding tower. Jackdaws were persuaded to nest inside an empty oil barrel, suspended at a considerable height. A Great Tit family in a nestbox were removed from a tree, transported across the garden and relocated on the side of a shed, which had been erected specially for the purpose. It was big enough to accommodate a cameraman, or indeed a presenter. Peter nearly missed the start of one show because he'd got locked in with the tits!

First-time-ever live pictures of newly hatched Kingfishers were achieved by a similar technique to the woodpeckers, except that instead of sawing a slice off a tree trunk, Simon dug a pit in a riverbank. Viewers were enthralled when the tiny, blind and naked chicks made their historic debut, but by morning they were incensed and distressed by the news that, later that evening, the parent birds had been spooked by a band of boisterous locals on a Treasure Hunt, which had involved a deal of shouting and splashing up and down the river. The chicks were left unbrooded for maybe 'only' an hour or two, but they chilled, and by morning they were dead.

Misfortune also befell Woody Woodpecker. We had often worried that his regular flight path involved flying across the nearby busy road. His typical woodpecker undulating flight style meant that at the highest point he was safe, but at the lowest he was definitely potential roadkill. One day, the inevitable happened. Or so we believe. A lorry driver came to see us and – with a sad and guilty face – confessed: 'I think I've just run over your woodpecker.' We tried to console him by saying that it might not be Woody, but we all knew it was. Especially because he was never seen again. Peter and I rhetorically asked the viewing public whether or not we should provide extra food for Winnie and her rapidly growing brood. These days the question would have been literal: 'Shall we save them by putting out mealworms? Or shall we let nature take its course? You decide!' A bowl of mealworms was placed just below the nest hole, so near that all Winnie had to do was lean out and grab a beakful. As the chicks grew, they learnt to do the same. They survived, and the viewers rejoiced just as they had wept for the Kingfishers.

Bird in the Nest was dubbed 'an avian soap opera', and great accolades were bestowed on the BBC by the national press. But I can't help thinking: it's a good job they didn't find out how some of it was done!

...''PAINT ʸ̷ THEM BLACK.

CHAPTER TWELVE

Anthropothingy

Anthropomorphism. Some people can't say it. Some people can't spell it. And some people can't stand it. Especially when the presenter of a wildlife film or TV programme starts giving creatures human voices, thoughts, opinions and emotions. I first realised that it was frowned upon by 'serious naturalists' when I attended my very first Wildscreen many, many years ago. The commentary on one of the films involved a slight tinge of the 'Johnny Morrises', which the majority of the audience received with what I could only describe as a collective sneer! I did not condone this derision, as must have become clear from the fact that on my own programmes I have rarely resisted dabbling in the anthropomorphic myself.

Why? Because it is challenging – one might call it acting – fun to do and, hopefully, to hear. It may simply be diverting, rather like that fanciful question: 'If you were an animal what would you be?', or it might help to illuminate animal behaviour. Watching Black Grouse on a lek, I found myself giving them dialogue like a couple of hard lads taunting each other, hoping to impress the girls by their bravura, while never actually coming to blows. 'Right mate, you want some do you?' 'Think you're well 'ard don't ya?' Anticipating any accusations of trivialisation, my producer – bless him – provided the perfect defence, by confirming that such a 'ritual' stand-off was exactly what the cock grouse were doing. What's more, to add to the anthropomorphic accuracy, a couple of disinterested hens stood at the side muttering: 'I don't fancy yours much!' The only complaint I got was that, though the lek was in Scotland, I gave them all cockney accents.

The lads and lasses at a club could validly be compared with what happens at a Black Grouse lek – and vice versa – and there are a few more basic urges, needs and experiences shared by both humans and animals, such as hunger, starvation, pain, eating, sleeping and sex. However, it is attributing subtler human emotions and characteristics to wildlife, such as jealousy, nostalgia, depression or happiness, that is usually deemed 'dangerous' by scientists. 'Dangerous' because it may well be wrong or at least not provably right!

Where anthropomorphism really comes into its own is when the words and thoughts are being put into the heads, mouths or beaks of animals in fiction. How authentic they are is the author's decision. It is accepted that *The Wind in the Willows* celebrates Kenneth Grahame's love of the river and its wildlife, but don't look to it as a compendium of accurate animal behaviour! Badger lives alone, real badgers live in groups. Moley potters around in daylight, real moles are strictly nocturnal. Ratty is clearly a Water Vole, and toads are slow, secretive and almost silent. No wild creature rows a boat or drives a vintage car. None of them talk. Grahame's creativity and characterisation were inspired by observing his fellow men, not just wildlife.

The fact is that animals and humans are a formidable combination. From fables to films, they provide the looks, we provide the words! A few of us provide the talent to draw, paint or animate. Consider the number of cartoons – full length and 'shorts' – that feature eloquent animals as the principal characters who, by the way, effortlessly upstage the humans. Is there anybody who considers Mowgli to be the star of *The Jungle Book*? And can you imagine anyone else – animal or human – performing 'Bear

Necessities' better than Baloo? I happily admit that few moments delight me more than when a cartoon animal character bursts into song. Even better if they dance, and better still if they are joined by a chorus. Surely we would all echo Dr Dolittle: 'If I could talk to the animals… And they could talk to me.' Except I would change that to 'sing'!

I believe that many of the greatest works of art – or entertainment? – are what I would call 'animated anthropomorphism' (though I might not be able to say it after a couple of double Scotches). Wild creatures may be fascinating and photogenic but, let's face it, they are not particularly creative! They may make us laugh and go 'aw', but they don't intend to, and – as far as we know – they have no imagination. I'll own up, I prefer my rabbits to tap dance and play the banjo (though I reckon that Bugs Bunny is really a hare). I am happy when my bluebirds harmonise on 'Zip-a-dee-doo-dah', and when I saw my first real Roadrunner and it didn't go 'beep beep', I felt like complaining to the Creator.

However, let me be clear, I am not giving up wildlife and, if any creature is feeling under-appreciated, let me remind us all of one thing. Without animals, there would be nothing to be anthropomorphic about.

Indeed, there would probably have been no human creativity at all. No music, dance, art, literature, drama, animation, nor even any high definition or 3D! In all things, man was surely inspired by nature. There was nothing else.

CHAPTER THIRTEEN

I Know That Tune

Everyone knows that the playback speed of recorded sound makes a difference to its pitch. Fast equals high pitch, slow equals low. Mind you, it is not so easy to demonstrate on a CD or an MP3. It was much easier with vinyl. Play a 45rpm at 78rpm and it sounded like Pinky or Perky. Play it at 33rpm and it became the voice of God. Is it just a bit of aural fun, or does it have deeper implications?

A couple of years ago, I visited the studios of Andy Sheppard, a world-class jazz saxophone player, who is also renowned for incorporating natural sounds in his music. He told me that his initial fascination was born of irritation. He had been playing at a club in Germany, and such is a jazz musician's nocturnal schedule, he finally got to bed as dawn was breaking and the birds were beginning to sing, including a Blackbird that was so loud it kept Andy awake. However, such was the loveliness of the song, that instead of cursing it he recorded it, which was such a relaxing process that he nodded off.

On waking many hours later, Andy reached out of bed and clicked on his tape recorder. What he heard literally scared him to death. Instead of the mellifluous melody of a Blackbird, his earphones were filled with a low rumbling roar, 'like dinosaurs in the movies!' He didn't recall recording the soundtrack of *Jurassic Park*. What he'd done was accidentally playback the Blackbird at a much slower speed, which transformed it into a *T. rex*! He increased the speed – not a huge amount – and the dinosaur turned into a whale. A little faster again, and it became a dolphin, until – back at normal speed – it reverted into a Blackbird.

As Andy altered the speed and pitch, I listened with my eyes closed. Every sound was exactly as he'd said. Finally, I asked him to speed up a recording of actual whale song. It sounded like a Blackbird!

I am not going to attempt any scientific theory or analysis of natural sounds, what they mean, why they are as they are, and whether they are random or rational. For that I refer you to *The Great Animal Orchestra* by Bernie Krause. Krause often refers to the work of British sound recordist Chris Watson. I have worked with Chris for many years and have heard many extraordinary things 'before my very ears'.

For example, the day he turned me into a Wren. I have the figure – small and dumpy – but what about the voice? A Wren's song is not long, but it is very fast, packed with notes and incorporating a characteristic trill. There was no way I could whistle or sing it. Then Chris slowed it down. What amazed me was that many of the notes swooped, whooped and bent, more in the manner of a dolphin or a gibbon. What to our ears was a single note was in fact several. The trill – unsingable for a human – became a slow-paced *tuk katuk katuk katuk*, which I reckoned I could get my larynx around. I prepared to sing like a Wren.

For half an hour, I listened, learnt and practised. Then Chris recorded me doing my slow-speed Wren impression. He played it back and I sounded somewhere between a scat singer and a human beatbox. Then, the moment of truth, to play it back at Wren speed. It became faster and higher-pitched. You only have my word for it, but it wasn't half bad! I was so confident, I perched on a gatepost, miming to the recording. At least one Wren sang back, but we drew the line at mating.

CHAPTER FOURTEEN

Don't Look Now

So there I was, nibbling my croissant, when in storms this enormous American woman. 'Mr Oddie, Mr Oddie! The swans are attacking the Canada Geese!' I was of course taken aback. It's not often I meet anyone feeling sorry for Canada Geese. Added to which, what did she want me to do? 'You've got to stop them!' Did she seriously want me to go swan wrestling? Wasn't she aware of the folklore? 'They can break a man's arm, you know.' Not that I have ever heard of one that did. Nevertheless, I bet they could make mincemeat of a Canada Goose! But I didn't tell the lady that. Instead, I resorted to euphemisms.

I explained that 'Mute Swans are very "territorial", as well as "protective" and "faithful". All admirable qualities, I think you'll agree.' She didn't. 'But they are killing the Canadas!' I countered that the appropriate word was not 'killing', but 'deterring'. 'They are just trying to make the geese go away by…'

'By killing them!' I was not winning. Clearly I would have to resort to the adjective that will brook no censure. 'Madam, what those swans are doing is entirely *natural*.' For a moment, she was silent, no doubt unable to resist her reverence for the blessed 'N' word. Her next pronouncement was not what I expected:

'Well, it may be natural, but I don't want to see it!'

'So don't look!' I suggested.

As she stomped out of the café, the thought struck me: I bet she doesn't watch many wildlife programmes!

Most of what wildlife programme-makers call 'animal behaviour', in a human context would be '*mis*behaviour'. Such content in a drama is preceded by a warning. (Or is it a promise?) 'The following programme contains scenes of a sexual nature, violence and bad language from the start.' The same ingredients in a wildlife programme are just what the audience expects to see, and certainly what the production team loves working on. A wildlife cameraman would kill for a kill, an editor loves cutting a chase sequence, the sound recordist revels in capturing every roar, and the director can't wait to add some Barry White to the soundtrack for mating hippos. The final cut – the broadcast version – is approved by the producer, or someone even higher, so if viewers disapprove, that's who to complain to!

But you can't edit a live programme. I recall several times on *Springwatch* when there was adverse audience reaction. The pair of House Sparrows that was guilty of exhibitionist coupling; the Blue Tit that brandished the corpse of its dead chick, before ejecting it from the nestbox; and the famished adolescent Barn Owl who staved off starvation only by gobbling up his baby brother. Yes, there were some complaints, but it was nobody's 'fault'. The show was live. We didn't know what was coming. But if we *had* known, would they have been shown? I suspect they would. But there was one that definitely wasn't.

It was on *Wild in Your Garden*, live, from Bristol. There were cameramen everywhere, secreted behind bins and fences, and in sheds and hides. One of them was Dave (not his real name). It was only when I saw him in the supper queue that I remembered he'd been staked out near a birdtable all day. Obviously, the control room had completely forgotten he was there! 'It's a pity,' he grumbled, 'because I got some great Sparrowhawk action.' He invited me to watch a playback. It started with the hawk perched on a fence. Then it took off. Dave followed its every twist and swoop until it grabbed a Starling in midair. It then flapped off to a fence post and – holding the Starling down with one foot – and gripping its frantically flailing wings with the other, it proceeded to rip at the Starling's chest with a bill like a meat hook, and began eating it alive!

What did that lady say? 'It might be natural, but I don't want to see it.' Nobody did.

INFINITE VARIETY

One ... two ... three - Are they Starlings or Passenger Pigeons?

CHAPTER FIFTEEN

Out for the Count

'The hobby that dare not speak its name.'

Well, that's how it used to be. By the time I was seven, I knew I was a birdwatcher. I didn't admit it till I was 10. The response of my peers was puzzlement, derision and mockery. 'Birdwatching? How soppy! Why can't you go scrumping apples and pulling girls' pigtails like us normal schoolboys?' Adults were just as indifferent, but men could rarely resist coming out with that most tedious of 'bird jokes': 'Oh yes. I'm a bit of a birdwatcher too! Two-legged kind, eh? Eh?' I endured that several hundred times, before I finally discovered the deserved riposte, which is: 'All birds have two legs. Unless they've been in an accident and lost one, in which case it's very distasteful to laugh at crippled creatures.'

The 'I'm a bit of a birdwatcher too' quip is still going pathetically strong, but the joyous truth these days is that many people *are*. 'What, the feathered kind?' Yes. Indeed, things have changed so much since I were a lad that, instead of being an esoteric minority activity, birdwatching is arguably the fastest-growing leisure pursuit in the world. Well, that's what I read in the business section of an American Airlines in-flight magazine about five years ago. It has probably been overtaken since by ballroom dancing and tweeting, but nevertheless it is undeniable that birdwatchers are no longer alone. We are out – outdoors that is – and proud. No longer are little lads and lasses teased about their hobby. Parents encourage them. A lot of them join in.

However, birdwatchers are not all unified as one harmonious band, but that is no bad thing. One of the delights and allures of birds is that they can be enjoyed in so many ways. Some people draw and paint them. Others photograph and film them. Some record their songs. Others 'twitch'. By the way – press and media please note – 'twitcher' is not simply a synonym for 'birdwatcher'. In the same way that a sprinter is an athlete, but an athlete is not necessarily a sprinter, a twitcher is a birdwatcher, but a birdwatcher is not necessarily a twitcher. Twitching is the often rather frantic pursuit of rare birds. We've all been on an occasional twitch, but a serious, knowledgeable birdwatcher who is not obsessed with his or her 'list' would prefer to be called 'a birder'. I am a birder.

I am not a 'bird spotter', an expression that belongs in pre-War Boy Scout manuals and I-Spy books. Nor would I claim to be an 'ornithologist', a title which implies scientific knowledge, a capacity for protracted study, an understanding of graphs, figures and statistics, and possibly a doctorate. Finally, at the opposite – but not bottom – end of the birdwatcher's league are people who put out bird food in their gardens, may not even be able to identify all the species, but simply enjoy having them there. Let's just call them bird lovers. Actually, we are all bird lovers aren't we? Birdwatchers, twitchers, ornithologists, birders, even bird spotters (if they are not extinct), we need you all.

At various times of the year, the RSPB, the BTO, the Wildlife Trusts and others organise surveys and events which you can take part in whatever you call yourself! Visit the websites for full details, including help with identification.

Facts, figures and fun.

This piece helped to publicise the RSPB's annual Big Garden Birdwatch.

'SCILLY? I should say I am.
I'm supposed to be in Argentina!!'

CHAPTER SIXTEEN

Blowing in the Wind

'Twitchers flock to see rare bird!' So says the headline above a
photo of a couple of hundred bearded blokes with binoculars.
But what actually constitutes rarity? Well, in this context we are
not talking 'endangered' (apart from being trampled by twitchers)
nor does it refer to a scarce breeding species. The rare bird that
hits the headlines and attracts the crowds is usually on its own,
and probably confused. A rare bird is a lost bird. Alternative
names confirm just that: an 'accidental', a 'vagrant', a 'drift
migrant'. That one sounds almost romantic, but it isn't. A bird's
migratory journey is a risky enough business, without wandering
off-course and ending up where it didn't mean to go. Not
surprisingly, it mainly happens to long-distance migrants. The
ones that boggle us by the distances they fly and the routes they
take, across oceans, deserts, mountains, forests and cities. Why do
they get lost? Sometimes it is a malfunction of their navigation

system. A dodgy satnav. Mainly, it is the effect of extreme weather. Sometimes extremely *good* weather.

In spring, a migrant flying north may get literally carried away by the ease and joy of soaring in clear blue skies on a warm southerly breeze and unwittingly overshoot its intended destination. A warbler that meant to nest in France may end up in Shetland. It won't find a mate. It won't find its way back either. It is lost, it is rare, it may well get twitched.

In autumn, it is most likely to be strong winds that are the problem. Migrants get blown off-course. Powerful air streams from the east, from Europe and beyond may transport birds from as far away as central Russia or Siberia. Birdwatchers call these birds 'sibes'.

But most of our wind comes from the west, sometimes originating in America and crossing the Atlantic, heading for the UK. On 6 September, I was heading for the Isles of Scilly, off Cornwall. At the same time, racing north-east off the coast of North Carolina, was Hurricane Irene, or was it Kate? Or Katia? I don't remember her name, but she was a fast lady. In not much over a day she swept across 'the pond', expending so much energy that she was demoted to a 'tropical storm', and then veered north to give the Hebrides and western Scotland a good lashing and a gigantic cold shower.

In Scilly, we only felt Katia's tail-end, but that was frisky enough to make my walking against the wind far more authentic than anything Marcel Marceau ever achieved. I headed for calm in the lee of a hill, suspecting that any sensible birds would do the same. I felt barely a breeze as I leant on a five-bar gate and scanned the field in front of me. It was a grassy field. Not long grass, but not very short either. Bisecting it was what looked like a wide bare earth path, which I later discovered was the aftermath of recent pipe burying. The scar was sandy, with a few pebbles and a shallow puddle. 'Wheatear habitat,' I predicted as I scanned. But there were no wheatears. 'OK, then, wagtails.' Sure enough, a White Wagtail trotted out and duly wagged its tail. 'And, what is that?' A little bundle of pearly-edged feathers. Asleep? Exhausted, more like. A Buff-breasted Sandpiper. Just flown in – or blown in – from America. Or rather from Arctic Canada. That is where Buff-breasts breed. Most of them migrate south to Argentina down the

Great Plains flyway, but most years a few reach Britain and Ireland, and Scilly.

As this fragile little traveller sighted the islands it must have sought out somewhere it felt comfortable, somewhere that reminded it of home, a tiny patch of surrogate tundra, a scratchy path scoured by the local pipe-layer, and a puddle just like the ones left by melting snow. OK, not exactly the Yukon, nevertheless comfortingly familiar. If only it had carried on for another mile or two to the island of St Mary's and checked out the airport, it would have found lashings of close-mown grass and another seven Buff-breasted Sandpipers! Next day, it joined them. Eight Buff-breasts together! That's not a vagrant, it's a flock!

Which makes me wonder, do they really all get blown over, and then find each other by luck? Or do they mean to come the transatlantic route, having prearranged a rendezvous? Great Plains? Boring! See you in Scilly.

I'm still wearing a flippin' aerial..

call me old fashioned, but I prefer the good old Aluminium ring..

CHAPTER SEVENTEEN

Puffin Billy

Back in the 1990s, an American friend and his wife came over from New York to spend Christmas in Britain. In early December, he rang me and announced: 'We have decided to give ourselves an early Christmas present. We want to see a Puffin. So, your present to us is to tell us where to go, as it were (some Americans *do* do irony). Can you do that?' 'No,' I replied firmly. He was understandably taken aback. Was divulging the whereabouts of Puffins a threat to national security perhaps? He confessed he'd been doing some research. 'What about Lundy island? *Lundi* means Puffin doesn't it?'

'Yes, but you won't see any there.'

'Shetland?'

'No.'

'The Fern Islands?'

'Farne Islands. Best place in Britain to get really close to seabirds.'

'So can't we go there?'

'You can, but you won't see any Puffins. Not at Christmas. But if you can stick around till Easter…' At which point, he figured it out. 'Ah, so Puffins breed in Britain, but they don't winter there.'

'You got it.'

'So where do they winter?'

'I don't know. Nobody knows. Presumably out in the ocean. Probably in the Atlantic.'

'Only probably?'

'We are not even sure about that. The truth is we simply have no idea where Puffins – and other seabirds – go in winter. Not that we haven't been trying to find out.'

Flashback to 1957. It is nearly Easter, and the seabirds are returning to the Farne Islands. Guillemots are gathering, lining up on the ledges like fluffy toys on rocky shelves. Razorbills cluster in crannies where they think they can't be seen. There are Puffins everywhere. Flying on wings so rapid that they blur, and zipping past me like miniature missiles, before crash-landing with less control than a manic schoolboy tumbling into the long jump pit. Like, for example, myself, in my mid-teens, 'intermediate' school athletics champion and temporary member of a Puffin-ringing expedition from Monks' House Bird Observatory on the Northumberland coast. In charge was a man with a figure like Mr Pickwick and a chuckle like Tommy Cooper, one of the greatest and most charming naturalists, artists and mentors a budding birder could wish to have. Dr Eric Ennion. They don't make 'em like that any more.

Dr E. led us nimbly over the spongy turf of Inner Farne, through what one might have assumed was an extensive rabbit warren, but was actually the Puffins' Underground City, with each subterranean apartment as snug and safe as a fall–out shelter, unless the booted foot – of say, a schoolboy like me – accidentally crashed through its grassy roof. What cruel irony if a bird that had survived six or seven months being buffeted on stormy oceans had found his way back to the very same burrow he had occupied last summer, and was now sitting there waiting for his faithful lady love to join him, paternal instincts trembling and hormones rising, when suddenly 'splat' – he is flattened by a boot from above, as unceremoniously as by Monty Python's giant foot.

Fortunately, the first hole was unoccupied, but my forfeit was that Dr Ennion appointed me as principal Puffin catcher. I was issued with a large pair of thick leather motorcycling gauntlets, which suggested that Puffins might not be as sweet and docile as they looked. Especially if they were relishing the arrival of a sexy female Puffin, but instead were molested by the leather-clad fingers of a nervous schoolboy. Believe me, it is terrifying sticking your hand into a pitch dark tunnel, not knowing whether or not there is something alive in there. It is scary if there is nothing, and even scarier if there is. You will soon know if the burrow is occupied, because the Puffin will try to pull you down there with it!

You now have two choices: you can let go, and apologise to both the Puffin and to your now derisive fellow Puffineers, or you can grab the bird with one hand and try to wrestle it to the surface, where you can use your other hand to grab its beak, which could surely snip off a finger as neatly as a pair of secateurs severing a twig. Thus deprived of its most lethal weapon, the bird appears to accept its fate and seems calm, content and even curious as you flick the gauntlet from your free hand so you can rummage in your shoulder bag for your notebook, ringing pliers and, of course, rings. You even risk relaxing your grip on the rainbow-coloured finger lopper. Such a pretty beak! And so ingeniously capable of holding more than a dozen slippery sandeels. Surely this Puffin will not peck me. Indeed it won't. But it will lacerate your wrists and forearms with its needle-sharp little claws.

It was easy to tell which of us had been on Puffin Posse duty. We looked like a bunch of extras from *True Blood*. Nevertheless, we bore our scars with pride. After all, we were contributing to science. Each bird was fitted with a lightweight metal ring inscribed with a number and the request 'Inform British Museum'. This was not so that the curators could come and recover their lost exhibit; it was an instruction to whoever found what was left of it. Most so-called 'recoveries' came from decidedly ex-Puffins: mainly tideline corpses, murdered by a Great Skua or a Great Black-backed Gull, choked by an oil spill, poisoned by pollution, strangled by a fishing net, or even – just a few – finally succumbing to old age.

Puffins can live for 35 years or more. That was something we had learnt from ringing, which also taught us that Puffins are faithful both to nest site – the very same burrow if it is available – and also to their mate. We have also compiled all kinds of data about what is often nominated as Britain's favourite bird, and which is undeniably fascinating and photogenic, and seems as relentlessly addicted to funny walks and pratfalls as Charlie Chaplin. But Puffins also have a dark side. Literally. They spend an awful lot of time underground, but – thanks to such up-to-date technology as endoscope cameras and minuscule microphones –we know a lot about their private life. However, until recently, there was still one thing we didn't know – where do they go in winter?

Fast-forward to 2013. I am on the Island of Skomer, off Pembrokeshire, South Wales. It is Easter, early spring. It's Puffin Time. Again I am in the presence of authority, but it is not a warden and his team of leaden-footed schoolboys, this time it is a revered scientist and his young French female assistant, whose footwork is as delicate as a ballerina's. A change for the better. There is another change, today's Puffins do not suffer the indignity of being dragged out of their burrows by hand. Instead, they are yanked out by foot, with a sort of miniature walking stick. Or they catch themselves in a small almost invisible 'mist net', from which they are disentangled by the scientist, or his lovely assistant, so deftly and rapidly that they barely have time to wonder what's happening.

Then comes the biggest change of all. The temporarily captive bird is not merely fitted with a ring on its leg. In addition, attached to the ring is what looks like a miniature radio. I assumed that this was some kind of tiny transmitter which would send signals back from wherever the Puffin ventured, but I was told that it was more like a midget computer. 'A sort of Puffin satnav?' I suggested.

'No,' said the scientist. 'A satnav tells you how to get somewhere.'

'Allegedly,' I interjected.

'While this device tells you where you have been', continued the scientist.

'Or rather where the Puffin's been,' I commented, sensing an impending historic revelation. 'So, does this mean we now know where Puffins go in winter?' In my head, I heard accelerating chimes building the tension. 'So what's the answer? Is it a yes or a no?'

'Well, Bill, it is… a… yes!' Blimey, cue audience applause! But hang on, this is a scientist talking. Scientists never completely commit. I bet there'll be an 'on the other hand', or a 'mind you', or – at the very least – a 'but'. Indeed there was a 'but', but it was a pretty incredible 'but'.

'We now know some of the places they go in winter, *but* they don't all go to the same place. For example, we have data that proves that some Skomer Puffins winter mainly off Portugal, while others winter off Newfoundland.'

'Birds from the same colony winter in different places?'

'Exactly. In fact, we had two birds in adjacent burrows. One went to Portugal, while next door went to Newfoundland.'

Now, I was full of questions.

'Do they go to the same place every year? Do male and female go to the same place? Will they meet up with Farne Island Puffins? And come to think of it… why? Why?!'

The answer was inevitable: 'We don't know. Yet!'

That evening I emailed my friend in New York. 'Hi Harvey, remember you wanted to see Puffins for Christmas and you were going to come over to Britain? Well, if only we'd known: you only had to go to Newfoundland!' He responded immediately: 'Christmas in Newfoundland! You gotta be kidding me! No way!'

'OK,' I replied, 'how about Portugal?' I attached a link to 'Winter Breaks in the Algarve'. The brochure had pictures of girls in bikinis, bottles of Mateus rosé, sardines on toast, and even a pair of White Storks, but no Puffins. Somebody should tell the tourist board. Harvey still hasn't seen one.

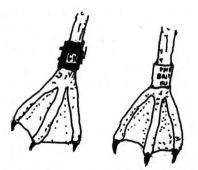

WHY NOT MIX & MATCH?

BIG GAME WATCHING
FROM HOT AIR BALLOON

CHAPTER EIGHTEEN

Flying Tonight

You know when tourists float across the African savanna looking down on the wildlife from the basket of a hot-air balloon? It has always bothered me. Not that I have had personal experience. The only balloon flight I have ever taken was over Loch Lomond in Scotland but, as it turned out, I was pretty bothered by that one too. It was both scary and farcical. The wind was very light. We took off vertically upwards, drifted slowly out over the water, and then began plummeting vertically downwards, seemingly destined to pitch in the drink. There were quips about being eaten by salmon and maybe even beavers (surely they have been reintroduced up there?). Such jests were lost on me. I can't swim.

Fortunately, our pilot (they do it by willpower!) managed to steer us back over land at the last minute, where we plonked unceremoniously down in a field so glutinously boggy that a local farmer had to be summoned to pull us out with his tractor. However, no sooner had he attached a rope from his vehicle to the basket than the balloon began to rise again, so abruptly that it lifted the tractor clean off the ground, with the farmer still sitting in the driving seat! It was a scene worthy of a Buster Keaton movie (or dare I say *The Goodies*?) but became less laughable when we realised that the dangling tractor, the farmer, the balloon, the basket and us were now being swept directly towards an electricity pylon and power lines. Happily, the breeze dropped just enough for the ever-increasing crowd from the village to stop laughing, slurp across the bog, grab hold of the tractor and pull us all back to safety.

But what has this to do with wildlife, apart from the fact that we were filming for the Natural History Unit (so much for health and safety!)? The point is this: while we were noiselessly floating over the farm fields, the animals below seemed to barely notice us. However, when the balloon went for a 'burn', horses, cows and sheep scattered and panicked as if they feared imminent attack from a giant winged predator. A balloon burn emits a roar that a *T. rex* would be proud of. Of course, the wildlife of the Serengeti and the Masai Mara is well used to roaring sounds, so maybe the balloon burns don't bother them, especially since hopefully Kenyan balloons are less prone to plummeting than our Scottish version and are therefore considered less of a threat. Nevertheless, I am still sufficiently bothered by the African balloon safari ride to have never taken one.

I have, however, had a Kenyan aerial experience that was surely much more memorable. I was taking part in a 48-hour sponsored bird race. Our challenge was to record as many species as possible in two days. All modes of transport were allowed and, as darkness fell on the first evening, four of us crammed into a tiny four-seater aircraft (plus one more for the pilot) and took off for the coast where we would search for seabirds at dawn the next day.

We were all pretty exhausted, and within 10 minutes most of us were asleep. Then suddenly we were startled from our slumbers by an almost deafening crack of thunder. Seconds later, the cabin and the sky around us were illuminated by sheet lightning, followed by another gargantuan explosion, and the sort of strobe lighting you are warned not to look at in nightclubs for fear it might trigger an epileptic fit. At the same time, the plane was rattling and rearing as if it were in the fist of King Kong. It was both terrifying and thrilling. People pay good money for this sort of ride at Disney World or Universal Studios. All it lacked was a computer-generated dragon to loom up in the windscreen.

Suddenly, there it was. Not a dragon. A bird. A big bird. For a few seconds, it flailed its raggedy wings as it nearly crashed into the windscreen. Then it veered away in a final flash of lightning.

'What was that?' I yelled. One of our Kenyan team members replied confidently: 'Crowned Eagle.'

'Have we had Crowned?' I asked.

'No. It's a new one!'

A cheer went up. The plane went down. Then steadied, and headed into the storm, and on to the Kenyan coast.

Balloons? They're for kids!

CAPPER ? CRAPPER MORE LIKE !

CHAPTER NINETEEN

The Call of Nature

A bogey bird is a bird you haven't seen but should have. A bogey bird may not be rare but it is elusive. For many years, my bogey bird was Capercaillie – the male is as big as a turkey, makes an unmistakable sound and its location is often well known or even signposted.

Such was the case in the Spey Valley in Scotland when Stephen Moss and I were working on an early episode of *Birding with Bill Oddie*. We endured a six-hour, decidedly unmagical mystery tour of the forest trails hoping for at least a glimpse of a Capper, which was 'definitely here somewhere'.

We found a feather and a small pile of probable poo, which was later reidentified as 'dog' by a man from the RSPB, who declared himself 'happy that we didn't see any Cappers, because that meant they were safe in the forest!'. We found it hard to share his happiness. Fortunately, another man from the RSPB had told us that if we had trouble – if! – there were two or three Capper cocks seen regularly near the Osprey Visitor Centre at Loch Garten.

'They are not actually visible from here,' explained the warden, as we poked telescopes and telephoto lenses through the viewing slots. 'But we have got a CCTV camera on the edge of the wood that's giving us great pictures.' To prove it, he switched on what I had assumed was a telly. Two male Cappers strutted across the screen and squared up to each other, like mythical creatures about to do battle. 'Is this a video?' I asked. 'No, no it's live. *Now*.' he emphasised proudly. 'They are only about 50 metres away, but they're behind the trees. You won't see them.'

'But I already have!' I countered. 'OK, they are on a screen, but they are live! So does that count?' I am sure the warden wanted me to 'lay my bogey', as it were, but rules is rules. 'You can't tick a bird on the telly. Unless you keep a telly list.'

'Which many birders do,' I reminded him. 'Maybe I should start a CCTV list?' But as if in protest, the screen went blank and the birds disappeared behind a snowstorm of interference. The picture returned, but they didn't.

More Capperless years went by, during which I clung to the consolation that one day we would return to Scotland and try again, but Stephen and I didn't like repeating ourselves. What we did enjoy was going somewhere different, for example, Sweden. We weren't even making a programme, but had been invited to witness and eulogise about the enormous spring gathering of cranes, of which the people are justly proud, and will be even prouder if the experience becomes a world-famous tourist attraction. It has all the ingredients: the birds look good and sound good, they are enormous, in huge numbers, spectacular as a flock and entertaining as family groups or in pairs, and they dance. Instant gratification guaranteed. Just what tourists need.

Stephen and I, however, had negotiated something a little more challenging. 'Have you had enough?' asked our Swedish host. 'We need to get you into the forest.'

The light was verging on crepuscular as we veered off the road and clattered along an ever narrowing forest track. Then we stopped. 'OK, you get out now. You get in the hide, quickly. I need to leave before the birds see us or they will not come. I shall be back in the morning. Maybe 10 o'clock. By then you will have seen the Capercaillies.' As he revved into a three-point turn he muttered something inaudible. Was it 'good luck'? Or 'fat chance'? The car's engine churred into the distance like a giant Nightjar, leaving us engulfed in a forest that was getting blacker every minute. The thick carpet of pine needles suffocated every sound. It was as silent as a graveyard. We shuffled towards our coffin.

The hide was neither cosy nor comfy. It was basically a large box with a narrow viewing slit at the front, and sackcloth curtains at the back, as the entrance and exit. We unrolled our sleeping bags, no doubt both deducing that a modicum of physical intimacy would be mathematically unavoidable. To minimise the risk, we constructed a low wall between the bags with our boots and rucksacks. Before long, darkness enveloped everything and eventually – after a few minutes of inevitable blokish banter – we both fell asleep.

We were woken not by the imperceptible brightening of the sky, but by a soft 'chucking' sound, not unlike water being poured from a bottle. We knew what it was. Every birder knows, whether they have heard it or not. The 'song' of the Capercaillie is one of the most surprising and comical songs in the bird world. The bottle-pouring sound isn't just repeated monotonously, it rises in speed and pitch and punctuates its climax with a resounding 'pop', similar to a champagne cork or a finger pulled out of a cheek. It would be silly enough if it were made by a small bird, but coming from an enormous plump Pickwickian creature it is as hilarious as it is unexpected.

It is not difficult to impersonate, so I did. Another bird answered. It wasn't far away. I contorted myself and ricked my neck peering out of the slot. My eyes climbed up a still unlit tree trunk. There – 9 or 10 metres up – hunched on a horizontal branch was my first unambiguous, in the flesh, not on a screen, male Capercaillie. At that moment, it was just a huge black ragged silhouette, but it wouldn't be long before it flopped down to the forest floor and engaged in some ritual sparring and popping with any other males in the area. All we had to do was to stay in our hide, keep still and quiet, and wait.

At which point, Stephen whispered in the sort of tone that normally indicates ensuing panic: 'Bill, I need to go!' He avoided my incredulous stare by crawling towards the exit. I verbally dragged him back. 'You can't!'

'But I need to.'

I was not sympathetic. 'Look, we've been in here – what? – 10 hours! We've only seen a silhouette. If you go outside, it'll be off! And it won't come back.' I could see that he was distressed. 'Just pee in the corner. It'll just soak in. I'll move my boots.' But he didn't move.

'That won't work,' he winced.

'Why not?'

'Because…' His hesitation spoke volumes. Talk about mixed emotions: annoyance, sympathy, confusion and a little bit of laughter!

If Stephen ever runs out of ideas for writing books or producing programmes – which he won't – there is a career for him as a commando. How he crawled through the sackcloth, did whatever was required, and crawled back again, I shall never know. I shall never know because I couldn't look for fear of laughing out loud and disturbing the Capper, which was still hunched up on its lofty perch. I was willing it to go back to sleep until Stephen had crawled back by my side. 'Please don't go. Please wait till it's light. Please find a rival and strut around going "pop".' It did. With two more. Which is why I now have to nominate another bogey bird.

Sorry? What do you mean I can't count it 'cos it was Swedish!

CHAPTER TWENTY

Black and White

A friend of mine works for the RSPB. One morning, he answered a call from a lady who asked him: 'I wonder if you could help me. I have just seen a strange bird in my garden.' If you are ever asked to identify a 'strange bird', there are two cardinal rules: first, assume it is a common species. Second, ask what it is doing. In this case, the lady offered that information anyway: 'It is eating the seeds on my birdtable. It's got a very pointy beak.'

'Ah yes,' responded my friend, as if he had already deduced or indeed anticipated what the bird was. 'What colour was it?' he asked. 'Er, sort of pale,' she replied. 'Pale brown? Pale grey?'

'Both really.'

'Buff? Pale buff, OK? And any other colours?'

'Yes, on its head, a bit of red, and I think a bit of black.'

It was time for the third cardinal rule: whatever the bird is, sound excited and share the joy. 'Oh, great,' he said. 'You've got a Goldfinch!' Her response surprised and perturbed him. 'It was definitely *not* a Goldfinch.'

'Is it still there?' he asked.

'I'll have to go and look through the kitchen window.'

There was a pause while she did. 'Yes, still there,' she announced. 'Still on the birdtable. Well, not actually on it. Standing by it. Pecking at the seed.'

Curioser and curioser! 'So, it's standing by the table and reaching up?'

'No, down. It's taller than the table.'

'What?! Heron size?'

'Maybe bigger. But sort of heron shape.'

'But it's definitely not a heron?'

'Of course not. I told you, it has a buffy body and red and black on its head.'

'And it's bigger than a heron. Blimey! It can't be!'

At which moment my friend remembered another cardinal rule: never make assumptions. The bird was not a Goldfinch. It was a crane!

The incident illustrates a couple of popular birdwatching adages: anything can turn up anywhere, and a rare bird is often a lost bird. One of the major factors is the weather, especially strong winds by which seabirds may be whisked inland and unceremoniously dumped somewhere bizarrely incongruous. For example, the Little Auk that made the front page of the *Birmingham Mail* by pitching into the 'Bullring' in the 1950s, when I was an embryo birder and the Bullring was a characterful open-air market, though still not typical Little Auk habitat. Little Auks belong in the far north of the Arctic, not in the English Midlands. They look like miniature penguins, but they can fly, and are prone to winter wandering round the North Sea, from which they may be plucked by easterly gales and end up 'wrecked', which is, by the way, the ornithological term for a bird being blown off-course, not for being sozzled on a Saturday night. Which takes me back to my friend at the RSPB. (No offence, you'll soon see the relevance.)

This time the distressed caller wasn't so much interested in identification as in emergency first aid. 'I have just found a bird lying on my patio. I think it may be injured. I've put it in a shoebox.' My friend applied the relevant rule: don't immediately say it is the RSPCA's problem (even though it is!), show compassion and concern. 'Oh dear, it's still alive is it?'

'It was when I last looked,' she said with no great conviction.

'That's good. In fact, that's excellent,' he added sounding almost excessively effusive. 'There have been a few Little Auk wrecks reported lately.'

'Oh, I don't know any of the birds,' interrupted the caller, 'except Blue Tits.'

'But this bird isn't blue is it?'

'No, it's black and white.'

'Good, good. And quite dumpy?'

'Well, yes. But quite little.'

'Exactly. Fantastic! I can drive over and pick it up, in about an hour.'

'Oh, that's so kind. Should I leave it in the shoebox?'

'Well, what it really needs is to get back to water. Tell you what... Run a cold bath, and put it in there.'

'Should I feed it?'

'Er, if you've got any tins of anchovies or sardines?'

'In tomato sauce?'

'No. I'll bring some fish. I'll be as quick as I can. And thank you *so* much for calling!'

Forty-five minutes later, they were climbing the stairs to the bathroom, discussing the patient's condition. The lady was clearly upset. 'It doesn't seem as lively as it was,' she whispered. My friend slipped into reassuring doctor mode, tinged with that tingle of anticipation every birdwatcher feels when they are on the brink of a close encounter with a rare bird. But as the bathroom door swung open, anticipation turned to disappointment, which turned to horror.

There, floating in the bath, was the bird. Black, white, soggy and obviously totally lifeless. She knew the answer, but she had to ask: 'Is it all right?'

'No. It is not what I hoped – I mean expected – it to be either. It is not actually a Little Auk. It is a Great Spotted Woodpecker!'

'A woodpecker? Shouldn't it be in a tree? Oh, poor little thing.'

'Yes, but it obviously wasn't well when you found it. I might have had to put it out of its misery anyway.'

The lady was not consoled. 'Maybe,' she snapped, 'but not by drowning it!'

SEPARATED AT BIRTH?

CHAPTER TWENTY-ONE

Between the Devil
and the BBC

In 2005 I was involved in a pair of programmes for BBC1 called *The Truth About Killer Dinosaurs*. As befits the grandiose title and the creatures themselves the production was on a pretty large scale. I was on the cover of the *Radio Times*, overacting between the jaws of a huge metallic model of a *T. rex*, every tooth as lethal as a javelin. Most of the show was filmed in an enormous studio that was also used to crash-test cars. We used it to crash-test dinosaurs, for example, one elaborate experiment involved propelling half a *Triceratops* on a motorised trolley straight into a brick wall until its skull shattered and its horns fell off, with a view to judging whether charging head to head with another dinosaur would have had the same effect. It would.

My personal favourite sequence was when we tested the clobbering effectiveness of an *Ankylosaurus*'s segmented club-ended tail by releasing a carefully calculated swipe at a frozen turkey. If you are having trouble envisaging that, think of the tail as a golf club and the turkey as a ball. Or the dinosaur as the equivalent of a medieval knight whacking people's heads off with his mace.

My personal close encounter with a killer was slightly less spectacular since it was achieved by the device of blue – or in this case green – screen, and involved me having to pretend to be terrified by two brooms leant against a kitchen chair, which – by the wonder of computer trickery – would eventually be replaced by an undeniably scary *T. rex*. When I saw the effect I was impressed, though I could barely resist shouting out 'It's not a killer dinosaur, it's a mop!'

Frankly, the technology made for tedious filming, but it was alleviated by gales of laughter, especially from one of our American palaeontologists whose job was to translate my commentary into a language that American viewers could understand! They say that Brits and Americans are divided by a common language. Maybe, but giggling sure brings us together! And believe me, playing 'whack the frozen turkey' is a real ice-breaker (pun slightly intended).

Talking of Americans, further proof of a generous budget and a major personal attraction was that the schedule included three days in Texas! One of the things I love about visiting different American states is that each one has its own clichés. No sooner had we left the airport than we were driving through oilfields, passing diners advertised by giant cowboys saying 'Howdy Pardner', and calling at gas stations where you could fill your tank for the price of a cup of tea. Best of all, the birds were Texan too. High in the glaringly blue sky, the 'buzzards' were circling just like they do in cowboy movies, though in fact they are not buzzards, they are Turkey Vultures. Whirring wings over the roadside meadows were – what else? – meadowlarks, and along the field margins were birds that looked like a cross between a lark and a sparrow. Lark Sparrow? Yep, you got it. Perched on wires and fence posts was a species I last saw in spring 1965 flitting around magnolia blossoms in Louisiana, and one that still gets my vote as one of the world's most elegant birds: Scissor-tailed Flycatcher. Even better, my eye was diverted by a creature scuttling along about 20 metres ahead of us as if daring us to catch up. 'A hare?'

suggested our driver. Nope. A Roadrunner. Just like in the cartoon, except they don't go 'beep beep'!

Pretty soon I could stand no more. Nature called. Our car stopped and I leapt out and disappeared behind a small clump of trees. 'How long will you be?' shouted our producer. 'Half an hour,' I called back, 'maybe a bit longer. Would an hour be OK?'

'Forty minutes. No more.'

It is, of course, not usual to haggle over how long an emergency stop is going to take, but I'm sure he'd realised that I was desperate to seek relief not from my bladder but from my frustration at being in a brand new location and not being able to do a bit of proper birding.

I was patiently stalking a Lark Sparrow – a new bird for me – when I was reminded of the reason we were in Texas. My binoculars followed the bird as it shuffled into what was clearly a completely dry riverbed. An ex-creek, I guess, in Texan. I noticed that what I'd assumed to be pebbles were all shell-shaped. Closer inspection revealed that this was because they *were* shells. Or rather they had been. A very, very long time ago. The more I looked, the more I found. Cockle fossils, mussel fossils, little fossils, big fossils. Very big fossils! You bet.

They call it Dinosaur Valley. There is a river, much wider than a creek, but especially after a dry period, the water can be very shallow or indeed absent. We set up the camera at the top of the bank, I looked down and we recorded my reaction. Wow! There below me, criss-crossing the riverbed, and as clear as if they had been stencilled overnight, were huge footprints. Two very obvious lines, and another area where the pattern was less orderly. We carried on down the slope and onto the shoreline, where we realised that what looked like sand was in fact hard flat rock. I waded into the shallows, and literally followed in the dinosaur's footsteps.

The true size of anything under water is, of course, hard to judge, but now I could measure each print in 'hands' (I needed more than two). Clearly, the producer's notion of me leaping from one print to another wasn't going to happen. An Olympic long jumper wouldn't have made it. Instead, I splashed around a bit and attempted to convey a word picture of what the palaeolithic scene might have looked like. This was obviously a drinking and bathing place. There were clearly different species visiting it, and experts have identified them. Some were relatively small, others were enormous. Some were harmless grazers, others fearsome carnivores, including the killer dinosaurs featured in our programmes.

We left the location astonished by what we had seen and delighted with what we had filmed. Incontrovertible evidence of life on ancient Earth, so different from now, and yet with many similarities to the modern world. Who among us would not be impressed? Quite a few it seems.

As we returned to the valley's main gateway, I veered towards a large white wooden-slatted building, which on the way in I had assumed was an information centre and gift shop. I was looking forward to buying fluffy dinosaurs for my granddaughters and a bag of assorted fossils for my grandson, and for me. However, as I approached the door I realised that it was not a shop; it was a church. The preacher and his congregation, far from celebrating dinosaurs, would be cursing them, if indeed they believed in their existence at all. Even more abhorrent was the concept of 'evolution', especially the suggestion that man himself is descended from 'lower forms', which is considered not merely a fallacy, but an iniquitous falsehood, a heresy and a sin. Such are the convictions and the creed of the 'Creationist' churches. There are an awful lot of them in the States, especially down south.

I have to admit that when you compare the two basic theories of the origins of life on Earth – either that it evolved over millions and millions of years or that God created it in six days – I personally find it hard to believe either of them. But Creationists v Evolutionists isn't just a matter of opinion or amiable rivalry. As you exit under the Dinosaur Valley Archway, the very first building is that church, challenging you to choose between confrontation and salvation. I could almost hear the preacher's voice: 'OK, you jest go ahead and look at them so-called din-ee-saw prints if you like, but after that, you'd better git in church and repent, for you have looked upon a lie! May the Lord forgive your sins.'

Sir David Attenborough told me that he was once on a lecture tour of the US, talking about prehistory and, of course, dinosaurs. Every show was a sell-out success – until he went down South. The hall was full, and the audience weren't actually hostile, but they were less than enthusiastic. When David had finished there wasn't the usual storm of applause. There was a mere trickle. Then everyone filed out in silence. David thanked them and withdrew to the wings where the theatre owner was waiting to escort him from the building, and possibly out of town. The man was uncomfortably silent, so David spoke: 'Er, was that all right? Only it didn't seem to go terribly well... did it?' The theatre owner took a deep breath and said – in that southern drawl that slips so easily from hospitality to menace – 'Folks round here don't care to think about that kind of thing.'

We couldn't possibly do a programme promising killer dinosaurs without featuring velociraptors. Perhaps the phrase 'The Truth About' implied that we were going to mollify – if not obliterate – their fearsome reputation, as established so chillingly in *Jurassic Park*. Well, maybe so. Scientific research has concluded that they were quite small and that they hunted in packs, probably seeking out prey that was already injured or sick. To demonstrate the relatively unthreatening nature and modest stature of *Velociraptor*, my producer had the quaint notion of comparing it to a turkey. Not totally inappropriate, since it is often mooted that birds evolved from dinosaurs. The idea was that I would crouch a little, thus approximating the size of a *Velociraptor*, with the similar-sized turkey standing beside me.

Our assistant producer was sent to procure a performing – or at least docile – turkey. There are Wild Turkeys wandering the woods in Texas, but they tend to betray their wildness by hiding or running away very fast (behaviour that has no doubt evolved as a response to being frequently shot at). The assistant producer phoned a turkey farm. The phone was answered by what sounded like a southern belle.

Farm owner: Hi y'all. How can we help you today?

Assistant producer: Er, we are looking for a turkey.

Owner: Well, mam, you sure come to the right place. Would you be wanting that plucked, or unplucked, or would you be fixin' to kill it youself? You can take 'em dead or alive!

Assistant producer: We want it alive. We want it for a television show.

Owner: A TV show? A show about turkeys! Well I never. You want a whole bunch of 'em? I can get you some real lively ones.

Assistant producer: No, we only want one. And we don't really want it lively.

Owner: And what kinda show is this?

Assistant producer: We're from the BBC.

Owner: The BBC! Oh my Lord! Hey Reuben, The BBC! *Doctor Who*, *Downtown Abbey*, Benny Hill! Oh my, we *love* the BBC. Oh my my. One of our turkeys gonna be on the BBC. Praise the Lord. We are so honoured! Tell me, mam, what kinda show is this?

Assistant producer: It's about dinosaurs.

There was a moment's silence as her voice snapped into menace mode.

Owner: Listen, lady, I don't care who you from. We are not letting one of our turkeys appear on no programme about that e-vo-lution shit! No, mam.

Fortunately, we managed to get a Buddhist turkey flown in from Florida.

PS *The Truth About Killer Dinosaurs* was issued as a BBC DVD in 2005, and may still be available somewhere!

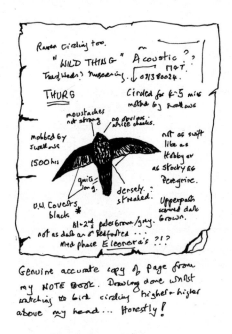

Raven circling too.

" WILD THING " Acoustic ? ?

Thur(Weds) museening. 071380024. MoT.

THURS   Circled for 4~5 mins
mobbed by swallows

moustaches not strong

no obvious white cheeks.

mobbed by swallows

1500 hrs

quite long.

densely streaked.

U.W. Coverts black *

Bl~2nd primaries Brown/grey.

not as dark as o' Redfooted ...
Mid phase Eleonora's ?!?

not as swift like as Hobby or as stocky as Peregrine.

Upperparts scorred dark Brown.

Genuine accurate copy of page from
my NOTE BOOK. Drawing done whilst
watching to bird circling higher + higher
above my head... Honestly!

CHAPTER TWENTY-TWO

One That Got Away

A birder friend of mine, while admitting that he had very little artistic ability, nevertheless reckoned that if he encountered an unfamiliar bird in the field, even the most rudimentary thumbnail sketch was worth more than several pages of notes, at which point he showed me his hasty pencil portrait of an as-yet-unidentified bunting. I commented that it certainly looked more like a thumbnail than a bird, which was only as unkind as it was true! Nevertheless, this certainly has not deterred him from sketching before writing and – for several reasons – I have to agree that that is the best way.

For a start, scribbling notes largely involves looking down at the page, not up at the bird. Indeed, there is a danger that concentrating on meticulous details of supercilia, tertials, primary tips, crown stripes and rumps can be so absorbing that by the time you have finally decided to scope it the bird has flown off when you weren't looking. Mind you, I can testify to the fact that there are some 'creative' twitchers who won't let a little thing like a fleeting or inadequate view of a 'possible' rarity stop them producing a two-page spread of field sketches from all angles and in a variety of poses, quite likely with little arrows indicating the diagnostic features. This, however, is not proof that they actually saw diagnostic details, but only that they know what they are. Whatever the truth, they are convincingly illustrated in their drawings, suitably labelled: 'Tail spread to reveal white outer tail feathers. Showed grey rump clearly on landing. Rufus streaking visible on flanks when bird is perching.' Which, of course, it is doing in the picture. By the way, I do hope you don't think I am insinuating there is such a thing as 'illustrated stringing'. I would prefer to call it 'enhanced field sketches', which as it happens is my personal favourite genre of bird art.

Some people sketch what they see. Others sketch what they want to see. Or perhaps wish they'd seen. I myself belong to the second camp, but only when I fancy doing a 'proper painting'. When faced with a suspected or even certain rarity I am with Mr Thumbnail. I draw – or rather scribble – while still looking at the bird through binoculars or telescope. What I produce is a tad more avian than a thumbnail, but it is barely recognisable as a bird. Ear coverts end up where undertail coverts should be, and the wing (no point in depicting two 'cos they're both the same!) may be completely detached. The overall result looks more like one of those puzzles in kids' comics, where you have a few apparently random lines, but when you join up the little numbers or dots it becomes something recognisable (though probably not a rare bunting).

So, I confess, my field sketches are a mess, but they do their job, which is to record enough detail to identify the bird. Once I have the identification sorted, I may attempt art. In fact, I only ever paint on holiday, so most of the species are Mediterranean rather than British. Golden Orioles, Woodchat Shrikes, Hoopoes, Azure-winged Magpies, Red-necked Nightjars and feral waxbills, from which miscellany you may deduce that I am a regular to southern Portugal. I am so familiar with the birds there that I feel I don't need them to pose. Instead, I set myself up in 'watercolour corner' (other family members paint other things) where I do a fairly rapid pencil sketch of my chosen bird or birds and colour in a few bits. It is all a bit cursory, because I am impatient to get on to the fun part, which I call 'designing the set and providing the props'. I rarely show a bird perched, feeding or doing whatever it is doing in the same context I saw it originally. For example, I saw the Woodchat on a wooden fence. I put it perching on barbed wire, with a few tufts of sheep's wool and a discarded fag packet snared on one rung and a half-eaten lizard on another. I also added a broken wine bottle – Mateus rosé – overgrown by thistles at the foot of the fence post. Some of my pictures look as though they were designed for a 'Take Your Litter Home' campaign. In fact, they often involve me taking other people's litter home. It is not easy to depict a Portuguese ice-cream wrapper from memory. By the end of the holiday, 'watercolour corner' is scattered with more detritus than a teenager's bedroom. I have considered entering it for the Turner Prize. With no due modesty, I admit I am proud enough of my little paintings to not mind people seeing them, or even bidding for them in a charity raffle. However, the same definitely does not apply to my field sketches.

Ironically, I may well have been intimidated by my first 'mentor' – the wondrous Dr E. A. R. (Eric) Ennion who was in charge of Monks' House Bird Observatory back in the 1950s. Many times as a teenager I sat with him on a Northumberland beach gazing out at the Farne Islands, while he dashed off instant drawings on the back of a fag packet, which he usually gave me to keep. Inevitably, alas, I didn't. The back of a fag packet was also the canvas of choice for another legendary field artist, R. A. Richardson, the Prince of Cley. He wasn't really a prince, of course, but he did habitually wear a suit of shining black leather and ride a proud and noble steed. A Harley Davidson I presume. As a teenager, I sat at the feet – or rather peered over the shoulder – of these two talented and incredibly nice men as they illustrated whatever birds we had been discussing or were watching. They were both generous and entertaining people as well as genius artists. If I had to establish a preference, as they say, I think I would have to favour Ennion, whose finished paintings somehow managed to retain the immediacy, movement and life of field sketches, despite his birds having jagged outlines that verged on impressionistic. It's a style that flourishes in the work of John Busby.

So, whether your motive is art or identification, field sketching is a talent to be envied and a skill to be learnt. If nothing else, if you are fortunate enough to find a rarity, a decent sketch, done while the bird was visible, will surely impress those who carry the poisoned chalice of judgement, such as the Rarities Committee. On the other hand, thanks to ever-evolving technology, it is now possible to capture a digital image on just about any implement from a phone to a 'tablet'. Even a camera! So ubiquitous are these devices that some rarities committees have announced that they will no longer accept any claims that don't have photographic evidence. Of course, in most cases, there is. But if there isn't, what about a decent, accurate sketch?

Do you sense a story of string or injustice about to unfold? The date was mid-September, a few years ago. The place: Tresco on the Isles of Scilly. It is early afternoon and it is warm and sunny. I am lounging almost on my back in our cottage garden. Hirundines are circling lazily on the thermals, along with a few gulls and the occasional raptor. One in particular catches my eye and makes me grab my binoculars. It is a falcon. Kestrel? No. Hobby? No. Peregrine? No. Merlin? Definitely not. That accounts for all the species I had seen on the island so far that week. This bird wasn't any of those.

The truth is that I knew what it was but I would need to prove it. I rapidly did a sketch, as it circled higher and higher and then drifted out of sight. As I scribbled a few notes, I found myself muttering: 'Black underwing-coverts. It's the only one.' All that remained was to flick to the falcons in a European field guide where I would surely confirm what I was actually sure of. However – I know it seems a bit arrogant – but I don't bother to take a field guide on a British holiday. Besides, there is usually one among the books in the accommodation, alongside the Ian Rankins and the various Shades of Grey.

However, the only bird book on our shelf was purely British and belonged back in the era of 'I-Spy'. Off I scampered towards the quay, keeping one eye on the sky in case the bird reappeared, while thinking: 'Perhaps I should get one of those new-fangled smartphones.' With my other eye, I spied two island kids kicking a ball around their garden. I assumed they were too young to know much about European raptors, so I asked: 'Is your mum in?' At which moment, mum appeared. On the mainland, she would no doubt have hustled the kids away from the strange man who was suspiciously panting with excitement. Instead, I simply got a typical Scilly greeting: 'Lovely day isn't it?' I agreed effusively, and asked: 'You don't happen to have a bird book do you?'

'Oh, I'm not sure,' she replied. 'I think we have. Do you want to come in and have a look?' That wouldn't happen on the mainland either.

Thirty seconds later, I was flicking through the pages of a relatively recent *Birds of Britain and Europe*. After another 10 seconds I was perusing a plateful of falcons and smiling at the first line of the text: 'The only European falcon with black underwing-coverts.' Eleonora's Falcon. Of course, I knew that, didn't I?

I telephoned the appropriate resident Scilly birder, knowing that he would spread the news. Next morning, I got a call myself. Somebody had reported what 'might have been' my bird over another island. There was also a rumour of an Eleonora's 'somewhere in Cornwall'. To cut a long, rather annoying, story short, in due course I submitted my claim, and a copy of my field sketch and scribbles. I added that I knew the species well from Majorca. Eventually, I got a reply, and a verdict. The letter stated that 'there seems to have been some confusion as to the age of this bird.' I had diagnosed it as a first-year male. It certainly wasn't a totally black adult. After looking at pages of photographs in specialist raptor books, I concluded that it might have been an intermediate morph or a dark female. Eleonora's Falcons notoriously come in various shades! But there is one feature that they all have and other species don't – black underwing-coverts!

My bird was rejected. I was dejected. But not corrected! I don't know what those other people saw, or what they said, but I know what I saw, and what I drew. Mind you, I have occasionally wondered: did those who passed judgement even look at my drawing? And another thing: if it had been drawn by Eric Ennion or Richard Richardson, or Killian Mullarney or Chris Rose, would they have accepted it then? Or would they have demanded a digital photo?

NOISY SCRUB-BIRD - THE WAY YOU'LL NEVER SEE IT!
Hardly worth it, is it? p.s. It is brown.

CHAPTER TWENTY-THREE

Invisible Bird

Some birds are hardly worth seeing. Their looks aren't what make them special. Which in some cases is just as well, since it is almost impossible to get even a fleeting glimpse of them. I rather feel that about Nightingales, and Cetti's or Grasshopper Warblers, and certainly about Quails. Nevertheless, they are all shameless show-offs compared with the Noisy Scrub-bird, an extremely rare Australian species. It is well named, in that its song is so loud that it can carry over a kilometre, and it does indeed live in 'scrub', more specifically in a small area of scrub at the very southern tip of Western Australia. However, it also qualifies for some kind of alternative name such as the 'might as well be invisible scrub bird'. This would also act as a warning to those birders intent on adding it to their list, such as, for example, myself. It must be a dozen or so years ago that I drove down from Perth to Two Peoples Bay with a trio of eminent Aussie 'birdos'. We say 'er', they say 'o'! We all say 'twitching'.

Since these fellas were part of a Save-the-Noisy-Scrub-bird-type project, they knew instantly which sections of the considerable expanse of thick vegetation held territory-holding males. Not that I wouldn't have figured it out for myself, when my ears were serenaded by a burst of birdsong that sounded rather like a Cetti's Warbler using a megaphone. 'Fruity' and 'explosive' would be apt adjectives, and of course 'loud', or indeed 'noisy'. A few seconds later, another one replied that was surely using a microphone and an amplifier. Then another song at even more volume. He had obviously turned his amp up to 11. My Aussie mates were clearly enjoying my slightly bewildered reactions. 'How many of them are there?' I asked. They smiled: 'Just one!'

Noisy Scrub-birds are real little teasers. Their song attracts your attention and lures you into the bush, much as sirens lure sailors onto the rocks. You creep forward, homing in on the dense and shady spot wherein surely lurks the hidden singer. Then there is a slightly longer silence, broken by a burst of song, further away and from a completely different direction. You state the obvious: 'It's moved!' Only to be corrected: 'Not necessarily. They are ventriloquists!'

'Oh. Have they got their dummies?' I quipped.

'You're the dummy, mate! No offence, but you'll never find them by following them. You've got to get them to follow you.' I guessed what was coming next.

Nowadays, it would be an MP3 player or a smartphone. Back then it would have been a portable cassette tape recorder. However, being a bit of a purist, I wasn't totally comfortable with 'tape-luring'. I always had a vision of the bird being really narked when it realised it was being flirted with or challenged by a machine. My compromise was to produce my Audubon bird caller, which is a small device that looks like a little wooden whistle, but is in fact 'played' by twisting it in your fingers so that the friction produces various squeaking noises that supposedly puzzle small birds enough to make them come closer to investigate. It's the equivalent of 'pishing', but without tingly lips. Neither technique is guaranteed to always work, but this scrub-bird found the Audubon squeaker irresistible. It ceased flaunting its ventriloquial skills, and its song got noisier and noisier and closer and closer, until I was convinced that the bird had to be in the middle of a small isolated bush, no more than a metre away. Even the Aussies were cautiously positive. Whispering ensued, and we literally surrounded the bird, so that it was equidistant from four keen-eyed, sharp-eared birders, armed with close-focus binoculars. We waited. Then it went quiet, or rather, it ceased to be noisy. Then it sang again, from what sounded like 100 metres away, but for all we knew it might as well have been under my boot. But when I lifted my foot, it wasn't there.

I have still not seen a Noisy Scrub-bird. Well, actually I did see one released – launched more like! – back into the wild from a 'captive-breeding' aviary. I saw it for barely three seconds, and only in flight, but well enough to confirm that it was yet another little brown bird. Hardly worth seeing? Well, that depends… can I count it?

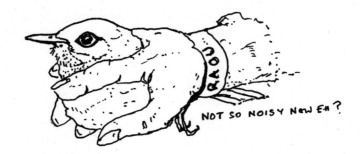

CURIOUSER AND CURIOUSER

CHAPTER TWENTY-FOUR

In the S**t

Back in the 1960s there was nothing I looked forward to more than a day out at a sewage farm. Young people today wouldn't know what a sewage farm was. 'They used to grow sewage? And harvest it?' No, they pumped it into lagoons. 'Lagoons of...?' Quite. 'Didn't it smell?' Oh yes. We always used to check the wind direction before we walked round. The birds loved it. In 1970, Wisbech Sewage Farm was declared the best place for migrant waders in Britain, if not in Europe.

Sewage is, of course, universal. Twenty-nine years ago I did my first proper wildlife series for the BBC. The producer's idea was to show what it was like for a British birder to be plonked down in a totally unfamiliar country. For example, Bill Oddie in Papua New Guinea. 'So, Bill,' he asked me, 'how would you go about finding the best birding places?' My reply would have been the same anywhere in the world: 'I'd ask if there was a local sewage farm.'

As it turned out, there was a beauty, just outside the capital city, Port Moresby. Locals rather poetically called it the 'S**t Pit'. As at all the best sewage farms, there were not only lagoons, but also reedbeds, ditches, damp grassland, hedges and trees, sprinklers and – at this one – a network of neatly trimmed grassy banks you could stroll along, while admiring relaxing ranks of wildfowl, egrets, herons, gulls and terns. Easy birding, and very easy filming. Unlike the rest of the trip, most of which was spent sloshing around in damp and gloomy rainforest, failing to find whatever we were looking for. I still smile at the irony of doing a series enticingly entitled *Oddie in Paradise*, which was mainly shot at the local sewage farm. A shame the producer didn't let me say so! Alas, since then, the S**t Pit has become the haunt of thieves and muggers and declared a no-go area.

However, there are no such dangers or delinquency at what may well be the best and possibly biggest sewage farm in the world, at Werribee in south-east Australia. Not only does it deal with the effluent of more than half of Melbourne, but it is also home to literally tens of thousands of birds, of nearly 300 species, including a colony of highly endangered Orange-bellied Parrots, which, by the way, do not mingle on the mud with the waders and wildfowl, but stick to the more manicured lawns and plantations.

Werribee Water Treatment Works (it sounds like a spa, but it's still a sewage farm!) is a king-size example of what Richard Mabey called 'unofficial countryside'. I'd amend that to 'incidental nature reserves'. Both phrases imply precarious impermanence, and to prove it Wisbech has been 'modernised', as has the nearby Cambridge Sewage Farm, another star venue in times gone by. Most others have gone the same way.

There is, however, one whose state remains a mystery. Perry Oaks Sewage Farm was too close to London's Heathrow Airport to be anything but an ear-shattering day out, but it was worth it. The birds ignored the planes, as did the birdwatchers – including myself – who slipped through, or even over, the security fence and scuttled around under cover of the embankments, occasionally popping up to scan a lagoon, flushing snipe and assorted shanks, plovers and sandpipers. I never did know whether or not Perry Oaks was private, but a terrorist threat to shoot down a British airliner assured that it definitely was. Thus, one of London's birding hotspots became totally inaccessible. It presumably still attracted birds, but no one was allowed to look at them.

Then, as the terrorist alert abated, another threat arose: Terminal 5! I am sure there were lots of objections to Terminal 5, but I doubt anyone pleaded that it would disturb or entirely obliterate Perry Oaks Sewage Farm. The truth is, I don't know if it did or not. Is there still a totally unwatched 'incidental nature reserve' down there? Or did they simply bury the sludge beds under the concrete of Terminal 5? Do you remember the film *Poltergeist* where a development had been built on the site of a cemetery, but 'they only moved the headstones!' thus desecrating the departed, whose spirits wreaked a terrible revenge?

Well, call me crazy, but every time I fly from Terminal 5, I swear I can hear the plaintive calls of Ringed Plover and Ruff, and I begin to feel a powerful force is trying to suck me down, down into a lagoon of... Now that's what I call a horror story.

It's the same with everything these days –
You can never get the flippin' lid off!

CHAPTER TWENTY-FIVE

Jewels in the Dark

I found an old lady in my lampshade last night
Of course she was dead, she'd been lured by the light
But her lace was unsinged, and her smock undefiled,
So I took her downstairs, and I called to my child…

The Old Lady was, of course, a moth. The child was my youngest daughter, Rosie. 'Why do you think it is called an Old Lady?' I asked. 'Because it looks like a lacy frock thingy.'

'A crinoline.'

'Whatever.' After a few more seconds of moth perusal, Rosie and I spoke in unison: 'And this affects me how?' This immortal expression of teenage indifference was first uttered in response to me showing Rosie a fox when she was about 13. She is now 24, and while she has hardly blossomed into a committed naturalist, she is appropriately appreciative of most of the wild things I draw her attention to. Meanwhile, the feigned disdain of 'and this affects me how?' has become a sort of family catchphrase. As indeed has the outraged cry of 'Dad! Oh my God!' indicating that someone has opened the fridge door and discovered that the egg rack's eggs have been replaced with small specimen jars. They may look like moth coffins, but I assure you the occupants are not deceased. They are sleeping, or rather in a torpor. When I release them in the garden their wings will start to shiver and quiver, until they fly off, hopefully avoiding the nimble and intelligent Robin who has learnt to recognise the appearance of my moth tray, moth book and moth jars as the promise of an easy meal.

I am an inveterate garden moth-er. This year it was 25 March when I first set up my trap. It is very basic. A wooden box, an especially bright light, two sloping sheets of clear plastic and – providing shade and warmth for anything that is lured in – a layer of egg boxes. I like to think that this means the moths are not so disorientated in the fridge. March 25th had been a record-breakingly warm day, but the night was chilly, so I wasn't too optimistic. Nevertheless, the morning inspection of the egg boxes did not draw a blank. It produced five moths of three species. Two Common Quakers, two Hebrew Characters and a Brindled Beauty. Add in the Old Lady, and you may deduce one of the reasons I love moths. Those names! Some, simply descriptive: Scalloped Hook-tip, Purple Treble-bar, Pinion-streaked Snout; others more playful: Maiden's Blush, True Lover's Knot; and a few almost fearsome: Death's-head Hawkmoth. All of them are testimony to the assiduousness and imagination of the Victorian naturalists who catalogued and named them.

Get into moths and you instantly become a member of a club. It may be literal – 'moth groups' abound – or it may seem more subversive or even slightly secretive. I first realised this when I filmed an item for *Bill Oddie Goes Wild*. My producer, Alex, had clearly grasped the atmosphere, and was determined to relish it. We convened at dusk and formed a circle round a single lamp while chanting: 'The first rule of Moth Club is you don't talk about Moth Club.' Then each member solemnly intoned their name and origin: 'Jack from Tewkesbury, Timothy from Chipping Norton, Bill from Hampstead', and each one stood by their traps, which incidentally were all home-made and collectively looked like an exhibition of outdoor scrap sculptures. There was a ritual synchronised turning on of mercury vapour lamps, followed by two or three hours of me talking to the camera and the club members quaffing red wine, an activity that continued well into the small hours as we all pored over identification books. Another rule of Moth Club: 'No moth goes unnamed.'

Alex's closing shot through the cottage window was of us crouched over a desk surrounded by wine glasses and empty bottles, all romantically lit by an oil lamp. You can just hear the lady of the house offering a choice of coffee or cocoa, while inebriated voices struggle with tongue-twisters like a Three-humped Prominent or a Triple-spotted Pug. At least one person had fallen asleep. It was one of those experiences that remind me that there is more to watching wildlife than the wildlife. Company, humour and shared enjoyment.

CHAPTER TWENTY-SIX

On the Fairway

Birdies, eagles, albatrosses. Am I talking wildlife or golf? Well, both actually.

The fact is that most naturalists – and birdwatchers in particular – are rather fond of golf courses, especially if they are sited by the sea, which many of them are. It means that many migratory birds' first landfall is on a golf course. The greens and tees may be a bit too velvety, manicured and possibly doused in insecticide, but the short-cropped fairways are much beloved of wheatears, pipits and larks, while warblers and thrushes lurk in ditches and any available scrub or bushes. What's more, landing in the 'rough' may be a nightmare for golfers but it is a joy not only for birds but also for small mammals, wildflowers and attendant insects, especially butterflies. Indeed, there are some golf courses that look as if they have been designed for nature. Some of them have.

A few years ago I was given a guided tour by the environmental manager of a holiday village in Suffolk. He showed me an area destined to become a golf course, but also a nature reserve. Islands of 'rough' had been left undisturbed and – encouraged by a little planting and management – were glowing on that May morning with heath-loving wildflowers, many of which had lain dormant until the construction work had emancipated them. These included some of the common orchids. If you hanker after less common varieties, there are few better sites than Sandwich Bay in Kent, or – to be more specific – the fringes of the Royal St George's Golf Course, sporadically home of the British Open and permanently home of Lizard Orchids.

So, is there a Ryder Cup of nature-friendly courses? Well, I have to admit that my most lavish experience of 'life on the links' – surely the title of a TV programme? – was in the US, at Walt Disney World, in Florida. There is a lot more to the Disney complex than Mickey Mouse, Thunder Mountain and Cinderella's Palace. An area almost the size of an English county is covered by woods and waterways, much appreciated by the usual brazenly tame Florida birds, such as herons, darters and ibises, plus the occasional alligator, and three kinds of chipmunks: real, animated and actors in furry suits.

There are also many golf courses. One of them became my temporary local patch for the week. I saw warblers and woodpeckers in the surrounding trees, kingfishers hovering and diving into what I assumed was a 'water hazard', but was also an ideal nesting beach for a small colony of Least Terns. I wondered if they ever ended up incubating a stray ball instead of their egg. Most fortuitous of all, it being a baking late August, the drought was drenched every morning by a cascade of sprinklers that left the greens and fairways soggy and soft and an ideal habitat for migrant waders, the passage of which varied entertainingly from day to day. When the golfers arrived the waders simply fluttered a few yards to another mini-marsh, both birds and golfers oblivious to the danger of a hooked tee shot bringing down a Semipalmated Sandpiper. At which point surely no golfer could possibly resist announcing: 'I got a birdie at the 12th!'

I see no reason why wildlife and golf courses should not co-exist. Nor, indeed, birders and golfers. Unless, of course, there is a rarity involved. This happened back in the 1980s in south Wales.

The bird in question was a Little Whimbrel (a Whimbrel is like a Curlew only smaller, a Little Whimbrel is even smaller) normally found in Australasia, and only twice seen in Britain. That is rare. It was first spotted within the bounds of Kenfig National Nature Reserve. However, just before dark, it flew to roost on the adjacent golf course. The news spread like wildfire. All night the twitchers of Britain travelled from far and wide. Before first light, several hundred of them were assembled – not at Kenfig Nature Reserve, where they were welcome, but at the end of the first fairway, where they weren't. Imagine the scene as, just after sunrise, the first golfer shuffled to the first tee, placed his ball on the pin, selected his driver, adopted his stance and peered down the fairway. At which point, 500 khaki-clad twitchers appeared over the horizen, plonked down their tripods, and pointed binoculars, cameras and bins apparently straight at him! Even Rory McIlroy would have sliced his shot.

'Eagle', 'albatross', why not 'little whimbrel'? It never has caught on.

CHAPTER TWENTY-SEVEN

Birth of an Island

Volcanoes are best viewed from a distance. This is not just a matter of health and safety, it is only from far away that you can appreciate the classic volcano shape of a massive inverted ice-cream cone, usually with the summit shrouded in cloud, which is quite reassuring if you had been considering a long trek to the top, because by the time you got there chances are you wouldn't have been able to see a flipping thing. I speak from experience.

If the volcano was active, you probably wouldn't want – or indeed be allowed – to approach the crater (TV presenters and film crews excepted, of course) which is fine by me, since the cosmic firework display of molten lava, elastic rock and cascades of fiery sparks looks so much more fun when you are gaping at it from way below, rather than fleeing for your life.

Eventually, of course, most volcanoes run out of steam, smoke and fire, and become habitable by wildlife, especially birds, some of which evolve to become either a new species or at least a volcanic 'race'. This often involves matching their plumage to the colour of their habitat in the interests of camouflage. Old, cold lava is, of course, black. This has led to some contradictions in our expectations of what colour some birds 'should' be. For example, the Seychelles has a 'black parrot' which, I'd say, contravenes the Trade Descriptions Act. The Galápagos have a Lava Heron and a Lava Gull, and a cormorant which is a common cormorant colour – black – but has also lost the power of flight. In case you are thinking that all this is the result of insular isolation, take a coach ride to the crater of the volcano just outside San José in Costa Rica and there you will find the Volcano Junco and the Sooty Robin, if you can spot them. Dark grey birds among dark grey rocks are not conspicuous.

Of course, evolution is a slow process. We can't literally watch it happening. However, 30km off the south coast of Iceland there is a sort of small-scale preview. The island of Surtsey rose from the sea in November 1963. It is therefore approaching its 50th birthday. Indeed, a celebratory conference is going on in Reykjavík even as I write. After eons of volcanic pregnancy, the birth began with several days of underwater contractions, followed by a spectacular eruption of water and smoke, which eventually cleared to reveal a newborn island. This provided a unique opportunity to observe its development, especially the arrival of life.

The only human beings allowed on Surtsey are 'licensed' scientists, and the BBC. Well, my film crew and I were. For a couple of hours, about 10 years ago. We were dropped by helicopter and left to tiptoe on hallowed ground. It wasn't spectacular. A few wisps drifted unthreateningly out of the crater, below which were slopes of slightly warm volcanic dust, as black and as powdery as pepper. At a glance they seemed lifeless, but then I realised they were speckled with tiny pinpricks of green. Seedlings. Not planted, but borne on the wind or on the feathers of birds. I sank to my knees to get a closer look, but it must've looked as if I was worshipping the advent of life itself.

My whimsy was interrupted by a bird zipping past me. A single Swallow, intent on becoming a pioneer perhaps? Or prospecting for a new nesting place, perhaps under the eaves of the scientists' hut? But he mustn't have liked it. Or maybe he couldn't find an equally adventurous mate. A recent survey of Surtsey's breeding birds records only 13 species. Swallow is not one of them. Most are seabirds.

The most numerous land bird – 12 pairs – is the Snow Bunting. There's an isolated population, living somewhat incongruously in a land of lava. Surely rife for a spot of evolution? Imagine the news: 'Surtsey's Snow Buntings turn black!' Darwin would love it.

first the black head, then the rest?

CHAPTER TWENTY-EIGHT

Hearing Test

Some years ago, what I would have called an 'elderly gentleman'–
until I became one myself – hailed me on Hampstead Heath
and asked: 'Where have all the Treecreepers gone?' Years of being
asked this sort of thing have taught me that it is impolite to
respond with: 'There's one just flown past you and landed on that
tree trunk,' because it could be interpreted as: 'It's not the
Treecreepers that have gone, it's your eyesight!' Instead, with the
blasé swagger of a relatively compos mentis 60 year old, I simply
replied: 'Well, actually, I saw a Treecreeper quite recently,' resisting
the urge to add, 'in fact, I am still looking at it!' I simply bade him
an encouraging 'good luck' and pottered off chuckling to myself
and muttering: 'You should've gone to Specsavers!'

At which point, I heard the Treecreeper start to sing. But the
gentleman didn't. It was at that moment it dawned on me that I
should've asked him: 'How's your ears?' I thought of calling back
to him, but I didn't. I was sure he wouldn't have heard me.

The truth is that what we call 'birdwatching' could just as appropriately be called 'bird listening'. Take a walk in the woods, and you will certainly hear more than you will see. Added to which, it is almost always a call or song that first attracts your attention. Treecreeper is a perfect example. They do exactly what it says on the tin: they creep up trees. A bark-coloured bird on bark. Unless and until they move, they are nigh on invisible, no matter how good your eyes. However, they have a sharp-edged 'peepy' little call, and a wispy down-the-scale song, with a debonair little flourish at the end. It is unmistakable, *if* you can hear it. The problem is that the call and song are very high-pitched – almost up in the range that would annoy bats – and human hearing almost invariably deteriorates from the top. Some people can't hear Goldcrests. Others can't hear Grasshopper Warblers. I once did a sponsored birdwatch with a friend who was losing both his hearing and his mobility. We had to carry him to within a few metres of a reeling 'gropper' which the youngest ears had detected half a mile away. His cry of 'I can hear it!' seemed genuine, but surprised us, because by then we couldn't! Never mind, it was for charity. The gentleman on the Heath I mentally christened 'The man who can't hear Treecreepers.' 'I wonder if he knows,' I mused. 'Shall I tell him? No. Let's face it, it'll come to us all.'

My personal moment of truth occurred about a year ago, in early spring, on top of Parliament Hill, which is generally recognised as one of the best places in London for 'viz mig' – visible migration. Some mornings, hundreds or even thousands of birds fly over. I – often accompanied by one or two other viz-mig aficionados – will stand on the hill for hours gazing at the skies and yelling out bird names. Members of the public probably think we belong to some weird esoteric cult, which in a way we do. Even our language is unintelligible to the uninitiated. 'Ten chaffs going north, four goldies, reed bunt west' (that's Chaffinches, Goldfinches and Reed Bunting). At this time of year there will also be many a cry of 'mipit!'

Meadow Pipits are small streaky brown birds that to me are the true harbingers of spring. More than Cuckoo, Swallow or the first warblers. Most British Meadow Pipits breed not so much in meadows as on moors. Tramp through the heather anywhere from Cornwall to Shetland and you will probably kick out a few 'mipits'.

However, a large percentage of the UK population winter in Spain and southern Europe. In early spring, they come flooding back. Some of them pass over Parliament Hill, flying fast and high.

Some of them are so high that they become 'inviz mig', but we know they're there, because they call. It is not an impressive sound. More of a short squeak, rendered phonetically in the books as *tsip*, but the consolation is that they call a lot. In fact, I don't think they are capable of flight without calling. A silent Meadow Pipit has surely lost its voice.

However, one morning in March 2011 my birdwatching chum Dave must have thought *I* had lost my voice. We were on the hill staring upwards. Every now and then, Dave called 'mipit!'. I didn't. I was silent, and – to me – so were the birds. I managed to spot a couple of dots at the sort of height and distance that everything looks much the same. 'Those two, Dave?'

'Mipits.'

'Did they call?'

'Yes. Several times. Couldn't you hear them?' I felt blighted, embarrassed and depressed. The answer was 'no!'

I am 70. I still get out on the Heath, and I still enjoy 'viz mig'. I can still pick up the flight calls of chaffs, goldies and reed bunts. But, just as my hearing is not what it was, neither am I. I am no longer 'the man who can identify all the bird calls', I have become 'the man who can't hear mipits!'

Ever had the feeling we don't really belong together?

CHAPTER TWENTY-NINE

Going Overboard

Some years ago I was offered the job of presenting *Breakaway* for
BBC Radio. I accepted, assuming that it would be tantamount to
a world tour subsidised by your licence fees. As it turned out, I
never got further than Tewkesbury. I reminded David, the
producer, that he had promised me one proper 'big trip'. Naturally,
he honoured his promise. The trip was big in distance but not in
length. Costa Rica for three days!

We flew to San José (presumably the same one that Dionne
Warwick asked the way to). The first morning, we took a taxi up
the local volcano. The higher we drove, the thicker the fog got,
until we arrived at the edge of the crater which was totally
invisible. 'Good job it's radio,' I muttered, and duly recorded my
reactions to an awesome landscape that I couldn't actually see. We
had our first sequence.

For the following day, David had planned an excursion that
was guaranteed to be much noisier and have the sort of

unpredictable excitement that comes over so well on radio. The
taxi dropped us off on a bridge. We were instantly aware of the
burbling and roaring of rushing water. Below us, a river – swollen
by recent deluges – was in turmoil. It sounded great, but looked
fearsome, especially as we were due to go white-water rafting. My
feeble plea of: 'Can't I just act it?' was rejected, and I was squeezed
into a wetsuit, along with David and half a dozen others – we had
a suit each of course. So did an attractive Amazonian blonde
American girl who stood astride the prow of our inflatable rubber
dinghy and took us through some synchronised paddle exercises.
'When I say "right", you guys stop paddling. When I say "left",
you guys…'

'Stop paddling?' I pre-empted.

'You got it!' she enthused. For 10 minutes we practised, until
we were as slickly drilled as a varsity boat-race crew. Then we
lowered the dinghy into the water.

There was instant mayhem, as the current swept us downriver,
dipping, tipping, swirling and buffeting. Paddle drill went haywire.
The Amazon barked: 'Left, right, left, *right*!' She might as well have
yelled: 'Everybody panic!' David was attempting to shove a
microphone in my direction, while protecting his precious tape
recorder from the spray. He began to interview me. 'Apparently
it's really good for wildlife along the river. Tell us what you can
see.' I was on the brink of blasphemy, when the Amazon called
our attention.

'Hold tight everybody (like we needed to be told)! Round this
corner yesterday there was a big boulder which could… Oh my
God! It's gone!' Judging from her tone, this was not good news.
Instead of a mighty boulder, there was now a cavernous hole,
down which the river was writhing like a maelstrom, as if Costa
Rica itself was going down the plughole. The boat tipped sidewise.
I fell out.

I remember being under water. I remember reaching upwards
and a hand grabbing mine, and I remember being hauled back on
board like a harpooned seal. I may have blacked out. I may have
fainted. How long I was 'gone' I shall never know. The next thing
I was aware of, I was kneeling at the prow proudly paddling along
Red Indian style. The river was now placid, and there was indeed

wildlife along the banks. But I was oblivious. My eyes were glazed. David asked me: 'Are you all right?'

'No,' I replied.

'Do you know who I am?' he continued.

'No.'

'I am David, from the BBC.'

'Oh.'

'Do you know where you are?'

'Er, no.'

'We are in Costa Rica. We're doing a radio piece for *Breakaway*.'

'Surely not!' I responded. 'We never go further than Tewkesbury.'

Half an hour later, we had moored by a charming riverside café. The dark skins and the colourful cloths and pottery were not typical of Tewkesbury. I told David that I was going to take a birding stroll round the garden, in the hope that whatever species I saw would help me reorientate. 'Mm, House Sparrow – could be anywhere these days.' Tennessee Warbler – North America? Montezuma Oropendola – only in South America. Chestnut-mandibled Toucans! I *was* in Costa Rica!

A few weeks later, I was back in London. David called me: 'I am afraid the falling in the river thing did spoil some of the recordings. I wonder, could we sort of knock up an ending? I don't like doing this but...'

'I do!' I responded.

So it was that we sat on a bench in the Rose Garden in Regent's Park, with a washing up bowl and a flannel, with which I simulated the lapping waters of a Costa Rican beach. I was about to bid my listeners a fond farewell, when a couple of Black-headed Gulls began squabbling over a discarded sandwich and started screeching loudly. 'We can't have that!' I pontificated. 'Why not?' asked David. 'They don't get Black-headed Gulls in Costa Rica. The BBC will get letters.'

I am sure they did.

HOW FRESH ARE THE PUGMARKS?
... VERY! ...

CHAPTER THIRTY

Beware of the Cat
(Dedicated to Dave)

No one has seen the Tiger, but we know he's there. There were pug marks along the main track and claw marks on a tree trunk, which he has been using as a scratching post, just like a domestic cat. Only these marks are four metres high. More than twice my height. A Tiger could reach up and sink its claws into an elephant's back. Even one as big as the alarmingly large-tusked bull that has just crashed out of the jungle 50m ahead, and now stands staring at us. Is he challenging us to approach or considering whether or not to charge? My Indian guide is clearly unnerved. In my experience, the local people are more wary of elephants than they are of Tigers. It is not surprising. Elephants don't hide. They don't skulk and there is usually more than one of them. A Tiger considers a human as food, but to an angry elephant we are enemies, or threats, especially if there are babies to be protected. It is, however, a small consolation that at least you see an elephant coming at you. You wouldn't see a Tiger. Ever. But we knew he was there.

Next morning there was more evidence. One of the lodge workers had been cycling to work when he noticed a small patch of flattened grass not far from the road. Not wisely, but probably mindful of earning a small bonus, he dismounted and swished towards the patch, shouting and flailing as he went. Tigers only function in silence, so he probably felt safe as he peered forward and saw what every safari guide and tourist is hoping for. A kill. A recent kill. Still bony, still bloody. A small deer, half-eaten, but half not. The Tiger would be back. So would we.

If I am ever asked: 'Where is the noisiest place I have ever filmed?' I would say: 'India, in town.' The quietest? India, in the countryside. Or at least, that part of Corbett National Park that morning. No rattle of distant vehicles, no rumble of planes, not even the throb of invisible airliners. A single crow of a Jungle Fowl – the ancestor of every barnyard rooster – and a neurotic yelp from a real wild Peacock, both evoked the grounds of an English stately home. The nearby trees weren't jungle, they were woods. The grassland reminded me of a deer park. Indeed, we had already seen deer, feeding nervously at the edge of the forest. They wouldn't wander out into the grassland. But we would.

We needed to find yesterday's kill. My elephant led the way, urged forward by the mahout who sat between its ears and steered by belting the animal over the head with an iron billhook. To me it looked horrendous, but to the elephant it was barely a tickle. I was perched on a wooden saddle, a foot or two lower than the highest claw scratches on that tree trunk. One cameraman stayed on the periphery, with his tripod as steady as a rock on the back of his open jeep. The second cameraman didn't have a tripod. He was shooting handheld, which should capture the reality and tension of the action. He had three angles: he could grab pictures of the animal (whatever it was), or shoot from my point of view (p.o.v.) so the camera saw what I saw, or he could shoot me and my reactions: anticipation, excitement or terror.

Slowly and inexorably we moved into the long grass, known as 'elephant grass', because that's how tall it grows. Once you are surrounded by it, it is scary. Whatever is in there you wouldn't see, unless it jumped up and waved at you. Or something worse. Against a background of silence, the only sound was the laboriously rhythmic swishing and the muffled 'flumps' of the elephant's footsteps. Now and then the mahout would apply the billhook, we would stop, and he would scan around us. Sometimes he would mutter something, presumably in Hindi. I didn't understand him, and he didn't understand me, except he recognised the word 'Tiger', which he would then repeat, with a point of a finger or a small flourish of his hand. I took this gesture to mean: 'There could be a Tiger crouching in the grass only a couple of metres away from us, and we won't see it because it is so brilliantly camouflaged. If it leaps up, it will have no trouble grabbing you and pulling you off the elephant. So let's just hope it came back last night and finished off the deer, in which case it won't be hungry any more, and is probably fast asleep somewhere in the forest.' Which was just what I was thinking! Amazing what you can convey in sign language.

For more than an hour I remained suspended between fear, anticipation and ultimately disappointment. We found the kill, and tried to convince ourselves that there were signs of recent gnawing – surely that bone was bigger yesterday? – but we couldn't be sure. We listened for the alarm bark of Spotted Deer, which is a sure sign that a Tiger is not far away. But everything was quiet. 'Almost too quiet', as they say in the movies. Another sign that the Tiger was still in the area? Maybe. Maybe not.

As the sun got hotter and the grass began to melt and shimmer with heat-haze, it was no longer Tiger time. The mahout's billhook engaged second gear and the elephant almost jogged over to the jeep, where the director was looking at the static cameraman's footage on a small screen. A wide shot of a benign landscape, bathed in gentle mist, and Bill going for a pleasant ride on an elephant. At that distance I certainly didn't look scared.

'So were you?' asked the director.

'What?'

'Scared.'

Before I answered, the soundman took off his earphones and handed them to me. I put them on. There was a noise like the gasping of a pair of industrial bellows, accompanied by a thumping drumbeat that would have filled a dance floor. 'That's you,' said the soundman. 'Breathing and heart beat.' The sound of fear.

I had never been so scared in my life. I still haven't.

LET'S FACE IT

CHAPTER THIRTY-ONE

Down on the Farm

When I was a kid my dad used to read me bedtime stories about friendly old Farmer Giles who was rosy-cheeked, straw-chewing, always cheery and above all caring and loving to not only the farm animals but also to the wildlife which he welcomed to his land. 'Good morning, Mr Badger, have a nice day.' The message in children's books was clear: farms are great for wildlife and that's how farmers wanted it.

However, as I grew into a young birdwatcher, I soon suspected that Farmer Giles had become extinct, if indeed he had ever existed. The farmers I was encountering on the outskirts of Birmingham were anything but rosy-cheeked and cheery. Some were blatantly belligerent, even physically violent. I once got clouted over the head with my own telescope while being ejected through a barbed wire fence. When I protested that I was only birdwatching, he clobbered me again. I tried explaining that his farm's sizeable pond with its miniature reedbed was something of a wildlife haven. His response was to bring in the bulldozers and fill it in.

This was not an isolated incident. Over the years, examples of some farmers' almost psychotic hatred of birdwatchers have passed into ornithological legend. Perhaps most notorious was the farmer whose fields were graced by the presence of an extremely rare bird with the pleasingly daft name of Black-winged Pratincole. It naturally attracted an ever-increasing audience of twitchers. The farmer was not welcoming. For a few days he tried to scare the bird and its admirers away by bellowing abuse in his Brian Blessed voice, followed by sporadic gunfire (presumably blanks), but the pratincole was too weary to move on – it should've been in Turkey or somewhere – while twitchers never give up unless things get really dodgy. Which they did. The farmer drove his tractor straight at them and sprayed them with what resembled – and probably was – raw sewage. A small price to pay for ticking off a Black-winged Pratincole.

For years, I considered the image of farmers to be possessive and paranoid. I admit I was often guilty of climbing fences or crawling under barbed wire, but this was what schoolboys did. What farmers did was yell at you and chuck you off. So much for Farmer Giles.

However, as I got older, I became aware of an escalating animosity that was – and continues to be – much more serious. There was clearly considerable friction and suspicion between farmers and conservationist organisations, particularly the RSPB. Probably because it had the highest profile, the largest membership and the most ideas about what was needed to conserve or create good wildlife habitat. Alas, its ideas were sometimes viewed with suspicion and construed as interfering, invasive or even threatening. They were met with the retort: 'I'm not having anyone telling me what to do with my land.' There was one farmer in Kent who every year defiantly damaged a small SSSI on his farm and every autumn spent two weeks in jail! As an isolated case, it might be amusing, but as a widespread attitude it is a disaster.

Maybe it was unavoidable. Those Farmer Giles books really didn't help. There is more to running a farm than chatting to the animals. What about the stuff about budgets and subsidies, and discussions with accountants, let alone the traumas of failed crops or diseased livestock. In a sense, farmers got lumbered with responsibilities maybe they didn't want, expect or realise. The accepted concept is that wildlife mainly lives in the countryside. Most of the countryside is farmland. Hence farmers become the custodians, whether they like it or not.

One of the most unfortunate results of the Badger cull has been the apparent taking of sides. The Government (Defra) is supported by the NFU that is 'protected' by the police. They line up against the NGOs that are largely supported by the public. This all too easily feeds a public perception of farmers as Badger killers (cullers). The truth is that some farmers support the cull, some don't. Similarly, while there certainly are farmers who are disinterested or even hostile towards wildlife and 'wildlife people', there are others who are willing to farm sympathetically, but need advice and a financial contribution. Worth their weight in gold are the farmers who know and love their wildlife, create special habitats, and even open their land for farm holidays including nature study.

It is often said that the only way of being 100 per cent certain that an area is totally wildlife-friendly is to own it. Hence the nature reserves owned and managed by such as the RSPB, the Wildlife Trusts, Wildfowl & Wetlands Trust, etc. Most of our countryside is owned by farmers. The way they manage it is absolutely crucial to the state of British wildlife. Does this government know that?

Or care?

CHAPTER THIRTY-TWO

Protecting What from Whom?

A friend of mine had just come back from a weekend in Scotland. He was excited but not totally confident, hence the question: 'Could we have seen a Golden Eagle?'

'Well, yes you *could* have done. Whereabouts in Scotland were you?'

'In the Cairngorms.'

'Well, there certainly are Golden Eagles in the Cairngorms. What was it doing?' 'We were driving. It flew across the road.'

'Are you sure it wasn't a Buzzard?'

'It was really big.'

Buzzards are big, but not as big as an eagle. Birdwatchers say that if you see an eagle but you are not sure, it is a Buzzard. But when you do see an eagle, you know! In Scotland they call Buzzards 'tourist eagles'. My friend was deflated; his wife said: 'Never mind, dear', and his daughter said: 'Told you so!'

That was about seven or eight years ago. Since then my friend has seen a lot of Buzzards, and he didn't have to go to Scotland.

He lives about 20 miles north of London and he sees Buzzards nearly every week. He doesn't mistake them for eagles, though he is getting confused by the ever-increasing number of Red Kites. It is not many years ago that both species were in trouble. In the late 1950s there were only half a dozen pairs of Red Kites and they were all deep in the Welsh Valleys. Buzzards were not as scarce as that, but they were very much birds of hills, mountains and moorlands. So much so that we assumed they needed such specialised habitat to survive.

Then, about 10 years ago, I went to the Netherlands. The polders in winter. The very epitome of flat farmland, with nary a hillock in sight. There were thousands of wild geese, and *lots* of Buzzards. Perched on posts, dawdling along dykes and most incongruously shuffling around in the grass feeding on earthworms. The conclusion was obvious: Buzzards needn't be confined to moors and mountains. The rhetorical question was inevitable: if they are happy in the Netherlands, why not in England?

And thus it has come to pass. Thanks to diminished use of poisons and pesticides, and less prejudice and persecution of raptors in general, 'tourist eagles' are proliferating. One of the secrets of maintaining what one might call their natural numbers is that they are not fussy eaters, which is just as well because they are hardly impressive hunters. They are not capable of the deadly dives of a Peregrine, or of the lightning interceptions of a Sparrowhawk, and their attempt at impersonating a Kestrel is more of a lollop than a hover. It is testament to their lack of skills that much of their 'live' food (rabbits, ducks, pigeons, etc) is already ill, or injured. Not surprisingly, Buzzards are prepared to risk their own lives by swooping on roadkill along with other scavengers such as crows, Jackdaws, Red Kites and Magpies.

So Buzzards are booming. So much so that I feared they would become victims of their own success. It is what often happens when a species becomes noticeably numerous. They will inevitably be blamed for the demise of other species, guilty or not. It happened to Magpies and Sparrowhawks – 'killing all our songbirds'. It is happening to parakeets – 'stealing all the nest holes', and now it is happening to Buzzards – accused of taking Pheasants!

Frankly, I could not believe it when the Government announced that it was sanctioning the destruction of Buzzard nests, by blasting them with a shotgun. How much blasting does it take to demolish a large platform of tightly woven twigs? And how do you make sure you avoid hitting the birds? Estate owners would also be allowed to 'remove' birds (how?) and commit them to captivity (where?).

I was not at all surprised that, within a couple of days, an enormous lobby of protest had been organised by individuals and the pertinent organisations, such as RSPB, the Wildlife Trusts and the League Against Cruel Sports.

I *was* surprised when, only a couple of days later, the Government announced that plans for the Battle of the Buzzards had been withdrawn. The fastest U-turn so far?

So what does this imply? That Defra – a department that has so much affect on our countryside and wildlife – bows to the wishes of the shooting lobby? Or that the Government really does take notice of public opinion?

Or, is it a cunning strategy? First, the Government comes up with some plan that is unthinkably absurd. Second, the public is outraged. Third, the PM makes a U-turn and drops the idea, which was so silly it would never have happened anyway. Fourth, the PM claims: 'See, we *do* listen!'

But where does that leave the wildlife? The Buzzards seem safe, for the time being. Meanwhile, the Pheasants – millions of them – are captive-bred to become living targets, to be blasted out of the sky in the name of 'sport'. Many of the birds can hardly fly and will inevitably be splattered and crushed on the road. What's left may well end up as 'Buzzard food'.

I will leave the last word to my friend: 'If they want to save Pheasants, ban traffic!' Look out for another U-turn!

CHAPTER THIRTY-THREE

Meet us, Don't Eat us

It is no secret that much of British wildlife is endangered. Fortunately, we – and our birds and mammals – are blessed by having several organisations working to conserve and protect them. Of course, this costs money, and much time and effort are inevitably spent on fundraising. However, recently I have been thinking that the wildlife benefits, but it doesn't contribute. So how's this for an idea to make wildlife pay for itself? First, you watch it, then you eat it! Let's face it; it happens already – Rabbit pie, venison, Pheasant. Wild creatures fulfilling two roles – entertainment and food. One does not detract from the other. Just because its parents are succulent doesn't mean a baby bunny is less cute, or a 'Bambi' less lovable, or even a male Pheasant less handsome. Most nature reserves have a café attached, so why not specialise in fresh local food. Very local. No transport costs, and much-needed income for conservation. Of course it needs a zappy publicity slogan. How about: 'View 'em, then chew 'em?'

I am, of course, joking. Bidding to become conservation's answer to Frankie Boyle perhaps? No, this outburst of satirical black humour was brought on by a recent visit to Iceland.

Within an hour of landing, we were taking a stroll around Reykjavík harbour. I literally could not believe what I saw. All along the quayside were kiosks and posters advertising whale-watching trips. Some of them even promised: 'If we don't see a whale, we will give you another trip – free.' There were also guarantees of sightings of porpoises, dolphins, and – arguably the northern hemisphere's most desirable bird – Puffins. Icelandic eco-tourism was obviously flourishing, which pleased me greatly since, only about 10 years ago, I had filmed, with the BBC on board, what was then the very first whale-watching boat. At the time, as one would have hoped, the commercial whaling industry seemed to be defunct, although there were rumours of its revival. But surely that was unthinkable? Whale-watching and whale butchering side by side? That must be a joke. A very sick joke.

However, less than a month ago, as I walked along Reykjavík waterfront, I realised that the 'joke' has become a reality. There were eight large ships moored side by side. The first six proudly bore the logo and name of whale-watching companies. The decks were fitted out for optimum viewing, with chairs, binocular and camera rests, and conspicuous identification charts. However, at the end of the row were two more boats, unmarked, and ominously functional. Each had a harpoon mount on the prow, a chain winch for hauling a wounded animal on board, and a big featureless grey open deck, space enough to butcher the whale. It was all too easy to picture it flooded with blood, intestines and body parts. Right now, the whaling ships were empty and silent, and some of the machinery was even a bit rusty. I even wondered if they were out of commission. Maybe the whalers had given up. Next morning, they were gone. Half an hour later, we found them again, moored even more conspicuously on the other side of the harbour. It was almost as if they were warning us: 'Oh yes, we can move, and we can kill whales. If we want to.'

The juxtaposition of whale-killing boats alongside whale-watchers was more than ironic. Iniquitous, more like. But it became almost surreal when I read the menu board outside a harbourside café. Halfway down the main dishes, it was recommending 'Whale Steak'. A rather swisher-looking restaurant was more specific – 'Minke Whale Steak'. Another one urged you to sample a sort of nautical hors d'oeuvre: a platter of 'Shag (like a Cormorant but smaller, and, I'd imagine, tougher!), Whale and Puffin'! I ask anyone who has been charmed or excited by these birds, and spent hours photographing them on the Farne Islands, or in Shetland, or indeed in Iceland, was your afterthought: 'Mmm, very cute, but I wonder what they taste like?' I think not.

But maybe I am being naïve. Maybe I should play devil's advocate. There was, of course, a time – and not that long ago – when a considerable part of people's staple diet was 'wildlife'. For thousands of years, that is all there was! Different geographical areas and different communities had their 'specialities'. Everyone knows that Iceland has always been a nation of seafarers and fishermen. Surely they have been whaling for centuries, and whale meat is a widely eaten traditional food? Well, the answer is 'no, they haven't, and no, it isn't.' Iceland only began commercial whaling in 1948, and a recent poll found that no more than 5 per cent of Icelanders regularly eat whale meat. It is certainly not considered to be a delicious 'local delicacy'. That is 'restaurant speak' to lure in the gourmets, or perhaps more likely the curious tourist rising to a dare. 'I bet you won't order blubber.' Or 'I believe in eating what the locals eat. You can't go to Iceland without eating whale, or Puffin, or Shag!' You can, actually.

I don't want to be a spoilsport, but I am afraid that seemingly frivolous attitude fuels some awful atrocities, involving willful slaughter and appalling cruelty. Order pâté de foie gras anywhere in Europe, including England, and you are condoning unspeakable torture to geese. In Cyprus, if you are offered *ambelopoulia*, just say 'no'. It looks like a jar full of pickled walnuts but its production is one of the reasons that Cypriot hunters annually slaughter literally millions of small songbirds, most of which are migrants. As indeed are many species of whale.

As it happens, Minke Whales (hunting of other species is illegal in Iceland) are thought not to be major travellers, but, like any creature that swims the oceans, they cannot be said to 'belong' to any particular country. At present, they are not endangered, but possibly only because there 'isn't much meat on them' compared to the really big ones, so they weren't considered to be worth hunting.

So are they worth hunting now? Only if there is a market for their meat, and that market is Icelandic restaurants. The demand comes largely from tourists. They have been drawn to a unique country of extraordinary landscapes, sea cliffs, bays, volcanoes, waterfalls, lakes and fresh clean air, where they can trek, ride, cycle, drive or sail, enjoying wildlife, watching birds and, of course, watching whales. If you see one surface, roll or dive, it will lift your heart. If you think of how it might die, it will break it.

There is no quick and painless way to kill a whale. It can't be dispatched with one 'good clean shot'. It will be pierced by several harpoons, dragged through the water gasping, writhing and unable to breathe. It is likely to have died through drowning before the final ignominy of being hauled out of the sea and onto that deck, soon to be awash with its blood.

As I wandered around Reykjavík, photographing menus and shop windows stuffed with literally hundreds of fluffy Puffins, I was overtaken by a couple of whales! Well, half whales actually. Both top halves. The legs belonged to young volunteers from IFAW (International Fund for Animal Welfare). They have a presence all over the world, wherever animals are in trouble. The job of this team is to intercept tourists who are returning from a whale-watching trip, explain the present situation in Iceland, ask whether or not they have tasted or intend to taste whale meat, and finally to get a signature on a 'postcard of protest', which will be added to the ever-growing pile already delivered to the government by IFAW. As the tourists return to their hotels (maybe to change their dinner order!), they are serenaded by the volunteers with a little whale song or rather 'whale chant': 'Meet us, don't eat us. Meet us, don't eat us.'

It is one of those moments that confirms my pet theory that care and kindness to animals brings out the best in humanity. Especially because the young volunteers are such a cosmopolitan bunch: French, Dutch, German, Croatian, Finnish, British, Swedish and a pair of Poles! Mind you, to be honest, everyone looks the same inside a whale costume!

My final fact-finding cruise was a day and a night on board IFAW's research vessel, a very handsome yacht called *Song of the*

Whale. She sails the world with her small crew of scientists, fully equipped with the latest technology for recording whales both at and below the surface, collecting data, and anticipating and investigating potential problems. The researchers enjoy the full trust and cooperation of the whale-watching companies, unlike the early days, when the initial response was to refer to IFAW personnel as 'terrorists', an unfortunate legacy of past anti-whaling protests that had involved a rather more buccaneering approach. No judgement, but that is not IFAW's way. On board the *Song of the Whale*, the atmosphere is anything but militant. The team are working almost non-stop, day and night, scanning with binoculars or cameras, checking video feeds and peering at computer screens. Every now and then a cry goes up, and so does a Minke Whale. It's a graceful animal. It moves with a glide rather than a leap, surfacing three or four times before sliding down to deeper waters, where the fish are. The sea is glassy calm. There is an air of concentration and contentment. This is another of those moments. The best of wildlife and the best of people.

Worth celebrating with a song. The Song of the Whale. All together now: 'Meet us, don't eat us. Meet us, don't eat us. MEET US, DON'T EAT US!'

OK, but I wouldn't mind a biscuit.

" FARMER FARMER PUT AWAY THAT DDT. now.
GIVE ME SPOTS ON MY APPLES
BUT LEAVE ME THE BIRDS AND THE BEES
PLEASE. Joni Mitchell, 1970

CHAPTER THIRTY-FOUR

The Way it's Gone

When it comes to environmental damage and desecration, there is nothing like the real thing. I had seen newsreels of oil spills, but it wasn't until 1993 – when I stood on my favourite beach in Shetland and watched ebony waves as viscous as lava splurging out of the *Braer* and crawling up the sand like a giant satanic amoeba – that I understood the true disaster of an oil spill.

The concept of 'acid rain' was even more amorphous until, one afternoon driving along the M4 past Port Talbot in South Wales, I saw the cause and effect. Smoky plumes of heaven-knows-what chemicals, swirling upwards from the factories towards a line of silhouetted trees on the near horizon with no more foliage on them than the deadly chimneys themselves. Black misshapen skeletons. Memorials to pollution, or posthumous entries for the Turner Prize?

I had similar revelationary shocks when I gazed upon the rotting detritus littering the north Norfolk marshes after the floods of '93;

and when I witnessed the power of the Great Storm of 1987, which interrupted my filming schedule by toppling a lime tree so enormous we couldn't get into the Tower of London!

I was mulling such thoughts, as our plane approached Kota Kinabalu, the main airport of Sabah, in Borneo. I looked down for signs of the curse that I had been told was threatening to swallow the jungle below and its wildlife with it. Palm oil. This was my first visit to Borneo, and I had not yet seen palm-oil plantations for myself. Would they show up from the air? Looking down, I noticed a few obvious brown squares where forest had been recently cleared, presumably for timber or planting, but otherwise everything looked green and leafy. Several days after landing, I realised that oil palms are green and leafy!

At first sight, a plantation looks neither unsightly nor barren. After all, they are trees, not dissimilar to the coconut palms that provide shade on many a silver-sanded tropical beach. They are stately and shapely, and their giant fronds ripple and sway like a feathery leaved ocean. You can't help wondering: 'Why aren't these as attractive to wildlife as native forest?' The answer is because a palm-oil plantation is not a mixed community of different trees. It is a congested ghetto of one species, melded together so closely to prevent light getting to the understorey, and lacking in clearings or what we'd call trunks or branches. What's more, the fruit yield is so meagre – not much bigger than a bunch of grapes on each tree – that the only way to greater productivity is to plant more and more palms, which means clear more and more forest, and lose more and more wildlife. Primary forest supports 220 species of birds here, palm-oil forest has 12!

An industry that is clearly contributing a great deal of income to the country is not going to disappear, but an awful lot of wonderful and unique Bornean wildlife will, unless the planting is controlled and the animals protected. This requires cooperation between groups of people as diverse as the forest itself. In Borneo I saw this happening.

First – in no particular order, as they say on *The X Factor* – the conservationists. The small group I was travelling with were under the aegis of the World Land Trust. Based in Britain, its role is to raise funding to literally buy wildlife-rich areas, wherever in the world they may be for sale. The Trust does not own the land. It is passed on to be managed by a local NGO. In Borneo, there is HUTAN which, unlike most NGOs, is not a mnemonic. It is the local word for 'forest'. There is the rather more elaborately entitled LEAP, which stands for Land, Empowerment, Animals, People. Which is as good a recipe of the essential ingredients for conservation I have ever heard! Oh, NGO = Non-Governmental Organisation (a euphemism for 'charity'!).

However, there is one more element whose understanding and support is absolutely crucial to the success or failure of… well, just about everything! The Government. We were granted a far from cursory audience – nay, frank and free discussion – with the Director of the Forest Department. His knowledge and concern was convincing, his confidence was reassuring and his practicality was undeniable. 'It is only because of the income we get from palm oil that we are able to finance conservation,' he said, thus complementing the words I had heard at LEAP and HUTAN: 'No point in fighting the palm-oil industry, we must work with it.' And from what I saw in Sabah, that is what is happening.

Oh, in case you are wondering about the wildlife. We saw a delightful herd of 30 Pygmy Elephants bathing at dusk (they weren't as small as I'd hoped!), and honey-furred, squishy-nosed Proboscis Monkeys staring at us as we punted by. We heard a couple of distant choruses of gibbon song, and were given a meticulous demonstration of how to build a leaf-hammock by a venerable male Orangutan, which he finished off by adding a leafy, but probably leaky, roof! Impressive primates indeed, but – during this week at least – the most impressive primate of them all was man, and woman, and children, and maybe a politician! You know, I've always said it: when it comes to good people and good deeds, there is nothing like the real thing.

SO THERE I AM, ON THE CENTRE
COURT AT LAST. IT STARTS DRIZZLING
THEY CLOSE THE FLIPPING ROOF!
WITH ME INSIDE! SO I LAND ON
KOURNIKOVA'S SHOULDER, AND SHE
GIVES ME A STROKE! RESULT!

CHAPTER THIRTY-FIVE

Harris Hawks

I was recently waiting for a train at St Pancras station, when a fellow traveller approached me eagerly: 'Last week I saw a man here with an eagle on his arm,' he said. 'Are you sure it was an eagle?' I asked. 'Well, no, but it was some kind of big hawk.' He was obviously hoping I would provide a more specific identification. 'What colour was it?' I asked. 'Er, I didn't really notice the colour.' There speaks a non-birdwatcher, I thought, but didn't say! 'Was it perhaps dark grey, with chestnut shoulders, and a white tail, with a black band across the end?' He gasped with delighted bemusement, like an audience volunteer bamboozled by a mind reader. 'Yes, that was it. What was it?'

'That was a Harris Hawk,' I announced. 'It is just about the commonest bird of prey in falconry shows and zoos. They are not British, they are American, but so many of them have escaped from captivity they have recently qualified for a mention in the recent atlas of British breeding birds. If they keep escaping at this rate, they could become honorary UK citizens, like Ring-necked Parakeets.

'But why would a falconer walk his hawk at St Pancras station?' he asked. 'Almost certainly, to keep the pigeons away.' They used a Harris Hawk at last year's Wimbledon, though presumably not while they were playing. That'd put you off your serve! And the BBC used Harris Hawks to dissuade pigeons from pooing on the newly redecorated Broadcasting House. Not everyone approved, but a BBC spokesman promised that no pigeons would be harmed. Unfortunately, one hungry hawk couldn't resist pouncing on a particularly plump pigeon, flying off to the roof with it, and tearing it to pieces, before the horrified eyes of a number of BBC staff. What's more, the supposedly well-trained hawk refused to fly back to its handler. Of course, when it finally did so, it was fired. Actually, there is a fortuitous irony in that these days there are several pairs of wild Peregrine Falcons breeding in central London who dine almost exclusively on Feral Pigeons, and whose territory almost certainly includes several railway stations and Broadcasting House. So that should put an end to the scandalous business of overpaid American raptors coming over here to eat our birds, which, as it happens, are probably not to their taste anyway.

The fact is that Harris Hawks are not the deadly feathered Exocet missiles that Peregrines are. Indeed, back home they hunt at a rather leisurely pace, in cooperative groups. I don't mean feeding flocks, like some of the small falcons catching dragonflies and such. Harris Hawks go in for properly coordinated teamwork. Hunting parties are between two and six birds. One of them flies ahead to look for potential prey, more likely a Jackrabbit than a pigeon. Then a second bird moves up and takes over the searching. Once a victim has been spotted, they overtake each other until they have surrounded their supper, which understandably freezes with fear and – acknowledging that all escape routes are barred – surrenders to its fate.

I have seen wild Harris Hawks in the Arizona desert, swooping and plunging against a background of a burning blue sky, sagebrush and giant cacti. It struck me more as an aerial ballet than a hunting party. The local Jackrabbits, however, no doubt would not agree. Any more than a prehistoric lizard would welcome the attention of a team of velociraptors. At which point you may fairly ask: 'What on Earth have Harris Hawks got to do with dinosaurs?' I shall tell you.

Several years ago, I presented a short series called *The Truth About Killer Dinosaurs*. It inevitably featured velociraptors. In the film *Jurassic Park* they were depicted as quite big, which they weren't – they were about the size of a turkey – and rampantly vicious, which they may well have been. One thing was undoubtedly true: they hunted in packs, pursuing and surrounding prey, before pouncing, killing and eating it, very much in the manner of... Harris Hawks. It is, of course, now widely accepted that birds evolved from small dinosaurs. So there we are, from *Jurassic Park* to St Pancras station is not as long a journey as you might think! Pity it only goes one way.

CHAPTER THIRTY-SIX

First Mornings

Show-business people talk about first nights. Birdwatchers talk about first mornings. Here is a classic scenario. You have gone abroad for a holiday to somewhere new. You arrived at the hotel, lodge or resort in the evening when it was dark. This may be a little frustrating, but it is also tantalising. What is it going to be like out there when you can see and hear?

Over the years, I have had a few surprises when the sun came up! On my first trip to India we were escorted down a pitch-dark path into a concrete cabin and fell asleep with nary a clue what kind of terrain we were in. I staggered out at dawn and almost fell into a cesspit. The considerable consolation was that there were several Painted Snipe feeding on it, and, even better, the surrounding woodland was pleasingly open and full of birds, many of them species that occur in Britain but rarely (Bluethroats, Red-breasted Flycatchers, etc). They were easy to hear and easy to see.

This is rarely the case in rainforest, wherever it is. Heaven knows, I am not dissing its importance or the profusion of its biodiversity, but the fact is my worst ever first morning was in Papua New Guinea, when I tramped the jungle trails for three hours without seeing or hearing a single bird! My wife Laura accompanied me on that trip. As, indeed, she did to Kenya, where we shared a memorable first morning at Lake Baringo Lodge. I had been aware of occasional snufflings and grumping in the night, but had not expected to draw the curtains and find a hippo with its nose pressed against the window. At least I could say: 'See, it wasn't me snoring.'

Challenging though it may be, there are few experiences more daunting for a birdwatcher than emerging on the first morning and not being able to recognise a single song or call. Of course *seeing* the bird should help, but not necessarily, especially in Asia or South America where there are whole families that don't seem to bear any relationship to anything we have at home. Page 96 of *Birds of Brazil* includes reedhaunters, foliage-gleaners, Firewood-gatherer and barbtails. And guess what? They are all little brown birds.

So what was my best first morning ever? Rather bizarrely, it was at a 'Dude' Ranch in Arizona. We had arrived in darkness, made even more disorientating by clouds of dust kicked up by every vehicle. The Ranch 'Cookhouse' was like the buffet at a Holiday Inn, and our chalet – far from being rustic – was a stone edifice that strangely resembled a Henry Moore sculpture. None of us was happy. The cost of the accommodation was in return for my wife writing a flattering travel piece – so that could be awkward – and my daughter Rosie kept reminding us that she was the only 10-year-old girl on Earth who hated horses. I myself was suffering a period of low mood and not sleeping well.

However, my insomnia was a blessing in disguise. As soon as I sensed a glimmer of light, I slipped outside into what was in effect a giant rock garden. A small-scale version of the true Arizona desert where cowboys roam, the Coyotes howl, and the cacti reach for the sky. I intended to visit the real thing, but for the moment this would do nicely. The birds clearly agreed. There were Cactus Wrens everywhere, same shape as ours but huge and

stripy. There were woodpeckers – cactus peckers more like –
laughing as woodpeckers do, and popping and peeping in and out
of their prickly nest holes. A parade of Gambel's Quails danced
across the path sporting bouncy little quiffs on their heads. All
around me there were warblers, flycatchers, orioles, sparrows,
shrikes and raptors. All different from home, but just that little bit
the same. I think that was why I enjoyed that walk so much. As I
ambled down the path, the species revealed themselves one by
one. It wasn't overwhelming. I had time to take notes and do
sketches. I rifled through the field guide over breakfast, and
announced that I had seen more than 20 'lifers', including my first
Roadrunner.

The rest of the week was not so good. It was wet, cold and
almost birdless. Laura lied ('fab for families') and Rosie fell off a
horse.

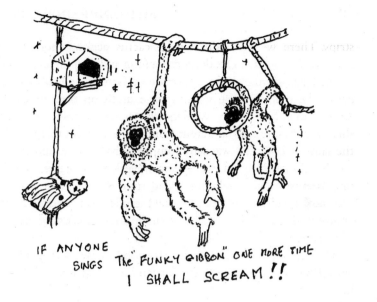

IF ANYONE SINGS THE "FUNKY GIBBON" ONE MORE TIME I SHALL SCREAM!!

CHAPTER THIRTY-SEVEN

Going Bananas

I'm no stranger to dressing up as a mammal or a bird. My first experience was at primary school when I was cast as a baby dragon in the school play. I do not remember the play, but I do remember the costume. It was like a scaly-patterned 'onesie'. It was tail-less, and I was therefore puzzled when our comely drama teacher asked me to spice up my exit with a vigorous wag. I protested that I had nothing to wag, but she insisted that I had. To this day, I am not sure if I was being dim or provocative. All I do know is that she finally had to resort to using the 'b' word, at which she blushed and the class fell about with joy. 'Miss! You said "bum"! Teehee.'

I was clearly traumatised by the experience, as I went through secondary school and three years at university without feeling any compulsion whatsoever to wear scales, fur or feathers. However, I more than made up for that during the 1970s, The Goodies Years as I like to think of them, though I am not of course insinuating that nothing else happened during the seventies. Actually, it was a decade in which wearing animal costumes was all too rife – reprehensibly, in the case of supermodels, and gleefully in the case of The Wombles. In the case of The Goodies, it was downright peculiar.

In the episode with the giant kitten, all three of us spent several days dressed as mice. I also gave solo performances as a Dalmatian dog, and as a Dodo (I did of course become extinct), and Tim and Graeme became intimate inside a pantomime horse, a role which I enjoyed greatly, since I got to ride them and give them a damn good thrashing with my whip. Comedy is rarely painless, but if I had to choose the least enjoyable animal costume I have ever had to wear it was when all three of us played giant rabbits and re-enacted extracts from *Watership Down*. Being run over by a lorry was pant-threateningly scary, but at least it was soon over (after seven takes!), unlike the seemingly never-ending, ever-worsening torture of being slowly broiled in our own sweat, leaving us so soggy and smelly that even our loved ones were repulsed.

So, if dressing up as a rabbit is uncomfortable, what about a gorilla? There must be plenty of opinions because – let's face it – unlike the magnificent animal itself, people in gorilla suits are not exactly an endangered species. One of the reasons is that costume hire companies don't know their primates. You can ask for anything from a Chimpanzee to a gibbon, but they'll always send you a gorilla. (You can imagine my pedantic strops when promoting 'The Funky Gibbon'.) You will see gorillas at Halloween, gorillas in panto, gorillas in tutus and gorillas in top hat and tails (which is ironic, 'cos they don't have tails. Any more than I did).

I don't think many people would disagree with the statement that as far as gorillas are concerned you can't have too many of them. It is a fair rule of comedy that 'more is funnier'. One dwarf is unremarkable, but seven are a hoot. One pantomime horse may get a smile, but a Grand National of them brings the house down. One gorilla is probably less than hilarious – no matter what it is wearing – but a whole rock band of five or six gorillas will keep an audience whooping for several songs before the truth becomes obvious – that it is almost impossible to play a guitar wearing a gorilla suit! More gorillas than half a dozen and the rule kicks in: the more the merrier!

The greatest gorilla gathering on Earth convenes in the region of Tower Bridge in London on a Saturday morning in late September, when there are more men and women in gorilla suits than there are endangered gorillas in the wild. The event is known as the Great Gorilla Run and it is indeed great. The laughter, good humour and waving of bananas at the start is truly uplifting. The state of the runners after an hour or two is something to be pitied. The effects of hopping in a rabbit suit are positively cosmetic compared with running as a gorilla. Rabbit-fur-induced perspiration is as fragrant as fine cologne compared with the fetid stench of gorilla sweat. Added to which, if the runner isn't instantly released from his or her costume, there is serious danger of being suffocated or drowned. One of the few consolations is that hair becomes so drenched that it can mimic the effect of gel or Brylcreem, which can look slick on gentlemen. Ladies should not wear make-up to avoid emerging like one of the Addams Family, unless you fancy going Goth.

By the way, the reason I know such details about the annual Great Gorilla Run is that I am a regular attendant. Indeed, I wouldn't miss it for the world. Nor of course would I dream of actually taking part. Such exertion would almost certainly prove terminal, and then I wouldn't be able to attend the following year, to send them off at the start and – even more fun – allow them to collapse on me at the finish, where I also adorn them with their well-earned gold medals. No silver, no bronze; they are all winners to me! That's what I tell them every year. Those who are still able to utter any coherent sound – apart from gasping, retching or weeping – usually greet that line with a howl of derision, signifying that, despite nearly killing themselves, their sense of humour is alive and well. The returning runners are molested by news cameras and reporters searching for statements of the obvious: 'Why do you do it?' 'Why is it important to save gorillas?' 'Aren't you tired?' In reply, the clichés also abound: 'Tired but happy'. 'No pain no gain'. 'Well, it's for a good cause isn't it?' I heartily agreed with the young lady who was both draped and dripping all over me, which wasn't surprising since she was dressed up as an elephant. As she flirtatiously nuzzled the tip of her trunk in my left ear, I was tempted to quote my old Python chums: 'This is getting silly!' Indeed, and all the better for it.

Alas, it is also getting serious for the gorillas. Please help.

WHY DO THEY CALL HIM A <u>GAME</u> KEEPER?
BECAUSE KILLING IS JUST A SPORT!

CHAPTER THIRTY-EIGHT

Crimes Against Nature

How do you kill a bird of prey? Shoot it. Trap it in a cage, then shoot it. Poison it, by putting out bait laced with a deadly chemical. Or wipe out a potential family by destroying the eggs or stealing them, and selling them to egg collectors or to foreign breeders who will hatch them and rear the birds for falconry. All these activities are – and have long been – illegal. All have been going on for many years. All are still rife.

In the majority of cases the crime is committed by a gamekeeper. His job is to protect the 'game' birds that are also, of course, destined to die, bagged by 'sportsmen' who will pay handsomely for the privilege. Not even the most myopically sentimental nature lover could deny that the diet of some birds of prey does include gamebirds and their chicks and even eggs. Predators are of course part of the 'natural balance' of things, but on a shooting estate the aim is to maintain an unnaturally large population of – literally – 'target' species. Therefore, we could hardly contradict a gamekeeper who argues that he is … just doing his job.

But there could be some aspects of the way he is doing the job that would make him a criminal, and if caught he would be liable to a fine, or possibly even a prison sentence. He may or may not lose his job, but if he does it would be iniquitous indeed, since whoever fires him, probably hired him and instructed him to 'control' – i.e. kill – raptors. He could certainly plead ... 'I was only carrying out orders.'

But he is still guilty as charged, and criminal justice is often rough. The street pushers are imprisoned, while the drug barons stay free. The 'hit men' take the rap, while the 'Godfather' is immune. On some estates, the gamekeeper gets caught, while the landowner feigns innocence or indignation. The truth is that it is he who should be facing prosecution.

It is generally agreed that the most productive wildlife locations are those where the land literally belongs to an owner with a genuine environmental ethic. It is why RSPB appeals are so often concerned with land purchase. Fortunately, there are many private landowners who are knowledgeable, conscientious, enterprising and generous. Unfortunately, there are still... *a lot who are not.* Some of them even regard the RSPB and other environmental NGOs as a sort of traditional enemy, as if they are engaged in some kind of deep-rooted sectarian war. It is the same mind-set that regards any bird with a hooked bill as 'vermin.' It is on or near those estates that you will hear the gunshots, or see the poison bait or snares, and witness the corpses, not just of birds of prey, but any other bird or mammal that might conceivably take a gamebird.

Many wildlife protection laws exist. Others, however, have been mooted, and yet have mysteriously stalled. The intention to criminalise possession of various poisons was announced five years ago, but as yet the names have not been specified. Why not? Everyone involved knows what they are. The police and the NGOs are doing a terrific – and often dangerous – job. There is widespread public approbation and cooperation. Offenders are being caught and punished. And yet the cruelty continues. Why? Because people with money are offering money and making money. Gamekeepers know they are not above the law, but there are landowners who may think they are. They must be named and shamed. A tabloid cliché perhaps, but it is what I believe should happen, even if the social status of some of the names may cause controversy and embarrassment.

When I first started birdwatching more than 50 years ago, many of Britain's birds of prey were very scarce. Red Kites were down to a few pairs, restricted to Wales. There were even fewer Marsh Harriers, only in East Anglia. Peregrine Falcons could only be found on craggy sea cliffs and were not common. Neither were Golden Eagles. And Hobbies and even Buzzards were a rare sight. There was a single pair of Ospreys at Loch Garten, and White-tailed Eagles were unknown as a breeding bird, although I did see one sitting in a field in Norfolk in 1958. (The eagle was sitting in the field, not me.)

The scarcity of these species had been caused by widespread DDT poisoning, though it was not specifically aimed at them but was an ingredient in various pesticides used by farmers. No doubt there was also some intentional poisoning, and certainly much gamekeeping 'control'. Fortunately, outrage, research and legislation began to get the situation under control and slow down the declines. RSPB schemes, creating habitats, pioneering reintroductions and tirelessly pursuing criminal elements, not only increased the numbers of birds, but also seemed to encourage some species to immigrate in larger numbers. Ospreys are now almost as ubiquitous in Britain as they are around the world. Marsh Harriers are now to be found building nests in tiny patches of reeds or crops, illustrating the principle that when a species increases its numbers it can't afford to be so fussy about its habitat. Peregrines have moved into cities. Of course, the once extremely rare species that most people have now seen, even if it's only swooping over a motorway, is the Red Kite. In parts of Scotland you are probably more likely to see a White-tailed Eagle than a Golden Eagle, or possibly both species circling on a thermal.

Alas, though, you are almost equally likely to find one dead. The battle continues.

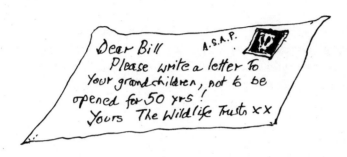

Dear Bill   A.S.A.P.
Please write a letter to
your grandchildren, not to be
opened for 50 yrs!
Yours The Wildlife Trusts xx

CHAPTER THIRTY-NINE

Talking About your Generation

Letter to my grandchildren, as requested by the Wildlife Trusts on their 100th anniversary (not to be opened for 50 years, unless you can't wait).

My dearest grandchildren

I am writing this in 2012. I am 70. Not as old as the Wildlife Trusts, but old enough to have seen a lot of changes. Throughout my teenage years and beyond, I was an obsessive birdwatcher. If you had asked me then: 'What is the state of the British countryside and wildlife?' I would have said: 'It seems OK to me.' I saw lots of birds on farmland, flowers in the meadows, frogs and fish in the streams, marine life in the rock pools, seabirds on the cliffs and so much more, and it all seemed fine. Looking back now, I was surely dwelling in blissful ignorance. I wasn't the only one. The principal agenda of a naturalists' club was to enjoy fun and fascination, not to fret over problems and dilemmas.

Then, in the 1970s and 1980s, I – and everyone else – had to learn a whole new vocabulary. 'Nature study' became 'environmental studies'. Surveys and analyses begat figures and facts, which spawned such ominous words as 'declining', 'threatened', 'endangered', and – gloomiest of all – 'extinct'. The grim truth was emerging that there was nary a species nor habitat that was not cause for concern. Knowing this, it was inevitable that for many naturalists their hobby became a crusade.

Now kids, at this point you are probably expecting me to apologise on behalf of my generation, but I am not going to. The state of the wild nation wasn't our fault, except in so far as we might have been a bit slow to notice. But that is often how it is with change. Like Joni Mitchell sang: 'You don't know what you've got till it's gone.' She was singing about woodland ('they've taken all the trees and put them in a tree museum') but the same could apply to heathland, downland, wetland, or any kind of land, or to any of the creatures that live there. At least we realised what we'd got. Maybe just in time.

People of my age are apt to comfort themselves and try to impress young folk by revelling in the (almost) unarguable achievements of the 1960s and 1970s. Ah, to be a teenager with The Beatles and The Stones, to witness the birth of satire, to be buying records during the decade of the great seminal LPs, and to be a viewer during what will likely be judged as the golden age of television. Frankly, kids, we never had it so good – and you certainly haven't – and I am proud to have been part of it. But we old folk have one more claim to fame. Or is 'fame' too ephemeral, too frivolous? 'Satisfaction' is a nobler sensation. Yes, the sixties and seventies gave us magical music and terrific telly, but it also saw the proliferation of environmental awareness. Knowledge.

No longer could polluters, poisoners or desecrators claim that they didn't realise that what they were doing was wrong, or that they didn't know how it could be put right. It continues to be true today. Even on a massive global scale, we are aware of both the problems and the solutions. Whether knowledge leads to action depends on the resources – the money! – the will and the passion, and above all the power.

Now, kids – and your kids if you have any (two maximum please) – I don't know if you care about the natural world, but if you do and you want to actually get things done rather than just have an opinion, then please never forget those two words: 'passion' and 'power'. The power can refer to 'people power', public opinion and protest. Never let it be underestimated, but its limitation is that while we punters may influence the lawmakers, we do not draft, pass or enforce the laws. You – and I – have the passion, but not the power. What the world needs are more people with both. Genuinely, honestly. Not a pretence, the real thing.

Do you get my drift? I am trying to give you a little career guidance. Not just to you kids, but to anyone. Assuming you love and care about wild things and wild places, what kind of job should you aim for? A warden of a nature reserve? No. In the PR Department of an NGO? No. A farmer? Mm, better. Prime Minister? Yes! Minister for the Environment. Now you're talking. The minister of anything? Any MP? Yes. A housing developer? A town planner? CEO of a multinational oil company? Richard Branson? Rupert Murdoch? Simon Cowell?

Or am I just being silly? Well, all that lot have the power. If any one – or better still three or four – of them had a passion for wildlife, I think it would help. Don't you? Oh, I don't suppose you remember any of them! Lucky!

Keep it natural.

Love,

The Green Grandad

PS Did they ever build HS2?
PPS Did they ever reintroduce Wolves?
PPS Did they ever have to cull the kites?

GRANDAD BIRD WATCHING IN HIS YOUNGER DAYS.

FALLING OFF A BLOG

TWEETS   PODCASTS   FACE BOOK
      BLOGS   INSTAGRAM   YOU TUBE
  BUT I HAVEN'T GOT ANYTHING TO SAY
THAT DOESN'T STOP EVERYBODY ELSE!

This is a message to anyone who used to follow my blog on my website – I am sorry that I gave up doing it, but at least I hope the rest of this book brings back pleasant memories, so you won't mind reading it again. If you didn't enjoy these 'posts' the first time, I can only plead that you give them a second chance. If you are not aware that I ever had a blog, that is good, because this means that these pieces will be entirely new to you. I hope you enjoy them.

By the way, the reason – or excuse – for giving up blogging was not because of laziness, forgetfulness or lack of interesting incident in my life. It was simply that it got too much for me once I started writing a monthly page for *BBC Wildlife*, providing quotes for NGOs' press releases, tweeting about everything from badger culls to Manchester United, and discovering that fans of Reading Football Club sing 'Bill Oddie, Bill Oddie, rub your beard all over my body!' When I heard this, I was flattered yet fearful. I warned them it could be a curse. It was. They were relegated. But they will be back. And some day, so will I.

Meanwhile, here is a selection of what I called News of the Wild. Note the often slightly salacious headings to each paragraph. They were intended as a tribute to the Rupert Murdoch school of journalism.

I DONT CARE IF ACORNS ARE MORE "NATURAL" I PREFER BIRD SEED!

BLOG ONE

News of the Wild

Unnatural urges

I have a small dilemma (ooh, missus!). The title of this blog, 'News of the Wild', is, of course, a deft and ironic reference to a recently defunct Sunday newspaper famed for featuring smut and scandal undiluted by accuracy or truth. It rarely covered wildlife or the environment; hence the irony. However, as I hinted in last month's blog (still available on archive) I am developing a tendency to become more diversified myself. To put it bluntly, less wild and more news, whatever the topic. I confess I feel a bit as if I am rejecting the religious in favour of the secular, but it's a decision brought about by two things: first, I now have my very own page each month in the unarguably authoritative and sumptuously illustrated magazine *BBC Wildlife*, which satisfies my 'natural' urges, as it were. Second, I feel justified in making this and future blogs as random, as frivolous or as contentious as I like. Hence, my dilemma is should I now call it 'News of the World'?! Am I allowed to? Or would I be in trouble with Rupert Murdoch? Actually, he might well be grateful to me for taking the name off his hands. But then I'd probably get investigated for phone tapping. I think I'll stick with 'News of the Wild'. Apropos of which…

Dig

I have been conducting a little Grey Squirrel experiment. Don't worry, nothing unpleasant. We all know that Grey Squirrels (and Red ones) gather up acorns at this time of the year and then bury them all over the place – especially in my lawn – so that if the winter gets harsh and food gets short, they can dig up their hidden stash. I am sure all of us have wondered whether or not they are clever enough to remember exactly where the acorns are buried, or do they just scamper around digging more holes until they get lucky? The answer is 'no' and 'yes.' No, they don't remember and, yes, it's just potluck if they find any acorns, which is why they bury so many.

Lovely acorns

Nevertheless, I have to agree it is a pretty enterprising strategy that benefits many hungry squirrels and plants a few new oak trees at the same time. Which brings me to my experiment. The nearest oak tree to my house is about half a mile away, and to get to and from it entails crossing two or three busy roads, whether you are a human or a rodent. I decided to make life easier for my garden squirrels. Thus, I returned from my morning saunter on Hampstead Heath having collected a bulging pocketful of acorns. I went out into the back garden – causing two squirrels to panic and fall off the bird feeders – and I placed the acorns carefully and conspicuously on a dilapidated birdtable that I have not thrown away in case it comes in handy for scientific experiment, like this one. I uttered a lilting cry, such as was once used by cockney street vendors: 'Get your lovely acorns. Sweet and succulent, straight from the oak tree!'

Tails atwitching

Even as I retreated indoors, there were two curious squirrels peering over the garden fence with tails atwitching. I peeped out through the back window. Squirrels on the fence. Acorns on the table. How long would it be before they descended on their personally delivered breakfast? I waited half an hour. Squirrels on bird feeders. Acorns still on table. I went up to my office and did a couple of hours' writing. I came down again and looked out of the back window. Squirrels gone. Acorns hadn't. I went outside and counted them: 35. One more than I put out! I recounted: 34. OK, the same as I put out. Later in the day, there were still 34. As dusk fell, the same. Next morning: three squirrels now, but still 34 acorns. Two days later, and the pile appeared still intact, though my count revealed that two acorns were missing. I found them on the floor.

Repugnant

This morning, after four days, about half of the acorns have gone, been disturbed, or in some cases slightly nibbled. I suspect Jays. So what do I deduce from this experiment? That Grey Squirrels don't like acorns at all? Indeed, the very aroma of them is so repugnant that they bury them rather than tolerate it. Only as a very last resort, in winters when starvation is nigh, will they dig them up and endure the ghastly taste of emergency rations.

Or is it that Grey Squirrels prefer good-quality bird food? I could help them there!

Marketing ploy?

Talking of bird food, I was in my local garden centre the other day when I happened to accidentally peruse the range of bird foods produced by a company whose brand name shall remain unrevealed, but wasn't Haith's or me. What caught my eye was the fact that nearly every one of a large number of bags bore a picture of a different species and that the claim on the bag was that the food therein would attract the species depicted. There was a specific food for Robins, Blackbirds, Song Thrushes, Blue Tits, Great Tits, Goldfinches, 'finches', swans, ducks (what happened to geese?) and sparrows (meant to be House Sparrows but the picture was of a Dunnock). Now, I am not insinuating that this is some kind of marketing ploy, and certainly not that the product is below par, but let me assure you that you don't have to purchase a dozen or more different foods to attract a good selection of birds. There are certain groups: ground feeders, seed-eaters, soft-food eaters, but beyond that, put it this way: Blackbirds, Song Thrushes and Robins have much the same tastes. As do Greenfinches and Chaffinches, and so on.

Of course, the Grey Squirrels will eat anything that isn't meant for them!

Done it again

Well, I've done it again! I allude to a blog full of laughter and lasciviousness and end up writing about garden wildlife. Next time, next time; I promise.

Are you sitting comfortably?

But before I migrate south for a few days to the Isles of Scilly… The other morning I was having brekky in our local tea-room. At a nearby table, a Hampstead mum was reading a ToyTown book to her toddler-aged son. He wasn't toddling then, he was sitting and listening intently, and I admit so was I. Imagine my surprise when mum showed a picture to the boy and said: 'Look, Noddy's got a satnav!' Unfortunately, mother and child departed, plus the book, and I hadn't the nerve to call after her: 'Noddy's got a satnav! Is that true?'

I hurried home, not certain which was shocking me most, that Noddy's car had had a 21st-century makeover, or that I'd started hearing voices about updating children's stories. As luck would have it, my wife, Laura, writes for children's television. She would not only know about such modernisations, but may even be responsible for some of them.

Disaster

It probably wasn't the first question she expected to hear when I got home: 'Laura, does Noddy have a satnav?' She had to think about it. Then she made a pronouncement that I felt had just a tinge of defensiveness about it, almost as if I had insulted the integrity of her profession. 'I am sure Noddy doesn't have a satnav. We don't change traditional characters. Of course, Bob the Builder has a mobile. And in one series he did have a laptop, but that was a disaster.'

I bet it was. And as for Winnie-the-Pooh getting hooked on World of Warcraft… And have you seen Angelina Ballerina's Facebook page?

SATNAV! BORING! I'VE GOT FREEVIEW. I WATCH "TOPGEAR" WHEN I'M DRIVING!

What do you mean:
"you hate the tadpoles?!"
Daisy..?

Not 'hate' —
I said, 'ATE!
mmm mm..

BLOG TWO

Frogs' Porn

Who's been eating my frogspawn?

I know it is only a small pleasure, but a few weeks ago I was so happy when one morning I pottered into my garden and discovered that the smallest and shallowest of my five ponds contained not one but two tightly clustered dollops of frogspawn. I was not only delighted but also surprised, since I was yet to see a frog in the garden this spring. However, a few minutes later, a telltale plop and ripple revealed there were in fact two frogs in the slightly larger pond about half a metre away. I must have overlooked them, which is understandable since that pond is not only larger but also much deeper. By the way, if you'd prefer more precise dimensions, the spawn pond is about a metre long and a couple of inches deep, while the larger one is maybe a centimetre more in length, but is a veritable garden Loch Ness, with a depth of at least a foot. While I'm at it – for the completists among you – my third pond is perched in the rockery like a diminutive mountain lake, and, like many real mountain lakes, is devoid of wildlife. Number four is ready-made, moulded and rather dull. It is adjacent to the bird feeders and is consequently used mainly for drinking and bathing. By the birds, that is. The waters are continually agitated by a small fountain, which sprays out unpredictably and randomly, but intentionally as I have amended the 'spout' by fixing a small piece of hollow wood over it, which is riddled with holes and therefore expels water all over the place, especially when the whole fragile arrangement is knocked skew-whiff by a clumsy pigeon (is there any other kind?).

The big pond

Finally there is the 'big pond' at the end of the garden. This used to be the one I dutifully dug out when we first moved into the house about 30 years ago. The previous owners had built a raised concrete patio in about the daftest available site which – due to a canopy of vast trees in surrounding gardens – received no sun whatsoever. It would also have been a pretty lousy place for a flowerbed. One might have thought that the same shivering shadows that prevented anything blooming or blossoming would also have deterred anyone wishing to bask, read or snooze in a deckchair. To be honest, when I first saw the supposed patio it didn't look as if anything living had visited it for years, except the snails, centipedes and woodlice that lurked or scuttled under the pile of old plant pots.

But I knew what I was going to do with it. I had never had a garden pond. In fact, I'd never really had what you might call a garden. Now that I had, I was overwhelmed by a pioneering spirit. Anyone who can remember the day they dug their own pond will no doubt recall the many emotions. The exhilaration, the anticipation, the stress, the throbbingly aching limbs from the digging, and the ever-worsening feelings of exhaustion and nausea that come from being hunched over for however long it takes to create a hole long, wide and deep enough. In my view, it should take a day. It might take less, but it must not take more. It is a matter of pride to be able to announce: 'I've built a garden pond!', whereupon you will be asked: 'How long did it take you?' To which the imperative answer is a nonchalant: 'Oh about a day. Well, less than a day actually. About a morning.'

Your audience will be impressed and doubly so when you amend the time scale to: 'Well less than a day actually, not much more than a morning.' Hopefully this will encourage, challenge or indeed oblige them to have a go in their garden. If they do that's great, but if they don't, it is your next duty to make them feel guilty. 'It'll take less than a morning, honestly. Garden ponds are really important. Not just for frogs. All sorts of things.'

Hosepipes ahoy!

My big pond was a major feat of engineering, involving the wielding of two sledgehammers, the gouging out of several weighty bucketfuls of London clay, and the laying of a butyl liner (butyl is rubbery waterproof stuff), and the final filling up process (no hosepipe bans in those days) which was carried out at least three times, until I finally got the water level level, if you see what I mean. It was a lot of work, requiring a degree of expertise, which I didn't have, but it was indeed basically completed within one day, albeit the final filling had to be conducted after dark by the glow of a couple of garden lamps. I also left the back door open so that music from my hi-fi drifted out which, coupled with the burbling hosepipe and the flashing lighting (I fixed the dodgy wiring later in the week), combined to create a passably impressive 'son et lumière'.

There is, alas, a slightly ironical postscript to the story of my big pond.

It is still there, but not in its original form. The butyl lining lasted for a couple of decades until it started to leak and the water began to seep away into the clay. I immediately resolved to repair or replace. However, after 20 odd years, the butyl lining wasn't the only thing that had deteriorated. So had I. My sledgehammer and digging days were over. I had by then created my several little ponds. I'd dug one, but for the others I had used those moulded plastic substitutes you can buy at the garden centre. Once put in place (I recommend a spirit level) and furnished with a few aquatics, they rapidly attracted a modicum of wildlife, most notably, of course, the frogs. So the question now was: how big a moulded pond can I get? The answer was 'flipping enormous'. To get one home in a car, to quote *Jaws*: I was gonna need a bigger car! Or a smaller pond. Hence the size of my new big pond was dictated by what I could get into my Renault Clio.

Prefers full sunshine

It was a bit sad placing a plastic pond in the hole left by what had been a 'natural' one, but by the time I had disguised the edges with rocks and branches and put a few little pots of aquatics on the ledges, it looked reasonably authentic. A slightly more powerful fountain than I had on the 'bird-feeder pond' added a classic running water sound, just like on the meditation CDs, while the permanent cascade almost qualified it as a 'water feature', like Alan Titchmarsh talks about. But of course this wasn't a 'water feature', it was a 'wildlife pond'. A title it totally merits, except for one thing. At no stage during its first two decades as a natural pond, nor during the several years since it went plastic, has my big pond attracted anything that could be judged to be wildlife! There are probably a few woodlice under the damper logs, but I have never ever seen anything truly aquatic, either in or on the water. There is, of course, an obvious reason. Just as a corner that never gets the sun is a pretty useless place to put a patio, or a flower bed, it is also a pretty unproductive site for a pond!

Dollops!

On the other hand, a small shallow pond, created by sacrificing a little patch of lawn that is in the sun almost all day, is 'frog paradise' and 'spawn city'. The double dollop was only the start. Next morning, there were two or three more portions; the next day the quantity had doubled, even if the frog count hadn't. Most springs there is one, usually rainy and mild, night, when it seems that all the frogs in a particular region feel the primal urges rising in their froggy loins and set off to their ancestral mating ground, or pond, where they indulge in what can only be called an orgy. It is not romantic, and it doesn't even look enjoyable, as males grab and grapple with females, until some of them are literally suffocated or drowned. One is tempted to comment: 'I've heard of a bit of rough but this is ridiculous!' Slightly disturbing though it be, I rejoice at the yearly gang-bang when my littlest pond is one day a seething cauldron of amphibian lust, and the next morning a very large helping of tapioca. This year, however, it wasn't like that.

The spawn bank

Or rather, there was only half of the equation. I never did see more than two or three frogs, and the only coupling was a soft and sensual demonstration of the request: 'be gentle with me'. And yet every day the spawn bank got bigger and bigger, until the pond was quite literally full! At this point, the frogs decided their work was at an end – as well they might – and I have not seen them, or any others since.

The circle of life

What I did witness was the beginning of one of the few life cycles that, as they say, every schoolboy (and girl) knows, and has probably witnessed. It wasn't long before several of the spawn clusters began the process, as the little black dots got a bit less little, and acquired a smidgeon of a tail shape. One particularly sunny morning stimulated the first wrigglers, and gave me a hint of what a tureen of life and energy my pond would eventually become, not to mention the hopping hordes of froglets that would invade my lawn.

It was going so well

Then something puzzling happened. They all disappeared. Dots, tiny tadpoles and spawn. The lot. All gone. No, I exaggerate. In fact, after swishing my hand gently in the weeds and water I disturbed one single tiny tadpole. I caught it in a cup and plopped it into a small tank along with a dozen others that I was rearing as exhibits to entertain my grandchildren. And myself. As I did so, it struck me that the ones I had rescued were still alive and well. Whatever had happened to the others, hadn't happened to them. But what had happened? I rummaged on the internet, but basically only confirmed what I had figured out for myself. Was it infertility, or was it what one might call lack of manpower? Male frogs don't impregnate the female and leave her to lay eggs, job done. She produces the spawn, and he then has to do the rounds, fertilising as much of it as he can. I sympathised with the male in my garden. There was a veritable spawn mountain, and possibly only him to fertilise it. Maybe he ran out of juice, as it were, or energy. I would not have blamed him, but the evidence didn't fit the theory.

I had noticed that some of the dots in the eggs had turned milky white and were presumably dead. That was most likely the result of a couple of days of late cold weather, which even included snow. In addition, some of the 'jelly' was limp and lifeless and could have been infertile, or rather unfertilised. But by no means all. Out of a pond full of spawn, and thousands of potential tadpoles, some casualties are to be expected, but there was no sign of any escalating epidemic or impending massacre. The depletion I had seen so far seemed perfectly natural. Until that morning, when *everything* disappeared. Except my little sample colony. They were fine in their tank. Whatever had got everything else hadn't got them. Surely that meant it was neither freeze nor disease.

An acquired taste
Was it possible that the whole pondful had been eaten? Or should that be drunk? To be honest I have never really thought of tadpoles as food or prey, but think of them as aquatic worms or slugs, or indeed small frogs, and they must surely get gobbled up by, for example, birds. I had noticed a queue of the usual suspects lurking and lunging by or even in the pond. Magpies and Jays were circumstantially guilty, but the only species I actually saw grab a 'taddy' and devour it was a Robin! No doubt quite a number slid down into that plump little scarlet tummy, but surely not all of them! And what about the glutinous globules? Imagine pecking at a pile of transparent jelly. It would take birds a week to get through it. Or had there been an enemy within, under the water? I don't think so. I keep no fish and I have never seen a newt in the garden.

So whodunnit?
A possible clue awaited me down by the shed. I confess I have a bit of an aversion to throwing away household chattels and furniture. This isn't for environmental reasons. I could, of course, take it to the recycling centre. However, I would rather incorporate suitable items into the decor of the garden, as it were. Thus, there are a number of mirrors and picture frames secreted among the foliage, and a lilac tree is decorated with kitchen utensils, such as knives and forks, cheese graters and whisks. Recently, a bamboo beaded door curtain became redundant and, since it was already

organic and indeed almost 'jungly', I fixed it up by the garden shed where it hung down and masked the dustbin, while also looking as if it shrouded a mysterious portal through the fence into a wild and magic land. Or something like that. Anyway, I liked it. But someone or something else didn't.

Temper, temper

Already mourning the desecration at the pond, I was now further appalled by an act of blatant vandalism. My beaded curtain had not only been pulled down to the ground, every single strand had been pulled off, and most of them were twisted and tangled, as if they had been shaken in a fit of temper, violent enough to also leave a scattering of bamboo and beads all round the shed. But though vanishing tadpoles puzzled me, destructive delinquency didn't. I knew instantly who was guilty. This was the work of Foxy.

There's gratitude for you

Heaven knows, I love to see urban Foxes in the garden, but it has to be said that our local representative is a bit of a hooligan. In recent times, he has chewed a gnome in half, beheaded a plaster pig, disembowelled a plastic Lapwing and pulled one of my water pumps out of the pond and gnawed at the flex. I trust he is grateful that I apprehended him before he electrocuted himself, but obviously not, or he wouldn't have destroyed my beaded curtain. Or eaten my tadpoles.

Dining at Oddie's

OK, I am not 100 per cent certain. I wouldn't risk taking him to court. But I have now heard from a few other people who have witnessed such a thing, and it does makes sense physically, as it were. Think of Foxy taking a wander through the Hampstead gardens, feeling peckish, imagining the well-healed householders picking at their Weight Watchers vol-au-vents and sipping their Pinots. 'I could do with a nibble,' he's thinking. 'Nothing too heavy. And a wee sip of pond water would go down nicely. I know, Oddie's.' So he slinks across a couple of lawns, leaps up on the Ivy-covered fence, trots along the top as daintily as a tightrope walker, and leaps off into Oddie's. Only to find himself trussed up in a bamboo curtain, which he can only disentangle himself from by tearing it to shreds. Not a lot of things spook old Foxy, but for a second there he thought he'd been trapped in some kind of net, and – own up – he panicked. 'Blimey, I need a stiff drink. Oddie's pond water! Not out of that horrible pretend pond; you can taste the plastic. The littlest pond. He fills that from the water butt. Pure rainwater, none more natural.'

From a sip to a slurp

So he takes a sip, and finds his nose covered in jelly! Maybe he's not sure what it is and tastes it and quite likes it. Or perhaps in Fox world frogspawn is a bit of a delicacy. My pond is like a huge bowl of caviar, or an enormous dish of tapioca or sago. There are little black wriggly things in there, too, not much meat on them, but quite an intriguing flavour. 'Reminds me of frog. Oh, of course, silly me – frogspawn. An acquired taste, but – you know what? – I think I have just acquired it.'

Whereupon, he slurps the lot.

Or was it?

Well, that's my theory, and I am sticking to it. The better news is that the tiny tadpole team that I decanted into the fish tank are doing fine, and some are looking distinctly froggish. And another glimmer of good news. Maybe Foxy is innocent after all, because I have just seen another possible culprit crouching on a garden chair and swiping his paws at the tadpole tank, which he won't get into 'cos I have put a lid on it. 'Come back for more, have you, Timmy?' Next door's cat! I know he had my Blue Tits, so I bet he thought: 'I'll have his tadpoles too!'

And I can't even do what I usually do to him. Flippin' hosepipe ban!

I DONT MIND THE OCCASIONAL FROG
BUT THAT STUFF IS REVOLTING !!

BLOG THREE

Whodunnit?

Suspense

OK, I'm sorry, I'm sorry, I'm sorry. Six weeks since my last blog. Six weeks waiting and wondering if my few remaining tadpoles have survived. How could I keep you in suspense like this? Don't I realise the pain of unrequited anticipation? Yes, yes; I do, I do. I felt the same about the next episode of *Homeland*, and *The Bridge*, and Manchester City's horribly inevitable last-minute goal. I even felt a twinge of tension before Pudsey, the dog, was quite rightly acclaimed as the most talented thing on television. And talking of television, I can't even use work as an excuse for not blogging. Well, not working on telly anyway, or doing anything I get paid for, well not yet anyway, though I am owed a small fistful of fees by the BBC and Channel 5 and half a dozen theatres. But I have been very, very busy.

Oh yeah! Doing what?

Well, there were those half-dozen gigs – oh ok, 'shows', talks, 'evenings with' type things. The 'with' being me and my longtime BBC TV producer Stephen Moss. Well, he isn't just mine; he's done lots of stuff on his own too. Anyway, we treat the audience to an evening of the 'best of' wildlife clips from over 10 years' worth of my own natural history series, introduced by and garnished with anecdotes and revelations. It is called 'Bill Oddie Unplucked', which means nothing but is further evidence that I wish I had been a musician (as in 'Unplugged', geddit?) It went rather well and we will probably do it again, so watch this space, as they say. So, that is a week 'on the road' accounted for, plus a couple of days recovering for me, while Stephen wrote another couple of books, no doubt now available from the appropriate website or even a real bookshop.

Tweet tweet

Writing is something else that has taken up quite a bit of my time. I have been tweeting with a regularity and occasionally an enthusiasm that has even surprised me. Anyone who has been following me will know that even my obsessions show little consistency, and the range of topics and targets could be described as 'scattergun'. Anything from the Queen's Speech to leaf blowers, via recent music releases, sport and, of course, conservation and animal rights.

My Twitter page is called Bill Oddie Official, to distinguish it from the disturbingly large number of tweeters pretending to be me. OK, it's maybe only two or three but it's still weird.

BBC

At rather greater length than 140 characters, I have produced two more monthly pages for *BBC Wildlife Magazine*, composed a letter from PETA to the Beeb protesting at the *Great British Menu* featuring recipes using foie gras (which involves hideously cruel force-feeding of geese, and in any case is not British). I also wrote a foreword for a forthcoming book called *The Dog That Survived the Titanic*, featuring heroic birds and mammals, both wild and domestic. It is hardly erudite but it is fun.

Daisy Daisy

During the time I have not been performing, writing or watching Chelsea do unlikely things to teams that are obviously better than them (but congratulations, especially to Big Drog) or keeping up with Nordic thrillers or English talent shows (not so thrilling), I have quite often ventured outside; proper outdoors, that is. The most distant excursions were to Norfolk. First, to the splendid Pensthorpe (for two years the home of *Springwatch*) for a delightful day celebrating the local River Wensum. I was accompanied by my new friend Daisy, who is yellow and has instant rapport with little children, even though they have not met her before. I am not sure exactly what species Daisy is. She says she is a Nature Bug, but as one precocious infant announced: 'She is not real!' Mind you, this didn't stop him wanting a cuddle. Daisy is a dispenser of awesome hugs which the kids accepted gleefully. Unlike my daughter Rosie, who at the age of four was introduced to Mickey Mouse at Disney World and instantly screamed and dived under the table at the 'Character Breakfast'. By the time she emerged it was time for the Character Lunch! I admit Rosie had my sympathy; my instinct was to do exactly the same. Out-of-work actors in character costumes with enormous heads but no voices give me the creeps. Daisy is not like that at all. Check her out. Check us both out.

Happy birthday

After the Pensthorpe day I drove up to Cley on the north Norfolk coast in the role of a sort of roving ambassador for the Wildlife Trusts, which were 100 years old in mid-May. That stretch of coastline is one of the most impressive demonstrations of what organised conservation can achieve. From the Wash to Cromer is in effect one continuous nature reserve, with various segments owned and managed by different but cooperating groups, such as the RSPB, the Norfolk Ornithologists' Association, Natural England, the National Trust and the Norfolk Wildlife Trust. Ah, if only the whole British coastline was protected like this! And the rivers, and the sea and – oh everything!

Dream on.

Simon, Sir David and me

The Trusts' birthday celebrations continued back in London. In the morning, at Gunnersbury Triangle, an urban reserve threatened by further encroachment of blocks of flats. That was the serious side of the day. In the evening, came the fully fledged 'posh do'. It was held at the Natural History Museum in South Kensington (maybe my favourite building in London). In the Great Hall, a massive towering dinosaur skeleton stands astride the orderly phalanxes of sparklingly coordinated round tables, bedecked in black and silver and each one sprouting a bouquet of wild flowers at the hub, which we were allowed – nay encouraged – to take home. The 'we' consisted of representatives past and present of sundry departments of the Wildlife Trusts and other NGOs (non-governmental organisations, i.e. charities). Neatly staged in natural breaks during the meal, we were treated to a sepia-tinted slide show of 'the old days'. Followed by words of wisdom from Sir David Attenborough (I don't think he knows any other kind of words!), a rallying cry by the current president, Simon King, and a quirky if perhaps slightly puzzling declamation from me of a letter I had been asked to write for my grandchildren to read in 50 years' time! By then they would be in their sixties. I just wouldn't be. A couple of people later told me that they found my performance 'inspiring'. Maybe because it proved it is possible to take a totally confusing concept and make it sound as if it makes sense. Perhaps they were politicians.

Talking of politicians

Guess where I was on the evening of Tuesday 22 May? The Chelsea Flower Show? No, I was there in the afternoon. In the evening I was at the Houses of Parliament! No, not sitting on the pavement with a placard. Nor haranguing the House during Prime Minister's question time. To be honest, I don't know what the bit we were in was called, but it took clearing several security checks and clattering down endless stone corridors to get there. I do know that if you go out on the balcony you overlook the Thames, which was nice. I had been asked to arrive at 8.30pm-ish, by which time I assumed that the MPs would have been let out of school and would now be guzzling and gorging in the tuck shop. Actually, I passed a whole corridor of 'tuck shops', or small dining rooms, each one harbouring a table groaning with wine, spirits and food, with a clientele of gentlemen groaning from having gobbled it all down too quickly. Meetings, receptions, committees, gatherings, piss-ups, jollies? Whatever they were, one component was blatantly almost missing. Women. Happily, this was not the case in our room. I am pleased – nay smug! – to be able to say that gender equality is exemplary in the world of conservation and animal welfare. If anything, I dare say women predominate, which I consider totally a good thing.

Cruel sports

Unfortunately, the other side tend to be largely men. What do I mean by 'the other side?' I can best elucidate by telling you more about that particular evening. The event was convened by The League Against Cruel Sports. It was to celebrate the appointment of a team of 10 investigators, whose task it is to track down people breaking animal-rights laws, and gather enough evidence to lead to convictions. This is what one might call the dark and dangerous side of the sort of work done by the RSPCA. I could recount distressing details, but suffice it to say that there is an escalating amount of cruelty occurring in Britain, much of it under the sickeningly inappropriate heading of 'sport'. Despite the ban on hunting with dogs, clandestine meets still take place, with a degree of attendant savagery. Even more shocking, there is a revival of the sort of practices that one might have thought became extinct during the Dark Ages. Badger-baiting, hare-coursing, cock-fighting and dog-fighting. The activities are, of course, illegal, as well as appallingly cruel. The perpetrators are also involved in betting on the outcomes of the fights, and also in many cases in drug-dealing, robbery and so on. These people are criminals. They are also almost without exception men. The League Against Cruel Sports operates on the front line. Other organisations fight their battles with political weapons: eloquence, argument, integrity, honesty, legality, unity of purpose and perhaps – most important of all – public opinion.

Cull, destroy, trap

Ironically, just as politicians are our allies –'our side' – so too are they often our enemies – 'the other side'. That evening, a small

contingent of MPs supporting the Countryside Alliance had duly
announced their presence with the sort of heckling and jeering
which seems to constitute the language of debate at Westminster.
It sounds more like a farmyard than an assembly of honourable
gentlemen. Rather appropriate I thought. By the time I gave my
speech the room was much quieter. Maybe they'd been taken
home to bed, or maybe they didn't think I was worth heckling.
Actually, I was rather disappointed not to have the opportunity of
talking to some of the other side. I wanted to know why this
Government is still minded to support the culling of Badgers. And
why they are granting estate owners the right to destroy Buzzards'
nests and to trap and remove the birds, illegal measures sanctioned
in the name of protecting the pheasant-shooting industry.

And?

I could go on. I already have done. No doubt I will again.
Meanwhile, if you are curious or incensed enough to want to
find out more, you know what to do: visit those websites. Listen
to the 'fors' and the 'againsts'. Examine your own beliefs and
emotions. And ask yourself one of the most fundamental questions
in life and folk song: 'Which side are you on?'

What's been eating my spawn?

Oh blimey! I have just realised! Here I am, utterly immersed in a
swamp of contention and lost in a labyrinth of polemics, and I
have forgotten to answer the one question that has been keeping
you on tenterhooks for six weeks of sleepless nights. *What
happened to my tadpoles?* For anyone who does not have the
story indelibly and permanently emblazoned on their
consciousness, may I suggest that you click on my last blog (yes, I
know it was the middle of April, sorry, sorry) and remind yourself
of the story. For those who can't be arsed, I shall rapidly reiterate
for you.

Small pond in my garden. Overflowing with frogspawn. One
morning, all gone! My theory: a Fox had swallowed the lot. Sort
of Fox sushi. However, I had rescued about a dozen taddies and
put them in a fish tank on the garden table. For a while, doing
fine. Then one morning, fish tank devoid of life. Taddies on table
nearby, dead or dying! What did that? Surely not a Fox! Surely a

bird, but why didn't it eat them? Sheer devilment? Which bird? Chief suspects, all seen on table now and then: Magpie, Jay, Great Tit, domestic pigeons, Wren, Blackbird, Robin. Only one species actually caught in the act of tadpole dipping. The Robin! But surely he didn't have all the spawn as well? Expert comment by Simon King: 'I can believe the Robin, but not the Fox.' So, Simon, what *did* take all the frogspawn? 'I honestly don't know,' said Simon.

That is the mark of true authorities – when they don't know something, they admit it.

Politicians take note.

CAUGHT RED-BREASTED....!

Weather Report

Seen it, hate it

I feel as if I ought to write about the weather, 'cos everybody else does. Of course by the time you read this we could be sloshing around in floods caused by a sudden thaw, but for the moment the view from my window is as bleak, white and icy as the Arctic. It's not the least bit pretty, and it wasn't even after the first fall, which was about a week ago although it feels more like a year. In fact, it is as if January's weather has linked up with December's and the whole of spring, summer and autumn never happened. At least I enjoyed it in January. I did slip over three times on Hampstead Heath's notoriously treacherous pathways and cracked a rack of ribs – mine, not from the butchers – but I still had a backdrop of a white wonderland and an audience of some of the biggest and best dressed snowmen I have ever seen. This year, though, there are no snowmen, and everyone is trudging around with a doleful expression that says: 'Snow? Seen it. Hate it.'

Flustered

At chilly times like these it is customary to ask 'what about the wildlife'? Any day now the RSPB will be exhorting us to 'feed the birds, and don't forget to provide unfrozen water', while the classier Sunday papers will carry artfully photographed snowscapes, with shadows, silhouettes and deer or ponies. At least, hopefully, we will no longer have to stomach seasonal scenes of stampedes of scarlet-clad 'country folk' eager to match the red of their coats with the blood of a terrified Fox. Talking of which, I have just witnessed something rather striking in my garden. No, the Hampstead Hunt hasn't just galloped through, but I did see their quarry. At midday, in broad daylight, a truly handsome fellow peered down from my shed roof as if he had just that second risen from beneath a blanket of snow as white as his own chin. His nose shone, his eyes twinkled and his coat glowed so brightly it looked as if you could warm your hands on it. If only. Even as I made a flustered grab for my camera, he popped down out of sight, and popped up again on our next-door neighbour's shed roof, which – unlike my flat one – has a steep slope, down which Foxy duly slid. He dropped – well, OK, tumbled – behind a privet hedge, hopefully in a nice soft snowdrift.

Dangle

I have yet to notice any of my garden birds looking unusually hungry. This is because they are continuously gorging themselves on the three kinds of high-class birdseed I put out for them, or on the top grade peanuts, or the extra-nutritious fat balls, or the three bowls of live mealworms. Not that they look terribly alive in these temperatures. I wonder if mealworms feel the cold? Never mind, they'll soon be snug and warm inside a Blackbird's tummy. Or a Song Thrush's, or a Robin's, or any one of three species of tits, or a Jay's or a Magpie's. Jays and Magpies aren't supposed to dangle. Especially not on small plastic feeders with conical lids on them to deter larger birds such as, for instance, Jays or Magpies, both of which have in my garden learnt to dangle almost as deftly as the Blue Tits to get at the mealworms. Mind you, it took them a bit of practice before they got the idea, and a lot of frantic wing flapping and falling off, which I have to admit gave me hours of enjoyment. Let's face it, Jays and Magpies are such cocky blighters they could do with losing their dignity now and then.

Clammy

So how are the rest of my garden critters reacting to the mini ice age? Foxy looked fine. The squirrels are, if anything, even more hyperactive, especially when they leap onto a snow-covered branch and give themselves a cold shower. The effect is even more spectacular when they jump straight onto a hanging bird feeder so that their weight pulls on the wire, releasing a veritable avalanche of snow from the tree above. It's like one of those rope and bucket showers intrepid campers set up, only they are probably in a clammy jungle, not a frozen garden.

Scare

The local Wood Mice really don't care for this weather at all. I know there's at least one living in the shed, because I have been putting out a bowl of seed, which is duly eaten every night. I know it's a mouse because of the teeny black droppings around the bowl. Also because I had a right old scare the other day when a plastic bag started to rustle and move across the floor, and when I plucked up courage to touch it a Wood Mouse literally leapt out vertically as if it had been fired from a catapult. The shed is not warm. I reckon the spring-heeled leaper really is the only mouse in there. Why? Because the rest of them are inside our house!

Goodies

It has happened before. Even at times when it hasn't been so cold. In fact, I am not convinced that it is the inclement weather that causes my Wood Mice to move into our living space. I think they just like it. I know they enjoy shredding the paper covers off my irreplaceable collection of Goodies' vinyl singles, which I had understandably banished into the corner of a dark cupboard. Just the sort of place mice love. Another one, or possibly two, completely stripped a pink fluffy plant-pot cover my wife had been given as a birthday present. She had not been grateful to the donor, but she was grateful to the mice for ruining it. She also loved the idea of a brood of baby mice being raised in a pink fluffy nest.

Unsavoury

However, the mice's favourite bit of our house is what we call the TV room, because the only thing we do in there is watch TV. It is quite a big TV (HD but not 3D), in quite a small room, but there is just enough space to accommodate a large cosy couch and a slightly dilapidated armchair. The armchair is mine. A detective could tell it belongs to a man of grandad age, because the carpet in front of it is stained with blotches of spilt wine and takeaway curries, plus a scattering of crisp crumbs, and the occasional grape or blueberry. This unsavoury – or maybe savoury – detritus is no doubt the mouse equivalent of a help-yourself buffet, so it's not surprising they are frequent visitors. Not that I ever see them for long.

Climax

Their appearances are almost subliminal, but their timing is ruthlessly impeccable. There I will be, slouched on my greasy yet comfy

I KNOW I DON'T BELONG IN HERE..
BUT I CAN'T GET BROADBAND IN THE WOODS.

cushions, enjoying *Match of the Day* or *Live at the Apollo*. A climax is nigh. The centre forward is bearing down on goal, or the 'stand-up' comic is just about to deliver his punchline, when... zip! What was that? I am distracted for barely a second, but by the time I turn back to the screen, the ball is nestling in the back of the net or the audience is screaming with laughter. As is also, I suspect, the mouse. I know he does it on purpose. He hides under the settee, checks out what's on the telly, waits for a vital moment, then propels himself across the hearthrug and vanishes behind the waste-paper basket. There is no point in me creeping over and peering round, under or in the basket. He won't be there. And he won't be anywhere else I look either. Frankly, I could strip the whole room of every piece of furniture, and I still won't find him. Like as not, I won't even find any potential mouse holes that he may have escaped down either. A magic mouse? I needed to know. So...

Paranoid

Late one night last week, I missed a vital wicket in the Test Match because just as the bowler was running up, the bottom of the curtain moved and I looked away from the screen. The triumphant cry of 'Owzat!' seemed aimed personally at me. I imagined a gleeful mouse, hiding behind the curtain, revelling in his mischief. 'Ha-ha. Gotcha Oddie!' But hang on. Was it a mouse that had got me, or my own imagination? The fact was, I hadn't seen anything at all. Except the curtain moved. Or did it? Was I becoming paranoid? Was it a hallucinatory mouse, or a real mouse? Before I retired for the night, I set a small humane trap – baited with Haith's finest birdseed – right in front of the telly.

We shall see

So what did I find the next morning? A cute little mouse! I admired and photographed him (or her), and released him in the street's communal garden. About 100 metres down the road. 'Not far enough,' several regulars at our local coffee shop have told me. 'You have to take them at least a mile away, otherwise they'll just come back.' Well, we shall see, because before he leapt to freedom, I anointed this little fellow's feet with green food dye. He is a marked mouse.

Watch this space.

< ITS VERY NICE OF THEM TO DIG US A NEW POND —
BUT WHAT'S IN IT FOR THEM ??

Mine all Mine

Hey ho, hey ho

I'm sorry, I'm sorry. I know I haven't blogged for several weeks, but I was in no fit state. Actually, I was in Zambia, East Africa. Oh yeah, swanning around the luxury safari camps in my lightweight linens, I dare say you assume. Well, as a matter of fact, for the first four days I was done up in overalls, wellies and a hard hat. Not the ideal garb when the temperature is high and the humidity is higher, but obligatory if you are dodging diggers, bulldozers and falling rocks, or seeking refuge down a mine shaft. A mine shaft where a large section of the tunnel ceiling was being contained from collapsing by what looked like a giant rope hairnet. In fact it *had* collapsed only a week before, but we were assured that the net meant that that bit was safe now. Of course, no one could vouch for the rest of the tunnel. There was much nervous banter about Chilean miners, being rescued by Lassie, and: 'Please can we get back above ground as quickly as possible?' This we did, only to find ourselves careering through a dust cloud, crammed into a rattling Land Rover, precariously descending into what looked like a massive volcanic crater but was in fact the work of the diggers and bulldozers that had gouged out this giant quarry. At the bottom, a small team of workers were scrabbling in the mud and staring intently downwards, as if all of them had coincidentally lost their contact lenses. The truth was that keen eyesight was essential to their task. They were searching for emeralds.

Emerald city

Now, I have to admit that gemstones and jewellery are not high on my list of interests, nor indeed do I consider them 'precious stones' because they look dazzling, but simply because they are worth a lot of money. Rather like a lot of contemporary art, the value of an emerald seems to be dictated only by what some extremely rich person is prepared to pay. Whatever the price paid, that is what the stone is worth. Until it gets sold to another rich dealer, whereupon it becomes worth even more. During the course of our visit we were frequently enlightened by lectures, demonstrations, PowerPoint presentations, and one-sided conversations about the complexities of the international gem market. To be honest, I understood barely a word. What I did grasp, though, was that the management of this mining company was doing well enough to be able to contribute a considerable sum of money to 'good causes'. In fact, they already were providing medical and schooling facilities for the local people, and – and here at last comes the reason for me donning a hard hat and braving an African mine shaft – they had also subsidised an elephant conservation project in India. They were now anxious to support their own Zambian wildlife, and we were anxious to let them. 'We' were a small deputation representing the World Land Trust, led by their Chief Exec, John Burton. To find out more about the excellent work they do please visit their website: www. worldlandtrust.org.

Show me the money

I have known 'purist' conservationists baulk at the idea of accepting funding from big industrial companies, especially ones that have the potential to destroy or ruin habitats. I remember 50ish years ago when large oil companies, such as Shell and BP, first began espousing wildlife and ecology by funding the publication of new bird books, and maintaining nature trails and reserves and so on, there was a widespread suspicion that it was 'guilt money', and the offers were not always accepted. To put it bluntly, the majority of conservationists nowadays take a more pragmatic attitude to industry, development, etc. The policy is: make sure they do as little damage as possible and hand over as much money as you can get! To be fair, many of these companies are genuinely anxious to appear both responsible and generous.

Trust the Trust

Of course, mining – for emeralds or anything else – is potentially a great wrecker of habitat, especially if it is open-cast. I well recall the state parts of Northumberland and Wales were left in after the ravages of open-cast coal-mining. Fortunately, nowadays there is an obligation to repair the damage. Indeed, excavation can be ultimately constructive. One generation's quarries can become the next generation's lakes, marshes and reedbeds. Just add water! This is already happening in Zambia at the emerald mine we visited. Further negotiations with the World Land Trust are continuing, even as I blog. I will keep you posted.

All Greek to me

All that sounds pretty constructive, doesn't it? So why did I start this blog off with a whinge? Ah, well, I am afraid our emerald-mining hosts made one mistake. On the last night they took us to a Greek restaurant. Not what you'd expect in Zambia, and indeed the food was not so much Greek as sort of Italian. Oh, let's face it, it was a pizza house. Instead of doing the prudent thing, like leaving, at least three of us chose dishes that involved fish or prawns. At some point during coffee, it was pointed out that we could hardly be further away from the sea, in a country probably not renowned for its rapid refrigerated transportation. The consequences were inevitable, unpleasant and lasted throughout the three days we spent at a delightful lodge in Luangwa. Alas, my condition was anything but delightful. A dawn safari drive is not the best thing to calm a queasy tummy and loose bowels. Erratic movement on rutted roads has much the same effect as being tossed around in a rowing boat in a squall, while being caught short leaves you with some pretty insidious choices. You can ask the driver to stop so you can nip behind a bush, but you risk antagonising a family of resting Lions. One can't imagine they would be pleased! Or you can try and hold it in till you get back to the lodge. You can try, but you may not succeed. In case you are wondering… you really don't want to know. And you certainly don't want me to describe it!

Would I recommend Zambia for an African adventure? Yes, yes and yes. Just don't eat the Greek pizza.

Tubby little singers

News from my garden. I am happy to say the Wrens are back. If indeed they ever went away. Certainly, a month ago there wasn't a Wren to be seen or heard in my neighbourhood and I feared that they had been hit very hard by the coldest part of the winter. Then, at the end of March, it was if someone had switched on 'Radio Wren'. Now there must be half a dozen tubby little singers belting it out on what was previously the silent circuit. So did they go, or just go quiet? Some of our birds do perform what are known as 'weather movements' if the weather gets too nasty. Lapwings, Skylarks, some pipits and finches fly off south-west and maybe even over to southern Ireland where it is milder. But Wrens? Surely not? Maybe they have learnt how to hibernate. Anyway, I am very happy they are back.

Shock!

As it happens, I was recently browsing the results of the RSPB's Big Garden Birdwatch. I noticed that Wrens were down at number 20. A considerable slide for a bird that has been regarded as Britain's most numerous. The top two also surprised me: House Sparrow and Starling, though that doesn't mean that they are increasing in number. I have seen neither in my garden for years. Another shock result, no Blackbird in the top 20! And Blue Tit appeared twice at both three and four until the RSPB scorer corrected the mistake and inserted Blackbird at number four where it belonged. Phew! Just in time to head off a 'Save our Blackbirds' campaign on Twitter.

Right then. I am due to cross the Atlantic in a fortnight's time. Going to South Carolina to meet some gibbons. Honestly. All will eventually be revealed. The only downside is that I will miss The Wedding. It will serve them right for not inviting me. They seem a nice young couple. I wonder if she feeds the birds instead of shooting them? It would be great to see a royal setting a good example wouldn't it? After all, it is the *Royal* Society for the Protection of Birds.

TREE BEES OFTEN TAKE OVER OLD NEST BOXES | WHERE IT IS COLD AND DAMP. | THEY'RE WELCOME!

Blow me Down

It's a twister!

Blimey, doesn't time fly, especially when I have been – flying that is. If I remember rightly – it's so long ago – I concluded my last blog by bidding you farewell before boarding a plane bound for Charleston, South Carolina, USA. There I would proceed to Summerville to visit the headquarters of the International Primate Protection League (IPPL), and also the residence of 30-odd gibbons. I was looking forward to it very much. The only small frisson of trepidation was triggered by news of extensive tornado damage in the south-eastern states of the US, including South Carolina. I scared myself even more by logging on to the American Weather Channel, which featured a continuous stream of video clips of ever blacker, ever bigger, and ever more destructive 'twisters'. These had all been sent in by viewers who invariably added a live commentary along the lines of: (please imagine a southern accent) 'I sure seen some twisters in my time, but damned if I seen one big as this!' Or – as if to top that – 'God damnit if there were not just one twister, but two of 'em! Like a pair of angry twins coming straight at us. I'm thinking, Lord, between 'em they gonna lift up the house. All we could do was sit tight and pray. So we did. And you know what? Just before they hit the house, them twister twins split either side of us. One of 'em clean lifted my wife's Chevy off the front drive, and the other one grabbed my pick-up from the back, threw it in the air, spinning like a top, and let it drop bang slap in the Reverend Millhouse's prize rose garden. And God damnit if there weren't four or five other vehicles already been pitched there by the twister, and they were on their sides, on their backs, wheels still spinning, like snapper turtles that had been tipped over by the kids. And I'm thinking, Lord, this is truly hell, when all of a sudden, the wind stops roaring and the rain stops pouring, and I figure we are right in the eye of the tornado, 'cos the sky is all still and calm and empty. No more pieces of fenders and trash cans and picket fences flying through the air. Nothing. Except, God damnit, I do believe it started to snow! But, of course, it weren't snow, it was rose petals! Floatin' down, pink and red and yellow and... Well, it was like it was showering down bits of rainbow. I gotta tell you it was beautiful. And now I'm thinking, if this ain't hell, maybe it's heaven. Only one thing spoilt it. Suddenly Reverend Millhouse comes out of his house, sees what's happened to his prize roses, and boy is he pissed! He starts cussin' and hollerin' and yellin' right up at the sky, like he's complaining to the Lord himself. I swear he called him a "holy mother f*****!" Sure weren't words you expect to hear from a man of God.'

Very scary

I admit I have embroidered that account a wee bit, but I promise you, there was some very scary footage of twisters and the appalling damage they cause. Nevertheless, I have to admit that a little bit of me was rather hoping I would get to see a twister myself. From a safe distance.

But I didn't. During the eight days I was in South Carolina, I experienced two light showers and some morning mist. Otherwise, it was blue skies every day.

But I did see some gibbons

The IPPL sanctuary is not a zoo. It is not open to the public. It is simply a safe home for some gorgeous animals that have previously lived in inappropriate or indeed horrendous conditions. They are 'rescue' gibbons. Some spent years being used for 'research' in laboratories. Others were saved from incompetent private owners or substandard zoos. They can never be returned to the wild, but at least at Summerville they are safe, cared for, and, most clearly of all, very much loved. To get to know them better and to learn more about primates and their problems I recommend visiting the IPPL website – www.ippl.org – and also do a bit of gibbon Googling. There are some great photos, but believe me, you haven't really experienced the best of a gibbon until you've seen it and heard it swinging and singing.

Buzz

Meanwhile, back in London. Something completely different, and to me completely new, though very close to home. Very close. In a tree just outside the back door. It is a slightly straggly lilac, which has become an extension of what I call 'the magic tree' in that I have chosen to festoon it with a kaleidoscope of wind chimes, fragments of coloured glass, beads, fake butterflies and an ornamental bird-box that is painted yellow with a red roof, and has never been used. But it has now. But not by birds. A small colony of bees has moved in. This sort of thing has happened before in my garden. I was once cleaning out a box and got stung by a 'solitary bee' that wanted to be alone. Another year, the same box was commandeered by a few White-tailed Bumblebees, which are quite tubby and slow and bumbly and therefore not too hard to identify. They are not, however, the only species that has a white tail. For instance, the bees in my magic box. They appeared to also have a largely black body and a gingery shawl (yes, I know, I should use all the scientific words for insect parts but I can never remember them). In fact, I was having trouble getting a decent view because they wouldn't keep still. Every now and then, one would zoom in or out of the hole in the nestbox, but the most conspicuous action was a small party that just kept swirling around outside the box, bouncing, dipping and diving, as if they were dancing. A rather unruly square dance perhaps?

Let it bee

Next step, consult the literature. In my pre-computer days I was pretty addicted to the excellent laminated identification charts produced by such organisations as the Wildlife Trusts. I also have a few favourite books on garden wildlife. So I searched. But I could not find my mystery bees.

However, it just so happened that later in the week I was due to attend an event at which Buglife would launch its 'Get Britain Buzzing' campaign (for more on that visit www.buglife.org.uk). I had barely entered the room when my eyes fell on an illustrated leaflet about 'bees in your garden', and there, among other species I knew well, was a photo of my bee! It was labelled Tree Bumblebee. Never heard of it! But my bees were in a tree. I soon collared a bee expert – not difficult at Buglife! – and quizzed him about Tree Bumblebees. What he told me was instantly conclusive. 'They often nest in old bird-boxes.' Like mine. 'They have this behaviour of dancing outside the nest.' Exactly like mine! 'They arrived from the Continent about five or six years ago.' Which explains why they are not in the books. 'Any problems with them?' I asked. 'No. In fact it's good to report that we have another pollinator in Britain. That's what this Buglife campaign is all about.' Exactly. So, I've got Tree Bumblebees! Welcome.

Dead parrots?

Another thing I've got in my garden is parakeets. There are, of course, parakeets all over London and beyond and there have been for years. There are probably more than 50,000 of them out there in the wild and they are now accepted as British birds.

It has therefore caused a right old kerfuffle that the government, with the support of the RSPB, has decided to 'cull parakeets'! Thus ran the headline in several national newspapers a few weeks ago. The article was often accompanied by a picture of a parakeet, just like the ones in my garden. The bird in question is a Ring-necked (or Rose-ringed) Parakeet.

On the face of it, this is a pretty unbelievable decision. Kill more than 50,000 birds! That's not a cull, that's slaughter. And it is surely impossible. Added to which, people – well most people – have grown rather fond of the old Ring-necks. And the RSPB approves! Outrageous!

Get it right!

Hang on, hang on! Remember the irrefutable adage by which we should all temper our opinions: 'Don't believe everything you read in the papers.' In the case of some papers, this could be amended to: 'Don't believe *anything* you read in the papers.' To which I would add: don't assume that they've got the right pictures in the papers. I sadly report that at least two so-called 'quality' papers proudly printed photos of Ring-necked Parakeets, alongside the 'parakeets to be culled' story. Wrong!

Monks' menace?

The proposed cull refers to Monk Parakeets, which are quite different from the Ring-neckeds, have a much smaller population and potentially do far more damage. There are thought to be about 100 to 150 birds on the loose (mainly round London) and the problem is that – unlike the Ring-neckeds, which live in tree holes – the Monks build an enormous nest of twigs and branches, which may be in a small colony, so that half a dozen nests meld together in a huge clump which can be the size of a small car! Unfortunately, this construction is often perched on a telegraph pole or electricity pylon and woven into the wires. In the US this has been known to cause blackouts.

I am not going to comment any further, but in case you were about to convene a Save Our Parrots campaign, please make sure you've got the right one. And don't depend on the papers for the facts. Although sometimes…

Chinese crackers

Did you see the story about the Chinese watermelon farmers who overdosed their crop on a chemical 'growth accelerator' and arose one morning to find their fields erupting with hundreds of exploding melons? What a wonderful image! It's at times like this I wish I was still doing a comedy show!

BEWARE ANT & DEC & CELEBRITY CHEFS.
ONE MAN'S ~~FOOD~~ IS ANOTHER MAN'S WILDLIFE.

BLOG SEVEN

Shall We Dance?

Strictly

I could have been Ann Widdecombe. Or am I more Russell Grant? So what weird fantasy is this? Have I decided to come out and confess my secret desire to be on *Strictly Come Dancing*? Well, the fact is I could've been. No, honestly, a couple of months ago the *Strictly* office rang me and asked if I would like to come in and discuss my being on this year's show. I decided to go into the office if only because it gave me an excuse to get all nostalgic about the old studios at BBC TV Centre, which are due to be sold off rather than plastered in blue plaques and preserved for ever as a shrine to the great BBC shows of yesteryear. There was also the small possibility that I might bump into one of the bosses who might recognise me and remember that I used to appear a lot on BBC Two, and could do so again. If they asked me. I can dream.

Pan's People

But here was a dream that could come true. Or would it be a nightmare? It was up to me. The people in the *Strictly* office were really nice, and it wasn't long before we were giggling together, as we acknowledged that I would be cast as the little fat one who couldn't really dance. Vanity forced me to inform them that I had danced on Broadway and won rave reviews, and had frequently been choreographed by the lovely – and sadly now late – Flick Colby, the mentor of Pan's People no less. On the other hand – or should it be other foot? – my style was strictly *not* ballroom. This was partially because the mention of quicksteps and foxtrots brought back painful memories of the Sixth Form Dance, where I was an eternal wallflower, sitting forlornly in my ill-fitting dinner suit, wishing that my bow tie would finally asphyxiate me and put me out of my misery.

Writhing

That's another thing. Costumes. Imagine me in a sky blue silk trouser suit, with a neckline plunging to the waist, revealing a belly that could compete with a Christmas pudding. Actually, I *wouldn't* imagine that if you want to sleep tonight. As for the combination of fake tan and facial hair! My head would look like a sweet chestnut. The chief interviewer lady attempted to shatter my objections by pointing out that back in the 1970s I had shamelessly cavorted in The Goodies in everything from a miniskirt to a mouse costume, and that silk trousers, hippy waistcoats and bling was my standard dress when I went clubbing. I couldn't deny that, but I pointed out that the dancing in those days consisted of little more than rhythmic writhing, which took place largely in the dark. 'The truth is,' I explained, 'I have never ever done any ballroom dancing.'

'Well, that is exactly the point!' the lady countered. I couldn't deny that either.

Perfect

To be perfectly honest, I could see all too well why I was an ideal choice for *Strictly*. I was totally unsuited. Perfect. What's more, we'd shared a nice pot of tea, biscuits and some merry banter and

I didn't want to disappoint them. 'You'll love it,' they assured me. 'Everybody who's done it has.' Maybe, but what about those watching? Like – for example – my family. I decided to give *them* the vote.

Hate

My middle daughter, Bonnie, who is a dance teacher and choreographer and therefore knows about these things, was practical in the extreme. 'It'll kill you,' she said. 'It's very hard work, and you are not very fit, and let's face it, you are a bit overweight.' My wife, Laura, who abhors negativity, immediately spotted a positive slant. 'You won't go on a diet, so if you lost weight that'd be good.' Then she added, almost as an afterthought: 'But not if it kills you.' She clearly felt it incumbent on her to come up with some of my more cerebral flaws. 'You are very bad at learning things.'

'You hate being taught,' agreed Rosie, daughter number three. 'When you tried to learn guitar for that BBC Two programme you made your teacher cry!' Kate – daughter number one – agreed totally. 'You'll say what you think and upset someone, and then you'll say you hate ballroom dancing anyway, and all the viewers will be thinking "so why is he doing it then?", and they'll all hate you too.'

OK, I'd got the message. 'So I'll take that as a "no" shall I? Kate, no. Rosie, no. Bonnie, no. And Laura?'

'You must do what you want to do. But … no.'

'So, that's four nos!'

Even as I spoke those words, the truth dawned on me.

'You know what? I want to watch *The X Factor*.'

Celeb

Oh dear, half a blog gone and I haven't mentioned wildlife. I promise I will. Meanwhile, let me tell you why I turned down *I'm a Celebrity… Get Me Out of Here*, twice. As it happens I reckon this is one of the 'best' of the 'reality shows', in so far as there has been some genuine interaction between an unarguably diverse bunch of people, and nobody could deny that it is physically and psychologically challenging. The costumes are of course much more my style, and even without my binoculars I would surely spy some interesting Australian rainforest fauna. Indeed, when I was first approached, somebody commented: 'It should be easy for you, you go to that sort of place all the time. Just carry on watching the wildlife.'

Cockroaches

Watching it, yes, but not eating it. Call me a soppy old insect lover if you like, but chewing live grubs and grasshoppers, or crunching through barrels of cockroaches, is not my idea of animal welfare. Maybe all the contestants should be forced to watch Attenborough's *Life in the Undergrowth*, before being handed a plateful of beetles to swallow. Insects are not some kind of lesser life. Here's a thought: the most malevolent and the most beneficial wild creatures in the world are insects. Take malaria-carrying mosquitoes and pollen-carrying bees. Bad or good, I find the idea of any living thing being sacrificed for laughs on a TV show – what's the word? – distasteful.

Serious

Talking of dodgy food, it is this time of the year that weekend newspapers and colour supplements are likely to carry articles on gathering, cooking and eating wild fungi. One word of advice: don't! The article will no doubt include a warning along the lines of: 'Make absolutely certain that the mushroom you have picked really is edible.' Yes, and how do we do that? Look it up in a mushroom identification book, or on the Internet, I presume. The warning further informs us: 'Many poisonous fungi look very similar to an edible species and vice versa.' If you want to confirm that: also look in the book. Peruse the pictures – whether photos or illustrations – and you will find pages and pages of apparently identical fungi. Many are the same colour, though in some species the colour may vary. So too may the shape and size. Some can only be safely identified by dissecting them! Others, you'd probably have to eat to be sure what they are. It's either that one – 'edible when fresh' – or that one – 'causes severe stomach pains and vomiting, and can be occasionally fatal'. If you think I am just scaremongering or have recently joined the Mushroom Liberation Front, get a book or two, find some fungi and try and sort them out for yourself. But before you fry 'em in butter and garlic, remember a mistake could have serious consequences. I repeat my advice: don't!

No advertising

And finally… I am often asked which binoculars I use and which 'outdoor clothing' I wear. Such secrets must never be revealed on BBC TV – no advertising knowingly allowed – but I can tell you here.

I use Swarovski optical equipment, and I am kept snug and dry by Country Innovation. And neither of them is paying me to say that.

I am now to be found monthly in the sumptuous and vastly informative *BBC Wildlife* magazine. And they *are* paying me, but that's for writing the articles.

Just stay in the shed ... ..till you can fly better.

This Just in

I thought you were ill

Who was it said: 'News of my death has been greatly exaggerated?' Was it Mark Twain? Whoever it was, it was some time ago, so presumably it isn't exaggerated any more. However, I am beginning to know what he or she meant... As far as I am aware, I am yet to appear prematurely in an obituary, but I am gathering evidence that people are assuming I am in worse shape than I actually am. For example, my agent has reported that on more than one occasion when he has been peddling his client (i.e. me) to a TV company or a producer, he has met with the response: 'Bill Oddie? I thought he was ill.' The operative word in that statement is 'was'. Past tense. Back in 2009, I was indeed floored by a deep and dangerous depression, however – happily – illness was duly followed by recovery, which has – even more happily – not been followed by relapse, and – more happily still – this state of 'not being ill' has been maintained for more than two years, as friends, family, neighbours, acquaintances and various medical authorities will testify.

Chunky blonde or quirky sweater?

During this time, I have done a fair amount of travelling, and have spent many enjoyable hours, days and even weeks in the company of those who work for the many terrific NGOs concerned with conservation, animal welfare, alternative energy, child care and mental health. I am proud to be able to help however I can. These people are truly inspirational, and a lot of fun, even though the dilemmas they deal with often aren't. I have also done quite a bit of writing, and have given interviews to several magazines and newspapers. I've done a lot of work in my little garden, listened to a lot of new music, watched a great deal of sport on the telly, become addicted to Nordic thrillers and *Homeland*, and developed old-age crushes on three heroines, though the quirky blonde in *The Bridge* does frighten me a bit. *The Killing*'s Sarah Lund I admire for her undistractable concentration, and her chunky sweater, which is very like the ones worn by fishermen in Shetland, which is one of my favourite places. I used to have one myself. *Homeland*'s Carrie Mathison (Claire Danes) is of course bipolar – as am I – so naturally I have empathy for her. And vice versa? If only.

Healing the well

Anyway, I put it to you that these are the activities of a normal, healthy man. I admit I do take a certain amount of medication, and I have occasional check-ups with my GP, but I no longer attend a shrink, nor belong to any kind of therapy group. I am not knocking them, I am simply pointing out that my health regime is much the same as that of anyone else: get some exercise, lose some weight, cut out the chocolate and cut down on the booze. One might call them remedies for the well people. So, that is my message to anyone out there who might be curious, concerned or indeed totally apathetic: *I am not ill.*

I hope you are all OK too.

Self-interest

Meanwhile, what's going on in my garden? A veritable Robin fest, that's what. In spring I had a pair of Robins trusting enough to take mealworms from my hand. This was not only entertainment for my granddaughters – and for me – it was also my way of hopefully encouraging them to nest in my Ivy, or in one of my nestboxes. Call it bribery and self-interest if you like, but it was also altruistic, as I tried to assure them each morning. Yes, I talk to the Robins. 'You guys nest in my garden and you'll have enough mealworms never to have to bother rummaging around looking for caterpillars or tiddly little worms. You'll be able to feed your chicks, and yourselves, without flying more than a few yards from your nest. Surely that's an offer you can't refuse?'

Not natural

But it was. As the soggy weeks of spring passed by, I had to choke back the pang of disappointment at seeing the pair gathering moss from my rockery and flitting over the fence with it. I was forced to face the rather hurtful fact that my Robins were nesting next door. This was particularly ungracious, since I would not call my neighbour a natural nature lover. (He nags me nearly every day: 'When are they going to shoot those bloody parakeets?')

Knackering

However, after a couple of largely Robinless weeks, suddenly things got a bit livelier. I knew instantly what had happened. The egg had hatched. And where did the parents immediately go in search of food? My garden! I do not hold grudges and I was not bitter, but as I tipped extra mealworms into my feeders, I could not resist letting the faithless parents know some of my feelings. 'Oh hello, so who's hungry then? You two? I expect it's because you're so busy feeding those babies, you don't have time to feed yourselves. How many have you got? Three? Five? The last Robins that nested here – in *my* Ivy, as it happens – had four. Course it was no problem. All mum and dad had to do was flit down onto the feeder – well three feeders actually, all with mealworms – so they could keep the kids full up, take a break while they digested their worms, and have a snack whenever they felt like it.

Of course, I would've done the same for you, but apparently you prefer to live next door, where there are no bird feeders, but there is a cat, and that bloke ranting on about the parakeets, and you have to keep flapping backwards and forwards over the fence. Yes, I am sure it *is* knackering, but it's what you wanted. Anyway, perhaps at least you'll bring the kids to see me when they fledge.'

They're leaving home
But Robins – and most small birds – don't work that way. Yes, you've seen *Springwatch*, when there has been a family of Blue or Great Tits lined up on a branch, and they shiver their wings and one of the parents feeds them, but it doesn't last long. It is essential that young birds learn to feed themselves as rapidly as possible. If they are reluctant, mum or dad is likely to give them a push, quite literally. No good protesting: 'I can't fly very well yet.'

'Yes you can, I've seen you. Now off you go, before I give you a good pecking.' Almost overnight, maternal affection turns to belligerence. Perhaps we humans should try it when the teenagers won't leave home.

Irresistible
Now, let's fast forward to just over a week ago. I go out in the garden for my morning routine. Fill up one feeder with sunflower hearts, and another with peanuts (both equally irresistible to finches, tits, squirrels, a Great Spotted Woodpecker and a dozen parakeets). Then, I put handfuls of mealworms in four plastic feeders: two hanging and two stuck on the window. These are meant for little birds, but neither Magpies nor Jays are beyond dangling and contorting themselves and gobbling up greedy beakfuls. I often lie on the couch by the backroom window, listening to records with my eyes closed. Believe me, it is quite disconcerting to be woken by tapping and scuffling and to look up to a Jay apparently trying to peck through the glass inches above my face.

Little visitor
The final task of the morning round is to check my moth trap. This is a very basic 'light and box' affair. The night had been damp and chilly. I didn't expect much and there wasn't. But no sooner

had I chivvied a Willow Beauty onto a little plastic jar and put it on the garden table, than I became aware of a little visitor perched on the nearby railing. A newly fledged Robin. A riot of spots. A fluffball with measles! It couldn't yet fly too strongly, but boy could it hop. It hopped straight towards me. It hopped onto the table and pecked at the moth in the jar, but – just like at the supermarket – the food was sealed in plastic so rigid it was unopenable. Fluffball cocked his or her head towards me, then hopped off the table and onto my foot!

Good behaviour
Since then he has perched on my lap and on my shoulder. When I hold out a handful of mealworms, he hovers above it for a moment as if selecting the one he fancies, then grabs it in his bill and retires to a shady spot, swallows it and comes back for more. At the risk of confessing to soppiness I admit this little bird cheers me whenever we meet; his behaviour – as the scientists say – also intrigues me. Why so tame so quickly? Last year, I managed to get an adult Robin to take food from my hand. Could that have been one of Fluffball's parents? Could tameness be hereditary? He certainly hadn't had time to learn this behaviour by copying either a parent or me.

There's more
A few days later, not one but two adult Robins appeared in the garden. Mum and dad coming to conscientiously – or guiltily – check on their progeny? Or were they just hungry? I presumed the latter, as one of them swooped in for a mealworm, only to be immediately repelled by a flurry of wings, beak and feet and be literally chased away by its own offspring. There was no fight, no defence, no retaliation, and it happened with both adults. Conclusion: juvenile Robins show zero tolerance to their own parents. Interesting.

Or to their siblings. A couple of days ago I was wondering if I was seeing double. Or was Fluffball playing hide-and-seek? Or… Oh, the fact is that there is not just one young Robin in my garden – there are two. Plus mum and dad hop in now and then, and – for a couple of days – we had a visit from another adult in such a tatty state of moult it was probably embarrassed to be photographed. So that's a quota of five Robins. There has been no great violence, but there have been a few skirmishes, and the siblings are yet to show the slightest affection for one another. The nearest I have observed to a truce is when they perched on the same branch only about a metre apart, though it was raining heavily, so presumably they had agreed to share the shelter till it stopped.

Worry
Anyway, it was bucketing down again last night, and so far today I haven't seen any of them, so I'd best go and check that they are OK. That's the trouble, they may not be my kids, but I do worry about them.

WHO AM I?

Do They Mean Me?

Angry

Do you recognise this person? More to the point, do I recognise this person?

In the mid-1960s, he was quite an angry man and had to leave Rochdale due to violence and drinking. He ended up in a hippie commune in London. His metal (sic) health doctor encouraged him to channel his anger into humour. He still has a bad temper and was reported to have struck John Craven with a tripod over a disagreement about tea!

Who is it?

That's me that is, apparently, according to some website I accidentally visited the other day when I was idly passing a spare five or six hours Googling myself (all celebs do it). Most of it is simply inaccurate or untrue. The mid-1960s were one of the happiest times of my life, when I was appearing on Broadway with John Cleese and Tim Brooke-Taylor, and beginning a relationship with the lady who became my first wife. I had long left Rochdale. I left when I was six! Presumably not due to violence or drinking. Well, not mine anyway. The hippie commune bit has a smidgeon of truth in that during the 1970s a number of friends lived in a big house together. We had a cooking rota, but we weren't hippies, and I didn't 'end up' there; I owned it! I like the idea of a 'metal health doctor'! Heavy metal I presume, or was he a robot? Either way, I was never advised to channel anger into humour, though it is not bad advice, and may indeed have been what I subconsciously did do, but no one put it that way until I visited a psychotherapist relatively recently. As for still having a bad temper, that's not up to me to judge, but I have never ever even thought about striking John Craven, let alone with a tripod, and certainly not over a disagreement about tea!

Fight!

I would, of course, love to know where – or who – all this nonsense comes from, but what really intrigues me is what exactly was the disagreement? Were John and I squabbling?

'You're drinking my tea.'

'No I'm not, it's mine.'

'No it isn't.'

'Yes it is.'

Or were we arguing about what kind of tea we had been given?

'I love a cup of Earl Grey, don't you?'

'Yes, but this is Darjeeling.'

'It's Earl Grey.'

'It is Dar-bloody-jeeling!'

Or was it simply an age-old tribalism?

'Of course, I am a coffee man myself.'

'Well I am a tea man.'

'No, no, you can't beat coffee.'

'Tea.'

'Coffee.'

'Tea.'

The truth is I do like coffee. But I also like tea. But which is best? Of course, there was only one way to find out. *Fight!* At which point I clouted John with my tripod.

Give it to him

And where did this assault take place? The fact that I had a tripod with me suggests that it was either a photographic or birding context. Maybe he was a guest on one of my shows, or I was a guest on his. I have certainly met and several times worked with John Craven, but I like and admire him, and I hope the feeling is mutual. Indeed, I would go so far as to say that were we to find ourselves when there was only one cup of tea left in the pot, I would gladly give it to him. Or does he prefer coffee?

Slapper

The tripod myth baffles me, unless it stems from the time the two of us were broadcasting from the Chelsea Flower Show, and I got a bit too playful with a bunch of gladioli while impersonating Dame Edna. I admit I started it, but John did retaliate by giving me a damn good thrashing with a Red Hot Poker.

By the way, this paragraph is as fictitious as the stuff on the website.

And another thing

While I'm at it, I have been implicated in several other urban myths (why just urban? Does that imply that people are less gullible in rural areas? Of course those townies will believe anything!).

I have read and been told several times that I live in Norfolk. I don't, nor ever have, but I can understand why people think I should. In fact, I have lived in London for 50 years. Before that I lived in Birmingham, and it is true that I went to King Edward's School, Birmingham. However, the story that on the day of the Queen's visit I moved all the bollards and rerouted the whole royal convoy through the school is not true. But I wish it was. Finally, it is a matter of rock and roll legend that The Goodies once beat up John Peel after he gave the 'Funky Gibbon' a bad review. No, they didn't.

Index